THE WISDOM OF THE JEWISH PEOPLE

THE WISDOM OF THE JEWISH PEOPLE

EDITED BY LEWIS BROWNE

JASON ARONSON INC.
NORTHVALE, NEW JERSEY
LONDON

10 9 8 7 6 5 4 3 2 1

Library of Congress Cataloging-in-Publication Data

Wisdom of Israel.
The Wisdom of the Jewish people.

Includes index.
Reprint. Originally published: The Wisdom of Israel. New York: Random House, 1945. Pt. 3 of original text omitted.
1. Judaism–History–Sources. 2. Ethics, Jewish.
3. Jewish Literature. I. Browne, Lewis, 1897–1949.
II. Title.
BM40.W53 1987 296.1 87-24101
ISBN 0-87668-985-3

Manufactured in the United States of America.

There are two kinds of readers of serious books. The first is like unto a man who squeezes grapes with his fingertips, extracting from them mere watery juice. When the stuff fails to ferment, he forthwith blames the grapes. The second is like unto a man who crushes grapes thoroughly, extracting from them all their richness. Such a one is never moved to complain, for the stuff he lays down will readily ferment, and he is left with most excellent wine.

Midrash Ribesh Tov

CONTENTS

ACKNOWLEDGMENTS

Appleton D.-Century Company, Inc.:
For "The Philosophy of Felix Adler," from *The Reconstruction of the Spiritual Ideal* by Felix Adler.

Associated Talmud Torahs:
For "The Shulhan Arukh of Rabbi Karo," from *An Anthology of Medieval Hebrew Literature,* translated by Louis Feinberg.

Behrman House:
For "Wisdom from the Gemara," "Wisdom from the Midrash," and "Sayings from the Zohar," from the *Talmudic Anthology,* translated by Louis I. Newman and Samuel Spitz; "Three Kinds of Education," translated by Maurice Samuel; "The Law According to Hanane'el," from the *Jewish Anthology,* translated by Maurice Samuel; "The Duty of the Jew," "How to Be a Jew," "Concerning Assimilation," and "The Jew of the Future," from *Israel* by Ludwig Lewisohn.

Bloch Publishing Company:
For "The Wisdom of Ibn Gabirol," translated by Rev. A.

Cohen; "Responsa of Rabbi Luria," translated by Simon Hurwitz; "Yiddish Humor," translated by Rufus Learsi.

Chicago University Press:
For selections from *The Complete Bible,* translated by Smith and Goodspeed.

Columbia University Press:
For "The Improvement of the Moral Qualities," translated by Stephen S. Wise; "The Wisdom of a Yemenite," from *Bustan Al-Ukul,* translated by David Levine.

Commission on Jewish Education:
For "The Oath of Amatus," "A Responsum of Rabbi Lublin," "Leon of Modena on Gambling," and "Ten Commandments for a Wife," from *The Jew in the Medieval World,* by Jacob R. Marcus.

E.P. Dutton & Co., Inc.:
For "The Contentions of Judah Halevy," from *Ketab Al-Khazari,* translated by Hartwig Hirschfield.

L.B. Fischer Publishing Corp.:
For "The Words of Heinrich Heine," translated by Hermann Kesten; "Reflections of Jacob Klatzkin," from *In Praise of Wisdom,* translated by Abraham Ragelson.

Harper & Bros.:
For "Some Opinions of Ludwig Lewisohn," from *The Island Within* and *Mid-Channel* by Ludwig Lewisohn.

Reverend Moses Hyamson:
For "The Ethics of Bahya," from *Duties of the Heart,* translated by Reverend Moses Hyamson.

The Jewish Publication Society of America:
For excerpts from *Hebrew Ethical Wills* and *Book of Delight and Other Papers*, translated by Israel Abrahams; *Gabirol's Selected Poems*, translated by Israel Zangwill; *Post-Biblical Hebrew Literature*, translated by B. Halper; *Selected Essays of Ahad Ha-Am*, translated by Leon Simon; and *Mesillat Yesharim*, translated by Mordecai M. Kaplan.

Mordecai M. Kaplan:
For "Ethics of a Conservative Jew," from *Judaism as a Civilization* by Mordecai M. Kaplan.

Alfred A. Knopf, Inc.:
For "The Wit of Sholom Aleichem," from *The World of Sholom Aleichem* by Maurice Samuel.

The Macmillan Company:
For excerpts from *That Man Heine* by Lewis Browne; *The War for the World, Italian Fantasies,* and *Chosen Peoples* by Israel Zangwill.

G.P. Putnam's Sons:
For "The Religion of Sholom Asch," from *What I Believe* by Sholom Asch, translated by Maurice Samuel.

Charles Scribner's Sons:
For "Sayings of the Baal Shem Tov," "Sayings of the Bratzlaver," and "Hasidic Tales and Teachings," from the *Hasidic Anthology*, translated by Louis I. Newman and Samuel Spitz.

FOREWORD

Lewis Browne, editor of *The Wisdom of the Jewish People,* has accomplished the formidable task of reducing to one volume the vast wisdom of the Jews as handed down over nearly six millennia. The breadth and depth of Browne's research, the incisiveness of his selections, and the discerning eye with which he separates "wisdom" from learning have allowed him to produce an immense yet compact anthology, an outstanding work of scholarship.

Browne's definition of "wisdom"–those qualities shown in the traditional "wisdom literature" (Proverbs, Job, and Ecclesiastes)–emphasizes the practical over the mystical, the universal over the particular, and the known over the learned. These criteria for wisdom have helped Browne to narrow his material and to cull the ancient, medieval, and modern Jewish literature to create an anthology that encapsulates without trivializing an immense subject.

All the writings in this book, from the ancient Torah, Talmud, and Midrash to the modern works of Moses Mendelssohn, Heinrich Heine, and Mordecai Kaplan, are part of the rich heritage of the Jewish people. The selections clearly and accurately reflect not only the philosophical, ethical, and moral history of a creative people, but also the deep humor and love of wisdom that have sustained them over the centuries.

The numerous subjects upon which Jewish wisdom has been brought to bear are represented in Browne's selections. *The Wisdom of the Jewish People* contains selections from the Bible, the Apocrypha, the Mishnah, and the Zohar; the sayings of Nahmanides, Maimonides, the Baal Shem Tov, and the Hasidim; and the humor, wit, and reflections of Sholom Aleichem, Isaac Peretz, and Israel Zangwill. The views of countless Jewish luminaries on good and evil, faith and apostasy, education and ignorance, love and hate, shine upon the modern reader with a gentle, inextinguishable light.

The Wisdom of the Jewish People affords today's readers easy access to the most enduring ideas conceived by the mind of man. The precepts of the Bible, the universalistic teachings of the prophets, and the continuing spiritual dedication of leading Jewish thinkers and teachers have given the world a philosophy that has proven itself invincible by withstanding waves of persecution and by refusing to be humiliated.

THE WISDOM OF THE JEWISH PEOPLE

PART I

THE BIBLE

INTRODUCTION

The most sacred collection of Jewish documents is Kitve HaKodesh *(The Holy Writings), also called TaNaKH, a combination of the initials of Torah, Nevi'im, and Ketuvim (Five Books of Moses, Prophets, Writings). It comprises twenty-four books–according to the Rabbinic canon. They are more than a haphazard collection of tales and fiats, more than a disjointed miscellany of hymns, visions, chronicles, and harangues. Essentially they form a coherent epic–"the immortal epic of a people's confused, faltering, but indomitable struggle to achieve a nobler life in a happier world."*[1]

[1] *The Graphic Bible,* by Lewis Browne (New York, Macmillan, 1928), p. 16.

SECTION ONE

THE TORAH

The Jewish Bible begins with the Torah set down in the so-called Five Books of Moses; and it is here that one finds the core of Israel's most ancient wisdom. It is made up of a number of different elements reflecting the widely divergent social and moral attitudes of many different periods in Jewish history.

Modern students have been able to distinguish at least four main elements: (1) the Jahvistic, deriving originally from the Hebrew tribes settled in the south of Palestine, and so named because among them the deity was known as Jahweh (Jehovah). This element shows the clearest traces of the primeval religion developed by those tribes while still in the desert. (2) The Elohistic, derving from the tribes settled in the north, where the deity was known as Elohim. Here, in a region primarily agricultural rather than pastoral, the tribes were compelled to abandon their desert way of life, and with it, many of their original beliefs and taboos. (3) The Deuteronomic, a far more advanced code compiled, it is thought, under the influence of the early Prophets, and adopted in 622 B.C.E. (4) The Priestly, apparently a still later code reflecting the influence of the priest-ridden Babylonians in whose midst the Judeans were held captive for fully a half century before being allowed to return home in 536 B.C.E. The Torah can yield more than a little that will impress even the most modern mind as wise. Part of that little is displayed in the following representative passages:[1]

[1]Throughout this section, I use (with permission) the admirable "American Translation" published by the University of Chicago. Its authors–chiefly Professors J. M. Powis Smith and Edgar J. Goodspeed–use an English that, if less rhetorical than that of the standard version, is far more understandable.

CHAPTER 1

THE TEN COMMANDMENTS

The core of Israel's wisdom lies in the Torah, the Law, and the chief seed in this core is the Decalogue, or Ten Commandments. Probably no single document has exercised a more pervasive influence on the religious and moral life of all mankind. Certainly, there is none to compare with it for brevity, comprehensiveness, forcefulness, and–considering its age–high ethical character. Two versions are given in the Bible, one in Exodus (20:2–14), and the other in Deuteronomy (5:6–21), but both appear to be elaborations of an original code that probably consisted of nothing more than ten stark affirmations. Scholars are inclined to believe that the basic affirmations may have read as follows:

Because I, the Lord, am your God, who brought you out of the land of Egypt, out of a state of slavery, you must have no other gods beside me.

You must not carve an image for yourself in the shape of anything that is in the heavens above or that is on the earth below or that is in the waters under the earth . . . .

You must not invoke the name of the Lord your God to evil intent.[1] . . .

---

[1]It is difficult to decide what was the original purpose behind this prohibition. Possibly it was to prevent necromancy, because the name of

Be careful to keep the Sabbath day holy. . . . Six days you are to labor and do all your work, but on the seventh day . . . you must not do any work at all, neither you, nor your son, nor your daughter, nor your male or female slave, nor your ox, nor your ass, nor any of your cattle, nor the alien in your employ who lives in your community.[2] . . .

Honor your father and mother . . . that you may live long and prosper. . . .

You must not commit murder.

You must not commit adultery.

You must not steal.

You must not bring a false charge against your fellow.

You must not lust after your neighbor's wife, nor covet your neighbor's house,[3] his fields, his male or female slaves, his ox, his ass, or anything at all that is your neighbor's. (Deuteronomy 5:6–21)

---

the deity was believed to have tremendous magical power. On the other hand, perhaps, it was to discourage the taking of malevolent or reckless vows.

[2]Some historians suggest that the Jewish word Sabbath is derived from the far more ancient Babylonian *shabbatum,* which was likewise set apart from other days. Significantly, however, the Babylonians regarded it as an evil day to be spent in fending off the demons, not as a holy one, to be dedicated to rest. See *This Believing World* by Lewis Browne, p. 73 ff.

[3]The version in Exodus, apparently following a more ancient and primitive text, mentions the house before the wife.

CHAPTER 2

THE BOOK OF THE COVENANT

Once the Israelites ceased to be a wandering folk of herdsmen and settled in Canaan as tillers of the soil, they necessarily had to adopt new customs and laws. These they must have learned largely from the Canaanites, who themselves had long been under the influence of the Babylonians. Characteristically, however, the Israelites gave a distinct ethical bias to the statues they adopted, as is evidenced by the following quotations from the so-called Book of the Covenant found in Exodus. There is no record of any other nation that attained such a high level of humaneness–and what else is wisdom?–at so early a date.

When you buy a Hebrew slave, he is to work for you for six years, but in the seventh year he is to go free without paying anything. If he came in single, he shall go out single; if he was married, his wife shall go out with him. . . . But if the slave declares, "I am fond of my master, my wife, and my children; I will not go free," his master shall bring him up to God; he shall bring him up to the door or the doorpost, and his master shall pierce his ear with an awl; he shall then be his slave permanently.[1] . . .

[1]Anthropologists are in considerable doubt as to the precise meaning of this ceremony. Sir James George Frazer (*Folk-lore in the Old Testament,*

If a man strikes his male or female slave with a stick, so that he dies under his hand, he must be avenged. . . .

If a man strikes the eye of his male or female slave, and destroys it, he must let him go free in compensation for his eye; if he knocks out the tooth of his male or female slave, he must let him go free in compensation for his tooth. . . .

Whoever strikes another, so that he dies, must be put to death; if, however, he did not lie in wait for him, but God let him fall into his hands, I will designate a place for you to which he may flee. If a man wilfully plans to murder another treacherously, even from my altar you must take him, that he may be put to death.

Whoever strikes his father or mother must be put to death. . . .

Whoever reviles his father or mother must be put to death. . . .

Whoever kidnaps a man, and sells him, or holds him in his possession, must be put to death.

You must not ill-treat a resident alien, nor oppress him; for you were once resident aliens yourselves in the land of Egypt. You must not wrong any widow or orphan. If you ever wrong them and they cry aloud to me, I will be sure to hear their cry, and my anger will blaze, and I will slay you with the sword; thus shall your own wives become widows and your children orphans.

If you lend money to my people, to any poor person among you, you must not behave like a creditor toward him; you must not charge him any interest. If you ever take another's cloak in pledge, you must return it to him by sunset; for that is

---

London, 1918, vol. III, p. 269) suggests that "according to the laws of primitive logic you can assure your control of a man by the simple process of cutting his ear and drawing a few drops of his blood. This conception may explain the treatment of a Hebrew slave . . . on whom his master might not unnaturally desire to possess some securer hold than the slave's own profession of good will and attachment."

his only covering; it is his cloak for his body. What else could he sleep in? And if he should cry to me, I would respond; for I am kind. . . .

You must not give false, hearsay evidence; do not join hands with a wicked person by being a malicious witness. You must not follow the majority by doing wrong, nor give evidence in a suit so as to pervert justice, by turning aside with the majority. Neither must you favor a poor man in his suit.

You must never take a bribe; for a bribe blinds the open-eyed, and subverts even a just case. . . .

If you chance upon your enemy's ox or ass going astray, you must be sure to take it home to him. If you see the ass of one who hates you lying prostrate under its load, you must refrain from deserting him; you must be sure to help him raise it up. . . .

For six years you may sow your land and gather in its crops, but during the seventh year you must leave it alone and let it lie fallow, so that the poor of your people may eat of it, and what they leave the wild beasts may eat. (Exodus 21:2–23:11)

CHAPTER 3

THE CODE OF HOLINESS

This code is imbedded in the Book of Leviticus (Chapters 17–26), and is traditionally ascribed to Moses, and establishes the Hebrews as pioneers in the field of enlightened legislation.

The Lord said to Moses,

You must be holy; for I, the Lord your God, am holy. You must each revere his father and mother, and you must keep my Sabbaths, since I, the Lord, am your God. Do not turn to unreal gods, nor make yourselves molten gods, since I, the Lord am your God. . . .

When you reap the harvest of your land, you must not reap your field to the very corners, nor gather the gleanings of your harvest; you must not glean your vineyards bare, nor gather the fallen fruit of your vineyard; you must leave them for the poor and the resident alien, since I, the Lord, am your God.

You must neither steal, nor cheat, nor lie to one another. You must not take a false oath in my name, and so profane the name of your God, of me, the Lord.

You must not defraud your fellow, nor rob him; the wages

of a hired laborer are not to remain all night with you until morning.

You must not curse a deaf person, nor place an obstacle in the way of a blind person; you must stand in awe of your God, of me, the Lord.

You must not do injustice in a lawsuit, neither showing partiality to the poor, nor deferring to the powerful, but judging your fellow fairly.

You must not play the part of a talebearer against your people; you must not secure yourself by the life of another, because I am the Lord.

You must not cherish hate against your fellow countryman; you must be sure to reprove your fellow, and not incur sin because of him. You must not avenge yourself, nor bear a grudge against the members of your own race, but you must love your fellow as one of your own, because I am the Lord. (Leviticus 19:1–5, 9–18)

You must not practice augury or soothsaying. . . .

You must not degrade your daughter by making a harlot of her, lest the land fall into harlotry, and become full of lewdness.

You must keep my Sabbaths, and stand in awe of my sanctuary, because I am the Lord.

Do not turn to mediums or magicians; do not defile yourselves with them by consulting them, because I, the Lord, am your God.

You must rise in the presence of the hoary-headed, and defer to the aged, and so stand in awe of your God, of me, the Lord.

If a convert is residing with you in your land, you must not mistreat him; you must treat the convert who resides with you like the native born among you, and love him as one of your own, because I, the Lord, am your God; for you were once aliens yourselves in the land of Egypt. (Leviticus 19:26–34)

CHAPTER 4

DEUTERONOMY

According to tradition, this book contains the discourses delivered by Moses just before his death; but modern commentators believe it must have been composed at a much later date. Its language and spirit show the distinct influence of the succession of prophets beginning with Amos, and external evidence indicates that the document was published for the first time in 622 B.C.E. There is a striking lack of emphasis on the ritual laws, and an even more striking insistence on the importance of the moral ones. God is described not as a tribal deity, gluttonous for flatteries and sacrifices, but as a Universal Ruler demanding most of all that men show kindness toward one another. If to be humane is a mark of wisdom, then this book is one of the wisest in the entire literature of mankind. For, as the following selections will make plain, Deuteronomy is–considering its age–phenomenally humane.

CONCERNING GOD'S DEMANDS

And now, O Israel, what does the Lord your God require of you but to stand in awe of the Lord your God, walk in all His ways, love Him, serve the Lord your God with all your mind and heart, and keep the commands of the Lord and His statutes that I am commanding you today, for your good. . . . Do not be stiff-necked any more, for the Lord your God is the God of gods, and Lord of lords, the great, mighty, and awful God, who is never partial, and never takes a bribe, who secures justice for the orphan and the widow, and loves the resident alien in giving him food and clothing. So you should love the resident alien; for you were once resident aliens yourselves in the land of Egypt. (Deuteronomy 10:12–20)

CONCERNING JUSTICE

In all communities which the Lord your God is giving you, you are to appoint judges and officials for your various tribes, to judge the people aright. You must not pervert justice; you must show no partiality, nor take a bribe; for a bribe blinds the eyes of the learned, and subverts even a just case. Justice, and justice only, you must strive for, in order that you may live, and take possession of the land which the Lord your God is giving you. (Deuteronomy 16:18–20)

CONCERNING FALSE WITNESSES

A single witness shall not convict a man in the case of any crime or offense of any kind whatsoever that he has committed; it is only on the evidence of two or three witnesses that a charge can be sustained.

If a plaintiff with a grudge appears against a man to accuse him falsely, the two parties who have the dispute must appear before the Lord, that is, before the priests and the judges that are in office at that time; the judges shall make a thorough investigation, and if it turns out that the plaintiff is false, having falsely accused his fellow, you must do to him as he meant to do to his fellow. Thus shall you eradicate the wicked person from your midst; and when those that are left hear of it, they will be afraid, and never again do such a wicked thing as this in your midst. (Deuteronomy 19:15–20)

CONCERNING SOCIETY

You must not learn to imitate the abominable practices of the [heathen] nations. There must not be found among you anyone who makes his son or his daughter pass through fire, a diviner, a soothsayer, an augur, a sorcerer, a charmer, a medium, a magician, or a necromancer. For anyone given to these practices is abominable to the Lord. . . . You must be absolutely true to the Lord your God; for while these nations whom you are to conquer give heed to soothsayers and diviners, the Lord your God has not intended you to do so. Instead, the Lord your God will raise up a prophet for you from among yourselves. (Deuteronomy 18:9–15)

CONCERNING MILITARY EXEMPTION

When you go out to do battle against your enemies . . . then the officers shall say to the people "Whoever has built a new house, but has not dedicated it, may leave and return home, lest he die in the battle, and another dedicate it. Whoever has planted a vineyard, but has not had the use of it, may leave and return home, lest he die in the battle, and another get the use of it. Whoever has betrothed a wife, but has not married her, may leave and return home, lest he die in the battle and another marry her." The officers shall say further to the people, "Whoever is afraid and fainthearted must leave and return home, so that his fellows may not become fainthearted like him." (Deuteronomy 20:5–8)

When a man is newly married, he is not to go out with the army, nor be counted with it for any duty; he is to be free at home for one year, to enjoy himself with his wife whom he has married. (Deuteronomy 24:5)

CONCERNING FEMALE WAR PRISONERS

When you go out to battle against your enemies, and the Lord your God delivers them up to you, and you make them prisoners, if you see among the prisoners a beautiful woman upon whom you set your heart, you may take her for a wife. When you bring her into your home, she shall uncover her head, and pare her nails, and throw off her prisoner's garb. She shall remain in your house, and bewail her father and mother for a whole month. After that you may have intercourse with her. You shall be her husband, and she shall be your wife. If you lose interest in her, you must let her go absolutely free; you must not sell her, nor mistreat her, because you have humiliated her. (Deuteronomy 21:10–14)

CONCERNING LOST PROPERTY

You must not see your fellow countryman's ox or sheep go astray without showing concern for it; you must be sure to take it home to your fellow countryman. If, however, your fellow countryman is not a tribesman of yours and you do not know him, you must take it home with you, and keep it until he claims it; then you must give it back to him. You must do the same with his ass, with his garment, and with anything lost by a fellow countryman of yours, which he has lost and you have found; you are not to be without concern for it.

You must not see your fellow countryman's ass or ox foundered on the road without showing concern for it; you must be sure to help him to raise it up. . . .

If you should happen to come upon a bird's nest in any tree, or on the ground, with young ones or eggs, and the mother sitting on the young or the eggs, you must not take the mother with the young. You must rather let the mother go, and only take the young, that you may prosper, and live long.

When you build a new house, you must make a parapet for your roof, that you may not bring the guilt of blood upon your house, in case anyone should fall from it. . . .

You must not plough with an ox and an ass yoked together. (Deuteronomy 22:1–10)

CONCERNING SEDUCTION AND RAPE

If there should be a girl who is a virgin betrothed to a husband, and a man chances upon her in the city and lies with her, you must take them both out to the gate of that city, and stone them to death; the girl, because she did not call for help although in the city, and the man, because he seduced another's bride. Thus shall you eradicate the wicked person from your midst. If, however, it is in the open country that the man chances upon the betrothed girl, and the man seizes her, and lies with her, then simply the man alone shall die. You must do nothing to the girl, since no sin deserving of death attaches to the girl; for this case is like that of a man attacking his neighbor and murdering him, since it was in the open country that he chanced upon her, [and] the girl may have called for help, but there was no one to save her. (Deuteronomy 22:23–27)

SUNDRY HUMANE LAWS

You must not turn a slave over to his master when he has escaped from his master to you; he shall live right in your midst with you, in any place that he chooses in one of your communities as being advantageous to him. You must not mistreat him. (Deuteronomy 23:15)

When you enter your neighbor's vineyard, you may eat your fill of the grapes, as much as you wish; but you must not put any in your bag.

When you enter your neighbor's grain field, you may pull off some heads with your hand; but you must not put a sickle to your neighbor's grain. (Deuteronomy 23:24–25)

No one is to take a handmill or an upper millstone in pledge; for he would be taking a means of livelihood in pledge. . . .

When you make your neighbor a loan of any sort, you must

not go into his house to take his pledge; you must wait outside, and the man to whom you are making the loan shall bring the pledge outside to you. If he is a poor man, you must not sleep in the garment that he has pledged; you must be sure to return it to him at sunset, that he may sleep in his cloak, and so be grateful to you. It will stand to your credit with the Lord your God.

You must not defraud a hired laborer who is poor and needy, whether he is one of your fellow countrymen, or one of the aliens residing in your land. You must pay him his wages by the day, before the sun sets (for he is poor and is expecting it), so that he may not cry to the Lord against you, and you incur guilt.

Fathers are not to be put to death with the children, nor are children to be put to death with their fathers. Everyone is to be put to death for his own sin.

You must not pervert the justice due the resident alien, or the orphan, nor take a widow's garment in pledge. You must remember that you were once a slave yourself in Egypt, and the Lord your God rescued you from there; that is why I am commanding you to do this.

When you reap your harvest in your field, and forget a sheaf in the field, you must not go back to get it; it is to go to the resident alien, the orphan, and the widow, that the Lord your God may bless you in all your enterprises. When you beat your olive trees, you must not go over them a second time; that is to go to the resident alien, the orphan, and the widow. When you pick the grapes of your vineyard, you must not go over it a second time; that is to go to the resident alien, the orphan, and the widow. You must remember that you were once a slave yourself in the land of Egypt; that is why I am commanding you to do this. (Deuteronomy 24:6–22)

You must not muzzle an ox when he is treading out the grain. (Deuteronomy 25:4)

CONCLUSION

For this charge which I am enjoining on you today is not beyond your power, nor is it out of reach; it is not in the heavens, that you should say, "O that someone would ascend to the heavens for us, so that we might observe it!" Nor is it beyond the sea, that you should say, "O that someone would cross the sea for us, and get to know it for us, and then communicate it to us, so that we might observe it!" No, the matter is very near you, in your mouth and in your mind, for you to observe.

See, I put before you today life and prosperity, along with death and misfortune. If you heed the commands of the Lord your God which I am giving you today, by loving the Lord your God, by walking in his ways, and by keeping his commands, statutes, and ordinances, then you shall live, and multiply, and the Lord your God will bless you in the land which you are invading for conquest. If, however, your heart turns away, and you give no heed, but are enticed to pay homage to alien gods and serve them, I tell you today that you shall most certainly perish. . . . I call heaven and earth to witness against you today that I have put life and death before you, the blessing and the curse; therefore, choose life that you as well as your descendants may live, by loving the Lord your God, by heeding His injunctions, and by holding fast to Him, for that will mean life to you. (Deuteronomy 30:11–20)

SECTION TWO

THE PROPHETS

The ancient Hebrews were never anything but a tiny folk occupying a mere crumb of a homeland, but they did produce those extraordinary characters called the prophets. Once the Hebrews overran the Land of Canaan, they naturally tended to forsake their stark old desert way of life. Formerly, they had all been poor and, therefore, equal; but now, settled in fertile places, some among them grew rich, and sharp social distinctions resulted. Formerly, they had been remote from civilization, so their wants had been simple and their morals correspondingly stern; but now, surrounded by citified races, they learned to crave luxuries, and their standards grew more and more lax. It was apparently these things that first made the prophets anxious to maintain the old religion. They became the voice of Israel's conscience, the chronic troublers in the land; and though ideologically reactionaries, practically speaking, they proved themselves revolutionists.

CHAPTER 5

THE ORACLE OF SAMUEL

Here, for example, is the traditional account of how a prophet living in the eleventh century B.C.E. *is supposed to have spoken when the Hebrews, wishing to be "like all the nations," insisted on getting themselves a king.*

This will be the procedure of the king who shall reign over you: he will take your sons and appoint them for himself for his chariots and for his horsemen; and they shall run before his chariots; and he will appoint for himself commanders of thousands and commanders of hundreds, and some to do his plowing and to reap his harvests and make his implements of war and the equipment for his chariots. He will take your daughters for perfumers, for cooks, and for bakers. He will take the best of your fields and your vineyards and your olive orchards, and give them to his courtiers. He will take the tenth of your grain crops and of your vineyards and give it to his eunuchs and to his henchmen. He will take your male and female slaves, and the best of your cattle and your asses, and make use of them for his work. He will take a tenth of your flocks; and you yourselves will become his slaves. Then you will cry out on that day because of your king whom you will have chosen for yourselves; but the Lord will not answer you on that day. (I Samuel 8:11–18)

CHAPTER 6

THE PARABLE OF NATHAN

Here is another instance of how an early prophet is reported to have spoken. The occasion was the scandalous episode involving King David and the lovely Bathsheba. This woman was the wife of a foreign mercenary, and the monarch had apparently considered it no more than his royal prerogative to invite her to his couch. Later, however, discovering that she was pregnant with his child, he became sufficiently perturbed to arrange to have her husband killed off in battle. Whereupon a certain prophet named Nathan felt himself called upon by God to go to David and say:

There were two men in a certain city, the one rich, and the other poor. The rich man owned very many flocks and herds. But the poor man had nothing but a single little ewe lamb, which he had bought. He reared it and it grew up with him and with his children. It would eat from his plate and drink from his cup, and it lay in his bosom, and it was like a daughter to him. Now there came a traveler to the rich man, and he refused to take from his own flock or his own herd to make ready for the wayfarer who had come to him, but he took the poor man's lamb and prepared it for the man who had come to him.

[Hearing this tale] David's anger became furious, and he said to Nathan: "As the Lord lives, the man that does this is worthy of death; he shall restore the lamb sevenfold, because he did this and because he showed no pity."

Whereupon Nathan cried to David: "*You* are the man! Thus says the Lord God of Israel: 'I anointed you king over Israel and I delivered you out of the hand of Saul, and I gave you your master's house and your master's wives into your bosom; I also gave you the house of Israel and of Judah, and if that were too little, I would add in this or that way. Why have you despised the Lord by doing that which is evil in my sight? You have slain Uriah the Hittite with the sword, and you have taken his wife to be your wife, having slain him with the sword of the Ammonites. Now, therefore, the sword shall never depart from your house!" (II Samuel 12:1–10)

CHAPTER 7

THE WORD OF AMOS

With Amos, who lived in the first half of the eighth century B.C.E., *the evolution of the Hebrew prophet from conjurer to reformer becomes complete. He was apparently the first whose greatness was seen to lie primarily in what he had to say, and whose words were therefore remembered to the exclusion of almost all else about the man. The little book containing his utterances is one of the marvels of literature because of both its subject matter and its style. Amos was no more than a peasant by calling, a casual laborer in a remote hill-country; yet he managed to voice ideas so startlingly advanced for his day that he deserves to be ranked with the supreme sages of all time. Briefly, his ideas were these: (1) God cares for all peoples, not just the Israelites; (2) God will show the latter no special favor unless they show special diligence in following His ways; (3) God's ways are the ways of righteousness, and they can be followed only by doing good, not by performing rites; (4) unless the Israelites do follow them, and at once, God Himself will devour their land.*

Leaving his flocks, Amos went down into the fat valley-lands where the people had become most corrupt, and he cried:

Thus says the Lord. . . .
"I will send a fire upon Judah,
And it shall devour the palaces of Jerusalem. . . .
Because they have rejected the instruction of the Lord,

And have not kept his statutes. . . .
For the three transgressions of Israel,
And for the four, I will not hold back (my wrath);
Because they have sold the innocent for silver,
And the needy in exchange for a pair of shoes;
They trample upon the heads of the poor,
And push the humble out of the way. . . .
Garments taken in pledge they spread out
Beside every altar;
And the wine of those who have been fined
They drink in the houses of their gods. . . .
Therefore, behold, I am going to make a groaning under you,
As a wagon groans that is loaded with sheaves.
Flight shall fail the swift,
And the strong shall not exert his strength. . . .
He who handles the bow shall not stand firm,
Nor shall he who rides on horseback save himself;
And the stoutest of heart among the warriors
Shall flee away naked on that day. . . ."

Hear this word which the Lord speaks
Against you, O Israelites, against the whole
Family that I brought up from the land of Egypt. . . .
"Because you hate him who protests in the public square,
And loathe him who speaks the truth. . . .
Though you have built houses of hewn stone,
You shall not dwell in them;
Though you have planted fair vineyards,
You shall not drink their wine. . . ."

Hear this, you cows of Bashan,[1]
You who oppress the weak, who crush the needy,
Who say to your husbands, "Bring that we may drink!"

---

[1]I.e., women. The cows bred in Bashan were famous for their fatness.

The Lord God has sworn by his holiness
That there are days coming upon you
When they will drag you away with grappling hooks,
And what is left of you with fishhooks;
And through the breeches you will go, each straight ahead,
And you will be flung upon the refuse heap. . . .
I am no prophet, nor am I a member of a prophetic order;
But I am a shepherd and a dresser of sycamores.
And the Lord took me from behind the flock,
And the Lord said to me,
"Go, prophesy to my people Israel."
And now hear the word of the Lord:
"Seek good and not evil that you may live, and that the Lord,
  the God of hosts, may be with you. . . .
Hate evil, and love good
And establish justice at the gate. . . ."

Behold, the Lord says:
"I hate, I spurn your feasts,
And I take no pleasure in your festal gatherings.
Even though you offer me your burnt offerings,
And your cereal offerings, I will not accept them;
And the thank offerings of your fatted beasts I will not look
  upon.

Take away from me the noise of your songs;
I will not listen to the melody of your lyres.
But let justice roll down like waters,
And righteousness like a perennial stream. . . .
Perhaps then the Lord, the God of hosts,
Will be gracious to a remnant of Joseph."

CHAPTER 8

THE WORD OF ISAIAH

Not all the prophets were of lowly origin like Amos. Some came from the upper class, most notably Isaiah, who served as a sort of spiritual statesman in Judah throughout the last third of the eighth century B.C.E. *He too denounced the folly of a crudely sacerdotal religion and the menace of a grossly unjust social order. He too was convinced that the God of Israel ruled over all the earth, and that righteousness alone could win His favor. For all these reasons he too was in the profoundest sense a revolutionist.*

Here are a few excerpts from the collection of Isaiah's sermons to be found in the first 39 chapters of the book that bears his name:

Hear the word of the Lord, you rulers of Sodom;
Give ear to the instruction of our God, you people of Gomorrah!
"Of what use is the multitude of your sacrifices to me," says the Lord;
"I am sated with burnt offerings of rams and the fat of fed beasts;
In the blood of bullocks and lambs and he-goats
I take no delight.
When you come to visit me,
Who demands this of you – the trampling of my courts?

Bring no more worthless offering! The odor of sacrifice is an abomination to me.
New Moon and Sabbath, the holding of assemblies –
Fasting and feasting I cannot endure.
My whole being hates your New Moons and your festal seasons;
They are a burden upon me; I am tired of them.
So, when you spread out your hands, I will hide my eyes from you;
Even though you make many prayers, I will not listen. . . .
Wash yourselves clean! Put away the evil of your doings from before my eyes;
Cease to do evil, and learn to do good!
Seek justice, and restrain the oppressor! (Isaiah 1:10–17)

Woe to you who join house to house,
And add field to field,
Till there is no more room,
And you are left to dwell alone
In the midst of the land!
Therefore the Lord of hosts has sworn in my hearing:
"Of the truth shall many houses become a desolation,
Houses great and goodly, without an inhabitant;
For ten acres of vineyard shall wield but a bath,
And a homer of seed shall yield but an ephah."

Woe to those who rise up early in the morning
To run after strong drink;
Who sit late into the twilight
Till wine inflames them;
Whose feasts are lyre and harp,
Timbrel and flute and wine;
But the doing of the Lord they heed not,
And the work of his hands they see not!
Therefore, my people are gone into exile,

For want of knowledge;
Their nobility is famished with hunger,
And their rabble is parched with thirst.
Therefore Sheol has enlarged her appetite,
And opens her mouth without limit;
And down go the rank and the rabble of Zion,
And all who rejoice in her. . . .
Then lambs will graze as on their pasture,
And fat kids will feed among the ruins.

Woe to those who draw guilt on themselves with cords of ungodliness,
And the penalty of their sin as with cart-ropes;
Who say, "Let his work speed on, make haste,
That we may see it;
Let the purpose of the Holy One of Israel drew near and come,
That we may know it!"

Woe to those who call evil good,
And good evil;
Who count darkness as light,
And light as darkness;
Who count bitter as sweet,
And sweet as bitter!

Woe to those who are wise in their own eyes,
And in their own light intelligent!
Ah! the heroes at drinking wine,
And the warriors at blending liquor;
Who acquit the guilty for a bribe,
And wrest the rights of the innocent from him!
Therefore, as a tongue of fire licks up stubble,
And hay sinks down in the flame,
Their root will become like rottenness,
And their blossom will go up like dust! (Isaiah 5:8–24)

CHAPTER 9

THE WORD OF MICAH

Micah was a contemporary of Isaiah, and perhaps a disciple. His aim, however, seems to have been to influence the people rather than their rulers, for he took pains to express himself in a language that the very simplest folk could understand. If he lacked originality in what he said, he more than made up for it by the brilliance with which he said it. For example, read this perfect summation of the prophetic teachings:

With what shall I come before the Lord,
And bow myself before God most high?
Shall I come before him with burnt offerings,
With calves a year old?
Will the Lord be pleased with thousands of rams,
With myriads of streams of oil?
Shall I give my first-born for my transgression,
The fruit of my body for the sin of my soul?
You have been told, O man, what is good,
And what the Lord requires of you:
Only to do justice, and to love mercy,
And to walk humbly with your God. (Micah 6:6–8)

CHAPTER 10

THE WORD OF JEREMIAH

Next in the succession of major prophets is Jeremiah of Anatot, who was born in 650 B.C.E., and who dedicated his entire life to moral agitation. For years he labored to try to save the tiny Kingdom of Judah from blundering into the fate that had already overwhelmed the Kingdom of Israel. And when he knew he had failed–Judah was ravaged by the Babylonians in 586 B.C.E.–he still refused to rest. Now that the people of Judah had been robbed of their independence, he sought to brace their will so that they might at least preserve their identity. It may, therefore, have been in part because of Jeremiah that the tribesmen of Judah, though far fewer in number, managed to survive. Here is how he counselled them:

These are the words of the letter that Jeremiah the prophet sent from Jerusalem to the elders among the exiles, and to the priests, the prophets, and all the people whom Nebuchadnezzar had carried into exile from Jerusalem to Babylon. . . .

"Thus says the Lord of hosts, the God of Israel, to all the exiles whom I carried into exile from Jerusalem to Babylon: 'Build houses, and live in them; plant vineyards, and eat the fruit of them; take wives, and beget sons and daughters; take wives also for your sons, and give your daughters to husbands, that they may bear sons and daughters; so let your numbers increase, and not diminish. And seek the welfare of the land to which I have carried you into exile, and pray to the Lord on its behalf; for in its welfare shall you find your welfare' " (Jeremiah 29:1, 4–7)

CHAPTER 11

THE WORD OF THE SECOND ISAIAH

The temptation to lose themselves in Babylonia was very strong among the bedraggled exiles from Judah; but more prophets arose to carry on Jeremiah's work, and thanks to them the temptation was resisted. One of these was a supremely eloquent man whose name is unknown, but whose utterances are preserved in the latter part of the Book of Isaiah. For that reason, modern scholars usually speak of him as the Second Isaiah. The mission of this prophet was apparently threefold: first, to keep his people from succumbing to the idolatry all around them; second, to remind them that righteousness, not ritualism, was what their God desired; third, to assure them that soon they would be restored to their homeland and that they would then be raised to a glory infinitely greater than any they had known before.

THE FOLLY OF IDOLATRY

The makers of idols are all of them inane, their precious products are good for nothing, and their devotees are without sight or sense. . . . The workman in iron works it over the coals, and shapes it with hammers, working it with his strong arm. . . . The workman in wood draws a measuring-line over it, outlines it with a pencil, works it with planes, shapes it with compasses, and makes it into the likeness of a man, with a beauty like that of the human form–to sit in a house!

A man cuts down a cedar, or takes a plane or an oak, or lays hold of some other tree of the forest, which the Lord planted and the rain has nourished for man to use as fuel. He takes part of it and warms himself, he kindles a fire and bakes bread; then he makes a god and worships it, he molds an image and prostrates himself before it. Half of it he burns in the fire, and on its embers he roasts flesh; he eats the roast and is satisfied; he also warms himself, and says, "Ha! ha! I am warm, I feel the glow." And the rest of it he makes into a god–his idol!–prostrates himself before it, worships it, and prays to it, saying, "Save me, for thou art my god!"

They have no knowledge and no intelligence; for their eyes are besmeared so that they cannot see, and their minds are dulled so that they cannot understand. No one has sense or knowledge or intelligence to say, "Half of it have I burned in the fire, and on its embers have I baked bread, and I am roasting flesh and eating it; and the rest of it shall I make into an abomination, and prostrate myself before a block of wood?"

Feeder on ashes! A deluded mind has led him astray, so that he cannot save himself, or confess, "Am not I holding to a delusion?" (Isaiah 44:9–20)

TRUE AND FALSE FASTING

If on your fast day you pursue your own business,
And press on with all your labors;
If you fast for the sake of strife and contention,
And to smite with godless fist;
You fast not on such a day
As to make your voice heard on high.
Can such be the fast I choose–
A day for a man to humble himself,

To bow down his head like a bulrush,
To grovel in sackcloth and ashes?
Will you call this a fast,
A day of pleasure to the Lord?

Is not *this* the fast I choose–
To loose the bonds of wickedness,
To undo the knots of the yoke,
To let the oppressed go free,
And every yoke to snap?
Is it not to share your bread with the hungry,
And the homeless poor to bring home;
When you see the naked, to cover him,
And to hide not yourself from your own flesh? . . .

If you remove from your midst the yoke,
The finger of scorn, the mischievous speech,
And share your bread with the hungry,
And satisfy the craving of the afflicted,
Then shall your light shine out in darkness,
And your gloom shall be as noonday.
And the Lord shall guide you continually,
And shall satisfy you with rich nourishment;
And your strength shall he renew,
And you shall be like a well-watered garden,
Or like a spring of water,
Whose waters fail not.
And your people shall rebuild the ancient ruins,
You shall raise up the foundations of many generations;
And you shall be called "the rebuilder of broken walls,
The restorer of streets to dwell in." (Isaiah 58:3–12)

GOOD NEWS TO THE LOWLY

The spirit of the Lord God is upon me,
For the Lord has anointed me;

He has sent me to bring good news to the lowly,
To bind up the broken-hearted,
To proclaim liberty to the captives,
And release to the prisoners;
To proclaim the year of the Lord's favor,
And the day of our God's vengeance;
To comfort all mourners,
To provide for the mourners of Zion,
To give them a crown instead of ashes,
Oil of joy instead of a garment of mourning,
A song of praise instead of a drooping spirit,
That they may be called oak trees of righteousness,
The planting of the Lord, with which he may glorify himself.

Then shall they rebuild the ancient ruins,
They shall raise up the desolations of old;
They shall renew the wasted cities,
The desolations of age after age. . . .

No more shall you be named "Forsaken," nor your land be named "Desolate";
But you shall be called "My delight is in her," and your land "Married";
For the Lord delights in you, and your land shall be married.
As a young man marries a maiden, so shall your Builder marry you;
And as a bridegroom rejoices over his bride, so shall your God rejoice over you.

Over your walls, O Jerusalem, I have appointed watchmen,
Who never keep silent by day or by night.
You who are the Lord's remembrances, take no rest for yourselves,
And give him no rest, until he establish
And make Jerusalem a praise in the earth!

The Lord has sworn by His right hand, and by His strong arm:
"No more will I give you grain to be food for your enemies,
Nor shall aliens drink your vintage for which you have labored;
But those who have garnered the grain shall eat it, and praise the Lord,
And those who have gathered the vintage shall drink it in my holy courts.
Pass through, pass through the gates, prepare the way of the people,
Grade up, grade up the highway, clear it of stones; raise a signal over the peoples.
See! The Lord has made proclamation to the end of the earth:
"Say to the daughter of Zion, 'See! your salvation has come;
See! His reward is with Him, and His recompense before Him.'
They shall be called 'the holy people, the redeemed of the Lord.' " (Isaiah 61:1–6, 62:4–12)

SECTION THREE

THE WRITINGS

This, the third main section of the Bible, contains–among other documents–at least three that are in the classic sense Books of Wisdom. They are entitled Proverbs, Job, and Ecclesiastes, and though traditionally ascribed to very ancient authors, all three are apparently of late origin. In their present form they belong to the period following 332 B.C.E., the year Alexander the Great overran Palestine.

Long before that date we find a new class of spiritual advisers emerging in Judea: the so-called hahamim, sages. These are not the hereditary priests who laid down the Law, nor the inspired prophets who uttered the Word of God; they are instead the rational men of learning who gave shrewd counsel. They took their stand in the market place, or by the city gates, and proffered instruction to the people by means of parables. They collected disciples in their homes, and discoursed to them in strophes and proverbs. They thus resembled the early Greek philosophers, and once direct contact was established with the Greek-speaking world, this resemblance increased. That world had already amassed a great store of wisdom literature, and it was only natural for the Jewish sages to covet a like store of their own. This led to more and more imitation of the Greek writings, and eventually considerable assimilation of the Greek ideas.

By the time that happened, however, the basic slant of the Jewish outlook on life had already become fixed; so Jewish wisdom was merely enriched, not unmade, by this new trend. The books that now began to be produced in Judea may have had a Greek coloring and texture, but the stuff inside them was still Hebraic through and through. Their abiding emphasis was still on God as the source of all things, and on morality as the way to all good. Wisdom, in them, was no vague mystical emanation, or recondite intellectual hypostasis. It was simply righteousness. First and last, it was nothing but a sort of sanctified human decency.

CHAPTER 12

THE BOOK OF PROVERBS

Despite its opening line, this book clearly belongs to the period when kings were no more than a romantic memory in Judea. Its earliest sections date back perhaps to around the year 400 B.C.E. and its latest to around 200 B.C.E.. This is made plain by the sort s of problems that are discussed and even more by those that are left unmentioned. No reference is made to the danger of idolatry, which so exercised the Prophets, nor to the value of the Temple ritual, which the Priests were so emphatic about. No time is spent discussing purely national matters–the name Israel does not occur even once in the Proverbs themselves–and the counsel throughout is universalistic. There is a frank appreciation of the good things of this earth–its prizes, honors, riches, and pleasures–and much canny advice as to how these can best be attained. Monogamy is taken for granted, commerce is ranked above husbandry, and prudence, thrift, and enterprise–characteristically urban virtues–are praised without stint. All of which indicates a relatively advanced social life.

The underlying tone, however, is still the one to be found in the more ancient Hebrew books. Though salvation is almost equated with prosperity in this document, the way to attain it is still righteousness.

EXHORTATIONS[1]

INTRODUCTION

The proverbs of Solomon, the son of David, king of Israel:
That men may gain wisdom and instruction,
May understand words of intelligence;
That they may receive instruction in wise conduct,
In rectitude, justice, and honesty;
That sense may be imparted to the simple,
Knowledge and discretion to the inexperienced–
The wise man also may hear and increase his learning,
The man of intelligence acquire sound principles–
That they may understand proverb and parable,
The words of the wise and their epigrams. . . .

A FATHER'S WARNING

Hear, my son, your father's instruction,
And reject not your mother's teaching;
For a graceful garland will they be for your head,
And a chain for your neck.
My son, if sinners entice you, consent not.
If they say, "Come with us, let us lie in wait for the honest,
Let us wantonly ambush the innocent;
Let us swallow them up alive and sound in health,
As Sheol swallows up those who go down to the Pit!
All kinds of precious wealth shall we find,
We shall fill our houses with spoil;

[1]Chapters 1–9 form a section containing hortatory discourses rather than proverbs, and it is probably one of the latest portions of the Book of Proverbs. Modern scholars are inclined to ascribe it to the middle of the third century B.C.E.

Cast in your lot with us,
We will all have one purse"–
My son, walk not in the way with them,
Keep your foot clear of their path;
For their feet run to evil,
They hasten to shed blood. . . .

THE FRUIT OF WISDOM

My son, if you receive my words,
And store my commands within you,
Inclining your ear to wisdom,
And applying your mind to reason;
If you appeal to intelligence,
And lift up your voice to reason;
If you seek her as silver,
And search for her as for hidden treasures–
Then will you understand reverence for the Lord,
And will discover the knowledge of God. . . .

For when wisdom finds a welcome within you,
And knowledge becomes a pleasure to you,
Discretion will watch over you,
Reason will guard you–
Saving you from the way of evil men.

THE WORTH OF WISDOM

How happy is the man who finds wisdom,
The man who gains understanding!
For her income is better than income of silver,
And her revenue than gold.

She is more precious than corals,
And none of your heart's desires can compare with her.
Long life is in her right hand,
In her left are riches and honor.
Her ways are ways of pleasantness,
And all her paths are peace.
She is a tree of life to those who grasp her,
And happy is every one who holds her fast.

The Lord by wisdom founded the earth,
By reason he established the heavens;
By his knowledge the depths are broken up,
And the clouds drop down dew.

My son, keep guard on wisdom and discretion,
Let them not slip from your sight;
They will be life to you,
And an ornament round your neck.
Then you may go your way in security.
Without striking your foot on a stone;
When you rest, you will not be afraid,
When you lie down, your sleep will be sweet;
You will fear no sudden terror,
Nor the storm that falls on the wicked;
For the Lord will be your confidence,
And will keep your foot from the snare.

WISE COUNSELS

Withhold not help from the needy,
When it is in your power to render it.

Say not to your neighbor, "Go, and come again;
Tomorrow I will give," when you have it beside you.
Plot no mischief against your neighbor,
When he lives in confidence beside you.
Do not idly quarrel with a man,
If he have done you no harm.

REPROOF TO THE LAZY

Go to the ant, O sluggard,
Study her ways, and learn wisdom;
For though she has no chief,
No officer, or ruler,
She secures her food in the summer,
She gathers her provisions in the harvest time.
How long will you lie, O sluggard?
When will you rise from your sleep?
[You say] "A little sleep, a little slumber,
A little folding of hands to rest"–
So will poverty come upon you like a footpad,
And want like an armed man.

WHAT THE LORD HATES

Six things the Lord hates,
Seven are an abomination to Him:
Haughty eyes, a lying tongue,
And hands that shed innocent blood;
A mind that plots mischievous schemes,
Feet that are quick to run after evil;
A false witness who utters lies;
And he who sows discord among brothers.

APHORISMS[2]

A wise son makes a glad father;
But a foolish son is a grief to his mother.

Treasures unjustly acquired are of no avail;
But honesty saves from death.

The Lord will not suffer the righteous to hunger;
But He will thwart the desire of the wicked.

A slack hand brings poverty;
But the hand of the diligent brings wealth.

He who reaps in summer acts wisely;
He who sleeps in harvest acts shamefully.

A wise man will take commands;
But a prating fool will fall.

He who walks honestly walks safely;
But he who walks crookedly will be found out.

He who winks with the eye makes trouble;
He who frankly reproves makes peace.

The mouth of the righteous is a fountain of life;
But the mouth of the wicked is filled with violence.

Hatred stirs up strife;
But love draws a veil over all transgressions.

---

[2]This miscellany is culled from what are probably the two oldest sections of the Book of Proverbs, i.e., Chapters 10–22 and 25–29.

On the lips of a sensible man wisdom is found;
But a man without sense needs a rod for his back.

A rich man's wealth is his fortress;
The ruin of the poor is their poverty.

He who pays heed to instruction is on the way of life;
But he who rejects admonition goes astray.

Righteous lips cover up hatred;
But he who lets out slander is a fool.

Where words abound, sin will not be wanting;
But he who holds his tongue acts wisely.

The tongue of the righteous is choice silver;
The mind of the wicked is of little worth.

To a fool it is like sport to do wrong;
But it is hateful to a man of sense.

What the wicked man dreads will befall him;
But the desire of the righteous will be granted.

As the whirlwind passes, so the wicked man vanishes;
But the righteous one is rooted forever.

As vinegar to the teeth, and as smoke to the eyes,
So is the sluggard to those who send him on an errand.

False scales are an abomination to the Lord;
But a just weight is His delight.

When pride comes, scorn comes;
But with the modest is wisdom.

When righteous men prosper, the city exults;
And when wicked men perish, there is jubilation.

The senseless man pours contempt on his neighbor;
But the intelligent man keeps silent.

A talebearer reveals secrets;
But a trustworthy man keeps a confidence.

For want of guidance a people will fall;
But safety lies in a wealth of counselors.

He who becomes surety for a stranger will suffer for it;
But he who hates giving pledges is secure.

A gracious woman wins respect;
And diligent men win riches.

A kindly man does good to himself;
But a cruel man does himself harm.

The wicked man earns illusive wages;
But he who sows righteousness has a true reward.

Like a golden ring in the snout of a sow
Is a beautiful woman lacking in taste.

One man spends, and grows still richer;
Another holds back his due share, only to bring himself to want.

The generous man will be enriched;
And he who waters will himself be watered.

He who holds back grain will be cursed by the people;
But blessing will be upon the head of him who sells it.

He who seeks what is good will win favor;
But he who aims at what is harmful will bring it upon himself.

A good wife is a crown to her husband;
But one who acts shamefully is like rot in his bones.

Better a man of low rank, who works for his living,
Than he who puts on grand airs, yet has nothing to eat.

A righteous man cares for his beast;
But the mercy of the wicked is cruel.

He who tills his ground will have plenty of food;
But he who follows empty pursuits lack sense.

The way of a fool is right in his own eyes;
But a wise man listens to advice.

Wealth acquired by scheming will dwindle;
But he who gathers little by little will increase his store.

Hope deferred makes the heart sick;
But desire fulfilled is a tree of life.

He who walks with wise men will become wise;
But the companion of fools will smart for it.

He who spares his rod hates his son;
But he who loves him seeks to discipline him.

The wise woman builds up her house;
But the foolish one tears it down with her own hands.

The scoffer seeks wisdom, and finds it not;
But to the man of intelligence, knowledge is easy.

Leave the presence of a fool;
You will gain no knowledge from his talk.

Guilt has its home among fools,
Good will, among the upright.

Every man knows his own bitterness,
And in his joy no stranger can share.

Even in laughter the heart may be aching,
And the end of joy may be sorrow.

The simple man trusts everything;
But the sensible man pays heed to his steps.

The wise man is cautious, and keeps away from trouble;
But the fool is blustering and confident in himself.

A man of quick temper acts foolishly;
But a man of discretion is patient.

The poor man is hated even by his neighbor;
But the rich has many friends.

He who despises his neighbor sins;
But happy is he who is kind to the poor.

In all labor there is profit;
But mere talk leads only to penury.

A tranquil mind is health for the body;
But passion is a rot in the bones.

Righteousness exalts a nation;
But sin is a people's ruin.

A gentle answer turns away wrath;
But harsh words stir up anger.

The eyes of the Lord are in every place,
Keeping watch on the evil and the good.

A soothing tongue is a tree of life;
But wild words break the spirit.

A glad heart makes a bright face;
But through sadness of heart the spirit is broken.

For the miserable man is unhappy every day;
But the cheerful man enjoys an incessant feast.

Better a little, with reverence for the Lord,
Than much treasure, and anxiety with it.

Better a dish of herbs, where love is,
Than a fatted ox, and hatred with it.

When no counsel is taken, plans miscarry;
But when there are many advisers, they succeed.

An apt utterance is a joy to a man;
And a word in season – how good is it!

The righteous man studies what he should answer;
But the mouth of the wicked pours out evil.

Bright eyes gladden the heart;
Good news fattens the bones.

All the ways of a man are pure in his own eyes;
But the Lord weighs the motives.

Better a little, with righteousness,
Than great revenues with injustice.

How much better it is to get wisdom than gold,
And more desirable to get understanding than silver.

Pride goes before destruction,
And a haughty spirit before a fall.

It is better to be humble with the lowly
Than to share spoil with the proud.

The laboring man's appetite labors for him,
For his hunger urges him on.

A fickle man sows discord;
And a whisperer separates friends.

He who shuts his eyes is hatching some crooked scheme;
He who tightens his lips concocts some mischief.

Gray hairs are a glorious crown,
Which is won by a righteous life.

A forbearing man is better than a warrior;
He who rules his temper better than one who takes a city.

Better a morsel of dry bread, and peace with it,
Than a house full of feasting, with strife.

He who mocks the poor insults his Maker;
He who rejoices at their calamity will not go unpunished.

Children's children are the crown of old men;
And fathers are the pride of their children.

Lordly words are not fitting for a fool;
Much less are lying words for a lord.

He who overlooks an offense promotes good will;
He who repeats a tale separates friends.

A rebuke sinks deeper into a man of intelligence
Than a hundred lashes into a fool.

Better be met by a bear robbed of her cubs
Than by a fool in his folly.

He who returns evil for good–
Evil will never depart from his house.

Of what use is money in the hand of a fool–
To buy wisdom, when he has no sense?

A friend is friendly at all times;
But a brother is born for adversity.

A man devoid of sense is he who pledges himself,
And becomes security in the presence of his neighbor.

He who begets a fool does it to his sorrow;
And the father of a dolt will have no joy of him.

A happy heart is a healing medicine;
But a broken spirit dries up the bones.

He who spares his words has true wisdom;
And he who holds his temper is a man of sense.

Even a fool is counted wise if he keeps silent,
Intelligent if he shuts his lips.

The recluse seeks his own selfish interests;
He quarrels with every sound principle.

He who is slack at his work
Is brother to him who destroys.

A rich man's wealth is his fortress,
And like a high wall are his riches.

A brother helped by a brother is like a fortified city;
He holds firm as the bar of a castle.

There are friends who play at friendship;
And there is a friend who sticks closer than a brother.

Better a poor man, who walks in his integrity,
Than one who is crooked in his ways although he is rich.

Wealth adds many friends;
But the poor man is estranged from his friend.

Many pay court to the noble;
Everyone is a friend to him who gives gifts.

A foolish son is his father's ruin;
And a quarrelsome wife is like a constant drip.

House and wealth are an inheritance from fathers;
But a sensible wife is a gift from the Lord.

Wine is a mocker, strong drink a brawler;
None who reels under it is wise.

The sluggard will not plow in autumn;
So in harvest he seeks a crop in vain.

Even a child is known by his deeds,
According as his conduct is crooked or straight.

Love not sleep, lest you come to poverty;
Keep your eyes open, and you will have plenty of food.

"Bad, bad!" says the buyer;
But when he has gone, then he boasts.

Bread won by fraud tastes sweet to a man;
But afterward his mouth will be filled with gravel.

A talebearer reveals secrets;
So have nothing to do with a gossip.

Say not, "I will pay back evil!"
Wait for the Lord to help you.

The glory of young men is their strength,
And the beauty of old men is their gray hair.

The doing of right and justice
Is more acceptable to the Lord than sacrifice.

It is better to live in a corner of the housetop
Than to share a spacious house with a quarrelsome wife.

He who closes his ear against the cry of the poor
Will himself also call and not be answered.

The lover of pleasure will come to want;
The lover of wine and oil will not grow rich.

A wicked man puts on a bold face;
But an upright man pays heed to his ways.

A good name is more desirable than great riches,
A good reputation, than silver and gold.

The rich and the poor meet face to face–
The Lord is the creator of them both.

A sensible man foresees danger and hides from it;
But the simple pass on and are punished.

Train up a child in the way he should go,
And even when he is old, he will not depart from it.

What your eyes have seen
Report not hastily to the mob.

Like apples of gold in a setting of carved silver
Is a word that is aptly spoken.

Like an earring of gold or a necklace of fine gold,
Is a wise man's reproof on a listening ear.

Like a draught of snow-cooled water in the time of harvest
Is a faithful messenger to those who send him.

Like clouds with wind that bring no rain
Is the man who boasts of gifts that are not given.

By forbearance a ruler is pacified;
And a soft tongue breaks the bones.

If you find honey, eat no more than you need,
Lest you be sated with it and vomit it up.

Set your foot but sparingly in your neighbor's house;
Lest he be sated with you and give you a cool reception.

Like one who drops vinegar upon a wound
Is he who sings songs to a sorrowful heart.

If your enemy be hungry, give him bread to eat;
And if he be thirsty, give him water to drink.

To eat much honey is not good;
Therefore, be sparing of your compliments.

Like a city breached and defenseless
Is a man who has no control of his temper.

Like snow in summer or rain in harvest,
Honor is unseasonable for a fool.

Like a sparrow flitting, a swallow fluttering,
The curse that is groundless will not reach home.

A whip for the horse, a bridle for the ass,
And a rod for the back of fools.

Answer not a fool according to his folly,
Lest you also become like him.

He cuts off his feet, drinks in disaster,
Who sends a message by a fool.

Like a thorn-stick brandished by a drunkard
Is a parable in the mouth of fools.

The master workman does everything himself;
But the fool hires a passer-by.

Like a dog returning to his vomit
Is a fool repeating his folly.

You see a man wise in his own eyes?
There is more hope for a fool than for him.

The sluggard is wiser in his own eyes
Than seven men who can give an apt answer.

Like a man who seizes a dog by the ears
Is the passer-by who meddles with a quarrel not his own.

Like a madman who hurls deadly firebrands and arrows
Is he who deceives his neighbor and then says, "Was I not joking?"

Where there is no wood, a fire goes out;
And where there is no whisperer, a quarrel dies down.

He who digs a pit will fall into it;
And he who rolls a stone–it will come back upon him.

A lying tongue brings destruction to itself;
And a flattering mouth works its own ruin.

Boast not of tomorrow;
For you know not what a day may bring forth.

Let another man praise you, and not your own mouth–
A stranger, and not your own lips.

A stone is heavy, and sand is weighty;
But the annoyance caused by a fool is heavier than both.

Wrath is ruthless, and anger a torrent;
But before jealousy who can stand?

Better is open rebuke
Than hidden love.

Sincere are the wounds of a friend;
But deceitful are the kisses of an enemy.

He who is sated with food disdains the honeycomb;
But to the hungry man, every bitter thing is sweet.

Like a bird that strays from her nest
Is a man who strays from his home.

Better is a neighbor near at hand
Than a brother far away.

As face reflects face in water,
So the mind of man reflects man.

As the smelter is for silver, and the furnace for gold,
So a man is tested by his praise.

The wicked flee when no man pursues;
But the righteous are as bold as a lion.

A man who is proud and oppresses the poor
Is like a lashing rain that leaves no food.

He who reproves men will get more thanks in the end
Than he who flatters with the tongue.

He who robs his father or his mother, saying, "There is no wrong in it,"
Is companion to him who destroys.

He who stiffens his neck against many reproofs
Will suddenly be broken beyond repair.

He who loves wisdom gladdens his father;
But he who keeps company with harlots wastes his substance.

The rod of correction gives wisdom;
But a child who is left to himself brings disgrace on his mother.

When the wicked are in power, crime increases;
But the righteous will see their downfall.

QUATRAINS[3]

Rob not the poor because he is poor,
And crush not the needy in the gate;
For the Lord will defend their cause,
And will rob their robbers of life.

Form no friendship with a hot-tempered man,
And go not with a man of passion;
Lest you learn his ways,
And get yourself into a snare.

Toil not to become rich, nor seek needless wealth;
Scarcely have you set your eye upon it, when it is gone!
For riches make themselves wings,
Like an eagle that flies toward the heavens.

Dine not with a miserly man,
And lust not after his dainties;

[3]These somewhat elaborate quatrains are taken from a section (Chapters 22–29) that appears to be of relatively late origin.

For they will be like phlegm in the throat,
And nausea in the gullet.

"Eat and drink," he says to you,
But in his heart he begrudges you;
You must spit out the morsel you have eaten,
And lose your good things.

Remove not the widow's landmark,
Nor enter the fields of orphans;
For their champion is strong,
And he will defend their cause against you.

Apply your mind to instruction
And your ear to words of knowledge.
Withhold not chastisement from a child;
For if you beat him with the rod, he will not die.

Listen, my son, and be wise,
And keep straight on the way.
Be not found among winebibbers,
Or gluttonous eaters of flesh.

Look not on wine when it is red and sparkles in the cup;
It may go down smoothly,
But at the end it bites like a serpent
And stings like an adder.

You will see strange sights,
And will utter weird words;
You will be like a man asleep at sea,
Asleep in the midst of a violent storm.

A wise man is better than a strong man,
And a man of knowledge, than a man of might;

For by wise guidance you wage war,
And victory lies in a wealth of counselors.

Rejoice not when your enemy falls,
Nor exult when he stumbles;
Lest the Lord see it and be displeased,
And withhold His anger from him.

Fret not over evildoers,
Nor be envious of the wicked;
For the evil man will have no future,
The lamp of the wicked will be put out.

Bear not unfounded witness against your neighbor,
Nor deceive with your lips;
Say not, "I will do to him as he has done to me,
I will requite the man according to his work."

DISCOURSES[4]

ON THIS AND THAT

There are three things too wonderful for me,
Four that I cannot understand:
The way of a vulture in the air,
The way of a serpent on a crag,
The way of a ship in the heart of the sea,
And the way of a man with a woman.

---

[4]These gnomic discourses are to be found in the section (Chapters 30–31) that scholars consider to be the very latest in the Book of Proverbs.

Under three things the earth quakes,
Under four it cannot bear up:
A slave when he becomes a king,
A fool when he is sated with food,
An unpopular woman when she is married,
And a maidservant when she supplants her mistress.

There are four things on earth that are small,
And yet are exceedingly wise:
The ants – they are no strong folk,
Yet they lay up their food in the summer;
The marmots – they are no mighty folk,
Yet they make their home in the crags;
The locusts – they have no king,
Yet they march all in ranks;
The lizard – she holds on by her forefeet,
Yet she finds her way into the king's palace.

There are three things that are lordly in stride,
Four that are stately in gait:
The lion, which is mightiest among beasts,
And turns not back before any;
The strutting cock, and the he-goat,
And the king at the head of his people.

If you have been foolish in exalting yourself,
Or if you have hatched a scheme,
Lay your hand upon your mouth!
For, as the pressing of milk brings forth curds,
And the pressing of the nose brings forth blood,
So the pressing of anger brings forth strife.

ADVICE TO A KING

What, O my son? O son of my womb?
What, O son of my vows?

Give not your strength to women,
Nor your love to those who are the ruin of kings.
Nor be it for kings, O Lemuel,
For kings to drink wine,
For princes to quaff strong drink;
Lest, as they drink, they forget the law,
And violate the rights of any in trouble.
Give strong drink to him who is perishing,
And wine to the bitter in heart;
That as he drinks he may forget his poverty,
And think no more on behalf of his misery.
Open your mouth on behalf of the dumb,
In defense of the rights of all who are suffering;
Open your mouth on the side of justice,
And defend the rights of the poor and the needy.

THE WOMAN OF VIRTUE

If one can find a good wife,
She is worth far more than corals.
Her husband puts his trust in her,
And finds no lack of gain.

She brings him good, and not harm
All the days of his life.
She sorts out wool and flax
And works it up as she wills.

She is like the ships of the merchant;
She brings her food from afar.
She rises while it is still night
And gives her household food,
With a portion for her maidens.

She examines a field and buys it;
With her earnings she plants a vineyard.
She girds her loins with strength,
And she makes her arms strong.

She perceives that her work is profitable
So her lamp goes not out at night.
She lays her hand on the distaff;
Her fingers grasp the spindle.

She stretches her hand to the poor,
She extends her arms to the needy.
She is not afraid of the snow for her household;
For her household are all clothed in scarlet.

She makes coverlets for herself,
Her clothing is linen and purple.
Her husband is known at the gates,
As he sits among the elders of the land.

She makes linen vests and sells them.
She supplies the merchants with girdles.
She is clothed with strength and dignity,
And she laughs at the days to come.

She opens her mouth in wisdom,
And kindly counsel is on her tongue.
She looks well after her household,
And eats not the bread of idleness.

Her children rise up, and bless her–
Her husband also, and praises her:
[Saying] "Many women have done well,
But you have excelled them all."

Charms are deceptive, and beauty is a breath;
But a woman who reveres the Lord – she will be praised.
Give her the due reward of her work;
And let her deeds bring her praise at the gates.

CHAPTER 13

THE DRAMA OF JOB

The Book of Proverbs, despite its occasional flashes of cynicism, is essentially an orthodox document, for its whole philosophy is based on the conviction that the righteous and the wicked are rewarded or punished according to their just deserts. By contrast, the Book of Job is essentially unorthodox, for it starts out by insisting that such a conviction is not borne out by the facts of life. Consequently, critical scholars believe the document must have been composed at a relatively late date–perhaps the third or even second century B.C.E.–when their own bitter experience plus Greek influence combined to make the Jews less naive than in earlier times.

In form this book is a philosophical symposium built into the framework of what may have been an old folktale. It deals with the most perplexing of human problems: Why do the innocent suffer? According to the story, Job was a virtuous old sheik, a man "perfect and upright, who feared God and shunned wickedness." Nevertheless, of a sudden all manner of evils befell him: his seven sons and three daughters were killed, all his flocks were destroyed, all his slaves were slaughtered, and he himself was smitten with leprosy. His first reaction was to suffer in silence. When his wife, a less patient soul, urges him to "curse God and die," he answers:

"You speak as one of the foolish women might speak. Should we, indeed, receive good from God, and should we not receive evil too?" (Job 2:10)

Eventually three of his friends come to comfort him as he sits on an ash-heap and scrapes his sores; but when they seem unable to find words to express their sympathy, the strain proves too much for Job. He suspects that they, being conventional folk, probably imagine that God is punishing him for some sin he has committed. Whereupon he bursts forth bitterly:

"Why did I not die at birth,
Come forth from the womb and expire? . . .
For then I might have lain down and been quiet,
I would have slept and been at rest. . . .
Why is light given to the miserable,
And life to the embittered in spirit,
Who long for death, but it comes not. . . .
And who would be delighted if they could [but] find the grave?" (Job 3:11, 13, 21–22)

This naturally shocks his friends, and they begin to argue with him. The first insists that God is probably disciplining Job for his own good. Says this friend:

"Happy, indeed, is the man whom God reproves;
So don't reject the instruction of the Almighty.
For He wounds, but He binds up;
He smites, but His hands heal.
He will rescue you from six troubles,
Yes, in seven no harm will touch you." (Job 5:17–19)

Job, however, answers that he does not stand in need of any such disciplining. Addressing God, he cries:

"Have I sinned? What do I unto Thee, O thou keeper of man?
Why does Thou make me a target for Thyself?" (Job 7:20)

Whereupon the second friend begins to upbraid Job, saying:

"How long will you utter such things? . . .
Does God pervert justice?

Or the Almighty pervert the right? . . .
If you were but pure and straight,
Then indeed he would bestir himself in your behalf." (Job 8:2, 6)

To which Job replies:

"Nevertheless I will make complaint freely.
I will speak my own bitterness,
I will say unto God, 'Do not condemn me;
Tell me why Thou dost quarrel with me. . . .
Why shouldst Thou search for my sin,
Although Thou knowest that I am not guilty'?" (Job 10:1, 6)

Thereupon, the third friend is so outraged that he cries:

"Shall your boastings put men to silence?
And when you scoff, is no one to rebuke you?
For you have said, 'My teaching is pure,
And I am clean in [God's] sight.'
But would that God might speak,
That He might open His lips against you,
And tell you the secrets of wisdom! . . .
For then you would know that God is exacting less of you than your guilt deserves." (Job 11:3–6)

Thus, the argument continues on and on. Job readily admits that God is omniscient and omnipotent, but he insists that neither of these attributes proves God to be just. Says he:

"Lo, God destroys the blameless as well as the wicked,
If a scourge slays suddenly,
He mocks at the despair of the innocent!
The earth is given into the hand of the wicked. . . .
If it is not He [who does these things], then who is it?" (Job 9:22–24)

God, it would seem , is deliberately seeking to put Job in the wrong:

"I know that . . . I am slated to be guilty. . . .
If I should wash myself in the snow,
And clean my hands with lye,
Even then wouldst Thou plunge me into the mire,
So that my own clothes would abhor me. . . .
O that there were an umpire between us,
Who would lay his hands on both of us. . . .
Then I might speak and not be afraid that God is dishonest
toward me." (Job 9:28–35)

In spite of all that his friends may say to the contrary, Job insists that God deals most unfairly with human beings:

"When I think of it, I am amazed,
And shuddering lays hold of my flesh.
Why do the wicked live,
Grow old, and amass wealth?
Their descendants are established with them in their sight,
And their offspring before their very eyes.
Their houses are safe from terror,
And the rod of God is not upon them. . . .
Though they say to God, 'Get away! . . .
Who is the Almighty, that we should serve Him?
And what good does it do to pray to Him?" (Job 21:6–15)

Thus does Job hold forth, challenging all that is taken for granted by his orthodox friends, until finally God himself enters into the debate. He speaks out of a whirlwind, hurling one question after another at Job, completely overwhelming him.

"Who is this that obscures counsel
By words without knowledge?
Gird up now your loins like a man,
That I may question you, and do you instruct me.

"Where were you when I laid the foundation of the earth?
Declare, if you have insight.
Who fixed its measurements?—if you should know.
Or who stretched a line over it?
Upon what were its bases sunk,
Or who laid its cornerstone,
When the morning stars sang together,
And all the heavenly beings shouted for joy?

"Who enclosed the sea with doors,
When it burst forth, issuing from the womb,
When I made the cloud its covering. . . .
And said, 'Thus far shall you come and no farther,
And here shall your proud waves be stayed'?

"Have you ever in your life commanded the morning? . . .
Have you gone to the sources of the sea,
Or walked in the hollows of the deep?
Have the gates of death been revealed to you,
Or can you see the gates of darkness?
Have you considered the breadth of the earth?
Tell, if you know all this.

"Which is the way where light dwells,
And which is the place of darkness? . . .

"Gird up your loins now like a man;
I will ask you, and do you instruct me.
Will you, indeed, break down my right?
Will you make me guilty that you may be innocent?
Or have you an arm like God,
And can you thunder with a voice like His?
Deck yourself, now, with majesty and eminence,
And clothe yourself with glory and splendor.

Scatter abroad the rage of your wrath;
And look upon everyone that is proud and abase him.

Look upon everyone who is proud and bring him low;
And crush the wicked where they stand.
Bury them in the dust likewise;
Bind up their faces in the hidden place.
Then I indeed will praise you,
That your own right hand can deliver you. (Job 38:2–19; 41:6–14)

And thus, Job is made to realize at last the arrogance of his complaints. He becomes aware that the entire problem of human suffering is infinitesimally small when seen in relation to the entire cosmic scheme. Whereupon he is forced to confess:

"Lo, I am of small account.
What shall I answer Thee? . . .
I have uttered that which I did not understand,
Things too wonderful for me, which I did not know. . . .
I knew Thee only by hearsay,
But now my eye has seen Thee.
Therefore I retract and repent,
In dust and ashes." (Job 40:4; 42:2–6)

CHAPTER 14

ECCLESIASTES

This extraordinary little book is attributed to King Solomon and is a series of gentle admonitions.

ALL IS VANITY

Vanity of vanities. . . .
Vanity of vanities, all is vanity!
What does a man gain from all his toil
At which he toils beneath the sun?
One generation goes, and another comes,
While the earth endures forever.
The sun rises and the sun sets,
And hastens to the place where he rose.
The wind blows toward the south,
And returns to the north.
Turning, turning, the wind blows,
And returns upon its circuit.
All rivers run to the sea,
But the sea is never full;
To the place where the rivers flow,

There they continue to flow.
All things are wearisome;
One cannot recount them.
The eye is not satisfied with seeing,
Nor is the ear filled with hearing.
Whatsoever has been is that which will be;
And whatsoever has been done is that which will be done;
And there is nothing new under the sun.
Is there a thing of which it is said, 'Lo, this is new'?
It was already in existence in the ages
Which were before us.
There is no memory of earlier people;
And likewise of later people who shall be,
There will be no memory with those who are later still.

WISDOM IS VAIN

I, Kohelet, was king over Israel in Jerusalem; and I set my mind to search and to investigate through wisdom everything that is done beneath the heavens. It is an evil task that God has given the sons of men with which to occupy themselves. I have seen everything that has been done under the sun; and lo, everything is vanity and striving for the wind. . . .

I thought within myself thus: I am great and have increased in wisdom above all that were before me over Jerusalem; and my mind has seen abundant wisdom and knowledge. So I set my mind to knowing wisdom and to knowing madness and folly. [But] I am convinced that this too is striving for the wind.

For with more wisdom is more worry,
And increase of knowledge is increase of sorrow.

WEALTH IS VAIN

I said to myself: "Come now, let me test you with mirth; so enjoy yourself." But this also was vanity. . . . I made myself great works; I built myself houses; I planted vineyards for myself; I made myself gardens and parks. . . . I bought male and female slaves and . . . gathered for myself silver and gold, the treasure of kings and provinces. . . . And nothing that my eyes desired did I withhold from them. . . . Then I reviewed all my works which my hands had made, and the toil which I had expended in making them, and lo, everything was vanity and striving for the wind, and there was no profit under the sun. . . . So I hated life, for everything that is done under the sun seemed to me wrong, for everything is vanity and striving for the wind. (Ecclesiastes 1:2–2:18)

LIFE IS VAIN

For there is one fate for both man and beast . . . as the one dies, so dies the other. The same breath is in all of them, and man has no advantage over the beast; for everything is vanity. All go to one place; all are from the dust, and all return to the dust. Who knows that the spirit of man goes upward and that the spirit of the beast goes downward to the earth? . . .

I considered once more all the oppressions that are practiced under the sun: for example, the tears of the oppressed, with none to comfort them, and the strength in the hands of their oppressors, with none to comfort them. So I congratulated the dead who were already dead, rather than the living who are still alive. And happier than both of them did I regard him who had never been, who had not seen the wicked work which is done under the sun. . . . (Ecclesiastes 3:19–4:4)

And so I have seen wicked men carried to the tomb and praised from the holy place and lauded in the city where they had acted thus. . . .

There is a vanity which is wrought upon the earth, namely, that there are righteous men to whom it happens in accordance with what should be done to the wicked, and there are wicked men to whom it happens in accordance with what should be done to the righteous. I say that this too is vanity.

EAT, DRINK, AND BE MERRY

So I commend mirth; for there is nothing good for man under the sun except to eat, drink, and be merry; for this will stay by him in his toil during the course of his life which God gives him under the sun. (Ecclesiastes 8:10, 14–15)

Go, eat your food with gladness, and drink your wine with a happy mind. . . . Enjoy life with the wife whom you love all the days of your empty life, which He has given you under the sun, all your empty life. (Ecclesiastes 9:7, 9)

CONCLUSION

Thus declared the gentle cynic who wrote this little book. But the pious editor has the final word, for most piously he adds:

The conclusion of the matter, all having been heard: Fear God and keep His commands. For this concerns all mankind, that God brings every work into judgment with regard to everything concealed, whether it be good or evil. (Ecclesiastes 12:13)

CHAPTER 15

PSALMS

In Hebrew the Book of Psalms is called simply Tehillim–Praises–*and that explains why only a little of it can be included in this anthology. Its primary orientation is toward God rather than man, and its prevailing appeal is to the heart rather than the mind. Nevertheless, as the following excerpts make plain, some of the Psalms do have that mundane, humane, ethical emphasis that I have taken to be the hallmark of Wisdom.*

PSALM 1

How happy is the man who has not walked in the counsel of
 the wicked,
Nor stood in the way of sinners,
Nor sat in the seat of scoffers!
But his delight is in the Law of the Lord,
And in His Law does he study day and night.
For he is like a tree planted by streams of water,
That yields its fruit in its season,
And whose leaf does not wither;
And whatever it bears comes to maturity.

The wicked are not so;
But are like the chaff which the wind drives away.
Therefore, the wicked will not stand in the judgment,
Nor sinners in the assembly of the righteous.
For the Lord knows the way of the righteous.
But the way of the wicked will perish.

PSALM 15

Who may sojourn in the pavilion, O Lord?
Who may dwell upon Thy holy hill?
"He who walks blamelessly, and does right,
And speaks truth from his heart.
He is not hasty with his tongue.
He does no wrong to his fellows;
Nor does he take blame upon himself because of his neighbor.
In his eyes a bad man is despised;
But he honors those who fear the Lord.
He swears to his own hurt and does not retract.
He does not put out his money on interest,
Nor take a bribe against the innocent.
He who does such things will never be moved."

PSALM 37

Fret not yourself because of evildoers,
Be not incensed because of wrongdoers;
For they will soon wither like grass,
And fade away like the green herb.

Trust in the Lord and do good;
Inhabit the land and feed in security.

Take your delight in the Lord,
And He will give you the desire of your heart.

Commit your way unto the Lord,
And trust in Him; and He will act.
He will bring forth your right like the light,
And your just cause like the noonday.

Wait patiently for the Lord and hope in Him;
Fret not yourself because of him who makes his way prosper,
Him who succeeds in his plans.

Cease from anger, and forsake wrath;
Fret not yourself; it does nothing but harm.
For evildoers shall be cut off;
While those who wait upon the Lord shall possess the land.

Yet a little while and the wicked shall be no more;
Though you look hard at his place, he will not be there.
But the meek shall possess the land,
And rejoice in abundant prosperity.

Though the wicked plot against the innocent,
And gnash his teeth at him,
The Lord laughs at him;
For He sees that his day will come

The wicked draw the sword and bend their bow,
To bring down the poor and needy,
To slay those whose way is right.
Their sword shall enter their own hearts,
And their bows shall be broken.

Better is the little of the righteous
Than the wealth of many wicked.

For the resources of the wicked shall be broken,
But the Lord supports the righteous.

The Lord knows the days of the innocent,
And their possession abides forever.
They shall not be put to shame in bad times,
And in the time of famine they shall be satisfied.

For the wicked shall perish;
And the enemies of the Lord,
Like a brand in the furnace,
Shall vanish in smoke.

If the wicked borrows, he does not pay back;
But the righteous is generous and gives.
Those who bless him shall possess the land,
But those who curse him shall be cut off.

The steps of a man are from the Lord,
And He establishes him with whose way He is pleased.
Though he fall, he shall not lie prostrate,
For the Lord holds his hand.

I have been young, and now I am old;
But I have not seen the righteous forsaken,
Nor his descendants begging their bread.
He is always generous and ever lending,
And his descendants become a blessing.

Shun evil and do good,
So shall you abide forever,
For the Lord loves the right,
And He does not desert His saints.

They are kept forever,
But the descendants of the wicked are cut off.

The upright shall possess the land,
And shall dwell therein forever.

The mouth of the upright utters wisdom,
And his tongue speaks justice.
The law of his God is in his heart;
His steps do not slip.

When the wicked spies upon the upright,
And seeks to kill him,
The Lord will not deliver him into his hand,
Nor will He declare him guilty when he is brought to trial.

Wait for the Lord, and keep His way;
And He will exalt you to possess the land.
You shall gaze upon the destruction of the wicked.

I saw the wicked triumphing,
And towering aloft like the cedar of Lebanon;
But I passed by—and lo, he was not!
When I sought for him he was not to be found.

Watch integrity and look upon right;
For there is a posterity for the man of peace.
But lawbreakers are wholly destroyed;
The posterity of the wicked is cut off.

The help of the innocent comes from the Lord;
Their strength is He in time of need.
The Lord helps them and rescues them;
He rescues them from the wicked and makes them victorious,
Because they trust in Him.

PSALM 49

Hear this, all you peoples;
Give heed, all you dwellers in the world,

Sons of men, and all mankind,
Both rich and poor.
My mouth speaks wisdom,
And my heart's meditation is insight.
I incline my ear to proverb;
I solve my riddle on the lyre. . . .
Even wise men die;
The fool and the brutish alike perish,
And leave their wealth to others.
Their graves are their everlasting home,
Their dwelling throughout the ages,
Though lands are named after them.
But man is an ox without understanding;
He is like the beasts that perish.
This is the fate of those who are self-sufficient,
And the end of those who are satisfied with their own words.
Like sheep they are appointed to Sheol. . . .

PSALM 133

Lo, how good and lovely it is
When brethren dwell together as one.
Like the goodly oil upon the head,
Which flows down upon the beard, Aaron's beard,
That flows down upon the edge of his robes,
So is the dew of Hermon that flows down upon the mountains of Zion;
For there has the Lord commanded the blessing:
Life for evermore.

CHAPTER 16

SOLOMON'S DECISION

The following excerpt is from I Kings, 3:16–28 and is quoted here only because it is so distinctly an example of wisdom literature.

Then two women of ill fame came to the king and stood before him, and the one woman said: "O, my lord, this woman and I dwell in the same house; and I gave birth to a child while she was there. Then, on the third day after I was delivered, this woman also gave birth to a child and we were together, there being no stranger present. But the child of this woman died in the night and she took my child from my side while I slept, and laid it in her bosom and laid her dead child in my bosom. Thus, when I arose toward morning to nurse my child, behold, it was dead; but when I was able to examine it closely in the morning, behold, it was not my child which I had borne."

Whereupon the other woman said: "No, but the living child is mine and the dead child is your child."

But the first woman was saying at the same time: "No, but the living child is mine and the dead child is your child."

Thus they spoke before the king.

Then the king said: "This one declares, 'This is my child, the living one, and your child is dead.' And the other declares, 'No; but your son is the dead and my son is the living.' So get me a sword."

And they brought in a sword before the king. The king then said: "Cut the living child in two and give half to one and half to the other."

But the woman to whom the living child really belonged spoke to the king–for her motherly tenderness was aroused for her son–and she said: "O, my lord, give her the living child, and by no means slay it."

The other, however, interrupted: "It shall be neither mine nor yours! Divide it!"

Then the king answered and said: "Give her [the first woman] the living child, and by no means slay it, for she is its mother."

Now when all Israel heard of the judgment that the king had rendered, they stood in awe of the king; for they perceived that the wisdom of God was in him to administer justice. (I Kings, 3:16–28)

PART II

THE POST-BIBLICAL PERIOD

INTRODUCTION

The literature belonging to the post-biblical period was as rich in content as it was varied in form. It was written in three languages, thus giving the greatest proof of the extent to which the Jews had broadened their cultural contacts. Most of the documents were naturally couched in Hebrew, which was still Israel's holy tongue. Others, however, were set down in Aramaic, a Mesopotamian dialect that had belatedly become the vernacular throughout Palestine. Still others were written in Greek, the language most familiar to the millions of Jews who were now living all around the Mediterranean.

It is difficult to classify all that was produced in these three languages. The bulk of the literature was in a sense scriptural, since it was modeled on the writings that had already become sacred to the Jews. A number of the new documents came to be actually included in the Septuagint, the first Greek version of the Jewish Scriptures, and later in the Vulgate, the first Latin version. They formed what was eventually called the Apocrypha–a sort of semi-sacred appendix to the Bible.[1]

[1]The Apocrypha is included in *The Complete Bible,* translated into "American" and published by the University of Chicago Press–thus making it possible for this anthology to continue quoting from that source.

In addition, a significant body of rabbinical teaching emerged during this period. This made no pretensions to being scriptual–it was not even written down until much later–yet it seems to have made a far deeper impression on the Jews and certainly acquired in the end incomparably more sanctity.

Finally, there was the beginning of strictly secular writing on the part of Jews, all of it in Greek, and much of it intended for general, not just Jewish, consumption.

Much that deserves to be regarded as wisdom was present in all three types of literature; so selections are given from each in turn.

SECTION ONE

THE APOCRYPHA

The canon of the Jewish Scriptures had already been effectually closed. It was impossible for any new work to become absolutely sacred. But some could still become at least semi-sacred. And that actually happened to a considerable number of books written during this relatively late period.

Most of those books cannot concern us here, since they were primarily mystical, not ethical, and dealt more with the future world than the present. They claimed to be apocalypses that offered a comfort that was altogether delusory, and they were, therefore, bound in the end to cause only harm, not good. They were opiates lulling the people into a blind belief that a miracle would soon and suddenly save them. Consequently, they can hardly be counted books of wisdom. The latter are necessarily stimulants, not opiates, for they tell men to look and do, not shut their eyes and wish.

However, such books, too, were produced during this period, and they were of conspicuous quality, as the following selections will demonstrate.

CHAPTER 17

THE APHORISMS OF BEN SIRA

This document, called in Latin Ecclesiasticus, *closely resembles the* Book of Proverbs. *It is, however, the work of a single author, and–this is without parallel–it bears his own name. In addition, being a somewhat later product, it shows more obvious traces of Hellenic influence. The customs described in it are typically Greek rather than Hebrew, and so are many of the attitudes. The author shares the taste of the Epicurean philosophers for bitter topics like the uncertainty of happiness, the unreliability of friends, and most of all the frailty of women. That, it seems, was the chief reason why the book, despite its strain of deep religiosity and stern moral tone, was never allowed to become part of the Bible.*

Nothing is known about the author except that he must have lived in Palestine early in the second century B.C.E., *was a lay scholar, had evidently traveled, and wrote in Hebrew. (This last fact, curiously, was not established until after 1896, when fragments of the original Hebrew text were discovered in a synagogue attic in Cairo.) His maxims show him to have been adequately disillusioned about men, completely distrustful of women, yet at the same time a warm advocate of social justice and moral probity.*

WISE COUNSEL CONCERNING MEN

Do not quarrel with a powerful man,
Or you may fall into his hands.

Do not contend with a rich man,
Or he may outweigh you.
Gold has been the destruction of many,
And has perverted the minds of kings.
Do not quarrel with a garrulous man,
And do not add fuel to the fire.
Do not make sport of an uneducated man,
Or you may dishonor your own forefathers.
Do not reproach a man when he turns from his sin;
Remember that we are all liable to punishment.

Do not treat a man with disrespect when he is old,
For all of us are growing old.
Do not exult over a man who is dead;
Remember that we are all going to die.
Do not neglect the discourse of wise men,
But busy yourself with their proverbs,
For from them you will gain instruction,
And learn to serve great men.
Do not miss the discourse of old men,
For they learned it from their fathers.
From them you will gain understanding,
And learn to return an answer in your time of need.
Do not kindle the coals of a sinner,
Or you may be burned with the flame of his fire. . . .

Do not lend to a man who is stronger than you,
Or if you do, act as though you had lost it.
Do not give surety beyond your means,
And if you give surety, regard it as something you will have to pay.

Do not go to law with a judge,
For in view of his dignity they will decide for him.
Do not travel with a reckless man,

So that he may not overburden you.
For he will do just as he pleases,
And you will perish through his folly.

Do not fight with a hot-tempered man,
And do not travel across the desert with him,
For bloodshed is as nothing in his eyes,
And where there is no help, he will strike you down.
Do not take counsel with a fool,
For he will not be able to keep the matter secret.
Do not do a secret thing before a stranger,
For you do not know what he will bring forth. . . .

SHARP COUNSEL CONCERNING WOMEN

Do not be jealous about the wife of your bosom,
And do not teach her an evil lesson, to your own hurt.
Do not give your soul to a woman,
So that she will trample on your strength.
Do not greet a prostitute,
Or you may fall into her snares.
Do not associate with a woman singer,
Or you may be caught by her wiles.
Do not look closely at a girl,
Or you may be entrapped in penalties on her account.

Do not give yourself to prostitutes,
So that you may not lose your inheritance.
Do not look around in the streets of the city,
And do not wander in the unfrequented parts of it.
Avert your eyes from a beautiful woman,
And do not look closely at beauty that belongs to someone else.
Many have been led astray by a woman's beauty,

And love is kindled by it like a fire.
Do not ever sit at table with a married woman,
And do not feast and drink with her,
Or your heart may turn away to her,
And you may slip into spiritual ruin.

APHORISMS ON FRIENDSHIP

Do not forsake an old friend,
For a new one is not equal to him.
A new friend is new wine;
When it grows old, you will enjoy drinking it.
Do not envy the glory of a sinner;
For you do not know what disaster awaits him.

Do not indulge in too much luxury,
Do not be tied to its expense.
Do not be impoverished because of feasting on borrowed money
When you have nothing in your purse.
A workman who is a drunkard will never get rich;
The man who despises little things will gradually fail;
Wine and women make men of understanding stand aloof;
And the man who is devoted to prostitutes is reckless. . . .

If you never repeat what you are told,
You will fare none the worse.
Before friend or foe do not recount it,
And unless it would be sinful of you, do not reveal it.
For someone has heard you and watched you,
And when the time comes he will hate you.
If you hear something said, let it die with you,
Have courage, it will not make you burst! . . .

Question a friend; perhaps he did not do it;
Or if he did, so that he will not do it again. (Ben Sira 18:32–19:13)

One man keeps silence and is considered wise;
While another is hated for his loquacity.
One man keeps silence because he has nothing to say;
And another keeps silence because he knows it is the time for it.
A wise man will keep silence till his time comes,
But a boaster and a fool miss the fitting time.
The man who talks excessively is detested,
And he who takes it on himself to speak is hated. (Ben Sira 20:5–8)

APHORISMS ON GOOD MANNERS

If you sit at a great table,
Do not gulp at it,
And do not say, "How much there is on it!"
Remember that an envious eye is wrong.
What has been created that is worse than the eye?
That is why it sheds tears on every face.
Do not reach out your hand wherever it looks,
And do not crowd your neighbor in the dish;
Be considerate of him of your own accord,
And be thoughtful in everything.
Eat like a human being what is served to you,
Do not champ your food, or you will be detested.

Be the first to leave off for good manners' sake,
And do not be greedy, or you will give offense.
Even though you are seated in a large company,
Do not be the first to help yourself.

How adequate a little is for a well-bred man!
He does not have to gasp upon his bed!
Healthy sleep results from moderation in eating;
One gets up in the morning, in good spirits.
The distress of sleeplessness and indigestion
And colic attend the greedy man.
If you are compelled to eat,
Get up in the middle of the meal and stop eating.
Listen to me, my child, and do not disregard me.
And in the end you will find my words true. (Ben Sira 31:12–22)

FOLLY AND WISDOM

A proverb on the lips of a fool will be refused.
For he will not utter it at the proper time.
One man is kept from sinning through poverty,
So his conscience does not prick him when he goes to rest.
Another loses his own life from sheer embarrassment,
And destroys it by his senseless expression.
Another out of embarrassment makes promises to his friend,
And so makes him his enemy for nothing.
A lie is a bad blot on a man;
It is continually found on the lips of the ignorant.
A thief is better than a habitual liar,
But they are both doomed to destruction.
Dishonor is habitual with a liar,
And his shame attends him continually.
A man who speaks wisely makes his way in the world,
And a man of good sense pleases the Great.
The man who cultivates the soil makes his heap high,
And the man who pleases the Great atones for wrongdoing.
Gifts and presents can blind the eyes of wise men,
And avert reproofs like a muzzle on the mouth.

Hidden wisdom and concealed treasure –
What is the use of either of them?
A man who conceals his folly is better
Than a man who conceals his wisdom. (Ben Sira 20:20–31)

COUNSEL CONCERNING SIN

My child, if you have sinned, do not do it again,
And pray over your former sins.
Flee from sin as from the face of a snake;
For if you approach it, it will bite you.
Its teeth are lion's teeth,
And destroy the souls of men.
All iniquity is like a two-edged sword;
A blow from it cannot be healed.
Terror and violence lay waste riches;
So the house of a proud man will be laid waste.
The prayer from a poor man's mouth reaches his ears.
And his judgment comes speedily.

A man who hates reproof is walking in the sinner's steps,
But he who fears the Lord will turn to Him in his heart.
A man who is mighty in tongue is known afar off,
But a thoughtful man knows when he slips.
The man who builds his house with other men's money
Is like one who gathers stones for winter.
An assembly of wicked men is like tow wrapped together;
For their end is a blazing fire.
The way of sinners is made smooth with stones,
But at the end of it is the pit of Hades.

WISDOM CONCERNING WISE MEN AND FOOLS

The man who keeps the Law controls his thoughts,
And wisdom is the consummation of the fear of the Lord.

The man who is not shrewd will not be instructed,
But there is a shrewdness that spreads bitterness.
A wise man's knowledge abounds like a flood,
And his counsel is like a living spring.
The heart of a fool is like a broken dish;
It will hold no knowledge.
If a man of understanding hears a wise saying,
He commends it and adds to it;
A self-indulgent man hears it, and it displeases him,
And he throws it behind his back.

The discourse of a fool is like a burden on a journey;
But enjoyment is found on the lips of a man of understanding.
The utterance of a sensible man will be asked for in an assembly,
And what he says they will think over in their minds.
To a fool wisdom is like a ruined house,
And the knowledge of a man without understanding is stuff that will not bear investigation.
To the foolish man, instruction is fetters on his feet
And handcuffs on his right hand.
A fool raises his voice when he laughs,
But a shrewd man will smile quietly.
To a sensible man, instruction is like a gold ornament
And like a bracelet on his right arm. (Ben Sira 21:1–21)

CHAPTER 18

THE ADMONITIONS OF TOBIT

The Book of Tobit is a quaint didactic novelette written originally perhaps in Greek by a devout Jew living–again perhaps–in Egypt, some time in the second century B.C.E. *The following passage taken from Chapter 4 (verses 3–19) is typical of the wisdom literature that was so popular in Israel throughout this period.*

So Tobit called to his son and said:

"My boy, when I die, bury me, and do not neglect your mother; provide for her as long as you live. Do what is pleasing to her, and do not grieve her in anything. Remember, my boy, that she faced many dangers for you before your birth, and when she dies, bury her beside me in one grave. All your life, my boy, remember the Lord, our God; do not consent to sin and transgress His commands. Act uprightly all your life, and do not walk in the ways of wrongdoing.

"For if you do right, prosperity will attend your undertakings. To all who act uprightly, give charity from your property, and do not let your eye begrudge what you give to charity. Do not turn your face away from any poor man, and God's face will not be turned away from you. Give to charity in proportion to what you have; if you have little, do not be afraid to give sparingly to charity; for then you will lay up a good treasure for yourself against a day of adversity; for charity will save you from death, and keep you from going down into darkness. Charity is a good offering in the sight of the Most High for all who give it.

"My boy, beware of any immorality. First, take a wife who is of the stock of your forefathers; do not marry an alien, who does not belong to your father's tribe, for we are the sons of the prophets. Remember, my boy, that Noah, Abraham, Isaac, and Jacob, our forefathers of old, all married wives from among their kindred, and were blessed in their children, and their posterity will possess the land. Now, my boy, love your kindred, and do not disdain your brothers and the sons and daughters of your people and refuse to marry one of them. F or such disdain leads to ruin and great distress, and worthlessness brings loss and great want, for worthlessness is the mother of famine. The wages of any man who works for you, you must not retain overnight, but you must pay him immediately. If you serve God, you will be rewarded. Take care, my boy, in all that you do, and be well disciplined in all your conduct. Do not do to anyone else what you hate.[1] Do not drink wine to the point of intoxication; drunkenness must not go with you on your way. Give some of your bread to the hungry and of your clothes to the naked. Give all your surplus to charity, and do not let your eye begrudge what you give to charity. Scatter your bread on the graves of the upright, but do not give to sinners.

"Ask advice of every wise man, and do not think lightly of any useful advice. Always bless the Lord God, and ask Him to make your ways straight and your paths and plans prosper."

---

[1]This is one of the earliest appearances of the Golden Rule in Jewish literature.

CHAPTER 19

THE TWELVE TESTAMENTS

One of the most illuminating books belonging to this period is a work called The Testament of the Twelve Patriarchs. *It purports to record the last words and exhortations of the twelve sons of Jacob and was probably written either in Hebrew or Aramaic toward the close of the second century* B.C.E.

REUBEN'S WARNING AGAINST UNCHASTITY

Hear ye the words of Reuben, your father. Pay no heed to the face of a woman, nor associate with another man's wife, nor meddle with affairs of womankind. Therefore, pay no heed, my children, to the beauty of women, nor set your mind on their affairs; but walk in singleness of heart in the fear of the Lord, and expend labor on good works, and on study and on our flocks, until the Lord give you a wife, which He will. . . .

For a pit unto the soul is the sin of fornication, separating it from God, and bringing it near to idols, because it deceives the mind and understanding, and leads young men down into Hades before their time. For many has fornication destroyed; because, though a man be old or noble, or rich or poor, he brings reproach upon himself with the sons of men and derision with Belial. For hear ye regarding Joseph: how he guarded himself from a woman, and purged his thoughts from all fornication, and found favor in the sight of God and men. For the Egyptian woman did many things unto him, and summoned magicians, and offered him love potions, but the purpose of his soul admitted no evil desire. Therefore, the God of your fathers delivered him from every evil [and] hidden death. For if fornication overcomes not your mind, neither can Belial overcome you.

For evil are women, my children; and since they have no power or strength over man, they use wiles by outward attractions that they may draw him to themselves; and whom they cannot bewitch by outward attractions, him they overcome by craft. For moreover, concerning them the angel of the Lord told me, and taught me, that women are overcome by the spirit of fornication more than men, and in their heart they plot against men; and by means of their adornment they deceive first their minds, and by the glance of the eye instill the poison, and then through the accomplished act they take them captive. For a woman cannot force a man openly, but by a harlot's bearing she beguiles him. Flee, therefore, fornication, my children, and command your wives and your daughters that they adorn not their heads and faces to deceive the mind; because every woman who uses these wiles has been reserved for eternal punishment. . . .

SIMEON'S WARNING AGAINST ENVY

Now, my children, hearken unto me and beware of the spirit of deceit and of envy. For envy rules over the whole mind of a man, and suffers him neither to eat nor to drink, nor to do any good thing. But it ever suggests [to him] to destroy him that envies; and so long as he that is envied flourishes, he that envies fades away. . . .

For envy makes savage the soul and destroys the body; it causes anger and war in the mind, and stirs up unto deeds of blood, and leads the mind into frenzy, and causes tumult to the soul and trembling to the body. For even in sleep some malicious jealousy, deluding him, gnaws, and with wicked spirits disturbs his soul, and causes the body to be troubled, and wakes the mind from sleep in confusion; and as a wicked and poisonous spirit, so appears it to men. . . .

LEVI COMMENDS FEAR OF GOD

Now, my children, I command you: Fear the Lord your God with your whole heart, and walk in simplicity according to all His law; and do ye also teach your children letters, that they may have understanding all their life, reading unceasingly the law of God. For every one that knows the law of the Lord shall be honored, and shall not be a stranger whithersoever he goes. . . .

Work righteousness, therefore, my children, upon the earth, that ye may have [it] as a treasure in heaven. And sow good things in your souls, that ye may find them in your life. But if ye sow evil things, ye shall reap every trouble and affliction.

Get wisdom in the fear of God with diligence; for though there be a leading into captivity, and cities and lands be destroyed, and gold and silver and every possession perish, the wisdom of the wise naught can take away, save the blindness of ungodliness, and the callousness [that comes] of sin.

For if one keep oneself from these evil things, then even among his enemies shall wisdom be a glory to him, and in a strange country a fatherland, and in the midst of foes shall prove a friend.

Whosoever teaches noble things and does them, shall be enthroned with kings, as was also Joseph my brother.

JUDAH CONDEMNS DRUNKENNESS AND AVARICE

Now I command you, my children, hearken to Judah your father. . . . Be not drunk with wine; for wine turns the mind away from the truth, and inspires the passion of lust, and leads the eyes into error. For the spirit of fornication has wine as a minister to give pleasure to the mind; for these two also take away the mind of man. For if a man drink wine to drunkenness, it disturbs the mind with filthy thoughts leading to fornication, and heats the body to carnal union; and if the occasion of the lust be present, he works the sin, and is not ashamed. Such is the inebriated man, my children; for he who is drunken has reverence for no man. . . .

Observe, therefore, my children, the [right] limit in wine; for there are in it four evil spirits–of lust, of hot desire, of profligacy, of filthy lucre. If ye drink wine in gladness, be ye modest with the fear of God. For if in [your] gladness the fear of God departs, then drunkenness arises and shamelessness steals in; but if you would live soberly, do not touch wine at all, lest ye sin in words of outrage, and in fightings and slanders, and transgressions of the commandments of God, and ye perish before your time. Moreover, wine betrays the mysteries of God and men . . . and is a cause both of war and confusion. . . .

Beware also, my children, of fornication and the love of money, and hearken to Judah your father. For these things withdraw you from the law of God, and blind the inclination of the soul, and teach arrogance, and suffer not a man to have compassion upon his neighbor. They rob his soul of all goodness, and oppress him with toils and troubles, and drive away sleep from him, and devour his flesh. . . .

My children, the love of money leads to idolatry; because, when led astray through money, men name as gods those who are not gods, and it causes him who has it to fall into madness. . . .

Know, therefore, my children, that two spirits wait upon man–the spirit of truth and the spirit of deceit; and in the midst is the spirit of the understanding of the mind, to which it belongs to turn whithersoever it will; and the works of truth and the works of deceit are written upon the hearts of men, and each one of them the Lord knows; and there is not time at which the works of men can be hid; for on the heart itself have they been written down before the Lord; and the spirit of truth testifies all things, and accuses all; and the sinner is burnt up by his own heart, and cannot raise his face to the judge. . . .

ISSACHAR COMMENDS SINCERITY

Now, hearken to me, my children, and walk in singleness of your heart, for I have seen in it all that is well-pleasing to the Lord. The single-minded man covets not gold, he overreaches not his neighbor, he longs not after manifold dainties, he delights not in varied apparel. He does not desire to live a long life, but only waits for the will of God.

The spirits of deceit have no power against him, for he looks not on the beauty of women, lest he should pollute his mind with corruption. There is no envy in his thoughts, nor malicious person makes his soul to pine away, nor worry with insatiable desire in his mind. For he walks in singleness of soul, and beholds all things in uprightness of heart, shunning eyes [made] evil through the error of the world, lest he should see the perversion of any of the commandments of the Lord.

Keep, therefore, my children, the law of God, and get singleness, and walk in guilelessness, not playing the busybody with the business of your neighbor; but love the Lord and your neighbor, have compassion on the poor and weak. Bow down your back unto husbandry, and toil in labors in all manner of husbandry, offering gifts to the Lord with thanksgiving. . . .

ZEVULUN URGES COMPASSION

Now, my children, I bid you to keep the commands of the Lord, and to show mercy to your neighbors, and to have compassion toward all, not toward men only, but also toward beasts. . . . Have, therefore, compassion in your hearts, my children, because even as a man does to his neighbor, even so also will the Lord do to him. . . .

I was the first to make a boat to sail upon the sea, for the Lord gave me understanding and wisdom therein; and I let down a rudder behind it, and I stretched a sail upon another upright piece of wood in the midst; and I sailed therein along the shores, catching fish for the house of my father until we came to Egypt; and through compassion I shared my catch with every stranger; and if a man were a stranger, or sick, or aged, I boiled the fish, and dressed them well, and offered them to all men, as every man had need, grieving with and having compassion upon them. Wherefore also the Lord satisfied me with abundance of fish when catching fish; for he that shares with his neighbor receives manifold more from the Lord. . . .

Now I will declare unto you what I did. I saw a man in distress through nakedness in wintertime, and had compassion upon him, and stole away a garment secretly from my father's house, and gave it to him who was in distress. Do ye, therefore, my children, from that which God bestows upon you, show compassion and mercy without hesitation to all men, and give to every man with a good heart; and if ye have not the wherewithal to give to him that needs, have compassion for him in bowels of mercy. . . .

Observe the waters, and know when they flow together, they sweep along stones, trees, earth, and other things; but if they are divided into many streams, the earth swallows them up, and they become of no account. So shall ye also be if ye be divided. Be not ye, therefore, divided into two heads, for everything which the Lord made has but one head, and two shoulders, two hands, two feet, but all the remaining members.

DAN CONDEMNS ANGER

Hearken to my words, ye sons of Dan; and give heed to the words of your father. I have proved in my heart, and in my whole life, that truth with just dealing is good and well-pleasing to God, and that lying and anger are evil, because they teach man all wickedness. . . .

Now, my children, behold I am dying, and I tell you of a truth, that unless ye keep yourselves from the spirit of lying and of anger, and love truth and long-suffering, ye shall perish. For anger is blindness, and does not suffer one to see the face of any man with truth. For though it be a father or a mother, he behaves toward them as enemies; though it be a brother, he knows him not; though it be a prophet of the Lord, he disobeys him; though a righteous man, he regards him not; though a friend, he does not acknowledge him. For the spirit of anger encompasses him with the net of deceit, and blinds his eyes, and through lying darkens his mind, and gives him its own peculiar vision. And wherewith encompasses it his eyes? With hatred of heart, so as to be envious of his brother. . . .

He who is wrathful, if he be a mighty man, has a threefold power in his anger: one by the help of his servants; and a second by his wealth, whereby he persuades and overcomes wrongfully; and third, having his own natural power, he works thereby the evil; and though the wrathful man be weak, yet has he a power twofold of that which is by nature; for wrath ever aids such in lawlessness. This spirit goes always with lying at the right hand of Satan, that with cruelty and lying his words may be wrought.

Understand ye, therefore, the power of wrath, that it is vain.

For it first of all gives provocation by word; then by deeds it strengthens him who is angry, and with sharp losses disturbs his mind, and so stirs up with great wrath his soul. Therefore, when any one speaks against you, be not ye moved to anger, and if any man praises you as holy men, be not uplifted: be not moved either to delight or to disgust. For first it pleases the hearing, and so makes the mind keen to perceive the grounds for provocation; and then being enraged, he thinks that he is justly angry.

If ye fall into any loss or ruin, my children, be not afflicted; for this very spirit makes [a man] desire that which is perishable, in order that he may be enraged through the affliction; and if ye suffer loss voluntarily, or involuntarily, be not vexed; for from vexation arises wrath with lying. Moreover, a twofold mischief is wrath with lying; and they assist one another in order to disturb the heart; and when the soul is continually disturbed, the Lord departs from it, and Belial rules over it.

Observe, therefore, my children, the commandments of the Lord: Keep His Law, depart from wrath, and hate lying, that the Lord may dwell among you, and Belial may flee from you. Speak truth each one with his neighbor, so shall ye not fall into wrath and confusion; but ye shall be in peace, having the God of peace, so shall no war prevail over you. Love the Lord through all your life, and one another with a true heart. . . .

The things which ye have heard from your father, do ye also impart to your children that the Redeemer may receive you; for he is true and long-suffering, meek and lowly, and teaches by his words the law of God. Depart, therefore, from all unrighteousness, and cleave unto the righteousness of God, and your race will be saved for ever.

NAPHTALI COMMENDS STEADFASTNESS

Be ye, therefore, not eager to corrupt your doings through covetousness or with vain words to beguile your souls; because if ye keep silence in purity of heart, ye shall understand how to hold fast the will of God, and to cast away the will of Belial. Sun and moon and stars change not their order; so do ye also change not the Law of God in the disorderliness of your doings. The Gentiles went astray, and forsook the Lord, and changed their order, and obeyed stocks and stones, spirits of deceit; but ye shall not be so, my children, recognizing in the firmament, in the earth, and in the sea, and in all created things, the Lord who made all things, that ye become not as Sodom, which changed the order of nature. In like manner the watchers also changed the order of their nature, whom the Lord cursed at the flood, on whose account He made the earth without inhabitant and fruitless. . . .

GOD URGES BROTHERLY LOVE

Now, my children, hearken to the words of truth to work righteousness, and all the Law of the Most High, and go not astray through the spirit of hatred, for it is evil in all the doings of men. Whatsoever a man does the hater abominates him: and though a man works the Law of the Lord, he praises Him not; though a man fears the Lord, and takes pleasure in that which is righteous, he loves Him not. He dispraises the truth, he envies him that prospers, he welcomes evil-speaking, he loves arrogance, for hatred blinds his soul. . . .

Beware, therefore, my children, of hatred; for it works lawlessness even against the Lord Himself. For it will not hear the words of His commandments concerning the loving of one's neighbor, and it sins against God. For if a brother stumbles, it delights immediately to proclaim it to all men, and is urgent that he should be judged for it, and be punished and be put to death; and if it be a servant it stirs him up against his master, and with every affliction it devises against him, if possibly he can be put to death. For hatred works with envy also against them that prosper: so long as it hears of or sees their success, it always languishes.

For as love would quicken even the dead, and would call back them that are condemned to die, so hatred would slay the living, and those that had sinned venially it would not suffer to live. For the spirit of hatred works together with Satan, through hastiness of spirit, in all things unto men's death; but the spirit of love works together with the Law of God in long-suffering unto the salvation of men.

Hatred, therefore, is evil, for it constantly mates with lying, speaking against the truth; and it makes small things to be great, and causes the light to be darkness, and calls the sweet bitter, and teaches slander, and kindles wrath, and stirs up war, and violence, and all covetousness; it fills the heart with evils and devilish poison.

These things, therefore, I say to you from experience, my children, that ye may drive forth hatred, which is of the devil. . . . Love ye each one his brother, and put away hatred from your hearts; love one another in deed, and in word, and in the inclination of the soul. . . . Love ye one another from the heart; and if a man sin against thee, speak peaceably to him, and in thy soul hold not guile; and if he repent and confess, forgive him; but if he deny it, do not get into a passion with him, lest catching the poison from thee he take to swearing and so thou sin doubly. Let not another man hear thy secrets when engaged in legal strife, lest he come to hate thee and become thy enemy, and commit a great sin against thee; for ofttimes he addresses thee guilefully or busies himself about thee with wicked intent; and though he deny it and yet have a sense of shame when reproved, give over reproving him. For he who denies may repent so as not to wrong thee again; yea, he may also honor thee, and fear and be at peace with thee; but if he be shameless and persists in his wrongdoing, even so forgive him from the heart, and leave to God the avenging.

If a man prosper more than you, do not be vexed, but pray also for him, that he may have perfect prosperity. For so it is expedient for you; and if he be further exalted, be not envious of him, remembering that all flesh shall die; and offer praise to God, who gives things good and profitable to all men. Seek out the judgments of the Lord, and thy mind will rest and be at peace; and though a man become rich by evil means, even as Esau, the brother of my father, be not jealous; but wait for the end of the Lord. For if He take away [from a man] wealth gotten by evil means He forgives him if he repent, but the unrepentant is reserved for eternal punishment. For the poor man, if free from envy he pleases the Lord in all things, is blessed beyond all men, because he hath not the travail of vain men. Put away, therefore, jealousy from your souls, and love one another with uprightness of heart. . . .

ASHER ON VICE AND VIRTUE

Hearken to your father, ye children of Asher, and I will declare to you all that is upright in the sight of God. Two ways has God given to the sons of men, and two inclinations, and two kinds of action, and two modes of action, and two issues. Therefore, all things are by twos, one over against the other. For there are two ways of good and evil, and with these are the two inclinations in our breasts discriminating them. Therefore, if the soul take pleasure in the good inclination, all its actions are in righteousness; and if it sin, it straightway repents. For, having its thoughts set upon righteousness, and casting away wickedness, it straightway overthrows the evil, and uproots the sin; but if it incline to the evil inclination, all its actions are in wickedness, and it drives away the good, and cleaves to the evil, and is ruled by Belial; even though it work what is good, he forces the issue of the action into evil for him, seeing that the treasure of the inclination is filled with an evil spirit.

A person, then, may with words help the good for the sake of evil, yet the issue of the action leads to mischief. There is a man who shows no compassion upon him who serves his turn in evil; and this thing has two aspects, but the whole is evil; and there is a man that loves him that works evil, because he would prefer even to die in evil for his sake; and concerning this it is clear that it has two aspects, but the whole is an evil work. Though, indeed, he have love, yet is he wicked who conceals what is evil for the sake of the good name, but the end of the action tends unto evil. Another steals, does unjustly, plunders, defrauds, and withal pities the poor: this too has a twofold aspect, but the whole is evil. He who defrauds his neighbor provokes God, and swears falsely against the Most High, and yet pities the poor: the Lord who commands the law he sets at nought and provokes, and yet he refreshes the poor. He defiles the soul, and makes gay the body; he kills many, and pities a few: this, too, has a twofold aspect, but the whole is evil. Another commits adultery and fornication, and abstaineth from meats, and when fasts he does evil, and by the power of his wealth overwhelms many; and notwithstanding his excessive wickedness he does the commandments: this, too, has a twofold aspect, but the whole is evil. Such men are hares; for they are half-clean, but in very deed are unclean. For God in the Tables of the Commandments has thus declared.

As for good men, they are of single face . . . and are just before God. To destroy the wicked is to do two works, of good and evil; but the whole is good, because it uproots and destroys that which is evil. To hate the unjust man who yet gives charity, and the man who commits adultery but fasts: this, too, has a twofold aspect, but the whole work is good, because it follows the Lord's example, in that it accepts not the seeming good as the genuine good. . . .

Ye see, my children, how that there are two in all things, one against the other, and the one is hidden by the other: in wealth [is hidden] covetousness, in conviviality, drunkenness, in laughter, grief, in wedlock, lechery. Death succeeds to life, dishonor to glory, night to day, and darkness to light; and all things are under the day, just things under life, unjust things under death; wherefore also eternal life awaits death; but it may not be said that truth is a lie, or that right is wrong; for all truth is under the light, even as all things are under God. . . .

JOSEPH COMMENDS UNITY

Love one another, and with long-suffering hide ye one another's faults. For God delights in the unity of brethren, and in the purpose of a heart that takes pleasure in love. . . .

If ye walk in the commandments of the Lord, my children, He will exalt you there, and will bless you with good things forever and ever. And if any one seeks to do evil unto you, do well unto him, and pray for him, and ye shall be redeemed of the Lord from all evil. . . .

BENJAMIN COMMENDS PURITY OF HEART

Let your mind be unto good, for he that has his mind right, sees all things rightly. Fear ye the Lord, and love your neighbor; and even though the spirits of Belial claim you to afflict you with every evil, yet shall they not have dominion over you. . . .

See ye, therefore, my children, the end of the good man? Be followers of his compassion, therefore, with a good mind, that ye also may wear crowns of glory. For the good man has not a dark eye; for he shows mercy to all men, even though they be sinners; and though they devise with evil intent concerning him, by doing good he overcomes evil, being shielded by God; and he loves the righteous as his own soul. If any one is glorified, he envies him not; if any one is enriched, he is not jealous; if any one is valiant, he praises him; the virtuous man he lauds; on the poor man he has mercy; on the weak he has compassion; unto God he sings praises; and him that has the grace of a good spirit he loves as his own soul.

If, therefore, ye also have a good mind, then will both wicked men be at peace with you, and the profligate will reverence you and turn unto good; and the covetous will not only cease from their inordinate desire, but even give the objects of their covetousness to them that are afflicted. If ye do well, even the unclean spirits will flee from you; and the beasts will dread you. For where there is reverence for good works and light in the mind, even darkness flees away from him. For if any one does violence to a holy man, that one repents; for the holy man is merciful to his reviler, and holds his peace; and if any one betrays a righteous man, the righteous man prays: though for a little he be humbled, yet not long afterward he appears far more glorious, as was Joseph my brother.

The inclination of the good man is not in the power of the deceit of the spirit of Belial, for the angel of peace guides his soul; and he gazes not passionately upon corruptible things, nor gathers together riches through a desire of pleasure. He delights not in pleasure, he grieves not his neighbor, he sates not himself with luxuries, he errs not in the uplifting of the eyes, for the Lord is his portion. The good inclination receives not glory nor dishonor from men, and it knows not any guile, or lie, or fighting, or reviling; for the Lord dwells in him and lights up his soul, and he rejoices toward all men always. The good mind has not two tongues, of blessing and of cursing, of contumely and of honor, of sorrow and of joy, of quietness and of confusion, of hypocrisy and of truth, of poverty and of wealth; but it has one disposition, uncorrupt and pure, concerning all men. It has no double sight, nor double hearing; for in everything which he does, or speaks, or sees, he knows that the Lord looks on his soul. And he cleanses his mind that he be not condemned by men as well as by God; and in like manner the works of Belial are twofold, and there is no singleness in them.

CHAPTER 20

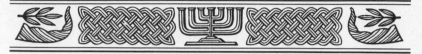

THE STORY OF BEL

The following is from a diverting tract in the Apocrypha known as Bel and the Dragon. The document may have been written originally in Aramaic during the second century B.C.E., *but was almost certainly based on a legend dating from a much earlier time. I include it in this anthology because it is so typical of the tales with which the Jews–like all other pious nations–loved to regale themselves.*

When King Astyages was gathered to his fathers, Cyrus the Persian succeeded to his kingdom; and Daniel was a companion of the king, and was distinguished above all his other friends. Now the Babylonians had an idol called Bel, and every day they bestowed on it twelve bushels of fine flour and forty sheep and fifty gallons of wine. The king revered it and went every day to worship it, but Daniel worshiped his own God; and the king said to him, "Why do you not worship Bel?"

Daniel said, "Because I do not revere artificial idols, but the living God, who created heaven and earth and is sovereign over all mankind."

The king said to him, "Do you not think that Bel is a living

God? Do you not see how much he eats and drinks every day?"

Daniel laughed and said, "Do not be deceived, O king, for it is only clay inside and bronze outside, and never ate or drank anything."

Then the king was angry and called Bel's priests, and said to them, "If you cannot tell me who it is that eats up these provisions, you shall die, but if you can show me that Bel eats them, Daniel shall die, because he has uttered blasphemy against Bel."

Daniel said to the king, "It shall be as you say."

Now the priests of Bel were seventy in number, besides their wives and children. So the king went with Daniel to the temple of Bel; and the priests of Bel said, "See, we will go outside, and you, O king, must put the food on the table, and mix the wine and put it on, and shut the door and seal it with your signet; and when you come back in the morning, if you do not find that it is all eaten up by Bel, we will die; or Daniel will, who is making these false charges against us." For they scorned him, because they had made a secret entrance under the table, and through it they used to go in regularly and devour the offerings.

So it happened that when they had gone, the king put the food for Bel on the table. Then Daniel ordered his servants to bring ashes, and they scattered them over the whole temple, in the presence of the king alone. Then they went out, and shut the door, and sealed it with the king's signet, and went away; and the priests came in the night as usual, with their wives and children, and ate and drank it all up.

The king rose early the next morning, and Daniel came with him, and the king said, "Are the seals unbroken, Daniel?"

Daniel said, "They are unbroken, O king."

As soon as he opened the doors, the king looked at the table and shouted loudly, "You are great, O Bel, and there is no deception at all about you."

Daniel laughed and held the king back from going in, and said to him, "Look at the floor and observe whose footprints these are."

The king said, "I see the footprints of men, women, and children!"

Then the king was enraged, and he seized the priests and their wives and children, and they showed him the secret doors by which they got in and devoured what was on the table. So the king killed them, and he turned Bel over to Daniel, and he destroyed it and its temple. (Bel and the Dragon, 1:1–22)

CHAPTER 21

THE DISPUTE OF THE COURTIERS

The following tale is from the apocryphal First Book of Ezra, a work compiled originally in Greek, and belonging in its present form perhaps to the first century B.C.E. *It serves there as the core of a didactic—and of course spurious—history of the return of the Jews from the Babylonian Exile under Ezra.*

Now King Darius made a great banquet for all his subjects . . . from India to Ethiopia; and they ate and drank, and when they were satisfied, they went home; but Darius the king went to his bedroom and fell asleep, and then awoke. Then the three young men of his bodyguard, who kept guard over the person of the king, said to one another,

"Let us each say what one thing is strongest, and Darius the king will give rich presents and great honors to the one whose words seem the wisest, and have him dressed in purple, and drink from gold plates, and sleep on a gold bed, and give him a chariot with gold bridles, and a linen headdress, and a necklace around his neck, and because of his wisdom he shall sit next to Darius, and be called Darius' kinsman."

Then each wrote his own answer and put his seal on it, and put them under the pillow of King Darius, and said,

"When the king wakes up, they will give him the writing, and the one whose choice the king and the three princes of Persia judge the wisest, shall be considered the victor in what he has written."

The first, wrote "Wine is strongest."

The second wrote, "The king is strongest."

The third wrote, "Women are strongest, but truth prevails over everything."

So when the king awoke, they took the writing and gave it to him and he read it. . . .

He said: "Summon the young men, and let them show their reasons."

They were summoned, and came in; and they said to them, "Explain to us about what you have written."

So the first one, who had told of the strength of wine, began and said,

"Gentlemen, how supremely strong wine is! It leads the minds of all who drink it astray. It makes the mind of the king and the mind of the fatherless child alike; the mind of the menial and the freeman, of the poor and the rich. It turns every thought to mirth and merrymaking, and forgets all grief and debt. It makes all hearts rich, and forgets kings and governors and makes everybody talk in thousands. When they drink, they forget to be friendly to friends and brothers, and very soon they draw their swords; and when they recover from their wine, they cannot remember what they have done. Gentlemen, is not wine supremely strong, since it forces them to act so?"

When he had said this, he stopped.

Then the second, who had told of the king's might, began to speak:

"Gentlemen, are not men strongest, because they control land and sea, and all that is in them? However, the king is supremely strong, and is lord and master of them, and every command he gives them they obey. If he orders them to make war on one another, they do so; and if he sends them out against the enemy, they go, and surmount mountains, walls, and towers. They kill and are killed, but they do not disobey the king's command. If they are victorious, they bring everything to the king, the spoils they take and all the rest. Among those who do not go to war or fight, but till the soil, again, when they sow and reap, bring it to the king, and they compel one another to pay taxes to the king. He is only one man; but if he orders them to release, they release; if he orders them to strike down, they strike; if he orders them to lay waste, they lay waste; if he orders them to build, they build; if he orders them to cut down, they cut down; if he orders them to plant, they plant. So all his people and his troops obey him. Besides, he reclines at table, he eats and drinks and sleeps, and they keep watch about him, and they cannot any of them go away and look after their own affairs, or disobey him at all. Gentlemen, how can the king not be the strongest, when he is so obeyed?"

He stopped.

Then the third, who had spoken of women and of truth – his name was Zerubbabel – began to speak:

"Gentlemen, is not the king great, and are not men many, and is not wine strong? Who is it then that rules over them and masters them? Is it not women? Women have borne the king and all the people, who are lords of sea and land; from them they are sprung, and they brought them up, to plant the vineyards, from which the wine comes. They make men's clothes, they make men's splendor, and men cannot exist without women. Why, if men amass gold and silver, and everything of beauty, and then see one woman remarkable for looks and beauty, they let all these things go, and gape at her, and stare at her with open mouths, and would all rather have her than gold or silver or any thing of beauty. A man will leave his own father, who brought him up, and his own country, and be united with his wife. With his wife he ends his days, and remembers neither his father nor his mother nor his country. Hence, you must recognize that women rule over men. Do you not toil and labor, and bring it all and give it to your wives? A man takes his sword and goes out on expeditions to rob and steal, and to sail the sea and the rivers; he faces the lion and walks in the darkness, and when he steals and robs and plunders, he brings it back to the woman he loves. So a man loves his wife better than his father or mother. Many have lost their heads completely for the sake of women, and have become slaves for their sakes. Many have perished, or failed, or sinned for the sake of women. Now do you not believe me? Is not the king great in his power? Do not all lands fear even to touch him? Yet I have seen him with Apame, the king's concubine, the daughter of the noble Bartacus, sitting at the king's right hand, and taking the crown from the king's head, and putting it on her own, and she slapped the king with her left hand. At this the king stared at her open-mouthed. If she smiled at him, he laughed; if she grew angry at him, he flattered her, so that she might be reconciled to him again. Gentlemen, how can women not be mighty, when they act like that?"

Then the king and the nobles looked at one another; and Zerubbabel began to speak about truth:

"Gentlemen, are not women mighty? The earth is vast, and heaven is high, and the sun is swift in its course, for it circles about the heavens and hastens back to its own starting-point in a single day. Is it not great that does these things? So truth is great, and mightier than all other things. The whole earth calls upon truth, and heaven blesses her; all his works quake and tremble, there is no wrongdoing with him. Wine is not upright, the king is not upright, women are not upright, all the sons of men are not upright, and all their doings, all such things, are not upright; there is no truth in them, and through their unrighteousness they will perish; but truth endures and is strong forever, and lives and reigns forever and ever. There is no partiality or preference with her, but she does what is right, rather than all that is wrong and wicked. All men approve her doings, and there is no injustice in her judgment. To her belong power and the royal dignity and authority and majesty in all the ages; blessed be the God of truth!"

When he stopped speaking, all the people shouted and said, "Truth is great and supremely strong."

Then the king said to him, "Ask whatever you please, beyond what is written here, and we will give it to you, since you have been found the wisest. You shall sit next to me, and be called my kinsman. (I Ezra 3:1–4:42)

CHAPTER 22

THE APOCALYPSE OF EZRA

The following is a short passage form the so-called Second Book of Ezra, an apocryphal document of doubtful date but unmistakable meaning. The author—supposedly the ancient scribe, Ezra—seeks to solve the age-old problem of why Israel, of all nations, is the most afflicted. The answer, given in a series of visions, is twofold: first, God's ways are inscrutable, and Israel must, therefore, be patient; second, God's justice is sure, and Israel's patience, if sufficient, will be soon and wonderfully rewarded.

"For I have gone all about the nations, and I have seen them abounding in wealth, yet unmindful of your commandments. Now, therefore, weigh our iniquities and those of the inhabitants of the world on the scales; and which way the movement of the pointer turns will be found out. Or when did the inhabitants of the earth not sin in your sight? Or what nation has kept your commandments so well? You will find names of men who have kept your commandments, but you will not find nations."

And the angel who had been sent to me, whose name was Uriel, answered and said to me, "Your mind has utterly failed in this world and do you expect to understand the way of the Most High?"

I said, "Yes, my lord."

He answered me and said, "I was sent to show you three ways, and to set three figures before you. If you can solve one of these for me, I will show you the way you want to see and teach you why the heart is wicked."

I said, "Go on, my lord."

He said to me, "Come, weigh me the weight of fire, or measure me a measure of wind, or call back for me the day that is past."

I answered and said, "Who that is born can do that, that you should ask such things of me?"

He said to me, "If I had asked you, 'How many dwellings are there in the heart of the sea, or how many streams at the source of the deep, or how many ways above the firmament, or what are the ways of leaving Paradise?' perhaps you would have said to me, 'I have never gone down into the deep, nor into Hades, nor have I ever climbed up into the heavens.' But now I have only asked you about fire and wind and the day, through all of which you have passed, and without which you cannot live, and you have given me no answer about them!" Continuing, he said to me, "Your own things that grow up with you, you cannot understand; and how can your frame grasp the way of the Most High, or one already worn out by the corrupt world understand incorruption?"

When I heard this, I fell on my face and said to him, "It would have been better that we should not be here than to come here and live in ungodliness, and suffer, without understanding why."

He answered me and said, "I went to a forest of trees of the field, and they took counsel and said, 'Come, let us go and make war on the sea, so that it may retire before us, and we may make more forests for ourselves.' In like manner the waves of the sea themselves also took counsel and said, 'Come, let us go up and conquer the forest of the field, so that there also we may win ourselves more territory.' The thought of the forest was in vain, for the fire came and consumed it; so was the thought of the sea waves, for the sand stood firm and stopped them. Now if you were their judge, which of them would you have undertaken to justify, and which to condemn?"

I answered and said, "It was a foolish plan that both formed, for the land is given to the forest, and the place of the sea is given it to bear its waves."

He answered me and said, "You have judged rightly; and why have you not judged so in your own case? For just as the land is given to the forest, and the sea to its waves, so those who live on the earth can understand only the things that are on the earth, and those who are above the heavens, the things that are above the height of the heavens."

Then I answered and said, "I beseech you, sir, to what end has the capacity for understanding been given me? For I did not mean to ask about ways above, but about those things which pass by us every day: why Israel is given up to the heathen in disgrace; the people whom you loved are given up to godless tribes; and the law of our forefathers is made of no effect, and the written agreements are no more. We pass from the world like locusts, and do not deserve to obtain mercy; but what will he do for his name, by which we are called? It is about these things that I have asked."

Then he answered me and said, "If you live, you will see, and if you survive, you will often marvel; for the age is hurrying fast to its end."

SECTION TWO

THE FIRST RABBIS

The Hebrew term rabbi, *meaning "my master," did not become current until somewhat later than this period; but those men to whom it was applied were essentially hahamim, sages, who believed that all truth had already been revealed to the Jewish people. A rabbi believed that everything worth knowing was contained in the Torah, the Law; so instead of presuming to write novel books of wisdom, he devoted himself entirely to studying the ancient classical literature of the TaNaKH. He applied himself day and night to expounding what he believed the Torah really said.*

This occupation probably started in the fifth century B.C.E. *when the Pentateuch was finally established by Ezra the Scribe as Israel's immutable code of law. Thereafter,* interpretation *became indispensable, because life kept changing, and a way had to be found to expand the scope of the code without amending its text. The result was the gradual formation of the Oral Law—an unwritten code consisting of all the concepts and precepts deduced from or read into the Written Law. Its creators were all pious men, and their prime interest was rigidly sectarian. However, they were not nearly so narrow as is commonly imagined, and they were capable of uttering the most liberal sentiments. Despite their sectarianism, they were often inclined to voice the most universal ideals. The proof is to be seen in the sayings they left as memorials to the spirit in which they labored.*

CHAPTER 23

SAYINGS OF THE FATHERS

As has already been stated, the first rabbis did not carry that title. Those who lived before the third century B.C.E. *were known only as "Men of the Great Assembly," and their successors until well into the first century* C.E. *were called simply the "Fathers." Who the foremost of those Fathers were, and what famed maxims they uttered, is recorded in that most popular of all Rabbinic documents entitled* Pirke Avot, *Chapters of the Fathers, or more traditionally, Ethics of the Fathers. It is to be found in the Talmud, and also in the Orthodox Jewish prayer book. (Its six chapters are read on successive Sabbaths, between Passover and the Jewish New Year, as part of the regular afternoon ritual.) Only fragments of the first two chapters are given here, since these alone refer to characters belonging to this early period.*[1]

Moses received the Law on Mount Sinai and handed it down to Joshua, who handed it down to the Judges, who handed it down to the Prophets, who handed it down to the Men of the Great Assembly. They used to say three things: "Be deliberate in passing judgment, and raise up many disciples, and build a hedge [i.e., defenses] around the Law."

[1]Selections from the remainder of *Pirke Avot* will be found in "Wisdom from the Mishnah." There, as here, I give my own translation, the standard ones being somewhat archaic.

Simeon the Just [died approximately 270 B.C.E.] was one of the last members of the Great Assembly. His favorite saying was: "The world is established on three things–on Law, on Worship, and on Generosity."

Antigonos of Socho received the Torah from Simeon the Just. His favorite saying was: "Don't be like those servants who work solely for pay . . . and let the awe of Heaven be upon you."

[Next came] Yose ben Yoezer and Yose ben Yohanan. The former used to say: "Let your house be a gathering-place for the wise, cover yourself with the dust of their feet, and drink in their words thirstily." The latter used to say: "Open your house wide, and let poor folk have a place in it, and don't talk too much to a woman." He meant [one should not talk too much] to one's own wife; therefore, how much the more certainly not to a friend's wife. . . .

[Next came] Yehoshuah ben Perakhyah and Nittai the Arbelite. The former used to say: "Get yourself a teacher, or find yourself a comrade, and judge every man according to his true merit." The latter used to say: "Stay away from an evil neighbor, steer clear of wicked companions, and never doubt that there is retribution."

[Next came] Shemayah and Avtalyon. The former used to say: "Love work, hate tyranny, and don't become [too well] known to the authorities." The latter used to say: "You wise men, watch what you say, lest you err and are exiled to a place of evil waters, and your disciples drink and die, and the name of Heaven be profaned."

[Next came] Hillel. . . .

CHAPTER 24

THE WISDOM OF HILLEL

The greatest of all the Rabbinic fathers was the famed Hillel, who began teaching around 30 B.C.E. He was born in Babylonia–where a large Jewish community had maintained itself ever since the Exile in the sixth century B.C.E.–and migrated to Palestine in order to perfect himself in the knowledge of the Torah. There, despite poverty and other obstacles, he succeeded in becoming the foremost of all the Pharisaic masters, and founded a relatively liberal type of rabbinism that dominated Jewish life for more than five centuries. The many traditions concerning his life and character are strikingly in harmony with the maxims recorded in his name.

Here are some of the utterances of and about Hillel as recorded in various rabbinic sources.

Hillel used to say: "Be among the disciples of Aaron, loving peace, cherishing mankind, and bringing [people] ever closer to the Law." [Also] he would say: "He who advertises his name, loses it; he who does not increase [knowledge], diminishes it; he who refuses to learn, merits extinction; and he who puts his talent to selfish use, commits spiritual suicide." [Also] he would say: "If I am not self-reliant, on whom shall I rely? But if I am selfish, what [good] am I? And if [the time for action is] not now, when [is it]?" (Pirke Avot 1:1–14)

Hillel [also] said: "Don't keep aloof from the people; and don't be [too] sure of yourself until the day you die; and don't condemn your comrade until you are in his place; and . . . don't say 'I shall study when I find the time,' because then you may never find it."

He [also] said: "A boor does not fear sin, and a vulgar man cannot be a saint. A bashful man cannot learn, an ill-tempered man cannot teach, and one who preoccupies himself with worldly affairs cannot impart wisdom. Moreover, in a place where there are no men, show yourself a man."

On one occasion he saw a skull floating, and he said: "Because you drowned others, you were drowned, and in the end they that drowned you shall likewise be drowned."

He used to say:
"More flesh, more worms;
More wealth, more worry;
More women, more witchcraft;
More concubines, more lechery;
More slaves, more thievery.
(But) More Law, more life;
More study, more wisdom;
More counsel, more enlightenment;
More righteousness, more peace.

He who acquires a good name, acquires it for himself;
He who acquires knowledge of the Law acquires life in the World-to-Come. (Pirke Avot, 2:5–8)

Hillel said: "Among those who stand, do not sit, and among whose who sit, do not stand. Among those who laugh, do not weep; and among those who weep, do not laugh." (Tosefta Berakhot, 2)

Once when Hillel left his disciples, they said to him, "Where are you going?" He replied, "To do a kindness to a guest in the house." They said, "Have you every day a guest?" He replied, "Yes, is not the soul a guest in the body? Today it is here, tomorrow it is gone."

Once when Hillel left his disciples, they said to him, "Where are you going?" He replied, "To do a pious deed." They said, "What may that be?" He said, "To take a bath." They asked, "Is that a pious deed?" He answered, "Yes, for if the man who is appointed to tend and wash the images of kings which are set up in the theaters and circuses receives his rations for so doing, and is even raised up to be regarded as among the great ones of the kingdom, how much more is it obligatory on me to tend and wash my body, inasmuch as I have been created in the image of God." (Leviticus Rabbah, 34:3)

A man once laid a wager with a friend that he could make Hillel lose his temper. If he succeeded he was to receive 400 *zuzim,* but if he failed he was to forfeit this sum. The Sabbath eve was approaching, and Hillel was engaged in his ablutions, when the man passed his door and shouted: "Where is Hillel?"

Wrapping his robe about him, Hillel sallied forth to ask what the man wished.

"I wish to ask thee a question," was the reply.

"Ask, my son," said Hillel

"I wish to know why the Babylonians have such round heads," said the man.

"A very important question, my son," said Hillel. "The reason is that their midwives are not skillful."

Several times this procedure was repeated, and finally the man said: "I have many more inquiries, but you will lose patience with me and become angry."

"Ask whatever you wish," replied Hillel.

The man, in vexation, said: "May there not be many like

thee in Israel, O Chief Justice! Through thee I have lost 400 *zuzim* on a wager that I could harass thee out of temper."

"Be warned for the future," said Hillel. "Better it is that thou shouldst lose 400 *zuzim* and 400 more after them than have it said of Hillel that he lost his temper." (Shabbat, 31a)

A heathen came to Shammai,[1] and said to him, "Accept me as a convert on the condition that you teach me the whole Law while I stand on one foot." Then Shammai drove him away with the rod which he held in his hand. Whereupon he went to Hillel, who received him as a convert and said to him, "*What is hateful to you, do not to your fellow: that is the whole Law; all the rest is its interpretation. Go and learn!*"[2] (Shabbat, 31b)

The schools of Hillel and Shammai disputed two and one-half years whether it would have been better if man had or had not been created. Finally they agreed that it would have been better had he not been created, but since he had been created, let him investigate his past doings, and let him examine what he is about to do. (The meaning is, "Let him live a righteous life.") (Eruvin, 13b)

Said Rav Abba in the name of Samuel: "For three years the schools of Hillel and Shammai have maintained a controversy, each school asserting that the decision should be given in accordance with its opinion. At last a [heavenly] voice descended in Yavneh and cried out: "The words of both these and these are the words of the living God, but the decision should follow the school of Hillel."

---

[1]Shammai was Hillel's foremost colleague, and also most consistent opponent in rabbinic issues. Tradition describes him as a contentious and impatient man, and his decisions prove him to have been ultra-conservative.

[2]This version of the Golden Rule is not original even with Hillel. It clearly echoes Tobit 4:15, which in turn echoes Leviticus 19:18.

It was asked: "If the words of both are those of the living God, why was the decision granted to the school of Hillel?"

The reply was: "Because the members of the school of Hillel are amiable of manner and courteous; they teach the opinions of both, and furthermore, they always give the opinion of their opponents first."

This teaches us that whosoever abases himself, God exalts. (Eruvin, 13b)

SECTION THREE

THE HELLENIZED JEWS

During this period more and more Jews were leaving Palestine to settle in the great trading ports along the Mediterranean Sea; among these the natural tendency was to become more and more Hellenized. Greek became their native tongue, and Greek ways and thoughts an increasing part of their culture. This process of assimilation was of course resisted from without as well as from within. Though the prevailing spirit in these commercial centers was relatively tolerant, it was far from being comradely. As a result a vicious cycle of exclusion and seclusion got under way, leading to friction, sparks, and sometimes explosions.

CHAPTER 25

THE ADMONITIONS OF PHILO

One of the foremost of the Hellenistic Jewish writers was a philosopher known as Philo Judaeus. He was born about 20 B.C.E. at Alexandria, Egypt, and wrote a number of works in which he sought to fuse Greek wisdom with Jewish tradition. This task seemed to him proper as well as feasible, since he was convinced that all that wisdom had originally been expounded by the ancient Hebrew prophets. Unfortunately, they had expounded it orally, and that was why, he argued, no memory of it had survived in Israel. Their pagan disciples, on the other hand, had written everything down, so Philo insisted he was merely recovering what was rightfully Israel's own in drawing on Greek books to buttress the Hebrew Scriptures.

The following brief selections are taken mainly from this author's voluminous allegorical exegesis of the Jewish Scriptures.

AGAINST OVERWEENING PRIDE OF BIRTH

We should blame those who spuriously appropriate as their own merit that which they derive from others – namely, good birth – and such people should justly be regarded as enemies not only of the Jewish race, but of all mankind; of the Jewish race, because they engender indifference in their brethren, so that they despise the righteous life in their reliance upon their ancestors' virtue; and of the Gentiles, because they would not allow them their reward even though they attain to the highest excellence of conduct, simply because they have not commendable ancestors. I know not if there could be a more pernicious doctrine than this: that there is no punishment for the wicked offspring of good parents, and no reward for the good offspring of evil parents. The Law judges each man upon his own merit, and does not assign praise or blame according to the virtues of the forefathers. . . . God judges by the fruit of the tree, not by the root; and in the divine judgment the proselyte will be raised on high, and he will have a double distinction, because on earth he deserted to God, and later he receives as his reward a place in Heaven. (De Exsecr. 6, 2:433)

AGAINST ASCETICISM

Truth will properly blame those who without discrimination shun all concern with the life of the state, and say that they despise the acquisition of good repute and pleasure. They are only making grand pretensions, and they do not really despise these things. They go about in torn raiment and with solemn visage, and live the life of penury and hardship as a bait, to make people believe that they are lovers of good conduct, temperance, and self-control. Therefore, be drunk in a sober manner. (De Fuga, 5 ff.)

ON THE TREATMENT OF SLAVES

Behave to your slaves as you pray that God may behave to you. For as we hear them, so shall we be heard, and as we regard them, so shall we be regarded. (Fragments ex Antonio, 2:672)

AGAINST TAMPERING WITH PIETY AND CUSTOMS

In the same way, if we add anything great or small to piety, which is the Queen of Virtues, or take anything away, we mar it and change its form. Addition will engender superstition, and diminution impiety–and thus true piety will disappear. Since true piety is the cause of the greatest of good, inducing in us a knowledge of our conduct toward God, which is a thing more royal and kingly than any public office or distinction, we should seek it above all other goods. . . .

Further, Moses lays down another general command, "Do not remove the boundary stone of thy neighbor, which thy ancestors have set up." This, methinks, does not refer merely to inheritances and the boundary of land, but it is ordained with a view to the preservation of ancient customs. For customs are unwritten laws, the decrees of men of old, not carved indeed upon pillars and inscribed upon parchment, but engraved upon the souls of the generations who through the ages maintained the chosen community. Children should accept the ancestral customs as part of their inheritance, for they were reared on them, and lived on them from their swaddling days, and they should not neglect them merely because the tradition is not written. The man who obeys the written laws is not, indeed, worthy of praise, for he may be constrained thereto by fear of punishment; but he who holds fast to the unwritten laws gives proof of a voluntary goodness and is worthy of our eulogy. (De Just, 2:360)

AGAINST OSTENTATION IN WORSHIP

If a man practices ablutions and purifications, but defiles his mind while he cleanses his body; or if, through his wealth, he founds a temple at a large outlay and expense; or if he offers hecatombs and sacrifices oxen without number, or adorns the shrine with rich ornaments, or gives endless timber and cunningly wrought work, more precious than silver or gold–let him none the more be called religious. For he has wandered far from the path of religion, mistaking ritual for holiness, and attempting to bribe the incorruptible, and to flatter Him whom none can flatter. God welcomes genuine service, and that is the service of a soul that offers the bare and simple sacrifice of truth, but from false service, the mere display of material wealth, He turns away. (De Ebr. 40)

CHAPTER 26

THE CONFESSIONS OF JOSEPHUS

Flavius Josephus (born about 37 C.E.) came from a distinguished Jewish family in Palestine and rose to be one of the commanders of the heroic little army that tried to defend that country from the Roman invader. After fighting several engagements, he was trapped with some forty of his men, and apparently in a fit of panic, sacrificed all but one of them in order to save himself. From then on, he spent the rest of his life writing books glorifying the history and defending the religion of the Jews.

Something of the torment that must have gone on in his mind can be gathered from the following selection. It is the speech that Josephus puts into the mouth of one of his fellow commanders who remained loyal to the last.

BLESSED ARE THE HEROES

As for those who have died in the war, we should deem them blessed, for they are dead in defending, and not in betraying, their liberty: but as to the multitude of those that have submitted to the Romans, who would not pity their condition? Who would not make haste to die before he would suffer the same miseries? Where is now that great city, the metropolis of the Jewish nation, which was fortified by so many walls round about, which had so many fortresses and large towers to defend it, which could hardly contain the instruments prepared for the war, and which had so many myriads of men to fight for it? Where is this city that God himself inhabited? It is now demolished to the very foundations; and has nothing but that monument of it preserved, I mean the camp of those that have destroyed it, which still dwells upon its ruins. Some unfortunate old men also lie upon the ashes of the Temple, and a few women are there preserved alive by the enemy for our bitter shame and reproach.

Now, who is there that revolves these things in his mind, and yet is able to bear the sight of the sun, though he might live out of danger? Who is there so much his country's enemy, or so unmanly and so desirous of living, as not to repent that he is still alive? I cannot but wish that we had all died before we had seen that holy city demolished by the hands of our enemies, or the foundations of our holy Temple dug up after so profane a manner. But since we had a generous hope that deluded us, as if we might perhaps have been able to avenge ourselves on our enemies, on that account, though it be now become vanity, and hath left us alone in this distress, let us make haste to die bravely.

Let us pity ourselves, our children, and our wives, while it is in our power to show pity to them; for we are born to die, as well as those whom we have begotten; nor is it in the power of the most happy of our race to avoid it. For abuses and slavery and the sight of our wives led away after an ignominious manner with their children, these are not such evils as are natural and necessary among men; although such as do not prefer death before those miseries, when it is in their power to do so, must undergo even them on account of their own cowardice. (Wars of the Jews, 7:8)

AGAINST APION

There was considerable anti-Semitism in the Greco-Roman world, especially among the pagan intellectuals, who could not understand the stubborn religiosity of the Jews. One of those intellectuals, a certain Apion who was a popular lecturer and publicist in Alexandria, wrote a scurrilous attack on the Bible, and Josephus replied with two vehement essays from which the following passages have been excerpted.

THE RELIGION OF MOSES

Now there are innumerable differences in the particular customs and laws that hold among all mankind, which a man may briefly reduce under the following heads: Some legislators have permitted their governments to be under monarchies, others put them under oligarchies, and others under a republican form; but our legislator had no regard to any of these forms, but he ordained our government to be what, by a strained expression, may be termed a theocracy, by ascribing the authority and the power to God, and by persuading all the people to have a regard to Him [God] as the author of all the good things enjoyed either in common by all mankind or by each one in particular, and of all that they themselves obtain by praying to Him in their greatest difficulties. He informed them that it was impossible to escape God's observation, either in any of our outward actions or in any of our inward thoughts. Moreover, he represented God as unbegotten and immutable through all eternity, superior to all mortal conceptions in form, and though known to us by His power, yet unknown to us as to His essence.

I do not now explain how these notions of God are in harmony with the sentiments of the wisest among the Greeks. However, their sages testify with great assurance that these notions are just and agreeable to the divine nature; for Pythagoras and Anaxagoras and Plato and the Stoic philosophers that succeeded them, and almost all the rest profess the same sentiments, and had the same notions of the nature of God; yet dared not these men disclose those true notions to more than a few, because the body of the people were prejudiced beforehand with other opinions. However, our legislator, whose actions harmonized with his laws, did not only prevail with those who were his contemporaries to accept these notions, but so firmly imprinted this faith in God upon all their posterity that it could never be removed.

The reason why the constitution of our legislation was ever better directed than other legislations to the utility of all is this: that *Moses did not make religion a part of virtue, but he declared other virtues to be a part of religion*–I mean justice, and fortitude, and temperance, and a universal agreement of the members of the community with one another. All our actions and studies are part of piety toward God, for he has left none of these in suspense or undetermined. There are two ways of arriving at any sort of learning and morality: the one is by instruction in words, the other by practical exercises. Now, other lawgivers have separated these two ways in their opinions, and choosing the one which best pleased each of them, neglected the other. Thus did the Lacedemonians and the Cretans teach by practical exercises, but not by words; while the Athenians and almost all the other Greeks made laws about what was to be done, or left undone, but had no regard to exercising them thereto in practice.

But our legislator very carefully joined these two methods of instruction together; for he neither left these practical exercises to be performed without verbal instruction, nor did he permit the learning of the law to proceed without the exercises for practice; but beginning immediately from the earliest infancy and the regulation of our diet, he left nothing of the very smallest consequence to be done at the pleasure and disposal of the individual.

Accordingly, he made a fixed rule of law, what sorts of food they should abstain from, and what sorts they should use; as also what communion they should have with others, what great diligence they should use in their occupations, and what times of rest should be interposed, in order that, by living under that law as under a father and a master, we might be guilty of no sin, neither voluntary nor out of ignorance. For he did not suffer the guilt of ignorance to go without punishment, but demonstrated the law to be the best and the most necessary instruction of all, directing the people to cease from their other employments and to assemble together for the hearing and the exact learning of the Law–and this not once or twice or oftener, but every week; which all the other legislators seem to have neglected.

THE LAWS OF MOSES

Education of children

Again the Law does not allow the birth of our children to be made occasions for festivity and an excuse for drinking to excess. It enjoins sobriety in their upbringing from the very first. It orders that they shall be taught to read, and shall learn both the laws and the deeds of their forefathers, in order that they may imitate the latter, and, being grounded in the former, may neither transgress nor have any excuse for being ignorant of them.

Funeral ceremonies

The pious rites which it provides for the dead do not consist of costly obsequies or the erection of conspicuous monuments. The funeral ceremony is to be undertaken by the nearest relatives, and all who pass while a burial is proceeding must join the procession and share the mourning of the family. After the funeral, the house and its inmates must be purified (in order that anyone guilty of murder may be very far from thinking himself pure).

Honor of parents and other regulations

Honoring parents is ranked by the Law as second only to honoring God. If a son does not respond to the benefits received from them – for the slightest failure in his duty toward them – the Law hands him over to be stoned. It requires respect to be paid by the young to all their elders, because God is the most ancient of all. It allows us to conceal nothing from our friends, for there is no friendship without absolute confidence; in the event of subsequent estrangement, it forbids the disclosure of secrets. A judge who accepts bribes suffers capital punishment. He who refuses to a supplicant the aid which he has power to give is accountable to justice. None may appropriate goods which he did not place on deposit, lay hands on any of his neighbor's property, or receive interest. These and many similar regulations are the ties which bind us together.

Attitude toward aliens

The consideration given by our legislator to the equitable treatment of aliens also merits attention. It will be seen that he took the best of all possible measures at once to secure our own customs from corruption, and to throw them open ungrudgingly to any who elect to share them. To all who desire to come and live under the same laws with us, he gives a gracious welcome, holding that it is not family ties alone which constitute relationship, but agreement in the principles of conduct. On the other hand, it was not his pleasure that casual visitors should be admitted to the intimacies of our daily life.

Humanity of the Law

The duty of sharing with others was inculcated by our legislator in other matters. We must furnish fire, water, food to all who ask for them, point out the road, not leave a corpse unburied, show consideration even to declared enemies. He does not allow us to burn up their country, or to cut down their fruit trees, and forbids even the despoiling of fallen combatants. He has taken measures to prevent outrage to prisoners of war, especially women. So thorough a lesson has he given us in gentleness and humanity that he does not overlook even the brute beasts, authorizing their use only in accordance with the Law, and forbidding all other employment of them. Creatures which take refuge in our houses, like supplicants, we are forbidden to kill. He would not suffer us to take the parent birds with their young, and bade us even in an enemy's country to spare and not to kill the beasts employed in labor. Thus, in every particular, he had an eye to mercy, using the laws I have mentioned to enforce the lesson, and drawing up for transgressors other penal laws admitting of no excuse. (Against Apion, II, 204–218)

ENCOMIUM ON THE TORAH

Upon the laws it was unnecessary to expatiate. A glance at them showed that they teach not impiety, but the most genuine piety; that they invite men not to hate their fellows, but to share their possessions; that they are the foes of injustice and scrupulous for justice, banish sloth and extravagance, and teach men to be self-dependent and to work with a will; that they deter them from war for the sake of conquest, but render them valiant defenders of the laws themselves; inexorable in punishment, not to be duped by studied words, always supported by actions. For actions are our invariable testimonials, plainer than any documents. I would therefore boldly maintain that we have introduced to the rest of the world a very large number of very beautiful ideas. What greater beauty than inviolable piety? What higher justice than obedience to the laws? What more beneficial than to be in harmony with one another, to be a prey neither to disunion in adversity, nor to arrogance and faction in prosperity; in war to despise death, in peace to devote oneself to crafts or agriculture; and to be convinced that everything in the whole universe is under the eye and direction of God? Had these precepts been either committed to writing or more consistently observed by others before us, we should have owed them a debt of gratitude as their disciples. If, however, it is seen that no one observes them better than ourselves, and if we have shown that we were the first to discover them, then the Apions and Molons and all who delight in lies and abuse may be left to their own confusion. (Against Apion, II, 291–295)

PART III

THE TALMUDIC PERIOD

INTRODUCTION

The supreme crisis in the history of the Jews occurred in the year 70 C.E., when their holy city, Jerusalem, was razed by the Romans, and they were left without a home either for themselves or their God. Wrecked now as a nation, it looked as though Israel would soon be destroyed even as a people.

The rabbis came to the fore and created what came to be called the Talmud. The Jews were able not merely to survive as a people, but even thrive.

The Mishnah is the first portion of the Talmud and is written in Hebrew. The Gemara comprises the second part of the Talmud and includes clarifications and discussions on the Mishnah. The Gemara is written in Aramaic. Together the Mishnah and the Gemara comprise the Talmud.

The Talmud, despite its diffusiveness, was primarily a legalistic anthology. Its compilers tried hard to include in it only such discussions as related more or less directly to the statutes and customs that a Jew must observe in daily life. Once the Talmud was completed, other material was gathered together, and a series of works appeared called the Midrashim, the "Expositions." Though these date from the sixth century onward, their contents are essentially contemporaneous with the Talmud itself, and they are therefore included in this section.

CHAPTER 27

WISDOM FROM THE MISHNAH

Being entirely a sectarian law code, the Mishnah contains little that can be aptly included in this anthology. That little, however, is of enormous worth, since it consists of the tractate entitled Pirke Avot, Chapters of the Fathers (or more traditionally, Ethics of the Fathers) from which excerpts have already been quoted.[1] *The passages following constitute the bulk of the tractate and throw striking light on the ethics of the Rabbis living during the first two centuries of the Common Era.*

Rabban Gamliel[2] used to say: "Get yourself a teacher, and keep away from doubtful matters, and never tithe by guesswork."

Simeon, his son, said: "All my life I have grown up among the wise, and I have found nothing better than silence. The chief thing is not to study but to do. And he who says too much, encourages sin."

Rabban Simeon ben Gamliel said: "The world rests on three things–Truth, Law, and Peace."

---

[1]See above: "Sayings of the Fathers" and "The Wisdom of Hillel."

[2]Grandson of Hillel.

Rabban Gamliel, the son of Rabbi Judah the Prince, said: "It is good to follow a workaday occupation as well as to study the Torah, for between the two one forgets to sin.[3] . . . Beware of the authorities, for they make no advances to a man except for their own purposes. They seem friendly when it is to their advantage, but desert a man when he is in trouble."

Rabban Yohanan ben Zakkai used to say: "Don't feel self-righteous if you have learned much Torah, because that is what you were created for." He said to his disciples: "Go and discover what [best helps] a man to find the right way of life." Rabbi Eliezer answered: "A good eye." Rabbi Yehoshuah answered: "A good comrade." Rabbi Yose answered: "A good neighbor." Rabbi Simeon answered: "Foresightedness." Rabbi Elazar answered: "A good heart." Rabban Yohanan then said to them: "I prefer Rabbi Elazar's answer, for his words include all of yours."

Rabbi Eliezer said: "Let your comrade's honor be as dear to you as your own; and do not be quick to get angry; also repent before it is too late. Warm yourself at the fire of the learned, but beware of their glowing coals, lest you get scorched. The bite of the learned is like the bite of a fox, their sting is like a scorpion's, their hiss like a serpent's, and all their words are like coals of fire."[4]

---

[3]The term "Torah" had many meanings to the Rabbis: the Pentateuch, the entire Bible, any learning based on the Bible, and sometimes all learning in general. It should be noted, incidentally, that the advice given in this maxim was widely accepted. As a rule the rabbinic sessions were conducted toward the close of the day, the majority of scholars being tradesmen or artisans.

[4]Rabbi Eliezer (born in Jerusalem about 40 C.E.) was the foremost learned man of his time, but his quarrelsome disposition eventually led to his excommunication. It was probably resentment at this treatment by his colleagues that led him to make such remarks about their "bite" and "sting."

Rabbi Yehoshuah said: "The evil eye and the evil desire and hatred of humanity cut a man off from the world."

Rabbi Yose said: "Let the property of your comrade be as dear to you as your own. And set yourself to learn Torah, for you can never inherit it. And let all your actions be for the sake of Heaven."

Rabbi Simeon said: "Don't pray mechanically, but let your prayer be a [heartfelt] plea and entreaty before God."

Rabbi Elazar said: "Be avid to learn Torah, and know how to refute a disbeliever."[5]

Akavya ben Mahalalel said: "Keep three things in mind, and you will escape the toils of wickedness–know whence you came, whither you are going, and before whom you will have to give a strict account of yourself. Whence did you come?–from a fetid drop [of sperm]. Whither are you going?–to a place of dust, worms, and maggots. Before whom will you have to give a strict account of yourself?–before the King of Kings, the Holy One, blessed be He."

Rabbi Hanina, deputy of the priests, said: "Pray for the stability of the government, because were it not for fear of the government, men would swallow each other alive."

Rabbi Hananyah ben Teradyon said: "When two sit together and fail to discuss Torah, lo, that is the 'seat of the scornful' but when two sit together and do discuss Torah, the *Shekhinah,* the Holy Spirit, rests on them."

Rabbi Simeon said: "If three have eaten at one table and failed to speak words of Torah during the meal, it is as if they had eaten of the sacrifices to dead [spirits]."

Rabbi Hanina ben Hachinai said: "He who stays up all night, and he who keeps to himself, and he who devotes his mind to idle thoughts, lo, such a one ruins his own well-being!"

---

[5]The Hebrew word is *Epikuros*–from the Greek, of course.

Rabbi Jacob said: "He who is walking alone and studying, but then breaks off to remark, 'How lovely is that tree!' [or] 'How beautiful is that fallow field!'–Scripture regards such a one as having hurt his own well-being."

Rabbi Hanina ben Dosa used to say: "When one's deeds are even greater than one's knowledge, the knowledge is effective; but when one's knowledge is greater than one's deeds, the knowledge is futile." He would also say: "The spirit of God is pleased with one whom the spirit of man finds pleasing."

Rabbi Dosa ben Horkinas said: "Sleep in the morning, wine during the day, childish talk, and association with boors; all these destroy a man's life."

Rabbi Elazar HaModai said: "Whoever profanes sacred things, or despises the holy days, or shames his comrade in public, or voids the covenants of the patriarch Abraham, or misinterprets the Torah, even though he have much learning and many virtuous deeds, he still has no place in the World-to-Come."

Rabbi Ishmail said: "Be obedient to a superior, affable to a petitioner, and friendly to all mankind."

Rabbi Akiva said: "Jesting and ribaldry lead a man to lewdness. Tradition protects the Torah, tithes protect wealth, vows protect virtue, and silence protects wisdom."

Rabbi Elazar ben Azariah said: "Where there is no Torah there is no refinement, and where there is no refinement there can be no Torah. Where there is no wisdom there can be no reverence, and where there is no reverence there can be no wisdom. Where there is no knowledge there can be no insight, and where there is no insight there can be no knowledge. Where there is no food there can be no Torah, and where there is no Torah, there can be no food."

Ben Zoma said: "Who is wise? He who can learn from every man. Who is strong? He who can control his passions. Who is rich? He who can feel satisfied with his lot. Who is honored? He who honors mankind."

Ben Azai used to say: "Despite no man, and consider nothing impossible, for every man has his hour and everything its place."

Rabbi Levitas of Yavneh said: "Be extremely humble, for the destiny of mortal man is the worm."

Rabbi Yohanan ben Berokah said: "He who profanes God in secret will be punished in the open, and this is true whether he commits the profanation out of ignorance or malice."

Rabbi Yose said: "He who honors the Torah is honored by mankind."

Rabbi Yonathan said: "He who fulfills the Torah amid poverty will in the end fulfill it amid wealth, and he who neglects the Torah amid wealth will in the end neglect it amid poverty."

Rabbi Meir said: "Be less busy with business and more busy with the Torah. . . . If you start neglecting the Torah, you will find more and more reasons to continue neglecting it."

Rabbi Elazar ben Shammua said: "Let the honor of your disciple be as dear to you as the honor of your colleague, the honor of your colleague as dear as your respect for your teacher, and your respect for your teacher as dear as your awe of God."

Rabbi Yehudah said: "Be cautious in teaching, for an error in teaching may lead to wilful sin."

Rabbi Simeon said: "There are three crowns – the crown of learning, the crown of priesthood, and the crown of royalty. But greater than any of these is the crown of a good name."

Rabbi Nehorai said: "Move to a place where there is learning, because you cannot expect learning to move to you."

Rabbi Jannai said: "It is beyond our power to explain either the prosperity of the wicked or the afflictions of the righteous."

Rabbi Matityah ben Heresh said: "Be first in greeting all men, and be rather a tail to lions than a head to foxes."

Rabbi Jacob used to say: "This world is no more than the

vestibule of the world to come, so get ready in the vestibule to enter the banquet hall. [However] one hour of repentance and good deeds in this world is better than a lifetime in the World-to-Come, and one hour of bliss in the World-to-Come is better than a lifetime in this world."

Rabbi Simeon ben Elazar said: "Don't try to calm your comrade when he is in a rage, or console him when he is in despair, or question him when he is vowing; and don't try to see him in the hour of his disgrace."

Rabbi Samuel the Younger said: "Don't rejoice when your enemy falls, or be glad when he stumbles."

Elisha ben Abuya[6] said: "If one learns as a child, to what is it comparable? To writing on clean paper. And if one learns as an old man, to what is that comparable? To writing on blotted paper."

Rabbi Yose bar Yehudah of K'far HaBavli said: "He who learns from the immature, to what is he comparable? To one who eats unripe grapes and drinks wine fresh from the winepress. But he who learns from the aged? He is comparable to one who eats ripe grapes and drinks old wine."

Rabbi[7] said: "What is the proper path for a man to follow? Any that seems honorable in his own sight and that wins him honor from his fellowmen." [He also said:] "Don't look at the pitcher but at what it contains. Sometimes a new pitcher is full of old wine, and an old pitcher is empty even of new wine."

Rabbi Elazar HaKappar said: "Envy, cupidity, and ambition drive a man from the world."

Yehudah ben Tama used to say: "At the age of five one is ready to study the Bible, at ten to study the Mishnah, at

---

[6]Although one of the most brilliant of the Talmudic sages, Elisha ben Abuya (born about 80 C.E.) was denied the title of Rabbi, perhaps because he eventually turned freethinker.

[7]Judah the Holy One, or the Prince, is commonly referred to simply as "Rabbi" because of his distinction as final compiler of the *Mishnah.* He is said to have been born in 135 C.E..

thirteen to observe the Commandments, at fifteen to study the Talmud, at eighteen to get married, at twenty to start earning a livelihood, at thirty to enter into one's full strength, at forty to show discernment, at fifty to give counsel, at sixty to start feeling old, at seventy to turn white, at eighty for travail and trouble, at ninety for senility; and at one hundred . . . for death."

Ben Bag-Bag said: "Study it [the Torah] over and over again, for everything is in it. Grow gray and old studying it, and never forsake it, for there is no better path for a man to follow."

This is the way of the studious life: eat a crust with salt, drink measured water, sleep on the floor, endure much hardship, and wrestle with the Torah. If you do all that, you will be happy and it will be well with you – that is, you will be happy in this world, and it will be well with you in the World-to-Come.

Don't try to be a great one, and don't look for more honor than your learning merits. Don't crave to sit at the table of kings, for your own table is better than theirs, and your crown likewise.

Rabbi Yose ben Kisma said: "Once, while on a walk, I met a man, and after we had exchanged greetings he said to me, 'Rabbi, whence do you hail?' I answered, 'From a great city where there are sages and scribes.' So then he said, 'If you agree to stay with us here, I'll give you a thousand thousand gold coins, as well as precious stones and pearls.' Whereupon I answered, 'If you were to offer me all the silver and gold and precious stones and pearls in creation, I'd still refuse to stay in any place where there is no study of the Torah!' "

There are seven traits in a wise man:
He does not speak in the presence of one wiser than himself;
He does not interrupt when a colleague speaks;
He does not rush out with a rejoinder;

He asks questions that are relevant, and gives answers that are logical;
He deals with first things first and last things last;
He readily admits when he does not know about a matter;
He acknowledges the truth.
The opposites of these traits mark the boorish man.

There are four types among men:
The ordinary one says: "What is mine is mine, and what is yours is yours.
The ignorant one says: "What is mine is yours, and what is yours is mine."
The saintly one says: "What is mine is yours, and what is yours is yours."
The wicked one says: "What is mine is mine, and what is yours is also mine."

There are four types of temperaments:
Easty to provoke and easy to calm. Here the fault is cancelled by the virtue.
Hard to provoke, but hard to calm. Here the virtue is cancelled by the fault.
Hard to provoke, and easy to calm. This is the temperament of a good man.
Easy to provoke, but hard to calm. This is the temperament of a wicked man.

There are four kinds of disciples:
Quick to learn, but quick to forget. In him the gift is cancelled by the failing.
Slow to learn, but slow to forget. In him the failing is cancelled by the gift.
Quick to learn and slow to forget. His is a fortunate lot.
Slow to learn and quick to forget. His is an evil plight.

There are four kinds of almsgivers:
He who gives, but doesn't want others to do so.
He who wants others to give, but won't do so himself.
He who gives and wants others to do likewise.
He who neither gives nor wishes others to give.

CHAPTER 28

WISDOM FROM THE GEMARA

There are two Talmuds. One is known as the Jerusalem Talmud and grew up in Palestine, where a remnant of Israel continued to maintain itself despite the most harrowing afflictions. The other, the Babylonian Talmud, was created in Babylonia where the Jews were safe from Roman oppression, and rabbinical studies could be carried on unhindered. This second work is naturally the superior one—so much so that it is commonly referred to as the Talmud. The following miscellany is culled from both works, the initials "J.T." being used to distinguish the quotations from the Jerusalem Talmud.[1]

The Torah is likened to salt, the Mishnah to pepper, but the Gemara to spices. The Torah is likened to water, the Mishnah to wine, but the Gemara to spiced wine. (Sofrim, 14a)

ON GOD

The elders in Rome were asked, "If your God takes no pleasure in the worship of idols, why does He not destroy them?"

[1]The translations—with some few exceptions—are those given in Montefiore and Loewe's admirable *Rabbinic Anthology* (London, Macmillan & Co., 1938) and Newman and Spitz's even more comprehensive *Talmudic Anthology,* published by Behrman's Jewish Book House in New York.

They replied, "If men had worshipped the things which the world does not need, He would certainly have destroyed them. But they worship the sun, moon, stars and planets. Is He to destroy His world because of the fools?"

The questioners replied, "Then He ought at least to destroy the things which the world does not need, and leave the others."

The elders said, "Then the worshippers of the stars, sun, and moon would be strengthened in their idolatry, for they would say, 'Behold, these verily are true gods, for they have not been destroyed.' " (Avodah Zarah, 54b)

It happened that when Rabbi Samuel went to Rome, he chanced to find a bracelet belonging to the queen. A crier went about the kingdom and announced: "Whoever returns the bracelet within thirty days shall receive such and such a reward, but if it is found upon him after thirty days, his head will be cut off." Nevertheless Rabbi Samuel would not return it until after the thirty days had elapsed. When he finally did, the queen asked him: "Did you not hear the proclamation?" He answered, "Yes." So she said: "Then why did you not return it within the thirty days?" "In order," he answered, "that you should not say I feared you, for I returned it only because I feared God." Whereupon the queen cried: "Blessed be the God of the Jews." (J.T. Baba Metzia, 2:5)

ON PRAYER

[In a time of drought] it was revealed to Abbahu in a dream that if a certain Pentekaka [i.e., man of five sins] were to pray for rain, then rain would fall. Abbahu sent for him and asked what his occupation was. Pentekaka replied, "Five sins I commit daily: I make assignations for harlots; I deck their theater; I take their garments to the baths; I clap and dance before them; and I beat the drum for their orgies."

Abbahu said to him, "Have you ever done one good deed?"

The man answered, "Once I was decking out the theater when a woman came up and wept behind one of the pillars. I asked her why she was weeping, and she told me that her husband was in prison, and that she was going to sell her body to obtain his ransom. So I pawned my bed and coverlet and gave her the money, and said, 'Go, redeem thy husband, and sin not.' "

Abbahu said to him, "Worthy art thou to pray and to be answered." (J.T. Ta'anit, 1:4)

Rabbi Meir said: "A man's words should always be few when addressing God." (Berakhot, 61a)

Rabbi Hiyya ben Abba said in the name of Rabbi Yohanan: "Whoever prolongs his prayer, and calculates on it (i.e., anticipates its fulfillment as a reward for its length), will eventually come to pain of heart" (Berakhot, 32b)

Rav said: "He whose mind is not quieted should not pray. Rabbi Hanina was wont not to pray when he was irritated." (Eruvin, 65a)

Rabbi Yohanan said: "He who recounts the praise of God more than is fitting will be torn away from the world." (Megillah, 18a)

Rav said: "Whoever has it in his power to pray on behalf of his neighbor, and fails to do so, is called a sinner." (Berakhot, 12b)

ON MAN'S INDIVIDUALITY

Even one ear of corn is not exactly like another. (J.T. Sanhedrin, 4:9)

One solitary man was brought forth at the time of Creation in order to establish God's greatness, for when a human being uses one die to stamp many coins, they come out all alike; but God stamped all men with the die of Adam, yet each is different. Therefore every man has a right to say, "For my sake was the world created." . . . It was done also in order to teach that whoever destroys a single life is as guilty as though he had destroyed the entire world, and whoever rescues a single life earns as much merit as though he had rescued the entire world. (J.T. Sanhedrin, 4:5)

ON EQUALITY AMONG MEN

One man alone was brought forth at the time of Creation in order that thereafter none should have the right to say to another, "My father was greater than your father." (J.T. Sanhedrin, 4:5)

Why was man created a solitary human being, without a companion? So that it might not be said that some races are better than others. (Sanhedrin, 37a)

The life of one man may not be sacrificed to save the life of another man. (Ohalot, 7b)

Formerly the deceased of the wealthy were buried in fancy caskets, and those of the poor in cheap coffins. The Rabbis have decreed, however, that now all who die, whether rich or poor, should be buried in inexpensive caskets. (Moed Katan, 27a)

A man came to Raba and said, "The prefect of my town has ordered me to kill so and so, or he will kill me." Raba replied, "Let him kill you; do you commit no murder. Why should you think that your blood is redder than his? Perhaps his is redder than yours." (Pesahim, 25b)

It was a favorite saying of the rabbis of Yavneh: I am a creature [of God], and my neighbor is also his creature; my work is in the city, and his in the field; I rise early to my work, and he rises early to his. As he cannot excel in my work, so I cannot excel in his work. But perhaps you say, I do great things, and he does small things. We have learned that [it matters not whether] a man does much or little, if only he directs his heart to heaven." (Berakhot, 17a)

ON ISRAEL

All Israelites are responsible for one another. (Shevuot, 39a)

Rabbi Yohanan said: "The Israelites are compared to an olive tree, because as the olive yields its oil only by hard pressure, so the Israelites do not return to righteousness except through suffering. (Menahot, 53b)

Israel is likened to a vine: the householders are the branches, the learned men are the fruit, and the unlearned the leaves. (Hullin, 92a)

Israel is like a vine. A vine is trodden underfoot, but later its wine is placed on the table of the king. So, too, does Israel, at first oppressed, eventually come to greatness. (Nedarim, 49b)

Only when you [Israelites] conduct yourselves like children of God are you deserving to be called his children. (Kiddushin, 36a)

The kind works of non-Jewish people remind God of Israel's sin. If those who did not receive the Torah perform deeds of kindness, how much the more should Israel, who accepted the Torah! (Baba Batra, 10a)

Rabbi Oshaya said: "God was charitable to Israel when He dispersed the Children of Israel among many nations."[2] (Pesahim, 87b)

God scattered His people over the earth, for only so could all the nations be gained for His service. (Pesahim, 87b)

ON GENTILES

Blessed art thou, O Lord our God, King of the universe, who hast given of thy wisdom to *all* flesh and blood. (Berakhot, 58a)

Whoever renounces idol worship may be called a Jew. (Megillah, 13a)

Even an idolator who studies Torah is like the High Priest. (Baba Kamma, 38a)

Rabbi Meir said: "A Gentile who lives a goodly life is like a High Priest." (Avodah Zarah, 3a)

God says: "Both the Gentiles and the Israelites are my handiwork, therefore how can I let the former perish on account of the latter?" (Sanhedrin, 98b)

Antoninus, the emperor, once asked Rabbi Judah, the patriarch: "Will I have a share in the World-to-Come?" Rabbi Judah replied: "Yes." "But is it not prophesied," the heathen demanded, "that none shall be left of the house of Esau?" "Yes," came the quick reply of Rabbi Judah, "but that applies only to those who commit Esau's acts of violence!" (Avodah Zarah, 10b)

The Jew is urged to resort to the aid of Gentiles in administering the affairs of his community. (J.T. Gittin, 5:9)

---

[2]When one nation persecutes a community of Jews, those in another nation can aid them.

Said Rabbi Tanchuma: "If a non-Jew bless thee, respond, "Amen," as it is written: 'Thou shalt be blessed by all peoples.'" (J.T. Berakhot, 8b)

In a city where there are both Jews and Gentiles, the collectors of alms collect both from Jews and Gentiles, and feed the poor of both, visit the sick of both, bury both, comfort the mourners whether they be Jews or Gentiles, and restore the lost goods of both. (J.T. Demai, 6:6)

To cheat a Gentile is even worse than cheating a Jew, for besides being a violation of the moral law, it brings Israel's religion into contempt and desecrates the name of Israel's God. (Baba Kamma, 113b)

He who steals from a non-Jew is bound to make restitution to the non-Jew; it is worse to steal from a non-Jew than to steal from an Israelite because of the profanation of the name of God. (J.T. Baba Kamma, 10:15)

Once the Roman Senate planned to adopt a law prohibiting the observance of the Sabbath and the performance of the circumcision rite.

Rabbi Reuben decided to outwit the oppressors, so he disguised himself as a Roman, came before the Senate, and said: "You hate the Jews, yet you will enable them to become richer if you make them labor seven days a week instead of six." So the Senate voted down the first prohibition.

Rabbi Reuben continued: "You will also keep them from weakening themselves if you forbid the rite of circumcision." So this prohibition, too, was voted down. (Megillah, 17a)

ON PROSELYTES

The Rabbis say: If anyone comes nowadays, and desires to become a proselyte, they say to him: "Why do you want to become a proselyte? Do you not know that the Israelites are harried, hounded, persecuted, and harassed, and that sufferings befall them?" If he says, "I know it, and I am not worthy," they receive him without further argument. (Yevamot, 47a)

One who desires to become a proselyte from love of a Jewess or of a Jew is not accepted. Nor are would-be proselytes from fear, or because of worldly advantage, received. But Rab said: They are to be received; this is the *halakhah* [i.e., the established rule]: they *are* to be considered as proselytes; they are not to be repelled, as would-be proselytes are repelled at the outset [to test their sincerity], and they must have friendly treatment, for perhaps after all they have become proselytes in purity of motive. (J.T. Kiddushin, 4)

Proselytes are as difficult for Israel as an ailment of the skin. (Yevamot, 47b)

ON KINDNESS

The highest wisdom is kindness. (Berakhot, 17a)

Deeds of kindness are equal in weight to all the commandments. (J.T. Pe'ah, 1:1)

"Thou shalt love thy neighbor as thyself." This is the great general rule in Torah. (J.T. Nedarim, 9:4)

The beginning and the end thereof [Torah] is the performance of loving-kindness. (Sotah, 14a)

Kindness says to Torah: Thou art beautiful only if I beautify thee. Thou art like unto a beautiful woman who needs a maidservant to watch over her beauty. (Hakdamah to Halakhot Gedolot)

If two men claim thy help, and one is thy enemy, help him first. (Baba Metzia, 32b)

Almsgiving and deeds of loving-kindness are equal to all the commandments of the Torah, but loving-kindness is greater. Almsgiving is exercised toward the living, but deeds of loving-kindness toward the living and the dead; almsgiving only to the poor, deeds of loving-kindness to the poor and to the rich. Also almsgiving is done with a man's money, deeds of loving-kindness with his money and in other ways. (Sukkah, 49b)

ON FRIENDLINESS

Better is he who shows a smiling countenance than he who offers milk to drink. (Ketubot, 111b)

Whoever gives a small coin to a poor man has six blessings bestowed upon him, but he who speaks a kind word to him obtains eleven blessings. (Baba Batra, 9b)

Once a disciple of Rabbi Akiva became ill, and no one visited him. Rabbi Akiva, however, entered the sick man's room, arranged that it be swept and cleaned, placed the pillow in order, and the like. All this assisted the recovery of the disciple. He exclaimed, "O Master, thou hast revived me." When Rabbi Akiva departed, he said: "Whosoever neglects to visit a friendless, sick person is as if he shed his blood." (Nedarim, 40a)

A man should always be alert in the fear [of God]–which means giving the soft answer that turns away wrath, increasing peace with all men, even the heathen in the street, so that he may be beloved above and on earth. (Berakhot, 17a)

He who has a claim for money upon his neighbor and knows that the latter is unable to pay, must not keep crossing his path. (Baba Metzia, 75b)

Rabbi Baruka of Huza frequented the market of Lapet. One day Elijah appeared to him there, and Rabbi Baruka asked him: "Is there among the people of this market any one that is destined to share in the World-to-Come?" Elijah replied, "There is none." But then two men appeared on the scene, and Elijah said to Rabbi Baruka, "No, here are two who will share in the World-to-Come."

Rabbi Baruka then asked them, "What is your occupation?" They said, "We are merrymakers. When we see a man who is downcast, we cheer him up; also when we see two people quarreling, we endeavor to make peace between them." (Ta'anit, 22a)

ON COMRADESHIP

People say: If two logs are dry and one is wet, the kindling of the two will kindle the wet log as well. (Sanhedrin, 93b)

People say: Either companionship or death. (Ta'anit, 23a)

A torch in the hands of one who walks alone at night is like one companion; moonlight is like two companions. (Berakhot, 43b)

In choosing a friend, go up a step. (Yevamot, 63a)

He who entreats aid for his comrade, though he himself is in need, is answered first. (Baba Kamma, 92a)

It is better for a man to cast himself into a flaming oven than to shame his comrade in public. (Berakhot, 43b)

Two dogs tending a flock were always quarreling. When the wolf attacked one, however, the other thought: "If I do not help my neighbor today, the wolf may attack me tomorrow." Thereupon the two dogs settled their differences, and together they killed the wolf. (Sanhedrin, 105a)

When Ulla ben Kosheb was hunted by the [Roman] government, he took refuge in Ludd with Rabbi Joshua ben Levi. The soldiers came and threatened to lay the entire city waste unless the fugitive was surrendered, whereupon Rabbi Joshua persuaded him to give himself up. Now the Prophet Elijah had been in the habit of appearing to this rabbi in visions, but from then on he never came again. So the rabbi fasted many days, and at last Elijah did reappear, but only to say, "Would it be right for me to show myself to informers?" (J.T. Terumot, 8:10)

If a company of Jews on a journey are overtaken by heathen bandits who say, "Deliver up one of your number, or we shall slay all of you"–then they must all be slain, for no Israelite may be delivered up to the heathen. . . . (Sanhedrin, 84a)

ON THE SOCIAL CONSCIENCE

Rabbi Jeremiah said: "He who occupies himself with the affairs of the community is as one who studies the Law." (J.T. Berakhot, 5:1)

If the community is in trouble, a man must not say, "I will go to my house, and eat and drink, and peace shall be with thee, O my soul." But a man must share in the trouble of the community, even as Moses did. He who shares in its troubles is worthy to see its consolation. (Ta'anit, 11a)

Honi HaMa'aggel once saw on his travels an old man planting a carob tree. He asked him when he thought the tree would bear fruit. "After seventy years," was the reply.

"Dost thou expect to live seventy years and eat the fruit of thy labor?"

"I did not find the world desolate when I entered it," said the old man, "and as my fathers planted for me before I was born, so do I plant for those who will come after me." (Ta'anit, 23a)

A man was removing stones from his own to public property. A sage noted this and said: "O man, why dost thou remove stones from the property of others to thine own?" The man, however, laughed at him.

Time passed. The man sold his field one day, and as he was walking away, he stimbled over some of the stones he had thrown into the roadway. He said to himself: "The sage was truly right when he declared that I was casting stones from the property of others upon mine own. That which belongs to all, belongs to each." (Baba Kamma, 50b)

ON THE GIVING OF CHARITY

The command to give charity weighs as much as all the other commandments put together. . . . he who gives alms in secret is greater than Moses. (Baba Batra, 9b)

Two disciples of Rabbi Hanina, who, like their master, disbelieved in the power of sorcerers, went into the forest to chop some firewood. They met an astrologer, who read their horoscope and predicted that they would not return alive. This, however, did not deter them from going on their way. They met an old man who accosted them and asked for food. They had only a single loaf of bread, but they divided it with him. When they returned, people who had heard the prediction asked the astrologer, "Is then your astrology false?"

He invited the two disciples to unwrap the bundles of wood which they carried. In each of them half a snake was found.

"What did you do," asked the astrologer, "to merit escape from sure death?"

"We know of nothing," they answered, "except that we gave half a loaf of bread to an old man."

Whereupon the astrologer cried: "What can I do if the God of the Jews is placated with half a loaf of bread?" (Sanhedrin, 39b)

Charity knows neither race nor creed. (Gittin, 61a)

Rabbi Johanan said: "So long as the Temple was in existence, the altar used to atone for Israel, but now a man's table atones for him." [The poor may be fed from his table, or he may have them as guests.] (Berakhot, 55a)

Rabbis Eliezer, Joshua, and Akiva went to the neighborhood of Antioch to make a collection for needy scholars. A certain Abba Judah lived there who was very liberal in giving. However, he had lost all his wealth, and when the rabbis came, he was ashamed and went home, and his visage was dejected. His wife said to him, "Why do you look so dejected?" He replied, "The rabbis have come here, and I do not know what to do."

His wife, who was even more pious than he, then said to him, "You still own one field. Sell half of it, and give them the proceeds." He did so, whereupon the rabbis prayed for him and said, "May your needs be supplied."

When they left, the man went to plow the half of the field that was still his, and as he did so, his cow stumbled and broke her hoof. He bent down to help her up, and God opened his eyes, and he found a treasure. Then he said, "Surely for my benefit has this cow broken her hoof."

When the rabbis came again, they asked how Abba Judah fared. The reply was, "Who can see Abba Judah? So rich is he in cattle and sheep and camels. He is as wealthy as he was before." Then Abba Judah himself came to the rabbis, and he greeted them, and said, "Your prayer has produced fruit upon fruit." Then they said, "Though on the last occasion others gave more than you, see, we put your name at the head of our list!" And they took him with them, and made him sit next to them at their dinner, and they applied to him the verse in Proverbs 18:16, "A man's gift makes room for him and brings him before great men." (J.T. Horyot, 3:7)

If a man sees that his means are straitened, let him give alms; and all the more if his means are large. He who cuts down his property, and gives alms is preserved from the judgment of hell. It is like two sheep swimming over a stream. The one is shorn, the other not. The shorn sheep crosses in safety, the other is swept away. (Gittin, 7a)

Let a man be generous in his charities, but let him beware of giving away all that he has. (Erchin, 28a)

He who lends without interest is more worthy than he who gives charity, and he who invests money in the business of a poor man is the most worthy of all. (Shabbat, 63a)

Rabbi Jonah said: It is not written, "Happy is he who gives to the poor," but, "Happy is he who *considers* the poor" (Psalm 41:1), that is, he who ponders how to fulfill the command to help the poor. How did Rabbi Jonah act? If he met a man of good family, who had become impoverished, he would say, "I have heard that a legacy has been left to you in such a place; take this money in advance, and pay me back later." When the man accepted it, he then said to him, "It is a gift." (J.T. Pe'ah, 9:21b)

Rabbi Elazar saw an impoverished colleague approaching, so he let a coin drop on the ground. When the other wished to return it, Rabbi Elazar said: "I lost it some time ago and despaired of finding it. It is, therefore, legally yours." (J.T. Baba Metzia, 2)

A rabbi saw a man give a penny to a beggar publicly. He said to him: "Better had you given him nothing than put him thus to shame." (Hagigah, 5a)

Mar Ukva was accustomed to throw four *zuzim* every day through a hole in his neighbor's door and walk away unseen. Once the poor recipient wished to know his benefactor and ran out of his home to detect him; but he was too late.

Rabbi Abba would drop a kerchief with coins among the poor. He was careful, however, to chase away rogues. (Ketubot, 67b)

One day when Rabbi Yohanan and Rabbi Simeon ben Lakish went to bathe in the public baths of Tiberias, they met a poor man who asked for charity. "When we come back," they told him.

But by the time they returned, he was already dead. Whereupon they said, "Since we showed him no charity when he was alive, let us attend to him now that he is dead." On laying him out for burial, however, they found a purse full of silver pieces upon him. Then they remembered what Rabbi Abbahu had said, "We must show charity even to the deceivers, for were it not for them, a man might be asked for alms by one who is truly a poor man, and he might refuse and be punished." (J.T. Pe'ah, 8:9)

The sage Nachum was called "Gimzo" because, no matter what befell him, he would say, "This too (*gam zeh*) is for the best."

It is related of him that he was blind in both eyes, crippled in both hands, that he had lost both his feet, and that the whole of his body was covered with leprosy. He lay stretched out in a tottering house, and his legs were thrust into pots of water so that the ants might not be able to get to him. One day his pupils said to him: "If you are so just a man, why do all these evil things overtake you?"

"My children," he answered, "I have brought them all on myself. One day as I was going to the house of my father-in-law, leading with me three donkeys, one laden with provisions, one with wine, and one with rare fruits, I chanced on a poor man who stopped me and said, 'Master, give me something to eat.'

"Wait," I said, "until I have unloaded my donkey." But before I could finish doing that, the man gave up the ghost. Then I went and threw myself upon him, saying: "May my eyes, which had no pity on your eyes, lose their sight; may my hands, which had no pity on your hands, be crippled; may my feet, which had no pity on your feet, be cut off." My spirit was not at rest until I had said: "May my whole body be covered with leprosy."

His pupils replied: "Woe to us, that we see you in this condition."

But he said: "Woe to me if you were not to see me." (Ta'anit, 21a)

ON THE TAKING OF CHARITY

Akiva said: "Rather make your Sabbath a workday than need the charity of your fellowman." (Pesahim, 112a)

He who eats of another's bread fears to look at him. (J.T. Pe'ah, 1:3)

He who does not need charity but takes will not die before he really needs help from others. He who is in need and yet does not take will not die before he will be able to help others. He who is neither lame nor blind, but pretends to be so, will not die before he becomes really lame and blind. (J.T. Pe'ah, 8:9)

Mar Ukba was accustomed to send a sum of money to a poor neighbor before Yom Kippur. Once his son, who took the money, reported: "The man was indulging in old wine, so I did not give him the money." His father retorted: "Nay, he must have seen better days if he has such dainty tastes. I will double the amount of my gift." (Ketubot, 67b)

ON STUDY OF THE TORAH

The Torah says: "If thou forsakest me for a single day, I shall forsake thee for two days." (J.T. Berakhot, end)

Rabbi Huna asked his son why he would not study under Rabbi Hisda, who was said to be a brilliant teacher. The son replied, "When I go to him, he speaks of vulgar things – about the functions of the digestive system, and how one should behave with regard to them."

His father replied: "Rabbi Hisda deals with the life of God's creatures, and you call that vulgar! All the more should you go to him." (Shabbat, 82a)

It was asked: "How could Rabbi Meir permit himself to learn from a heretic?" [By way of answer] Rabbi Meir took a pomegranate, ate the inside and threw away the peel. (Hagigah, 15b)

One day, at the close of the fig harvest, Rabbi Tarfon was walking in a garden, and he ate some figs which had been left behind. The custodians of the garden came up, caught him, and began to beat him unmercifully. Then Rabbi Tarfon called out, and said who he was, whereupon they let him go. Yet all his days did he grieve, saying, "Woe is me, for I have used the crown of the Law for my own profit." For the teaching ran: "A man must not say, I will study so as to be called a wise man, or rabbi, or an elder, or to have a seat in the college; but he must study from love. The honor will come of itself." (Nedarim, 62a)

A scholar who has abandoned the study of the Torah is like a bird that has abandoned its nest. (Hagigah, 9b)

Rabbah bar Rab Huna said: "He who has knowledge of the Law, but no fear of God, is like a keeper of a treasury who has the inner keys but not the outer keys. He cannot enter." (Sabbath, 31b)

ON THE MASTERS OF THE TORAH

A learned man is better than a prophet. (Baba Batra, 12a)

Six things are a disgrace to an educated person:

1. To walk on the street perfumed.
2. To walk alone by night.
3. To wear old, worn out shoes.
4. To talk with a woman overlong in the street.
5. To sit at a table with illiterate men.
6. To be late at the synagogue. (Berakhot, 43b)

A scholar is recognized by his conduct as regards money and drinking; also by the control of his temper, by his dress, and, some say also, by his speech. Four things are unseemly for a scholar: to walk out at night, to smell of scent in the street, to be among the last to enter the synagogue, to dally much with the boorish. Let the scholar be seemly and quiet in his eating, drinking, bathing, anointing, tying his shoes, his gait, his dress, his voice, and in his charitable deeds. (Derekh Eretz Zuta, 5:2, 3; 6:1; 7:2)

Even the profane talk of a disciple of the sages needs to be studied. (Sukkah, 21b)

If a great man has said something seemingly illogical, laugh not at it, but try to understand it. (Berakhot, 19b)

He who does not permit a scholar to share in the enjoyment of his property will have no blessing from it. (Sanhedrin, 92a)

If a sage dies, everyone is his kinsman, and should mourn for him. (Shabbat, 105b)

He who sees a sage die is as if he saw a Scroll of the Torah burn. Rabbi Abbahu said: "I fast on such a day." (J.T. Moed Katan, 3)

Rabbi Hiyya bar Abba asked the patriarch Judah for a letter of recommendation because he wished to leave Palestine on business. The patriarch wrote: "Behold, the bearer is a great man. His greatness consists in the fact that he is not ashamed to admit, when asked something he has not learned, that he has not heard this from his teachers. He is our representative and has equal authority with us while away." (J.T. Hagigah, 1)

Some rabbis had to transact business with a [Roman] lady with whom all the great ones of the city used to consort. They said, "Who shall go?" Rabbi Joshua said, "I will go." So he went with some disciples. When they got near her house, he took off his phylacteries and went in and shut the door behind him. When he came out, he bathed, taught his disciples, and said to them, "When I took off my phylacteries, of what did you suspect me?"

"We thought the master felt that holy objects should not be brought into an unclean place."

"And when I shut the door?"

"We thought perhaps you had a matter of state business to transact with her."

"And when I bathed?"

"We thought perhaps the spittle from her mouth might have fallen on your clothes."

He replied, "Thus it was, and as you judged me favorably, so may God judge you favorably." (Shabbat, 127b)

As the kernel of a nut is not despised, even though the shell be marred, so it is with the scholar. (Hagigah, 15b)

The emperor's daughter once said to Rabbi Joshua ben Hanania [who was very ugly]: "How is it that your God saw fit to put such glorious wisdom in so hideous a vessel!"

He replied: "Why does thy father keep wine in an earthen pitcher?"

"How else should we keep it?" she asked.

"People of your rank," said the rabbi, "should keep their wine in vessels of gold or silver."

Thereupon the princess persuaded her father to transfer the wine from earthen to gold and silver vessels. The wine, however, turned sour. The emperor summoned the rabbi and inquired why he had given such poor counsel.

Rabbi Joshua answered: "I did so to show to thy daughter that wisdom like wine is best kept in a plain vessel."

"But," the girl objected, "are there not handsome scholars as well?"

"Yes," answered the rabbi, "but they might have been greater scholars had they been ugly." (Ta'anit, 7a)

A scholar on whose garment a soiled spot is found is deserving of censure. (Shabbat, 114a)

Reside not in a town whose mayor is a disciple of the wise. He will have no time to attend to municipal affairs, being preoccupied with his studies. (Pesahim, 112a)

Rav Ashi, the teacher of Ravina, sent a message to the latter on a Friday afternoon, asking him for a loan as a deposit on a piece of land. Rabina replied to the messenger: "Please prepare the document and have witnesses."

When Rav Ashi came, he asked: "Couldst thou not trust even me?"

"Thee especially I could not," answered Ravina. "Thy mind is always full of the Law, and therefore thou art more likely than some one else to forget the loan." (Baba Metzia, 75b)

An aged scholar, who through no fault of his own forgets his learning, shall be deemed as holy as the Ark (of the Covenant). (Kiddushin, 33b)

Rabbi Yohanan said: "The words of the Torah abide only with him who regards himself as nothing." (Sotah, 21b)

One coin in a bottle rattles, but a bottle full of coins makes no sound. Similarly, the scholar who is the son of a scholar is modest; but the scholar who is the son of a yokel trumpets his knowledge all around. (Baba Metzia, 85b)

Rabbi Elazar, son of Rabbi Simon, while returning from the academy of Migdal Guedor, rode on his donkey along the bank of the river and was filled with pride because he had learned much Torah. There crossed his path a very ugly man who said, "Peace unto you, Rabbi Simon." But the rabbi, instead of returning the greeting, said, "Tell me, are all the men of your city as ugly as you?" The other replied, "I do not know. Go and say to the craftsman who made me: 'How ugly is this, the vessel Thou hast made!' "

When Rabbi Elazar saw that he had sinned, he went down from his donkey, prostrated himself before the man, and said, "Forgive me, I pray you!" The other replied, "I will not forgive you until you say to the craftsman who made me, 'How ugly is this, the vessel Thou hast made.' "

And the rabbi walked behind him, until they came to the village. The men of the village came out to meet the rabbi and said, "Peace be to you, our rabbi, our teacher!" The man said, "Who is he whom you call rabbi and teacher?" They said, "The man who is walking behind you."

"If he be a teacher," said the man, "may there be few like him in Israel!" They asked him why he said this, and he told them what had happened. "Forgive him nevertheless," they said, "for he is a man great in the Torah." So finally the man said, "For your sakes only I will forgive him, but let him never act in like fashion again."

Rabbi Elazar soon came to the school, and taught that day: "A man should be yielding, like the reed; not hard, like the cedar." (Ta'anit, 20a)

ON TEACHERS AND DISCIPLES

He who learns and does not teach is like a myrtle which grows in the desert: no one receives enjoyment from it. (Rosh Ha Shanah, 23a)

As with perfume, any one who desires may be made fragrant by it, so the scholar should be willing to teach any one who desires to profit by his learning. In such a case, his learning will be retained by him. (Eruvin, 54a)

As a little wood can set light to a great tree, so young pupils sharpen the wits of great scholars. Hence, said Rabbi Hanina:

"Much Torah have I learned from my teachers, more from my colleagues, but from my students most of all." (Ta'anit, 7a)

If a disciple knows that his teacher is able to answer him, he may ask. Otherwise he may not ask. (Hullin, 6a)

If a disciple sits at a trial, and sees that his master errs, he must interfere. (Sanhedrin, 6b)

Rabbah bar Bar Hana said: "Why are the words of Torah likened unto fire (Jeremiah 23:29)? It is to teach that as the fire from a single piece of wood does not give forth heat, so the Torah of a single student likewise does not give forth warmth."

Rav Hanina bar Idi said: "Why is the Torah likened to water (Isaiah 55:1)? It is to teach that just as one who is thirsty is not too lazy to seek water, so a disciple who has the thirst for knowledge does not hesitate to seek out a teacher." (Ta'anit, 7a)

Rav Hisda said: "To learn Torah it is best to go to one teacher; to discuss it, it is better to go to several teachers. The many different explanations will help to give you understanding." (Avodah Zarah, 19a)

If you see a student to whom his studies are as tough as iron, it is because his teacher has not explained them properly. (Ta'anit, 8a)

Rabbah would open his discourse with a jest and let his hearers laugh a little. Then he would become serious. (Shabbat, 30b)

ON WISE MEN AND FOOLS

Rabbi Yohanan said: "The Holy One, blessed be He, gives wisdom only to him who has wisdom." (Berakot, 55a)

Once a Roman lady put this question to Rabbi Yose ben Halafta: "Is it a fact that all God's praise consists in his 'giving wisdom to the wise?' It should rather be by giving wisdom to fools!"

Yose said to her, "Have you any jewels?"

She answered, "Certainly."

"If someone comes and wishes to borrow them, will you lend them to him?"

She said, "Yes, I will, if he is a man of responsibility."

"Then," said Yose, "you will not lend your jewels save to a worthy borrower, and shall God give his wisdom to fools?" (Berakhot, 55a)

He who has understanding has everything. (Nedarim, 41a)

The wise man knows at the commencement of a matter what its end will be. (J.T. Sotah, 5 end)

ON HONORING PARENTS

There are three partners in man: God, his father, and his mother. (Kiddushin, 30b)

In what does reverence for a father consist? In not sitting in his presence, and in not speaking in his presence, and in not contradicting him. Of what does honor for parents consist? In providing for them food and drink, in clothing them, in giving them shoes for their feet, in helping them to enter or leave the house [or, possibly, to spend and to earn]. Rabbi Eliezer said: "Even if his father orders him to throw a purse of gold into the sea, the son should obey him." (Kiddushin, 31b)

Rabbi Abbahu said, "My son Abimi fulfilled the command, 'Honor thy father and mother.' " Abimi had five sons ordained as rabbis in his father's lifetime, but whenever his father came and called out at his gate, Abimi would run to open the door, and call, "Yes, yes, I am coming to you." One day his father asked him for some water. When he brought it, his father had fallen asleep. Abimi bent over him, and stood there until his father woke up. (Kiddushin, 31b)

Rabbi Meir would show respect for an aged man even if he was a boor, for he argued, "Not for nothing is one able to attain a long life." (J.T. Bikkurim, 3:3)

Rav Joseph, hearing the step of his mother as she entered, would say: "I must stand up, for the Shekhinah (Holy Spirit) enters." (Kiddushin, 31a)

Once a man gave his father several fat chickens. The father asked: "My son, can you afford this?"

The son replied: "Eat what you are given and ask no questions."

Another man was grinding meal. An official came to conscript a member of the family to do forced labor for the government. The son said: "Do the grinding, my father, and I shall go. Thus will you avoid the discomforts of forced labor."

The Sages said: "The first fed his parent well, yet his lot will be in Gehenna. The second made his father perform hard work, yet his lot will be in Eden." (J.T. Pe'ah, 1a)

ON WOMEN

Why is it easier to appease a male than a female? Because the first male was created out of soft dust, but the first female out of hard bone. (Niddah, 31)

The Rabbis say that if a male and female orphan have to be maintained, the female takes precedence, for a man can beg, but a woman cannot. It is the same as regards marriage; the female should be married first, for the shame of a woman is greater than the shame of a man. (Ketubot, 67a)

People say if a male dog barks at thee, enter; if a female dog, depart. (Eruvin, 86a)

A woman recognizes the worth of a guest quicker than a man. (Berakhot, 10)

A bride who has fine eyes is fine throughout. (Ta'anit, 24a)

ON MARRIAGE

A man should not marry a woman with the thought in mind that he may divorce her. (Yevamot, 37b)

He who weds for money will have delinquent offspring. (Kiddushin, 70a)

There is no marriage settlement wherein there is no quarrel. (Shabbat, 130a)

A man once said: "When our love was strong, we could sleep in a bed no wider than the edge of a sword; but now that our love has waned, a bed sixty feet across seems too narrow for us." (Sanhedrin, 7a)

Rav said: "Be careful not to hurt your wife, because woman is prone to tears and sensitive to wrong." Rabbi Helbo said: "Be careful about the honor of your wife, for blessing enters the house only because of the wife." (Baba Metzia, 59a)

Rabbi Yohanan said: "If a man's first wife dies, it is as if the Temple were destroyed in his day."

Rabbi Alexandri said: "If a man's wife dies, the world becomes dark for him."

Rabbi Samuel ben Nachman said: "For everything there is a substitute except for the wife of one's youth."

Rabbi Akiva said: "He is wealthy who possesses a virtuous wife." (Sanhedrin, 22a)

The emperor said to Rabban Gamliel: "Your God is a thief, for did He not cause Adam to fall asleep and then steal one of his ribs?"

At this the rabbi's daughter interrupted and cried to the emperor to send for the police.

"What has happened?" asked the emperor.

"A thief entered my house last night," she replied, "and took away a silver pitcher, but left a gold one in its place."

The emperor said: "Would that such a thief would come to me every night."

Whereupon the daughter of Rabban Gamliel replied: "Why then do you decry our God? Did he not steal a rib from Adam only to enrich him with a wife?" (Sanhedrin, 22b)

A certain woman used to go to the synagogue each Friday evening to hear Rabbi Meir address the general congregation. One evening his sermon was so lengthy that the lamp in her home went out before she could return. This angered her husband (because the Law forbade kindling a light on the Sabbath) and when she told him where she had been, he cried: "Never shall you reenter this house until you have spat in the eyes of the preacher."

Now Rabbi Meir, aided by the Holy Spirit, saw what had happened, and immediately pretended that there was something wrong with his eyes. He announced, "Any woman who knows how to whisper a spell against pains in the eyes, let her come and whisper it."

Hearing this, the neighbors said to the woman: "Now at last

you can return to your house. Pretend that you are going to whisper a spell, and then spit in the rabbi's eyes."

So she went to him, but when he asked her whether she could whisper a spell, she could not bring herself to say yes. Thereupon he said, "Spit seven times into my eyes, for that will heal them."

This she did do, and then the rabbi said: "Now go and tell your husband, 'You told me to spit once, and I have spat seven times.' "

Thereupon the disciples cried to their master: "Should the Law be thus made contemptible? If you had told us, we would have sent for the man, and lashed him with rods till he had made it up with his wife." He, however, answered: "Shall it not be with the honor of Rabbi Meir as with the honor of his Maker? If the Holy Name may be washed away in water, in order to make peace between a man and his wife, how much more is this true of the honor of Rabbi Meier!" (J.T. Sotah, 16:45)

ON FAMILY LIFE

A man rejoices when he dwells in his own home. (J.T. Moed Katan, 2:4)

He who loves his wife as himself, who honors her more than himself, who rears his children in the right path, and who marries them off at the proper time in life, concerning him it is written: "Thou wilt know that thy home is at peace." (Yevamot, 62b)

Do not inspire overmuch fear among the members of thy household. (Gittin, 6b)

Anger in a home is like rottenness in fruit. Immorality in a home is like a worm in fruit. (Sotah, 3b)

The Torah teaches us a lesson: first build a home, then marry. (Sotah, 44a)

Can a goat live in the same barn as a tiger? In the same fashion, a daughter-in-law cannot live with her mother-in-law under the same roof. (Ma'aseh Torah, 4)

The life of the mother takes precedence over the life of the unborn child. (Ohalot, 7)

A man should not marry a pregnant widow or a divorcee until after the child is born. (Yevamot, 36b)

Most bastards are wise, and a fool is worse than them. (J.T. Kiddushin, end)

Three things make a man cheerful: a good home, a good wife, and good enough possessions. (Berakhot, 57b)

ON CHILDREN

As my fathers planted for me, so do I plant for my children. (Ta'anit, 23a)

Do not threaten a child. Either punish or forgive him. (Semahot, 2:6)

If thou must strike a child, strike it with the string of a shoe. (Baba Batra, 21a)

A child is inclined to exaggerate his own importance. (Sukkah, 21a)

Rabbi Zera said: "One must not promise to give something to a child, and not give it to him, because thereby he is taught to lie. (Sukkah, 46b)

He who gives food to a small child, must tell its mother. (Shabbat, 10b)

It is important for the development of a growing child that he be given things to break. Rabbah often bought imperfect earthenware for his little ones to break if they wished. (Hullin, 24)

The father's obligations to his son are: he must circumcise him, redeem him, teach him Torah, teach him a trade, and help him secure a wife. Some say he should also teach him to swim.

Rabbi Judah ben Ilai said: "A man who does not teach his son a trade, teaches him robbery." (Tosefta Kiddushin, 1:11)

TEACHING THE YOUNG

The world itself rests upon the breath of the children in the schoolhouse.

Rabbi Hamnuna said: "Jerusalem was destroyed only because the children did not attend school and loitered in the streets." (Shabbat, 119b)

Take care of the children of the poor for they are the ones who advance science. (Nedarim, 81a)

Encourage the children of the peasants, for it is they who increase knowledge. (Sanhedrin, 96a)

Whoever teaches his son teaches not his son alone, but also his son's son, and so on to the end of all generations.

Rabbi Hiyya ate no breakfast until he had taught a boy a bit of Scripture, repeating with him what he had learned the day before, and teaching him a new bit. Rabbi Huna ate no breakfast until he had taken a boy to school. (Kiddushin, 30a)

A calf may wish to suckle, but the cow wishes even more to give suck. [The teacher wishes to teach even more than the pupil wishes to learn.] (Pesahim, 112a)

Raba said: "If there are more than twenty-five children in a class for elementary instruction, an assistant should be appointed. If there are fifty children in a class, two competent instructors should be in charge."

Rav Dimi said: "A teacher who teaches less than his fellow instructors should be dismissed. The other teachers will become more diligent both out of fear of dismissal and out of gratitude.

"If a teacher is to be appointed, preference should be given to him who teaches thoroughly, not to him who teaches much superficially; for an error once learned is difficult to unlearn." (Baba Batra, 21a)

We read: "My doctrine shall drop as the rain, my speech shall distil as the dew" (Deuteronomy 32:2). Commenting on this the rabbis said: "If a teacher is incompetent, his words seem to the pupils as harsh as falling rain; but if he is competent, his teaching is distilled gently like dew." (Ta'anit, 7a)

He who studies and does not repeat his lessons is as one who plants and does not enjoy the fruit. (Sanhedrin, 90)

He who understands the why and wherefore of what he learns does not forget it quickly. (J. T. Berakhot, 5:1)

ON POVERTY

Poverty is more grievous than fifty plagues. (Baba Batra, 116a)

Three lives are no lives: he who lives off others; he who is ruled by his wife; he whose body is overcome by sufferings; and some say, he who has only one shirt! (Betzah, 32b)

People say: When food is lacking in the larder, quarrel knocks at the door. (Baba Metzia, 59a)

Rabbi Kahana, who was forced to peddle baskets in order to make a living, was once urged by a Gentile housewife to come and sin with her. He put her off by saying, "First let me go and get ready." Then, ascending to the roof, he jumped.

Elijah came and caught him in time, but complained, saying: "I had to rush 400 miles to catch you." Whereupon Kahana answered: "Had it not been for my poverty, I might never have been put into a position where I had to jump." So then Elijah gave him a potful of gold coins. (Kiddushin, 40a)

All the members of the body depend upon the heart, and the heart depends on the purse. (J.T. Terumot, 8, end)

ON THE DIGNITY OF LABOR

No labor, however humble, is dishonoring. (Nedarim, 49b)

Artisans are not required to stand up from their labor when a sage passes by. (Kuddushin, 33a)

Rabbi Judah would enter the House of Study carrying a jug [which he himself had made], and Rabbi Simeon carrying a basket [which he himself had woven]. They said, "Great is handicraft, for it honors those who engage in it." (Nedarim, 49b)

A man is obliged to teach his son a trade, and whoever does not teach his son a trade teaches him to become a robber. The person who has a trade in his hand is like a vineyard which is fenced in, so that cattle and beasts cannot get in, or passers-by eat of it. (Tosefta Kiddushin, 1:2)

The Law declares that for stealing an ox one must repay fivefold, but for a lamb only fourfold (Exodus 22:1). Rabbi Meir said, "See how God loves a worker! Why must the thief repay fivefold for an ox? Because the ox is a worker and his work was interrupted. But for the lamb, which is not a worker, the thief needs to repay only fourfold." (Tosefta Baba Kamma, 7:10)

Hire yourself out to a work which is beneath you rather than become dependent on others. (J.T. Sanhedrin, 11, f. 30b)

Greater even than the pious man is he who eats that which is the fruit of his own toil; for Scripture declares him twice-blessed. (Berakhot, 8a)

ON THE WAGES OF LABOR

The right of the workingman always has precedence over that of his employer. (Baba Metzia, 77a)

Rabbi Yohanan gave to his slave a portion of everything he himself atc. He said: "Did not He who made me also make him? Did not One fashion both of us in the womb?" (J.T. Ketubot, 5)

The son of Rabbi Yohanan ben Matthias hired several laborers and promised them their meals. His father said: "It would have been better had you given them their full hire in money, and let them buy their own meals . . . for a worker is entitled to eat what he himself prefers." (Baba Metzia, 86b)

Said Rabbi Huna: "The waiter should have his portion after the meal is over; but if fat meat or old wine is served, he must receive it immediately so that he may be spared the pain of longing for it." (Ketubot, 61a)

The gait of the ass is according to the amount of barley he receives. (Shabbat, 51b)

ON THE TREATMENT OF ANIMALS

Rabbi Judah said in the name of Rav: "A man is forbidden to eat anything until he has fed his beast." (Gittin, 62a)

The patriarch, Rabbi Judah I, suffered from a toothache for many years. Why was he thus punished? Because he once saw a bound calf being taken to the slaughter. The calf bleated and appealed for his aid, but the rabbi said: "Go, since it is for this that thou hast been created."

How was the patriarch cured? He once saw a litter of mice being carried to the river to be drowned. He said: "Let them go free, for it is written, 'His mercies are over all His works.' " (J.T. Kilaim, chapter 9)

Once Rabbi Judah the Prince sat and taught the Law before an assembly of Babylonian Jews in Sepphoris, and a calf passed before him. It came and sought to conceal itself, and began to moo, as if to say, "Save me." Then he said, "What can I do for you? For this lot alone [i.e., to be slaughtered] were you created." As a result Rabbi Judah suffered toothache for thirteen years. . . . At the end of that time a weasel chanced to run past his daughter, and she wanted to kill it. He said to her, "Let it alone, for it is written, 'His mercies are over all His works.' " So then it was decreed in Heaven, "Because Rabbi Judah had pity, pity shall be shown to him." Thus, his toothache ceased. (Baba Metzia, 85a)

No man may buy a beast, an animal, or a bird until he has provided food for it. (J.T. Yevamot, 15:3)

ON SICKNESS AND HEALTH

Zunin met Rabbi Akiva and said: "Rabbi, there is a thing that perplexes me greatly. Scores of sick and ailing people come and testify: 'We have worshipped in this or that temple of an idol and we have been cured.' "

Rabbi Akiva replied: "I shall explain it to you by means of a parable. In a certain town there lived a trustworthy person who owned a strong safe, and people would let him store their valuables without either witness or a receipt. Once a man came with witnesses for his deposit. He followed this routine many times, but finally on one occasion brought no witnesses.

"The wife of the trustworthy man said to him: 'Let us teach this fellow a lesson since he mistrusts us. When he asks for his deposit, deny that we have received it.'

"Her husband answered: 'Because this man does not act correctly, shall I do likewise?'

"So it is with sicknesses. When God sends them, He places a limited time upon them. Would it be right for these ailments to betray their mission, and not depart from their victims when their time is passed, merely because those victims have been superstitious and behaved like fools?" (Avodah Zarah, 55a)

Rabbi Ishmael ben Rabbi Yose said: "The cold stones on which we sat in our youth caused us disorders in our old age."

Rabbi Jonah told his disciples never to sit on the outer steps of the schools because these were certain to be cold.

When Rabbi Joseph felt chilly, he would work in a mill to warm himself.

Rabbi Sheshet, in such a case, would drag logs, saying: "Great is labor, it warms up the laborer." (J.T. Shabbat, 14:3)

More people die from overeating than from undernourishment. (Shabbat, 33a)

If you have a fine meal to consume, enjoy it in a good light. (Yoma, 74b)

If a man chews well with his teeth, his feet will find strength.

Food is better for a man up to the age of forty; after forty, drink is better. (Shabbat, 152a)

Uncleanness of the body brings illnesses of the skin; of the garments, madness; of the head, blindness. (Nedarim, 81a)

ON PHYSICIANS

The proverb says: "Pay homage to the physician before you need him." (J.T. Ta'anit, 3:5)

A physician who takes no fee is worth no fee. (Baba Kamma, 85a)

A physician from afar has a blind eye. [The family physician understands your case better.] (Baba Kamma, 85a)

ON GOVERNMENT

He who rebels against his Sovereign deserves to die. (Sanhedrin, 49a)

The law of the country is the law [to be observed by Jews]. (Baba Kamma, 113a)

As the fish die when they are out of water, so do people die without law and order. (Avodah Zarah, 4a)

Rabbi Isaac said: "A ruler is not to be appointed unless the community is first consulted." (Berakhot, 55a)

ON LEADERS AND LEADERSHIP

In the place where there is already a leader, do not seek to become a leader; but in the place where there is no leader, strive thou to become a leader. (Berakhot, 63a)

Greatness seeks out the man who runs away from greatness. (Eruvin, 13b)

The years of him are shortened who runs after leadership. . . . Why did Joseph die before his brothers? Because he was imperious and ruled over them. (Berakhot, 55a)

"Before I was elected to head the court, I would have thrown to the lions anyone who would have suggested to me to become a candidate. After my election, I would throw boiling water on anyone who would suggest that I resign." (Menahot, 109)

Happy the generation where the great listen to the small, for it follows that in such a generation the small will listen to the great. (Rosh HaShanah, 25b)

Like generation, like leader. (Erchin, 17)

What can the great ones do if their generation is evil? (Ta'anit, 24b)

Woe to the ship whose captain has been lost. (Baba Batra, 91b)

ON THE CONDUCT OF JUDGES

Commenting on the text, "Thou shalt not take a bribe," the rabbis say: this means not merely a money-bribe, but every other kind. Thus, on one occasion, when Rabbi Samuel was getting on a ferry, a man rushed up to give him a hand. Rabbi Samuel asked him why he was so attentive, and the man replied, "I have a lawsuit in your court." Thereupon Samuel said: "I am forbidden to be your judge." (Ketubot, 105b)

Mar bar Rav Ashi said: "I cannot try the case of a student of the law because I love him as myself, and no one can see a fault in himself." (Shabbat, 119a)

A judge who has made a loan from a man on trial may not sit in judgment over him. (Sanhedrin, 105b)

Two scholars who dislike each other shall not sit together as judges at a trial. (Sanhedrin, 29a)

After a trial has been concluded, no one of the judges on leaving the court may say: "I acquitted him; my colleagues convicted him. What could I do? They outvoted me." Of such a one it is written, "Thou shalt not go about as a talebearer among thy people"; and "He that goes about as a talebearer reveals secrets" (Leviticus 19:16; Proverbs 11:13). (Sanhedrin, 31a)

A man may not accuse himself of a crime. (Yevamot, 25b)

A man cannot be declared guilty in his absence. (Ketubot, 11a)

Silence is equivalent to confession. (Yevamot, 87b)

Judgment delayed is judgment voided. (Sanhedrin, 95a)

ON SINCERITY

The whole worth of a benevolent deed lies in the love that inspires it. (Sukkah, 49b)

It is not external rites that win forgiveness, but inward sincerity. (Ta'anit, 16a)

It matters not whether a man gives little or much, if only his heart goes out with it to his Father in Heaven. (Berakhot, 17a)

The essence of goodness is good intent. (Megillah, 20a)

If a man intended to perform a good deed, but was prevented, he is regarded as though he had actually carried it out. (Kiddushin, 40a)

"And it came to pass when Moses held up his hand that Israel prevailed, and when he let down his hand, Amalek prevailed" (Exodus 17:11). Commenting on this, the rabbis said: "Could the mere position of the hand of Moses influence the battle? The true meaning of the verse is that at such times as the Israelites directed their thoughts on high, and kept their hearts sincerely turned to their Father in heaven, they prevailed. At all other times they suffered defeat." (J.T. Rosh HaShanah, 3:8)

There are seven kinds of thieves, but the worst kind is he who deceives his fellowman. For example, he who urges his neighbor to be his guest when in his heart he does not really want to invite him. Or he who presses gifts on his neighbor when he knows the other will not accept them. (Tosefta Baba Kamma, 7:8)

ON THE VIRTUE OF SILENCE

For every affliction, silence is the best remedy. (Megillah, 18a)

Press thy lips together and be not in a hurry to answer. (Avodah Zarah, 35a)

If silence be good for the wise, how much the better for fools. (Pesahim, 98b)

ON PRIDE AND HUMILITY

Why was man created on the sixth day? To teach that if he is ever swollen with pride, it can be said to him: A flea came ahead of thee in creation. (Sanhedrin, 38a)

Rabbi Hanina bar Idi said: "Why are the words of the Torah likened unto water (Isaiah 55:1)?" The answer is: Just as water forsakes a high place and travels to a low one, just so do the words of Torah find a resting place only in a man of humble spirit.

Rabbi Oshaya said: "Why are the words of the Torah likened to water, wine, and milk (Isaiah 55:1)?" The answer is: Just as these liquids are kept only in the simplest of vessels, so the holy words are preserved only in the man of humble spirit. (Ta'anit, 7a)

O Bush of Moses! Not because thou art tall, but because thou art lowly, did God reveal Himself in thee. (Shabbat, 67a)

The proud man is not loved even in his own household. (Baba Batra, 98a)

Absalom was proud of his hair and, therefore, was he hanged by his hair. (Sotah, 9b)

God says concerning the man of pride: "I and he cannot abide together." (Sotah, 5)

Once Rav Nahman bar Isaac seated himself among the young students; another rabbi went over to him and said: "Will you not be good enough to take a place more toward the front, where I am seated?"

Rav Nahman bar Isaac replied: "The place does not honor the man, but the man honors the place. When the Shekhinah was on Mount Sinai, no one was allowed to approach the Mount, but when the Shekhinah departed, everyone was allowed to ascend it." (Ta'anit, 21b)

Because of three types of men the Almighty weeps daily; and of these three the worst is the presiding elder who acts haughtily toward his congregation. (Hagigah, 5b)

ON GOOD MANNERS

He who is versed in Scripture, Talmud, and good manners will not easily fall into sin – as it is said, "A threefold cord is not easily torn" (Ecclesiastes 4:12). He who has none of the three is not a civilized man. (Kiddushin, 1:10)

He who eats in the street is like a dog. (Kiddushin, 40)

The saying goes: "After you have paid your fine in court, sing a song to yourself and walk away." (Baba Kamma, 7)

One must not ask the price of a thing if one has no intention of buying it.

One must not say to a man who has repented [and changed his way of life], "Remember your former deeds."

If a man is a descendant of proselytes, one must not say to him, "Remember the deeds of your ancestors." So the Mishnah. The Gemara enlarges: If a proselyte wants to study the Law, one must not say, "What! A mouth which ate forbidden food and creeping abominations wants to learn the Law which was spoken by the mouth of God!"

If sufferings and sickness befall anyone, or if his children die, one must not say to him, as Job's friends said to Job, "Who ever perished being innocent?"

If there is a case of hanging in a man's family, never say to him, "Hang this fish up for me." (Baba Metzia, 59b)

Rabbi Hanan ben Raba said: "Everyone knows why a bride enters the bridal chamber; but if a man sullies his lips by speaking of it, then even if seventy years' prosperity have been decreed for him, it is reversed."

Rabbah ben Shela said, in the name of Rabbi Hisda: "If a man sullies his mouth with ribaldry, hell is deepened for him. Wounds and boils follow lasciviousness . . . dropsy is its mark." (Shabbat, 33a)

A little praise of a man may be uttered in his presence, but fulsome praise in his presence is forbidden. (Eruvin, 18b)

Great is hospitality; greater even than early attendance at the House of Study, or than the reception of the Holy Spirit. (Shabbat, 127a)

Who is a despicable guest? One who brings along another guest, or who creates unusual bother. (Derekh Eretz Zuta, 8)

ON THRIFT

Eat vegetables and fear no creditors, rather than eat duck and hide. (Pesahim, 114a)

A penny added to a penny creates in the end a large sum. (Sotah, 8b)

The improvident man who refuses to live within his means, and seeks to be supported by charity, must not be helped. (Ketubot, 67b)

He who has inherited much and desires to lose his inheritance should clothe himself in linen and use glassware. (Baba Metzia, 29b)

Sell thyself to a work beneath thee rather than beg favors of Me. (J.T. Berakhot, 9:2)

ON PRUDENCE

Rabbi Yannai would not board a ferry until he had examined it as to its safety. Rabbi Zeira would not pass between trees on a windy day. Rav and Samuel would not use a shortcut which passed by a ruined wall, even though that wall had stood for many years. Rabbi Yannai said: "A person should never take chances in a place of danger and expect to be rescued miraculously. Even if a miracle does occur, his reward in the World-to-Come is thereby lessened. (Shabbat, 32a)

Rabbi Hiyya bar Abba asked Rabbi Assi: "Why do the sages in Babylonia dress in so distinguished a manner?"

Rabbi Assi replied: "Because they are minor scholars, they desire to be respected because of their attire."

Rabbi Yohanan overheard him and said: "Thou art wrong. They dress well because they are immigrants there; and the popular saying runs: 'In my own town I am respected for the name I have achieved; in a strange town I am respected because of my raiment.' " (Shabbat, 145b)

People say: "Make use of a costly vessel today, and enjoy it, for it may be taken from you tomorrow."(Berakhot, 28a)

Eat a third, drink a third, and leave the remaining third of your stomach empty. Then, if anger overtakes you, there will be room in it for gas, and you will not suffer from apoplexy. (Gittin, 70a)

Teach thy tongue to say: "I do not know," lest thou invent something and be trapped. (Berakhot, 4a)

ON HONESTY

When man appears before the Throne of Judgment, the first question he is asked is not: "Have you believed in God?" or "Have you prayed and observed the ritual?" He is asked: "Have you dealt honorably and faithfully in all your dealings with your fellowman?" (Shabbat, 31a)

Once the tradesman has made up his mind to take a certain price for his goods, he may not raise it even if he has the chance. (Kuddushin, 30b)

Nor may the tradesman demand twice the amount of his debt, in order that he may the more easily recover the true amount. (Shevuot, 31a)

ON GREED AND USURY

Why are men like weasels? A weasel hoards and knows not for what purpose. So it is with men. (J.T. Shabbat, 13:1)

There are persons who are chained to gold and silver. (Shabbat, 54a)

He who walks in perfection is the man who does not lend on interest either to Jew or Gentile. (Makkot, 24a)

Mark the blind folly of the usurer. If a man were to call him a scoundrel, he would fight him to the death; and yet he takes pen, ink, and paper, and in the presence of witnesses solemnly writes himself down a rogue, and a denier of Israel's God. (Baba Metzia, 71a)

ON SIN

Rabbi Hanina ben Hama said: "Everything is in the power of Heaven except the fear of Heaven. God in His providence determines beforehand what a man shall be and what shall befall him, but not whether he shall be righteous or wicked." (Niddah, 16b)

If a man guard himself against transgression once, twice, and thrice, God guards him henceforth. (J.T. Kuddushin, 1, end)

When a man commits the same offense twice, it seems to him already permissible. (Yoma, 87a)

If a man makes a harness for his beast, how much the more should he fashion a harness for his impulses, which may prompt him to lead a good or evil life. (J.T. Sanhedrin, 10:1)

To what may a sinner be likened? To one who beholds open handcuffs and places his hands in them. (J.T. Nedarim, 9:1)

When Rabbi Yohanan ben Zakkai was sick unto death, his disciples came to visit him, and before leaving him they said: "Master, give us thy farewell blessing."

He said to them, "O that the fear of God may be as much upon you as the fear of man."

His disciples remarked: "Should we not fear the Lord more than man?"

He replied: "If you should fear to sin in private, where God alone is aware of it, as much as you fear to sin in public, why should more be desired?" (Berakhot, 28b)

No man sins for someone else. (Baba Metzia, 8a)

Rabbi Meir was sorely vexed by some neighbors, and fervently prayed that God take them from the earth. His wife,

Beruriah, reasoned with him, however, and said: "It is written, 'Let sin cease to be and the wicked will be no more.' Pray, therefore, on their behalf, that they may be led to repentance, and those who are wicked will be evil no more." (Berakhot, 9b)

Frankincense has an evil odor, and yet it is included among the ingredients of the holy incense. This teaches us that thou shalt not hesitate to include sinners among the congregation that worships. (Keritot, 6b)

ON THE EVIL IMPULSE[3]

This is the trick of the Evil Impulse: Today it says to you, "Do this"; tomorrow, "Do that"–and finally it says, "Worship an idol." Moreover, you actually do that. (Shabbat, 105b)

The Evil Impulse desires only that which is forbidden. Rabbi Mena (on the Day of Atonement) went to visit Rabbi Haggai who was ill.

Rabbi Haggai said, "I am thirsty."

Rabbi Mena said, "You may drink" [despite that it is a fast day]. After an hour he came again and said, "How about your thirst?"

The sick man answered, "No sooner did you permit me to drink than the desire left me." (J.T. Yoma, 6:4)

If the Evil Impulse says to thee: "Sin and God will forgive," believe it not. (Hagigah, 16a)

The greater the man, the more powerful his Evil Impulse. (Sukkah, 52a)

The Evil Impulse seduces in this world and accuses in the next. (Sukkah, 52b)

---

[3]This is one of the translations of the Hebrew term *Yetzer HaRa.*

The Evil Impulse is sweet in the beginning and bitter in the end. (J.T. Shabbat, 14:3)

It can be proved by the Torah, the prophets, and the other sacred writings, that man is led along the road which he wishes to follow. (Makkot, 10b)

ON LUST

Lustful thoughts are even worse than lustful deeds. (Yoma, 29a)

Rabbi Ammi said: "He who gives himself up to sensual thoughts is not allowed to draw near to the Presence." (Niddah, 13b)

Rabbi Yochanan said: "There are three whose virtue the Holy One, Blessed be He, Himself proclaims daily. These are, the bachelor who lives sinless in a city, the poor man who restores lost property to the owner, the rich man who pays tithes secretly."

Now Rabbi Safra was a bachelor who lived in a city, and it happened that a sage once taught this very passage in his presence. Rabbi Safra blushed; whereupon one of his colleagues said to him: "The saying does not apply to bachelors like you, but to bachelors like, for example, Rabbi Hanina and Rabbi Oshaya, who were shoemakers in Palestine, and who dwelt in the harlots' street, making shoes for them and carrying them to their houses. While the women inspected the shoes, those rabbis never raised their eyes to glance at the women. That is why people used to swear by the lives of those holy Rabbis of Palestine." (Pesahim, 113b)

God cursed the snake, but it finds sustenance everywhere. God cursed the woman, but all men pursue her. (Yoma, 75a)

What are the tactics of a rooster? Before he approaches a hen, he promises her a present, saying, "Come to me and I shall give thee a gown of many colors." Afterward he says, "May I lose my comb if I have the money to buy it!" (Eruvin, 100b)

ON DRINKING

Rabbi Isaac said, quoting Proverb 23:31: "Wine makes the faces of the wicked red in this world, but pale in the world to come."

Rabbi Meir said: "The tree of which Adam ate was a vine, for it is wine that brings lamentation to man." (Sanhedrin, 70a)

A sale by a drunken man constitutes a sale, and a purchase by him, a purchase. If he has committed a capital crime, he is to suffer death. The rule is that he is equivalent to a sober man in all things. (Eruvin, 65a)

Just as it is forbidden to permit that which is prohibited, so it is forbidden to prohibit that which is permitted. (J.T. Terumot, 5 end)

ON QUARRELING

A quarrel is like a stream of water. If it has once opened a way, it becomes a wide path. (Sanhedrin, 7a)

When two quarrel, he who yields first displays the nobler nature. (Ketubot, 71b)

All lies are forbidden unless uttered in order to make peace. (Baraita Perek HaShalom)

ON DECEPTION

Stealing a man's thought [deception] is the worst form of theft. (Tosefta Baba Kamma, 7:8)

Rabbi Yohanan said: "Jerusalem was destroyed because the people observed the Law, and yet acted evilly." The following story serves as an illustration: A former apprentice who had become rich was enamored of his master's wife. She returned his love and often visited him by stealth. Once the master needed money and informed his erstwhile apprentice of this. The latter offered to lend him the money and suggested that the master send his wife for it. They remained together for three days, and just as she left her lover, the husband arrived, inquiring for his wife.

"She left me within the hour of her arrival," said the apprentice, "but I have heard a rumor that she has been unfaithful to you."

"What shall I do?" asked the master.

"Divorce her," said the apprentice.

"But her dowry was large, and were I to divorce her on the strength of a mere rumor, I would have to return the money."

"I shall advance it to you," said the apprentice.

No sooner was the divorce arranged than the paramour married the woman, and then he sued her ex-husband for the money that had been advanced. The latter, being unable to pay the sum, was compelled to agree to work off his debt by labor. He became a menial of the wicked couple, and tears would often trickle down his cheeks and fall into the cups of wine he was serving them.

Then was the decree sealed in heaven that Jerusalem should be destroyed. No actual crime had been committed. The wrong had been entirely legal, yet it merited a harsher penalty than any actual crime. Justice may not be deliberately blind. (Gittin, 58a)

There are many persons who eat and drink together, yet they pierce each other with the sword of their tongues. (Yoma, 9b)

ON GOSSIP AND SLANDER

He who slanders, who listens to slander, and who testifies falsely, deserves to be thrown to the dogs. (Pesahim, 118a)

Slander is worse than the weapons of war: the latter damage from near, the former from afar. (J.T. Pe'ah, 1:1)

A good man of evil speech the Rabbis aptly likened to a palace built next to a tannery; the one defect destroys all his grandeur. (Shabbat, 56b)

Why have fingers been made flexible? So that we may stop our ears with them when evil is being spoken. (Ketubot, 5b)

The animals will one day remonstrate with the serpent and say, "The lion treads upon his prey and devours it; the wolf tears and eats it. What profit hast thou in biting?"

The serpent will reply, "I am no worse than a slanderer." (Ta'anit, 8a)

Hot coals, which are cooled on the outside, grow cool within, but gossip and slander, even if cooled outwardly, do not cool inwardly. (J.T. Pe'ah, 1:1)

People say: That which a child speaks he has heard from his father or mother. (Sukkah, 56b)

ON ANGER

All the divisions of Hell rule over the angry man. (Nedarim, 22a)

Rabbi Simeon ben Eleazar said: "He who rends his garments, breaks a vessel, or scatters his money in a moment of anger, shall be regarded as if he worshipped idols." (Shabbat, 105a)

He who raises his hand against a fellowman, even though he does not smite him, is called a man of wickedness. (Sanhedrin, 58a)

Do not attempt to pacify a man at the height of his anger. (Berakhot, 7a)

ON HATRED

Rabbi Yohanan ben Torta said: "Why was the first Temple destroyed? Because the Israelites were guilty of idolatry, lewdness, and murder; but in the days of the second Temple they were earnest about the Torah and careful about tithes; so why was that one likewise destroyed? The answer is because they . . . hated each other. This teaches that hatred of one's fellowman is a sore sin in God's sight, and as grave as idolatry, lewdness, and murder." (Tosefta Menahot, 13:22)

It is written, "Thou shalt not hate thy brother in thy heart." A man might think, I must not strike my brother, or lash him, or curse him [but I am allowed to hate him]. Therefore, it is written, "*in thy heart.*" (Erchin, 16b)

Rabbi Huna said: "Hate is like a channel made by a burst of water: it widens continually." Abbaye the Elder said: "Hate is like the plank of a landing bridge which, once it is put in position, remains." (Sanhedrin, 7a)

The Temple was destroyed because of unfounded hatred. (Yoma, 9b)

ON MEN OF VIOLENCE

If you are a man of the sword, then you cannot lay claim to be a man of the book; if you are a man of the book, you will not be a man of the sword. (Avodah Zarah, 17b)

People say: "The maker of arrows is often slain by the very weapons he fashions. (Pesahim, 28a)

ON THEFT

It is a more grievous sin to rob men than God. (Baba Batra, 88b)

To rob one's fellow of a penny is as bad as robbing him of his life. (Baba Kamma, 119a)

Stealing is as wicked as shedding blood and revering idols. (Semahot, 2:1)

Why does the Torah say that he who has stolen a beast, slaughtered it, and sold the meat, should be fined four or five times its value? Because he has become rooted in offending. (Baba Kamma, 68a)

Do not steal back your property from a thief, lest you likewise appear to be a thief. (J.T. Sanhedrin, 8:3)

The thief becomes law-abiding when he can steal no more. (Sanhedrin, 22a)

Rabbi Zeira, while walking with Rabbi Haggai, passed a man with a load of wood. Rabbi Zeira said: "Bring me, I beg you, a sliver of wood to cleanse my teeth." At once, however, he called Rabbi Haggai back and said: "Do not do this. If every one took but a sliver, the man's livelihood would be gone." Was Rabbi Zeira unreasonably scrupulous in this instance? No. Being a famous person, it was incumbent on him to act according to the spirit of our Creator's laws, not just the letter. (J.T. Demai, 3)

ON CATCHING THIEVES

No man shall put his hand out to steal, for he will surely betray himself by his actions.

Once when Mar Zutra the Pious sojourned at an inn, one of the guests stole the innkeeper's silver beaker. Mar Zutra watched the actions of the guests, and when he saw one of them wash his hands and wipe them on the robe of another who was not present, he advised the landlord to search through that man's effects. And lo, the beaker was discovered! Thereupon Mar Zutra said, "He who does not care for the property of another betrays that he is a dishonest man." (Baba Metzia, 24a)

Following a wave of crimes, the chief of the police received orders to round up all suspects. Rabbi Elazar ben Rabbi Simeon went to him and said: "Let me show you how to detect the true culprits. If at ten o'clock in the morning you perceive a person with a wine cup in his hand who acts as though he had had no sleep, investigate him. If he is a student, a night-laborer, or the like, he is innocent; if not, he has spent the night in revelry."

When this counsel was reported to the governor, he promptly appointed the rabbi as chief of the police. (Baba Metzia, 83b)

ON PENITENCE

Who is the penitent man? Rabbi Judah said, "The man who refrains from sinning even though the same opportunity to sin occurs more than once." (Yoma, 86b)

Rav said: "Whoever commits a transgression, and is filled with shame thereby, all his sins are forgiven him." (Berakhot, 12b)

Rabbi Yohanan said: "How foolish is the man who, having consorted with a harlot, gives alms to a beggar on the way out, and then says to himself, 'If it had not been God's will to offer me atonement for my sins, He would not have sent me this chance to do charity.' God answers him, 'Learn from the Proverbs: "The wicked shall not be unpunished."' " (Berakhot, 13a)

A twinge of conscience in a man's heart is better than all the floggings he may receive. (Berakhot, 7a)

ON EXCESSIVE PIETY

Who is a man of piety and yet a fool? He, for example, who sees a woman drowning, but says, "It is unseemly for me to touch her, and, therefore, I cannot pull her out." (Sotah, 21b)

Who is the pious fool? He who sees a child struggling in the water, and says, "When I have taken off my phylacteries, I will go and save him," and while he does so, the child breathes his last. (J.T. Sotah, 3:4)

ON THE SABBATH

Rabbi Hisda and Rabbi Hamnuna said that it is permissible to make plans for good deeds on the Sabbath.

Rabbi Eleazar said that one may arrange about alms for the poor on the Sabbath.

Rabbi Yohanan said: "One may transact business which has to do with the saving of life or with public health on the Sabbath, and one may go to synagogue to discuss public affairs on the Sabbath." Rabbi Jonathan said: "One may even go to theaters and circuses on the Sabbath for such a purpose."

In the school of Manasseh it was said that one may talk about the future marriage of one's children on the Sabbath, or about the children's education, or about teaching them a handicraft, for the Scripture forbids only "*thy* business." Whatever is God's business is permitted. (Shabbat, 150a)

ON ASCETICISM

Rabbi Ishmael ben Elisha said: "Now that the Roman government has power over us . . . and seeks to prevent the circumcision of our sons, should we ordain that no one marry and beget children? No, for then the descendants of Abraham would die out. Therefore, we must allow Israel to marry." (Baba Batra, 60b)

Rabbi Jeremiah ben Abba said in the name of Resh Lakish: "A scholar is not allowed to impose fasts upon himself because it makes him lessen his holy work." (Ta'anit, 11b)

Because of the Roman oppression, Rabbi Simeon ben Yochai and his son hid in a cave, and there for many years spent all their days in study and contemplation. One day they came out of the cave and observed people tilling the soil. Turning to his pupils, Rabbi Simeon remarked: "These men neglect eternal life and busy themselves with momentary needs." Thereupon all that they looked at was immediately destroyed by fire. After which a heavenly voice was heard to say to them: "Did you come out to destroy my world? Return to your cave!" (Shabbat, 33b)

One who causes himself pain by abstinence from something he desires is called a sinner. (Nazir, 19a)

Self-imposed abstinence is disapproved by many rabbis. Rabbi Isaac said: "Are not the things prohibited you in the Law enough for you, that you wish to prohibit yourself still other things?" (J.T. Nedarim, 41)

Rav said: "On the Judgment Day a man will have a demerit on his record for each thing he beheld with his eyes and declined to enjoy." (J.T. Kiddushin, 4)

In the World-to-Come, a man will be asked to give an account for that which, being excellent to eat, he gazed at and did not eat. (Kiddushin, end)

Rabbi Yose said: "A private individual must not fast excessively lest he become a burden on the public, and the public be forced to support him." (Tosefta Ta'anit, 2:12)

A hired laborer must not starve himself or undergo privations, for that lessens his value to his employer. (J.T. Demai, 7:4)

ON MIRACLES

One day Rabbi Eliezer brought up all possible arguments in the course of a legal dispute, but his colleagues refused to heed him. Finally he said: "If the law is as I teach it, let this carob tree give a sign." The carob tree moved back two hundred cubits, but the others said: "A carob tree proves nothing." So he said: "If the law is as I teach it, let the water in this channel give a sign." The water in the channel flowed upward instead of downward. The others said to him: "The waters of a channel prove nothing." Then he said: "If the law is as I teach it, let the walls of the school decide." The walls of the school leaned over as to fall; but Rabbi Joshua cursed the walls saying: "When the pupils of the sages dispute a point of law, what business is that of yours?" Thereupon a Divine echo thundered, "What ails you? Why do you harass Rabbi Eliezer? The law has always been what he teaches it to be." But Rabbi Joshua, rising to his feet, exclaimed: "It is not in Heaven!" (Deuteronomy 30:12.)

What did he mean by those words? He meant that the Torah is no longer in Heaven. Having been given to us from Mount Sinai once and for all, we need no longer pay heed to any heavenly voice. For in the Torah, given at Sinai, it is written: "The opinion of the majority shall prevail."

The prophet Elijah appeared to Rabbi Nathan who asked him: "What was God doing at that moment [when Rabbi Joshua denied the value of miracles]?" The prophet replied: "God was laughing and saying: 'My children have outwitted Me, My children have outwitted Me.' " (Baba Metzia, 59b)

MISCELLANEOUS APHORISMS

He who blows at the foam in his glass is not thirsty. (Sanhedrin, 100b)

People are accustomed to say: "When a dog is hungry, he will eat leftovers." (Baba Kamma, 92b)

Snatch and eat, snatch and drink, for this world is like a wedding. (Eruvin, 54a)

If a man has no money, he should not bid. (Baba Metzia, 58b)

When a fox has his hour of importance, bow to him. [If the unimportant man has authority, do not dispute it.] (Megillah, 16b)

Those who breathlessly run after a livelihood rarely overtake it. (Shabbat, 32b)

A man sees every disease of the skin except his own. (Negaim, 2, 5)

Shame not and you will not be shamed. (Moed Katan, 9b)

This is the penalty for the liar: even when he tells the truth, no one believes him. (Sanhedrin, 89b)

The ox fell; sharpen the knife. [Strike while the iron is hot.] (Shabbat, 32a)

There is no remedy for a fool. (Gittin, 70b)

A single coin in a crock makes much noise; but if the crock is full of coins, it is silent. (Baba Metzia, 85b)

When a debater's point is not impressive, he brings forth many arguments. (J.T. Berakhot, 2:3)

A pearl is a pearl anywhere. If it be lost, it is lost only to its owner. (Megillah, 15a)

People say: "Throw no stone into the well from which thou drinkest." (Baba Kamma, 92b)

An ornament looks beautiful only on a beautiful body. (J.T. Nedarim, 9)

Old men sometimes dye their hair, but the roots remain white. (Nazir, 38b)

As the larger among fish swallow the smaller, so among men. (Avodah Zarah, 4a)

Silver purifies the bastards. (Kiddushin, 71a)

People say: In my own town I am respected because of the name I have made for myself; in another town I am respected for the rich garments which I wear. (Shabbat, 145b)

Let thine ears hear what thy mouth speaketh. (J.T. Berakhot, 2:4)

He who hears himself abused and is silent will be preserved from many abuses. (Sanhedrin, 7a)

Sufficient unto the hour is its tribulation. (Berakhot, 9a)

SUNDRY SAYINGS

The chief merits are: at a wedding, to cause merriment; among mourners, to keep silent; at a lecture, to listen; at a session, to arrive early; at teaching, to concentrate; in time of fasting, to give charity. (Berakhot, 6b)

God loves these three: the person who does not get angry; the one who does not get drunk; and the one who does not insist upon his privileges.

God hates these three: the person who says one thing with his mouth and thinks otherwise in his heart; the person who could give evidence in another's favor, but does not do so; and the person who, being alone, sees his neighbor sin, and gives unsupported testimony against him.

There are three types of men whose life is not worth living: he who is prone to rage; he who is too soft-hearted; and he who is too fastidious. (Pesahim, 113a)

There are three types of men whose life is not worth living: he who must eat at another's table; he whose wife rules over him; and he whose body is racked by pain. (Betzah, 32b)

Three things tranquilize a man's mind: a pleasant melody, a pleasant scene, and a fragrant odor. Three things broaden a man's mind: a fine house, a handsome wife, and beautiful furniture. (Berakhot, 57b)

Three things are good in a little measure and evil in large: yeast, salt, and hesitation. (Berakhot, 34a)

Four classes of men will never see God's face: the scoffer, the liar, the slanderer, and the hypocrite. (Sotah, 42a)

Of eight things a little is good and much is evil: travel, mating, wealth, work, wine, sleep, spiced drinks, and medicine. (Gittin, 70a)

There are eight warnings: Let not a man be awake among those who sleep, or sleep among those who are awake, or weep among the joyful, or be joyful with those who weep. Let him not sit when others stand, or stand when others sit, or read Scripture when others are reading Mishnah, or Mishnah when others read the Scripture – in fine, the principle is, "Let not a man depart from the conduct or usages of his environment." (Derekh Eretz Zuta, 5:5)

CHAPTER 29

WISDOM FROM THE MIDRASH

The midrashic compilations, unlike the Mishnah and the two Talmuds, are essentially non-legalistic, and contain the utterances of the rabbis in the synagogues rather than the academies. They are usually organized in the form of homiletic commentaries on various books or passages in the Bible and are exceedingly rich in folklore as well as ethical teaching. While ranked as of secondary importance by the learned in Israel, these works were always held in the highest favor by the plain folk.[1]

Rabbi Abbahu and Rabbi Hiyya ben Abba came to the same town at the same time. Rabbi Hiyya delivered a scholarly discourse on the Law, while Rabbi Abbahu delivered a Midrashic sermon. Thereupon all the people left Rabbi Hiyya and came to Rabbi Abbahu.

Rabbi Hiyya was greatly discouraged, but his colleague said to him: "I will tell thee a parable. Two men once entered the same town, the one offering for sale precious stones and pearls, the other tinsel. To whom do you think people thronged?

---

[1]In this, as in the previous section, I have drawn heavily on Montefiore and Loewe's *Rabbinic Anthology,* and Newman and Spitz's *Talmudic Anthology.*

Was it not to him who sold the tinsel, seeing that that was what they could afford to buy?" (Sotah, 40a)

Let not the simple parable seem trivial in thine eyes, for through it thou acquirest an insight into the complex Law. (Shir HaShirim Rabbah, 1, 8)

ON GOD

Rabbi Akiva said: "Do not act toward the Lord as other nations act toward their gods. They honor them solely when times are good; but when misfortune befalls them, they curse their gods. You who belong to Israel should offer praise no matter whether the Lord brings you good times or evil." (Mekhilta to Shemot, 20:30)

The Emperor Hadrian, having returned from conquering the world, called his courtiers and said to them, "Now I demand that you consider me God."

Hearing this, one of them said, "Be pleased then, Sire, to aid me in this hour of need."

"In what way?" asked the emperor.

"I have a ship becalmed three miles out at sea, and it contains all I possess."

"Very well," Hadrian said. "I will send a fleet to rescue it."

"Why bother to do that?" asked the courtier. "Send merely a little puff of wind."

"But whence am I to get the wind?"

"If you do not know," the courtier retorted, "then how can you be God who created the wind?"

Hadrian went home highly displeased. (Tanhuma Bereshit, 7:10)

ON PRAYER

Rabbi Abbahu said in the name of Rabbi Yohanan: "If a man seeks to praise God excessively, he is banished from the world, as it is said, 'Who can utter the mighty acts of the Lord, and show forth all His praise?' " (Psalm 106:2); (Midrash Tehillim, 29:1)

It is said that Antoninus once asked Rabbi Judah HaNasi: "What is your opinion with respect to prayer at every hour?"

"It is forbidden," was the reply, "lest a man become accustomed to calling upon the Almighty falsely."

Antoninus did not appreciate the force of the answer until the rabbi presented himself once every hour, beginning in the early morning, and greeted him nonchalantly, "Good morning, Emperor! Your good health, King!"

The emperor became indignant: "How dare you treat royalty with such disrespect?" he demanded.

Rabbi Judah replied, "If you, a mere mortal king, object to being saluted every hour, how much more the King of Kings!" (Tanhuma Buber, Miketz, 11)

ON ISRAEL

Is then a Jew anywhere an alien? Wherever he goes, his God is with him. (Devarim Rabbah, 2, 16)

Why is Israel compared to a dove? All other birds, when tired, rest upon a rock or upon the branch of a tree. Not so the dove. When the dove tires, she does not cease flying; she rests one wing and flies with the other. (Bereshit Rabbah, 39:10)

Why is Israel like sand? As in the sand thou diggest a pit, and in the evening thou findest it filled up, so too is it with Israel. (Pesikta Buber, 139)

Israel is likened to the dust and the sand. As nothing can grow without the dust of the soil, so the nations of the world cannot exist without Israel, through whom they receive their blessing.

As sand mixed in bread injures the teeth, so those who persecute Israel suffer for it. (Pesikta Rabbati, 11:5)

Israel is likened to sand. As sand is moved from place to place without a sound, so Israel is exiled from place to place without complaint. (Introduction to Tanhuma Buber, 134)

As everyone treads on dust, so does every nation tread on Israel; but as dust lasts longer than metal, so shall Israel outlast all nations. (Bereshit Rabbah, 41:9)

As the myrtle is sweet to him who smells it, but bitter to him who bites into it, so Israel brings prosperity to the nation which grants it kindness, and depression to the people which afflicts it with evil. (Esther Rabbah, 6, 5)

God said to Moses and Aaron: "My children are often obstinate, often angry, often tiresome. With this knowledge accept for yourselves My mission, but be prepared for curses and stones." (Shemot Rabbah, 7)

Rabbi said: "Great is peace, for even if the Israelites worship idols yet maintain peace, God says: 'I can do nothing to them.' " (Bereshit Rabbah, 38:6)

"And they shall stumble, one man with his brother" (Leviticus 26:37). This means that one man will stumble because of the sin of his brother. Hence, learn that every Israelite is surety for every other. (Sifra, 112b)

It is said (Exodus 32:9): "I have seen this people, and behold, it is a stiff-necked folk." Commenting on this, Rabbi Yohanan said: "There are three impudent creatures: among beasts, it is the dog; in birds, it is the cock; among people, it is Israel." Rabbi Ammi added: "Do not suppose that this is said in blame. It is said in praise, for to be a Jew means a readiness to suffer crucifixion." (Shemot Rabbah, 42:9)

Rabbi Aha said: "When the Jew is reduced to eating the wretched fruit of the carob tree, then he repents. Poverty suits the Jew as a red bridle suits a white horse." (Bamidbar Rabbah, 13:4)

He who loveth My children will rejoice with My children. (Shemot Rabbah, 18)

When trouble comes into the world, Israel feels it first; when good comes, Israel feels it first. (Eikhah Rabbah, 2, 3)

When the Jews prosper, the Gentiles say: "We are your cousins." When the Jews suffer tribulation, the Gentiles add to it. (Bereshit Rabbah, 37)

One empire comes and another passes away, but Israel abides forever. (Derekh Eretz Zuta, Perek HaShalom)

The scourge that smites Israel will meet an evil end. (Mekhilta Beshallah)

Whatever robberies Gentiles commit against Jews, they do not consider to be crimes but acts of justice. (Bamidbar Rabbah, 10:2)

ON GENTILES

The falling of rain is an event greater than the giving of the Law, since the Law is for Israel only, but rain is for the entire world. (Midrash Tehillim, 117:1)

The just among the Gentiles are priests of God. (Eliahu Zuta, 20)

He who acknowledges idols repudiates the whole Torah, but he who repudiates idolatry is like one who accepts the whole Torah. (Sifre Deuteronomy, Re'eh, 54:86b)

A man cannot become a priest or a Levite, no matter how he might wish it, unless his father was one. But he can become righteous, even though he be a heathen, because righteousness does not depend on ancestry. To become righteous entails only the resolve to do good and love God. (Midrash Tehillim, 146:8)

I call heaven and earth to witness that whether a person be Jew or Gentile, man or woman, manservant or maidservant, according to his acts does the Divine Spirit rest upon him. (Tana d've Eliahu, 207)

Israelites are enjoined to deal kindly with all whom they encounter. (Midrash Tehillim, 52:6)

The heathen is thy neighbor, thy brother; to wrong him is a sin. (Tana d've Eliahu, 284)

If thou hast habituated thy tongue to speak evil of Gentiles, thou wilt end by speaking evil of Israelites. (Devarim Rabbah, 6:9)

Shimon ben Shetah was occupied with preparing flax. His disciples said to him, "Rabbi, desist. We will buy you an ass, and you will not have to work so hard."

They went and bought an ass from an Arab, and a pearl was found on it, whereupon they came to him and said, "From now on you need not work any more."

"Why?" he asked.

They said, "We bought you an ass from an Arab, and a pearl was found on it."

He said to them, "Does its owner know of that?"

They answered, "No."

He said to them, "Go and give the pearl back to him."

"But," they argued, "did not Rabbi Huna, in the name of Rav, say all the world agrees that if you find [not steal] something which belongs to a heathen, you may keep it?"

Their teacher said, "Do you think that Shimon ben Shetah is a barbarian? He would prefer to hear the Arab say, 'Blessed be the God of the Jews,' than possess all the riches of the world. . . . It is written, 'Thou shalt not oppress thy neighbor.' Now thy neighbor is as thy brother, and thy brother is as thy neighbor. Hence, you learn that to rob a Gentile is robbery." (Tana d've Eliahu, 74)

ON PROSELYTES

The Holy One loves the proselytes exceedingly. To what is the matter like? To a king who had a number of sheep and goats which went forth every morning to the pasture, and returned in the evening to the stable. One day a stag joined the flock and grazed with the sheep, and returned with them. Then the shepherd said to the king, "There is a stag that goes out with the sheep and grazes with them, and comes home with them."

The king loved the stag exceedingly. And he commanded the shepherd, saying, "Give heed unto this stag, that no man hurt it." He also ordered that when the sheep returned in the evening, the stag too should be given food and water.

Finally the shepherd said, "My Lord, thou hast many goats and sheep and kids, and thou givest us no directions concerning them; but concerning this stag thou givest us orders day by day."

Then the king replied: "It is the custom of the sheep to graze in the pasture, but the stags dwell in the wilderness, and do not venture into cultivated places. Therefore, it behooves us to be grateful to this stag for having left the great wilderness, where many stags and gazelles feed, to come to live among us."

Thus also spake the Holy One: "I owe great thanks to the stranger, in that he has left his family and his father's house, and has come to dwell among us. Therefore, I declare in the Law: 'Love ye the stranger.' " (Bamidbar Rabbah, Naso, 8:2)

God commanded the Israelites to do good to proselytes and to treat them with gentleness. (Sifre Bamidbar, 78: f. 21a)

Dearer to God is the proselyte who has come of his own accord than all the crowds of Israelites who stood around Mount Sinai. For had the Israelites not witnessed the thunder and lightning, the quaking mountain and sounding trumpets, they would not have accepted the Torah; but the proselyte, who saw not one of these things, came and surrendered himself to the Holy One, blessed be He, and took the yoke of Heaven upon himself. Can anyone be dearer to God than this man? (Tanhuna Buber, 6, f. 32a)

ON THE CHIEF COMMANDMENT

It is related that an ass-driver came to Rabbi Akiva and said to him, "Rabbi, teach me the whole Torah all at once."

Akiva replied, "My son, Moses our teacher stayed on the Mount forty days and forty nights before he learned it, and you want me to teach you the whole Torah at once! Still, my son, this is its basic principle: What is hateful to yourself, do not to your fellowman. If you wish that nobody should harm you in connection with what belongs to you, you must not harm him in that way; if you wish that nobody should take away from you what is yours, do not take away from another what is his."

The man rejoined his companions, and they journeyed until they came to a field full of seed-pods. His companions each took two, but he took none. They continued their journey and came to a field full of cabbages. Again each took two, but he took none. They asked him why he refrained, and he replied: "Thus did Rabbi Akiva teach me: What is hateful to yourself, do not to your fellowman. If you wish that nobody should take from you what is yours, do not take from another what is his."[2] (Avot d'R. Natan (verse II), 26, f. 27a)

ON THE WAY OF GOODNESS

The way of goodness is at the outset a thicket of thorns, but after a little distance it emerges into an open plain; while the way of evils is at first a plain, but presently runs into thorns. (Sifre on Deuteronomy, 11:6)

Isaiah said, "Sovereign of the Universe, what must a man do to be saved from the doom of Hell?" God said to him, "Let him give charity, dividing his bread to the poor, and giving his money to scribes and their students; let him not behave haughtily to his fellowmen; let him busy himself in the Torah and in its commandments; let him live in humility and not speak in pride of spirit. If he humbles himself before all creatures, then will I dwell with him, as it says, 'I dwell with him that is of a humble spirit' (Isaiah 57:15). I testify that he who has these qualities will inherit the future life; whoever has Torah, good deeds, humility, and fear of Heaven, will be saved from doom. (Pesikta Rabbati, 198a)

---

[2]Akiva's teaching was not new. Hillel had already taught: "What is hateful to you, do not to your fellow creature" (*Shabbat* 31 a); and he in turn was echoing Tobit 4:15 and Leviticus 19:18.

Rabbi Levi in the name of Rabbi Simeon ben Lakish, said: "The gazelle is the animal best beloved of God. When she gives birth to a fawn, God sends an herb to heal her. When she is thirsty, she digs her horns into the ground and moans. God hears her plea and aids her to find water in the deep pits. When she goes forth to drink, she is at first in terror of the other beasts, but God imbues her with courage. She stamps with her feet and uses her horns. The beasts then flee from her. Why does God love her? Because the gazelle harms no one, and never disturbs the peace." (Midrash Shmuel, 9)

See that thou dost not say: "Inasmuch as I have been despised, my comrades shall be despised with me; inasmuch as I have been cursed, my comrades shall be cursed with me."

Rabbi Tanhuma said: "If thou dost this, reflect whom thou dost despise, for it is written: 'In the image of God He made him.' " (Bereshit Rabbah, 24:7)

There is no absolute good without some evil in its midst. (Tanhuma, Introduction, 9)

ON FORGIVING THE ENEMY

Learn to receive blows, and forgive those who insult you. (Avot d'R. Natan, 41)

Rabbi Abba said in the name of Rabbi Alexandri: "He who hears himself cursed, and is able to stop the curser, yet remains silent, he makes himself a partner with God. Does not God hear how the nations blaspheme Him, yet remain silent? (Midrash Tehillim, 86:1)

God loves the persecuted and hates the persecutors. (Pesikta Rabbati, 193b)

If others speak ill of you, let the worst they say seem to you trifling; but if you speak ill of others, let each trivial remark seem to you enormous.

If you have done much good, let it be in your own eyes as little; but a small benefit from others should seem to you very great.

If *A* says to *B*: "Lend me your scythe," and *B* refuses, and the next day *B* says to *A*: "Lend me your shovel," and *A* replies, "I will not, seeing that you refused to lend me your scythe"–that is revenge [which the Law forbids].

If *A* says to *B,* "Lend me your spade," and *B* refuses, and the next day *B* says to *A,* "Lend me your scythe," and *A* replies, "Here it is, for I am not like you, who would not lend me your spade"–that is bearing a grudge [which also is forbidden]. (Sifra, 89b)

Who is the bravest hero? He who turns his enemy into a friend. (Avot d'R. Natan, 23)

ON BROTHERLINESS

When the year has been prosperous, people become brotherly toward each other. (Bereshit Rabbah, 89:4)

If a man knows any evidence in favor of the defendant, he is not at liberty to keep silent regarding it, for thus he may become responsible for the man's death. If a man sees another in mortal danger by falling into a river, through an attack by robbers, or some other evil, he is duty-bound not to stand idly by, but must come to the rescue. Moreover, if he sees one man pursuing another to kill or to ravish, he is duty-bound to try to prevent the crime, if need be by taking the life of the pursuer. (Sifre Kedoshim, Perek 4)

It is easy to acquire an enemy, but difficult to acquire a friend. (Yalkut Shimoni on Pentateuch, 845)

A man should not say: "I will love the learned and hate the unlearned," but rather shall he say: "I will love them all." (Avot d'R. Natan, 16)

If a man gives to his fellow all the good gifts of the world with a dour countenance, the Scripture regards it as if he had given nothing; but if he receives his fellow cheerfully, the Scripture regards it as if he had given him all the good gifts in the world. (Avot d'R. Natan, 13)

What should be done if one of two wayfarers in the desert has a little water, and the other has none? Were one of them to drink all the water, he would be able to survive, but were they to divide it, both would die. Ben Paturi said they should both drink, and die, for it is written: "And thy brother shall live with thee." (Sifra on Vayikra, 25:36)

ON THE SOCIAL CONSCIENCE

Rabbi Simeon ben Eleazar said: "If a man sits in his place and keeps silent, how can he pursue peace in Israel between man and man? So let him leave his place and roam about in the world, and pursue peace in Israel. Seek peace [not alone] in your own dwelling place, but pursue it everywhere." (Avot d'R. Natan, 12:26a)

It is to the glory of the righteous that, even when they are on the point of death, they do not think of their own affairs, but concern themselves with the needs of the community. Thus, when God told Moses that he must die, the latter's first concern was that God should appoint a leader in his place. (Sifre Bamidbar, 138, f. 52a)

If the man of learning participates in public affairs and serves as judge or arbitrator, he gives stability to the land; but if he sits in his home and says to himself: "What have the affairs of society to do with me? Why should I concern myself with the lawsuits of people? Why should I trouble myself with their voices of protest? Let my soul dwell in peace!"–if he does this, he overthrows the world.

When Rabbi Ammi's hour to die was at hand, his nephew found him weeping bitterly. He said: "Uncle and Teacher, why dost thou weep? Is there any Torah which thou hast not learned and taught? Is there any form of kindness which thou hast not practiced?–and thou hast never accepted a public office or sat in judgment."

The rabbi replied: "It is for this very reason that I weep. I was given the ability to establish justice in Israel, but I never tried to carry it out." (Tanhuma to Mishpatim)

What shall a man do to be of use in the world if he is not inclined by temperament to be a scholar? He should devote time to public affairs and to the public welfare. (Vayikra Rabbah, 25)

If a man takes in his hands a number of reeds bound together, can he break them? Only if they are separated, each from the other, can they be broken. (Tanhuma Nitzavim, 1)

To illustrate the truth that no man can sin for himself alone, Rabbi Simeon ben Yohai said: "A number of men were seated in a boat, and one of them took an augur and began boring a hole beneath him. His comrades exclaimed: 'What are you doing there?'

He replied, 'What concern is it of yours? Am I not boring a hole beneath my own seat?'

"They replied: 'Surely it is our business, for the water will swamp the boat and all of us with it.' " (Vayikra Rabbah, 4:6)

ON THE TRIBULATIONS OF GOOD PEOPLE

Rabbi Jonathan, commenting on the text, "The Lord tries the righteous" (Psalm 11:5), said: "The potter does not test cracked vessels. It is useless to tap them even once, because they would break. He does, however, test the good ones, because no matter how many times he taps them they do not break. Even so God tests not the wicked but the righteous."

Rabbi Yose ben Hanina said: "The flax dealer who knows that his flax is good pounds it, for it becomes more excellent because of the pounding. The more he beats it, the more it glistens; but when he knows that his flax is bad, he does not dare to pound it, for it would split. So God bears down not on the wicked, but the righteous."

Rabbi Eleazar said: "A man had two cows, one strong and one weak. Upon which will he lay the yoke? Surely upon the strong. So God does the same with the righteous." (Bereshit Rabbah, 32:3)

ON CHARITY

The door which is not open to a mendicant will have to open for a physician. (Pesikta Rabbati, 42b)

It is narrated that one day Rabbi Yohanan ben Zakkai was walking outside Jerusalem, accompanied by his disciple, Rabbi Joshua. At the sight of the Temple in ruins, Joshua exclaimed: "Woe to us, for the place where Israel atoned for its iniquities is destroyed!"

Rabbi Yohanan replied: "Do not grieve, my son, for we have means of atonement which are equally good–namely, deeds of mercy. For the Scripture says: 'I desire mercy and not sacrifice.' " (Hosea, 6:6; Avot d'R. Natan, 4:5)

A blind beggar accosted two men walking on the road. One of the travelers gave him a coin, but the other gave him nothing. The Angel of Death approached them and said: "He who gave to the beggar need have no fear of me for fifty years, but the other shall speedily die."

"May I not return and give charity to the beggar?" asked the condemned man.

"No," replied the Angel of Death, "a boat is examined for holes and cracks before departure, not when it is already at sea." (Midrash, quoted in "Meil Tzedakah.")

Thou shalt not harden thy heart against thy poor brother. If you do not give to him, in the end you will have to receive from him. (Sifre on Deuteronomy, 116)

Bar Kappara was once walking on the cliff overlooking the sea at Caesarea when he saw a Roman proconsul struggling to shore from a shipwreck. He hastened to aid the official, took him home, and gave him food and drink and also money with which to go on his way.

Some time afterward, certain Jews were wrongfully imprisoned by the provincial administrator, and knowing that Bar Kappara was in favor with the Romans, they gave him a purse of 500 gold coins with which to appease the oppressors. On reaching the capital, Bar Kappara encountered the proconsul whom he had rescued, and the latter rose up and greeted him with the words: "Why have you troubled to come hither?"

"To beg your mercy for those Jews," replied the rabbi.

"Do you not know," said the other, "that the government will do nothing for nothing?"

"I have brought 500 gold pieces," answered Bar Kappara. "Take them and be appeased."

Thereupon the official said, "Keep these 500 gold coins as a reward for the five silver pieces you once gave me, and let those Jews be set free in return for the food and drink. Now go home in peace and honor."

Thus is established the saying (Ecclesiastes 11:1), "Cast thy bread upon the waters." (Ecclesiastes Rabbah, 28a)

He who gives alms–a blessing is upon him; but he who lends is even better; and he who gives a poor man money to trade with, or who becomes a partner with him, is better than either. (Avot d'R. Natan, 41:66a)

Better is he who gives little to charity from money honestly earned that he who gives much from wealth gained through fraud. (Kohelet Rabbah, 4)

ON JUSTICE

Once the great Alexander visited a king in an outlying corner of the world. The king acted as a magistrate and invited his guest to sit beside him. Two men came before the court. One said: "I have bought a house from this man, and while repairing it, a treasure was found. I offered to return it to him, but he refuses to accept it." The other said: "I knew nothing of the treasure, so it does not belong to me. Having sold him the house and the lot, the treasure is his own."

The king said to the first man, "Have you a son?" The answer was yes. He asked the second man, "Have you a daughter?" Again the answer was yes. "Then," continued the king, "let them marry and keep the treasure as their dowry."

Alexander smiled and remarked: "In our country the law is that the king takes unto himself whatever is found."

His host looked at him in astonishment and said: "Does the sun shine in your land? Does the rain ripen grain and fruits?"

"Yes," responded Alexander.

"Are there beasts in your land?" the king inquired.

"Yes," answered Alexander.

"Then surely, the sun and rain come to your land for the sake of the innocent beasts; not for the sake of unjust men. In our land, however, the sun shines and the rain descends for the sake of men, and the beasts receive their food for our sake." (Introduction to Tanhuma Buber, 152)

Rabbi Akiva said that a court which has pronounced a sentence of death should taste nothing all that day, for the Torah declares, "Ye shall not eat anything with the blood." (Leviticus 19:26; Sifra, 90b)

"God came down to see [the Tower of Babel]" (Genesis 11:5); but did He need to come down? Is not all patent and revealed to Him who "knoweth what is in the darkness, and with whom light dwells" (Daniel 2:22)? The answer is that God did this to teach to mankind not to pass sentence, yea, not even to utter a single word, on hearsay, but to look with their own eyes. (Tanhuma Noaf, f. 23b)

"In righteousness shalt thou judge thy neighbor" (Leviticus 19:15). You must not let one litigant speak as much as he wants, and then say to the other: "Shorten thy speech." You must not let one stand and make the other keep his seat. (Sifra, 89a)

Let a case involving a small matter be as important to you as a case involving a grave matter. A dispute over a penny is as important as a dispute over great wealth. (Avot d'R. Natan, 10:22a)

Shimon ben Shetah said: "When you are judging, and there come before you two men, one rich and the other poor, do not say: "The poor man's words are to be believed, but not the rich man's.' Just as you listen to the words of the poor man, so listen to the words of the rich man, for it is written, 'Ye shall not respect persons in judgment.' " (Deuteronomy 1:17; Avot d'R. Natan, 20:22a)

If there be no officer to enforce the law, of what avail is the judge? (Tanhuma Shoftim, 2)

The case is like that of a king who had some empty goblets. He said: "If I put hot water in them, they will burst. If I put in cold water, they will crack." So the king mixed cold and hot water together, and poured it in, and the goblets were uninjured. Even so God said, "If I create the world with the attribute of mercy, sin will multiply; if I create it with the attribute of justice, how can it endure? So I will create it with both, and thus it will endure." (Bereshit Rabbah, 12:15)

ON HOSPITALITY

When Job's distress came upon him, he said: "Have I not fed the hungry, given drink to the thirsty, and clothed the naked?"

God replied: "Thy hospitality does not equal Abraham's. Thou didst sit in thy house and thus thou didst attend the incoming guests. Thou didst ask them regarding the food to which they were accustomed: if one usually ate wheaten bread, thou gavest it to him; if not, thou gavest him oaten. If he was accustomed to meat and wine, thou gavest it to him; otherwise, he received coarse food. Abraham, however, went outside to welcome his guests. He gave them the best bread, meat, and wine, even to those who had never enjoyed such good food. In fact, he never inquired from anyone what should be given him. He put the best viands and drinks on long tables, so that all who wished might come and drink and eat. 'Good enough for the poor' was not the way of Abraham." (Avot d'R. Natan, 7)

When a man's family is polite, if a poor man stands at the door and asks: "Is your father in?" they reply: "Yes, enter." Then, hardly has he entered, before the table is prepared, and he sits down and eats, and blesses God.

When they are ill-tempered, they reply: "No," and they rebuke him, and drive him away with an outcry. (Avot d'R. Natan, 7:17b)

It is the custom of the world that when a guest arrives, he is given on the first day a calf slaughtered in his honor; on the second day, a sheep; on the third day, at most a fowl. (Midrash Tehillim, 23:3)

ON HUMILITY

Great is the man who ignores his own dignity and is not angered at affronts. (Midrash Gadol u-Gedolah, 15)

As the vine has large and small clusters of grapes, and the larger cluster hangs down lower than the smaller, so it is among Israel. The greater the man, the humbler he is. (Vayikra Rabbah, 36:2)

They say to fruit-bearing trees: "Why do you not make any noise?" The trees reply: "Our fruits are sufficient advertisement for us." (Bereshit Rabbah, 16, 3)

The proverb runs: "How great that man would be, were he not so arrogant." (Kallah Rabbati, 3)

King Solomon received from the Lord a wondrous gift, namely, a silken carpet which flew through the air. The king and his associates would take breakfast in Damascus and supper in Media, carried to and fro on the magic carpet.

Once the king passed an ant hill. Because he understood the speech of all living creatures, he overheard the queen-ant order the subject-ants to hide from Solomon.

"Why hast thou said this?" the king called down.

"Because I was afraid they might look up to thee, and learn from thee pride in place of humility, diligence, and praise for their Maker."

"Let me ask thee a question," Solomon said.

"Take me up to thee, then," answered the queen-ant.

When he took the little creature in his palm, the king asked: "Is there anyone in the world greater than I?"

"Yes," answered the ant, "I am greater, since God has sent thee to carry me." (Midrash Vaayosha, end)

When King David had completed the Book of Psalms, he felt exceedingly proud, and said: "Lord of the Universe, hast Thou a creature that proclaimeth more praises of Thee than I?"

God thereupon sent to him a frog, which said: "David, take not such pride in thyself. I chant the praises of my creator more than dost thou. Moreover, I perform a great virtue in that when my time comes to die, I go down to the sea and permit myself to be swallowed up by one of its creatures. Thus even my death is a deed of kindness." (Yalkut Shimoni, ii, 889)

God loves nothing better than humility. (Pesikta Rabbati, 185b)

Let a man be ever humble in learning and good works, humble with his parents, teacher, and wife, with his children, with his household, with his kinsmen near and far, even with the heathen in the street, so that he become beloved on high and respected on earth. (Tana d'be Eliahu, 197)

Do not be like a large door, which lets in the wind, or a small door, which makes the worthy stoop. Instead, be like the threshold on which all are able to tread, or like a low peg on which all can hang their belongings. (Tana d'be Eliahu, 193)

ON KINDNESS TO ANIMALS[3]

If men make a sea voyage, and take cattle with them, should a storm arise, they jettison the animals to save mankind, because people do not love animals as much as they love human beings. Not so is God's love. Just as He is merciful to man, so is He merciful to the beasts. You can see this from the story of the Flood. When man sinned, and God determined to destroy the world, He treated man and beast alike. But when He was reconciled, He was reconciled to both, and He pitied both, man and beast alike, as we read in the narrative, "God remembered Noah and the animals that were with him in the ark." (Genesis 8:1; Tanhuma Buber, Noah, 17a)

---

[3]Cruelty to animals was given a special term by the Rabbis, *tza'ar ba'alei haim,* which literally means: "Afflicting anything possessed of life."

Rabbi Tanhuma ben Abba cited Proverbs (11:30), "He that is wise, wins souls." The Rabbis said: "This refers to Noah, for in the Ark he fed and sustained the animals with much care. He gave to each animal its special food, and fed each at its proper period, some by day and some by night. Thus, he gave chopped straw to the camel, barley to the ass, vine tendrils to the elephant, and grass to the ostrich. So for twelve months he did not sleep by night or day, because all the time he was busy feeding the animals." (Tanhuma Buber, Noah, 15a)

While Moses was feeding the sheep of his father-in-law in the wilderness, a young kid ran away. Moses followed it until it reached a ravine, where it found a well to drink from. When Moses reached it, he said, "I did not know that you ran away because you were thirsty. Now you must be weary." He carried the kid back. Then God said, "Because thou hast shown pity in leading back one of a flock belonging to a man, thou shalt lead My flock, Israel." (Shemot, Rabbah, 2:2)

ON THE STUDY OF THE TORAH[4]

The Fathers said, "Build a fence around the Torah" (Avot, 1:1), for a vineyard with a fence is safer than one without a fence; but a man should guard against building the fence too high, for then it may fall in and crush the plants it is supposed to guard. (Avot d'R. Natan, 1:2a)

Words of Torah are like golden vessels, the more you scour and polish them, the more they glisten and reflect the face of him who looks at them. So with the words of Torah; whenever you repeat them, they glisten and illumine one's face.

Words of Torah are compared to garments of fine wool

---

[4]As has already been noted, the word *Torah* means not merely the Law, but all learning.

which are difficult to acquire, but easy to tear. Just so, words of Torah are hard to learn but easy to forget. Words of folly, on the other hand, are like sackcloth: easy to buy, but hard to tear. Just so, words of folly are easy to acquire and hard to lose. (Avot d'R. Natan, 31:34b)

As water is free for all, so is the Torah free for all. As water is priceless, so is the Torah priceless. As water brings life to the world, so the Torah brings life to the world. As water brings a man out of his uncleanness, so the Torah brings a man from the evil way into the good way. As wine cannot keep good in vessels of gold and silver, but only in cheap earthenware vessels, so the words of the Torah keep good only with him who makes himself lowly. Like wine, the words of the Torah rejoice the heart. As wine grows better by keeping, so the words of the Law become better as a man grows older. (Sifre Deuteronomy, Ekev, 48, f. 84a)

Rabbi Yohanan went for a walk from Tiberias toward Sepphoris, and Rabbi Hiyya ben Abba was at his side. They came to a field, and Rabbi Yohanan said: "This field was mine, and I sold it to enable me to study the Law." They came to a vineyard, then to an olive garden, and at each Rabbi Yohanan said the same. Rabbi Hiyya began to weep. "Why do you weep?" asked Rabbi Yohanan. Rabbi Hiyya replied: "Because you have left nothing for your old age."

Then Rabbi Yohanan said: "Is it a light thing in your eyes, what I have done? I have sold what was created in six days, and acquired what was given in forty days, as it is said: 'Moses was there with the Lord forty days and forty nights.' " (Leviticus Rabbah, Emor, 36:1)

Teach the Law gratis and take no fee for it: for the words of the Law no fee must be taken, seeing that God gave the Law gratis. He who takes a fee for the Law destroys the world. (Derekh Eretz Zuta, 4:2)

Do the words of the Law for the doing's sake; speak of them for their own sake. Do not say: "I will learn Torah so that I may be called wise, or sit in the college, or gain long days in the world to come." (Sifre Deuteronomy, Ekev, 48: f. 84b)

ON THE VALUE OF LEARNING

A man who has gold but no knowledge – what has he? (Kohelet Rabbah, 1, 6)

If thou lackest knowledge, what hast thou acquired? If thou acquirest knowledge, what dost thou lack? (Bamidbar Rabbah, 19:3)

A scholar on board a ship with many other merchants was asked: "What merchandise have you?"

He answered: "The best merchandise in the world."

They looked in the hold of the ship, but finding nothing save what they themselves had put on board, they laughed at him. The ship was wrecked, and all of its freight was lost. The merchants barely escaped with their lives, and finally reached a strange port. The scholar sought out the local synagogue and asked permission to deliver a discourse. When it was seen that he was a greater scholar than anyone in the city, he was appointed head of the school, and was given a seemly stipend. When the scholar departed from the synagogue, the most important men of the community accompanied him. The impoverished merchants came to him and begged for aid. He secured for them their passage money home, and they said to him: "You were right. Our merchandise has been lost, but yours endures." (Tanhuma to Terumah)

Commenting on the verse, "He who associates with the wise becomes wise" (Proverbs 13:20), the rabbis said: "It is like a man who goes into a scent shop. Even if he does not buy anything, the sweet smell clings to his clothes, and does not depart all day." Concerning the verse, "The companion of fools shall be destroyed," they said: "If a man goes into a tannery, though he buys nothing, he and his clothes are fouled, and the evil smell does not leave him all day long." (Avot d'R. Natan, 11:14b)

ON EDUCATION

If you do not teach the ox to plow in his youth, it will be difficult to teach him when he is grown. (Midrash Mishle, 22)

Rabbi Judah said: "Let a man always acquire his first knowledge of Torah in the form of general principles, for if he acquires it in the form of many details, they will weary him, and he will not know what to do [with them]. It is like a man going to Caesarea and needing a hundred or a couple of hundred shillings for expenses. If he takes them as separate coins, they will weary him, and he will not know what to do, but if he changes them for crown pieces, he can take them from place to place at will. (Sifre Devarim, 306)

A Persian came to a certain rabbi and said: "Will you teach me the Torah?"

The rabbi agreed and showed him the letter *aleph.*

The Persian said: "How can you prove to me that this is an *aleph*?"

The rabbi pulled his ear, and the other cried: "Oh, my ear! my ear!"

"How will you prove to me that this is your ear?" asked the rabbi.

"Everyone knows that."

"By the same token everyone knows that this is an *aleph,*" was the rabbi's reply.

The Persian laughed and became a proselyte. (Kohelet Rabbah, 7)

He who learns receives but one-fifth of the reward that goes to the one who teaches. (Midrash Shir HaShirim)

Rabbi Yose bar Hanan narrated the following: Once as I walked on the road, I beheld a distinguished personage in costly garments approaching me. I fell back in agitation, thinking he might be an angel. Then, collecting myself, I ran after him and cried: "Rabbi, what is thy name?"

He answered: "Isaac ben Huna."

"Art thou a scholar in the Law or general learning?"

"In neither," he replied.

"What then may thy occupation be?"

"I have none."

"Has God then fashioned a human being who does no work whatsoever?"

"I teach children," he replied.

"Art thou married?"

"No," he answered.

"Be cursed then, thou rogue," I said. "Thy kind goes to homes to teach, and misleads the matrons of the household."

Unmarried teachers, our Sages tell us, are as arrogant in their hearts as kings, and their minds are like those of children. To greet them is to greet an idolater. He who respects them inherits Gehenna. He who says on their death, "Blessed be the Righteous Judge," shall have no share in the World-to-Come. (Pirke de-Rabbenu HaKodash, 7)

ON THE LEARNED ONES

Happy is he whose deeds are more than his learning. (Eliahu Rabbah, 17)

Once when Rabbi Yannai was taking a walk he encountered a young man who was dressed like a student, so he invited him to his house. He tried to engage him in learned discourse during the meal, first on the Scriptures, and then on the Mishnah, the Midrash, and the Talmud, but found the guest ignorant on all these subjects. Finally the rabbi said, "Take the wine cup and offer the blessing."

The other replied, "No, the host should say the blessing in his own house."

Yannai said, "Can you, at least, repeat what I shall say?"

"Yes."

"Then repeat, 'A dog has eaten Yannai's bread.' "

At this the guest leaped up and seized Yannai, and the latter cried, "What merit have you that you should eat at my table?"

"This," replied the other, "that I never went out of my way to be churlish, nor did I ever see two men quarreling without trying to make peace between them."

Thereupon Rabbi Yannai cried: "Woe, that I should have called such a one as you a dog!" (Vayikra Rabbah, 9:3)

If a scholar has no good taste, he is lower than an animal. (Tana d've Eliahu, 33)

A carcass is better than a scholar without common sense. (Vayikra Rabbah, i, 15)

If a scholar engages in business and is not too successful, it is a good omen for him. God loves his learning and does not wish to enrich him. (Midrash Shmuel, 29)

If you wish to be charitable, select for your beneficence those who labor in Torah. (Kohelet Rabbah, 11, 1.)

No table is blessed from which a scholar is never fed. (Tana d've Eliahu, 9)

I call heaven and earth to witness that every scholar who eats of his own, and who enjoys the fruits of his own labor, and who is not supported by the community, belongs to the class who are called happy; as it is written, "If thou eat the fruit of thy hands, happy art thou" (Psalm 128:2; Tana d've Eliahu, p. 91)

ON FOOLS

To the wise a wink, and to the fool a fist. (Midrash Mishle, 22)

The fool thinks every one else is a fool. (Kohelet Rabbah, 10)

It is a shame for a man to send a fool as his messenger. (Tanhuma Tissa, 25)

As an ass cannot ascend a ladder, so a fool cannot become wise. (Otzar Midrashim, 191)

The only thing to do with an idiot and a thorn is to get rid of them. (Shemot Rabbah, 6, 5)

One fool can ask a question that a thousand wise men cannot answer. What one fools spoils, a thousand wise men cannot repair. (Torat HaKenaot, 42; Bet Jonathan, 8)

Were all people fools, they would not be known as fools. (Midrash T'rumah, 2)

When you flog a fool, by the time it takes you to raise the whip a second time, he has already forgotten the first blow. (Tanhuma Noah, 24)

He who passes judgment on fools is himself judged to be a fool. (Pesikta Eikhah Rabbati, 14)

ON THE IMPORTANCE OF WORK

If a man works, he is blessed. (Midrash Tehillim, 23)

He who needs the blaze must fan it. (Midrash Shmuel, 9)

If a man does not plow in the summer, what will he eat in the winter? (Midrash Mishle, 6)

A man should not say: "I shall eat and drink while I may, and Heaven will have compassion upon me." Rather must he work for his sustenance. (Tanhuma Vayetze, 13)

The Rabbis said: "Do not think that the blessing will be yours even if you stand idle. Oh no! God's blessings rest only 'on all that thou doest'–on all that thou shalt labor" (Sifre, Re'eh, 99b)

A man must not depend on the work of his ancestors. If a man does not do good in this world, he cannot fall back on the merit of his fathers. No man will eat in the Time-to-Come of his father's works, but only of his own. (Midrash Tehillim, 146:3)

It is written, "The Lord will bless thee in all the work of thy hands" (Deuteronomy 2:7). Rabbi Jacob said: "One might think that He will bless us even if we are idle; therefore it says, 'in all the *work* of thy hands.' If a man works, he is blessed; if not, he is not blessed." (Midrash Tehillim, 23:1)

A man can quickly die if he has nothing to do.

Rabbi Simeon ben Elazar said: "Even Adam did not taste

food until he had done work; as it is said, "The Lord God took the man, and put him into the Garden of Eden to till it and keep it' (Genesis 2:15), after which He said, 'Of every tree of the garden thou mayest eat.' "

Rabbi Tarfon said: "Even the Holy One, blessed be He, did not cause his Spirit to alight upon Israel until they had done work; as it is said, 'Let them make for me a sanctuary, and then I will dwell among them." (Exodus 25:8; Avot d'R. Natan, 11:23a)

Emperor Hadrian, on his way to war, rode past a garden where he observed a very old man planting a fig tree. He halted his horse and asked: "Why in your old age do you labor so zealously? Do you expect to eat the fruit of the tree you are planting?"

The old man replied: "If it be the will of God, I shall eat of it; if not, my sons will enjoy it."

Three years later the emperor passed the garden again. The same old man approached Hadrian with a basket of figs, and, handing it to him, said: "My master, be good enough to receive this gift. I am the man to whom you spoke three years ago."

The emperor was touched, and commanded that the basket be filled with gold pieces and returned to the diligent old man.

The wife of a neighbor chanced to be in the gray-beard's home when he returned with the gold. She heard his story and immediately commanded her husband to take the emperor a large basket filled with varied fruits. "He loves the fruit of this region," she said, "and he may, as a reward, fill your basket with gold pieces."

Her husband followed her advice, and bringing the fruit to the emperor, said: "Sire, I have heard that you are fond of fruit, and I have brought these for your enjoyment."

On hearing the whole story, the emperor became incensed at the man's impudence, and gave orders to his soldiers to throw the fruit at his face. Bruised and half-blinded, the schemer returned to his home.

"How did you fare?" asked his wife greedily.

"I fared excellently," replied her husband. "Had I taken citrons, I would have died of the blows." (Vayikra Rabbah, 25)

Abba Joseph, though a rabbi, was a builder's laborer. While at his work one day he was accosted by a man who wished to drag him into a theological discussion. The rabbi refused: "I am a day laborer," he said, "and cannot leave my work. Say quickly what you would and go." (Shemot Rabbah, 10, 1)

He who buys and sells in truth and fidelity is regarded as if he had fulfilled the whole Law. (Mekhilta Vayetze, 158)

ON LEARNING A TRADE

A man should learn a trade, and God will send him sustenance.

He who has a trade is like a woman who has a husband, and like a vineyard which has a fence. (Kohelet Rabbah, 10, 6)

Together with thy knowledge of Torah, acquire a trade. (Kohelet Rabbah, 9)

Rabbi Judah said: "If a man does no work, people speak about him and say, 'How does so-and-so manage to eat and drink?' It is like a woman who has no husband, but who decks herself and goes into the street, and people speak about her."

Rabbi Meir said: "He who does not work in the week will end by working on the Sabbath. How is this? If a man is idle for two or three days, he will have nothing to eat, and he will steal. They will catch him, hand him over to the government, and cast him into prison, where he will have to work on the Sabbath."

Rabbi Elazar ben Azariah said: "Great is work, and each craftsman should walk abroad with the implements of his calling, and be proud of them. Thus the weaver should appear with a shuttle in his hand, the dyer with wool in his arms, and the scribe with his pen behind his ear. All have a right to be proud of their craft. Even God speaks of His own work (Genesis 2:2); how much more should man!" (Avot d'R. Natan, 21:23a)

ON THE RIGHTS OF LABOR

Rabbi Yose chanced to overhear his wife blaming her maid-servant for something she did not do.

"How can you blame her if you are not certain of her guilt?" he asked his wife.

"But you should not have reproved me in her presence," said she.

"Nay," answered the rabbi. "She ought to know that her rights are not despised." (Bereshit Rabbah, 48)

ON MARRIAGE

Before a man marries, his love goes to his parents; after he marries, his love goes to his wife. (Pirke d'R. Eliezer, 32)

Rabbi Jacob said: "He who has no wife lives without good, or help, or joy, or blessing, or atonement." Rabbi Joshua of Sikhnin (Sogane), in the name of Rabbi Levi, added that such a man is also without life. Rabbi Hiyya ben Gammada said that he is not really a complete man, and some say that he diminishes the Divine Likeness. (Bereshit Rabbah, 17:2)

There was once a pious man who was married to a pious woman, and they had no children. They said, "We are no profit to God." So they divorced one another. The man went and married a bad woman, and she made him bad. The woman, on the other hand, went and married a bad man, and she made him good. This proves that all depends upon the woman. (Shemot Rabbah, 17:7)

The bridegroom should not enter the marriage chamber until the bride gives him leave. (Pesikta Rabbati, 17b)

There is no greater adultery than when a woman, while her husband has intercourse with her, thinks of another man. (Tanhuma Buber, Naso, 13:16a)

A Roman matron asked Rabbi Yose, son of Chalafta: "In how many days did the Holy One, blessed be He, create the world?"

"In six days," he replied.

"What has He been doing ever since?"

"Making marriages."

The woman asked, "Is that all He does? I could do as much myself. I have male and female slaves, and in one little hour I can marry off all of them."

"Though it may appear easy in your eyes," said the rabbi, "yet every marriage means as much to the Holy One, blessed be He, as the dividing of the Red Sea."

What did the woman do when Rabbi Yose was gone? She took a thousand male slaves and a thousand female slaves, placed them in two ranks, and said: "Let this one take that one, let this one take that one"–and in a single night she married all of them off.

The next morning the women came to the house of their mistress. One had a cracked head, another a bruised eye, a third a broken limb.

"What ails you all?" the mistress asked.

And they replied, each one, "I will not live with this one . . . I will not live with that one. . . ." Then the woman sent for

Rabbi Yose, and said to him: "There is no God like your God, and your Torah is beautiful and praiseworthy, for you were in the right." (Bereshit Rabbah)

Rabbi Idi said: "There was a woman in Sidon, who lived ten years with her husband, and had borne no child. They went to Rabbi Simeon ben Yohai, and asked to be divorced. He said to them, 'As your coming together was with a banquet, so let your separation be with a banquet.' They agreed, and made for themselves a holiday and a banquet, and she made her husband drink more than enough. When his mind returned to him, he said to her, 'My daughter, see what is most precious to you in my house, and take it, and go to your father's house.'

"What did she do? When he had gone to sleep, she beckoned to her servants and handmaids, and said to them, 'Carry him on the mattress to my father's house.' In the middle of the night, he woke up and he said to her, 'Whither have I been brought?' She said, 'To the house of my father.' He said to her, 'But why?' She replied, 'Did you not tell me last night to take what was most precious to me from your house and to go with it to the house of my father? There is nothing in the world more precious to me than you.'

"After that they went back to Rabbi Simeon ben Yohai, and he prayed for them, and they were given a child." (Shir HaShirim Rabbah, 1:4)

King Solomon had a most beautiful daughter, concerning whose fortune he was exceedingly anxious. He prayed that he be shown her intended mate, and it was revealed to him in a dream that her mate was a youth born of the poorest of the poor in Israel.

"Let me test God's intentions," thought the King [to see if they cannot be foiled].

He built a palace on an island and erected round about it a high wall. He took to it his daughter and her servants, left provisions with them, locked the gate, and departed with the key.

A poor youth was wandering one cold night on a deserted road and lost his way. Observing the open carcass of a large bull, he crept between the ribs for warmth and fell asleep. A huge bird snatched up the carcass, flew away with it, and deposited it on the roof of the palace. When the princess went up to the roof, as was her daily morning custom, she beheld the youth. She commanded that he be bathed and properly clad, and lo, he was the handsomest youth she had ever seen! She commenced to converse with him and found him to be cultivated and amiable. The inevitable happened: they fell in love and were married in the presence of the servants. When the king arrived on his periodic visit and beheld his son-in-law, he rejoiced greatly and exclaimed: "Blessed be the Lord!" (Introduction to Tanhuma Buber, 136)

ON FAMILY LIFE

Every man is king in his own home. (Avot de-R. Natan, 28)

There was once a man who made a will saying that his son should inherit nothing of his until he became a fool. Two sages went to consult Rabbi Joshua ben Karha about this matter, and as they approached his dwelling, they were shocked to see him crawling on his hands and knees with a reed in his mouth, playing with his little son. They waited in hiding till the game ceased, and then drew near and asked the rabbi's opinion about the will.

He laughed and said, "That father must have meant for his son to marry and have children. Behold, once a man begets young ones, he acts like a fool!" (Midrash Tehillim, 92:4)

He who brings up the child is to be called its father, not he who gave him birth. (Shemot Rabbah, 46:5)

A man's father is his king. (Pirke d'R. Eliezer, 39)

Rabbi Joshua ben Ilem dreamed that his neighbor in Paradise would be Nanas, the butcher. He visited this Nanas to inquire what good deeds he was performing to deserve a high place in Paradise. The butcher replied: "I know not, but I have an aged father and mother who are helpless, and I give them food and drink, and wash and dress them daily."

The Rabbi said: "I will be happy to have thee as my neighbor in Paradise." (Midrash quoted in Seder HaDorot)

The rabbis asked: "What is meant by the phrase 'May the Lord bless thee and watch over thee'? One of them answered: "The meaning is: 'May He bless thee with sons and may He watch over thy daughters.' " (Bamidbar Rabbah, 11:13)

Rabbi Shimon ben Gamliel said: "He who makes peace in his house, the Scripture reckons it as if he made peace for every single Israelite in Israel. But he who brings jealousy and strife into his house, it is as if he brought them among all Israel." (Avot d'R. Natan, 28:43a)

"Be of the disciples of Aaron, loving peace" (Avot, 1, 12). Commenting on this text, the rabbis declared that whenever a man quarreled with his wife, and turned her out of the house, then Aaron would go to the husband and say, "My son, why did you quarrel with your wife?"

The man would say, "Because she acted shamefully toward me."

Aaron would reply, "I will be your pledge that she will not do so again."

Then he would go to the wife and say to her, "My daughter, why did you quarrel with your husband?" And she would say, "Because he beat me and cursed me."

Aaron would reply, "I will be your pledge that he will not beat you or curse you again."

Aaron would do this day after day until the husband took her back. Then in due course the wife would have a child, and she would say, "It is only through the merit of Aaron that this son has been given to me" (and she would call the boy Aaron).

Some say that there were more than three thousand Israelites called Aaron. That is why, when Aaron died, the Scripture says *all* the congregation mourned for him. But when Moses died, it says that those who wept were the children of Israel, not *all* the children of Israel. (Numbers 20:29, Deuteronomy 34:8; Avot d'R. Natan 25:25b)

If a man sins against those of his own household, he will inevitably come to sin against his neighbor. (Tana d've Eliahu, 289)

ON BASTARDS

A bastard can have a place in the World-to-Come. (Kohelet Rabbah, 4:3)

Who is referred to in the text (Ecclesiastes 4:1): "Behold the tears of the oppressed who have no comforter!"? These are the bastards who suffer in many ways through no fault of their own. God says: "I shall be their comforter in the World-to-Come." (Vayikra Rabbah, 32)

ON POVERTY

There is nothing more painful than poverty. . . . Certain of the Sages said: "Put all other sufferings in one scale, and poverty in the other, and the two would balance." Others said: "The scales containing poverty would be even heavier." (Shemot Rabbah, 31:12, 14)

A Jew became tired of life and wrote to Hadrian: "If thou dost hate the circumcised, why dost thou not persecute the Ishmaelites? If thou dost hate those who keep the Sabbath, why dost thou not persecute the Samaritans? It is not religion, but hatred of Israel that moves thee. May the God of Israel repay thee for this!"

Hadrian sent for the Jew and said: "Thou deservest death, but I am eager to know why thou dost court it."

The Jew replied: "Because I hoped thou wouldst save my soul from three worries."

"What are they?" asked the emperor.

"My soul wishes food and cannot obtain it; my wife and my child also are in want."

"Let him go," commanded the cruel ruler. "Life will be a greater punishment for him than death." (Kohelet Rabbah, 2)

ON PRUDENCE

He who risks his life needlessly, even for the sake of Torah, will not have his name mentioned when his legal decisions are cited. (Baba Kamma, 61)

He who eats of his own bread is like a child reared at his mother's breast. (Avot d'R. Natan, 31)

He who leases one garden eats birds; he who leases many gardens is eaten by birds. (Kohelet Rabbah, 4:9)

Make not a fence more expensive [or more important] than the thing that is fenced. (Bereshit Rabbah, 19:3)

Eat less than you can afford, dress less fittingly, but see that you live in a good dwelling. (Bereshit Rabbah, 20:12)

A man should not place all his money in one corner. (Bereshit Rabbah, 76:3)

If a man combats the wave, it overpowers him. If he permits it to roll over him, the wave passes on. (Pesikta-Zutarti Bereshit, 32:5)

Run not too far, for thou must then return the same distance. (Kohelet Rabbah, 11:9)

If a man travels in a strange country, and has all his provisions with him, he should nevertheless put them aside, and buy his wants from the shopkeepers, in order to improve trade. (Tanhuma Buber, 61b)

A man may flatter his wife for the sake of marital peace; his creditor for the sake of obtaining a respite; and his teacher for the sake of obtaining more attention. (Otzar Midrashin, 224)

ON BEING SHREWD

Rabbi Yudan said: "The gypsies are shrewd at begging. One of them came to a woman and said to her, 'Have you an onion? Give it to me.' When she gave it to him, he said, 'Can one eat an onion without bread?' When she gave him the bread, he said, 'Can one eat without drinking?' Thus he got both food and drink."

Rabbi Aha said: "Some women are shrewd at asking for things, and some are not. The shrewd one comes to her neighbor, and though the door is open she knocks and says, 'Peace be with you, neighbor. How fare you? And your husband? How are your children? May I come in?' The other answers, 'Come in. What do you want?' Thereupon the first says, 'If you happen to have such and such an article, I wish you would give it to me.' The other naturally replies, 'Here, take it.' But the woman who is not shrewd goes to her neighbor, and if the door is shut, she abruptly opens it, and calls out, 'Have you such and such an article?' The reply is, 'No!' "

Rabbi Hanina said: "Some tenant-farmers are clever at asking, some are not. The clever one, when he sees he is failing, plucks up courage, combs his hair, launders his clothes, and with a bright countenance, stick in hand and rings on his fingers, goes straight to his landlord. The latter asks him, 'How is the land? Will you be able joyfully to eat of its fruits? How are the oxen? Will you be able to enjoy their fat? How are the goats? Will you be able to fill yourself up with the kids? What do you want?'

"Thereupon the farmer says, 'If you happen to have ten dollars on you, I could do with them.' To which the landlord replies, 'You can have twenty, if you need them.'

"But the fellow who does not know how to ask will go to the landlord with tousled hair, dirty clothes, and a hangdog look on his face. When he is asked, 'How is the land?' he will answer, 'Would that it might yield what we have put into it.' When asked, 'How are the oxen?' he will answer, 'They are doing poorly.' Then, when the question comes, 'What do you want?' he whines, 'Can you spare me a couple of dollars?' Whereupon the landlord says, 'First pay me what you already owe me.' " (Vayikra Rabbah, 8)

ON OFFICE-HOLDERS

Office seeks out the man who runs away from office. (Tanhuma Vayikra, 4)

He who accepts office in order to profit by it is no better than an adulterer. (Pesikta Rabbati, Aseret HaDibrot, 2–4)

Woe to high position, for it takes the fear of Heaven from him who occupies it. (Midrash HaGadol, 412)

When a man is appointed an official on earth, he becomes a man of evil in Heaven. (Midrash Haser We-Yater, 39)

There are folk who, before rising to greatness, will always greet other people; but when they attain to greatness, their spirit becomes haughty, and they pay no heed at all to their fellow-citizens. (Tanhuma Buber, 90b)

A legislator who wishes that the law which he has helped to enact should be observed should himself be the first to observe it. (Shemot Rabbah, 43:4)

When the shepherd blunders on his way, his flock blunders after him. (Pirke d'R. Eliezer, 42)

ON SIN

We should not tempt even an honest man to sin, much less a thief, for the Sages say this is like putting fire next to hemp. (Tanhuma Buber, 26b)

He who transgresses a light commandment will end by violating a weighty one. If he neglect, "Thou shalt love thy neighbor as thyself" (Leviticus 19:18), he will soon transgress the command, "Thou shalt not hate thy brother in thy heart" (Leviticus 19:17), and "Thou shalt not avenge nor bear a grudge against the children of thy people" (Leviticus 19:18). Having transgressed these, he will go on to violate the command, "And thy brother shall live with thee" (Leviticus 25:36); for he will have been impelled to shed blood. (Sifre Devarim, 187)

Rabbi Akiva said: "In the beginning, sin is like a thread of a spider's web; but in the end, it becomes like the cable of a ship." (Bereshit Rabbah, 22:6)

He who cleaves to sinners, even if he does not imitate them, shares in their punishment. (Avot d'R. Natan, 30)

To cause another to sin is even worse than to slay him; it is to compass his death not only in this world but in the next. (Bamidbar Rabbah, 21)

It is forbidden to pray that a wicked man should die. Had Terah died while he worshipped idols, his son Abraham would not have come into the world. (Midrash HaNeélam, i, 105a)

He who aids his fellowman to do a wicked thing is as if he had murdered him. (Midrash HaGadol, 300)

Rabbi Shimon said: "How can it be shown that to cause another to sin is worse than to murder him? Because if you murder him, you kill him as regards this world, but a portion may remain for him in the World-to-Come. However, if you cause him to sin, you deprive him of both worlds." (Vayikra Rabbah, 21:4)

From the hour that a man thinks in his heart to commit a sin, he is faithless to God. (Vayikra Rabbah, 8:5)

Rabbi Nehemiah said: "If a man purpose to commit a sin, God does not reckon it to him until he has done it; but if he purpose to fulfill a command, then although he has had no opportunity to do it, God writes it down to him at once as if he had done it." (Midrash Tehillim, 30)

Rabbi Ishmael said: "As long as a man does not sin, he is feared; as soon as he sins, he himself is in fear." (Pesikta, Buber, 44b–45a)

The commandment against murder corresponds to the commandment that we believe in God, for in God's image has He created man.

The commandment against adultery corresponds to the one against idolatry; for both are forms of infidelity.

The commandment against stealing corresponds to the commandment against perjury, for the first leads to the second.

The commandment against false testimony corresponds to the commandment to observe the Sabbath, which was given to us in order that we may testify that God is the Creator.

The commandment against coveting corresponds to the one enjoining us to honor our parents, for the coveting of one's neighbor's wife results in divorce and prevents children from honoring their parents. (Pesikta Rabbati, 21:18)

ON THE EVIL INCLINATION

It is written: "We are the clay, and thou art our Father" (Isaiah, 64:8). Therefore, Israel argues, "Even though we sin, and Thou art angry, Thou shouldst not forsake us. If the potter makes a jug and leaves a pebble in the clay, it is not inevitable that the jug should leak? Behold, Thou didst create in us from our childhood the Evil Inclination, as it is said, 'The inclination of man's heart is evil from his childhood' (Genesis 8:21). Therefore, we beseech thee, cause the inclination to pass away from us that we may do thy will." God replies, "I will do so in the Time-to-Come." (Shemot Rabbah, 46:4)

Rabbi Samuel ben Nahman, commenting on the text, "And behold it was very good" (Genesis 1:31), declared that this refers to the Evil Impulse. Is then the Evil Impulse good? Yes, for were it not for the Evil Impulse, no man would build a house, nor marry a wife, nor beget children, nor engage in trade. Solomon said (Ecclesiastes 4:4): "All excelling work is the result of a man's rivalry with his neighbor" (Kohelet Rabbah, 3:11)

Like iron, out of which man can fashion whatever implements he pleases when he heats it in the forge, so the Evil Impulse can be subdued to the service of God, if tempered by the word of the Torah which is like fire. (Avot d'R. Natan, Perek 16)

ON UNCHASTITY

When the Israelites sinned against the second commandment, they were forgiven [as in the crucial case of the Golden Calf], for there is nothing concrete or real in idols. Idolatry merely provokes God's jealousy. However, when the Israelites sinned at Shittim, in that they committed unchastity, then there fell of them 24,000 men. This teaches that in unchastity there is something very concrete and real. (Shemot Rabbah, 30:21)

Rabbi Akiva's chief disciple, the one who sat at the head of all the four and twenty [thousand] students, happened one day to traverse the street of the harlots, and he saw one whom he passionately desired. So he sent a go-between to her and arranged an assignation for that evening.

Before the hour arrived, the harlot went up on the roof of her house and spied the disciple sitting at the head of all the other students, looking like a prince, and with the Angel Gabriel at his right hand. Whereupon she cried to herself: "Such a great one! Like a king he is! Shall I then bring him to ruin, and as a result go to Gehenna when I die?"

So when the disciple did finally appear, she sought to discourage him, saying: "My boy, why lose all chance of life in the World-to-Come for sake of one hour in this world?" Nevertheless his ardor was not cooled, so she cried, "My boy, what you want to do is the foulest of all things!" Then at last he was brought to his senses, and from that day forth he remained chaste; and a heavenly voice went forth and announced: "This woman and this man are assured life in the World-to-Come!" (Tana d've Eliahu, 39)

Rav Huna said: "There was once a sage who opened a perfumery shop for his son in the street of the harlots. Between the merchandise, the location, and the son's youthfulness, he naturally went astray. His father, catching him with a harlot, became greatly enraged, crying: 'I shall put you to death!' But another sage intervened, saying to the father: 'You yourself caused that young man to go astray, so how can you blame him? Of all occupations, you had to make him a perfumer, and of all places to set him up, you had to pick the street of the harlots!' " (Shemot Rabbah, 43:7)

ON DRINK

Drink wine, and you will condemn the innocent, and acquit the guilty. Therefore, it has been said, "A judge who has drunk a quart of wine may not sin in judgment, and a rabbi who has drunk a quart may not teach. . . .

When wine comes in, knowledge goes out. . . .

If a man has drunk one quart of wine, a quarter of his intelligence is gone. If he has drunk three quarts, then three-quarters of his intelligence is gone, and his mind is so confused that he begins to say unseemly things. If he drinks a fourth quart, then all his intelligence goes, his mind becomes addled, and he can no longer talk, for his tongue has become paralyzed. (Vayikra Rabbah, 1:4, 8)

When Noah was about to plant the vine, Satan came and stood before him, and asked what he was planting. Noah said: "A vineyard." Satan said: "What is its nature?" Noah replied: "Its fruits are ever sweet, whether moist or dry, and from them one makes wine that 'rejoices the heart of mortals' " (Psalm 104:15). Satan then said: "Come and let us collaborate, the two of us, in this vineyard." Noah said to him: "Very good."

So Satan brought successively a lamb, a lion, a pig, and an ape, which he slaughtered, and with their blood he fertilized the vineyard. This is a sign that before a man drinks wine, he is weak as a sheep. . . . If he drinks just enough, he becomes as strong as a lion. . . . If he drinks more than enough, he becomes like a pig that wallows in the mire; and when he becomes drunk, he dances like an ape, and utters folly before all, and knows not what he does. If all this could happen to Noah, the man whom God singled out for praise as 'righteous in his generation,' how much more surely will it happen to ordinary folk! (Tanhuma, 21b)

ON SLANDER

Rabban Gamliel commanded his slave, Tobi, to buy the best edible in the market. The slave brought home a tongue. The next day Rabban Gamliel commanded him to buy the worst thing in the market, and again Tobi brought home a tongue. When asked for an explanation, the wise slave replied: "There is nothing better than a good tongue, and nothing worse than an evil tongue." (Vayikra Rabbah, 33)

In the World-to-Come all sinners will be redeemed save the serpent, because it uttered slander. Therefore, the Scripture says, "Cursed art thou above all creatures." (Tanhuma Buber, 24a)

Slander is as serious as idolatry. Rabbi Joshua said: "Slander is as bad as murder. Slander is like unto idolatry and murder and incest." (Midrash Mishle, 6:12)

Rabbi Abbahu and Rabbi Simeon ben Lakish visited Caesarea. Rabbi Abbahu said: "Why enter so evil a city; its inhabitants are guilty of blaspheming God?"

Rabbi Simeon descended from his donkey and, picking up some gravel, threw it into the mouth of Rabbi Abbahu.

"Why have you done this?" exclaimed the latter.

"To teach you," said Rabbi Simeon, "that God dislikes men who slander." (Shir HaShirim Rabbah, 1)

A man had three daughters, all of good appearance but each with a defect: one was lazy, the second, a thief, the third was fond of slander. A friend proposed that the daughters marry his sons, and promised that he would cure them of their faults. He placed the lazy daughter in charge of many servants, and she had nothing requiring time or effort. He gave his keys to the thieving maiden, and told her to take whatever she wished at any time; she therefore had no reason to take anything in secret. As for the gossiper, he would ask her for her criticism, even before she began to speak words of slander.

When their father arrived, the first daughter said to him: "I can be as lazy as I wish, and I am happy here."

The second said: "I can take whatever I wish and I am happy."

The third one, however, said: "My father-in-law makes love to me."

She alone was not happy [for no one would believe her], and she had no opportunity to speak slander. (Midrash Aseret HaDibrot)

This is the way of gossipers: They commence with praise and end with derogation. (Tanhuma Shelah, 9)

Even if all the words of slander are not accepted as true, half of them are accepted. (Bereshit Rabbah, 56:4)

ON HATE AND ANGER

He who hates a man is as if he hated God. (Pesikta Zutarti Behaálotkha)

The spittle which a man throws upward will fall upon his own face. (Kohelet Rabbah, 7:9)

Rabbi Akiva said: "He who tears his clothes, and breaks his furniture in his passion and wrath, will in the end become an idolater, for such is the craft of the evil inclination: today it says, 'Tear your clothes,' and tomorrow it says, 'Worship idols.' " (Avot d'R. Natan, 3:8a)

ON USURY

He who takes usury has no fear of God. . . . God says, "He who lives on usury in this world shall not live in the World-to-Come." (Shemot Rabbah, 31:6)

The usurer breaks all the commandments; his sin is as flagrant as murder. . . . Usury is like slow-working poison. . . . Usury is like the bite of a poisoned snake; it is a small thing in itself, but its deadly effects are far-reaching. (Shemot Rabbah, 31)

A man who borrows of another, and merely for that reason takes care to greet him in the street, does a wrong act. He is guilty of paying usury in words. (Baba Metzia, 75b)

Far better that a man should take a small sum and trade with it, and earn his bread with difficulty, than get rich by moneylending. There is a taint clinging to the trade which no one who values comeliness and dignity of life will ignore. (Vayikra Rabbah, 3)

Man enters the world with closed hands, as if to say: "The world is mine." He leaves it with open hands, as if to say: "Behold, I take nothing with me." (Kohelet Rabbah, 5:14)

ON THEFT

He who steals men's confidence is chief among thieves. (Mekhilta Mishpatim)

The disciples of Rabbi Yohanan ben Zakkai once asked their master: "Why does the Law prescribe that the thief pay twofold and more, but that the robber pay only what he has taken by violence?"

"Because," replied the rabbi, "the robber has demonstrated that he is as little afraid of man as he is of God; but the thief, who takes by stealth, shows that he is in fear of man but not of God."

Rabbi Meir related a fable he had heard in the name of Rabban Gamliel: "There were two weddings in a city. To one, a great many people were invited, but the governor was omitted; to the other, only the near relatives were invited and the governor was left out. Whose conduct showed disrespect to the governor? Clearly the man who invited many people." (Tanhuma, Noah, 4)

All thievery depends upon the receiver.

A magistrate was accustomed to imprison receivers of stolen goods and to release the thieves. He heard the people grumbling and ordered that every grumbler should come to the courtyard.

When they had arrived, he distributed portions of meat among a few weasels. The weasels hastened away with them to their hiding-places in the ground.

A little later, he commanded that the holes of the weasels be stopped up, and again distributed meat to the same weasels. When the little animals saw that they had no place to keep their meat safely, they brought it back.

"See then, my friends," remarked the judge, "if the thieves have no place to dispose of their stolen wares, they will not steal." (Vayikra Rabbah, 6)

ON PENITENCE

When the time comes for an accounting of a man's deeds, it is too late to do anything. (Bereshit Rabbah, 84:12)

If a wicked man abandons his wickedness and repents, do not despise him. (Midrash Mishle, 6:30)

Five classes of men will not be forgiven: he who repents repeatedly; he who sins repeatedly; he who sins in a righteous generation; he who sins with the intention of repenting; and he who profanes the Name of God. (Avot d'R. Natan, 39:58b)

When the wicked are in trouble, they are penitent; but when their trouble is ended, they return to their evil ways. (Tanhuma, Va'era, end)

ON ASCETICISM

After the Temple was destroyed, the ascetics increased in Israel; they ate no meat, and drank no wine. Then Rabbi Joshua went to them and said: "Why do you eat no meat and drink no wine?"

They said: "How can we eat meat when it was offered daily on the altar, or drink wine which was poured out on it? And now all this has ceased."

Rabbi Joshua said to them: "In that case we ought to eat no figs and grapes, for they were offered as first fruits; and we ought to eat no bread, because they used to bring two loaves on Pentecost, and the shewbread on every Sabbath; and we ought to drink no water, for there was a libation of water at the feast of Tabernacles." They gave no answer, so he continued: "Not to mourn at all is impossible, but to mourn much is also impossible . . . since only such decrees must be issued which the majority of the community can endure." (Midrash Tehillim, 137:5)

ON MOURNING THE DEAD

Man's exit from the world, as compared to and contrasted with his entry into it, is portrayed by Rabbi Levi thus: Of two vessels sailing on the high seas, the ship which has come into port is in the eyes of the wise much more an object of joy than the ship about to leave the harbor. Even thus should we contemplate man's departure from this world without sorrow or fear, seeing that at death he has already entered the harbor – the haven of rest in the World-to-Come. (Shemot Rabbah, 48:1)

Rabbi Meir sat discoursing on a Sabbath afternoon in the House of Study. While he was there, his two sons died. What did their mother do? She laid them upon the bed, and spread a linen cloth over them. At the outgoing of the Sabbath, Rabbi Meir came home and asked, "Where are my sons?"

His wife replied, "They went to the House of Study."

He said, "I did not see them there."

She gave him the wine cup, and he said the blessing for the outgoing of the Sabbath. Then he said again, "Where are my sons?"

She replied, "They went to another place, and now they have returned." Then she gave him to eat, and he ate and recited the blessing. Then the woman said, "I have a question to ask you."

"Ask it."

She said, "Early today a man came here and gave me something to keep for him; now he has come back to ask for it again. Shall we return it to him or not?"

Meir replied, "He who has received something on deposit must surely return it to its owner."

She replied, "Without your knowledge I would not return it." Then she took him by the hand, and brought him up to the bed, and took away the cloth, and he saw his sons lying dead upon the bed. He began to weep . . . but his wife said to him, "Did you not say to me that one must return a deposit to its owner? Does it not say, 'The Lord gave, the Lord took, blessed be the name of the Lord?' "

Thus she comforted him and quieted his mind. (Midrash Mishle, 31:10)

When Rabban Yohanan ben Zakkai's son died, Rabbi Eliezer ben Arak came to offer consolation. He said: "To whom may I liken you? To a man who has received for safekeeping a jewel from his king. As long as he has it beneath his roof, he is troubled with anxiety regarding it. When the king takes it back in the same good condition, the man rejoices. You, O Master, have received for safekeeping a dear soul. He studied much and well, and died without sin. You have returned it in perfection, and you should find comfort in the knowledge of this."

Rabban Yohanan thanked him heartily. (Avot d'R. Natan, 14)

SUNDRY SAYINGS

Three men become aged before their time: he who lives on an upper floor; he who endeavors to raise poultry for a livelihood; and he who gives orders but is not obeyed. (Otzar Midrashim, 166)

Four things cause a man to age prematurely: fright, anger, children, and an evil-natured wife. (Tanhuma, Hayye Sarah)

There are four classes of men who do not see the face of the Holy Spirit: the mockers, the hypocrites, the slanderers, the liars. (Midrash Tehillim, 101:7)

Four men are called wicked: he who lifts his hand against his fellowman to smite him; he who borrows and does not repay; he who is impudent of countenance; and he who is quarrelsome. (Bamidbar Rabbah, 18:12)

When Rabbi Meir saw a man go on a journey alone, he would say: "Greetings to thee, O thou who courtest death."

When he saw two walking forth, he would say: "Greetings to you, O ye who court quarrels."

If he saw three departing, he would say: "Greetings, O men of peace." (Kohelet Rabbah, 4)

When a human being is a year old, he is like a king; everyone loves and embraces him. At two, he is like a pig, wallowing in his dirt. During his boyhood, he is like a kid, dancing and laughing all day long. When he is eighteen, he is like a horse, rejoicing in his youth and strength. When he marries, he is like an ass, carrying a burden. Later, he becomes like a dog, unashamed to ask favors and to beg for a livelihood. In his old age, he is like a monkey; he becomes curious and childish, and no one pays any attention to his words. (Tanhuma Pekudei)

MISCELLANEOUS APHORISMS

The proverb says: The door that is closed to a good deed is open to a physician. (Shir HaShirim Rabbah, 6:1)

Offer not pearls for sale to those who deal in vegetables and onions. (Tanhuma, Behukotai, 3)

The stone fell on the pitcher? Woe to the pitcher. The pitcher fell on the stone? Woe to the pitcher. (Esther Rabbah, 7:10)

Thou has entered the city; abide by its customs. (Bamidbar Rabbah, 48:14)

A thread is always found on the tailor. (Introduction to Tanhuma Buber, 79)

Many candles can be kindled from one candle without diminishing it. (Sifre Beha'alotekh, 93)

In a field where there are mounds, do not tell secrets. (Bereshit Rabbah, 74:2)

If one man says to thee: "Thou art a donkey," do not mind; if two speak thus, purchase a saddle for thyself. (Bereshit Rabbah, 45:10)

A man can forget in two years what he has learned in twenty. (Avot d'R. Natan, 24:6)

A tree is cut down by an axe which is joined to a piece of the tree itself. (Eliahu Rabbah, 29)

When thorns burn, they give out much noise, as if to say: "We too are wood." (Kohelet Rabbah, 7)

A reconciliation without an explanation that error lay on both sides is not a true reconciliation. (Bereshit Rabbah, 54:3)

Bad neighbors count a man's income, but not his expenses. (Pesikta Rabbati, 31)

A man can live without spices, but not without wheat. (Midrash Tehillim, 2:16)

A carpenter who has no tools is not a carpenter. (Shemot Rabbah, 40:1)

A man has three friends: his sons, his wealth, and his good deeds. (Pirke d'R. Eliezer, 34)

When one dog barks, he soon finds other dogs to bark with him. (Shemot Rabbah, 31:9)

Better one bird that is tied than a hundred birds that are flying. (Kohelet Rabbah, 4:6)

When the ox falls, many are ready to slaughter him. (Eikhah Rabbah, 1:34)

It is unseemly for a lion to weep before a fox. (Eliahu Rabbah, 17)

In this world he who is a dog can become a lion, and he who is a lion can become a dog. (Rute Rabbah, 3:2)

All beginnings are difficult. (Mekhilta Yitro, 19:5)

People say: "All is well that ends well." (Pesikta Zutarta, Bereshit, 47:28)

How many pens are broken, how many ink bottles are consumed, to write about things that have never occurred? (Tanhuma Shoftim, 18)

He who destroys any useful thing is guilty of a sin. (Midrash Aggadah Shoftim)

Truth is heavy; therefore, few wear it. (Midrash Shmuel on Avot, 4)

SOME ANECDOTES

The salesman of idols

Once Terah left his son Abram in his shop to sell the idols which he had fashioned. An old man wished to buy a fresh idol for his birthday. Abram said: "Here is a new idol, completed this very day. Do you not think that you are of more importance than a god a day old?" The graybeard left in confusion, and Abram did not sell the idol.

"You are incompetent as a salesman," said Terah. "I shall try you out as a priest." Abram asked his mother to prepare a tasty dish for the idols. He then took a large axe, smashed all the idols with the exception of the largest one, in whose hand he placed the axe. When Terah returned, Abram said: "The large idol became incensed at the presumption of the others in wishing to partake of the food before him, and he smashed them." Terah was angry at this conduct on the part of his son and informed King Nimrod that the youth had desecrated the temple.

Nimrod asked Abram: "Why do you not worship my god?"

Abram replied: "Is it an idol of wood or stone that you mean? If so, how can I worship that which I have seen made before my own eyes?"

"Nay, those are for fools," said Nimrod. "My god is the consuming fire that gives light and destroys."

"But how can fire be god if water quenches it?" asked Abram.

"Then worship water," commanded the king.

"But a cloud is mightier, carrying water where it wills."

"Worship the cloud then."

"But wind is stronger, for it disperses the clouds."

"Then worship wind."

"But man withstands wind, and I cannot worship man because death overcomes him." (Bereshit Rabbah, 38:19)

A wise will

A wealthy Jew and his slave went to trade in a foreign country. There he sickened and when near to death he commanded a scribe to write down his last will and testament. He dictated these provisions: "To my faithful slave who brings this document I leave all my property. To my only son whom I have left in Judea I leave any one thing of my possessions which he may choose."

The slave returned with all the wealth of his dead master and showed the will. A rabbi said to the son: "It is a most sagacious will. If your father had left everything to you, the slave would have fled with the wealth. Now he has brought everything safely to you, and you may choose him, according to provision of the will: for all the property of a slave belongs to his master." (Tanhuma Bereshit, Lekh Lekha)

Alexander and the women

Alexander the Great came to a city inhabited only by women. He would have made war on them, but they said: "If thou slayest us, they will say: 'He conquered women.' If we slay thee, they will say: 'What a king that was! Women slew him!' "

Then he said: "Bring me bread." They brought him a loaf of gold on a table of gold. He asked them: "Can I eat gold?"

They answered: "If it was bread thou didst need, was there none in thy kingdom that thou hadst need to set out to so far a place?"

He went thence, having written on the gate of their city: "I, Alexander, was a madman, having come to Africa to be taught by women." (Tanhuma Buber)

The not-so-smart crook

It once happened that a man deposited a hundred *dinarii* with a certain Bartholomew, and when he asked for them back, the latter declared: "I have already returned them to your hand." The man demanded that Bartholomew come to the synagogue and repeat the declaration under oath; to which the other agreed. First, however, he hollowed out a cane, put the hundred coins therein, and pretended to use it for a walking-stick. On arriving at the synagogue, he said to the plaintiff:

"Here, hold this cane while I swear." He went on: "By the lord of this good place, I swear that that which was entrusted into my hand I have given back into yours."

The other man was so shocked at this that he dropped the cane, whereupon all the coins fell out. Then Bartholomew, trying to brazen it out, smiled and cried: "Pick them up, pick them up, for it is your own that you pick up." (Pesikta Rabbati, 12b)

PART IV

MEDIEVAL NOON

INTRODUCTION

The aim of the creators of the Talmud was to preserve the homeless Jews by surrounding them with a Wall of Law no matter where they might be forced to roam. In this they succeeded, and though the price was religious totalitarianism and cultural isolation, it proved well worth paying at the time. The ensuing centuries witnessed the high tide of the barbarian incursions, and all Europe and the Near East were plunged into turmoil. The Roman Empire collapsed, carrying with it all semblance of order, and countless races, nations, and sects vanished from sight. But not Israel. Huddled behind its ramparts of ritual, Israel was able to hold fast to its identity, and when those "Dark Ages" passed, Israel was still alive.

But thereafter the need for seclusion became less pressing, and then the Jews began to tire of their confinement. This occurred first in Babylonia, which had now become the seat of a new Mohammedan Empire. Eventually it spread to North Africa and Spain and wherever else the Arabic-speaking races had started reviving civilization. In all these lands many Jews ceased to believe it was sufficient if their Wall of Law was merely solid and towering. They came to feel that it ought to let in light as well as shut out hate; that it ought to encourage venturesomeness, and not just provide safety.

The result was a cultural revolution in Israel. For centuries the scholars had sought wisdom solely in their own ancestral scriptures; but now they took to rummaging for it in the secular writings of infidel folk. Their favorite mine was the rediscovered literature of the classic Greeks, and what they found there seemed to them immeasurably precious. It was Reason—and this, they argued, was a thing the Jews had too long neglected. For it was not inherently hostile to faith. On the contrary, when interpreted aright, reason could produce the clearest arguments to buttress faith.

That was no new line of argument. Philo Judaeus had used it many centuries earlier. Moreover, he had offered very beguiling evidence to back it up. He had insisted that Socrates had actually been a disciple of the prophet Ahitophal, that Plato had studied under Jeremiah, and that Aristotle had sat at the feet of Rabbi Simon the Just. Consequently he had seen high virtue, not wickedness, in any interest a Jew might show in the writings of those great pagans.

What Philo had said was now repeated, but with emphasis and vast elaboration. A long succession of scholars arose in Israel, all of them intent on reconciling Greek logic and Hebrew belief. What they accomplished was immensely significant. Beginning early in the ninth century of the Common Era, and continuing on until the close of the twelfth, they effected a cross-fertilization of ideas, which produced a harvest that fed the mind of mankind.

CHAPTER 30

THE SPECULATIONS OF SAADIA

The first of the medieval Jewish rationalists was a certain Saadia ben Joseph (892-942) who held the title of gaon as head of the chief rabbinical academy in Babylonia. His very name reveals how conditions had changed. Saadia may have been adapted from the Arabic "Sa'id," and only a measure of intimacy between the two peoples could have made such an adaptation possible.

Saadia's first great work–completed at the age of 20!–was an exhaustive Hebrew-Arabic dictionary based on what were then the most advanced linguistic principles. Later he translated the Bible into Arabic, and still later a portion of the Talmud. His masterpiece, however, was a treatise on Jewish theology entitled Sefer Emunot V'Deot, *the "Book of Beliefs and Dogmas." In this he undertook the pioneer task of systematizing and interpreting his ancestral faith in the light of what the contemporary world was slowly rediscovering to be Reason. Though the influence of his Arabic contemporaries is clear in every line, the work became one of the most cherished in Israel, and remains to this day a prime text in erudite circles. I quote only three selections, two of them–for the sake of clarity–from a paraphrase rendered by a twelfth-century commentator named Berachya ben Rabbi Natronai HaNakdan.*

EIGHT SOURCES OF SKEPTICISM[1]

There are eight causes through which skeptical thoughts, doubts, and petulance are produced among human beings.

The *first* is inactivity, sloth, and the breaking away from the yoke of the Law. As soon as the sluggard, or the one who casts off the yoke of the Law, knows that he is bound to fulfill the precepts and statutes, he first becomes tardy of their fulfillment, and neglectful of their observance. The task becomes too difficult for him, and he endeavors through his love of idleness and inactivity to free himself from the precepts. Thus, the idle are continually saying, "Aha! The command is too difficult to observe, the truth is bitter, and the work is laborious; we cannot perform it. . . ."

The simple do not understand that, through their inactivity and gormandizing, they become paupers, bereft of clothing, hungry and thirsty, and that they will ultimately wander about without house or home.

The *second* is the foolishness which is bound up in the heart of murmurers, and the folly which rules over fools. They consequently err in their stupidity, and wandering astray like animals, declare in their folly that they have no Lord or master. . . . When these assert they have no god, they do not consider that, were they to practice such folly with regard to their kings, and adhere to stupidities and absurdities in relation to their princes, they would long have been destroyed, and have perished.

The *third* is the wicked desire and the evil inclination which obtain the mastery over some fools, permitting them to partake of all kinds of food and drink, and even forcing them to justify the acquisition of ill-gotten wealth, and the indulgence of their bestial desires. We see these foolish men continually exerting themselves and striving to loosen the bonds of the

[1] *Ethical Treatises of Berachya,* translated by Hermann Gollancz (London, 1902), pp. 2–5.

commandment, to break the yoke of the Law, and to permit themselves every kind of evil action, devoid of all knowledge or wisdom. . . .

The *fourth* is temper, shortness of spirit, and narrowness of mind which prevent a man from receiving, understanding, and searching into knowledge and wisdom, as it is right and proper. The petulant will, therefore, not wait until he becomes wise in his investigation of knowledge, nor will he have sufficient patience to grasp the force of an argument. He will neither remain long enough in his research, nor will he complete his examination; but, resting satisfied with a few proofs of individual instances and with partial explanations, he will say, "I have investigated and have examined, but could find nothing more than this. The truth of no theory whatsoever has been proved or made clear to me, except this conclusion. . . ."

The *fifth* is haughtiness and pride which are inherent in some men; for the proud man cannot sufficiently humble himself to learn wisdom, nor will his arrogance for one moment forsake him. . . . He does not understand that his pride and arrogance will avail him naught, when he wishes to write a book and he has not become learned, or when he wishes to engrave a seal; for how is it possible for the haughty to accomplish any work without study. . . .

The *sixth* cause is derived from the fact that a man has heard one single argument from some simple-minded, ignorant and confused persons, and having pleased him, it remained firmly established in his mind. It becomes part and parcel of his belief, and becomes so interwoven with his imagination, that he gives credence to it and observes it all the days of his life. . . . The simpleton does not consider that were man to occupy himself all the days of his life, as regards his desires and wants, with one action or with one principle, he would surely become a wandering mendicant. He does not understand that unless he believes in the truth of the possibility of two theories, or of two kinds of action, he will never be able to keep clear of snares, thorns, and heat, that they destroy him not.

The *seventh* source of doubt is found in an untenable proof, or a vitiated conclusion, which believers have heard from the lips of some students, and in consequence of which they ridicule and despise these students to such an extent that they despise all teaching, and hold up all the precepts to derision. They do not understand, that as regards things which in themselves are praiseworthy, although none other praises them, the praise does not cease; that the established truth does not thereby become nullified, because unbelievers deny it, and that with regard to the object which is beautiful to the eye of the intellect, neither will pollution besmirch it, nor foolishness diminish its beauty; just as the scant praise of the broker will not diminish the value of beautiful silk garments.

The *eighth* cause is found in the strife and contention arising between a man and those who observe the Law (Monotheists or those who declare the Unity of God). His perversity and waywardness, his hatred and enmity engendered by the quarrel, lead him to recklessness, so that he forsakes the way of truth, and the idea of God's Unity; and in order to carry out to the full his animosity against those who proclaim the Unity of God, and his hostility against the upright, he ends by abhorring the precepts, and forgetting his God. . . . He does not understand that his very enemy cannot injure him as much as he injures himself, for his adversary cannot cast him into Gehinnom, as he does himself.

THIRTEEN FALLACIOUS IDEALS[2]

These are the thirteen things which are made the objects of life by the various classes of mankind, and it is because of their devotion to them that they disregard (cast behind their backs)

---

[2] *Ibid.*, pp. 293–301.

the disgrace and blemish which often attach to them: (1) Contempt for the world, and avoiding a fixed abode (or social life); (2) Eating, drinking, and pleasuring; (3) Lust; (4) Delighting in the affection of one's fellow-creatures; (5) The love of amassing wealth; (6) The desire to have many children; (7) The love of cultivating the soil, and building; (8) The love of longevity; (9) Pursuit after greatness; (10) The love of revenge upon one's enemies; (11) The love of learning and prudence; (12) The uninterrupted service of God; (13) The love of rest and repose.

Contempt for the world. Many men say that it is our duty to bewail this world, as it is an empty and perishable world; it is full of vicissitudes for many, and does not remain in man's hands; for, while a man is at rest and at his ease, peaceful, flourishing, and joyful, his rejoicing is turned into mourning, his honor into disgrace, and his riches into poverty. Besides, all men's days are passed in lying and fraud, in oppression and forwardness; and it is for these reasons that some people say that it is proper to despise the world, and to live on, without building houses, or planting vineyards, or marrying and begetting children. We should (they say) rather make the mountain and the forest our dwelling-places, living on green herbs and grasses, until the day of death.

When I examined these statements, I found that although their way of stating had an element of truth in it, they had yet strayed from the right path, and forsaken the proper course. For what they desired to do was to give up a settled life altogether, and to keep aloof from marriage, so as not to have children. Now, if this had been the desirable course for man, surely God would have commanded that it should be so, and that everybody should act in such a manner. He, however, saw that if this were the case, the name of man would cease to exist, and the world become a waste; man's intellect would become blunted, and would change into the instinct of brutes, or he would altogether lose his reason; and, owing to the lack of good food, he would be seized with fits of melancholy, and other diseases would afflict him, so that he would at length die in bitterness of soul.

The golden mean is to despise the things of this world on occasions when it is proper to despise them. For instance, when a man sees before him some fine dainty food, and he remembers that the Law has forbidden him to partake thereof, then such food should appear in his eyes as abhorrent and defiled. When he sees a beautiful woman, and she is prohibited to him, let him keep at a distance from her; and so with money which is not his, let him fly from it, and not touch it with the idea of stealing it. In fine, let a man in all things ever place the fear of God before his eyes, as it is written: "In all thy ways acknowledge Him, and He shall direct thy paths" (Proverbs 3:6).

Eating, drinking, and pleasuring. Some people say that it is right for man to occupy himself with eating, drinking, and enjoyment, for these keep body and soul together. For when a man afflicts himself by fasting, his heart becomes weak, his strength fails, the light of his eyes becomes dim, and he becomes hard of hearing.

When I examined their contention, I found that they had gone wrong, inasmuch as they looked at the advantages but ignored the positive harm in these things. For by over-indulgence in food and drink the blood increases in the body, illness ensues, and the general system becomes weak; moreover, a man becomes like a dog which is never satiated, and in consequence of his foul throat, he becomes disgusting to everyone, and being subject to diarrhea, his body becomes like a sieve. . . .

The golden mean is that a man should eat and drink in moderation, in quantities sufficient to maintain his life, as it is said: "The righteous eateth to the satisfying of his soul" (Proverbs 13:25); "Hast thou found honey, eat so much as is sufficient for thee" (Proverbs 25:16).

The love of sensual pleasures. Many have thought it right to occupy themselves in this manner, because they say that the pleasure to be derived from their indulgence is most agreeable, adding to the enjoyments of life, removing the heaviness felt in the head and brain, and making man bright and intelligent.

When I tested their arguments, I found them erroneous; for such pleasures cause dimness of the sight, and trembling of the loins, and destroy true ambition and physical strength. For these reasons Solomon warned us: "Give not thy strength unto women" (Proverbs 31:3). Through such indulgence a man's heart becomes excited (or "divided"), as it is said, "Whoredom, wine, and new wine take away the understanding" (Hosea 4:11). Whosoever gives way to it will be unable to quench the flame of his fire; his learning will become brutish, his action will be despicable and abhorrent, and his disgrace will not be blotted out.

The golden mean is to indulge in this pleasure moderately and at stated intervals, with the object of having offspring by one's lawful and wedded wife.

Delighting in the affection of one's fellow creatures. If we observe mankind, we shall find that many human beings place love above all other considerations; for they hold that it elevates and rejoices the soul, gladdens the heart, and brightens the appearance. It seems to me, however, that those who say so are foolish and make a mistake, for the only love and affection we should have ought to be bestowed upon the partner in life that has fallen to our lot. . . .

The amassing of wealth. Man says: How good a thing it is in this world to toil in gathering riches for it is said that "Money answereth all things" (Ecclesiastes 10:19); by its means a man rises, attains power, and receives honors, as it is said, "Many will intreat the favor of the prince" (Proverbs 19:6); "The rich hath many friends" (Proverbs 14:20).

The examination we shall find that their utterances are not true; for "He that loveth silver will not be satisfied with silver"

(Ecclesiastes 5:10). All his days will be spent in pain, his heart will not be at ease, for fear of losing the wealth which he has gathered. Riches, indeed, very often prove the means of ruin to their possessor.

The golden mean is that a man should strive in moderation to obtain wealth, in proportion to the wants of his household; and he should cheerfully enjoy that which his Creator has graciously bestowed upon him, for it is "the Lord's blessing which maketh rich."

The desire to have children. Many say: "How good it is to have many children, for they are life's pleasures, and the delight of the eyes! It is through them that kindness and pity exist; through them that the name and remembrance of man endure; in them parents may find their support during old age."

But I say, "What is the use of a child that is a source of fear and shame to its parents? Better that it had never been born. . . ."

The love of cultivating the soil and building. See how many men there are whose whole heart is devoted to the thought of cultivating the earth, building houses, planting vineyards, and restoring the waste places. I considered the subject, and find it all vanity. For who can tell whether his son will inherit it; perchance, a man who has not labored upon it will inherit it.

The golden mean is to occupy yourself with building just to the extent of your living requirements; and with planting and sowing just enough to supply the means of subsistence for your household.

The love of longevity. Many say that a man should endeavor to lengthen his life, for "What profit is there to man after his death?"

The object of their words is to tell man that he must eat and drink incessantly, and gratify the desires of his heart, and avoid causes of fright and danger; but how about the experience, that many observe these prescriptions, and yet do not prolong their lives? Come and see how kings spend their days in pleasure, and yet do not live long. Even those people who do increase their days only thereby increase their anxiety, vexation, guilt, and sins.

The golden mean is to love this world with the object of doing good in life, and to aspire to the higher life in the world to come.

The love of authority. How many love authority and exalt themselves in the world! They act, nevertheless, foolishly. Do as our sages observe: "Love work and hate lordship." "Alas for the possession of authority, that buries its possessor!"

The golden mean is to gain authority and power, for the purpose of acting as the judge of what is right, of supporting the poor, and delivering the oppressed from the hands of the oppressor, of removing the spoiler, and driving off those who are perverse, as it is written: "Behold, a king shall reign in righteousness" (Isaiah 32:1).

The love of taking revenge. "How sweet it is," say some men, "to take revenge upon one's enemies; for revenge sets anger at rest, causes excitement to cease, and chases sorrow!"

Surely such men wander far away from what is sensible; for, as regards revenge, a man ultimately regrets it. Thus, too, says the philosopher: "Pardon the one who has done thee an ill, and give unto him who has refused thee." He continues: "If thou takest revenge, thou wilt sorrow; if thou forgivest, thou wilt rejoice."

The golden mean is that if thou must take revenge, then rather revenge thyself on those who corrupt their ways before God, as it is said: "I will early destroy all the wicked of the land" (Psalm 101:8).

The love of learning. Our Rabbis say: "Turn from all pursuits, and engage in knowledge, for thereby thou wilt come to understand all phenomena, and it will be a satisfaction to thy soul!"

These words are undoubtedly true as far as they go; but we have to take exception to the idea that we must occupy ourselves with knowledge to the exclusion of all else. For have not our sages remarked: "The study of the Law, together with worldly pursuit, is good." Also, "Where there is no meal, there is no Law." For you cannot possibly pursue knowledge without eating and drinking; and if man were to engage simply in the pursuit of knowledge and of the Law, the human species would die out, and the world would become a blank.

Which, then, is the golden mean? To engage but little in worldly occupations, just sufficient as is necessary for the world's demands, and to occupy yourself also with the Law. To eat and drink in moderation, so as to strengthen the body and support the heart, and not to impair by over-indulgence the subtle character of knowledge. We observe that God fed Israel for forty years with manna; whereas, if they had some heavier food, they would have been found neglecting the knowledge of the Law. On the other hand, He ordained tithes and gifts for the maintenance of the recipients, so that they should not neglect the study of the Law for want of the necessary nourishment.

The love of God's service. Many people remark that there is nothing better for man than to trust in God, and to serve Him day and night, in fact, to leave every other occupation in order to engage in the service of the Creator. God will in return fulfill his every desire, so that he shall lack no good thing.

All this sounds very well, but it is impracticable; for, if a man did not trouble himself about his means of livelihood, his body could not be kept up, and the consequence would be that this very service would have no existence, for he would die without issue; whilst the duty of serving God has been entrusted to him and to his offspring. . . . If, furthermore, a man separates himself from his fellow creatures and has no dealings with them, neither in weights nor measures, how can he possibly carry out such precepts as "Just balances . . . shall ye have" (Leviticus 19:36); "Ye shall not wrong one another" (Leviticus 25:14); "Ye shall judge righteously" (Leviticus

19:15)? And how can he observe the laws relating to cleanliness and uncleanliness, or to tithes and vows? And, lastly, we surely dare not rely on miracles, saying: "God will find me food, without my providing it."

Which is the golden mean? To engage both in the service of the Creator, and in making provision for the maintenance of his household and of himself. His chief striving, however, should be centered in the Torah, and in the service of God; and then it will be well within him, both in this world and in the world to come.

The love of rest. There are, again, many men who say that rest is better than anything else; for it produces a healthy mind, adds enjoyment to one's food, and helps to develop a vigorous frame. The object of all man's labor is, in truth, to find rest in later life. . . .

Now I looked well to understand the ideas of these men, and found them senseless; for they do not understand what is meant by rest. Rest has only a value when toil has preceded; for rest without toil is actually not rest, but rather indolence; and the sluggard never attains the wish of his heart, and the rest for which he craves. It is concerning such a person that it is said: "The desire of the slothful kills him" (Proverbs 21:25), for the indolent is not satisfied with the good he enjoys; he is lax in matters of divine worship, the study of the Law, and prayer. Furthermore, through too much rest the body grows torpid, the stomach gets inflated, and disease in the lower parts is engendered; there ensue sciatica and gout, diseases of the lower limbs, and even elephantiasis. So important is this consideration that even though a man may have all his requirements, he dare not sit idle; for the idle man will come to insanity and sickness; and his strength will become reduced; and this truth applies even to a king or ruler.

The golden mean is to realize that it is best to toil and labor in attending to one's occupation and work, and then rest will follow as a sweet and pleasant prize. No rest is worth having which does not follow toil; the only desirable rest is the one to be enjoyed in the World-to-Come; and this is an uninterrupted state of rest.

THREE KINDS OF EDUCATION[3]

There are three kinds of education, of which one is the most potent. The first and weakest consists in saying to the one to be educated: "Do this: do not do that," without making him understand the consequences of the command or the prohibition, whether he obey or refuse to obey.

The second kind consists in giving, together with the command or prohibition, the consequences of the path chosen. Thus: "Do this, and you will be rewarded: do not do that, or you will be punished." This method is better than the former, for it awakens the idea of happiness or of misery resulting from the path of conduct chosen by the individual.

The third kind of education, while it consists in giving command and prohibition, and in indicating the recompense or punishment that will follow, adds thereto the history of those people who have obeyed and were rewarded by salvation, and of those people who disobeyed and were punished by misery. This method is more effective than the other two, since it adds as it were the test and experience to the commands, and, to point the lesson, adduces the value of personal testimony.

Now God has revealed all three methods in the Bible, which is a book dedicated primarily to the education of his servants. He commands piety and prohibits sin; He announces the reward of good actions and the punishment of evil actions; and finally He gives the history of those who lived on earth before

[3]This selection is taken from the Preface to Saadia's *Commentary on the Pentateuch,* as quoted in *The Jewish Anthology,* by Edmond Fleg, tr. by Maurice Samuel (New York, Harcourt, Brace & Co., 1925).

us—the salvation of those who have been virtuous and the punishment of those who have been wicked. The divine Book therefore contains the three principal forms of education. . . .

But know furthermore, you who read this, that despite its inestimable worth, despite its high place, and despite the beauty of its language, which light up the darkness and the mystery of its contents, the servants of God would do wrong to believe that outside of the Bible there is nothing which would compel men to believe in the Eternal. Indeed, they are in duty bound to know that many other proofs exist.

CHAPTER 31

THE LAW ACCORDING TO HANANE'EL

Not all the learned Jews during this period were lured afield by the sun of Arab enlightenment. The majority acted with the grim caution bred of dread experience, and insisted on burrowing solely in their own traditional Jewish lore. Not for them the seductions of Greek philosophy and Arabic science; they sought to remain faithful in the strictest sense to the Torah.

Significantly, however, the strictest sense now was the reasonable, not the literal one. A typical instance is Hanane'el ben Hushiel, an Egyptian rabbi who lived during the first half of the eleventh century. He confined his studies entirely to the Bible and Talmud, writing commentaries on them which aimed to be illuminating yet at the same time orthodox. Here is a characteristic passage taken from his Commentary on the Pentateuch.[1] *It deals with the law of "an eye for an eye" (Exodus 21:24), and repeats a benevolent rationalization invented by the very earliest rabbinical authorities.*

According to the tradition of our teachers, this expression means the *value* of the eye, and not the eye itself. The proof thereof is found in a passage which precedes the one cited, according to which a man who wounds another bodily must pay for the time during which the wounded man is idle, and in

[1] Quoted in Edmond Fleg's *Jewish Anthology,* trans. by Maurice Samuel (New York, 1925), pp. 173–174.

addition the cost of the cure; and if the same wound is inflicted for punishment on the guilty man, how would he pay his victim, seeing he would himself be idle and would have to find payment for his own cure?

Furthermore, if the Law had intended that the man who tore out another man's eye should be punished in the same way, one would have to pause before the fact that some men are weaker than others, and perhaps the guilty man, being weaker, would die as a result of the punishment; but the Torah says: "An eye for an eye," and not: "A life for an eye. . . ."

Finally, it is impossible to inflict on the second man exactly the same wound as was suffered by the first, for the first wound was not measured exactly, as to its length, depth, and width. If, then, the ruling were to be observed: "As he did, so shall it be done to him," it would have to be the same, neither more nor less. . . . Reason, Scripture, and tradition, therefore, teach us that the words, "An eye for an eye" are not to be taken literally, but that what is meant is pecuniary reparation for the lost eye."

CHAPTER 32

THE TESTAMENT OF ELEAZAR THE GREAT

The trend toward rationalistic philosophizing was confined to the Jewish scholars who were in contact with the Arabs. Those living in the Christian hinterland of Europe, being forced to breathe an atmosphere of the most poisonous bigotry, kept their heads buried, and their eyes turned inward. Typical of them was a certain Eleazar ben Isaac, who served as rabbi of the town of Worms in the eleventh century, and whose labors as a teacher of Talmudic exegesis earned him the sobriquet HaGadol, "the Great." *The following passages are taken from the* tzava'ah, the will, *which he is reputed to have left for the guidance of his son. The document is one of the earliest examples of a type of simple ethical literature which grew to be extremely popular in the medieval Jewish ghettos.*[1]

My son, when thou wakest from thy sleep at midnight, converse with thy wife in chaste terms, using no indecent expression, even in jest. . . . If thou wakest at other hours, let not thine heart indulge in impure fancies, for evil thought leads to evil deed.

My son, keep a vessel of water always near thy couch. On rising at morn do not begin to dress before washing thy hands,

[1]*Hebrew Ethical Wills,* edited and translated by Israel Abrahams (Philadelphia, Jewish Publication Society, 1926).

nor receive thy garments from another in the same condition, for the spirit of uncleanness rests on the hands. Pass not thine unwashed hands over thine eyes, intending harm to an enemy, lest thy plot fail and thy gaze prove baneful to thy friends, though harmless to thy foes.[2]

My son, keep thy body pure, cleanse the abode of thy soul. Beware lest thou make it detestable, and thyself the cause of thine own rejection. . . . My son, be not impatient when I thus insist on this subject. Washing the hands is one of the sublime things which stand on the height of the world. Beware lest by neglect in this regard thou become as one excommunicated, and forfeit future bliss. For when thou washest thy hands thou art bound to stretch them on high in adoration of thy Maker; it were unseemly to do so with foul fingers.

My son, never dress thyself without benediction. Even as men should offer thanks for the enjoyment of food, so must they do for the gift of raiment. He who dresses without blessing shall wear worm and clod in the grave, and the worms cause as much pain to the dead as a needle in raw flesh. . . .

My son, in the house of learning speak no idle words, but incline thine ear to the discourse of the wise. Consider nothing negligible, and despise no man. For many pearls are found in the poor man's tunic.

My son, be zealous in visiting the sick, for sympathy lightens pain. Urge the patient to return as a penitent to his Maker. Pray for him, and depart! Do not fatigue him by staying too long, for his malady is heavy enough already. Enter cheerfully, for his heart and eyes are on those who come in.

My son, comfort the mourners, and speak to their heart. The companions of Job were held punishable merely because

---

[2]Unwashed hands were believed to harbor "unclean spirits," and a malevolent person could use them to equip himself with an "evil eye."

they reproached when they should have consoled him. Thus, it is written: "Ye have not spoken of Me the thing that is right, as My servant Job hath."

My son, join in bringing the bride to the canopy, help to gladden the bridegroom, for he who acts thus is as though he participated in the nuptial ceremony of the giving of the Law at Sinai.

My son, show honor to the poor man, and draw out thy soul unto him. Be punctilious to offer thy gift in secret, not in the public gaze. Give him food and drink in thy house, but do not watch him while he eats. His soul famishes, and perchance he pounces on the viands.

My son, crush not the poor man with harsh words, for the Lord will plead his cause. Such conduct rouses on high many accusers, to whom there is no defense. But he who treats the poor with good will and generosity acquires intercessors to plead his cause. . . .

My son, enter not thy house suddenly, still less enter thy neighbor's house without announcement. Make not thyself too much feared in thine home, for this is the cause of many evils.

My son, drive anger out of thine heart, "for anger resteth in the bosom of fools, and a strange god rests on their head."

My son, love the wise, and attach thyself to them. Seek to know thy Maker, for "that the soul should be without knowledge is not good." Salute all men and speak the truth.

My son, be chaste, and self-restrained in all thine actions. When thou sittest at thy table to eat, remember that thou art in the presence of the King. Be not a snatcher or a glutton. Wash thy hands before and after the meal, for both actions are essential. If thou drinkest while the rest are eating, do not obtrusively recite the benediction over the wine. Speak not during the meal, not even words of Torah.

Nevertheless, my son, never omit to discourse of the Torah afterwards, for a table whereat there is no discourse of Torah is full of filthy vomit, in that the All-Present is not in their thoughts.

My son, when thou visitest a sick man who is without means, go not to him with empty hands. When he awakes, be quick to offer refreshment to him, and he will esteem it as though thou didst uphold and restore his soul. The Lord will requite thee!

My son, reveal not thy secret to thy wife. Be of faithful spirit to all, betray not another's confidence even when thou art at strife with him.

My son, eat herbs rather than beg from others, and if thou beggest, ask only for thine absolute need. Prefer death to making thyself a burden on thy fellow creatures!

My son, it is incumbent on thee to beget children, and to rear them for the study of the Torah. For their sake wilt thou be worthy of eternal life.

My son, beware lest thy wife be overgenerous to her first son-in-law. Appoint not the latter as administrator over thy household. Approach not thy wife near her menstrual period. Avoid all grossness. Hold aloof from what is foul and from what has the appearance of foulness. . . .

My son, be on thy guard lest thou provoke one of the wise, for his anger is as a viper's venom, the poison of a basilisk which will not be charmed; but if there be death in such a one's wrath, there is life in his good will.

My son, walk not alone, judge not alone, testify not alone, nor be witness and judge at the same time. None may judge alone save One.

My son, be no cause of plaint to orphan or widow, for God is the father of the fatherless and judge of the widows. Rob them not, seeing that He hath already deprived them of all their happiness. Hence, "He will despoil of life those that despoil them."

My son, keep far from a wicked neighbor and from him

whose reputation is evil, for what they say of him below accords with what they say of him on high.

My son, "Rejoice not when thine enemy falleth, and let not thy heart be glad when he stumbleth, lest the Lord see it and it displease Him, and He turn away His wrath from him [to thee]." Yet, "if thine enemy be hungry give him bread to eat."

My son, be not as a fly o'er thy fellowman's sore, leaving the healthy parts and pouncing on the plague spot. Cover up thy neighbor's disease, and lay not his corruption bare to the world.

My son, haste to the performance of a duty, and let it not seem light in thine eyes. Say not, this is light, that is important, for thou knowest not the grant of reward for each. Let all thy deeds be done in the Name of Heaven!

My son, be not righteous overmuch, neither be thou overmuch wicked. Nor let thyself become overyielding to the extent of drinking water left over from the lips of thy friend. For the breath cometh out from within his throat, and thou art unaware who is suffering from disease. Be bashful in all matters, but efface not thyself at the cost of thy health. Yet in the House of Study be thou modest. Behave there as one unlearned, even though thy comrades laugh at thee for it.

My son, sit not in the company of calumniators and slanderers, for all is noted on high, and is recorded in a book; and all who are present are inscribed in the list of offenders.

My son, wed not an unworthy woman: woe to the tarnished who tarnishes his seed! Absalom and Adonijah, the offspring of such a union, wrought many evils to Israel. They were unchaste and stirred up rebellion. My son, have no marital intercourse with thy wife while she is suckling her child. Do not leave an infant in his cradle alone in the house by day or night, nor pass thou the night alone in any abode. For under such circumstances, Lilith seizes man or child in her fatal embrace.

My son, zealously bring up thy children in the study of the Law. Withdraw them not from it! For he who so acts shortens his life; the Holy One weeps over such a one day by day.

My son, drink no water that has been left uncovered overnight.

My son, give unto thy Creator His share of all thy food. This, God's portion, belongs to the poor. Therefore, select of the choicest viands on thy table and present them to thy Maker. "Thou shalt not curse the deaf, but thou shalt fear thy God."

CHAPTER 33

THE WISDOM OF IBN GABIROL

Solomon ben Judah ibn Gabirol ranks among the greatest of medieval Jewish luminaries. He was at once poet, philosopher, moralist, and grammarian, and brilliantly exemplifies the universalism which the wise in Israel can achieve when the pressure of bigotry is lessened.

Little is known of his life except that he was born in Moorish Spain about 1021, and subsisted there as a wandering scholar until his death when still in his thirties. According to legend, he was murdered by a Mohammedan who was jealous of Gabirol's poetic gifts, and was buried beneath a fig tree that thereupon began to bear fruit of extraordinary sweetness.

Altogether a Jew in his religious devotions–many of his hymns have become an integral part of synagogue liturgy–Gabirol belonged to the entire world in his philosophical outlook. Nor is this surprising, since in the relatively enlightened land in which he lived, this Jew could feel sufficiently safe to dare draw on the entire world for his ideas. The clearest proof is the fact that one of his earliest literary products was a collection of maxims derived almost entirely from non-Jewish sources. This small book, written originally in Arabic, was later rendered into Hebrew under the title Mivhar HaPeninim, *"The Choice of Pearls," in which version it acquired enduring popularity throughout Israel. Here are a few of those maxims.*[1]

[1]Translated by Rev. A. Cohen (New York, Bloch Publishing, 1925).

THE CHOICE OF PEARLS

CONCERNING WISDOM

A wise man's question is half of wisdom; a conciliatory attitude toward one's fellow creatures is half of intelligence; and systematic expenditure is half way to satisfying one's needs.

What sort of man is fit to rule? Either a sage who has been invested with power or a king who seeks wisdom.

I search not, said the sage [Aristotle], for wisdom with the hope of ever coming to the end of it or attaining it completely; rather do I search for it so as not to be a fool, and the intelligent man should have no other motive than this.

The sage was asked, "How is it thou hast more wisdom than thy fellows?" He replied, "Because I spent on (midnight) oil more than they spent on wine."

Man is only wise during the time that he searches for wisdom; when he imagines he has completely attained it, he is a fool.

Kings may be the judges of the earth, but wise men are the judges of kings.

The worth of every man is proportionate to what he knows.

The sage [Diogenes] was asked, "Who are greater, the wise or the rich?" He replied, "The wise." It was then objected, "If so, how is it that there are more wise men at the doors of the rich than rich men at the doors of the wise?" He replied, "Because the wise appreciate the advantage of wealth, but the rich do not appreciate the advantage of wisdom."

The first step in the acquisition of wisdom is silence; the second, listening; the third, memory; the fourth, practice; the fifth, teaching others.

Nobody is wise unless he possesses three qualities: never to despise an inferior (in learning) while he searches after wisdom; not to envy one who is more wealthy; and not to accept payment for his wisdom.

The finest quality in man is that he should be an inquirer.

When wisdom is lacking in the believer, he must seek it even from skeptics.[2]

The quest of wisdom in old age is like a mark made in the sand, but the quest of wisdom in youth is like an inscription on stone.

Poverty cannot disgrace the wise man, nor can lust enslave him.

Wisdom, about which there is no discussion, is like a hidden hoard from which nothing is withdrawn.

There are four mental types among human beings: the man who knows and is aware that he knows – he is wise, so inquire of him; the man who knows but is unaware that he knows – remind him and help him that he forget not (his knowledge); the man who is ignorant and knows that he is ignorant – teach him; the man who is ignorant but pretends to know – he is a fool, so keep away from him.

It is the practice of a fool, when he does wrong, to blame others; it is the practice of the seeker of instruction to blame himself; but it is the practice of the wise and pious man (so to act that he has occasion) to blame neither himself nor others.[3]

One who acts the part of a wise man, without possessing wisdom, is like an ass working the mill, going round and round without making progress.

Nobody can detect the error of his teacher until he knows varying opinions.

Four things will an honorable man not consider beneath his dignity to perform: stand up to greet his father; pay deference to his guests; inspect his carriages though he have a hundred servants; and honor the wise man to partake of his wisdom.

---

[2]Although this aphorism is derived from an Arabic source, it accords with Hebrew teaching. It receives illustration from the great talmudic sage, Rabbi Me'ir.

[3]This is a saying of Socrates.

Beware of a fool who is devout and a wise man who is a sinner.

Said the sage, "When I hear evil speech, I pay no attention." Somebody asked him the reason, and he replied, "Because I am afraid of hearing still worse."

To a fool silence is the best answer.

CONCERNING PATIENCE

A man came before a sage and said to him, "I perceive that human beings do harm, so my soul counsels me not to mingle with them." The sage replied, "Do not so, because thou canst not stand without them nor they without thee; they need thee as thou needest them. Nevertheless, be in their company a deaf man that can hear, a blind man that can see, and a dumb man that can speak."

Somebody insulted a wise man, and one of his disciples said to him, "Master, permit me to punish him." The sage replied, "He is not a wise man who gives another permission to do wrong."

Who cannot control his temper is defective in intellect.

Who is mighty? He who responds to folly in humility and subdues his temper.

Whoever cannot control his temper, how much less can he control others!

The beginning of the success of a humble man is that his fellows assist him because of his submissiveness.

I find humility a greater help to me than all my fellowmen.

CONCERNING FAITH

The sage was asked, "Why do we never perceive in thee a trace of anxiety?" He replied, "Because I never possessed a thing over which I would grieve had I lost it."[4]

---

[4]Another saying of Socrates.

He also said, "Everything requires a fence." He was asked, "What is the fence?" He answered, "Trust." "What is the fence of trust?" he was asked; and he replied, "Faith." To the further question, "What is the fence of faith?" he answered, "To fear nothing."

Who refuses to accept the decree of the Creator, there is no healing to his stupidity.

Who is the wisest of men and the most trusting? He who accepts things as they come and go.

CONCERNING FORTITUDE

I am astonished at the person who has not prepared patience for every misfortune and gratitude for every piece of good fortune.

Worry over what has not occurred is a serious malady.

To drink a deadly poison is better than worry.

There is a calamity which, when contrasted with another kind of calamity, appears fortunate. Sometimes a calamity becomes auspicious through fortitude.

Fortitude may be bitter, but it averts injury from those who possess it.

Who is honorable in the sight of the Creator? He who has met with adversity but bravely endures whatever befalls him

CONCERNING CONTENTMENT

Who seeks more than he needs hinders himself from enjoying what he has.

A king said to the sage, "Wert thou to make such a request of me, thou wouldst have sufficient for thy needs throughout thy life." The sage replied, "Why should I make such a request of thee, seeing that I am richer than thou!" The king asked, "But how art thou richer than I?" He answered, "Because I am more content with the little I possess than thou art with thy greater wealth."[5]

Who desires from the world only sufficient for his wants, the little that he has suffices him.

Contentment is better even than intellect.

Regulate the desire in accordance with the means, otherwise it will demand from thee more than thou canst supply.

Two things can never be associated together–contentment and covetousness.

CONCERNING PERCEPTION

He is not clever who carefully considers a matter after he has stumbled in it, but he who comprehends it and gives it close consideration so as not to stumble.

It is meet for an intelligent man to perceive (the spirit of) his age, guard his tongue, and attend to his business.

Which man is most likely to achieve his object? He who discards whatever is superfluous and takes the short road.

There is no limit to trials; but the clever man increases his knowledge by their means.[6]

Instruction removes bewilderment from the clever man, but increases the bewilderment of the fool. Exactly so does the day heighten the vision of those who have eyes but intensifies blindness for the bat.

Beware of the chief seat, because it is a seat that shifts.

It is easier to tolerate a whole fool than half a fool, that is, a fool who wishes to appear clever.

---

[5]Diogenes uses this reasoning to prove that he is richer than the King of Persia.

[6]A saying of Aristotle.

Know that when the people are capable of speaking (of revolt), they can accomplish it; strive, then, that they should not talk of it, and thou wilt be spared that which they can do.

CONCERNING COMPANIONS

A bad companion seeks a pretext for quarrel, not an explanation.

All love has reality, except the love of a stupid person.

The sage said to his son: "My son, exchange not an old companion for a new one while his heart is still true to thee; let not a solitary enemy seem trifling in thine eyes, nor a thousand friends too many."

A friendless man is like a left hand bereft of the right.

When the death of one of my companions occurred, one of my limbs perished.

It was asked of the sage, "Whom lovest thou more, thy brother or thy companion?" He replied, "I love not my brother unless he be my companion."

There are three classes of friends: Some are like food with which thou canst not dispense; others, like medicine which is needful occasionally; and others, like an illness which thou dost never want.

A man's best companion is his intellect; his worst enemy, his desire.

The best of animals needs the whip; the purest of women, a husband; and the cleverest of men, to ask advice.

A companion who tells thee thy faults privately whenever he meets thee is better for thee than a companion who hands thee a gold coin whenever he meets thee.

The eye of a needle is not narrow for two friends, but the world is not wide enough for two enemies.

Lovest thou thy companion, flatter him not; nor make inquiries about him, lest thou meet an enemy of his who will malign him to thee and cause an estrangement between thee and him.

Let not the friendship of the king deceive thee (into a sense of security) when his minister is thine enemy; but if thou art safe from the minister, be not afraid of the king.

Who is slothful among men? He who is too indolent to acquire friends; and still more indolent is he who possessed friends and loses them.

Beware against associating with one from whom thou canst learn nothing good.

How can an intelligent man test himself? When he endures the company of a bad wife.

A bad wife is like a wolf which may change its hair but not its nature.

If one brings suspicion on himself, let him not condemn anybody who thinks ill of him.

What is best for man? That he should possess intellect. If he lack intellect, then the best is money, for thereby he will be respected. If he lack money, then a wife who will conceal his faults. If he lack a wife, then silence which will hide his defects. If he lack silence, then the best thing for him is the grave.

Desirest thou to make a companion of a man, first provoke him to anger. If he admit the truth to thee in the time of his wrath, accept his companionship; otherwise abandon him.

Place no trust in the gratitude of a person to whom thou givest (what he asks) until thou deniest him (his request): for the patient man is the truly grateful, whereas the peevish man is ungrateful.

CONCERNING CONFIDENCES

Whatever thou wouldst hide from thine enemy, do not disclose to thy friend.

A man once revealed a secret to his friend, and then asked, "Didst understand?" He replied, "Yes, I understood, but I have forgotten."

The sage was asked, "What is keeping a secret?" He replied, "I repudiate the person who tells it to me and conceal what he told me."

The sage was asked, "How dost thou hide a secret?" He replied, "I make my heart its grave."

Never have I condemned a man who disclosed a secret of mine which I entrusted to him; rather have I condemned my own heart which was too narrow to hold it at the time I deposited it in his heart.

Thy secret is thy prisoner; but shouldst thou disclose it, thou becomest its prisoner.

A secret is that which is between two; but if it be between three it is no longer a secret.

CONCERNING SILENCE

If I utter a word, it becomes my master; but should I not utter it, I am its master.

I am better able to retract what I did not say than what I did say.

The pain of silence is better than the pain of loquacity; die of the disease of silence, but not of the disease of loquacity.

The best worship (of God) is silence and hope.

Through silence thou mayest experience one regret, but through loquacity, two regrets.

Treasure thy tongue as thou treasurest thy wealth.

Lackest thou instruction, cleave to silence.

The bait by which a man is caught lies concealed beneath his tongue; a man's deathtrap is between his cheeks.

It is related that a man from Arabia entered a company and preserved a lengthy silence. Somebody said to him, "Rightly do they call thee one of the noble men of Arabia." He replied, "My brethren, the portion of a man from his ear belongs to himself, but the portion of a man from his tongue belongs to others."

When thou speakest, say little; for the fewer the words of a man, the fewer his mistakes.

When thou speakest at night, lower thy voice; and when thou speakest by day, look around thee first.

CONCERNING SPEECH

To speak the truth is better than maintaining silence about it.

It is related that some men reviled speech in the presence of a king. He said, "God forbid (that I should agree with you); for he who is able to make a right use of speech is able to make a right use also of silence."

CONCERNING TRUTH

The wise enjoy themselves when they have discovered truth, but fools, when they have discovered falsehood.

A king ordered the execution of a certain wise man against whom a false charge had been brought. As he was led out to be executed, he perceived his wife weeping; so he said to her, "Why weepest thou?" She replied, "Why should I not weep, seeing that they are putting thee to death although thou hast done no wrong." He retorted, "Dost thou, then, prefer that they should execute me because I *have* done wrong?"

CONCERNING POVERTY

None is poorer than he who rejoices not in his portion and whose eye is never satisfied.

None is so poor as the man who is fearful of becoming poor.

When a man's wealth diminishes, even his children do not accept his opinion, but contradict his words and commands.

I have tasted the bitterness of all things, but I have found nothing so bitter as the taste of begging.

What is the wound which is incurable? When a noble-minded man has occasion to ask something of a mean person and is refused.

A man came to a sage and said to him, "Pray on my behalf to thy God that He never make me to need anything of my fellowmen." He replied, "It is impossible that thou shouldst never have recourse to others; but may God never make thee to ask anything of the worthless among men."

CONCERNING ENVY

Envy is to men like bodily ailments–it leads to consumption.

I have not seen one who hurts himself more than does the envious person; his mourning is unceasing, his soul grieves, his intellect deteriorates, and his heart is disquieted.

Everybody can eat with satisfaction except the man who envies good fortune; for he is only pleased by the misfortune (of others).

Every enmity has the possibility of cure, except the enmity of him who hates thee from envy.

Envy not thy brother for what he has; he enjoys his life whilst thou art sated with vexation and unrest.

Thou hast sufficient revenge of the envious person that he grieves over thy happiness and good fortune.

CONCERNING THE EVIL TONGUE

A certain person talked of his companion's failings in the presence of an eminent man. The latter said to him, "Thou hast indicated to me how numerous are thy failings by narrating at length the failings of another."

A man said to his companion, "I wish to avoid thee because people speak against thee." He replied, "Hast thou ever heard me speak against others?" "No," was the reply. "That being so," he retorted, "avoid those who speak against me."

A man condemned his companion because of something he had heard about him, and the latter defended himself. "But was it not a trustworthy person who told me?" exclaimed the other. "If he were a trustworthy person, he would not have told thee," was the retort.

Who carries calumny is himself the calumniator.

The sage was asked, "Which is the worst malady?" He replied, "A bad neighbor. If thou keepest close to him, he will cause thee trouble; if thou holdest aloof from him, he will speak against thee and narrate whatever is to thy discredit."

An eminent man was asked, "How didst thou attain all this honor, although thou art an Ethiopian?" He replied, "Through truthfulness and loyalty, by abstaining from artifice, and never asking for what was not essential to me."

THE IMPROVEMENT OF THE MORAL QUALITIES

The following excerpts are from a short treatise written in Arabic by Ibn Gabirol about 1045. It deals with ethics, not metaphysics, and its aim is to give a systematic account, the first by any Jewish author, of the various human impulses and the manner in which they can be trained so that they make for virtue, or neglected so that they lead to vice.[7]

ON HAUGHTINESS

The ancients say, "With him who is pleased with himself, many become displeased." A poet composed these lines concerning the blameworthiness of arrogance:

[7]The translation is from *Gabirol's Improvement of the Moral Qualities,* by Stephen S. Wise, Ph.D. (New York, Columbia University Press, 1902).

"Let him who shows great vanity concerning his beauty consider this! If men would but consider what is within them, neither young nor old would feel proud. Are there not in the head of every son of man five orifices from which come forth effluvia? The nose exudes snot, the ear gives forth an unpleasant odor, the eye sheds tears, and the mouth salivates. O son of earth, to be consumed of earth and on the morrow, desist from thy pride, for thou wilt be food and drink (to the earth)!"

It is told of Ardeshir,[8] the king, that he gave a book to a man accustomed to stand at his side, and said unto him, "When thou seest me become violently angry, give it to me." In the book (was written), "Restrain thyself, for thou art not God; thou art but a body, one part of which is on the point of consuming the other, and in a short while it will turn into the worm and dust and nothingness."

ON MODESTY

A wise man was asked, "What is intelligence?" and he answered, "Modesty." Again he was asked, "What is modesty?" and he replied, "Intelligence." . . . To every man of understanding the nobility of the intellect is patent, for it is the dividing line between man and beast, in that it masters man's natural impulses and subdues passion. With the help of intelligence man realizes the benefit of knowledge and gets to understand the true nature of things, he comes to acknowledge the Unity of God, to worship his Master, and to bear a striking resemblance to the character of the angels. Since this precious quality is of so noble a kind, it follows that modesty which resembles it is almost equally so. The proof of its being thus related is that thou wilt never see a modest man lacking intelligence, or an intelligent man devoid of modesty. This being so, man must direct all his efforts to the attainment of this wonderful and highly considered quality.

---

[8] Called an "Indian King" in the *Choice of Pearls* (No. 538).

ON LUST

Lust is preferred by foolish men only because of the immediateness of its delight and for the sake of the amusement and merriment and the hearing of mirthful songs which they get through it. They heed not the suffering and the wretchedness that follow in its train, and, therefore, incline in accord with their natural impulses to the attainment of present pleasure.

ON HATE

Thou shouldst know that he who hates men is hated by them, and when this quality takes firm hold of the soul, it destroys it, because it leads to the hatred of the very food and drink with which man sustains life. Besides, he suffers injury through the hostility of men. When excessive love is expended on other than divine things, it is changed into the most violent hatred.

ON HARD-HEARTEDNESS

This quality is exercised for the purpose of wreaking vengeance upon enemies. There is no harm in making use of it in this manner, although the intelligent man ought not endeavor to be avenged upon his enemies. For this is not befitting.

Plato, the author of the laws in regard to vengeance, said, "He who desires to be revenged upon his enemies should add (a degree of) excellence to himself."

ON GLOOM AND APPREHENSION

If it be impossible for a man to have what he desires, he must desire what he has. Let him not prefer continual gloom. We ought to strive to cure our souls of this evil (disease), in the same way as we must suffer hardships in trying to cure our bodies and to rid them of diseases by means of burning and cutting (fire and iron), and so forth. Rather must we gradually accustom ourselves to improve our souls through strength of purpose, and to endure a little difficulty in order that, as a result of this, we may pursue a praiseworthy course. We know, moreover, that if we represent to ourselves that no misfortune will befall us, it is as though we desired not to exist at all. Because misfortunes are a necessary condition of the passing of worldly things. If this were not, there could be no becoming. Therefore, to wish that no accident should come to pass is like wishing not to exist; but existence is (a part) of nature, and annihilation likewise is (a part) of nature. Then if we desire that this be not (a part) of nature, we desire the impossible; he who desires the impossible will have his wish denied, and he whose wish is denied is miserable.

We ought to be ashamed to give the preference to this quality–namely, grief–and we should yearn to rise unto a state of beatitude. Let him who would not mourn represent to his soul the things that lead to mourning, as though they already were; thus, for example, let man say, "A certain possession of mine will be destroyed and I will mourn for it," accounting it as already destroyed, or (considering) as already lost that which he loves.

Socrates was asked, "Why do we never perceive in thee any sign of apprehensiveness?" And he answered, "Because I have never possessed anything over the loss of which I would grieve."

Wherefore let the intelligent man consider that there is nothing in this world of all that grows, save it be insignificant at the outset, and afterwards develops, except grief, which is greatest on the day it comes into being, and the longer it continues the less it becomes, until it entirely disappears. The firm and resolute man is he who braces himself with all his might in the hour of his affliction.

Alexander, in order to console his mother about himself (in the event of his death), wrote to her as follows: "My mother, order a great and fortified city to be built when the news of Alexander's death reaches you. Prepare therein for eating and drinking, and gather together in it, on an appointed day, men from all lands to eat and drink. When that has been done and all the men are ready to eat and drink what the queen has prepared, let it be proclaimed at that moment that no man should enter her abode whom misfortune has befallen."

And thus she did upon the death of Alexander. But when she ordered that no one whom misfortune had befallen should enter her house, she noticed (that) no one (came). Then she felt sure that he had only wished to comfort her about himself.

ON WRATH

Let us begin by describing the useful side of this quality, although the latter is inseparable from its baneful aspect. There is no quality so reprehensible, but that it at times serves a use, even as no quality is so praiseworthy, but that it frequently becomes detrimental. Thus, thou knowest that silence is a commendable trait, but it becomes detestable when resorted to while listening to absurdities. Wrath is a reprehensible quality, but when employed to correct or to reprove, or because of indignation at the performance of transgressions, it becomes laudable. Therefore, the thoroughly wise and ethically trained man must abandon both extremes and set about the right mean.

ON GOOD WILL

This is one of the praiseworthy qualities, since it is rarely to be met with, except in the case of a noble-minded person, who accepts things just as they come to him and looks not for better ones. . . .

From this quality there branch out forbearance and forgiveness, which are of the attributes of the Creator, exalted is He and blest, and of the wise and noble man. The poet spake, "If I were not to pardon a brother's fault, and if I were to say that I would exact vengeance from him, where then would be the superiority? And if I were to cut myself from my brethren because of their sins, I would be alone, and have none with whom to associate."

ON ENVY

This quality is an offshoot of wrath. Most rational beings are not exempt from it: but it is in them all, for we see men seeking to imitate the actions of their companions. For instance, when one (man) sees that his friend has acquired some worldly gain, mineral, animal, or vegetable, or other possessions, he likewise endeavors to acquire similar things, although he be able to dispense with them or compensate himself with other things in their stead. Let him not protract his endeavor, nor set his heart upon attaining such possessions.

ON BEING ALERT

This is a commendable quality, and man ought to make use of it in whatsoever work of art or science he be engrossed. Was it not said of him (Proverbs 12:27), "The substance of a wide-awake man is precious."

The surest reason for the success of a man is (to be found in) the alertness with which he conducts his affairs, and the greatest sign of misfortune is his slothfulness with regard to them. The poet has said: "The pure and noble souls are wakeful, watchful, and sound of judgment, while the stupid and heavy souls are drowsy, mean, and low."

However, that intense wide-awakedness which leads to hastiness is culpable. Let the intelligent man beware of using it, for it is the very worst of evils. He who is hasty, rushes to destruction, and the man of hastiness is not secure from disappointment.

ON GENEROSITY

This quality, when it is employed with moderation and does not lapse into prodigality, is commendable. Man must prefer this quality to its antithesis–that is, the quality of niggardliness–since the great men who are renowned by reason of their excellence are convinced that niggardliness is not a praiseworthy quality. . . .

The unseemly side of generosity appears when a man wastes his substance needlessly and mismanages it–for instance, when he spends it in devotion to pleasures and in gratifying his lust. This is squandering and is not characteristic of the wise. A gift in the right place is a treasure put aside. It perisheth not in the course of time, but abideth with the ages. . . .

Man ought to know that if he be in a prosperous condition, then his generosity will not impair his prosperity, and if he be in a straitened condition, his adversity will not continue on that account. It is peculiar to this noble quality, that he who employs it never feels the want of anything; on the contrary, his abundance is much increased. . . .

Consider well when to yield and when to deny, when to grant and when to promise. For a gift after denying is better than denying after (promising) a gift and favor. Setting out to do after consideration is better than to abandon after setting out. Know that thou shouldst be more prompt to do what thou hast not promised than to promise what thou wilt not do. Therefore, beware of hastily promising what thou fearest thou mayest be unable to perform. Adorn thy promise with truth and thy deed with justice.

ON NIGGARDLINESS

Know thou that this is a reprehensible quality. Among the host of reprehensible qualities, there is none more abominable than this. For thou seest that he who is lavishly bountiful of his substance, although blameworthy, is satisfied with the pleasure he derives and men's goodly praise which is his. However, niggardliness is accompanied by evil repute without even the attainment of pleasure; and to be of evil repute is not one of the qualities desired by the excellent. The noble-minded man ought to shrink from this quality and not employ it on any occasion. . . .

The wise man ought not be niggardly in dealing out his knowledge, for knowledge is not lessened by imparting it (to others), as little as the brightness of the fire dies away when a light is kindled therefrom. The best rule with regard to the employment of this quality is to accustom one's self to beneficence toward kinsmen, until one gradually habituate one's self to benevolence toward strangers, and thus, train one's self to choose generosity.

ON COURAGE

The man who is large-hearted, full-veined, and long-armed will generally be the man of valor, especially if, combined with those physical advantages, he be master of the art of war. This quality is praiseworthy (in man), when it is manifested in his strength, and in accordance with his determination to be saved from what might befall him. However, when he departs from a moderate course and unites valor with the quality of folly, and it becomes the cause of a man's throwing himself into dangerous places, then it is reprehensible. . . .

This quality of valor never fails to be conspicuous in the souls of mighty men and courageous heroes. With reference to valor and patience in facing danger, the poet spake: "There came a day in the heat of which some people warmed themselves, but though there was no fire, they acted as if in the fire's midst. . . ."

Among the things which have been said in order to encourage the use of valor is: "Crave death, and life will be granted thee." The Arabs were accustomed to call the man of valor "safe." Among the things which have been said on the emboldening of the spirit in combat is the word of the poet: "I went to the rear to preserve my life (in battle), but I found that I could not preserve my life unless I went forward."

Thus the noble man must make use of this quality in such a way as not to overstep the middle path lest he be called foolhardy. The philosopher spake, "The extreme limit of valor is strength and endurance with respect to what thou abhorrest." Valor cannot go hand-in-hand with vanity (untruth), nor firmness with absurdity, nor patience with weariness, for these are of the qualities of asses and swine. Valor consists in persevering in the right and overcoming thy desires, until thou feel that to die in the best way thou hast found is more desirable than to live in the evil way, which the power of understanding may have revealed to thee.

ON COWARDICE

This quality is generally found in spirits that are abject and downcast, poor and wretched. It is a reprehensible quality. Let the wise man be on his guard against it, let him make no use of it, exert himself to keep away and abstain from it, since he derives no benefit from it; on the contrary, he reaps ill-repute, a vile record, and a diminution of praise. . . .

The coward is known to say: "I will not travel, for fear of

highwaymen and wild beasts. I will not engage in business, lest I meet with losses. I will not fast, lest I become ill. I will give no alms, lest I become poor," and similar words that put an end to all activity, until there remains nothing for him to do, but living on without moving from his place. . . .

However, in a case where escape is impossible, it is permissible for the quality of cowardice to come into play–as in the case of him, concerning whom it is said: "The king dispatched him to a dangerous place. He refused to go. The king reviled him, whereupon he said, 'It is better that thou revile me when living than bless me when dead.' "

THE ROYAL CROWN

Among his own people Ibn Gabirol came to be most revered as a writer of verse, one who–to quote a thirteenth-century admirer–"spread such a fragrance of song as was ne'er produced by any poet either before or after him." In keeping with poetic tradition, he experienced much suffering in his youth, being poor, without parents, and often friendless. As a result, his verses are prevailingly doleful, and dwell constantly on man's need of God's help. The following is taken from the most noted of his compositions, a lengthy philosophical tract in rhyme which he called Keter Malkhut, the Royal Crown.[9]

Man entereth the world,
And knoweth not why;
He rejoiceth
And knoweth not wherefore;
He liveth,
And knoweth not for how long.
In his childhood he walketh in his own stubbornness,
And when the spirit of lust beginneth in its season
To stir him up to gather power and wealth,
Then he journeyeth from his place

[9] *Gabirol's Selected Poems,* translated by Israel Zangwill (Philadelphia, Jewish Publication Society, 1923).

To ride in ships
And to tread in the deserts,
And to carry his life to dens of lions,
Adventuring in among wild beasts;
And when he imagineth that great is his glory
And that mighty is the spoil of his hand,
Quietly stealeth the spoiler upon him,
And his eyes are opened and there is naught.
At every moment he is destined to troubles
That pass and return,
At every hour evils,
At every moment chances,
On every day terrors.
If for an instant he stand in security,
Suddenly disaster will come upon him,
Either war shall come and the sword will smite him,
Or the bow of brass transpierce him;
Or the sorrows will overpower him,
Or the presumptuous billows flow over him,
Or sickness and steadfast evils shall find him,
Till he become a burden on his own soul,
And shall find the gall of serpents in his honey.

When his pain increaseth
His glory decreaseth,
And youth make mock of him,
And infants rule him,
And he becometh a burden to the issue of his loins,
And all who know him become estranged from him.
When his hour hath come, he passeth
From the courts of his house to the court of Death,
And from the shadow of his chambers to the shadow of Death.
He shall strip off his broidery and his scarlet
And shall put on corruption and the worm,

And lie down in the dust
And return to the foundation from which he came.

O man, whom these things befall,
When shall he find a time for repentance
To scour away the rust of his perversion?
For the day is short and the work manifold,
And the taskmasters irate,
Hurrying and scurrying,
And Time laughs at him,
And the Master of the House presses.

Therefore, I beseech Thee, O my God,
Remember the distresses that come upon man,
And if I have done evil
Do Thou me good at my latter end,
Nor requite measure for measure
To man whose sins are measureless,
And whose death is a joyless departure.

CHAPTER 34

THE ETHICS OF BAHYA

Bahya ben Yoseph ibn Pakuda, who flourished in Saragossa, Spain, during the first half of the eleventh century, ranks as one of the foremost of all Jewish philosophers. Nothing is known of his career save that he served as dayan (judge) of the local rabbinical court, and published a book towards the close of his life which swiftly became a classic. It was written in Arabic under the title, "Guide to the Duties of the Heart" (in Hebrew, Hovot Ha Levavot), and gave the first systematic presentation of Jewish ethics. Bahya's aim was to correct the tragic overemphasis on ritualism which had naturally resulted from Israel's absorption in the Talmudic writings. His people had become so wrapped up in outward observances that they had almost forgotten the immeasurably greater importance of inward faith. So he set himself the task of explaining the nature of that faith, and of describing the ethical impulses which it engendered.

Bahya's work was so Jewish in flavor that it became a treasury of devotion for his people throughout the Middle Ages. Passages from it are still regularly recited by pious Jews as part of the liturgy for the Penitential Days.

The book is divided into ten sections, or "gates," corresponding to what Bahya considered the ten fundamental elements of religious faith and practice. Only the first three passages are presented here.[1]

---

[1] *Duties of the Heart,* by Bahya ben Joseph ibn Paquda, translated from the Hebrew version by Rev. Moses Hyamson, B.A., LL.D. (New York, Bloch Publishing, 1941).

THE DIVISIONS OF WISDOM

The noblest of the gifts which God bestowed on His human creatures . . . is Wisdom. This constitutes the life of their spirit, the lamp of their intellect. It secures them the favors of God, and saves them from His wrath both here and hereafter. . . .

Wisdom falls into three divisions. The first division is the science of created things . . . and deals with the essential and accidental properties of material bodies. The second division consists of the ancillary sciences: for instance, arithmetic, geometry, astronomy and music. The third department is the science of theology, and treats of the knowledge of God, blessed be He, and of the knowledge of His law, and so forth.

All the sciences are gates which the Creator has opened to rational beings, through which they may attain to a comprehension of religion and of the world; but while some sciences are more adapted to the needs of religion, others are more requisite for secular interests. The sciences specially required in secular affairs form the lowest division; whereas the one essential to religion is the highest science, Theology. . . .

INWARD AND OUTWARD RELIGION

As the science of religion deals with two parts, external and inward religion, I studied the books of the ancient writers who flourished after the Talmud and who composed many works dealing with the precepts, in the expectation of learning from them the science of inward religion. . . .

I found however that this department of knowledge, the science of the Duties of the Heart, had been entirely neglected. No work had been composed which set forth its principles and divisions systematically. I was so greatly surprised that I said to myself, "Possibly this class of duties is not positively enjoined by the Torah. . . . Possibly it belongs to the class of supererogatory practices that are optional, for which we will not be called to account nor be punished if we disregard them. Therefore, our predecessors omitted to treat of it in a special work." A careful examination, however, by the light of Reason, Scripture, and Tradition, of the question whether the Duties of the Heart are obligatory or not, convinced me that they indeed form the foundation of all the precepts, and that if there is any shortcoming in their observance, no external duties whatever can be properly fulfilled.

First, the arguments from Reason. Man, we know, consists of body and of soul; both of them are marks of the Creator's goodness to us. One of these elements of our being is seen; the other, unseen. We are accordingly bound to render the Creator visible and invisible service. The outward service is the observance of practical precepts; for example, praying, fasting, almsgiving; learning the Torah and teaching it; erecting a booth for the Feast of Tabernacles and waving palm branches on the festival; wearing fringes, attaching the mezuzah to the doorposts; erecting a parapet on the roof; fulfillment of other precepts which call for the exercise of the physical organs. Inward service, on the other hand, consists of the fulfilment of the duties of the heart; for example, that we should acknowledge the Unity of God in our hearts; believe in Him and in His Laws and accept His service; revere Him, be humble and abashed before Him; love Him, trust in Him, and surrender our very lives to Him; abstain from what He hates, dedicate our activities to His name; meditate on the benefits He bestows and similar duties that are fulfilled in thought and by the exercise of inward faculties, but do not call for activity of the bodily organs.

THE PRIMACY OF INWARD RELIGION

I am certain that even the practical duties cannot be efficiently performed without willingness of the heart and desire of the soul to do them. If it should enter our mind that we are under no obligation to choose and desire the service of God, our bodily organs would be released from the obligation to fulfill the practical duties, since no work is complete without the assent of the soul. As it is clear that the Creator has imposed upon us external duties, it would be unreasonable to suppose that our mind and heart, the choicest elements of our being, should have been exempted from serving Him to the extent of their power, since their cooperation is requisite for the complete service of God. Hence, it is clear that we are under the obligation of inward as well as external duties; so that our service shall be perfect and complete, and shall engage mind as well as body.

When I became convinced of the necessity of inward duties on rational grounds, I said to myself, "Possibly these duties are so plain and so universally known, and all men are so attached to them, that a treatise on the subject was unnecessary." When, however, I studied human habits throughout the ages, as recorded in literature, I discovered that men were far from the knowledge or practice of these duties, with the exception of some pious and zealous individuals, according to what is reported of them; but as for the rest, how greatly did they stand in need of exhortation and instruction! . . .

After I had become convinced of the obligatory character of the Duties of the Heart and that, on grounds already mentioned, we are bound to observe them; after I had noticed that these duties had been neglected and that no book had been composed specially treating of them; and after I had further realized in what condition our contemporaries were as a result of their inability to comprehend, much less fulfill, these duties and occupy themselves with them; then I was moved by the grace of God to inquire into the science of inward duties.

THE REASON FOR THIS BOOK

I began to train myself in this science, and imposed on myself the task of studying and practicing those duties. The discovery of one duty revealed another related to it, which in turn suggested a third, until the subject matter assumed large dimensions and became difficult to retain in the memory. I feared that I might forget what I had already thought out, and that what had assumed solid shape in my mind might dissolve, especially because among our contemporaries there are so few fellow-workers in this line of research. I resolved, therefore, to write down my reflections and put them together in a work that would comprehend the general principles of the subject and include its subdivisions as well as many of the detailed applications; and so I would always be able to exhort myself to learn these duties and oblige myself to fulfill them. . . .

When I thought of proceeding to carry out my resolution in regard to this book, I saw that a man like myself was not fit to compose such a work. I felt that I was unequal to the adequate analysis of its various parts, the subject being too difficult, my knowledge too slight, my intellectual capacities too weak to grasp the topics. Moreover, I do not possess an elegant style in Arabic, in which the book would have to be written, as it is the language best understood by the majority of our contemporaries.[2] I feared that I would be laboring at a task which would expose my deficiencies, and that I would, thus, be exceeding the just bounds of discretion. I therefore determined to change my mind and give up my plan.

No sooner, however, had I thus resolved to abandon the project than I began to suspect myself of choosing repose, and of preferring to dwell in the abode of indolence, quietness, and security. . . . Many profitable undertakings, I also reflected, have failed through diffidence; numerous losses have resulted from fear. I recalled the maxim: "It is the part of prudence not to be too hesitant." If every one engaging in a good work, or wishing to teach the right and proper way, were to hold his

[2] Arabic had become the vernacular of the Jews throughout the Islamic lands.

peace and wait until his purpose had been completely fulfilled, not a word would be uttered by any one after the prophets whom God had chosen as His messengers and strengthened with His Divine aid. If every one desirous of acquiring all good qualities, and unable to do so, were, therefore, to neglect those that he could make his own, all the children of men would be lacking in virtues and deficient in graces of character. They would be forever running after deceptive hopes. The paths of goodness would be desolate and the abodes of kindness would be destroyed.

I further realized that while men have a strong desire to attain evil ends, they are negligent in the pursuit of that which is noble. They are tardy in seeking the good but dally in the paths of frivolity and pleasure. If a vision of lust appears to them and beckons to them, they invent falsehoods so that they may turn to it. They bolster its arguments to make its obliquities upright, its weaknesses strong, its loosenesses firm and compact. Even though the lamp of truth invitingly shines before them, they frame idle pretexts for refraining from turning to it. They argue against it, declare its courses misleading, and contradict its assertions, so as to make it appear inconsistent and, thus, have an excuse for keeping away from it. Thus, every man's enemy is beneath his own ribs. . . .

I, therefore, determined to force myself to undertake the laborious task of composing this treatise, and resolved to expound its topics in the language at my command, and in idioms that readily occurred to me, provided they conveyed the meaning. So, too, of the detailed particular duties of the heart, I shall only mention those that suggest themselves to me, and shall not trouble to adduce all of them, so as not to make the book too long.

THE SCOPE OF THE BOOK

My aim is to bring to light the root principles of our religion that are deeply fixed in the unsophisticated intellect—those pivotal principles of our Torah which are latent in our souls. Once we rouse our minds to meditate on them, their truth becomes clear to us inwardly and their bright rays will even be manifest in us externally. The following is an apt analogy. An astrologer went to a friend's courtyard and divined that it contained a hidden treasure. The man searched for it and found a mass of silver that had turned black and had lost its luster because of the tarnish with which it had become covered. He took some of the metal, scoured it with salt and vinegar, washed and polished it, until it had recovered its original luster, beauty and brightness. He then gave orders that the rest of the treasure should be similarly treated. I wish to do the same with the hidden treasures of the heart: namely, to bring them to light and exhibit their shining excellence so that any one who desires to draw near to God and cling to Him may do likewise.

When, my brother, you have read this book and apprehended its contents, take it as a reminder of your duties and of your shortcomings. Pass on yourself a true judgment. Read my book repeatedly; develop its thoughts. Bring it close to your mind and heart. If you see any error in it, correct the error; any omission, supply it. In studying the work, let your aim be the practical one of following its instruction and guidance, but do not let your object be to win a reputation or gain glory through its wisdom.

Though the benefits God bestows upon His creatures are all embracing, as Scripture saith (Psalm 145:9), "The Lord is good to all," the majority of mankind are too blind to recognize these benefits or comprehend their high excellence.

WHY MEN ARE BLIND

There are three reasons for this lack of comprehension.

(1) Men are too absorbed in secular affairs and pleasures, and they long too much for something they cannot get from this

world . . . because the sole hope on which their hearts are fixed is the satisfaction of their desires and fulfillment of their wishes. Whatever stage of success they attain, they seek to proceed higher and further. The numerous benefits enjoyed by them are, in their view, but few. The great gifts already conferred on them, they deem small, so that any advantage gained by another person, they look upon as having been taken from them. Happenings that come to them from God they regard as calamities that have befallen them. They do not reflect upon the works of the Lord that are for their benefit, as Scripture saith (Psalm 10:4), "The wicked, in his high arrogance, does not enquire. God is not in any of his thoughts."

(2) The second reason is that human beings when they come into this world are like foolish beasts and an ass's colt, as the wise man saith (Job 11:12), "Like a wild ass's colt is man when born." They grow up surrounded with a superabundance of divine favors which they experience continuously, and to which they become so used that they come to regard these as essential parts of their being, not to be removed or separated from themselves during the whole of their lives. . . .

In this respect they resemble an infant found in the desert by a kindhearted individual. The benevolent man took pity on the child, carried it to his home, brought it up, fed it, clothed it, and provided it generously with all that was good for it until it was old enough to understand and comprehend the many benefits it had received. The same philanthropist heard of a man who had fallen into the hands of his enemy and had for a long time been treated with extreme cruelty, starved, and kept naked. The benevolent man's compassion was aroused. He appeased the enemy so that the latter freed the prisoner and forgave him his debt. After his release, the philanthropist took the man home and showed him kindness, but to a smaller extent than that shown to the foundling. Yet the man was more appreciative of, and grateful for, what had been done for him than the child who had been surrounded with benefits from infancy. The reason was that the prisoner passed from wretchedness and destitution to a state of happiness and tranquillity at a time when his mental faculties were mature. Hence, he fully appreciated the goodness and kindness of his benefactor; but the foundling did not realize the value of the benevolence he had experienced, even after his powers of perception and understanding had become fully developed because he had been used to favors from earliest childhood. Still, no individual with intelligence will doubt that the kindness to the child was wider in scope and more clearly recognizable, and that consequently there was in its case a greater obligation of constant gratitude to the benefactor.

A similar thought is indicated in the text (Hosea 11:3), "And I dandled Ephraim, taking him in my arms, and he knew not that I healed him."

(3) The third reason is that human beings are subject in this world to various mishaps and damage in person and property, and do not understand that these misfortunes have beneficial results, not realizing the value of trial and discipline, as Scripture saith (Psalm 94:12), "Happy is the man whom Thou, O Lord, chastenest and teachest out of Thy Law." They forget that they themselves and all they have are benefits which the Creator in His generosity and lovingkindness has bestowed on them, and that His decrees are executed in justice and are in accordance with His wisdom. They are resentful when His judgment is visited upon them; but they do not praise him when His mercy and lovingkindness are manifested to them. Their foolishness leads them to deny the benefits and the Benefactor. Their folly may even induce many of them to indulge in sophistical speculations concerning God's work and its various products which He created for their improvement.

In this regard, how like are they to blind people who were admitted into an institution specially built for them and furnished with everything requisite for their comfort. Every single thing was in its right place and arranged for their advantage in the way that might best serve the specific purpose of improving their condition. Useful medicaments had also been provided and a skilled physician appointed to heal them by the application of these remedies so that their sight might be benefited. They, however, did not trouble about their treatment and paid no heed to the directions of the physicians who sought to cure them. They wandered about aimlessly in the institution, miserable because of their blindness. Often as they were walking, they would stumble over articles that had been placed there for their benefit, and fall on their faces. Some were bruised, others suffered broken limbs. Their pains and sufferings increased and multiplied. Then they burst forth in complaints against the builder and proprietor of the home, condemned his work, charged him with falling short in the fulfillment of his duty and condemned him as a bad manager. They persuaded themselves that his aim and purpose had not been to do them good and show them kindness, but to cause them pain and injury. This attitude of mind induced them at last to deny his goodness and kindliness, even as the wise man saith (Ecclesiastes 10:3), "Yea, also when a fool walketh by the way, his understanding faileth him and he declareth to everyone that he is a fool."

SEVEN EVIDENCES OF DIVINE WISDOM

The indisputable evidences of divine wisdom in the universe can be classified under seven heads. The first is to be seen in the order of the cosmos itself. The earth, we observe, is at the center; close to it and above it is water; close to the water is the atmosphere; above all is fire in a just and unchanging balance and measure. Each of these elements maintains the proper position appointed for it. The ocean bed, with the waters imprisoned therein, stays in its place and does not pass beyond its boundaries, notwithstanding the roaring of the waves and the raging of the winds, as it is written (Job 38:9-11), "And I prescribed for it my decree, and set bars and doors; and said: 'Thus far shalt thou come, but no further, and here shall thy proud waves be stayed.' "

The second evidence of wisdom is apparent in the human species – a universe on a small scale that completes the ordered series of creation, and constitutes its crowning beauty, glory, and perfection. David, peace be to him, referred to man when he exclaimed: "O Eternal, our Lord, how glorious is Thy name in all the earth."

The third evidence of wisdom is apparent in the formation of the individual human being – his physical structure, the faculties of his mind and the light of reason with which the Creator has distinguished him and, thus, given him superiority over other living creatures that are irrational. Man resembles the large universe, being like it fundamentally and in its original elements. . . .

The fourth evidence is seen in other species of living creatures, from the least to the greatest – those that fly or swim or creep or move on four feet, with their various qualities, pleasures and uses. . . .

The fifth is displayed in plants and other natural products [e.g., minerals] that have been provided for the improvement of the human race, because of their usefulness to man in various ways, according to their natures, constitutions and virtues. . . .

The sixth is discernible in the sciences, arts, and crafts which the Creator, blessed be He, provided for man, to contribute to his improvement, to enable him to obtain a livelihood and gain other benefits of a general and particular character. This mark of divine wisdom is referred to in the texts (Job 38:36), "Who hath put wisdom in the inward parts? Or who hath given understanding to the mind?" and again (Proverbs 2:6), "For the Lord giveth wisdom; out of His mouth cometh knowledge and discernment."

The seventh evidence is exhibited in the appointment of the Torah and its statutes, to teach us how to serve the Creator and secure for one who consistently lives according to their dictates, immediate happiness here, and recompense in the life to come hereafter. . . . To this should be added the customs by which the government of other nations is regulated together with their useful features. For those nations, these customs take the place of the Torah, though only in secular matters. . . .

Some are of the opinion that when the wise man said (Proverbs 9:1), "Wisdom hath built her house; she hath hewn out her seven pillars," he had in mind the seven evidences which we have just mentioned.

PHILOSOPHY IS MAN'S KNOWLEDGE OF HIMSELF

It is our first duty to study the beginning of a human being, his birth, the formation of the parts of his physical frame, the joining together of his limbs, the use of each limb and the necessity which caused his being made in his present form. Next, we should study man's advantages, his various temperaments, the faculties of his soul, the light of his intellect, his qualities – those that are essential and those that are accidental; his desires, and the ultimate purpose of his being. When we have arrived at an understanding of the matters noted in regard to man, much of the mystery of this universe will become clear to us, since the one resembles the other. Thus, some sages declared that philosophy is man's knowledge of himself; that is, knowledge of what has been mentioned in regard to the human being, so that through the evidence of divine wisdom displayed in himself, he will become cognizant of the Creator; as Job said (Job 19:26), "From my flesh, I see God."

MARKS OF PROVIDENCE IN THE INFANT

At the beginning of a human being's existence, the Creator appointed the mother's body to serve as a couch for the fetus so that it might abide in a safe place, a strongly guarded fortress, as it were, where no hand can touch it, where it cannot be affected by heat or cold, but is shielded and sheltered and where its food is ready for it. Here it continues to grow and develop, even becomes capable of moving and turning, and receives its nourishment without any effort or exertion. This nourishment is provided for it in a place where no one else can in any way reach it, and is increased as the fetus develops until a definite period. Then it emerges without any contrivance or help on its part, but solely by the power of the wise, merciful, and gracious One who shows compassion to His creatures. . . .

When the infant has emerged into the world–all its senses, except those of touch and taste, being weak–the Creator provides for it food from its mother's breast. The blood which had been its nourishment before it was born is now converted into milk in the mother's breast, pleasant and sweet, flowing like a gushing spring whenever needed. The milk is not so abundant that it might become burdensome to the mother and flow without suction, nor so scanty as to tire the child when taking the breast. Divine grace is also manifested in His having made the orifice of the nipple like the eye of a needle, not so wide that the milk would run without suction, in which case the child might be choked while being suckled, nor so narrow that the infant would have to exert itself in drawing its nourishment.

Later on the infant's physical faculties grow stronger, so that it is able to distinguish sights and sounds. God inspires the parents' hearts with kindness, love and compassion for their offspring, so that rearing it is not a burden to them. They are more sensitive to its needs in regard to food and drink than to their own requirements. All the labor and trouble involved in bringing it up, bathing and dressing it, gently leading it, and warding off everything harmful, even against its will, is of little account in their sight.

MARKS OF PROVIDENCE IN THE GROWING CHILD

The offspring passes from infancy to childhood. His parents do not tire of him nor become angry at his multitudinous wants and slight recognition of the burden which they bear in caring and providing for him. On the contrary, the solicitude they feel on his behalf increases until he reaches adolescence, when he has already learned to speak correctly and properly, and his physical senses and mental faculties have become strong enough to acquire wisdom and knowledge. Then he apprehends some physical phenomena with his senses, and some intellectual ideas with his mental faculties, as the wise King Solomon said (Proverbs 2:6), "For the Lord giveth wisdom; out of His mouth cometh knowledge and discernment."

It is of great benefit to a human being that during his childhood he is not a thinker and is unable to distinguish good from evil. For had he, while growing up, been endowed with a ripe intellect and mature powers of perception and had he been able to discern the superiority of adults, in their ability to manage for themselves, move freely and keep clean, and realized the contrast presented by his condition in all these respects, he would have died of grief and sorrow. Remarkable too it is that crying, as learned physicians state, is beneficial to an infant. For in the brains of infants there is a humor, which, if it remained there undischarged, would produce evil results. Weeping dissolves this humor and drains it away from the brain, and, thus, the infants are saved from its injurious effects. The Creator's abounding grace to man is also manifested in that the new teeth come out singly, one after another, and so the gradual falling out of the old teeth during the process of replacement does not interfere with mastication.

Later on he is subjected to diseases and meets with painful accidents, and so he gains knowledge of the world, the real nature of which is no longer hidden from him. Thus, he is put on his guard against artlessly trusting the world or permitting his lusts to have dominion over him, in which case he would become like the brutes that neither know nor understand; as it is written (Psalm 32:9), "Be ye not as the horse or as the mule which have no understanding."

THE MIRACLE OF THE BODY

One should then consider and reflect upon the uses of the limbs and organs and the various ways in which each of them functions for man's benefit—the hands serving for taking and giving; the feet for walking; the eyes for seeing; the ears for hearing; the nostrils for smelling; the tongue for speaking; the mouth for eating, the teeth for masticating; the stomach for digestion; the liver for purifying the food; the tubes for removing superfluities; the bowels for retention. The heart is the reservoir of natural heat and the wellspring of life. The brain is the seat of the spiritual faculties, the wellspring of sensation, and the root from which the nerves begin. The womb serves to preserve and develop the seed; and so it is with the rest of the bodily organs. They all have their specific functions, of which more are unknown than are known to us.

So, too, one who reflects on these matters will take notice of the natural processes by which the nourishment received by the body is apportioned to every one of its parts. . . . Thus, the food passes into the stomach through a tube that is absolutely straight without bend or twist. This tube is called the esophagus. The stomach grinds the food more thoroughly than the teeth had already done. Then the nutriment is carried into the liver through fine intermediate veins which connect these two organs, and serve as a strainer for the food, permitting nothing coarse to pass through to the liver. The liver converts the nutriment it receives into blood which it distributes all over the body, sending the vital fluid to all parts of the corporeal frame through conduits formed for this purpose, and resembling water pipes. The waste substances that are left are eliminated through canals specifically adapted to that purpose. What belongs to the green gall goes to the gall bladder. What belongs to the black gall goes to the milt (spleen); other humors and juices are sent to the lungs. The refuse of the blood passes into the bladder. Reflect, O my brother, on the wisdom of the Creator manifested in the formation of your body; how He set those organs in their right places, to receive the waste substances, so that they should not spread in the body, and cause it to become sick.

Then consider the formation of the vocal organs, and instruments of speech. The trachea, hollow for the production of sound; the lips, and teeth serving for the clear enunciation of consonants and vowels. These organs have other uses also. The air enters the lungs through the trachea; the tongue is the organ which enables one to taste savory victuals, and aids also in the deglutition of solid and liquid nourishment. The teeth serve to masticate solid food. The lips enable one to retain liquids in the mouth, and swallow the quantity desired, and only when one wishes to do so. In regard to the other organs, the uses of some are known to us; of others, unknown. . . .

THE MIRACLE OF THE MIND

Next consider the faculties of the soul and their place among the advantages bestowed on man – the faculties of thought and recollection, the power of forgetting, the feeling of shame, the faculties of understanding and speech. What would man's condition be if one of these were lacking? Take memory, for instance. How much loss a person would incur in all his affairs if he were unable to remember what he owned and what he owed; what he had taken and what he had given; what he had seen or heard; what he had said and what had been said to him; if he could not recall the one who had conferred a benefit upon him and the one who had wrought him harm; the one who had rendered him a service, or inflicted upon him an injury. Such a person would not recognize a road even if he had frequently traversed it, nor remember a science though he had studied it all his lifetime. Experience would be of no profit to him. He would not weigh any matter by what had happened in the past. Nor could he calculate future events by what was taking place in the present. Such a person would seem almost entirely divested of the qualities that make up a human being. Forgetting also has uses. For were it not for the ability to forget, a man would never be free from melancholy. No joyous occasion would dispel his sadness. The events that should delight him would afford him no pleasure when he recalled the troubles of life. Even from the realization of his hopes he could not hope to derive rest and peace of mind. He would never refrain from grieving. Thus, you see how memory and forgetfulness, different and contrary to each other as they are, are both endowments bestowed upon man, and each of them has its uses. Next consider the feeling of shame with which man alone has been endowed. How high is its value, how numerous are its uses and advantages! Were it not for this feeling, men would not show hospitality to strangers. They would not keep their promises, grant favors, show kindness, nor abstain from evil in any way. Many precepts of the Torah are fulfilled only out of shame. A large number of people would not honor their parents, if it were not for shame, and certainly would fail to show courtesy to others. They would not restore a lost article to its owner nor refrain from any transgression. For whoever commits any of the disgraceful acts which we have mentioned, does so only when he has cast off the vestment of shame. As Scripture saith: (Jeremiah 6:15), "Yea they are not at all ashamed, neither know they how to blush." (Zephaniah 3:5), "The unrighteous knoweth no shame."

THE BLESSINGS OF COMPREHENSION

The abounding goodness of God to us is manifested in the capacities of thought and perception with which he has uniquely endowed us and distinguished us from other living creatures. The value of these faculties in the care of our bodies and ordering of our activities is known to all, with the exception of those who have suffered a loss of these faculties as a result of cerebral injuries. . . .

A person whose understanding has failed him, loses all the excellences of a human being. Laws are no longer binding upon him; he is not amenable to reward or punishment.

Among the benefits of the understanding, it is to be noted that by its aid man obtains his knowledge of all things perceived by the senses or apprehended by the intellect. By his understanding, he discovers aspects of visible objects, undisclosed to the physical senses, as, for instance, the movement of the shadow on the sundial, or the action of a single drop of water on the flinty rock. By his understanding, man distinguishes between truth and falsehood, between excess and deficiency, between good and evil, between the laudable and despicable, between the necessary, the contingent and the impossible. By his understanding, man makes other living creatures work for his benefit and pleasure. By the use of this faculty, he recognizes the position of the stars, determines their distances and their movements in their orbits, comprehends the relations and analogies treated in the science of mathematics, the figures and modes of demonstration (syllogisms) set forth in logic, and other sciences and arts too numerous to mention. So, too, all the other faculties of man, if you study them, you will find, display the utmost perfection and are of the highest value to him, as we have shown is the case with the understanding.

THE BLESSINGS OF SPEECH

Reflect further on the benefits God has bestowed on man by the gift of speech and the orderly arrangement of words, whereby he gives expression to what is in his mind and soul and understands the conditions of others. The tongue is the heart's pen and the mind's messenger. Lacking speech, there would be no social relations between one person and another; a human being would be like the cattle. Speech makes manifest the superiority of an individual among his fellows. By means of speech, covenants are made among human beings and between God and his servants. By means of speech, a man turns away from his perversities and seeks forgiveness for his iniquities. Speech it is that demonstrates a man's worthiness or unworthiness. Man, it has been said, is heart and tongue, and this completes the definition of a human being. For a human being is defined as "a living rational mortal," and by speech, he is differentiated from the brute creatures.

Then consider the advantages derived from written characters and the art of writing. By their aid, the deeds and affairs of those who have passed away and of those who are still existing are recorded for the benefit of those who will come after them; communications reach the absent, and information is received concerning those far away and concerning relatives in another country; and it is possible that the receipt of this information may save their lives or deliver them from misfortune and mishaps. By this means, knowledge of the sciences is preserved in books; desultory thoughts are gathered together. Men write down their dealings with each other in commercial transactions, in loans, purchases, marriages, divorces.[3] The subject is too wide to be dealt with completely.

A crowning benefit bestowed on man is that he has been provided with hands and fingers, with which he can draw, write, embroider, kindle fire, and perform other acts and fine operations that are beyond the capacity of other living creatures, because these are not needed by them. I assert that there is not one of these organs the uses of which I have mentioned that does not show to one who reflects on them marks of divine wisdom in its structure, form, and combination with other organs. They furnish strong evidence and clear proof of the Creator's mercy toward us. Galen, in numerous treatises, has expounded the functions of the bodily organs. Were we to do so in the case of one of these, we would depart from the rules of conciseness. What we have adduced is sufficient to arouse anyone to whom the Creator will point out the way of his salvation.

ALL THINGS SERVE MAN

Among the benefits bestowed upon man, the following is to be noted. When you contemplate the marks of divine wisdom in created things, you will find that, besides testifying to the divinity and might of the Creator, they all without exception are in various ways useful to man and contribute to his improvement. While some of these uses are manifest, others are obscure. Take light and darkness, for instance. The benefits of light are obvious and evident, but those of darkness are hidden. For human beings are uncomfortable in the dark; their activities and movements are interrupted at its arrival; but were it not for the darkness of night, the physique of most living beings would be destroyed by their incessant toil and protracted movements. One interval of time is distinguished from another through the recurrence of night. It gives knowledge of periods which would otherwise be unknown (e.g.,

[3]The Arabic original adds the emancipation of slaves.

days and weeks) and determines the respective length or brevity of human lives.

If time were uniform (i.e., without alternation of day and night) there would be no ordinances for special seasons, such as Sabbaths, festivals or fasts; no appointments could be made for a definite date; most of the sciences related to time would be unknown. Even food would not be perfectly digested by any living creature. As man however needs light at night to do some of his work, and to nurse the sick, the Creator has provided him with a substitute in the light of fire which he can kindle at any time and extinguish whenever he pleases. Wondrous, too, it is that the hue of the sky belongs to the colors that strengthens the sight. For it inclines to black which has the special quality of gathering together and strengthening the light that enters the eyes. Had the color of the sky been white, it would have injured the eyes of living creatures and weakened them. Similarly, other marks of wisdom are exhibited by other created things. . . .

In considering secular affairs, it is proper that you should always look to the final outcome of hard experiences. You will discover the surprising fact that many untoward events turn out in the end to be to our advantage, and vice versa. A story is told of a company of travelers who lay down near a wall to rest overnight. A dog, passing by, wetted one of them. The man awoke and got up to wash off the uncleanliness. After he had gone some distance from his fellows, the wall fell down on his companions and killed them, while he alone escaped. Events frequently happen in similar or contrary fashion. . . .

A subject that you should also examine, and derive from it evidences of the divine wisdom and beneficence, is the agreement of human beings to buy and sell goods for gold and silver which, through God's mercy, they endeavor to accumulate and thus improve their positions, though their actual needs are not thereby satisfied. For when anyone is afflicted with hunger and thirst through want of food or lack of water, an abundance of gold and silver will not avail him or supply his wants; and if anyone suffers pain in any of his limbs, he will not be cured by silver and gold; for while other minerals are largely used for medicinal purposes, this is less so in the case of gold or silver.

A wondrous evidence of wisdom it also is that, while a few individuals possess large amounts of these precious metals, the majority of mankind have but little of them. If all human beings possessed them in abundance, they could not use them as a medium for obtaining what they desire. Some people have much and others have little. They are precious from one point of view and of little account from another, because intrinsically they are useless. This too is within the plan of the Creator's supreme wisdom.

CONCERNING MUTUAL AID

We assert, as a truth generally recognized, that if anyone benefits us, we are under an obligation of gratitude to him in accordance with his intent to help us. Even if he actually falls short, owing to some mishap which prevents his benefiting us, we are still bound to be grateful to him, since we are convinced that he has a benevolent disposition toward us and his intention is to be of use to us. On the other hand, should we obtain any benefit through one who had no such intention, the duties of gratitude to that person would cease and we are under no such obligation.

When we consider the benefits human beings render each other, we find that these fall into five classes: (1) a father's beneficence to his child; (2) a master's to his servant; (3) a wealthy man's beneficence to the poor for the sake of heavenly reward; (4) the beneficence rendered by human beings to each other in order to gain a good name, honor and temporal reward; and (5) the powerful man's beneficence to the weak, induced by pity for the latter and sympathy with his condition.

ALTRUISM IS ENLIGHTENED EGOISM

Let us now consider the motive in each of the classes mentioned: Is it disinterested, the sole aim being to help the beneficiary, or is it not so? First, a father's beneficence to his child: It is obvious that the father's motive in this is to further his own interest. For the child is a part of the father, whose chief hope is centered in his offspring. Do you not observe that in regard to its food, drink, clothing and in warding off all hurt from it, a father is more sensitive about his child than about himself? To secure ease for it, the burden of toil and weariness is lightly borne by him – the feelings of tenderness and pity for their offspring being naturally implanted in parents. Nevertheless, the Torah and reason impose upon children the duty of serving, honoring and revering their parents, as Scripture saith: "Ye shall, everyone, revere his father and his mother" (Leviticus 19:3); "Hear, O my son, the instruction of thy father and forsake not the law of thy mother" (Proverbs 1:8); further, "A son honoreth his father, and a servant his master" (Malachi 1:6). (And these duties are enjoined) notwithstanding that the father is impelled by a natural instinct and the benefaction comes from God, while the parent is only the agent.

The kindness of a master to his servant: It is obvious that the master's intent is to improve his property by an outlay of capital, since he needs his servant's work, and his sole motive is to further his own interest. Nevertheless, the Creator, blessed be He, imposes upon the servant the duties of service and gratitude, as it is said, "A son honoreth his father and a servant his master" (Malachi 1:6).

The rich man's beneficence to the poor man for the sake of a heavenly reward: He is like a merchant who acquires a great and enduring pleasure which he will enjoy at the end of a definite time by means of a small, perishable, and inconsiderable gift which he makes immediately. So the rich man only intends to win glory for his soul at the close of his earthly existence by the benefaction which God entrusted to him, in order to bestow it upon anyone who will be worthy of it. Yet, it is generally recognized that it is proper to thank and laud a benefactor. Even though the latter's motive was to gain spiritual glory hereafter, gratitude is, nevertheless, due to him, as Job said: "The blessing of him that was ready to perish came upon me" (Job 29:13); and futher, "If his loins have not blessed me, when he warmed himself with the fleece of my sheep" (Job 31:20).

Kindness men show each other for the sake of praise, honor and temporal rewards: This is as if one were to deposit an article in another's care or entrust him with money, because of the depositor's apprehension that he may need it later on. Although, in benefiting another person, the aim is to further his own interests, the benefactor is, nevertheless, entitled to praise and gratitude for his kindness, as the wise king said, "Many court the generous man, and everyone is a friend to him that giveth gifts" (Proverbs 19:6); and he also said, "A man's gift maketh room for him and bringeth him before great men" (Proverbs 18:16).

The kindness of one who has compassion on a poor man for whom he is sorry: The benefactor's motive is to get rid of his own distress that results from depression and grief for the one he pities. He is like one who cures a pain which has attacked him by means of the bounties that the Lord bestowed upon him. Nevertheless, he is not to be without due praise, as Job said, "Could I see any perish for want of clothing or any poor without covering? Did not his loins bless me, when he warmed himself with the fleece of my sheep?" (Job 31:19-20)

From what has here been advanced, it is clear that anyone who bestows benefits on others has first his own interest in mind – either to secure an honorable distinction in this world, or hereafter, or relieve himself of pain, or improve his material substance. Yet all these considerations do not absolve the beneficiaries of their duty of praising, thanking, respecting, and loving their benefactors and making them some return; and this, despite that the benefit was only loaned to the benefactors; that they were obliged to dispense it, as we have pointed out; and that their beneficence is not permanent, their generosity not prolonged, and their benevolence is mixed with the intent either to further their own interest or ward off injury. How much more then does a human being owe service, praise, and gratitude to Him who created the benefit and the benefactor, whose beneficence is unlimited, permanent, perpetual, without any motive of self-interest, or purpose of warding off injury, but only an expression of grace and lovingkindness emanating from Him toward all human beings.

We should, furthermore, bear in mind that a human being who renders a kindness to another in any of the modes above specified is not superior to the person whom he benefits, except in some casual detail, while in their humanity and essential characteristics they are alike and akin to one another, in substance and form, in physical conformation and figure (or mentality – Genesis 1:27) in their natures and in a larger part of what happens to them. Nevertheless the beneficiary, as we have set forth, is under an obligation of service to his benefactor; and if we thought that the beneficiary was extremely defective and imperfect in his physical conformation, figure and appearance (we would conclude that), the obligation of service on his part would be so much the greater. So also, if we should deem the benefactor the best and most perfect of all beings, while the beneficiary was the most defective of all things and the weakest of all creatures, reason would require that the service to the benefactor should be increased to an infinite degree.

CHAPTER 35

THE CONTENTIONS OF JUDAH HALEVI

Judah the Levite was born in Castile around 1085 and died en route to Jerusalem around 1140. He was the greatest Hebrew poet of the Middle Ages, producing love lyrics rivaling those of the Arab and Castilian minstrels, and liturgical hymns recalling the Book of Psalms. Serious by nature, he interested himself deeply in philosophy, but as a critic rather than a devotee. He was convinced that divine revelation was a far surer guide to truth than philosophical inquiry, and sought to prove it in a learned work written in Arabic and entitled Kitab al-Khazari. *This purported to give the arguments which finally convinced the head of the Crimean Kingdom of the Khazars that Judaism was more sensible than agnosticism, Christianity, and Mohammedanism. The work is in the form of a dialogue between the king and the rabbi and offers an excellent presentation of the case for Jewish traditionalism.*

The following excerpts are taken from some of the speeches made by the rabbi. They deal with matters of sufficiently universal interest to come within the range circumscribed for this anthology.[1]

WHO IS A PIOUS MAN?

The pious man is comparable to a prince in that he is obeyed by his senses, and by his mental as well as his physical

[1] *Judah Hallevi's Kitab Al Khazari,* translated from the Arabic by Hartwig Hirschfeld, Ph.D. (New York, E. P. Dutton, 1905).

faculties, which he governs corporeally, as it is written: "He that ruleth his spirit [is better] than he that taketh a city" (Proverbs 16:32). He is fit to rule, because were he the prince of a country he would be as just [to his people] as he is to his body and soul. He subdues his passions, keeping them in bonds, but giving them their due in order to satisfy them as regards food, drink, cleanliness, and so forth. He allows them all the freedom necessary for coping with material wants and for solving scientific problems; but not so much that he is betrayed into doing evil. He allows the senses their due according as he requires them for the use of hands, feet, and tongue, as necessity or desire arises. The same is the case with hearing, seeing, and the kindred sensations which succeed them: imagination, conception, thought, memory, and will power, which commands all these, but is, in turn, subservient to the will of intellect.

He does not allow any one of these limbs or faculties to go beyond its special task, or to encroach upon another. Having satisfied each of them (giving to the vital organs the necessary amount of rest and sleep, and to the physical ones the necessary motion and worldly occupation), he calls upon his whole being as a respected prince calls upon his disciplined army, to assist him in reaching the higher or divine degree which is to be found above the degree of the intellect. He arranges his being in the same manner as Moses arranged his people around Mount Sinai. He orders his will power to accept every command issued by him and to carry it out forthwith. He makes faculties and limbs to do his bidding without contradiction, forbids them evil inclinations of mind and fancy, forbids them to listen to them, or believe in them, until he has taken counsel with the intellect. If he permits, they can obey him; but not otherwise.

In this way his will power receives its orders from him, carrying them out accordingly. He directs the organs of thought and imagination, relieving them of all worldly ideas mentioned above, charges his imagination to produce, with the assistance of memory, the most splendid pictures possible, in order to resemble the divine things sought after. Such pictures are the scenes of Mount Sinai, Abraham and Isaac on Mount Moriah, the Tabernacle of Moses, the Temple service, the presence of God in the Temple, and the like.

He then orders his memory to retain all these and not to forget them; he warns his fancy and its sinful promptings not to confuse the truth or to trouble it by doubts; he warns his irascibility and greed not to influence or lead astray, nor to take hold of his will, nor subdue it to wrath and lust. As soon as harmony is established, his will power stimulates all his organs to obey it with alertness, pleasure, and joy. They stand without fatigue when occasion demands, they bow down when he bids them to do so, and sit at the proper moment. The eyes look as a servant looks at his master, the hands drop their play and do not meet, the feet stand straight, and all limbs are frightened and anxious to obey their master, paying no heed to pain or injury.

The tongue agrees with the thought, does not overstep its bounds, and does not speak in prayer in a mere mechanical way as the starling and the parrot; but every word is uttered thoughtfully and attentively. This moment of prayer forms the heart and fruit of his time, whilst the other hours represent the way which leads to it. He looks forward to its approach, because while it lasts he resembles the spiritual beings, and is removed from merely animal existence.

Those three times of daily prayer are the fruit of his day and night, and the Sabbath is the fruit of the week, because it has been appointed to establish the connection with the divine spirit, and to serve God in joy, not in sadness, as has been explained before. All this stands in the same relation to the soul as food to the human body. Prayer is for his soul what nourishment is for his body.

The blessing of one prayer lasts until the time of the next, just as the strength derived from the morning meal lasts until supper. The further his soul is removed from the time of prayer, the more it is darkened by coming in contact with worldly matters. The more so, as necessity brings it into the company of youths, women, or wicked people, when one hears unbecoming and soul-darkening words and songs which exercise an attraction for his soul which he is unable to master. During prayer, he purges his soul from all that passed over it and prepares it for the future.

According to this arrangement there elapses not a single week in which both his soul and body do not receive preparation. Darkening elements having increased during the week, they cannot be cleansed except by consecrating one day to service and to physical rest. The body repairs on the Sabbath the waste suffered during the six days, and prepares itself for the work to come, whilst the soul remembers its own loss through the body's companionship. He cures himself, so to speak, from a past illness, and provides himself with a remedy to ward off any future sickness. This is almost the same as Job did with his children every week, as it is written: "It may be that my sons have sinned" (Job 1:5).

He then provides himself with a monthly cure, which is "the season of atonement for all that happened during this period," that is, the duration of the month and the daily events, as it is written: "Thou knowest not what a day may bring forth" (Proverbs 27:1).

He further attends the Three Festivals and the great Fast Day, on which some of his sins are atoned for, and on which he endeavors to make up for what he may have missed on the days of those weekly and monthly cycles. His soul frees itself from the whisperings of imagination, wrath, and lust, and neither in thought nor deed gives them any attention. Although his soul is unable to atone for sinful thoughts–the result of songs, tales, and the like, heard in youth, and which cling to memory–it cleanses itself from real sins, confesses repentance for the former, and undertakes to allow them no more to escape his tongue, much less to put them into practice, as it is written: "I am purposed that my mouth shall not transgress" (Psalm 17:3). The fast of this day is such as brings one near to the angels, because it is spent in humility and contrition, standing, kneeling, praising, and singing.

All his phyiscal faculties are denied their natural requirements, being entirely abandoned to religious service, as if the animal element had disappeared. The fast of a pious man is such that eye, ear, and tongue share in it, that he regards nothing except that which brings him near to God. This also refers to his innermost faculties, such as mind and imagination. To this he adds pious works. (Part III, 2–5)

THE INDIVIDUAL AND SOCIETY

An individual who prays but for himself is like one who retires alone into his house, refusing to assist his fellow citizens in the repair of their walls. His expenditure is as great as his risk; but he who joins the majority spends little, yet remains in safety, because one replaces the defects of the other. The city is in the best possible condition, all its inhabitants enjoying its prosperity with but little expenditure, which all share alike.

In a similar manner, Plato styles that which is expended on behalf of the law, the "portion of the whole." If the individual, however, neglects this "portion of the whole" which is the basis of the welfare of the commonwealth whereof he forms a part, in the belief that he does better in spending it on himself, he sins against the commonwealth, and more against himself. For the relation of the individual is as the relation of the single limb to the body. Should the arm, in case bleeding is required, refuse its blood, the whole body, the arm included, would suffer. It is, however, the duty of the individual to bear hardships, or even death, for the sake of the welfare of the commonwealth. He must particularly be careful to contribute his "portion of the whole" without fail. Since ordinary speculation did not institute this, God prescribed it in tithes, gifts, and offerings, as a "portion of the whole" of worldly property. (Part III, 19)

CONCERNING ASTROLOGY

Whosoever strives by speculation and divining in the manner of astrologers to call down supernatural beings, or to manufacture talismans, such a man is an unbeliever. He may bring offerings and burn incense in the name of speculation and conjecture, but he is in reality ignorant of that which he should do: how much, in which way, by what means, in which place, by whom, in which manner, and many other details too numerous to mention. He is like an ignoramus who enters the surgery of a physician famous for the curative power of his medicines. The physician is not at home, but people come for medicines. The fool dispenses them out of the jars, knowing nothing of the contents, nor how much should be given to each person. Thus, he kills with the very medicine which should have cured them. Should he by chance have effected a cure with one of the drugs, the people will turn to him and say that he helped them, until they discover that he deceived them, or they seek other advice, and cling to this without noticing that the real cure was effected by the skill of the learned physician who prepared the medicines and explained the proper manner in which they were to be administered. They who are deceived by astrological and physical rules wander from law to law, from god to god. (Part I, 79)

CHAPTER 36

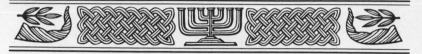

THE COUNSEL OF A NAMELESS POET

The following stanzas are taken from an anonymous Hebrew poem unearthed and translated by the late Dr. Hermann Gollancz, and published by him under the title, The Foundations of Religious Fear *(London, 1915). Its precise dating is unknown, but it clearly belongs to this period. Medieval Jewish literature is replete with such hortatory works couched in lush and orientally fragrant verse.*

Men of understanding have asked me to teach them the ways of instruction and wisdom, to give them rules whereby they might find life for their bodies while they are upon the earth, and help them toward the life of the soul on the day when they shall be called to ascend on high. . . .

Therefore, why shall I remain silent? Is it not well that I rouse the slumberers, and build up a habitation firm and exalted upon the mountain top whither my goal shall be? Indeed, as for the foundation of fear, I will establish it upon its true basis, and set it forth in chapters and stanzas.

Hearken unto me, and incline thine ears, attend with thy heart, and open thy eyes; rebel not against the words of my mouth and against my voice when I speak; accept my instruction, and I will argue and order my subject with the help of direct proverbs, clear and transparent.

Fear the Lord! This is the first and beginning of all wisdom: yea, its end and aim. In the first place, it ensures physical repose, wherein you forget sorrow and labor; and ultimately man is assured thereby of spiritual peace, a good name and reputation. . . .

Learning without religious fear is as a woman of contradictions, disobedient, and lacking in manners, one who makes her eyes look large by the use of rouge and eye-paint, and adorns herself with necklaces and earrings. What is the use of all her beauty and splendor, when her clothing is untidy, and her true nature is disclosed?

Learning without fear is as a house and a high tower which have no proper foundation. Today it is high and lofty as the heavens, as a row of hewn stone forming a citadel and fortress, but of what avail is it? Tomorrow the satyrs and children of destruction may dance upon its mounds. . . .

He who has learned in order to teach others, while his own soul loathes instruction and wisdom, will find that his . . . lessons will be but mists of empty wind, and showers of dust and earth upon the ground.

Obtain wisdom, and care not in whose hands it may be found, and how it will be regarded. Is the clay vessel reckoned according to its maker? . . . There are weeds which flourish like the lily, and through their flourishing men suffer them to rise at the very head of the garden.

Ask for information: why shouldst thou be ashamed? Surely it is more shame for thee that thou dost not know. Say not, "My own heart will teach me; I am quite sufficient in myself as regards counsel"; for then, when others will load thee, thou shalt be able to carry things which thou hast not before carried. . . .

The human frame without knowledge may be compared to a majestic vessel in the midst of the deep sea, moved and tossed about as a reed at every light or strong breeze; how can it possibly stand, if there be no one to handle the rudder, no sailor to spread the sail upward? . . .

Open the eye of thy heart, that thou mayest appreciate what thou seest with thy physical eye; for how many mortals are there who have their eyes open and look, yet see not; while many a closed eye sees all, and even that which is concealed is revealed to it! . . .

Endure things; muzzle yourself, and be silent; for if you answer a fool you will hear more things. 'Tis better that you should yourself in privacy tolerate unpleasantness than that others should hear it; your reply might only have the effect of disclosing some shady spot in your own career, which had hitherto been kept secret. . . .

Is it not better to endure that which you have neither strength nor the power to remove? What is better calculated to remove the worries and sorrows of a man than the power of endurance which comes to his aid? Herein lies the panacea for all mourning and grief, the healing of all the ills of the flesh. . . .

Drink from thine own well, and wander not about after deep waters. Rejoice in the wife of thy youth, and err not through strange and senseless beauty. Give not unto strangers thy strength, nor in folly spend thy earnings in an unknown house.

The attractive woman adorns herself in fine apparel so that she may be showy in her beauty, and she is as buoyant as a horse harnessed. You might think that in her love there is relief; but set your heart to understand her end, and you will find that the end is shame and reproach.

Are you dazzled by beautiful appearances and ostentation, by embroideries, by fine linen and purple garments? Why not consider whether she is "the well undefiled," or whether her chastity has been destroyed, and her vileness exposed? Think of the earthenware pot in the garden; it may be gilded over, indeed, but in reality there is the bad earthy odor clinging to it still.

See the strange woman who flatters with the words of her mouth; these are as drawn swords, to win over the simple and wanting in heart, who know not the right way; their feet are suddenly entangled and caught in the net and snare, and they have no rest.

The simple one goes after her as a lamb brought to the slaughter; and while sinners fall by her, the man good and righteous before God will always escape. Cleave, therefore, to thine own wife, rejoicing in her beauty and reveling in her love.

How much better it is to caress a lioness than a senseless woman! Better to kiss the lips of an adder or scorpion than foolishly to kiss her lips! You may think it pleasant to have her company to your heart's content; but understand, you'll have a full share of shame and disgrace to follow.

Love life's companion with a constant love, and then you may be assured of her love; and when you thrust her aside, thrust her aside with your left hand, but draw her near to you with your right. Otherwise your heart will flit about hither and thither; and while you are strict with her, be so with gentle patience, for then you will have peace at all hours and times.

Be glad, rejoice in the charms of the love destined for thee by heaven, so she forever will find her fullest joy, and delight with gladness in thee. Understand, too, there are times to embrace; but there is also a time when it is better to stay afar. . . .

Make thy dwelling as firm and fixed as a house of stone, and in it be thy hand open wide; then when thou sittest therein both in summer and winter, thou shalt have rest and security under the shade of thy roof; just as the bird of freedom dwelleth in her nest; and though the tempest be great, she findeth her rest.

Have several changes of raiment wherewith to clothe thyself decently, according to thy means; neither walk about half-dressed or in tatters, nor dress thyself in purple or embroideries; prepare thy supplies all in appropriate measure, and then things will be to thy honor and not to thy shame.

In whatever you do, act with a plan, and arrange your

outgoings methodically. Let your garments always be clean and the bread of your table sufficient; and neither deck yourself in the splendor of gold and fancywork, nor accustom yourself to partake of foods which are rich and sweet.

A man who is busy laboring and toiling to gather riches, and who is not satisfied the greater and richer he becomes . . . is like a thirsty man who drinks salted things. He increaseth his thirst to his own discomfort. . . .

Do you stare at fools who mount on high, and marvel when they triumph with their wealth? Does your heart mislead you, as you regard what seems their permanent power and influence, and their prosperous state? Then open your eyes, and see ahead the thick clouds gathering, and the storm passing over them, so that they are no more.

The fool, when he dresses in fine style, thinks to himself that he is sure to win favor, and presumes in his passion to enter high society, being devoid of prudence; but he is as the peacock, glorying in its beautiful feathers, while revealing its shame and reproach.

If a man be clever and his knowledge burn as a fire within him, why should you lay stress on his beautiful apparel? For when night cometh, he divests himself thereof, and you would not be ashamed to have respect for his frame. Choose of the nut the kernel, and cast away the husk and shell.

The fool carries all his greatness in the clothes on his back; and when he takes them off, he at the same time divests himself of all his glory. If then he be like an ass carrying burdens, will the name of ass be ever removed from him? However, the wise man, being precise as to his clothing, never while he lives, loses the respect due to him.

The fool will have dainty dishes and rich drinks, the choicest of fare; whatever is in season is prepared for him, one meal after another, day by day; but as for the man of knowledge, can he satisfy his hunger and dine off his knowledge, without bread and meat? . . .

Realize that regret and remorse are of no avail in the case of three things: A maiden when she has once lost her maidenhood; a stone when it has once been flung from the sling; and a dart when it has been shot from the bow. Thus also is it with the word of man; it cannot be recalled when it is once spoken.

Open the gates of thy heart before thou openest the floodgates of thy mouth, and reflect concerning matters what their effect may be, viewing the end of a thing at the beginning. For remember, that in the power of the tongue are bound up the instruments of both life and death.

Take thy friend into thy most secret counsel, but of a thousand, choose one. Then turn from thine own unto his advice, provided thy intellect be as clear and serene as his; for thou possibly wilt see only that which meets the eye, whilst he will see the matter from all sides.

Choose of thy fellows men of reliance, whose hearts will be closed by the bars thou'lt place upon them, and whose lips will be sealed by thy bolts, so that thou be not moved nor slip, by reason of any flaw in the construction of thy plans. Before thou dost store thy produce, dost thou not construct round about it a building, and cover it with plaster?

When thou openest thy heart unto a man to whom thou shouldst not reveal things, understand that thou hast thereby made him thy lord and master; thou hast become a slave after having been a freeman, having been entrapped in his net. Beware lest thou send away thy gift into the desert; thou hast no longer power over it to claim it.

See, if others entrust thee with their greatest secrets, why shouldst thou expose thy heart's defects by foolishly betraying such profound and hidden things. Better suffer the pangs of vomiting in the case of the morsel which thou hast swallowed, than help to bring to light the victim bound in the prison-house.

See, when thy friend consults thee and asks thy advice owing to his confidence in thee, give him the most loyal and upright counsel possible, as a true Israelite should; this is the kindness and consideration expected of thee. Furthermore, why shouldst thou play the hypocrite with thy tongue? Art thou able to conceal from God what is deep down in thy heart? . . .

For three things men are honored in life, but two of them have slippery edges. Men are honored either for their wealth or for their station, commanding strong positions; but does not such honor turn at the least change of fortune? What remains of it all but a stumbling block?

The third heritage of honor, however, is given to thee of God. This is the real honor; thou canst acquire it by God's service and by a lowly disposition, if you leadest it on gently; but in the day on which thy heart becometh proud, it vanisheth and departeth as the traveler at his first opportunity. . . .

Understand that he who pays daily visits will be regarded as of no account, nay, he will be considered a bore. How much better is it not to pay frequent and continuous visits! Let this be your guide and motto: "The rain which comes continuously makes people tired of it, whilst they welcome it with gratitude as soon as it is kept back."

How good it is to pay your calls (at intervals) for a few moments, for then you will become neither a bore nor a burden; but if you are sure that your company is agreeable, then have the courage to enjoy more of the honey according to the full limit. At New Moon it is customary to pronounce the benediction, because for a couple of days the moon has been hidden from view.

CHAPTER 37

THE WISDOM OF A YEMENITE

Yemen, in the extreme southwest of Arabia, was remote from the centers of Jewish life, yet even there Jewish learning had its ardent devotees. One of the most notable was Natanael ibn al-Fayyumi, Chief Rabbi of the Yemenite community, who in 1165 wrote an ethical treatise in Arabic entitled Bustan Al-Ukul, *"Garden of Wisdom." He intended it to be "a compendium for our youth," and with the eclecticism characteristic of most Jewish authors in the Arab world, he included much that was drawn from patently non-Jewish sources. His justification was the one offered by Philo almost twelve centuries earlier; namely, that all that was true in the writings of the Gentiles was originally derived from none other than the ancient Hebrew sages.*

The following passages are taken from a translation by David Levine, Ph.D., of a unique manuscript of the Bustan Al-Ukul *now in the Columbia University Library.*[1]

TWO OPINIONS OF THE WORLD

A pious man, when asked his opinion about this world, responded, "What can I say concerning a dwelling upon whose very threshold there is trouble, a dwelling which we

[1]New York, Columbia University Press, 1908.

must leave empty-handed? . . . When a man becomes rich in this world, he is ill at ease; and when he is poor, he is sad. One person works zealously for it, and it escapes him, while another sits still and it comes to him. . . .

While the pious man was thus blaming the world, another who was present said, "Do not disparage it offhand, for it is a dwelling of righteousness to him who lives righteously in it, a safe dwelling to the one who understands it, and a rich dwelling to the one who manages to get a bed in it. It is a place of divine revelation, the prayer house of his messengers, the mosque of his prophets and the marketplace of his favorites where they purchase Paradise, wherein they obtain mercy."

ON CALUMNIATORS

A shameless fellow abused a righteous man with the words, "Your mother did so and so." He replied, "If what you say is true, may God pardon her; and if what you say is false, may God pardon you."

It is also narrated that a calumniator came to a certain pious man with slander, whereupon the pious man retorted, "Slander is abominable. Were your charge true, verily we would search out what you added to it; and even if it turned out true, we would detest you; and if it proved to be false, we would punish you; but if you would have us pardon you, we shall pardon you." He replied, "Forgive me!" So he forgave him.

It is also narrated that a calumniator hastened to a certain king, whereupon the king queried, "Wouldst thou have us hear from thy rival concerning thee just as we have heard from thee concerning him?" He answered, "No, pardon me." So he pardoned him.

A certain king remarked, "Verily I esteem the sweetness of forgiveness above and beyond the sweetness of revenge."

ON INCURRING NEEDLESS DEBT

It is narrated that a pious man passed among people who sold portions of meat on trust for a certain length of time. They asked him to take a piece and offered to give him the same length of time to pay the price as they gave to other people. As he was loath to accept, they pressed him, telling him that they had put off the payment of the price twice as long as people usually do. Still he refused. He said unto them, "I have taken counsel of my soul, and it has offered to give me a respite from eating meat twice as long as the time you would postpone payment."

THE KING AND THE SAGE

It is narrated of a certain king that he passed by a pious man who failed to rise in his honor. When the servants of the king berated him, he retorted, "I will not rise in the presence of the servant of my handmaid."

The king thereupon stopped and asked, "How canst thou say that I am the servant of thy handmaid?"

The servant of God answered, "Dost thou not know that I cast aside the world which thou servest, and that whosoever abandons a thing has power over it? Truly I have forsaken it and its pleasures, whereas thou servest it and its pleasures. Hence, thou art indeed its servant."

The king, recognizing that here was a wise man, commanded his retinue to bestow upon him gold and silver. The sage, however, rejoined that if the king had something that he was unable to buy, he would not esteem it lightly. So the king said unto him, "I shall give thee delicious viands."

To which the sage responded, "Wherein is the king's means of satisfying himself superior to those of his subjects? He relieves nothing but his hunger."

Then the king added, "I will adorn thee with the most beautiful garments."

To this the sage also rejoined, "Would that thou couldst adorn the wise with wisdom, good works, abstinence from worldly things, and the fear of God in private and in public."

At this remark the king wept and rode away.

CHAPTER 38

THE TESTAMENT OF IBN TIBBON

Judah ibn Tibbon, born in Granada about 1120, occupies an important place in medieval Jewish history because of his prolific labors as a translator from Arabic into Hebrew. Like most other Jewish scholars of the period, he was a practicing physician, and this testament is addressed to his beloved–but apparently none too obedient–son who was being trained to follow the same profession.[1]

My son, listen to my precepts, neglect none of my injunctions. Set my admonition before thine eyes; thus, shalt thou prosper and prolong thy days in pleasantness.

Exert thyself whilst still young, the more so as thou even now complainest of weak memory. What then wilt thou do in old age, the time of forgetfulness? Awake, my son, from thy sleep; devote thyself to science and religion; habituate thyself to moral living, for "habit is master over all things." As the Arabian philosopher (Al-Ghazali) holds, there are two sciences, ethics and physics; strive to excel in both!

[1]The translation is taken from Israel Abrahams's *Hebrew Ethical Wills*, vol. 1, p. 62 ff.

Well art thou aware, my son, that the companionship of the ungodly is noxious, that their example cleaves like the plague. O "enter not into the path of the wicked!" Loiter not in the streets, sit not in the highway, go not with him whose society is discreditable. As the sage says: "He that walketh with wise men shall be wise." And also as Ben Mishle writes:

Choose upright men for friends, with them
  Take counsel, but the fool despise!
With the wise thou canst a rock o'erturn,
  And safety find 'gainst giants' rage!

My son, make thy books thy companions, let thy cases and shelves be thy pleasure grounds and gardens. Bask in their paradise, gather their fruit, pluck their roses, take their spices and their myrrh. If thy soul be satiate and weary, change from garden to garden, from furrow to furrow, from prospect to prospect. Then will thy desire renew itself, and thy soul be filled with delight! For, remember the lines of the poet [Judah HaLevi]:

The wise of heart forsakes the ease of pleasure,
  In reading books he finds tranquillity;
All men have faults, thine eyes can see them,
  The wise heart's failing is–forgetfulness!

Consult a man of sense and well-beloved,
  Put not thy trust in thine own device;
For if thou turnest to thy heart's desire,
  Desire will hide from thee the right;
Is it a yearned-for end? Thy heart
  Doth make thy lust seem fair before thee!

Contend not with men, and meddle not "with strife not thine own." Enter into no dispute with the obstinate, not even on matters of Torah. On thy side, too, refrain from subterfuges in argument, to maintain thy case even when thou art convinced that thou art in the right. Submit to the majority and do not reject their decision. Risk not thy life by taking the road and leaving thy city in times of disquiet and danger. Even where large sums are involved, travel only on the advice of men of mature judgment who are well disposed to thee; trust not the counsel of the young in preference to that of the old. Let not the prospect of great gain blind thee, to make light of thy life; be not as a bird that sees the grains but not the net. Remember what the sage, of blessed memory, said: "A wise man feareth and departeth from evil, but the fool behaveth overbearingly and is confident."

Show honor to thyself, thy household, and thy children, by providing decent clothing, as far as thy means allow; for it is unbecoming for any one, when not at work, to go shabbily dressed. Spare from thy belly and put it on thy back!

And now, my son, if the Creator has mightily displayed his love to thee and me, so that Jew and Gentile have thus far honored thee for my sake, endeavor henceforth so to add to thine honor that they may respect thee for thine own self. This thou canst effect by good morals and by courteous behavior; by steady devotion to thy studies and thy profession, as thou wast wont to do before thy marriage.

As Ben Mishle says:

In outside books oft meditate, thou'lt find
  What brings repute to its doer in the gates;
Will make thy voice respected 'mid the great,
  Thy name extolled o'er thine associates.

Let thy countenance shine upon the sons of men; tend their sick, and may thine advice cure them. Though thou takest fees from the rich, heal the poor gratuitously; the Lord will requite thee. Thereby shalt thou find favor and good understanding in the sight of God and man. Thus wilt thou win the respect of high and low among Jews and non-Jews, and thy good name will go forth far and wide. Thou wilt rejoice thy friends and make thy foes envious. For remember what is written in the "Choice of Pearls": "How shall one take vengeance on an enemy? By increasing his own good qualities."

My son, examine regularly, once a week, thy drugs and medicinal herbs, and do not employ an ingredient whose properties are unknown to thee. I have often impressed this on thee in vain when we were together.

My son, if thou writest aught, read it through a second time, for no man can avoid slips. Let not any consideration of hurry prevent thee from revising a short epistle. Be punctilious as to grammatical accuracy, in conjugations and genders, for the constant use of the vernacular sometimes leads to error in this regard. A man's mistakes in writing bring him into disrepute; they are remembered against him all his days. As our Sages say: "Who is it that uncovers his nakedness here and it is exposed everywhere? It is he who writes a document and makes mistakes therein." Be careful in the use of conjunctions and adverbs (particles), and how thou appliest them and how they harmonize with the verbs. I have already begun to compose for thee a book on the subject, to be called "Principles of Style," may God permit me to complete it! Whatever thou art in doubt about and hast no book to refer to, abstain from expressing it! Endeavor to cultivate conciseness and elegance; do not attempt to write verse unless thou canst do it perfectly. Avoid heaviness, which spoils a composition, making it disagreeable alike to reader or audience.

The same rules apply to poetry. The lines must not drag, verbosity must be eschewed. The words must be harmonious to the ear and light on the tongue. Use no rare constructions or foreign idioms or terms, for though the latter may be justified by analogy, they are none the less unnatural; and remember what I said to thee when thou didst make a blunder over an infinitive! Avoid all such faults; but choose what is sweet to thy palate and pleasant to those who hear thee.

See to it that thy penmanship and handwriting are as

beautiful as thy style. Keep thy pen in fine working order; use ink of good color. Make thy script as perfect as possible, unless forced to write without proper materials, or in a pressing emergency. The beauty of a composition depends on the writing, and the beauty of the writing on pen, paper, and ink; and all these excellences are an index to the author's worth. Do not get into the habit of contracting the characters or of running them together, but make each long, broad, straight.

For writing, as I said above, is an art among the arts, and the more care one takes, the better is the result. Be fastidious, too, in the alignment; the lines must be straight, and the spacing uniform, so that one does not go up and another down. May thy God prosper thee, and make thee straight in all thy ways!

Very important is it that thou shouldst fulfill my commands regarding thy diet. Slay me not before my time! For thou knowest my distress, my soul's sorrow, my fear for thee in thy sickness. . . . Yearly, as thou knowest, thou art visited with sickness (for my sins), and the chief cause of thy complaints is unwholesome food.

So now, O my son, by the God of heaven, by the obedience to me imposed by His law, by the gratitude due for my rearing and educating thee, I adjure thee to abstain, with all thy resolution, from noxious food! Experience has taught thee how much thou hast suffered from carelessness in this regard. Be content with little and good, and beware of hurtful sweets. "Eat no eating that prevents thee from eating."

Art thou not ashamed before thyself and the world when all know that thou art periodically sick because of thy injurious diet? There is no more disgraceful object than a sick physician, who shall forsooth mend others when he cannot mend himself. Ben Mishle says:

Turn from one who enjoins the doing
  Of right, but himself is a man of wrong!
How shall *he* heal the malady,
  Who himself suffers from its pain?

Say not in thy heart: "I will venture as before and will escape." For all the world knows that but for the mercy of God and for my nearness to thee, thou hadst been near to death. (May the Lord preserve thee in happy life!)–but not at every hour does a miracle happen! "Lo, all these things doth God work, twice, yea thrice, with a man, but not always."

My son, I command thee to honor thy wife to thine utmost capacity. She is intelligent and modest, a daughter of a distinguished and educated family. She is a good housewife and mother, and no spendthrift. Her tastes are simple, whether in food or dress.

The Arab philosopher says of women: "None but the honorable honoreth them, none but the despicable despises them." Ben Mishle also says:

> Pardon thy child and wife their failings,
>   And persevere in thine exhortations;
> As an armorer sharpens the edge of a sword,
>   By oft drawing it to and fro on the stone.

If thou wouldst acquire my love, honor her with all thy might; do not exercise too severe an authority over her; our sages have expressly warned men against this. If thou givest orders or reprovest, let thy words be gentle. Enough is it if thy displeasure is visible in thy look, let it not be vented in actual rage. Let thy expenditure be well ordered. It is remarked in the "Choice of Pearls": "Expenditure properly managed makes half an income." There is an olden proverb: "Go to bed without supper and rise without debt." Defile not the honor of thy countenance by borrowing; may thy Creator save thee from that habit!

My son, devote thy mind to thy children as I did to thee; be tender to them as I was tender; instruct them as I instructed; keep them as I kept thee! Try to teach them Torah as I have tried, and as I did unto thee, do thou unto them! Be not indifferent to any slight ailment in them, or in thyself (may God deliver thee and them from all sickness and plague), but if thou dost notice any suspicion of disease in thee or in one of thy limbs, do forthwith what is necessary in the case. As Hippocrates has said: "Time is short, and experiment dangerous." Therefore be prompt, but apply a sure remedy, avoiding doubtful treatment.

Examine thy Hebrew books at every New Moon, the Arabic volumes once in two months, and the bound codices once every quarter. Arrange thy library in fair order, so as to avoid wearying thyself in searching for the book thou needest. Always know the case and chest where the book should be. A good plan would be to set in each compartment a written list of the books therein contained. If, then, thou art looking for a book, thou canst see from the list the exact shelf it occupies without disarranging all the books in the search for one. Examine the loose leaves in the volumes and bundles, and preserve them. These fragments contain very important matters which I collected and copied out. Do not destroy any writing or letter of all that I have left; and cast thine eye frequently over the catalogue so as to remember what books are in thy library.

Never intermit thy regular readings with thy teacher; study in the college of thy master on certain evenings before sitting down to read with the young. Whatever thou hast learned from me or from thy teachers, impart it again regularly to worthy pupils, so that thou mayest retain it, for by teaching it to others thou wilt know it by heart, and their questions will compel thee to precision, and remove any doubts from thine own mind.

Never refuse to lend books to anyone who has not the means to purchase books for himself, but only act thus to those who can be trusted to return the volumes.

Take particular care of thy books. Cover the bookcases with rugs of fine quality; and preserve them from damp and mice, and from all manner of injury, for thy books are thy good treasure. If thou lendest a volume make a memorandum before it leaves thy house, and when it is returned, draw thy pen over the entry. Every Passover and Tabernacles call in all books out on loan.

My son, if thou hearest abuse of me from the lips of fools, be silent and make no reply. Take no notice of aught that they may say against me.

Show eagerness in honoring thy teachers and do them service. Attach thyself to their friends, make their foes thine. Treat them with respect in all places and under all circumstances, even though thou hast no need of them while they have need of thee, a thousand and a thousand times more if thou needest them.

But, my son, honor thy comrades, and seek opportunities to profit them by thy wisdom, in counsel and deed.

I enjoin on thee my son to read this, my testament, once daily, at morn or at eve. Apply thy heart to the fulfillment of its behests, and to the performance of all therein written. Then wilt thou make thy ways prosperous; then shalt thou have good success.

Now, my son, emulate wisdom, and endeavor to follow men of virtue! Let not thy heart be envious of sinners, but let it be zealous in the fear of God all day!

Behold a small cloud rising from the sea of science and learning, carried by the breeze of wisdom and understanding! If the cloud empty itself on a fertile soil, causing righteousness and faith to spring up, making pleasant knowledge to flourish – ripeness will come in due season, and the roots of wisdom will be made firm; the branches will bloom, its food will be for nourishment, its leaves for healing! The lovingkindness of the Lord will guard it, will water it every moment, and shield it from all mishap. May He who gives prudence to the simple and to young men knowledge and discretion, bestow on thee a willing heart and a listening ear! Then shall our soul be glad in the Lord and rejoice in His salvation!

CHAPTER 39

THE BOOK OF DELIGHT

The following quotations are from the Sefer Sashuim, *"The Book of Delight," an exuberant little mishmash in rhymed Hebrew prose by Joseph ben Meir ibn Zabara, who was born in Barcelona about 1140. Though much of the material is derived from Hindu and other Oriental sources, and the general tone shows strong Arab influence, the document deserves inclusion in this anthology, if only because of its prolonged popularity in Jewish circles.*[1]

ON THE WISDOM OF WIVES

A leopard once lived in joy and plenty; ever he found easy sustenance for his wife and children. Hard by there dwelt his neighbor and friend, the fox. The fox felt in his heart that his life was safe only so long as the leopard could catch other prey, and he planned out a method of ridding himself of this dangerous friendship. Before the evil cometh, say the wise, counsel is good. "Let me move him hence," thought the fox. "I will lead him to the paths of death; for the sages say, 'If one come to slay thee, be beforehand with him, and alay him instead.' "

[1]The translation is taken from Israel Abrahams's *The Book of Delight and Other Papers* (Philadelphia, Jewish Publication Society, 1912).

Next day the fox went to the leopard, and told him of a place he had seen, a place of gardens and lilies, where fawns and does disported themselves, and everything was fair. The leopard went with him to behold this paradise, and rejoiced with exceeding joy. "Ah," thought the fox, "many a smile ends in a tear." The leopard was charmed, and wished to move to this delightful abode. "But, first," said he, "I will go to consult my wife, my lifelong comrade, the bride of my youth."

The fox was sadly disconcerted. Full well he knew the wisdom and the craft of the leopard's wife. "Nay," said he, "trust not thy wife. A woman's counsel is evil and foolish, her heart hard like marble; she is a plague in a house. Yes, ask her advice, and do the opposite." . . . The leopard told his wife that he was resolved to go. "Beware of the fox," she exclaimed; "two small animals there are, the craftiest they, by far–the serpent and the fox. Hast thou not heard how the fox bound the lion and slew him with cunning?"

"How did the fox dare," asked the leopard, "to come near enough to the lion to do it?"

Then said the leopard's wife: The lion loved the fox, but the fox had no faith in him, and plotted his death. One day the fox went to the lion whining that a pain had seized him in the head. "I have heard," said the fox, "that physicians prescribe for headache that the patient shall be tied up hand and foot." The lion assented, and bound up the fox with a cord.

"Ah," blithely said the fox, "my pain is gone." Then the lion loosed him.

Time passed, and the lion's turn came to suffer in his head. In sore distress he went to the fox, fast as a bird to the snare, and exclaimed, "Bind me up, brother, that I, too, may be healed, as happened with thee."

The fox took fresh withes and bound the lion up. Then he went to fetch great stones, which he cast on the lion's head, and thus crushed him.

"Therefore, my dear leopard," concluded his wife, "trust not the fox, for I fear him and his wiles. If the place he tells of be so fair, why does not the fox take it for himself?"

ON THE WICKEDNESS OF WOMEN

Enan the Demon related: Once upon a time, in my wanderings to and fro upon the earth, I came to a city whose inhabitants dwelt together, happy, prosperous, and secure. I made myself well acquainted with the place and the people, but, despite all my efforts, I was unable to entrap a single one.

"This is no place for me," I said. "I had better return to my own country." I left the city, and, journeying on, came across a river, at the brink of which I seated myself. Scarcely had I done so, when a woman appeared bearing her garments to be washed in the river.

She looked at me and asked, "Art thou of the children of men or of demons?"

"Well," said I, "I have grown up among men, but I was born among demons."

"But what art thou after here?"

"Ah," I replied, "I have spent a whole month in yonder city; and what have I found? A city full of friends, enjoying every happiness in common. In vain have I tried to put a little of wickedness among them."

Then the woman, with a supercilious air, declared: "If I am to take thee for a specimen, I must have a very poor opinion of the whole tribe of demons. You seem mighty enough, but you haven't the strength of women. Stop here and keep an eye on the wash; but mind, play me no tricks. I will go back to the city and kindle therein fire and fury, and pour over it a spirit of mischief, and thou shalt see how I can manage things."

"Agreed!" said I. "I will stay here and await thy coming, and watch how affairs turn out in thy hands."

The washerwoman departed, went into the city, called upon one of the great families there residing, and requested to see the lady of the house. She asked for a washing order, which she promised to execute to the most perfect satisfaction. While the housemaid was collecting the linen, the washerwoman lifted her eyes to the beautiful face of the mistress, and exclaimed: "Yes, they are a dreadful lot, the men; they are all alike, a malediction on them! The best of them is not to be trusted. They love all women but their own wives."

"What dost thou mean?" asked the lady.

"Merely this," the washerwoman answered. "Coming hither from my house, whom should I meet but thy husband making love to another woman, and such a hideous creature, too! How he could forsake beauty so rare and exquisite as thine for such disgusting ugliness, passes my understanding; but do not weep, dear lady, don't distress thyself and give way. I know a means by which I shall bring that husband of thine to his senses, so that thou shalt suffer no reproach, and he shall never love any other woman than thee. This is what thou must do. When thy husband comes home, speak softly and sweetly to him; let him suspect nothing; and when he has fallen asleep, take a sharp razor and cut off three hairs from his beard; black or white hairs, it matters not. These thou must afterwards give to me, and with them I will compound such a remedy that his eyes shall be darkened in their sockets, so that he will look no more upon other lovely women, but cling to thee alone in mighty and manifest and enduring love." All this the lady promised, and gifts besides for the washerwoman, should her plan prosper.

Carrying the garments with her, the woman now sought out the lady's husband. With every sign of distress in her voice and manner, she told him that she had a frightful secret to divulge to him. She knew not if she would have the strength to do so. She would rather die first. The husband was all the more eager to know, and would not be refused. "Well, then," she said, "I have just been to thy house, where my lady, thy wife, gave me these garments to wash; and, while I was yet standing there, a youth, of handsome mien and nobly attired, arrived, and the two withdrew into an adjoining room: so I inclined mine ear to listen to their speech, and this is what I overheard: The young man said to thy wife, 'Kill thy husband, and I will marry thee.' She however, declared that she was afraid to do such a dreadful deed. 'O,' answered he, 'with a little courage it is quite easy. When thy husband is asleep, take a sharp razor and cut his throat.' "

In fierce rage, but suppressing all outward indication of it, the husband returned home. Pretending to fall asleep, he watched his wife closely, saw her take a razor to sever the three hairs for the washerwoman's spell, darted up suddenly, wrested the razor from her hands, and with it slew his wife on the spot.

The news spread; the relations of the wife united to avenge her death and kill the husband. In their turn his relatives resolved to avenge him; both houses were embroiled, and before the feud was at an end, 230 lives were sacrificed. The city resounded with a great cry, the like of which had never been heard.

ON SINGERS

My son, beware of singers, for they are mostly thieves; trust no word of theirs, for they are liars; they dally with women, and long after other people's money. They fancy they are clever, but they know not their left hand from their right; they raise their hands all day and call, but know not to whom. A singer stands on the platform, raised above all other men, and he thinks he is as lofty as his place. He constantly emits sounds, which mount to his brain, and dry it up; hence, he is so witless.

CHAPTER 40

THE SENTIMENTS OF AL-HARIZI

Judah ben Solomon, surnamed Al-Harizi, was a celebrated Hebrew poet of the early thirteenth century who lived in Spain and traveled in the Orient. Even more than his great predecessor, Judah HaLevi , his thought and style were influenced by the Mohammedans. His masterpiece, entitled Tahkemoni, *"The Wise One," is a rhymed account of his experiences during a long and painful voyage to Palestine. It reveals him a shrewd observer, a caustic wit, and a most dexterous weaver of biblical quotations, Talmudic allusions, Mohammedan fantasies, and barbarous quips. The following passage, translated by B. Halper, is from the nineteenth chapter of that work.*[1]

I was in the land of Pethor, the city of Balaam the son of Beor; and while I was walking by the riverside, under the shadows of plants and thickets of flowers, I perceived seven pleasant youths of the choicest society. They sat upon the bank of the river, making their hearts merry with words of rhetoric. One of them called out and said, "Which is the best quality that is more beloved than all other qualities and is the worthiest in the sight of God and man?"

[1] *Post-Biblical Hebrew Literature,* an anthology by B. Halper, M.A., Ph.D. (Philadelphia, Jewish Publication Society, 1921), pp. 156–160.

One then answered, "I know that all qualities are praiseworthy, but there is none as sublime as humility; for it conceals all faults, and reveals all that is beautiful; it causes one to forgive transgressions, and makes its possessor associate with the modest; it increases his lovers and friends, and causes him to inherit a precious and pleasant name. . . . Amongst man's good traits there is none like meekness: it is graceful and sublime to all the wise; it stirs up love in hearts of enemies, and covers a man's sins and transgressions."

Thereupon a second youth said: "Thou has strayed from the right path, and fed the wind. Humility is esteemed as naught when compared with promptness, for with that a man conquers souls, and finds favor and good understanding in the sight of God and men, and inherits much honor and greatness in this world and in the next. He who is never belated amasses increasing riches and houses full of all good things. . . . Truly, promptness has no equal, and happy is he who walks in its way. All other precious qualities are but handmaids, whereas this one is the queen."

His third companion said, "Thou too hast spoken foolishly, for there is no quality as good and precious as courage. With that a man subdues all his enemies, and does good to his friends; he joins himself unto the great, and will cry, yea, he will shout, he will prove himself mighty against his enemies. He will ascend the throne of excellence, so that they will proclaim before him, 'Cast up the highway!' . . . Verily, there is no precious trait in man like courage blended with strength; indeed with it a man subdues his foes, and brings them down with sorrow to the grave."

The fourth one said, "Thou in turn hast wandered out of the way, and hast been made to serve folly with a vengeance; for among all the qualities there is no quality as worthy as faithfulness; because with it a man lifts up his head, his soul becomes precious, he is honored in the sight of all flesh and blood, and finds favor and good understanding in the sight of

God and man. . . . Know there is no quality as worthy in God's sight as faithfulness; if prophecy assumed a mortal garb, it would appear like faithfulness in form."

The fifth one said, "There is no steadfastness in thy mouth, and thy speech is without understanding; for the most sublime quality is wisdom: it lifts up those of its adherents that are low, and raises its banners upon their heads. Wisdom preserves the life of him that has it; if not for wisdom, man would be no better than a beast. . . . In this our world there is no trait so sublime and glorious as wisdom. With it a man ascends the royal throne, and by dint of it the weary ones find strength."

The sixth one said, "A vain vision hast thou seen, and falsely hast thou testified; for there is no quality as good to any flesh as culture. It is for his culture that a man is honored by those that know him, and loved by those that hear him; they cover all his transgressions; his memorial is pleasant to all mouths, and his praise is like a tower built for an armory. Such a man is a delight to the heart, and his praises endure for ever and ever. . . . Culture is majesty and grace unto all flesh; for if a man possesses all charms, but has no culture, know that he lacks honor."

The seventh one said, "Thou trustest in vanity, and, following the east wind, feedest on air; for among all the qualities there is none as worthy as a good heart. Through it a man is beloved of all creatures, and is placed at the head of all guests; he is honored in the sight of those that hear him and see him, all that look upon him love him, and even his enemies praise him. Men laud him, and the angels of heaven remember him for good. . . . With a good heart a man will flourish like a watered garden; through it he will be beloved of his Maker, and will find favor and good repute in his sight."

An old man who had been sitting by and listening to their words, said unto them, "Ye are all perplexed, and walk in darkness; the right thing is hidden from you, and ye know not to choose the truth. For among all the qualities, there is no quality as good as generosity. All other qualities bow down at its feet, and it excels them all. Through it all sins are forgiven, and hatred is removed from the heart; with it a man attains desirable things that are far away, even if they are in heaven; through it he is counted among the pious, for with it he does righteous and kind deeds; with it he acquires a good name, and his memorial is like precious oil; but he who lacks generosity, his righteousness is counted as guilt, his kindnesses as errors, and his favors as sins. All his companions despise him, those who know him hate him, his friends remember him for evil, and they that dwell in his house and his maids count him for a stranger. The bountiful man, however, lifts up his countenance, for generosity covers all his sins, and blots out all his transgressions. Even his adversaries love him, and his enemies give him praise. . . . I have seen wicked men who commit evil deeds, but if they have a generous heart, their wickedness and guilt are covered up. . . . I have likewise seen men of faithfulness, prudence, and understanding, possessing all worthy qualities; but if generosity is not among them, fear of God becomes a sin, and humility, haughtiness; promptitude, impudence; prudence, folly; merit a fault; and understanding, lack of knowledge. Verily, all other good qualities bow down at the feet of generosity. . . ."

CHAPTER 41

THE PHILOSOPHY OF MAIMONIDES

Rabbi Moses ben Maimon (1135–1204), known also–from the initials of his full name–as RaMBaM, was the greatest of all the medieval Jewish sages. His writings constitute the last and brightest flare of the lamp of reason which Saadia had kindled almost 300 years earlier.

Born the son of a scholarly father, and reared in the cultured city of Cordova (Spain), Maimonides was naturally drawn to a life of learning. He had barely begun his studies, however, when a storm of reaction swept the Moorish lands, and he and his family were forced to become refugees. After years of wandering in Spain, they moved to Morocco, then to Palestine, and finally to Egypt. In Cairo the mighty Sultan Saladin was still maintaining the principle of tolerance, so there Maimonides found a safe haven at last.

He was thirty by that time, and thanks in part to his father and younger brother, who had been supporting him all these years, he had managed to acquire vast learning; but now they died, the latter in a shipwreck which carried away the fortune of the entire family–he was a jewel merchant–and Maimonides was suddenly forced to consider gainful occupation. Mindful of the Talmudic injunction never to make the Torah "a spade to dig with," he decided to become a physician. Like most learned Jews of the period, he had studied medicine as a matter of course, and it was not long before his extraordinary skill and conscientiousness won him wide renown. He was appointed personal physician to the Sultan and proved so competent that a court poet wrote of him ecstatically:

If the moon would submit to Abu Imram's [Maimonides'] art,
He would heal her of her spots,
Cure her of her periodic troubles,
And keep her from ever waning!

However, medicine was merely this man's means of livelihood, not his life. His supreme interest was Jewish lore, and his voluminous writings in this field eventually established him as the foremost rabbinic authority in the world. From far and wide, congregations wrote to him for his opinion on disputed points of dogma and ritual, for he had come to be considered "the second Moses." When he finally died at the age of 69, worn out by chronic illness and incessant activity, there was grief throughout Israel. In Cairo itself, both Jews and Moslems observed public mourning for three days, and in Jerusalem there was a general fast. His body was buried in Tiberias, on the Sea of Galilee, and the tomb there has remained a place of pilgrimage.

The greatness of Maimonides lay in his prodigious capacity not just for amassing knowledge, but also for sifting and assaying it. His first major work, a comprehensive commentary on the Mishnah, although begun when he was barely 23, already revealed the striking independence of his mind. In this, he heaped scorn on all who, "being ignorant of science and far away from knowledge," took every saying of the ancient rabbis literally. Many of those sayings, he insisted, were purely figurative. The same was true, he held, with respect to much that was in the Scriptures. Maimonides was a confirmed rationalist, and believed in believing only that which was—or could at least be so interpreted as to seem—reasonable.

This was the conviction animating all his subsequent writings, and it received its fullest expression in a great work entitled Moreh Nevuhim, *"The Guide for the Perplexed." (Maimonides, though a superb Hebraist, preferred to write in Arabic, his mother-tongue.) That work was the climax of his labors as a rationalizer of religion, and profoundly influenced the development of medieval scholasticism.*

The following passages are taken—with slight stylistic changes—from translations of various of his writings as cited in Rev. A. Cohen's excellent handbook on Maimonides.[1]

---

[1] *The Teachings of Maimonides* by Rev. A. Cohen, M.A., Ph.D. (London, Shapiro, Valentine & Co., 1927).

ON THE EXISTENCE OF EVIL

Men frequently think that the evils in the world are more numerous than the good things; many sayings and songs of the nations dwell on this belief. They say that a good thing is found only exceptionally, whilst evil things are numerous and enduring. Not only common people make this mistake, but even many who imagine they are wise. . . . The origin of the error is to be found in the circumstance that people judge the whole universe on the basis of what happens to one particular individual. An ignorant man is prone to believe that the whole universe only exists for him, and, therefore, if any disappointment comes to him, he immediately concludes that the whole universe is evil. If, however, he would take the whole universe into consideration, and realize how small a part of it he is, then he would know the real truth. . . .

The numerous evils to which individual persons are exposed are due to the defects existing in the persons themselves. We complain and seek relief from our own faults; we suffer from the evils which we, by our own free will, inflict on ourselves. Why then ascribe them to God, who has no part in them? . . .

The evils which befall men are of three kinds:

The first kind of evil is that which comes to man because he is subject to birth and death, being possessed of a physical body. . . . Now, it is in accordance with the divine wisdomthat there can be no birth without death, for unless the individuals die, how can the species continue? Thus, the true beneficence of God is proved. Whoever thinks he can have flesh and bones without being subject to external influences – to physical accidents, and so forth – unconsciously wishes to reconcile two opposites: that is, to be at the same time subject and not subject to change. If man were never subject to change, there could be no generation; there would be one single being, but no individuals forming a species. . . .

The second class of evils comprises such as people cause to

each other: for example, when some of them use their strength against others. These evils are more numerous than those of the first kind and originate in ourselves rather than in the outside elements. Nevertheless, against them too the individual is helpless. . . .

The third class of evils, however, comprises those which a man causes to himself by his own action. This is the largest class, and . . . originates in man's vices, such as excessive desire for eating, drinking, and love. Indulgence in these things in undue measure, or in improper manner, brings disease and affliction to body and soul alike.

The sufferings brought to the body are familiar. The sufferings of the soul are twofold: First, those directly due to the afflictions of the body, because the properties of the soul depend on the condition of the body. Second, the soul, when accustomed to superfluous things, acquires a strong habit of desiring things which are neither necessary for the preservation of the individual nor for that of the species. This desire is without a limit, whilst things which are necessary are few in number and restricted within certain limits. For example, you desire to have your vessels of silver, but golden vessels are still better; others have even vessels of sapphire, or perhaps they can be made of emeralds or rubies, or any other substance that might be suggested. Those who are ignorant and perverse in their thought are, therefore, constantly in trouble and pain, because they cannot get as much of superfluous things as others possess. They are wont to expose themselves to great dangers – for example, by sea-voyage, or service of kings – and all this for the purpose of obtaining that which is superfluous and not necessary; and when they incur the consequences of their folly, they blame the decrees and judgments of God! . . .

How many trials and tribulations are due to the lust for superfluous things! In our frantic search for them, we lose even those which are indispensable. For the more we strive after that which is superfluous, the less strength have we left to grasp that which is truly needed.

Observe how nature proves the correctness of this assertion. The more necessary a thing is for living beings, the more easily it is found and the cheaper it is; the less necessary it is, the rarer and dearer it is. For example, air, water, and food are indispensable to man. Air is most necessary, for if man is without air a short time he dies, whilst he can be without water a day or two; and is not air more abundant and easily obtained than water? Again, water is more necessary than food, for some people can be four or five days without food, provided they have water; and is not water more abundant everywhere, and cheaper, than food? The same proportion can be noticed in the different kinds of food: that which is more necessary in a certain place exists there in larger quantities and is cheaper than that which is less necessary. No intelligent person, I think, considers musk, amber, rubies, and emeralds as very necessary for man except perhaps as medicines; and they, as well as other like substances, can be replaced for this purpose by herbs and minerals. This shows the kindness of God to his creatures, even to us weak beings. . . . (Guide III, 12)

ALL THAT GOD MADE IS GOOD

I contend that no intelligent person can assume that any of the actions of God can be in vain, purposeless, or unimportant. According to our view and the view of all who follow the Torah of Moses, all actions of God are "exceedingly good." Thus, Scripture says, "And God saw everything that He had made, and behold, it was very good" (Genesis 1:31). That which God made for a certain thing is necessary, or at least very useful, for the existence of that thing. Thus, food is necessary for the existence of living beings; the possession of eyes is very useful to man during his life. . . . This is assumed also by the philosophers, for they declare that nothing in Nature is purposeless. (Guide III, 25)

WAS THE UNIVERSE CREATED FOR MAN?

Some people assume that the universe was created solely for the sake of man's existence, that he might serve God. Everything that is done they believe is done for man's sake; even the spheres move only for his benefit, in order that his wants might be supplied. . . .

On examining this opinion, as intelligent persons ought to examine all different opinions, we will discover that it is erroneous. Those who maintain it may be asked whether God could have created man without those previous creations, or whether man could only have come into existence after the creation of all other things. If they answer in the affirmative, insisting that man could have been created even if, for example, the heavens did not exist, then they must be asked what is the object of all those other things, since they do not exist for their own sake, but for the sake of something that could exist without them? Even if the universe existed for man's sake and man existed for the purpose of serving God, one must still ask: "What is the end of serving God?" He does not become more perfect if all His creatures serve Him; nor would He lose anything if nothing existed beside Him.

It might perhaps be replied that the service of God is not intended for God's perfection, but for our own. Then, however, the question arises: What is the object of our being perfect?

Pressing the inquiry as to the purpose of the Creation, we must at last arrive at the answer: It was the will of God; and this is the correct answer. . . . Logic as well as tradition proves clearly that the universe does not exist for man's sake, but that all things in it exist each for its own sake. (Guide III, 13)

CONCERNING GENTILES

The teachers of truth, our Rabbis, declared, "The pious of the Gentiles have a portion in the World-to-Come," if they have attained what is due from them to attain relative to a knowledge of the Creator, and corrected their soul with the virtues. There is no doubt about the matter that whoever corrects his soul with purity of morals and purity of knowledge in the faith of the Creator will assuredly be of the children of the World-to-Come. On that account our Rabbis stated, "Even the Gentile who occupies himself with the Torah of Moses is equal to the High Priest." (Responsa II, 23d et seq.)

CONCERNING ASTROLOGY

Do not believe the absurd ideas of astrologers, who falsely assert that the constellation at the time of one's birth determines whether one is to be virtuous or vicious, the individual being thus necessarily compelled to follow out a certain line of conduct. (Commentary on Mishnah, Eight Chapters VIII)

I know that nearly all men are led far astray in matters of [astrology], and think there is some reality in them. There are even good and pious men of our own faith who think there is sense in these practices, and refrain from them only because they are forbidden by the Torah. They do not understand that these things are hollow frauds, and that the Torah forbids us to practice them precisely as it forbids us to indulge in falsehood. (Commentary on Mishnah, Avodah Zarah 4:7)

Know, my masters, that the whole subject of astrology, whereby people say so-and-so will happen or not happen, and the constellation at a man's birth determines that he should be such-and-such, and this will befall him and not that—all these things are not science at all but folly; and I have irrefutable proofs with which to answer all their arguments. Not one of the true philosophers of Greece occupied himself with this subject, or wrote about it in his books. The mistake of calling it a science was made only by the Chaldeans, Egyptians, and Canaanites, to whom it was actually a religion. The wise men of Greece–and they were real scientists–offered convincing proofs to destroy all astrological theories, root and branch. Also the wise men of Persia believed that the astrology of the Chaldeans, Egyptians, and Canaanites was false. . . . Only fools and charlatans talk of astrology as having any worth. (Responsa II, 25b)

ON OTHER SUPERSTITIONS

We may not practice divination as do the heathen; as it is said, "Ye shall not practice divination" (Leviticus 19:26). What is divination? Here is an example: a person says, "Because a piece of my bread dropped from my mouth, or my stick dropped from my hand, I shall not go today to a certain place, for were I to go, my business would not be transacted"; or, "Because a fox crossed on my right side, I shall not go outside the door of my house today, for if I were to go out, a deceiver would meet me." Similarly those who listen to the chirping of birds and say that so-and-so will or will not happen, such-and-such is advisable to do and something else is not; or others who say, "Kill this cock which crowed like a raven, or kill this hen which crowed like a cock." So, also the man who makes omens for himself, saying, "If such-and-such a thing happen to me, I will do a certain thing, and if it should not happen to me, I will not do it"–like Eliezer, the servant of Abraham (Genesis 24). All divinations such as these are prohibited. . . .

All these are the false and fraudulent notions with which priests of old used to mislead the ignorant masses in order to exploit them. It is unthinkable that Jews, who are of a higher mental caliber, should succumb to such superstitions, or see the slightest validity in them. . . . All men of wisdom and culture know with absolute certainty that divination, so explicitly prohibited by the Torah, is nonsensical, and appeals only to the weak-minded. . . . (Yad, Akum XI, 4, 16)

You must beware of sharing the error of those who write amulets. Whatever you hear from them, or read in their works, especially with reference to the names which they form by combination, is utterly senseless. They call these combinations *shemot* ("names") and believe that their pronunciation demands sanctification and purification, and that by using them one is able to work miracles. Rational persons ought not to listen to such men, nor in any way believe their assertions. (Guide I, 61)

Whoever whispers a charm over a wound by quoting a verse from Scripture, or reads a scriptural verse over an infant that it be not terrified, or places a Scroll of the Torah or phylacteries on a child so that it should sleep – all such persons are not alone in the category of diviners and soothsayers, but they are also to be included in the class of those who deny the Torah. The words of Torah are intended to heal the soul, not the body. (Yad, Akum XI, 12)

WHO CAN BE A PROPHET?

Among those who believe in prophecy, and even among our co-religionists, there are some ignorant people who think as follows: God selects any person He pleases, inspires him with the spirit of prophecy, and entrusts him with a mission. It makes no difference whether that person be wise or stupid, old or young, so long as he is to some extent morally good. (They have not yet gone so far as to maintain that God might inspire even a wicked person with His spirit. They admit that this is impossible, unless God has previously caused him to improve his ways.)

The philosophers, on the other hand, hold that prophecy is a certain faculty of man in a state of perfection, which can only be obtained by study. Although the faculty is common to the whole race, yet it is not fully developed in each individual, either on account of the individual's defective constitution, or on account of some other external cause. . . . Accordingly, it is impossible that an ignorant person should be a prophet; or that a person being no prophet in the evening should, unexpectedly on the following morning, discover himself to be a prophet; but if a person, perfect in his intellectual and moral faculties, and also perfect, as far as possible, in his imaginative faculty, prepares himself in the manner which will be described, he must become a prophet because prophecy is a natural faculty of man. It is impossible that a man who has the capacity for prophecy should prepare himself for it without attaining it, just as it is impossible that a person with a healthy constitution should be fed well and yet not properly assimilate his food.

However, there is a third view taught in Scripture, and this forms one of the principles of our faith. It coincides with the opinion of the philosophers in all points except one. For we believe that, even if one has the capacity for prophecy and has duly prepared himself, it may yet happen that he does not actually prophesy. In that case the will of God keeps him from the use of the faculty. (In my own opinion, however, such a case would be as exceptional as any other miracle, since the laws of Nature demand that whoever has a proper physical constitution, and has been duly prepared as regards education and training, can be a prophet.) (Guide II, 32)

PROPHETS VS. SCIENTISTS

In the realm of science, the prophet is like the rest of men. If a prophet expresses an opinion in this realm, and a non-prophet likewise expresses an opinion, and should the former declare, "The Holy One, blessed be He, has informed me that my view is correct"–do not believe him. If a thousand prophets, all of the status of Elijah and Elisha, were to entertain an opinion, and a thousand plus one sages held the opposite, we must abide by the majority and reject the view of the thousand distinguished prophets. (Commentary on Mishnah, Introduction)

THE PURPOSES OF THE TORAH

The general aim of the Torah is twofold: the well-being of the soul and the well-being of the body. The well-being of the soul is promoted by correct opinions communicated to the people according to their capacity. Some of these opinions are, therefore, imparted in a plain form, others allegorically, since certain opinions, if given in their plain form, would be too burdensome for the capacity of the common people. The well-being of the body is established by a proper management of our conduct ourselves toward one another.

The latter object is required first, and is dealt with in the Torah most carefully and minutely, since the well-being of the soul is obtainable only after that of the body has been secured. . . . First, therefore, a man must have all his wants supplied as they arise–that is, food and other things for his body, for example, shelter, sanitation, and the like; but no one man can procure all this by himself. The physical wants can be procured only through collective effort, because man, as is well known, is by nature gregarious.

The spiritual perfection of man consists in his becoming an actually intelligent being; that is, he knows all that a person is capable of knowing. Such knowledge can be obtained not by mere virtue and righteous conduct, but through philosophical inquiry and scientific research. . . .

The true Torah–which is of course the Torah of our teacher

Moses – aims first to foster good mutual relations among men by removing injustice and creating the noblest feelings, and second, to train us in faith, and to impart correct and true opinions when the intellect is sufficiently developed. (Guide III, 27)

It is also the object of the perfect Torah to make man despise, reject, and reduce his desires as much as is in his power. He should give way to them only in so far as is absolutely necessary. Intemperance in eating, drinking, and sexual intercourse is what people most crave and indulge in; and these are the very things that do most to injure the well-being of the individual and disturb the social order of the country. For by yielding entirely to the domination of lust, as is the way of fools, man loses his intellectual energy, wrecks his body, and perishes before his natural time. Sighs are cares multiply, and there is an increase of envy, hatred, and warfare for the purpose of taking what another possesses. Fools, being steeped in ignorance, consider physical enjoyment an object to be sought for its own sake. God in his wisdom has, therefore, given us such commandments as would counteract that idea by keeping us . . . from everything that leads to excessive desire and lust. This is an important thing included in the objects of our Torah. (Guide III, 33)

The ordinances of the Torah are not a burden, but a means of ensuring mercy, kindness, and peace in the world. (Yad, Shabbat II, 3)

Every narrative in the Torah serves a certain purpose in connection with religious teaching. It either helps to establish a principle of faith, or to regulate our actions, and to prevent wrong and injustice among men. (Guide III, 50)

WHY THE DIETARY LAWS?

I maintain that the food which is forbidden by the Torah is unwholesome. . . . The principal reason why the Torah forbids swine's flesh is to be found in the circumstance that the swine's habits and food are very dirty and loathsome. It has already been pointed out how emphatically the Torah enjoins the removal of the sight of loathsome objects, even in the field and in the camp; how much more objectionable is such a sight in towns. If the eating of swine's flesh were permitted, the streets and houses would be dirtier than any cesspool, as may be seen at present in the country of the Franks.[2] A saying of our Sages declares, "The mouth of a swine is as dirty as dung itself."

The fat of the intestines makes us full, interrupts our digestion, and produces cold and thick blood; it is more fit for fuel than for human food.

Blood (Leviticus 17:12) and also the flesh of a diseased animal (Exodus 22:30), or of an animal that died of itself (Deuteronomy 14:21), are indigestible and injurious as food.

The characteristics given in the Torah (Leviticus 11 and Deuteronomy 14) of the permitted animals—that is, cud-chewing and divided hoofs for cattle, fins and scales for fish—are in themselves neither the cause of the permission when they are present, nor of the prohibition when they are absent. They are merely signs by which the recommended species of animals can be discerned from those that are forbidden. . . .

It is prohibited to cut off a limb of a living animal and eat it, because such an act would be cruel and would encourage cruelty. Besides, the heathens used to do that, for it was a form of idolatrous worship to cut a certain limb off a living animal and eat it.

---

[2]The Moslems, among whom Maimonides lived, shared the Jewish aversion to eating swine's flesh.

Meat boiled in milk is undoubtedly gross food and makes overfull; but I think that most probably it is also prohibited because it is somehow connected with idolatry, forming perhaps part of the service, or being used during some heathen festival. . . .

The commandment concerning the slaughter of animals is necessary since meat is a natural food of man–as any doctor knows full well–and the Torah, therefore, enjoins that animals should be put to death as mercifully as possible. It is forbidden to torment the animal by cutting the throat in a clumsy manner, by poleaxing it, or by cutting off a limb whilst the animal is alive. (Guide III, 48)

CONCERNING FREE WILL

Free will is granted to every man. If he wishes to direct himself toward the good way and become righteous, the will to do so is in his hand; and if he wishes to direct himself toward the bad way and become wicked, the will to do so is likewise in his hand. Thus, it is written in the Torah, "Behold, the man is become as one of us, knowing good and evil" (Genesis 3:22)–that is to say, the human species has become unique in the world in that it can know of itself, by its own wit and reflection, what is good and what is evil, and in that it can do whatever it wishes.

Let there not enter your mind the belief of the fools among other peoples and also of the many uninformed men among the Israelites, that the Holy One, blessed be He, decrees concerning the human being, from his birth, whether he is to be righteous or wicked. The matter is not so. Every man has the possibility of becoming as righteous as Moses our teacher, or as wicked as Jeroboam–wise or stupid, kind or cruel, miserly or generous, and similarly with all the other qualities. That is what Jeremiah said, "Out of the mouth of the Most High proceedeth not evil and good" (Lamentations 3:38), meaning, the Creator does not decree concerning a man that he should be either good or bad. It consequently follows that the sinner caused his own downfall, and it behooves him to weep and lament over his sins and for having done violence to his soul. . . .

This subject is a most important Principle of Faith; it is a pillar of the Torah and of the commandments. . . . If God decided whether a man is to be righteous or wicked . . . as the foolish astrologers imagine, how could He have commanded us through the prophets, Do this and avoid that, mend your ways and go not after your wickedness? If from the outset of a man's existence his fate had been decreed for him . . . what place would there have been for the whole of the Torah? And by what justice, or by what right, could God punish the wicked or reward the righteous? "Shall not the Judge of all the earth do justly?" (Genesis 18:25).

Do not say in surprise, "How can a man do all that he desires and his actions be under his control? Can he do anything in the world without the permission and will of his Creator; as Scripture declares, 'Whatsoever the Lord pleased, that hath He done in heaven and in earth' (Psalm 135:6)?" Know that even though everything is done according to God's will, our actions remain under our own control. How is this? In the same way that the Creator willed that . . . all created things should have the tendency which He desired, so did He desire that a man should be possessed of free will, that all his actions should be under his control, and that there should not be anything to compel or withhold him, but that of his own accord and by the mind with which God had endowed him, he should do all that man is able to do. For this reason is a man judged according to his actions. If he has done good, good is done to him; and if he has done evil, evil is done to him. (Yad, Teshuvah V, 1-4)

ON THE MESSIANIC AGE

Let it not enter the mind that anything in the world's system will cease to exist when the Messiah comes, or that any novelty will be introduced into the scheme of the universe. The world will go on as usual. The statement of Isaiah, "The wolf shall dwell with the lamb, and the leopard shall lie down with the kid" (11:6), is a metaphorical expression signifying that Israel will dwell in safety among the wicked of the heathens who are likened to wolves and leopards (Jeremiah 5:6). They will be converted to the true religion, and will no more plunder and destroy, but will live honestly and quietly like Israel. . . .

The sages and prophets did not long for the days of the Messiah for the purpose of wielding dominion over all the world, or of ruling over the heathens, or being exalted by the peoples, or of eating and drinking and rejoicing. Their desire was to be free to devote themselves to the Torah and its wisdom, without anyone to oppress and disturb them, in order that they might merit the life of the World-to-Come.

In that era there will be neither famine nor war, neither jealousy nor strife. Prosperity will be widespread, all comforts found in abundance. The sole occupation throughout the world will be to know the Lord; and men will then be very wise, learned in things that are now hidden; they will attain all the knowledge of the Creator that is within the capacity of mortals—as it is said, "For the earth shall be full of the knowledge of the Lord, as the waters cover the sea" (Isaiah 11:9). (Yad, Melakhim XI, 1; XII, 1, 4f)

WHEN WILL THE MESSIAH COME?

It is your duty to know that it is not proper for any man to endeavor to ascertain when the "end" will actually come. As Daniel explained, "The words are shut up and sealed until the time of the end" (12:9). True, some of the learned have indulged in much speculation on this question and imagined they had solved it; as the prophet foretold, "Many shall run to and fro, and knowledge shall be increased" (v. 4)–meaning, the opinions and conjectures on this point will be increased. The Holy One, blessed be He, had previously declared through his prophets that some men will calculate "ends" for the Messiah, but these will pass by without fulfillment. He warned us, moreover, not to despair on account of this, saying, "Do not distress yourselves if their calculation proves wrong; but however long the Messiah delay, heighten your hope in him." Thus, it is said, "For the vision is yet for the appointed time, and it declareth of the end, and doth not lie; though he tarry, wait for him because he will surely come, he will not delay" (Habakkuk 2:3). . . .

Daniel has explained to us the profundity of the knowledge concerning the "end," and that it was "shut up" and concealed. For that reason the sages forbade us to try to calculate the advent of the Messiah, since this raises false hopes among the masses, and ends by plunging them into despair. So the sages exclaimed, "A plague on those who make such calculations!" (Iggeret Teman, Responsa II, 5a)

WHAT CAN A MAN BELIEVE?

Know that it is not proper for a man to believe except these three things: (1) that for which the mind offers clear proof–for example, arithmetic, geometry, and astronomy; (2) that which he can grasp through the five senses – for example, he knows and sees that this is black and that red, and so forth, through the vision of the eye; or he tastes that this is bitter and that sweet; or he feels that this is hot and that cold; or he hears that this sound is clear and that blurred; or he smells that this is malodorous and that pleasant; and so on; (3) that which is received from the prophets and righteous men.

It is necessary that a man should be mentally able to classify in his mind all that he believes, and say, "This I believe because it is handed down from the prophets; this I believe from my senses; and this I believe from reason." But whoever believes anything which does not fall within these three categories, to him applies the dictum, "The thoughtless believeth every word" (Proverbs 14:15). (Responsa II, 25a)

He who wishes to attain to human perfection must first study logic, next the various branches of mathematics in their proper order, then physics, and lastly metaphysics. (Guide I, 34)

WHAT CAN A MAN KNOW?

I declare that there is a limit to man's capacity for knowledge, because so long as the mind is in the body, it cannot know what is beyond Nature. Therefore, when the mind essays to contemplate what is beyond, it attempts that which is impossible. However, it certainly can know and reflect on all that is in Nature, and should try its utmost to do so. (Responsa II, 23b)

There are three causes which prevent men from discovering the exact truth: first, arrogance and vainglory; second, the subtlety, depth, and difficulty of any subject which is being examined; third, ignorance and want of capacity to comprehend what might be comprehended.

There is a fourth cause: that is, habit and training. We naturally like whatever is familiar, and dislike whatever is strange. This may be observed amongst rustics. Though they can rarely take a bath, have few enjoyments, and live a life of wretchedness, they abhor city life. The privations with which they are familiar seem to them better than the comforts to which they are foreign. It would give them no satisfaction to live in palaces, to be clothed in silk, and to indulge in baths, ointments, and perfumes.

The same is true of the opinions to which a man has been accustomed from his youth. He likes them, defends them, and shuns the opposite views. This is likewise one of the causes which prevent men from finding truth, and which make them cling to their habitual opinions. (Guide I, 31)

MEN ARE NOT BORN GOOD OR EVIL

It is impossible for man to be endowed by nature from his very birth with either virtue or vice, just as it is impossible that he should be born skilled by nature in any particular art. It is possible, however, that through natural causes he may from birth be so constituted as to have a predilection for a particular virtue or vice, so that he will more readily practice it than any other. For instance, a man whose natural constitution includes toward dryness, whose brain-matter is clear and not overloaded with fluids, finds it much easier to learn, remember, and understand things than the phlegmatic man whose brain in encumbered with a great deal of humidity. But if one who inclines constitutionally toward a certain excellence is left entirely without instruction, and if his faculties are not stimulated, he will undoubtedly remain ignorant. On the other hand, if one by nature dull and phlegmatic, possessing an abundance of humidity, is instructed and enlightened, he will, though of course with difficulty, gradually succeed in acquiring knowledge and understanding.

In exactly the same way, he whose blood is especially warm has the requisite quality to become a brave man. But another whose heart is colder than it should be, is naturally inclined toward cowardice and fear, so that if he should be encouraged to be a coward, he would easily become one. If, however, it be desired to make a brave man of him, he can without doubt become one, providing he receive a proper training which would require, of course, great exertion.

I have entered into this subject so that thou mayest not believe the absurd ideas of astrologers, who falsely assert that the constellation at the time of one's birth determines whether one is to be virtuous or vicious, the individual being thus necessarily compelled to follow out a certain line of conduct. We, on the contrary, are convinced that our Torah agrees with Greek philosophy, which substantiates with convincing proofs the contention that man's conduct is entirely in his own hands, that no compulsion is exerted, and that no external influence is brought to bear upon him that constrains him to be either virtuous or vicious – except inasmuch as, according to what we have said above, he may be by nature so constituted as to find it easy or hard, as the case may be, to do a certain thing. That he must necessarily do, or refrain from doing, a certain thing is absolutely untrue. (Commentary on Mishnah, Eight Chapters VIII)

[Hereditary forces, therefore, are not the deciding factor of a man's conduct in life. Ultimately he himself determines his course, and the responsibility of choice is his alone. Commenting on the verse, "Be ye not as the horse or as the mule which have no understanding; whose mouth must be held with bit and bridle" (Psalm 32:9), Maimonides remarks:]

This means that what restrains beasts from doing harm is something external, as a bridle and a bit, but not so with man. His restraining agency lies in his very self, I mean in his human framework. When the latter becomes perfected, it is exactly that which keeps him away from those things which perfection withholds from him and which are termed vices; and it is that which spurs him on to what will bring about perfection in him, that is, virtue. (Commentary on Mishnah, Introduction to Helek)

THE VIRTUE OF THE MIDDLE COURSE

The right way is the middle course in every one of man's tendencies – in other words, the course which is no nearer one extreme than the other. The sages of old have therefore recommended that a man should always keep estimating his tendencies, calculating and directing them into the middle course, so that he may be perfect in his bodily constitution. How is this meant? He should be neither passionate and easily irritated, nor like a corpse which is without feeling. He should hold the mean between the two, not giving way to vexation except in some serious matter where it is proper for him to be vexed, in order that a similar thing may not be repeated. (Yad, De'ot I, 4)

Good deeds are such as are equibalanced, maintaining the mean between two equally bad extremes – the *too much* and the *too little.* Virtues are the dispositions which are midway between two reprehensible extremes, one of which is characterized by excess, the other by deficiency. Good deeds are the product of these dispositions. To illustrate, abstemiousness is a disposition which adopts a midcourse between inordinate passion and total insensibility to pleasure. Abstemiousness, then, is a proper rule of conduct, and the disposition which gives rise to it is an ethical quality; but inordinate passion, the extreme of excess, and total insensibility to enjoyment, the extreme of deficiency, are both absolutely pernicious.

Likewise, liberality is the mean between miserliness and

extravagance; courage, between recklessness and cowardice; dignity, between haughtiness and loutishness; humility, between arrogance and self-abasement; contentedness, between avarice and slothful indifference; gentleness, between irascibility and insensibility to shame and disgrace; and modesty, between impudence and shamefacedness. So it is with the other qualities.

It often happens, however, that men err as regards these qualities, imagining that one of the extremes is good and is a virtue. Sometimes, the extreme of the *too much* is considered noble, as when bravado is made a virtue, and those who recklessly risk their lives are hailed as heroes. Thus, when people see a man who runs deliberately into danger, intentionally tempting death, and escaping only by mere chance, they laud such a one to the skies, and say that he is a hero. At other times, the opposite extreme, the *too little,* is greatly esteemed, and the coward is considered a man of prudence, the loafer a man of contentment, and a bovine creature a man of moderation. In like manner, profuse liberality and extreme lavishness are erroneously extolled as excellent characteristics. This is, however, an absolutely mistaken view, for the middle course alone is praiseworthy, and everyone should strive to adhere to it at all times. (Commentary on Mishnah, Eight Chapters IV)

HOW CAN ONE BECOME GOOD?

A man ought to associate with the righteous and be constantly in the company of the wise, so that he may learn from their actions. He must likewise keep far from the wicked who walk in darkness, so that he should not learn from their actions. . . . Consequently, if he is in a region where the customs are evil, and the inhabitants walk in wickedness, he should move to another where the customs are righteous and the inhabitants conduct themselves in the way of good men.

If, however, the inhabitants of all the countries which he knows, and the report of which he has heard, conduct themselves in a way which is not good–as is the case in our own day–or if he be unable to go to a country where the customs are good, owing to sickness, or fear of brigands on the road, then he should lead a solitary life. And if his countrymen be so wicked and sinful that they do not allow him to dwell in that land unless he mingle with them and conform to their evil customs, he should repair to caves, thickets, and deserts rather than yield to them. (Yad, De'ot VI, 1)

[A second and more drastic method of acquiring virtue and eradicating vice is to undergo] a cure, exactly as he would were his body suffering from an illness. So, just as when the equilibrium of the physical health is disturbed, and we note which way it is tending in order to force it to go in exactly the opposite direction until it shall return to its proper condition, in exactly the same manner must we adjust the moral equilibrium.

Let us take, for example, the case of a man in whose soul there has developed a tendency toward great avarice, so that he deprives himself of every comfort in life–a tendency, by the way, which is one of the most detestable of all. To cure him we must not command him merely to practice deeds of generosity, for that would be as ineffective as trying to cure a patient burning up with fever by administering mild medication. We must instead order him to squander his money until his tendency toward avarice has totally disappeared. Then, when he reaches the point where he is about to become a spendthrift, we must teach him to moderate his conduct, and practice no more than common generosity, watching out thenceforth never to relapse into either profligacy or niggardliness.

If, on the other hand, a man is a squanderer, he must be directed to practice strict economy, and to repeat acts of niggardliness. It is not necessary, however, for him to perform acts of avarice as many times as the stingy man must go in for profligacy. (This we know from the science of medicine, which teaches us that it is easier for an apathetic man to be stirred to moderate enjoyment than it is for one burning with passion to curb his lusts.) In the same way, the coward requires exposure to danger more frequently than the reckless man needs to be coerced into prudence. All this is a fundamental principle of the science of curing moral ills, and is worth remembering. (Commentary on Mishnah, Eight Chapters IV)

CONCERNING ASCETICISM

When at times some of the pious deviated to one extreme by fasting, keeping nightly vigils, refraining from eating meat or drinking wine, abjuring sexual intercourse, clothing themselves in hairy garments, dwelling in the mountains, and wandering about in the wilderness, they did so partly as a means of restoring the health of their souls, and partly because of the immorality of their neighbors. When the pious saw that they themselves might become contaminated by association with evil men, they fled to the wilderness in order to avoid their society. . . .

When the ignorant observed saintly men acting thus, not knowing their motives, they considered such conduct virtuous, and blindly imitated it. They too chastised their bodies with all manner of afflictions, imagining that they thus acquired moral worth, and approached nearer to God–as if He hated the human body and desired its destruction. It never dawned on them that these actions were bad and resulted in moral imperfection of the soul.

Such imitators can be compared only to one who, ignorant of the art of healing, sees skillful physicians cure the sick by administering purgatives such as colocynth, scammony, aloe, and the like, and by depriving them of food, and, therefore, foolishly concludes that since these things cure sickness, they must be all the more efficacious in preserving health and prolonging life. If a healthy person should take these things constantly, treating himself as though he were sick, before long he would really be sick. Likewise those who are spiritually well, but have recourse to asceticism, will surely become morally ill.

The perfect Torah which leads us to perfection . . . recommends none of these things. On the contrary, it aims at man's following the path of moderation, in accordance with the dictates of Nature, eating, drinking, enjoying legitimate sexual intercourse, all in moderation, and living among people in honesty and uprightness, but not dwelling in the wilderness or in the mountains, or clothing himself in hair garments, or otherwise afflicting the body. (Commentary on Mishnah, Eight Chapters IV)

A man should never devote his entire wealth to religion. Such conduct transgresses the intention of the scriptural verse which states, "*Of* all that he hath" (Leviticus 27:28)–not "*all* that he hath"–as the sages point out. To give all to religion is not piety but folly, because it so impoverishes a man that he must become dependent on charity. We need show no compassion for such a man, because he belongs to the class described by the sages as "pious fools who destroy the world."

A man should devote at most one-fifth of his income to religion, and thus, show himself one "that ordereth his affairs rightfully" (Psalm 112:5) both in religious and worldly ways. Even in the matter of the sacrifices, which were mandatory, the Torah has consideration for a man's resources. How much more so, then, in matters where there is no absolute obligation should a man be careful to do only according to his means. (Yad, Arahin VIII, 13)

One who suffers from melancholia can sometimes rid himself of it by listening to singing and instrumental music, by strolling through beautiful gardens and splendid buildings, by gazing at beautiful pictures, and other such things that enliven the mind and dissipate gloomy moods. The purpose of all this is to restore the healthful condition of the body; but the real object in maintaining the body in good health is to acquire wisdom. Likewise, in the pursuit of wealth, the main design in its acquisition should be to expend it for noble purposes, and to employ it for the maintenance of the body and the preservation of life, so that its owner may obtain a knowledge of God, in so far as that is vouchsafed unto man. . . .

Our Rabbis of blessed memory say, "It is becoming that a sage should have a pleasant dwelling, a beautiful wife, and domestic comfort." One becomes weary, and one's mind is dulled, by constant worry over wants and discomforts. Thus, just as the body becomes exhausted by hard labor, and is reinvigorated by rest, so it is necessary for the mind to have relaxation by gazing upon pictures and other beautiful objects, that its weariness may be dispelled. (Commentary on Mishnah, Eight Chapters V)

RULES FOR PHYSICAL HEALTH

The well-being of the soul can only be obtained after that of the body has been secured. (Guide III, 27)

Know that the perfection of the body precedes the perfection of the soul, and is like the key which opens the inner chamber. Therefore, let the chief aim of your discipline be the perfecting of your body and the correcting of your morals, to open before you the gates of Heaven. (Ethical Will, Responsa II, 38a, b.)

Man's only design in eating, drinking, cohabiting, sleeping, waking, moving about, and resting, should be the preservation of bodily health. The reason for the latter is that the soul and its agencies may be in sound and perfect condition, so that a man can readily acquire wisdom, and gain moral and intellectual virtues, all to the end that he may reach the highest goal of his endeavors. (Commentary on Mishnah, Eight Chapters V)

Eat that you may live and condemn excess. Believe not that much eating and drinking makes the body grow, or enlarges the understanding, like a sack which is filled by what is put into it. Just the reverse is true. By moderate eating, the stomach acquires strength to receive food and, through the natural heat, to digest it. Then a man grows in physical health, and his mind is settled. But if he eat more than is necessary, the stomach cannot receive the food, and the natural heat cannot digest it, and he will be forced to vomit. "It is a vile thing; it shall not be accepted" (Leviticus 19:7). His body will become emaciated, his understanding enfeebled, and his purse empty. Take care, then, that you do not eat except what you can digest, because it is injurious to the body and purse, and it is the cause of most illnesses. (Ethical Will, Responsa II, 39a)

A man should never eat except when he is hungry, nor drink except when he is thirsty; and he should not delay the performance of the act of purgation. . . . He should not keep on eating until his stomach is filled, but leave about a fourth part of his appetite unsatisfied. He is not to drink water during a meal, but only a little water mixed with wine. When the food begins to digest, he may drink as much as is proper; much water, however, should not be drunk even when the food is digesting. He should not eat until he is completely assured that he has no need of performing his natural functions. He should not eat until he has walked before the meal a sufficient distance for the body to begin feeling warm, or do some kind of work, or take some other exercise. The general rule is, he should exercise his body and tire it daily in the morning, until it begins to feel warm, rest a little until he is refreshed, and then have his meal. To take a hot bath after exercise is a good thing, but then he should wait a little before eating.

One should always remain seated while eating, or recline on one's left side. One should not walk, ride, undergo exertion, or induce perspiration. One should not walk about until the food becomes digested. Whoever walks about, or exerts himself, immediately after a meal brings on himself serious illnesses.

Day and night being twenty-four hours, it is enough for a person to sleep a third part thereof, that is, eight hours. These hours should be toward the end of the night, so that there are eight hours from the beginning of his sleep to sunrise, and he consequently gets up from his bed before the sun rises. It is not proper to sleep lying on one's face or back, but on the side—at the beginning of the night on the left, and at the end of the night on the right side. He should not retire to sleep immediately after a meal, but wait about three or four hours. He should also not sleep during the day.

Things which are laxative, for example, grapes, figs, mulberries, pears, melons, and all kinds of cucumbers and gherkins, one may eat as appetizers, not partaking of them together with the food, but waiting a little while and then eating his meal. Costive things, such as pomegranates, quinces, apples and Paradise-pears, he may eat immediately after a meal, but should not overindulge in them.

If one wish to partake of poultry and meat at the same meal, one should eat the poultry first. Similarly in the case of eggs and poultry, one should eat the eggs first; lamb and beef, he should give precedence to the former. A person should always partake of the lighter food first and then the heavier.

During the summer he should eat cooling things and not take too much spice; but he may use vinegar. During the winter he should eat warmth-giving food, use much spice, and take a little mustard and asafetida. He should follow these directions in cold countries and hot, in each place according to the local conditions.

There are foods which are exceedingly harmful and a person should never eat them; for example, large, salted and stale fish, salted stale cheese, mushrooms and all fungi, stale salted meat, wine fresh from the press, and cooked food which has been standing until its flavor has gone. Likewise any food which is malodorous or excessively bitter to the body like a deadly poison. There are, on the other hand, foods which are injurious, though not to the same extent as the former; therefore, it is right that a person should indulge in them sparingly and at rare intervals. He should not accustom himself to the use of them as food, or frequently eat them with his food. In this category are large fish, cheese, milk which has stood more than 24 hours from the time of milking, meat of big bulls and rams, beans, lentils, chickpeas, barley bread, unleavened bread, cabbage, leek, onions, garlic, mustard, and radishes. All these are harmful foods of which one should eat but very little indeed, and only in winter. In summer one ought not eat them at all. Beans and lentils by themselves should not be eaten in summer or winter; gourds, however, may be eaten in summer.

There are some foods which are injurious though not to the extent of the above-mentioned; for example, waterfowl, small pigeons, dates, bread toasted in oil or kneaded in oil, fine flour which has been so thoroughly sifted as to leave not even a particle of bran, brine, and pickle. One should not overindulge in them; and the man who is wise, curbs his desire and is not carried away by his appetite, abstaining from them altogether unless he requires them as medicine.

A person should avoid unripe fruits, for they are like swords to the body. Similarly carobs are always harmful; likewise all sour fruits are bad and should be eaten only in small quantities in summer and in hot climates. Figs, grapes, and almonds are always beneficial, whether fresh or dried. One may eat of them as much as one needs, but not to excess, even though they are more beneficial than all other fruits of trees.

Honey and wine are bad for the young, but good for adults, especially in winter. One need eat in summer two-thirds of what one eats in winter. . . .

There is another rule stated in connection with the healthy condition of the body: As long as a person works and takes plenty of exercise, does not eat to excess, and keeps his bowels regulated, no ailment will befall him and his strength keeps developing, even if he eat unwholesome food; but whoever sits idle and does no work, or retards the natural functions, or is of a costive nature, even though he eat wholesome food and take care of himself according to medical regulations, he will suffer all his life, and his strength will diminish. Excessive eating is to the body of a man like deadly poison, and is the root of all diseases. Most illnesses which befall men arise either from bad food, or from immoderate indulgence in food, even of the wholesome kind. . . .

The rule about the bath is this: A man ought to enter the bathhouse each week, but he should not enter it immediately after a meal, nor when he is hungry, but when the food begins to digest. He should bathe the whole of his body in hot water, but not of a heat to scald the body. The head only is to be washed in very hot water. After that he should bathe in lukewarm water, then in water still cooler, until he finally bathes in cold water. The head, however, should not be immersed in lukewarm or cold water. One should not bathe during winter in cold water, nor take the bath until the whole body is in a state of perspiration and has been shampooed. He should not stay long in the bath, but as soon as his body perspires and has been shampooed, he should take a shower, and go out. . . .

When he leaves the bath, he should dress and cover his head in the outer room, so as not to catch cold; even in summer he must be careful. After leaving the bath, he should wait a while until his body has relaxed, and the heat has departed; then he may take a meal. If he can sleep a little on leaving the bath, before his meal, this is very beneficial. He should not drink cold water when he comes out of the bath, much less drink it while in the bath; but if he is thirsty on leaving the bath and cannot resist drinking, he should mix the water with wine or honey, and drink. If he anoint himself with oil in the bath, during winter after he has had a shower bath, it is beneficial.

A person should not accustom himself to constant bloodletting; he should only be cupped in a case of emergency. He should not undergo it either in summer or winter, but a little during the spring, and a little in autumn time. After fifty years of age one should never submit to bloodletting. Nor should a person be cupped and enter the bath on the same day, or go on a journey; nor should he be cupped on the day he returns from a journey. . . .

Whoever conducts himself according to the rules we have prescribed, I guarantee that he will not be afflicted with illness all his days until he reaches advanced age and dies. He will not need a physician, but will always enjoy good health, unless he was physically weak from birth, or gave way to evil habits from early youth, or some plague or drought befall the world. (Yad, De'ot IV, 1-18, 20)

WAYS OF GIVING CHARITY

Whoever closes his eyes against charity is called, like the idol-worshipper, impious. . . . Whoever gives alms to the poor with bad grace and surly looks, though he bestow a thousand gold pieces, all the merit of his action is lost. He must give with good grace, gladly, sympathizing with the mendicant in his trouble. If a poor man solicit alms of you and you have nothing to give him, console him with words. It is forbidden to upbraid the poor, or raise the voice against him, since his heart is broken and crushed. . . . Woe, then, to the person who shames the poor man! Be to him, rather, like a parent whether with funds or kindly words. . . .

There are eight degress in alms-giving, one lower than the other. Supreme above all is to give assistance to a fellowman who has fallen on evil times by presenting him with a gift or loan, or entering into a partnership with him, or procuring him work, thereby helping him to become self-supporting. Next best is giving alms in such a way that the giver and recipient are unknown to each other. This is, indeed, the performance of a commandment from disinterested motives; and it is exemplified by the institution of the Chamber of the Silent which existed in the Temple, where the righteous secretly deposited their alms and the respectable poor were secretly assisted.

Next in order is the donation of money to the charity fund of the community, to which no contribution should be made unless there is confidence that the administration is honest, prudent, and efficient.

Below this degree is the instance where the donor is aware to whom he is giving the alms, but the recipient is unaware from whom he received them. The great sages, for example, used to go about secretly throwing money through the doors of the poor. This is quite a proper course to adopt and a great virtue where the administrators of a charity fund are not acting fairly.

Inferior to this degree is the case where the recipient knows the identity of the donor, but not vice versa. For example, the great sages would sometimes tie sums of money in linen bundles and throw them behind their backs for poor men to pick up, so that they should not feel shame.

The next four degrees in their order are: the man who gives money to the poor before he is asked; the man who gives money to the poor after he is asked; the man who gives less than he should, but does it with good grace; and lastly, he who gives grudgingly. (Yad, Matanot Aniyim X, 1-14)

HOW A WISE MAN SHOULD BEHAVE

A wise man should not shout or be noisy when he speaks, but his conversation with all people should be quiet. He should be careful, however, not to overdo this, and give the impression of haughtiness. He should anticipate every man with his greeting, so that all are favorably disposed toward him. He should judge every man leniently, praising his friends, and not disparaging anyone. If he perceives that his words are helpful and listened to, he should continue talking; otherwise he keeps silent. For instance, he will never attempt to pacify his neighbor whilst the latter is angry, or question him concerning his vow at the time he made it. He waits until the other's mind has grown calm and composed. He does not comfort the mourner while the dead body still lies in his presence, because the mourner is too overcome before the burial; and so on. He does not enter the presence of his friend at the time of the latter's disgrace, but averts his eyes from him. He does not depart from his word, neither adding to it or subtracting from it, except when peace is involved. In general, he speaks only on scholarly subjects, or to practice benevolence. He does not converse with a woman in a public place, even if it be his wife, sister, or daughter.

A wise man should not walk with a haughty demeanor; nor should he walk with slow and measured gait like women and proud people; nor run about in public roads like madmen; nor stoop like a hunchback; but he should gaze downward as though standing in prayer, and walk in the street like a man occupied in business. From the manner of a man's walking it may be perceived whether he is wise and learned or foolish and ignorant.

The dress of a wise man should be suitable and clean. It is forbidden that stains or grease marks should be found on his garment. He should not wear the apparel of princes–for example, garments of gold and purple–to attract the attention of people; nor the clothes of paupers which bring disrespect to the wearer. His garments should be of a medium character and suitable for him. His flesh should not be visible through his apparel, like the very fine linen garments made in Egypt; nor should his dress drag along the ground like that of the haughty, but should only reach to the heel, and the sleeves to the tips of the fingers. He should not wear a conspicuously long prayer shawl, save on the Sabbath, and then only if he has no other in its place. He should not wear patched shoes in summer, but if he is a poor man he may wear them in winter. He should not go out into the street perfumed, nor with scented garments, nor use any perfume for his hair, but it is allowable if he anointed his body with perfume to remove the bad odor. He should not go out alone at night unless there be a fixed time when it is his habit to go out to attend to his studies. All these rules are intended to avoid suspicion.

A wise man measures his words with judgment, eats and drinks and supports his household according to his means, and does not encumber himself with unnecessary burdens. . . . The sages recommended that a man should spend upon food less than his means, upon dress up to his means, and expend in honor of his wife and children more than his means.

The course adopted by a man of intelligence is first to determine upon a means of livelihood, then to purchase a dwelling house, and then to marry. . . . But fools marry first, then if they can afford it, acquire a dwelling house, and afterward, when advanced in years, go about to find a trade, or have to be supported from charity. . . .

All the transactions of the wise man must be honest and done with integrity. His nay should be nay, his yea, yea. In financial matters, he must be strict with himself, but lenient with others. He pays the purchase-money immediately; he does not make himself a surety or responsible for others; nor does he undertake the responsibility of a power of attorney. In business, he does not enter into such obligations as the Torah has not imposed upon him, so that he may abide by his word and not depart from it. If others are legally indebted to him, he grants them an extension to pay, is forgiving, and lends graciously. He does not interfere with the business of his neighbors, and never acts harshly toward anybody. In general, he is rather of the persecuted than of the persecutors; of the offended, not of the offenders. (Yad, De'ot V, 7-13)

WHY ALL MEN CANNOT BE INTELLECTUALS

If all men were students of philosophy, the social order would be destroyed and the human race quickly exterminated, for man is very helpless and needs many things. It is necessary for him to learn plowing, reaping, threshing, grinding, baking, and how to fashion implements for these tasks, in order to secure his food. Similarly, he must learn spinning and weaving to clothe himself, the building art to provide a shelter, and craftsmanship to fashion tools for all these works.

But the life of Methuselah would not be sufficiently long to learn all these occupations which are indispensable to human existence. How then can all men find the leisure to study and acquire wisdom? It is, therefore, imperative for the majority of men to follow these productive occupations so that the few who devote themselves to learning may have their wants provided, and the human race maintained at the same time that wisdom is enriched. (Commentary on Mishnah, Introduction)

FOUR KINDS OF PERFECTION

The ancient and the modern philosophers have shown that man can acquire four kinds of perfection. The first kind, the lowest, in the acquisition of which people spend their days, is perfection as regards property: the possession of money, garments, furniture, servants, land, and the like. The possession of the title of a great king belongs to this class. There is no close connection between this possession and its possessor; it is a perfectly imaginary relation when on account of the great advantage a person derives from these possessions, he says, "This is my house, this is my servant, this is my money, and these are my hosts and armies." For when he examines himself, he will find that all these things are external, and their qualities are entirely independent of the possessor. When, therefore, that relation ceases, he that has been a great king may one morning find that there is no difference between him and the lowest person, and yet no change has taken place in the things which were ascribed to him. The philosophers have shown that he whose sole aim in all his exertions and endeavors is the possession of this kind of perfection, only seeks perfectly imaginary and transient things; and even if these remain his property all his lifetime, they do not give him any perfection.

The second kind is more closely related to man's body than the first. It includes the perfection of the shape, constitution, and form of man's body; the utmost evenness of temperaments, and the proper order and strength of his limbs. This kind of perfection must likewise be excluded from forming our chief aim; because it is a perfection of the body, and man does not possess it as man, but as a living being; he has this property besides in common with the lowest animal; and even if a person possesses the greatest possible strength, he could not be as strong as a mule, much less can he be as strong as a lion or an elephant; he, therefore, can at the utmost have strength that might enable him to carry a heavy burden, or break a thick substance, or do similar things, in which there is no great profit whatever from this kind of perfection.

The third kind of perfection is more closely connected with

man himself than the second perfection. It includes moral perfection, the highest degree of excellency in man's character. Most of the precepts aim at producing this perfection; but even this kind is only a preparation for another perfection, and is not sought for its own sake. For all moral principles concern the relation of man to his neighbor; the perfection of man's moral principles is, as it were, given to man for the benefit of mankind. Imagine a person being alone, and having no connection whatever with any other person, all his good moral principles are at rest, they are not required, and give man no perfection whatever. These principles are only necessary and useful when man comes in contact with others.

The fourth kind of perfection is the true perfection of man; the possession of the highest intellectual faculties; the possession of such notions which lead to true metaphysical opinions as regards God. With this perfection man has obtained his final object; it gives him true human perfection; it remains to him alone; it gives him immortality, and on its account he is called man. Examine the first three kinds of perfection, you will find that, if you possess them, they are not your property, but the property of others; according to the ordinary view, however, they belong to you and to others; but the last kind of perfection is exclusively yours; no one else owns any part of it. "They shall be only thine own, and not strangers' with thee" (Proverbs 5:17). Your aim must, therefore, be to attain this (fourth) perfection that is exclusively yours, and you ought not to continue to work and weary yourself for that which belongs to others, whilst neglecting your soul until it has lost entirely its original purity through the dominion of the bodily powers over it.

The prophets have likewise explained unto us these things and have expressed the same opinion on them as the philosophers. They say distinctly that perfection in property, in health, or in character, is not a perfection worthy to be sought as a cause of pride and glory for us; that the knowledge of God, that is, true wisdom, is the only perfection which we should seek, and in which we should glorify ourselves. Jeremiah, referring to these four kinds of perfection, says: "Thus saith the Lord, Let not the wise man glory in his wisdom, neither let the mighty man glory in his might, let not the rich man glory in his riches; but let him that glorieth glory in this, that he understandeth and knoweth me" (Jeremiah 9:22, 23). See how the prophet arranged them according to their estimation in the eyes of the multitude. The rich man occupies the first rank; next is the mighty man; and then the wise man; that is, the man of good moral principles: for in the eyes of the multitude, who are addressed in these words, he is likewise a great man. This is the reason why the three classes are enumerated in this order. (Guide III, 53)

OBITER DICTA

When I have a difficult subject before me–when I find the road narrow, and can see no other way of teaching a well-established truth except by pleasing one intelligent man and displeasing ten thousand fools–I prefer to address myself to the one man, and to take no notice whatever of the condemnation of the multitude. (Guide, Introduction)

A truth, once established by proof, neither gains force by the consent of all scholars, nor loses certainty because of the general dissent. (Guide II, 15)

It is in fact ignorance, or a kind of madness, to weary our minds with striving to discover things which are beyond our reach. (Guide II, 24)

He who has studied insufficiently, and teaches and acts according to his defective knowledge, is to be considered as if he sinned knowingly. (Guide III, 41)

Do not consider a thing as proof because you find it written in books; for just as a liar will deceive with his tongue, he will not be deterred from doing the same thing with his pen. They are utter fools who accept a thing as convincing proof simply because it is in writing. (Iggeret Teman, Responsa II, 5d)

The truth of a thing does not become greater by its frequent repetition, nor is it lessened by lack of repetition. (Tehiyat HaMetim, Responsa II, 9d)

It is through the intellect that the human being has the capacity of honoring God. (Commentary on Mishnah, Hagigah II, 1)

The wise man is a greater asset to a nation than is a king. (Commentary on Mishnah, Horayot III, end)

Wisdom is the consciousness of self. (Guide I, 53)

Let the truth and right by which you are apparently the loser be preferable to you to the falsehood and wrong by which you are apparently the gainer. (Ethical Will, Responsa II, 38c)

Moral conduct is a preparation for intellectual progress, and only a man whose character is pure, calm, and steadfast can attain to intellectual perfection – that is, acquire correct conceptions. (Guide I, 34)

A miracle cannot prove that which is impossible; it is useful only as a confirmation of that which is possible. (Guide III, 24)

It is of great advantage that man should know his station, and not erroneously imagine that the whole universe exists for him alone. (Guide III, 12)

It is to be feared that those who become great in riches and comfort generally fall into the vices of insolence and haughtiness, and abandon all good principles. (Guide III, 39)

It is in the nature of man to strive to gain money and to increase it; and his great desire to add to his wealth and honor is the chief source of misery for man. (Guide III, 39)

It is a natural phenomenon that we find consolation in our misfortune when the same misfortune or a greater one has befallen another person. (Guide III, 40)

It is, indeed, a fact that the transition from trouble to ease gives more pleasure than continual ease. (Guide III, 24)

PART V

MEDIEVAL NIGHT

INTRODUCTION

The great civilization of the Arabs faded out in the thirteenth century, and with it went the tolerance that had nurtured Israel's "Golden Age." Beset now by Turkish barbarism in the East, and Christian bigotry in the West, the Jews no longer dared look afield for wisdom. They felt they had to retreat to their old fortress of ritual, and try to live there off their own traditional lore.

How well they succeeded is made clear by what they produced during the next five hundred years. The quantity of their literary output remained as prodigious as ever, but the quality fell off. One original intellect to arise throughout this period was Spinoza, and he was promptly read out of the fold. It is safe to say that Maimonides would have met a similar fate had he appeared during these centuries, for we know what happened to his greatest book. The Guide for the Perplexed *was either reviled or ignored by all save the most intrepid scholars, and even these read it with trembling hearts. For that book urged them to gird up their intellects and follow the path of reason—which was a strange path leading no one knew where. It seemed safer in this time of darkness to take the hand of tradition and walk in the way of faith.*

So there was relatively little scientific inquiry now, or philosophical reflection. Instead there was dogged ardor for legalistic research, and flaring passion for theosophical speculation. A body of notions known as the Kabbalah, *which had been furtively growing in Israel for well over a thousand years, now suddenly burst into the open and captured innumerable scholarly minds. It claimed to contain the wisdom secretly "received" by successive generations of initiates from certain ancient Jewish mystics to whom it had been divinely "revealed."*

In at least one respect there was no decline, and that was in the insistence on the primacy of ethics. Despite the inordinate absorption in ritualism and mysticism which characterized these centuries, wisdom in the classic sense still survived. Though shut out by the world and walled in by themselves, though hounded and bloodied and all but exterminated, the Jews never ceased to ponder the problem of worthy morals.

CHAPTER 42

SAYINGS FROM THE ZOHAR

The Zohar ("Radiance") is an esoteric commentary on the Pentateuch which became the sacred handbook of the medieval Jewish mystics. It interprets the scriptural text in purely theosophical terms, and though ostensibly the product of a second-century miracle-working Rabbi, Shimon ben Yohai, it was almost certainly compiled by a thirteenth-century Spanish Kabbalist named Moses de Leon. Its ideas are drawn from many foreign sources, but most of all from Indian literature. The Zohar, indeed, tries to read into the Five Books of Moses a greater emphasis on practical ethics. With all his insistence on the primacy of ecstatic union with God, the compiler of the Zohar could not forget the importance of service to mankind. Apparently even to this impassioned theosophist, faith had meaning only insofar as it was supported by works.

Since the mystical is excluded by definition from this anthology, I quote here only from the ethical sayings in the Zohar.[1]

ON VIRTUE AND CHARITY

If a man walks in the ways of the Lord, but transgresses by accident, every creature below and above helps to conceal it. (Zohar, 3:101a)

---

[1]The majority of the quotations are taken from the *Talmudic Anthology* by Louis I. Newman and Samuel Spitz.

When a man steps down from his bed, he should say to himself: "Guard thy feet when thou walkest." (Zohar, 4:175b)

A good intention is accounted as a good deed. (Zohar, 1:28b)

Woe unto him against whom the poor man makes complaint to his Heavenly Master, for the poor man is nearest to the king. (Zohar, 2:86b)

He who lengthens the life of a poor man has his own life lengthened when his time to die arrives. (Zohar, 3:85a)

Neglect not thine own poor in order to give to strangers who are poor. (Zohar, 4:206a)

The world was created for the sake of those who are ashamed to do evil. (Tikkun Zohar, Introduction 12b)

ON PIETY AND PRAYER

Who are the pious? Those who consider each day as their last on earth and repent accordingly. (Zohar, 1:220a)

Why is Israel like a worm? Because the worm's sole strength lies in its mouth. So is it with Israel [for it has the power of prayer]. (Zohar, 1:178a)

Woe to him who carries on conversation in the synagogue. He shows us that he does not belong there; he diminishes the faith; he has no share in the God of Israel; he proves that he has no God. (Zohar, 1:256a)

Tears break through the gates and doors of heaven. (Zohar, 2:245b)

Not all tears come before the King. Sullen tears, and tears accompanying the petition for vengeance do not ascend on high; but tears of entreaty and patience, and tears beseeching relief, cleave the very heavens, open the portals, and ascend to the King of Kings. (Zohar Hadash to Ruth, 80a)

ON LOVE AND MARRIAGE

A man fell in love with a woman who resided in the street of the tanners. If she had not lived there, he would never have entered this evil-smelling section; but, since she dwells there, the street seems to him like the street of the perfumers. (Zohar, 3:116b)

He who loves without jealousy does not truly love. (Zohar, 3:245)

God creates new worlds constantly. In what way? By causing marriages to take place. (Zohar, 1:89a)

When a soul is sent down from heaven, it is a combined male and female soul. The male part enters the male child and the female part enters the female. If they are worthy, God causes them to reunite in marriage. This is true mating. (Zohar, 3:43b)

The Holy Spirit can rest only upon a married man, because an unmarried man is but half a man, and the Holy Spirit does not rest upon that which is imperfect. (Zohar Hadash, 4:50b)

A man should marry and have children so that he may not go alone to the World-to-Come. (Zohar Hadash, 5:59a)

A man should build himself a home, plant himself a vineyard, and then bring into the home a bride. Fools are they who marry while they have no secure livelihood. (Zohar Hadash, 1:4b)

ON PARENTS AND CHILDREN

Honor thy father and thy mother, even as thou honorest God; for all three have been partners in thy creation. (Zohar, 3:93a)

Because Esau respected his father, his descendants rule the world. (Zohar, 1:146b)

A man without children is like a piece of wood, which though kindled does not burn or give out light. (Zohar, 1:187a)

A man appreciates the love of his grandchildren more than the love of his children. (Zohar, 1:233a)

If a man has a son in this world, he does not feel lonely in the World-to-Come. (Zohar Hadash to Ruth, 84a)

Gehenna has no power over him who leaves a learned son to practice good deeds. (Zohar Hadash to Ruth, 89a)

ON LEARNING

Who is learned?
He who is never at a loss when he is asked a question.
Who is wise?
He who respects his teacher.
Who has understanding?
He who reads everything and knows more than his own specialty. (Zohar, 2:201a)

No one is so poor as he who is ignorant of the Torah and its commandments, for this is all that can be considered as wealth. (Zohar, 2:93a)

He who rears his son to study Torah, and takes him twice daily to the school, is as if he observed the Torah twice daily. (Zohar, 1:105a)

Sages are higher than prophets, for prophecy does not abide with a man continuously. Wisdom, however, remains with the sage at all times. (Zohar, 2:6b)

If a man praises himself, it is a sign that he knows nothing. (Zohar, 4:193)

A pseudosage is like a donkey that carries a load of books. (Zohar Hadash, Tikkun, 70)

ON SIN AND THE EVIL IMPULSE

The greatest sinner is he who regrets his previous goodness. (Zohar, 3:101a)

Why does a man have fear? Because his sins break his courage and he has no strength left. (Zohar, 1:202a)

This is the way of everyone who does evil: when he sees evil approaching him, he is terrified for the moment, but immediately after, he returns to his wickedness. (Zohar, 1:110b)

If a man sins in secret, God takes pity on him. If he repents, God forgives and forgets his sin; but if he does not repent, God causes his transgression to be known in public. (Zohar, 1:66a)

He who warns the wicked, even if his warning be unheeded, has rescued himself from blame; but the wicked will be caught in the snare of his own sins. (Zohar, 1:68a)

Even in the Millennium we can hope only for the weakening of the Evil Impulse, not for its total extinction. (Zohar, 1:128b)

When the Evil Impulse comes to thee, it is like iron as yet cold. If thou dost not drive it forth, it soon becomes molten within thee, as if transformed by fire. (Zohar, 5:267b)

To what may the Evil Impulse be compared? To a man who comes to a door, opens it, and if no one halts him, enters as if he were an invited guest. If no one still objects, he gives orders as if he were the master of the house. (Zohar, 5:267b)

The Good Impulse seeks the joy of the Torah; the Evil Impulse, the joy of women, wine and arrogance. (Zohar, 1:202a)

He is called a man who subdues his evil desires. (Zohar, 2:128a)

The Evil Impulse is like a cake of yeast. The yeast is placed at one spot in the dough, but it ferments throughout it. The Evil Impulse does likewise. (Zohar, 2:182a)

Had the Israelites not worshipped the Golden Calf and drawn upon themselves the Evil Impulse, they would have lost the desire to beget children, and there would have been no other generations henceforth. (Zohar, 1:61a)

It is forbidden us to pray to God that He send death to the wicked. If God had removed from the world the idolatrous

Terah before he begat Abraham, there would have been no Israel, no Torah, no Messiah, and no Prophets. (Zohar Hadash, 105)

VARIOUS ADMONITIONS

He who returns evil for good, shall not evil go forth from his abode? He who returns evil for evil acts wrongly. He should have patience, and God will give him help on this account. (Zohar, 1:201a)

Hunger overtakes the world when mercy is not found in justice. (Zohar, 1:81b)

There is no true justice unless mercy is part of it. (Zohar, 4:146b)

If there be quarreling among men, even God's anger does not frighten them. (Zohar, 1:76b)

If a man in his anger breaks something, the broken object represents a sacrifice on the altar of Satan. (Zohar, 2:163b)

He whose face is inflamed with anger shows that the Evil Spirit burns within him. (Zohar, 4:179a)

How shall a man know whom to bring near, or whom to keep far from himself? Let him watch people when they become angry, for then their true character becomes manifest. (Zohar, 2:182b)

What is the sign of a proud man? He never praises any one. (Zohar, 4:193b)

He who strives to attain that which is not for him loses that which was intended for him. (Zohar, 4:176a)

Regard thy table as the table before the Lord. Chew well, and hurry not. (Zohar, 4:246a)

A man should address another in the language which the latter understands. He should not use a literary form of speech to an uneducated person, and crude language to the learned. (Zohar, 2:80a)

A judge who listens to one litigant when the other is not present is as if he believed in an idol in addition to the true God. (Zohar, 1:179b)

He who withholds the hire of the poor worker is as if he had snatched the soul of a man and his family. He shortens their lives, and his own life too will be shortened. (Zohar, 3:85a)

As soon as the day's work was over, Rav Hammuna would gather his laborers and give them their pay, saying: "Here, take your souls."

If a laborer did not wish to take his money at that time, the rabbi would insist that he take it. He would say: "Thou canst not deposit with me thy body; how much the more thy soul!" (Zohar, 3:85)

God accepts repentance for all sins, except the sin of imposing a bad name upon another. (Zohar, 3:53a)

Do not praise a man if he deserve it not, for thus wilt thou cause him shame. (Zohar, 1:232b)

MISCELLANEOUS SAYINGS

A rich man who is afflicted with sickness is called a poor man; likewise, one who has lost his reason. (Zohar, 5:273b)

The ideal man has the strength of a male and the compassion of a female. (Zohar, 4:145b)

In the day of death, a man considers that he has lived but a single day. (Zohar, 1:98b)

What is the sign of a foolish man? He talks too much. (Zohar, 4:193b)

The eyes and ears of man are not always dependent upon man's willpower; but a man's tongue is always dependent upon his will. (Zohar, 1:195a)

Silence is restful. It gives rest to the heart, the lungs, the larynx, the tongue, the lips, and the mouth. (Zohar, 4:173a)

A man's soul testifies during the night whatsoever he does during the day. (Zohar, 1:92b)

There is no smoke without a fire. (Zohar, 1:70)

A river filled with water does not freeze as quickly as a river with little water. (The thoroughly learned will not grow cold to religion like the half-learned.) (Zohar, 1:152a)

The acts of the leader are the acts of the nation. If the leader is just, the nation is just; if he is unjust, the nation too is unjust and is punished for the sins of the leader. (Zohar, 2:47a)

Throw a bone to a dog and he will lick the dust on your feet. (Zohar, 3:63)

It is the way of a dog that if he is hit by a stone, he bites a fellow dog. (Zohar, 1:149)

There is no Sitra Ahara (unclean spirit) that has not a thin thread of the Sitra Kadisha (Holy Spirit). There is no fantasy without a kernel of wheat (truth) in the mass of chaff (untruths). (Zohar, Tosefta, 2:69b)

CHAPTER 43

THE ADMONITIONS OF JUDAH THE PIOUS

Judah ben Samuel HeHasid ("the Pious") was a renowned German Kabbalist and ethical writer who died in Regensburg in 1217. Though acquainted with the rationalistic philosophy cultivated by his colleagues in Spain and North Africa, he preferred to steep himself in mysticism, convinced that thus alone could he attain true wisdom and perfect solace. His chief claim to fame is his reputed authorship of a work entitled, Sefer Hasidim, *"Book of the Pious," a rambling treatise full of moral reflections, theosophical flights, and peasant superstitions. The following passage, translated by Prof. B. Halper, is typical of that work at its best.*[1]

SINFUL MEEKNESS

There is a kind of meekness which inherits Gehenna, and causes the heirs of the humble to inherit a burning fire in Gehenna; and what kind is that? If a man sees that his children, relatives, or pupils are of bad behavior, and it lies within his power to correct them, by reprimanding or by beating them, but he says to himself, "I shall rather be agreeable to them and not reprimand or beat them," most surely

[1] *Post-Biblical Hebrew Literature,* an anthology by B. Halper (Philadelphia, Jewish Publication Society, 1921), pp. 162–166.

then does he cause them to inherit Gehenna. For they will corrupt their way, and will do mischief even to their father and their mother, so that they will despise them, and curse the day wherein they were born. In connection with such a case it is written, "He that spareth the rod hateth his son" (Proverbs 13:24). It is also said that he who smites his grown-up son transgresses the injunction, "Put not a stumbling block before the blind" (Leviticus 19:14). But a son that is accustomed to reproofs of instruction, and is beaten while small, will not resent it if his father beats him when he is grown up . . .

There is another kind of meekness which likewise brings a man down to Gehenna. For instance, a man sits in a court of justice, and knows that the judges are in error, or a private man knows that the court is in error, but says, "How shall I go and put them to shame?" Or a man knows that the judges are not well versed in law, while he is well versed, and when they say to him, "Sit with us that we may not go astray," he replies, "I shall not take a seat, for ye are well versed." It is obvious that if they go astray, the sin is to be attached to him. Another instance is when a man hears that the congregation speak falsely, and he says, "Who am I that I should correct them?" Behold, it is written, "And in they majesty prosper, ride on, in behalf of truth and humility of righteousness" (Psalm 45:5). From this we infer that there is a kind of humility which is not righteousness.

SINFUL CHARITY

There is a kind of charity which is pernicious; and what kind is that? One who gives alms to adulterers or to a glutton or a drunkard . . . He who supplies weapons of destruction to murderers is regarded as if he himself had committed murder . . . He who gives food to robbers is like their accomplice. Similarly, he who gives alms to adulterers is regarded as though he had aided them and brought them together, for they take the money that is given to them, and offer it as a hire to harlots. It is also said that a man should give no alms at all rather than give it publicly. In a similar sense it is also said that if a man who cannot pay his debts gives alms, it is obvious that his charity is robbery.

SINFUL PIETY

There is a kind of piety which is bad. For instance, a man whose hands are unclean sees a holy book fall into the fire, and says, "It is better that it should be burned," and does not touch the book. Another instance has also been cited: a man sees a woman drown in the river, and says, "It is better that she should drown than that I should touch her."[2]

There is also false piety. For instance: a man brings out a Scroll of the Law into the public thoroughfare on the Sabbath on account of a fire; or when a man says: "How shall I save a man's life and profane the Sabbath?"

SINFUL KINDNESS

A favor sometimes turns out to be harmful and is regarded as an evil for its author and his offspring. In what manner is it? For instance, a man arranges for sinners to be permitted to dwell in the city. Since this is bad for the people of the city, it is evident that he and his offspring will stumble over them, and they will do mischief to his offspring . . .

Another instance: he who does a good deed in order to be honored, and to praise himself thereby.

---

[2]This refers to the taboo forbidding a male to touch any female during her menses.

CHAPTER 44

THE TESTAMENT OF NAHMANIDES

Moses ben Nahman (1194–1270), commonly known as Nahmanides, was a renowned Talmudist who served for many years as Chief Rabbi of Catalonia. Though well versed in philosophy and science, his inherent bent was toward mysticism, and this coupled with his overpowering reverence for tradition made him side with those who sought to excommunicate all disciples of Maimonides. Toward the close of his life, old Nahmanides took refuge in Palestine, and it was from there that he wrote the following letter of admonition to his eldest son.[1]

Hear, my son, the instruction of thy father, and forsake not the teaching of thy mother! Accustom thyself to speak in gentleness to all men at all times. Thus wilt thou be saved from anger, which is so fertile a cause of sin. As our Sages say: "Over the man of wrath rules every manner of Hell, and it is written: 'Remove anger from thy heart, and (thus) put away evil from thy flesh.' "

Being delivered from anger, there will arise in thy heart the quality of humility, which is better than all things good! . . . For it is humility that impels thee always to lay to thine heart

[1]The translation is from *Hebrew Ethical Wills* by Israel Abrahams, vol. 1, p. 95 ff.

the memory of whence thou didst come, and whither thou must go. It is humility that warns thee that in life thou art but a worm, and the more so in death. It is humility that warns thee that the One before whom thou must be judged and called to account is the King of Glory.

Accordingly, I will explain how thou must habituate thyself to humility in thy daily life. Let thy voice be low, and thy head bowed; let thine eyes be turned earthwards and thy heart heavenwards. Do not stare in the face of him whom thou dost address. Every man should seem in thine eyes as one greater than thyself. Whether he be wise or wealthy, it is thy duty to show him respect. If he be poorer than thee, or thou wiser than he, think in thy heart that thou art the more guilty, he the more innocent. If he sin, it is from error; if thou sin, it is with design.

Read this letter once a week, and be as regular in carrying out its injunctions. Walk by its aid forever after the Lord, blessed be He! Then wilt thou prosper in all thy ways, and be held worthy of all the good which is treasured up for the righteous!

CHAPTER 45

THE LAMENT OF JEDAIAH OF BÉZIERS

Jedaiah ben Abraham (1270–1340), poet, philosopher, and of course–physician, was a typical Jewish savant of southern France during this period. Reared in an atmosphere of relative enlightenment–Moorish Spain lay just across the Pyrenees–he became an ardent rationalist, and an eloquent partisan of the Maimonidean writings. During his middle years, however, the steady resurgence of obscurantism among the Jews–due directly to the sharp recrudescence of fanaticism among the non-Jews–seemed to induce a growing despair in his outlook on life. This is seen most clearly in a long didactic poem entitled Behinat HaOlam, *"The Examination of the World," which he composed shortly after all the Jews were ordered banished from France (1306). The following passage, translated by Prof. B. Halper, is taken from the eighth chapter of that work.*[1]

The world is a tempestuous sea of immense depth and breadth, and time is a frail bridge constructed over it, the beginning of which is fastened with the cords of chaos that preceded existence, while the end thereof is to behold eternal bliss, and to be enlightened with the light of the King's countenance. The width of the bridge is a cubit of a man, and

[1]*Post-Biblical Hebrew Literature,* an anthology by B. Halper (Philadelphia, Jewish Publication Society, 1921), pp. 183–187.

it lacks borders. And thou, son of man, against thy will art thou living, and art continually traveling over it, since the day thou hast become a man.

When thou considerest that thy path is narrow, and that there is no way to turn either to the right or to the left, shalt thou glory in position and fame? When thou seest that destruction and death are unto thee a wall on thy right and on thy left, shall thy heart endure or shall thy hands be strong? Even if thou pridest thyself on the desirable acquisitions and the abundance of possessions which thou hast amassed and discovered with thine arm, hast sought with thy bow, and hast gone down to possess with thy net, what wilt thou do against the tempest of the sea and the roaring thereof, when it rages, overflows, and sweeps on, so that even thy dwelling place is about to be broken? Glory thou over this immense sea in whose midst thou art; rule over the horsemen and chariots thereof; go out now, I pray thee, to fight against it. For even while thou reelest to and fro, and staggerest with the wine of thy rebellious arrogance which deceived thee, and with the juice of the pomegranates of thy haughtiness which misled thee, thou wilt soon incline slightly toward one side or another, and wilt perish in the terrible depths, and none will seek thy blood from them. Thou wilt go from abyss to abyss, perplexed in the depths of the sea, and none shall say, "Restore."

Shall I trust in falsehood, shall I rely upon the staff of the bruised reed, to consider a lodging place of wayfares like this as a strong fortress and a king's sanctuary, the wing of the flea as a point of diamond, a spider's web as coral and crystal? When thou seest that the days are pleasant, that time frisks and dances, that the moment goes on to give thee repose, and that the hour frolics and rejoices before thee in the world, thou wilt despise the latter days in thy heart. But it is in falsehood that thou trustest: thou seest the shadow of a gourd as though it were a high and lofty mountain. Is it for these things that thou hast cast the soul behind thy back, and hast turned thy way toward the pleasures of the flesh which cause grief? . . .

Why shall I covet the earth which is like Admah, and pleasure which is like Zeboim (Deuteronomy 29:22)? Her wrath is stored up in her company; her conspiracy is tightly fastened to her covenant; her sweetness and honeycomb are like chaff before the whirlwind; her end and conclusion are eternal disgrace and everlasting shame. Moreover, how can my flesh be delighted when it is announced to me that I shall live long, since there is no escape from the destruction of death? What avails the age of strength, since at the end thereof come wrath and the grave? What pleasure is there in eighty years, since by their side is the shadow of death? What cheerfulness is there in ninety years, since there is no salvation in their border? Shall ants that languish and perish, and creeping things that melt away like water, exalt themselves to reign? Even if they endure for a day or for two days, will they never be devoured with the sword? How can the fields of Sodom and the sheaves of Gomorrah prosper?

CHAPTER 46

THE PLAINT OF KALONYMOS

Kalonymos ben Kalonymos ben Meir, poet, philosopher and scientist, was born in southern France in 1286, and died there some time after 1328. Like his elder contemporary, Jedaiah of Béziers, he was reared in the rationalist tradition of the Arabs, and devoted much of his time to translating their works. Like the other, however, his attitude toward life became increasingly embittered because of the reactionary tendencies of his age. He seems to have tried to vent some of his despair in a lengthy prose poem entitled Even Bohan, *"Stone of Investigation," from which the following passage is taken.*[1]

O my heart, hearken unto this, and consider. Knowest thou not that youth lasts not forever, and that the end of man is to die? A brother cannot redeem, none has power, and the riches of the gold of Sheba and the heights of the mountains profit not. Even if I ascend into Heaven, or make my bed in Sheol, I shall never be able to redeem my life from destruction. Behold, a day is coming, a day of vengeance and a year of recompense, in which He will fill me with bitterness. There is no escape, for the snares of death will overtake me within the straits . . .

O my heart, if not now, when shall I seek rest for myself?

[1] *Ibid*, pp. 198–201.

Shall I do it in the days of hoary hair, when the strength fails? The branch of all mortals shall wither; even the tender and delicate shall be dried up and wither when they grow old; their skin shall shrivel. Will God create a new thing in me, that I may have youth after I have grown old? Behold, I was formed out of clay; nature fashioned me small in my dimensions; I have the face of a man, not the face of an eagle that renews its youth at the time of old age. . . .

My head which, while in its freshness, was as the most fine gold, and upon which brown hair was grown, has white branches now, because hoariness, snowing in its midst, is scattered over it. In the prime of my life, while still in its full strength, my hair was plucked and torn out, and was moved out of its place. Shall my stature, which was like a palm tree, and my back, which was straighter than a hedge, now be bowed down as a rush, so that none can raise it? My locks, which were curly and intertwined, fall out and are scattered. The tresses of my head, which were desirable as gold, and the hair thereof which was like purple, has become scanty, and through its departure has left breaches. What shall I do when God arises to seek my iniquity? For behold, my sins shall surely be found out.

CHAPTER 47

THE TESTAMENT OF JUDAH BEN ASHER

Judah ben Asher (1270–1349), noted German Talmudist, spent most of his life in Spain, where he served for many years as rabbi of Toledo. As had become the custom, he filled his last will and testament with ethical admonitions, and it is from this document that the following passages are taken.[1]

So I will open with a voice of thanksgiving, I, Judah, to the Rock whose works are awe-inspiring . . . and who, ere I was born, remembered me for good. My mother dreamed how she was told that she would bear a son, and was asked whether she wished him to be wise or wealthy. She chose wisdom; and though in reality dreams speak vain things, for I learned not wisdom, yet in a certain deceptive sense the dream was fulfilled. The world imagines that I am a scholar, one who giveth goodly words! Wealth, too, the Lord, blessed be He, hath bestowed on me beyond the ordinary, in that He hath made me content with my lot.

Now therefore, ye children, hearken unto me, for happy are they that keep my ways. Come, listen unto me, I will teach you the fear of the Lord. Look unto the rock whence ye were

[1]Translated in Israel Abrahams's *Hebrew Ethical Wills,* vol. 1.

hewn, and to the hole of the pit, whence ye were digged. Why, forsooth, were ye brought into this world? Not merely to eat and drink and wear fine linen and embroideries, but for the service of the God who hangeth the earth over nothing. . . . Food to a man is like oil to a lamp: if it have much, it shines; if little, it is quenched. Yet, sooner is the lamp extinguished by too much than too little oil. Therefore, be diligently on your guard against overfeeding. More heinous than homicide is suicide. Gross eating is as dangerous to the body as a sword—besides which it bars one from occupation with the Law of God and the reverence due to Him . . .

Make it your firm custom to study the Torah at fixed times, probe deeply into its contents, and endeavor to communicate daily a portion of the rabbinic law to others; for to accomplish this you will be compelled to make your own knowledge precise, moreover by the exposition orally it will be fixed in your memories. Always repeat, if possible going back to the beginning of the tractate. Our sages of blessed memory have said (with regard to perfect service): "He who repeats his chapter a hundred times cannot be compared to him who repeats it a hundred and one times." . . .

Think not in your heart that the Torah is an inheritance from your fathers and needs no personal effort to win it. The matter is not so. If ye toil not therein, ye shall not acquire, and more than ordinary will be your punishment, in that ye forsake your family tradition. So we read in tractate Nedarim: "Why do not learned fathers invariably beget learned children? Rabbi Joseph answered: 'So that people shall not say, Your Torah is inherited from your Fathers.' "

See to it diligently that ye be not among the four classes who behold not the divine presence: liars, scoffers, hypocrites, and slanderers.

(1) The class of liars: Let no falsehood or lying be found among you, but let truth and fidelity be a girdle round your loins. . . .

(2) The class of scoffers: From all levity and frivolity guard yourselves, for man is forbidden to fill his mouth with laughter in this world. Furthermore, play no game for money, for that is a form of robbery. . . .

(3) The class of hypocrites: Never flatter any man, nor show partiality to any in judgment. . . .

(4) The class of slanderers: Avoid this to the utmost, for slander leads to many sins, and most men are given to it. As our rabbis of blessed memory said, "Many are prone to theft, and a few to incontinence, but all to slander." Further they said: "Let no man praise another (too much), for it may result in disclosing something to his discredit." In all such matters I have not found anything better for a person than silence. Even, then, let a man bethink himself before he speak, uttering his words if they be profitable, suppressing them if they would profit nothing. Silent above all must he be if speech would actually harm. . . .

Be punctilious in honoring all men, for therein shall you find your own honor, for God Himself has declared: "them that honor me will I honor." People remarked to a sage: "We have observed that thou ever showest honor to every man"; and he replied: "I have never come across one in whom I failed to recognize superiority over myself; therefore, have I shown him respect. Were he older, I said he has done more good than I. Were he richer, I said he has been more charitable. Were he younger, I said I have sinned more. Were he poorer, I said he has suffered heavier tribulations. Were he wiser, I honored him for his wisdom. Were he not wiser, I said his fault is the lighter." Take this to heart and understand it.

CHAPTER 48

THE TESTAMENT OF ELAZAR OF MAYENCE

The following passages are taken from a last will and testament left, not by a rabbi, but by an ordinary pious Jew of the fourteenth century. The admonitions appear to have been fairly conventional, and help to explain why the Jews were able to survive the horrors of life in medieval Europe.[1]

These are the things which my sons and daughters shall do at my request. They shall go to the house of prayer morning and evening. . . . So soon as the service is over, they shall occupy themselves a little with the Torah, the Psalms, or with works of charity. Their business must be conducted honestly, whether in dealings with Jew or Gentile. They must be courteous in their manners, and prompt to accede to every honorable request. They must not talk more than is necessary, by this will they be saved from slander, falsehood, and frivolity. They shall give an exact tithe of all their possessions. They shall never turn away a poor man empty-handed, but must give him what they can, be it much or little. If he beg a night's lodging, and they know him not, let them provide him with

[1]Translated in Israel Abrahams's *Hebrew Ethical Wills*, vol. 1.

the wherewithal to pay an innkeeper. Thus shall they satisfy the needs of the poor in every possible way.

My daughters must obey scrupulously the rules applying to women; modesty, sanctity, reverence should mark their married lives. They should carefully watch for the signs of the beginning of their periods and keep separate from their husbands at such times. Marital intercourse must be modest and holy, with a spirit of restraint and delicacy, in reverence and silence. They shall be very punctilious and careful with their ritual bathing, taking with them women friends of worthy character. They shall cover their eyes until they reach their home, on returning from the bath, in order not to behold anything of an unclean nature. They must respect their husbands, and must be invariably amiable to them. Husbands, on their part, must honor their wives more than themselves, and treat them with tender consideration.

If they can by any means contrive it, my sons and daughters should live in communities, and not isolated. . . . Even if compelled to beg the money to pay a teacher, they must not let the young, of both sexes, go without instruction in the Torah. Marry your children, O my sons and daughters, as soon as their age is ripe, to members of respectable families. Let no child of mine hunt after money by making a low match for that object. . . .

As to games of chance, I entreat my children never to engage in such pastimes. During the leisure of the festival weeks they may play for trifling stakes in kind, and the women may amuse themselves similarly on New Moons, but never for money.

In their relation to women, my sons must behave continently, avoiding mixed bathing and mixed dancing and all frivolous conversation, while my daughters ought not to speak much with strangers, nor jest, nor dance with them. They ought to be always at home, and not be gadding about. They should not stand at the door, watching whatever passes. I ask, I command, that the daughters of my house be never without work to do, for idleness leads first to boredom, then to sin; but let them spin, or cook, or sew.

I earnestly beg my children to be tolerant and humble to all, as I was throughout my life. Should cause for dissension arise, be slow to accept the quarrel. Seek peace and pursue it with all the vigor at your command. Even if you suffer loss thereby, forbear and forgive, for God has many ways of feeding and sustaining his creatures. To the slanderer do not retaliate with counterattack; and though it be proper to rebut false accusations, yet is it most desirable to set an example of reticence. You yourselves must avoid uttering any slander, for so will you win affection. In trade be honest, never grasping at what belongs to another. For by avoiding these wrongs–scandal, falsehood, money-grubbing–men will surely find tranquillity and affection; and against all evils, silence is the best safeguard.

Now, my sons and daughters, eat and drink only what is necessary, as our good parents did, refraining from heavy meals, and holding the glutton in detestation. The regular adoption of such economy in food leads to economy in expenditure generally, with a consequent reluctance to pursue after wealth, but the acquisition of a contented spirit, simplicity in diet, and many good results. . . . Accustom yourselves and your wives, your sons and your daughters, to wear nice and clean clothes, that God and man may love and honor you. In this direction do not exercise too strict a parsimony. But on no account adopt foreign fashions in dress. After the manner of your fathers order your attire, and let your cloaks be broad without buckles attached.

Be on your guard concerning vows, and cautious as to promises. The breach of one's understandings leads to many lapses. Do not get into the habit of exclaiming "God!" but speak always of the "Creator, blessed be He"; and in all that you propose to do, today or tomorrow, add the proviso, "If the Lord wills, I shall do this thing." Thus, remember God's part in your life.

Whatever happiness befall you, be it in monetary fortune or in the birth of children, be it some signal deliverances or any other of the many blessings which may come to you, be not stolidly unappreciative, like dumb cattle that utter no word of gratitude. But offer praises to the Rock who has befriended you, saying: "O give thanks unto the Lord, for He is good, for His mercy endureth forever. Blessed art Thou, O Lord, who art good and dispensest good." . . .

Be very particular to keep your houses clean and tidy. I was always scrupulous on this point, for every injurious condition, and sickness and poverty, are to be found in foul dwellings. . . .

On holidays and festivals and Sabbaths seek to cheer the poor, the unfortunate, widows, and orphans, who should always be guests at your tables; their joyous entertainment is a religious duty. Let me repeat my warning against gossip and scandal; and as ye speak no scandal, so listen to none, for if there were no receivers there would be no bearers of slanderous tales; therefore, the reception and credit of slander is as serious an offense as the originating of it. . . .

I beg of you, my sons and daughters, my wife, and all the congregation, that no funeral oration be spoken in my honor. . . . Wash me clean, comb my hair, trim my nails, as I was wont to do in my lifetime, so that I may go clean to my eternal rest, as I went clean to the synagogue every Sabbath day. . . . At a distance of thirty cubits from the grave, they shall set my coffin on the ground, and drag me to the grave by a rope attached to the coffin. Every four cubits they shall stand and wait awhile, doing this in all seven times, so that I may find atonement for my sins. Put me in the ground at the right hand of my father, and if the space be a little narrow, I am sure that he loves me well enough to make room for me by his side. If this be altogether impossible, put me on his left, or near my grandmother, Yuta. Should this too be impractical, let me be buried by the side of my daughter.

CHAPTER 49

ABRAVANEL ON MONARCHISM

Don Isaac Abravanel (1437–1508) was one of those fascinating Jewish characters whose lives outromance the most romantic historical fiction. Scion of a distinguished line of Iberian Jewish statesmen–his father was the treasurer of Portugal–he spent his youth in religious and philosophical studies, and thereafter devoted his entire life to honest scholarship coupled with high finance. Succeeding to his father's office, he enjoyed both great honor and wealth until 1483, when a sudden shift on the throne compelled him to flee to Spain. There, after a spell of poverty during which he wrote an erudite work on Bible exegesis, he managed to win the favor of Queen Isabella of Castile–and amassed a second fortune. Again, however, his luck did not last, for he refused to convert to Christianity in 1492, and was once more forced to become a penniless refugee. This time he fled to Naples, where he acquired a third fortune as a royal treasurer, only to lose this in turn when the French captured the city. Years of wandering followed until finally, in republican Venice, he recouped his fortunes all over again–and died.

Here is a passage taken from one of the best known of his numerous writings, an extensive and very lucid commentary on the Bible. Though ostensibly an objective interpretation of a verse in Deuteronomy (17:15), it reflects more than a little of the author's bitter personal experience.[1]

[1]*Post-Biblical Hebrew Literature,* an anthology by B. Halper, (Philadelphia, Jewish Publication Society, 1921), pp. 221–223.

Behold, it behooves us to know whether a monarch is a necessity, inherently needed for the people, or whether it is possible to exist without him. The philosophers adopt the former opinion, and think that the service rendered by the king to the people in the political organization is the same as the relation of the heart to the body in animals possessing a heart, and as the relation of the First Cause to the entire universe.

Now if the investigators think that a government must be based on three things–first, unity; second, continuity; third, absolute power–then their conclusion as to the necessity of a monarch is indeed fallacious. For it is not impracticable that a people should have many leaders, united, agreeing, and concurring in one counsel, who should decide administrative and judicial matters. This militates against the first principle. Then, why should not their administration be for one year, or for three years, like the years of a hireling, or less than that?

When the turn of other judges and officers comes, these will be able to investigate whether the first ones have not failed in their trust, and whomever they condemn shall make good the wrong that was done. This militates against the second principle. Therefore, why should their power not be limited and regulated according to the laws and statutes? A common-sense principle tells us that when one man disagrees with the majority, the law is according to the majority. It is more likely that one man should trespass, through his folly, or strong temptations or anger, than that many men taking counsel should transgress. For if one of them turns aside from the right path, the others will protest against him. Moreover, since their administration is temporary and they must render account after a short while, the fear of man will be upon them.

What need is there of abstract arguments when experience is more forceful than logic? Behold the lands where the administration is in the hands of kings and you will observe their abominations and corruptions. Each king does that which is right in his own eyes, and the earth is filled with their wickedness. On the other hand, we see this day many lands where the administration is in the hands of judges. Temporary rulers are elected there, and over them is a chief against whom there is no rising up; they choose that which is right by definite regulations; they rule over the people, and decide concerning matters appertaining to war; none can withstand them. . . .

Dost thou not know, and has thou not heard, that there was a great country that had dominion over all the world? She conquered the whole earth and subdued it when her administration was in the hands of the numerous consuls who were faithful and held temporary office; but after an emporer was made to rule over it, it became tributary. . . . Even today Venice rules as a mistress, great among nations, a princess among the states; and the state of Florence is the glory of all lands. There are likewise other states, great and small, which have no king, and are governed by leaders elected for a fixed time.

Now in the elected governments in which there is nothing crooked or perverse, no man lifts his hand or his foot to commit any manner of trespass. They conquer countries with wisdom, understanding, and knowledge. All this proves that the existence of a monarch is not necessary; nay, it is harmful and a great danger. In a similar manner, Maimonides warned against the great dangers incurred in traveling on the seas and in serving kings, on account of the similarity that exists between the two in the possibility of danger, both being alike, the stormy wind on the ocean and the spirit of the ruler. . . .

I, therefore, think that kings were at first set up not by the people's elections, but by force. They made themselves masters, as if God, who is blessed, gave them the earth and the fullness thereof, and they leave it as an inheritance to their children after them and to their children's children forever, as if it were a plot of land which one acquires for money. . . .

CHAPTER 50

THE OATH OF AMATUS

Amatus Lusitanus (1511–1568) came of one of those innumerable Jewish families in Spain and Portugal which had converted to Christianity under duress during the late fifteenth century. Like most of the others, however, it had merely allowed itself to be baptized, not truly converted. Young Amatus was secretly reared in the faith of his ancestors, and given a good grounding in Jewish lore. He took up the profession of medicine, but fear of the Inquisition compelled him to flee his native land while still in his twenties. After many years of wandering, he settled in Rome, where his renown as a physician and scientist brought him the patronage of Pope Julius III. Eventually, however, he found it impossible to continue living the lie forced on him by Christian fanatacism, and took refuge in Salonica–then a Moslem city–where he was free at last to proclaim himself a Jew.

His voluminous medical records written in Latin contain the following statement of the spirit in which he carried on his work as a physician.[1]

I swear by the Eternal God and by His ten most holy commandments, which were given on Mount Sinai through Moses as lawgiver after the people had been freed from their bondage in Egypt, that I have at all times earnestly striven after

[1]Translated by Jacob R. Marcus, Ph.D., in his book *The Jew in the Medieval World* (Cincinnati, Sinai Press, 1938), pp. 317–319.

this one thing, namely, that benefit might spread forth to mankind; that I have praised no one, and censured no one, merely to indulge in private passions, unless zeal for truth demanded this. If I lie, may I incur the eternal wrath of God and his angel Raphael [the angel of healing], and may nothing in the medical art succeed for me according to my desires.

Concerning the remuneration, furthermore, which is commonly given to physicians, I have not been anxious for this, but I have treated many, not only zealously, but even without pay. I have unselfishly and unswervingly refused several rewards offered by many people, and have rather sought that the sick might, by my care and diligence, recover their lost health than that I might become richer by their liberality. All men have been considered equal by me of whatever religion they were, whether Hebrews, Christians, or the followers of the Moslem faith. [The Church law that Jews must not treat Christian patients was not always observed.]

As regards loftiness of station, that has never been a matter of concern to me, and I have accorded the same care to the poor as to those born in exalted rank. I have never brought about sickness. In diagnosis I have always said what I thought to be true. I have unduly favored no vendors of drugs, except, perhaps, those whom I knew to surpass the others by reason of their skill in their art or because of their natural qualities of mind. In prescribing drugs, I have exercised moderation in proportion as the powers of the sick man allowed. I have revealed to no one a secret entrusted to me; I have given no one a fatal draught. No woman has ever brought about an abortion by my aid; nothing base has been committed by me in any house where I was practicing. In short, nothing has been done by me which might be considered unbecoming an excellent and famous physician.

I have always held up to myself Hippocrates and Galen, the [ancient Greek] fathers of the medical art, as examples worthy of being followed by me, and the records of many other excellent men in the medical art have not been scorned by me. In my method of studying, I have been so eager that no task, however difficult, could lead me away from the reading of good authors, neither the loss of private fortune, nor frequent journeys, nor yet exile, which, as befits a philosopher, I have thus far borne with calm and invincible courage. The many students I have thus far had, I have always considered my sons, and have taught them very frankly, and have urged them to strive to conduct themselves like good men.

I have published my books on medical matters with no desire for profit, but I have had regard for this one thing, namely, that I might, in some measure, provide for the health of mankind. Whether I have succeeded in this, I leave to the judgment of others. At all events, I have held this always before me, and have given it chief place in my prayers.

Given at Thessalonica, in the year of the world 5319 [1559].

CHAPTER 51

THE SHULHAN ARUKH OF RABBI KARO

Persistent growth throughout the long centuries of persecution had finally made the holy Law so vast and complicated that it confused even the average learned Jew. Digests therefore became imperative, and eventually one was compiled which won acceptance throughout Israel. This was the work of an Iberian Jew named Joseph Karo (1488–1575) who, having been expelled from his native place because he would not submit to baptism, took refuge in the Near East. Karo's mind was extraordinarily ambivalent, being addicted, on the one hand, to the wildest mysticism, and on the other, to the most precise legalism. He claimed to be under the direct guidance of a heavenly mentor from whom he received instructions, and with whom he carried on discussions touching all sorts of personal matters. However, since the interpretation of the Law was supposed to be a strictly impersonal activity, he tried to carry that on without any occult intervention.

The climax of his lifelong labors as a legalist was the production of a popular digest entitled Shulhan Arukh *("Table of Order"), which codified all the rabbinic ordinances governing Jewish life and belief. It was immediately attacked by certain of his contemporaries, most notably a certain Rabbi Moses Isserles, who was the foremost authority in Poland. The latter objected to the book's exclusive emphasis on ancient ordinances, and neglect of the many later customs which were generally considered almost equally binding on the Jews. To prove his point, Isserles wrote a series of notes to the* Shulhan Arukh *supplying these omissions, and thus inadvertently made the book more attractive than ever. It was now so complete that not even the most carping critic could question its worth. Karo's text, with Isserles' glosses, remains to this day the definitive law code for Orthodox Jews throughout the globe.*

Despite that the Shulhan Arukh *is a purely nomistic work, the following brief excerpts will indicate to what an extent it is suffused with what is essentially ethical wisdom.*[1]

BLESSINGS OF THE CHARITABLE

No man is ever impoverished through giving alms, nor is evil or harm ever caused by it; as it is written, "And the work of righteousness shall be peace" (Isaiah 32:17).

Whosoever has compassion on the poor, the Holy One, blessed be He, has compassion on him.

(*Note by Isserles:* Let man realize that he himself is forever seeking sustenance at the hand of God, and just as God answers his prayer, so should he answer the prayer of the poor. Let him also realize that the world is a revolving sphere, and that eventually he or his son or his grandson may be reduced to poor circumstances.)

Charity prevents threatened punishment from Heaven, and in famine it delivereth from death. (Article 247:2–4)

OBLIGATIONS OF CHARITY

Everyone is obliged to contribute to charity. Even a poor man who is himself maintained by charity should give a portion of what he receives. If one gave less than his due, the court used to bring pressure to bear and punish him for contempt of court until he gave the amount assessed; and if he

---

[1]The passages are taken from a translation by Louis Feinberg as quoted in Abraham E. Millgram's *Anthology of Medieval Hebrew Literature* (Philadelphia, Associated Talmud Torahs, 1935), p. 295 ff.

persisted in his refusal, they would seize his goods to the amount (in his presence).

A man who gives more than his share to charity, or who straitens himself to pay the collector in order not to be embarrassed, from such a man it is forbidden to demand or claim his dues; and the *gabbai* who humiliates him by asking for it will be called to account in the future by the Holy One, blessed be He.

He who wishes to be deserving of divine reward shall conquer his evil inclinations and open wide his hand, and everything (done or given) in the name of heaven shall be of the best and the finest. If he build a house of worship, let it be more beautiful than his dwelling; if he feed a hungry one, let him give him to eat of the best and the sweetest on his table; if he clothe one naked, let him clothe him with one of his finest garments; if he consecrate anything, let him consecrate from the best of his property; and so, too, the Bible says: "All the fat is the Lord's." (Leviticus 3:16; Article 248:1, 7,8)

THE AMOUNT OF CHARITY

The amount of charity one should give is as follows: if one can but afford, let him give as much as is needed. Under ordinary circumstances, a fifth of one's property is most laudable. To give one-tenth is the average disposition; but to give less than one-tenth is niggardly. When the Rabbis said a "fifth" they meant a fifth of the property the first year only and a fifth of the profits in succeeding years.

(*Note by Isserles:* But a man should not give more than one-fifth for charity, so that he might not himself become a public charge. This refers only to his lifetime. Of course, at the time of death a man may leave for charity as much as he pleases.)

One should never give less than one-third of a shekel a year and if a man gives less than this, he does not fulfill the command to be charitable. (Article 249:1–2)

THE SPIRIT OF CHARITY

Charity should be given with a friendly countenance, with joy, and with a good heart; the giver should sympathize with the poor man, and should speak words of comfort to him. If he gives with a displeased countenance, he loses his reward.

If the poor man stretches out his hand and he has nothing to give him, he should not scold and raise his voice to him, but should speak gently to him and show him his goodness of heart; namely, that he wishes to give him something but cannot.

(*Note by Isserles:* It is forbidden to turn away a poor man entirely empty-handed. Let him give something, if only a fig, for it is written, "Oh, let not the oppressed return ashamed" (Psalm 74:21).)

If he can induce others to give, his reward is greater than the reward of the one who gives. (Article 249:3–5)

THE QUANTITY OF ALMS

How much is to be given to a poor man? Sufficient for his need in that which he lacks (Deuteronomy 15:8). Thus, if he is hungry, he should be fed; if he needs clothing, he should be clothed; if he lacks household utensils, they should be purchased for him; and even if he had been accustomed, before he was impoverished, to ride on horseback with a slave running before him, he should be furnished with a horse and a slave; and so each and every one should be supplied with what he needs. If it is fit to give him (merely) a slice of bread, give him a slice; if it is proper to give him dough, give him dough; if he ought to be provided with lodging, provide a bed for him. If it is fit to give him a warm meal, give him warm food; if cold lunch, then cold lunch. If he has to be fed (like an infant), then he must be fed. If he is unmarried and he comes to take a wife, the community should find him a mate; but first they should rent him a home, prepare him a bed, and furnish him with necessary household utensils, and then marry him off.

(*Note by Isserles:* It appears that all this applies to *gabbaim* over public funds or to many doing charitable work together, but every individual is not bound to satisfy all the needs of a poor man who may chance to come his way. What he ought to do is to arouse public interest in a worthy case; but if he lives far from men, he should give what he can afford.)

A poor woman who has an opportunity of marrying, shall receive not less than fifty *zuzim;* and if there is enough in the treasury, she should be maintained as honorably as is befitting her.

A pauper who begs from house to house should be given only a small sum from the *kupah.*

A poor man, who goes from place to place, shall receive not less than a loaf of bread. . . . If he remains overnight, he should be given a couch to sleep upon and a bolster under his head, and oil and small fruit; and if it is Sabbath, he should be provided with food for three meals, and oil, small fruit, fish and herbs; and if he is known (to be worthy), he should be given as much as it is befitting his honor.

If the poor in a city are numerous, and the rich say they should go and beg, and the middle classes say they should not beg but be supported by the members of the community in proportion to their wealth, the law is as the latter say. (Article 250:1–5)

THE DISTRIBUTION OF PUBLIC FUNDS

If a man and a woman ask for food, the woman is given the preference; and so, too, if they ask for clothing. So also, if two orphans, a man and a woman, come to be married, the woman is given the precedence.

If one comes and says, "Give me food,"no investigation is made to see that he is not an imposter, but he is given food at once. If he is destitute and asks for clothing, the case is investigated; and if he is found worthy, he is immediately furnished with raiment.

Two poor men who are required to give to charity, may pay their obligations by giving alms to one another.

(*Note by Isserles:* This refers to charity in the ordinary sense; but if, for some misdemeanor, the community imposes a fine upon them to give a certain sum to charity, they cannot give it to one another; for that would not be paying a fine.)

A congregation in need of a rabbi and a cantor, but unable to engage both, should give the preference to the former, provided he is a distinguished rabbi. . . . Otherwise, a cantor should be engaged.

(*Note by Isserles:* The rabbi should not be maintained out of the charity fund, as it is a disgrace both for him and for the city; but the community should provide him with another source of income. However, gifts of individuals are perfectly honorable.)

The community authorities may use even school funds, if necessary, for the payment of the annual per-capita tax to the commander of the city's troops because it is a matter of life and death; for if they will not come to terms with him now, many poor people, not having the wherewithal to pay, will be beaten and stripped naked. (Article 251:8, 10, 12–14)

WHO MAY RECEIVE CHARITY

One should always avoid charity and rather roll in misery than to depend upon the help of man. Thus, our Sages commanded, "Rather make thy Sabbath a weekday than be dependent on men." Even though he be scholarly and respectable, let him engage in some occupation, even an unpleasant occupation, so as not to need the help of man.

Whosoever is not in need of charity, but deceives the public and takes it, will be in actual need before his days are ended; and whosoever is so much in need of charity that he cannot live unless he receives it—as, for instance, a man who is old or sick or in constant pain—but takes none out of pride, is guilty of bloodshed and is responsible for his own life; so that he has nothing for his suffering, save punishment and sin. However, whosoever is in need of charity and suffers patiently and leads a pinched and humble life, so as not to become a burden to society, will live to help others some day; and it is with reference to such a person that the Bible says, "Blessed is the man that trusteth in the Lord" (Jeremiah 17:7; Article 255:1–2)

THE DUTY TO RANSOM CAPTIVES[2]

Ransoming captives comes before feeding or clothing the poor. There is no act of charity more meritorious than ransoming captives; therefore, money collected for any worthy purpose whatsoever may be used as ransom, even if originally collected for the erection of a synagogue. Further, even if the building materials have already been bought and the beams squared (which makes it a grave offense to sell them for any other purpose) nevertheless, it is permitted to sell them to raise a ransom. However, if the structure is already erected it should not be sold. . . .

He who shuts his eyes against the ransoming of captives transgresses the negative precepts, "Though shalt not harden

[2]Jewish soldiers captured in battle and Jews kidnapped by bandits or pirates were usually sold into slavery. Also, debtors who could not meet their obligations were, as a rule, sold into slavery. The number of such captured and enslaved Jews was often considerable. The public fund for *Pidyon Shevuim* (The Redemption of Captives) was, therefore, one of the most important institutions of medieval Jewish life.

thy heart," and "(Thou shalt not) shut thy hand"; also this, "Neither shalt thou stand against the blood of thy neighbor," and this, "He shall not rule with rigor over him in thy sight"; and he neglects the positive precepts, "Thou shalt surely open thy hand unto him," and "That thy brother may live with thee," and "Thou shalt love thy neighbor as thyself," and "Deliver them that are carried away unto death."

Every moment that one delays unnecessarily the ransoming of a captive, it is as if he were to shed blood.

Captives are not to be ransomed at an unreasonable cost, for the safety of society; otherwise, the enemies would exert every effort to capture victims; but a man may ransom himself at any price. So also, a scholar should be ransomed at a greater price, or even a student who gives promise of becoming a great scholar.

Captives should not be aided to escape for the sake of public safety; lest the enemies treat the captives with greater severity and confine them under closer custody.

He who sells himself as a slave to heathens, or who borrowed from them and is enslaved by them for nonpayment, should be ransomed the first time and the second time, but not if it happens a third time. . . . However, if his life is in danger, he must be ransomed immediately, no matter how many times it has happened before.

If a non-Jewish slave belonging to a Jew is made captive, he is to be ransomed like a captive Israelite, since he is regarded as a free man after he takes the required ritual bath and assumes the obligations of certain Jewish laws.

A woman is redeemed before a man. . . . If a captive man and woman threaten suicide, the man is rescued first.

If a man and his father and his teacher are captives, he himself comes before his teacher; and his teacher before his father; but his mother comes before all.

If a man and his wife are captured, the wife is ransomed first, and the court may seize his property to ransom her; and even if he protests, "Do not ransom her with my property," no attention is paid to him.

If a captive has property but does not wish to ransom himself, his ransom is paid against his will.

A father is obliged to ransom his son if the father has the means and the son has not. (Article 252:1–12)

CHAPTER 52

THE RESPONSA OF RABBI LURIA

Despite all efforts to codify the holy Law, the average rabbi was continually being confronted with cases which he found difficult to adjudicate. The custom, therefore, persisted of seeking the opinion of some colleague whose learning had earned him widely recognized authority. This led to the growth of an extensive literature of collections of She'elot U'Teshuvot *("Questions and Answers") left by individual scholars who had served as regional–and sometimes even world-wide–courts of appeal.*

One of the most famous of these collections was left by Solomon Luria (1510–1573), a Lithuanian rabbi who eventually settled in Lublin, Poland, where he served as head of a renowned Talmudic academy. He was apparently a man of sharp independence of mind, but his learning was so great that few dared challenge his opinions. That he was also endowed with considerable shrewdness is evidenced by the following typical fragments from his Responsa.[1]

The Case: Disagreement between a married couple reached so acute a stage that the wife, encouraged by her father, demanded a divorce. She complained that her husband was constantly making fun of religion.

---

[1]Paraphrased here from the version in Simon Hurwitz's *Responsa of Solomon Luria* (New York, Bloch Publishing, 1938).

Question: May the husband be forced to grant his wife a divorce on the ground that he is treating religion with scorn?

Answer: The husband cannot be forced to give his wife a bill of divorcement on such a charge. Even if the charge be true, or even if he were to become an apostate, yet still cared for his wife as the law requires of a Jewish husband, she could not compel him to give her a divorce.

However, neither can she be compelled to continue living with him. She has a right to take the dowry given to her by her father and return home. Should she do that, however, she would not have the right to take along any possessions given her by her husband.

In this particular case the court ought to find out from her parents, under the threat of excommunication, whether they advised her to make this accusation against her husband because she is in love with another man. Should such a conspiracy be discovered, she must forfeit even her dowry on quitting her husband's house. The same holds true should it be proved that violence is used to force the husband to grant her a divorce.

The Case: Evidence was taken against a man of Novogrodek (Province of Minsk) that he said to a woman who had refused to dance with him: "I know why you refuse me; it is because I do not want to pay you three *guldens.* You act likewise, I have been told, toward your own husband; you will not let him come near you unless he pays you three *guldens.*"

Question: What punishment should be meted out to the man for his vile language?

Answer: Were it even true that the woman had boasted of such behavior toward her husband, the man involved in this case should not go unpunished. Boasts of that sort should be taken with a grain of salt. It is a known fact that women, when gossiping among themselves, love to prattle about the power they have over their husbands. The court should, therefore, order the accused to stand before the Holy Ark in the synagogue with lighted candles in his hands, and beg God, the woman, and her husband to pardon him for his scurrility. He should also be made to sit on the outer threshold of the synagogue for four weeks as a mourner. Finally, he must pay all the expenses incurred by the husband in connection with this trial. In case the delinquent refuses to comply with this decision, he should be excommunicated.

Question: Is it permissible for a sick person to consult Gentile sorcerers?

Answer: If the patient is mortally ill, or appears to be so, or if a limb is in danger, such consultation is permissible, since sorcerers sometimes help through genuine remedies. However, when no such extremity is involved, this practice is prohibited, because sorcery in general is based on nothing but superstition and fraud.

CHAPTER 53

A RESPONSUM OF RABBI LUBLIN

Here is another highly quotable "question and answer," this one from the Responsa of Rabbi Meir Lublin (1558–1616), a Polish Talmudist whose fame reached to the ghettos of Turkey and Italy. In private life, he was a wealthy business man, and in his personal relations, rather arrogant. As an interpreter of the Law, however, his memorabilia show him to have been inclined to considerable leniency.[1]

Question: This case deals with a man of low spirit, a man of pains and sickness, mentally distraught because of an unfortunate incident which, as it were, God caused to happen to him in line with the old proverb: "From the wicked cometh forth wickedness" [I Samuel 24:13]. [The implication here is that he was stricken with disease because of his bad character.]

This happened during the time when there were disturbances in Volhynia due to the Tartar invasions. At this time, by command of the general and the officers, every man there was expected to be ready with his weapon in his hand to engage in battle and to fight the marauders.

---

[1]This selection is taken from Prof. Jacob R. Marcus's admirable source book, *The Jew in the Medieval World* (Cincinnati, Sinai Press, 1938), p. 327 ff.

It happened then on a certain day that the man in question was trying out his gun, as musketeers usually do. He was shooting with his weapon through a window in his house at a target that was fixed on the wall in his yard. Just then a man coming from the street into that yard, and wishing to enter that house, ran into the area just described and was unfortunately killed, without having been seen and certainly without having been aimed at, for the man who did the shooting had never seen the unfortunate fellow, as was later made clear by evidence offered in court on his behalf by people of his city. It was further testified that the Gentile who was the officer of the Jewish musketeer, and his superior–for he was in charge of ten men–had stationed himself outside to warn off any one who might wish to enter the yard. Indeed, he had done so in this case, too, for he had shouted at the intruder and had warned him not to enter there, as was made clear in court.

Now this musketeer has come to me, weeping and crying in the bitterness of his soul, and has willingly offered to take upon himself any penance for the calamity which, unfortunately, happened through him. [He wished to do penance by going into exile, although innocent.] Now, I saw that he was a sick man, for he had just recovered from a skin disease–may you never get it!–and that he was weak of foot, and that he did not have the strength to wander from town to town as would be required of a real penitent. In addition to this, he is burdened with sons and daughters who are dependent on him for their support, and he lives among Gentiles in a village. [There were no other Jews to look after his children.] Therefore I have set my mind to inquire and to search about and to find some support among the teachings of our rabbis, of blessed memory, as to how to lighten his exile.

Answer: Now, aside from any other reason or argument, the subject of our discussion is very much like a case of an unavoidable accident, for the person in question had relied on the guard who was stationed outside–even though he was a Gentile–to warn everyone who might enter, as indeed he did. That unfortunate victim, however, disobeyed at the cost of his life, as was testified.

Now considering these circumstances, and in view of his [the musketeer's] poor physical condition, I have seen fit to lighten his exile to the degree that he should wander about in the towns which are in his immediate neighborhood, as is indicated in the sheet of penance which I have written for him. In addition, on every Monday and Thursday [when there are special synagogue services], he must go, from the village where he lives, to the next largest Jewish community to recite the confessions of sin and to be whipped, all this as indicated in the next paragraph.

Namely, first he is to go to the holy community of Ostrog and to lie down at the threshold of the synagogue as everyone goes out, and then he is to be whipped and to make confession for his sins. [In the Middle Ages, both Jews and Gentiles employed these means of penance.] Afterwards, he is to go to the holy community of Vinnitsa, after that to Zaslavl, then to Ostropol, then to Sinyava, and finally to the holy community of Konstantinov, and shall also do that which is prescribed above. [These towns are in the Ukraine.]

On every Monday and Thursday thereafter, he must come on foot from the village in which he is living to the synagogue of the holy community of Konstantinov and sit behind the door. Then he is to be whipped and is to make confession and to fast every day [until evening] until a half year is passed, and he must frequently fast for three days and three nights straight.

However, when I saw that this was more than his strength could bear, for he was a sick man, I again lightened his penance to the effect that he should fast only three days in every seven, but that he should not eat meat or drink strong drink the entire week, except on the Sabbaths and holidays, nor sleep on mattresses and pillows on weekdays. Also, he was not to put on a clean garment, nor to take a bath, nor to cleanse his hair but once every month; nor was he to go to any feast or trim his hair. Now whatever I have lightened is because he is a man of pains and sickness and cannot walk from town to town and because he also has sons and daughters dependent on him for their support.

These are the words of the busily engaged Meir.

CHAPTER 54

LEON OF MODENA ON GAMBLING

Living in the relatively tolerant atmosphere of Renaissance Italy, Leon of Modena (1571–1648), though a rabbi, had little in common with his colleagues in more benighted lands. He was educated in science and philosophy as well as rabbinics, and could express himself as brilliantly in the vernacular as in the holy tongue. Even priests would flock to hear his sermons in the synagogue, and humanists from far and wide came to him for instruction. He was, of course, very liberal in his religious views, and wrote–among many other works–a pseudonymous treatise demolishing the very foundations of Orthodox Judaism.

Unhappily, however, his will was less powerful than his intellect, for he had an unconquerable passion for gambling. This weakness must have been in him even as a child, since his very first attempt at literary composition–written in superlatively classical Hebrew at the age of thirteen–was a long dialogue in which two disputants argue whether gambling is a sin or merely a pastime. The following is an excerpt from that dialogue.[1]

Eldad endeavors to prove that the gambler trespasses each one of the Ten Commandments, and Medad retorts.

---

[1]Quoted from *The Jew in the Medieval World* by Jacob R. Marcus, Ph.D. (Cincinnati, Sinai Press, 1938), pp. 418–421.

Eldad: If with all human effort you draw out words and arguments to institute a comparison between gaming and commerce, in order to prove that one is similar to the other, inasmuch as they both equally tend to increase or diminish one's possessions, wealth, and the coveted things of this world; I would still ask, how you could possibly defend this pursuit when it is understood that they who walk in its way are workers of iniquity? Each commits thereby an act of rebellion toward his Maker, and gradually estranges himself from Him, since he takes money from his fellowman by wicked and thievish methods, without giving him a *quid pro quo,* and without any labor on his part.

If you go into the matter thoroughly, you will see that the gambler trespasses all the Ten Commandments, the very foundation of the Law of Moses and of his prophecy, acknowledged not alone by the people of Israel, holy unto the Lord, but also by those nations among whom we dwell. First, with regard to those Commandments from the words [Exodus 20:2,8] "I am the Lord thy God" unto the fourth, "Remember the Sabbath Day." These all warn against the sin of idolatry; and beyond doubt he trespasses against each one of them. For, as soon as his star is unlucky, and he loses everything, he will be beside himself, will grow full of fury and anger; and it is clear to us that our Rabbis were right when they said that "the man of anger is like the idolator [in forgetting his God, Zohar, Genesis 27b]." They have expressed the same idea even more clearly when they remarked: "A gambler is an idolator," basing their dictum on the scriptural phrases: "And Sarah saw the [idolatrous] son of Hagar . . . playing [gambling]"; "And the people [after they made the golden calf, an idol,] sat down to eat and drink, and they rose up to gambol [gamble]" [Genesis Rabbah 53:15].

As regards the Third Commandment [Exodus 20:7]: "Thou shalt not take the name of the Lord thy God in vain," and so forth, it is self-evident to all, that at every moment during play, at every opportunity for sinning, or differences among players, a man will commit perjury; he will swear thousands of vain and false oaths, dragging his soul down to earth – a dark and dreary outlook.

How easily the Commandment referring to the Sabbath Day is broken! A man is playing on Sabbath Eve, near dusk; the loser, in the forlorn hope of winning back what he has lost; the winner, whose greed for gain is not satisfied, hoping to make more, suddenly find that the Sabbath has overtaken them, and they have infringed the sanctity of the day. In many other ways, too, this can happen to players.

The honoring of father and mother is equally jeopardized by this pursuit. Properly speaking, it is the duty of father and mother to correct and chastise the son who is addicted to gambling, in the endeavor to bring him back; but the son who is steeped in this sort of thing, which has become to him as second nature, will give them no ear. He answers them harshly, and this is a source of bitterness to their lives, for he has ignored the command [Leviticus 19:3]: "A man shall fear his mother and his father."

Furthermore, when a man realizes that he has lost his money, the fire of envy and hatred will burn within him against his fellowman; or he will seek a pretext to quarrel with him, remarking, "The game was not so," calling him a wicked scoundrel, anxious to rob him of his own. The other will retort, and the discussion, having become heated – we cannot predict where it will end. It may even be that each will draw his sword, so that one gets killed, and the command of the Lord [Exodus 20:13], "Thou shalt not murder," be transgressed.

A gambler will mix with loose women. In his rage he will utter obscene and filthy expressions, and concerning such a sin our rabbis have said [Shabbat 33a]: "The one who defiles his mouth with unhallowed words has no share in the bliss of the World-to-Come."

Words are the index to actions; the mouth makes the first move, and the organs of action do the rest. This is all contained in the prohibition [Exodus 20:13]: "Thou shalt not commit adultery."

Now, when he has been left destitute, left entirely without money, it is natural that all his thoughts are misdirected the livelong day. He broods upon how he may steal secretly, or rob his fellow creatures openly, hoping by this means to make up for his deficiencies, with the result that he will be like the chief baker, Pharaoh's servant, hanging between heaven and earth, for not having observed the warning [Exodus 20:13]: "Thou shalt not steal."

It may happen, too, in the course of a game with his friend, that they may form a compact to share the profits equally, and a misunderstanding arising, a third party is called in to arbitrate; but he, being a friend of one of the players, gives the decision in favor of that friend, to wit, unjustly; what becomes now of the command [Exodus 20:13]: "Thou shalt not bear false witness against thy neighbor"? It is thrown overboard.

It stands to reason that, if a man is not particular with regard to the law of stealing, he will be less careful as regards the prohibition [Exodus 20:14]: "Thou shalt not covet"; for whatever his eyes see, his heart will desire with a longing which will never satisfy the eye of covetousness.

Consider and answer now, whether the evil of this wicked pastime is not monstrous enough to reach unto heaven. . . . Surely the one who touches such a diversion cannot go unpunished!

Medad: You have employed many words to condemn this sport, but you have nevertheless said nothing effectual to cast a stigma upon it which might not apply equally to every other human pursuit. For [Ecclesiastes 7:9] "anger resteth in the bosom of fools" even in trivial matters, but the sensible man is patient at all times.

This is my experience. I saw a man yesterday losing 400

gold pieces, and he never uttered a word by way of cursing his luck; only once he exclaimed: "Thou, O Lord, art righteous!" On the other hand, I knew a man who, on receipt of the news that corn had depreciated in value–he was a corn- and wine-dealer–went up to the roof, threw himself down, and was killed.

Where will you find the occasion for more wicked and perplexing oaths than among merchants, which they employ to confirm their statements in the course of buying and selling?

With regard to your apprehension as to the violation of the Sabbath, this may apply as well to the tailor, shoemaker, and every other workman who is desirous of increasing his profits.

There are, furthermore, many other diversions which might lead to the breaking of the command to honor father and mother, or to the commission of murder and adultery.

The same is the case with stealing, which a poor fellow in straitened circumstances justifies by saying, it is not for stealing that he is hanged, but owing to his unlucky star and hard times.

As far as concerns false swearing, this may occur in any form of partnership; and covetousness, even outside gaming, is well known to reside naturally in the heart of man.

To sum up the matter: a perfectly righteous person will be as upright in commercial pursuits as in sport or anything else; whilst a wicked person will act wickedly in the one matter as in the other. Now, finally, I say, go and reflect upon this one point. If, as you insist, gambling is such robbery and an intolerable sin, why did not our rabbis of old prohibit it to us and our descendants in a clear, decisive, and expressive manner? Considering, too, as is well known, that their object was ever to keep us aloof, not alone from transgression and wickedness itself, but even from that which in a remote degree might lead to its commission; and they, therefore, in their exalted and perfect wisdom, instituted one fence and safeguard upon another to protect the law–what conclusion can we arrive at from the consideration that they never lifted up their voice against this diversion, but that they found therein nothing of vice or vanity, as you would have us believe?

CHAPTER 55

TEN COMMANDMENTS FOR A WIFE

The bulk of the Jewish literature of the Middle Ages was written in Hebrew, but because many Jews did not understand their ancient tongue, books were written for them in the ghetto vernacular, an archaic German encrusted with Hebrew words which eventually came to be called Yiddish. Most of these books were intended for women, although some were written also for the average man.

Some time before 1620, Isaac ben Eliakim of Posen, a Polish Jew who later lived in Prague, wrote a Yiddish ethical work which he called Lev Tov *("A Good Heart"). His purpose was to teach the ordinary man and woman the basic moral principles of Judaism, and to encourage a more fervent devotion to them. The book became enormously popular throughout the Judeo-German communities, and was reprinted some nineteen times during the following century.*

The following selection is taken from the chapter on marriage. It reflects the attitude of his generation toward the duties of a Jewish wife to her husband.[1]

This is the story of a queen who gave her daughter in marriage to a young king and then gave her the following instructions. Since she was sending the daughter away for her marriage, she said to her: "My dear child, I am giving you away and am turning you over to a stranger, and I don't know what sort of a person he is, so I am going to instruct you and

[1] *Ibid*, pp. 443–444.

give you ten rules. If you keep my instruction, everything will be well with you; but if you don't heed my advice, things won't go right with you. Therefore, take these ten rules to heart, and think of them day and night, early and late; and if you do this, your husband will love you as he does the heart in his body.

"The first, my dear daughter, is to beware of his anger, lest you enrage him. When he is cross, don't you be jolly; and when he is jolly, don't you be cross; and when he is angry, smile at him and answer him with kind, soft words, and speak pleasantly to him. Thus, you will still his anger.

"The second, my dear daughter, concerns his eating and drinking. Search and consider and reflect about his food, about that which he likes to eat, and let these be your words: 'My lord, wouldn't you rather have something else to eat?' Urge him. Try to have his meals ready at the proper time, for hunger does nobody any good. When he comes home and doesn't find his meal ready at the proper time, he'll get angry. Should he have gotten drunk, don't tell him what he did, or what he said in his drunkenness; and if he tells you to drink, you drink, but don't drink yourself drunk, lest he should see you in such a state and learn to hate you.

"The third, my dear daughter. When he sleeps, guard his sleep that he not be awakened, for if he doesn't get a good night's rest he may become very angry.

"The fourth, my dear daughter. Try to be thrifty and careful with your husband's money, and make an effort not to bring any loss to him. Don't give anything away without your husband's knowledge, unless it be a small thing which he wouldn't care about.

"The fifth, my dear daughter. Don't be anxious to know his secrets; and if you should know anything of his secrets don't confide them to anyone in the whole world; and those things, also, which he boasts about to you, tell to absolutely no one.

"The sixth, my dear daughter. Find out whom he likes and

like that person, too; and him whom he dislikes, you dislike, too. Don't like his enemies, and don't hate his friends.

"The seventh, my dear daughter. Don't be contrary with him. Do everything he tells you. If he tells you anything, let his words find favor with you. Don't say to him: 'You haven't said the right thing,' or 'My advice is better than your advice.'

"The eighth, my dear daughter. Don't expect of him anything that he considers difficult. He may take a dislike to you because you expect something of him which he believes is too hard.

"The ninth, my dear daughter. Heed the requests which he may make of you, and he will love you, be your slave, and serve you with joy.

"The tenth, my dear daughter. Be very careful to guard against jealousy. Don't make him jealous in any way. Don't say anything that might hurt him, and let him have his own way in everything. Make an effort in all things to do what pleases him and don't do what he doesn't like. If you treat him like a king then he, in turn, will treat you like a queen.

"Now, my dear daughter, take these ten rules of instruction with you as your provision, and let them be as a reminder to you throughout all your life."

CHAPTER 56

THE WISDOM OF SPINOZA

Baruch Spinoza (1632–1677), Dutch philosopher and Bible critic, is included in this section only out of chronological considerations. Intellectually, he belongs not to the medieval but the modern period in Israel's history.

He came of Spanish stock, but was born in Amsterdam, where there was a considerable settlement of Jewish refugees from the Iberian Peninsula. Their ancestors had been forcibly Christianized more than a century earlier, and these refugees, being free at last to profess their real faith, were inclined to profess it with especial ardor. Spinoza was reared in the strictest piety, receiving all his early education at the hands of religious teachers. He proved a diligent student, and was eventually enrolled in the local Talmudic academy, being apparently destined to become a rabbi.

To round out his learning, however, he was allowed to take lessons in Latin, philosophy, and the sciences from a free-thinking Gentile teacher, and the effect was disastrous to his piety. He became increasingly skeptical as to the truth of all traditional religion, and when this was finally discovered by the synagogue elders, and he stubbornly refused to abjure his doubts, there was so great an outcry against him that he was forced to flee from the ghetto. He took refuge in the house of a Christian friend in a near-by suburb, and while there received notification that he had been formally excommunicated as a Jew.

Spinoza was twenty-three at the time, and from then on never again had any intercourse with his own people. He took up lens-grinding for a livelihood, but spent most of his time in study and learned discussion with earnest young Christians. These were drawn to him because of the saintliness of his character as well as the profundity of his mind–most of them were Mennonites and sternly moralistic–and they eventually formed themselves into a circle of disciples. At their suggestion he began to put his ideas on paper, and when he died–apparently of tuberculosis at the early age of forty-five–they published a volume containing all his writings save two which had appeared in print during his lifetime.

Despite that he wrote so little, Spinoza exercised an extraordinary influence over the subsequent development of thought. His profoundest work, a treatise written in a geometrical form and entitled simply Ethics, *became a classic text of pantheistic philosophy. His most readable work, an essay entitled* Treatise on Theology and Politics, *provided the basic arguments for generations of warriors against religious obscurantism and political tyranny. The character of his writings can best be judged by the great men who have most admired them. These include Goethe, Hegel, Shelley, Byron, Renan, and Einstein. It is not too much to say that Spinoza lighted one of the brightest beacons pointing the way to the intellectual freedom.*

Some slight notion of the nature of ideas will perhaps be indicated by the following passages.[1]

ON DEMOCRACY

In a democracy, irrational commands are still less to be feared: for it is almost impossible that the majority of a people, especially if it be a large one, should agree in an irrational design: and, moreover, the basis and aim of a democracy is to avoid the desires as irrational, and to bring men as far as possible under the control of reason, so that they may live in peace and harmony. If this basis be removed the whole fabric falls to ruin.

Such being the ends in view for the sovereign power, the duty of citizens is, as I have said, to obey its commands, and to recognize no right save that which it sanctions.

---

[1]The translations are by various hands, chiefly R. H. M. Elwes, W. H. White, and A. Wolf.

It will, perhaps, be thought that we are turning citizens into slaves, for slaves obey commands and free men live as they like; but this idea is based on a misconception, for the true slave is he who is led away by his pleasures and can neither see what is good for him nor act accordingly: he alone is free who lives with free consent under the entire guidance of reason.

Action in obedience to orders does take away freedom in a certain sense, but it does not, therefore, make a man a slave; all depends on the object of the action. If the object of the action be the good of the state, and not the good of the agent, the latter is a slave and does himself no good; but in a state or kingdom where the weal of the whole people, and not that of the ruler, is the supreme law, obedience to the sovereign power does not make a man a slave, of no use to himself, but a citizen. Therefore, that state is the freest whose laws are founded on sound reason, so that every member of it may, if he will, be free; that is, live with full consent under the entire guidance of reason.

Children, though they are bound to obey all the commands of their parents, are yet not slaves; for the commands of parents look generally to the children's benefit.

We must, therefore, acknowledge a great difference between a slave, a son, and a citizen; their positions may be thus defined. A slave is one who is bound to obey his master's orders, though they are given solely in the master's interest; a son is one who obeys his father's orders, given in his own interest; a citizen obeys the orders of the sovereign power, given for the common interest, wherein he is included.

I think I have now shown sufficiently clearly the basis of a democracy. I have especially desired to do so, for I believe it to be of all forms of government the most natural and the most consonant with individual liberty. In it, no one transfers his natural right so absolutely that he has no further voice in affairs; he only hands it over to the majority of a society, whereof he is a unit. Thus, all men remain, as they were in the state of Nature, equals. (Tractatus Theologico-Politicus, Chapter 16)

ON FREEDOM OF THOUGHT AND SPEECH

If men's minds were as easily controlled as their tongues, every king would sit safely on his throne, and government by compulsion would cease; for every subject would shape his life according to the intentions of his rulers, and would esteem a thing true or false, good or evil, just or unjust, in obedience to their dictates. However, . . . no man's mind can possibly lie wholly at the disposition of another, for no one can willingly transfer his natural right of free reason and judgment, or be compelled to do so. For this reason, any government which attempts to control minds is accounted tyrannical, and it is considered an abuse of sovereignty and a usurpation of the rights of subjects to seek to prescribe what shall be accepted as true, or rejected as false, or what opinions should actuate men in their worship of God. All these questions fall within a man's natural right, which he cannot abdicate even with his own consent. . . .

However unlimited, therefore, the power of a sovereign may be, however implicitly it is trusted as the exponent of law and religion, it can never prevent men from forming judgments according to their intellect, or being influenced by any given emotion. It is true that it has the power to treat as enemies all men whose opinions do not, on all subjects, entirely coincide with its own . . . I grant that it is able to rule in the most violent manner, and put citizens to death for very trivial causes; but no one supposes it can do this with the approval of sound judgment. Nay, inasmuch as such things cannot be done without extreme peril to itself, we may even deny that it has the absolute power to do them. . . .

Since, therefore, no one can abdicate his freedom of judgment and feeling; since every man is by indefeasible natural right the master of his own thoughts, it follows that men, thinking in diverse and contradictory fashions, cannot, without disastrous results, be compelled to speak only according to the dictates of the supreme power. Not even the most experienced, to say nothing of the multitude, know how to keep silence. Men's common failing is to confide their plans to others, though there be need for secrecy, so that a government would be most harsh which deprived the individual of his freedom of saying and teaching what he thought; and would be moderate if such freedom were granted. . . .

The ultimate aim of government is not to rule, or restrain by fear, nor to exact obedience, but, contrariwise, to free every man from fear that he may live in all possible security; in other words, to strengthen his natural right to exist and work without injury to himself or others.

No, the object of government is not to change men from rational beings into beasts or puppets, but to enable them to develop their minds and bodies in security, and to employ their reason unshackled; neither showing hatred, anger or deceit, nor watched with the eyes of jealousy and injustice. In fact, the true aim of government is liberty. (Tractatus Theologico-Politicus, Chapter 16)

ON PERSECUTION

What greater misfortune for a state can be conceived than that honorable men should be sent like criminals into exile, because they hold diverse opinions which they cannot disguise? What, I say, can be more hurtful than that men who have committed no crime or wickedness should, simply because they are enlightened, be treated as enemies and put to death, and that the scaffold, the terror of evildoers, should become the arena where the highest examples of tolerance and virtue are displayed to the people with all the marks of ignominy that authority can devise?

He that knows himself to be upright does not fear the death of a criminal and shrinks from no punishment. His mind is not wrung with remorse for any disgraceful deed. He holds that death in a good cause is no punishment, but an honor, and that death for freedom is glory.

What purpose, then, is served by the death of such men, what example is proclaimed? The cause for which they die is unknown to the idle and the foolish, hateful to the turbulent, loved by the upright. The only lesson we can draw from such scenes is to flatter the persecutor, or else to imitate the victim.

If formal assent is not to be esteemed above conviction, and if governments are to retain a firm hold of authority and not be compelled to yield to agitators, it is imperative that freedom of judgment should be granted, so that men may live together in harmony, however diverse, or even openly contradictory their opinions may be. We cannot doubt that such is the best system of government and open to the fewest objections, since it is the one most in harmony with human nature. In a democracy (the most natural form of government) everyone submits to the control of authority over his actions, but not over his judgment and reason; that is, seeing that all cannot think alike, the voice of the majority has the force of law, subject to repeal if circumstances bring about a change of opinion. In proportion as the power of free judgment is withheld we depart from the natural condition of mankind, and consequently the government becomes more tyrannical. (Tractatus Theologico-Politicus, Chapter 20)

ON SUPERSTITION

Men would never be superstitious, if they could govern all their circumstances by set rules, or if they were always favored by fortune: but being frequently driven into straits where rules are useless, and being often kept fluctuating pitiably between hope and fear by the uncertainty of fortune's greedily coveted favors, they are consequently, for the most part, very prone to credulity. The human mind is readily swayed this way or that in times of doubt, especially when hope and fear are struggling for the mastery, though usually it is boastful, overconfident, and vain.

This as a general fact I suppose everyone knows. . . . Most people, when in prosperity, are so overbrimming with wisdom (however inexperienced they may be), that they take every offer of advice as a personal insult, whereas in adversity they know not where to turn, but beg and pray for counsel from every passer-by. . . . If anything happens during their fright which reminds them of some past good or ill, they think it portends a happy or unhappy issue, and, therefore, (though it may have proved abortive a hundred times before) style it a lucky or unlucky omen. Anything which excites their astonishment they believe to be a portent signifying the anger of the gods or of the Supreme Being, and, mistaking superstition for religion, account it impious not to avert the evil with prayer and sacrifice. Signs and wonders of this sort they conjure up perpetually, until one might think Nature as mad as themselves. . . .

Thus, it is brought prominently before us that superstition's chief victims are those persons who greedily covet temporal advantages; they it is, who (especially when they are in danger, and cannot help themselves) are wont with prayers and womanish tears to implore help from God: upbraiding reason as blind, because she cannot show a sure path to the shadows they pursue, and rejecting human wisdom as vain; but believing the phantoms of imagination, dreams, and other childish absurdities, to be the very oracles of heaven. As though God has turned away from the wise, and written his decrees, not in the mind of man but in the entrails of beasts, or left them to be proclaimed by the inspiration and instinct of fools, madmen, and birds. Such is the unreason to which terror can drive mankind!

Superstition, then, is engendered, preserved, and fostered by fear. . . . It springs, not from reason, but solely from the more powerful phases of emotion. We may readily understand, therefore, how difficult it is to maintain the same course men prone to every form of credulity. For, as the mass of mankind remains always at about the same pitch of misery, it never assents long to any one remedy, but is always best pleased by a novelty which has yet proved illusive.

This element of inconsistency has been the cause of many terrible wars and revolutions; for, as Curtius well says (Tractatus Theologico-Politicus 4, Chapter 10): "The mob has no ruler more potent than superstition," and is easily led, on the plea of religion, at one moment to adore its kings as gods, and anon to execrate and abjure them as humanity's common bane. Immense pains have, therefore, been taken to counteract this evil by investing religion, whether true or false, with such pomp and ceremony, that it may rise superior to every shock, and be always observed with studious reverence by the whole people. . . .

But if, in despotic statecraft, the supreme and essential mystery be to hoodwink the subjects, and to master the fear, which keeps them down, with the specious garb of religion, so that men may fight as bravely for slavery as for safety, and count it not shame but highest honor to risk their blood and their lives for the vainglory of a tyrant; yet in a free state no more mischievous expedient could be planned or attempted. Wholly repugnant to the general freedom are such devices as enthralling men's minds with prejudices, forcing their judgment, or employing any of the weapons of quasi-religious sedition; indeed, such seditions only spring up when law enters the domain of speculative thought, and opinions are put on trial and condemned on the same footing as crimes, while those who defend and follow them are sacrificed, not to public safety, but to their opponents' hatred and cruelty. If deeds only could be made the grounds of criminal charges, and words were always allowed to pass free, such seditions would be divested of every semblance of justification, and would be separated from mere controversies by a hard and fast line. . . .

I have often wondered that persons who make a boast of professing the Christian religion, namely love, joy, peace, temperance, and charity to all men, should quarrel with such rancorous animosity, and display daily toward one another such bitter hatred, that this, rather than the virtues they claim, is the readiest criterion of their faith. Matters have long since come to such a pass that one can only pronounce a man Christian, Turk, Jew, or Heathen, by his general appearance and attire, by his frequenting this or that place of worship, or employing the phraseology of a particular sect–as for manner of life, it is in all cases the same. Inquiry into the case of this anomaly leads me unhesitatingly to ascribe it to the fact that the ministries of the Church are regarded by the masses merely as dignities, her offices as posts of emolument–in short, popular religion may be summed up as a respect for ecclesiastics. The spread of this misconception inflamed every worthless fellow with an intense desire to enter holy orders, and thus the love of diffusing God's religion degenerated into sordid avarice and ambition. Every church became a theater, where orators, instead of church teachers harangued, caring not to instruct the people, but striving to attract admiration, to bring opponents to public scorn, and to preach only novelties and paradoxes, such as would tickle the ears of their congregation.

This state of things necessarily stirred up an amount of controversy, envy, and hatred, which no lapse of time could appease; so that we can scarcely wonder that of the old religion nothing survives but its outward forms (even these, in the mouth of the multitude, seem rather adulation than adoration of the Deity), and that faith has become a mere compound of credulity and prejudices – aye, prejudices too, which degrade man from rational being to beast, which completely stifle the power of judgment between true and false, which seem, in fact, carefully fostered for the purpose of extinguishing the last spark of reason! Piety – great God! – and religion are become a tissue of ridiculous mysteries; men, who flatly despise reason, who reject and turn away from understanding as naturally corrupt, these, I say, these of all men, are thought – Oh, lie most horrible! – to possess light from on High. Verily, if they had but one spark of light from on High, they would not insolently rave, but would learn to worship God more wisely, and would be as marked among their fellows for mercy as they now are for malice; if they were concerned for their opponents' souls, instead of for their own reputations, they would no longer fiercely persecute, but rather be filled with pity and compassion. . . . (Tractatus Theologico-Politicus, Preface)

ON THE INTERPRETATION OF SCRIPTURE

When people declare, as all are ready to do, that the Bible is the Word of God teaching men true blessedness and the way of salvation, they evidently do not mean what they say; for the masses take no pains at all to live according to Scripture, and we see most people endeavoring to hawk about their own commentaries as the word of God, and giving their best efforts, under the guise of religion, to compelling others to think as they do. . . .

If men really believe what they verbally testify of Scripture, they would adopt quite a different plan of life: their minds would not be agitated by so many contentions, nor so many hatreds, and they would cease to be excited by such a blind and rash passion for interpreting the sacred writings, and excogitating novelties in religion. On the contrary, they would not dare to adopt, as the teaching of Scripture, anything which they could not plainly deduce therefrom: lastly, these sacrilegious persons who have dared, in several passages, to interpolate the Bible, would have shrunk from so great a crime, and would have stayed their sacrilegious hands.

Ambition and unscrupulousness have waxed so powerful that religion is thought to consist, not so much in respecting the writings of the Holy Ghost, as in defending human commentaries, so that religion is no longer identified with charity, but with spreading discord and propagating insensate hatred disguised under the name of zeal for the Lord, and eager ardor.

To these evils we must add superstition, which teaches men to despise reason and nature, and only to admire and venerate that which is repugnant to both: whence it is not wonderful that for the sake of increasing the admiration and veneration felt for Scripture, men strive to explain it so as to make it appear to contradict, as far as possible, both one and the other. . . .

If we should separate ourselves from the crowd and escape from theological prejudices, instead of rashly accepting human commentaries for Divine documents, we must consider the true method of interpreting Scripture and dwell upon it at some length: for if we remain in ignorance of this we cannot know, certainly, what the Bible and the Holy Spirit wish to teach.

The method of interpreting Scripture should not differ widely from the method of interpreting nature. . . . For as the interpretation of nature consists in the examination of the history of nature, and therefrom deducing definitions of natural phenomena on certain fixed axioms, so scriptural interpretation should proceed from the examination of Scripture to the inference of the intention of its authors. . . . By working in this manner, everyone will always advance without danger of error—that is, if they admit no principles for interpreting Scripture, and discussing its contents save such as they find in Scripture itself—and will be able with equal security to discuss what surpasses our understanding, and what is known by the natural light of reason. . . .

As the highest power of scriptural interpretation belongs to every man, the rule for such interpretation should be nothing but the natural light of reason which is common to all–not any supernatural light nor any external authority; moreover, such a rule ought not to be so difficult that it can only be applied by very skillful philosophers, but should be adapted to the natural and ordinary faculties and capacity of mankind. (Tractatus Theologico-Politicus, Chapter 7)

ON THE IDEA OF A CHOSEN PEOPLE

Every man's true happiness and blessedness consist solely in the enjoyment of what is good, not in the pride that he alone is enjoying it, to the exclusion of others. He who thinks himself the more blessed because he is enjoying benefits which others are not, or because he is more blessed or more fortunate than his fellows, is ignorant of true happiness and blessedness, and the joy which he feels is either childish or envious and malicious. For instance, a man's true happiness consists only in wisdom, and the knowledge of the truth, not at all in the fact that he is wiser than others, or that others lack such knowledge: such considerations do not increase his wisdom or true happiness.

Whoever, therefore, rejoices for such reasons, rejoices in another's misfortune, and is, so far, malicious and bad, knowing neither true happiness nor the peace of true life.

When Scripture, therefore, in exhorting the Hebrews to obey the law, says that the Lord has chosen them for Himself before other nations (Deuteronomy 10:15); that He is near them, but not near others (Deuteronomy 4:7); that to them alone He has given just laws (Deuteronomy 4:8); and, lastly, that He has marked them out before others (Deuteronomy

4:32); it speaks only according to the understanding of its hearers who . . . as Moses testified (Deuteronomy 9:6–7), knew not true blessedness. For in good sooth they would have been no less blessed if God had called all men equally to salvation, nor would God have been less present to them for being equally present to others; their laws would have been no less just if they had been ordained for all, and they themselves would have been no less wise. The miracles would have shown God's power no less by being wrought for other nations also; lastly, the Hebrews would have been just as much bound to worship God if He had bestowed all these gifts equally on all men. . . . (Tractatus Theologico-Politicus, Chapter 3)

ON DIVINE HELP

By the help of God, I mean the fixed and unchangeable order of nature or the chain of natural events: for I have said before and shown elsewhere that the universal laws of nature, according to which all things exist and are determined, are only another name for the eternal decrees of God, which always involve eternal truth and necessity.

So that to say that everything happens according to natural laws, and to say that everything is ordained by the decree and ordinance of God, is the same thing. Now since the power in nature is identical with the power of God, by which alone all things happen and are determined, it follows that whatsoever man, as a part of nature, provides himself with to aid and preserve his existence, or whatsoever nature affords him without his help, is given to him solely by the Divine power, acting either through human nature or through external circumstance. So whatever human nature can furnish itself with by its own efforts to preserve its existence, may be fitly called the inward aid of God, whereas whatever else accrues to man's profit from outward causes may be called the external aid of God. (Tractatus Theologico-Politicus, Chapter 3)

ON MIRACLES

As men are accustomed to call Divine the knowledge which transcends human understanding, so also do they style divine, or the work of God, anything of which the cause is not generally known: for the masses think that the power and providence of God are most clearly displayed by events that are extraordinary and contrary to the conception they have formed of nature, especially if such events bring them any profit or convenience: they think that the clearest possible proof of God's existence is afforded when nature, as they suppose, breaks her accustomed order. . . .

The masses then style unusual phenomena "miracles," and partly from piety, partly for the sake of opposing the students of science, prefer to remain in ignorance of natural causes, and only to hear of those things which they know least, and consequently admire most. In fact, the common people can only adore God, and refer all things to his power by removing natural causes, and conceiving things happening out of their due course, and only admire the power of God when the power of nature is conceived of as in subjection to it. . . .

A miracle is an event of which the causes cannot be explained by the natural reason through a reference to ascertained workings of nature; but since miracles were wrought according to the understanding of the masses, who are wholly ignorant of the workings of nature, it is certain that the ancients took for a miracle whatever they could not explain. . . .

Nature preserves a fixed and unchangeable order and that God in all ages known and unknown has been the same;

further, the laws of nature are so perfect that nothing can be added thereto nor nor taken therefrom; and, lastly, miracles only appear as something new because of man's ignorance. (Tractatus Theologico-Politicus, Chapter 6)

ON FANATACISM

"You who assume that you have at last found the best religion, or rather the best teachers, and fixed your credulity on them, how do you know that they are the best among those who have taught other religions, or now teach or shall hereafter teach them? Have you examined all those religions both ancient and modern which are taught here and in India and all the world over? And even supposing you have duly examined them, how do you know that you have chosen the best?" (Letter to Burgh)

ON MAN AND NATURE

Let us imagine, with your permission, a little worm, living in the blood, able to distinguish by sight the particles of blood, lymph, and so forth, and to reflect on the manner in which each particle, on meeting with another particle, either is repulsed, or communicates a portion of its own motion. This little worm would live in the blood in the same way as we live in a part of the universe, and would consider each particle of blood, not as a part, but as a whole. He would be unable to determine how all the parts are modified by the general nature of blood, and are compelled by it to adapt themselves so as to stand in a fixed relation to one another. For if we imagine that there are no causes external to the blood, which could communicate fresh movements to it, nor any space beyond the blood, nor any bodies whereto the particles of blood could communicate their motion, it is certain that the blood would always remain in the same state, and its particles would undergo no modifications, save those which may be conceived as arising from the relations of motion existing between the lymph, the chyle, and so forth. The blood would then always have to be considered as a whole, not as a part.

But as there exist, as a matter of fact, very many causes which modify, in a given manner, the nature of blood, and are, in turn, modified thereby, it follows that other motions and other relations arise in the blood, springing not from the mutual relations of its parts only, but from the mutual relations between the blood as a whole and external causes. Thus, the blood comes to be regarded as a part, not as a whole. So much for the whole and the part.

All natural bodies can and ought to be considered in the same way as we here considered the blood, for all bodies are surrounded by others, and are mutually determined to exist and operate in a fixed and definite proportion, while the relations between motion and rest in the sum total of them, that is, in the whole universe, remain unchanged. Hence, it follows that each body, in so far as it exists as modified in a particular manner, must be considered as a part of the whole universe, as agreeing with the whole, and associated with the remaining parts. As the nature of the universe is not limited, like the nature of blood, but is absolutely infinite, its parts are by this nature of infinite power infinitely modified, and compelled to undergo infinite variations. . . .

You see, therefore, how and why I think that the human body is a part of nature. As regards the human mind, I believe that it also is a part of nature; for I maintain that there exists in nature an infinite power of thinking, which, in so far as it is infinite, contains subjectively the whole of nature, and its thoughts proceed in the same manner as nature – that is, in the sphere of ideas. Further, I take the human mind to be identical with this said power, not in so far as it is infinite, and perceives the whole of nature, but in so far as it is finite, and perceives only the human body. In this manner, I maintain that the human mind is part of an infinite understanding. (Letter to Oldenburg, 1665)

WE ARE AS WE ARE MADE

No one can bring a complaint against God for having given him a weak nature, or infirm spirit. A circle might as well complain to God for not being endowed with the properties of a sphere, or a child who is tortured, say, with stone, for not being given a healthy body, as a man of feeble spirit, because God has denied to him fortitude, and the true knowledge and love of the Deity, or because he is endowed with so weak a nature that he cannot check or moderate his desires. For the nature of each thing is only competent to do that which follows necessarily from its given cause.

That every man cannot be grave, and that we can no more command for ourselves a healthy body than a healthy mind, nobody can deny, without giving the lie to experience, as well as to reason. "But," you urge, "if men sin by nature, they are excusable"; but you do not state the conclusion you draw, whether that God cannot be angry with them, or that they are worthy of blessedness – that is, of the knowledge and love of God. If you say the former, I fully admit that God cannot be angry, and that all things are done in accordance with His will; but I deny that all men ought, therefore, to be blessed – men may be excusable, and nevertheless, be without blessedness and afflicted in many ways. A horse is excusable for being a horse and not a man; but, nevertheless, he must needs be a horse and not a man. He who goes mad from the bite of a dog is excusable, yet he is rightly suffocated. Lastly, he who cannot govern his desires, and keep them in check with the fear of the laws, though his weakness may be excusable, yet he . . . necessarily perishes. (Letter to Oldenburg, Feb. 7, 1676)

OF HUMAN BONDAGE

The impotence of man to govern or restrain the emotions I call bondage, for a man who is under their control is not his own master, but is mastered by fortune, in whose power he is, so that he is often forced to follow the worse, although he sees the better before him. (Ethics, Part 3)

ON VIRTUE

Since reason demands nothing which is opposed to nature, it demands, therefore, that every person should love himself, should seek his own profit—what is truly profitable to him—should desire everything that really leads man to greater perfection, and absolutely that every one should endeavor, as far as in him lies, to preserve his own being. This is all true as necessarily as that the whole is greater than its part. Again, since virtue means nothing but acting according to the laws of our own nature, and since no one endeavors to preserve his being except in accordance with the laws of his own nature, it follows: (1) That the foundation of virtue is the endeavor to preserve our own being, and that happiness consists in this—that a man can preserve his own being; (2) That virtue is to be desired for its own sake, nor is there anything more excellent or more useful to us than virtue, for the sake of which virtue ought to be desired. (3) That all persons who kill themselves are impotent in mind, and have been thoroughly overcome by external causes opposed to their nature. (Ethics, Part 4)

ON LAUGHTER

Laughter, like jesting, is mere pleasure, and, therefore, is in itself good, so it be not excessive. Surely 'tis but an ill-favored and sour superstition that forbids rejoicing. For why is it a better deed to quench thirst and hunger than to drive out melancholy? This is my way of life, and thus have I attuned my mind. No deity, nor anyone but an envious churl, hath delight in my infirmity and inconvenience, nor reckons toward our virtues weeping, sobs, fear, and other such matters which are tokens of a feeble mind; but contrariwise the more we are moved with pleasure, the more we pass to greater perfection; that is, the more must we needs partake of the divine nature. Therefore, it is the wise man's part to use the world and delight himself in it as he best may, not indeed to satiety, for that is no delight. A wise man, I say, will recruit and refresh himself with temperate and pleasant meat and drink, yea and with perfumes, the fair prospect of green woods, apparel, music, sports and exercises, stage-plays and the like, which every man may enjoy without any harm to his neighbor. For the human body is compounded of very many parts different of kind, which ever stand in need of new and various nourishment, that the whole body alike may be fit for all actions incident to its kind, and that by consequence the mind may be equally fit for apprehending many things at once. (Ethics, Part 4)

ON THE POWER OF LOVE

He who lives according to reason endeavors to the utmost of his power to outweigh another man's hate, anger or despite against him with love or highmindedness. . . . He who chooses to avenge wrong by requiting it with hatred is assuredly miserable; but he who strives to cast out hatred by love may fight his fight in joy and confidence; he can withstand many foes as easily as one, and is in nowise beholden to fortune for aid. As for those he doth conquer, they yield to him joyfully, and that not because their strength faileth, but because it is increased. (Ethics, Part 4)

ON ENFORCED ORDER

A commonwealth whose subjects rise not in arms because they are overcome by terror is rather to be spoken of as being without war than as enjoying peace. For peace is not mere absence of war, but an excellence proceeding from high-mindedness; since obedience is the constant will to perform that which by the common ordinance of the state ought to be done. Moreover, a commonwealth whose peace depends on the dullness of its subjects, and on their being driven like cattle, to learn nothing but slavery, is more fitly called a wilderness than a commonwealth. When, therefore, we say that the government is best under which men lead a peaceable life, I mean that life of man which consists not only in the circulation of the blood and other properties common to all animals, but whose chief part is reason and the true life and excellence of the mind. . . .

If slavery, rudeness, and desolation are to be called peace, then is peace the most wretched state of mankind. Truly there are more and sharper disputes between parents and children than between masters and slaves; and yet it were no good housekeeping to make the father into a master, and hold the children for slaves. It makes for slavery, not for peace, to confer unlimited power on one man. (Tractatus Politicus, Chapter 5)

ON FALSE GOODS

After experience had taught me that all things which frequently take place in ordinary life are vain and futile . . . I determined to inquire whether I might discover and acquire the faculty of enjoying throughout eternity continual supreme happiness. . . . The things which . . . are esteemed the greatest good of all, as may be gathered from their works, can be reduced to these three headings: to wit, riches, fame, and pleasure. With these three, the mind is so engrossed that it can scarcely think of any other good. . . .

There are many examples of men who have suffered persecution even unto death for the sake of their riches, and also of men who, in order to amass wealth, have exposed themselves to so many perils that at last they have paid the penalty of death for their stupidity. Nor are the examples less numerous of those who have suffered in the most wretched manner to obtain or defend their honor. Finally, the examples are innumerable of those who have hastened death upon themselves by too great a desire for pleasure.

These evils seem to have arisen from the fact that the whole of happiness or unhappiness is dependent solely on the quality of the object to which we are bound by love. For the sake of something which no one loves, strife never arises, there is no pain if it perishes, no envy if it is possessed by someone else, nor fear, nor hatred, and, to put it all briefly, no commotion of the mind at all: for all these are consequences only of the love of those things which are perishable, such as those things of which we have just spoken.

But the love toward a thing eternal and infinite alone feeds the mind with pleasure, and it is free from all pain; so it is much to be desired and to be sought out with all our might. . . . (Improvement of the Understanding, Part 1)

ON THE TRUE GOOD

One thing I could see, and it was that . . . the acquisition of money and desire for pleasure and glory are only in the way as long as they were sought for their own sakes and not as means to attain other things. But if they are sought as means, they . . . will help in the attainment of the end for which they are sought. . . .

I will at this point only briefly say what I understand by true good, and at the same time what is supreme good. In order that this may rightly be understood, it must be pointed out that good and bad are terms only used respectively: and, therefore, one and the same thing can be called good or bad according to the various aspects in which we regard it. . . . For nothing regarded in its own nature can be called perfect or imperfect, especially after we know that all things which are made, are made according to the eternal order and the fixed laws of nature. . . .

The greatest good is for man to attain . . . the knowledge of the union which the mind has with the whole of nature. This is the end to attain which I am striving, namely, to acquire such a knowledge, and to endeavor that many also should acquire it with me. It is part of my happiness that many others should understand as I do, and that their understanding and desire should be entirely in harmony with my understanding and desire; and in order to bring this to pass it is necessary to understand as much of nature as will suffice for the acquiring of such a knowledge, and moreover to form a society . . . enabling most people to acquire this knowledge with the greatest ease and security.

Attention must be paid to *moral philosophy* and the *theory for the education of children*, and inasmuch as health is not an insignificant means to this end, the whole of the science of *medicine* must be consulted, and finally, as many things which are difficult are rendered easy by skill and contrivance, and we can thus save a great deal of time and convenience in life, the art of *mechanics* must in no wise be despised. However, above all things, a method must be thought out of healing the understanding and purifying it at the beginning, that it may with the greatest success understand things correctly. From this, everyone will be able to see that I wish to direct all sciences in one direction or to one end, namely, to attain the greatest possible human perfection. (Improvement of the Understanding, Part 2)

CHAPTER 57

THE SAINTLY PATH OF MOSES LUZZATTO

Moses Hayim Luzzatto (1707–1747) was one of the last great Jewish savants to write entirely in the medieval spirit. Though born of wealthy Italian parents who schooled him thoroughly in Latin and the sciences, he soon envinced a passionate preference for Hebrew and piety. He became so ardent a believer in the Kabbalah, and so inveterate a receiver of Messianic revelations, that he alarmed many of his elders in the rabbinate, and in the end was forced to move to Palestine. His whole career is commonly regarded as one more proof of the persistence of medievalism in Jewish life, and this is no doubt justified.

The following excerpts are taken from Luzzatto's most famous work, Mesillat Yesharim, *"Path of the Upright," published in 1740.*[1]

PREFACE

If you will observe the present state of affairs, you will note that most of those who possess keen intellect concentrate all their study and thought upon the subtleties of the sciences, each according to the bent of his mind and natural taste. Some devote themselves to the physical sciences; others turn all their

[1]Translated by Mordecai M. Kaplan (Philadelphia, Jewish Publication Society, 1936).

thoughts to astronomy and mathematics; others, again, to the arts. Finally, there are those who penetrate into the innermost sanctuary of knowledge, which is the study of the holy Torah. . . . However, there are but few who study the nature of the love and the fear of God, of communion, or any other phase of saintliness.

Yet the neglect of these studies is not due to their being regarded as unessential. On the contrary, everyone would admit that these subjects are of cardinal importance, and that a man cannot be considered learned unless he finds himself thoroughly at home in them. But the reason they are neglected is that they are regarded as so familiar and commonplace as not to deserve that anyone should spend much time on them. Consequently, the pursuit of these studies is confined to people of limited mentality. Indeed, one who is saintly is inevitably suspected of being a dullard.

This fact has its evil consequences both for the learned and the unlearned. It is exceedingly hard to find saintliness among us, since neither the learned nor the ignorant are likely to cultivate it. The learned will lack saintliness because they do not give it sufficient thought; the ignorant will not possess it because their powers of understanding are limited, so that the majority of men will conceive saintliness to consist in reciting numerous psalms and long confessionals, in fasting, and in ablutions in ice and snow. Such practices fail to satisfy the intellect and offer nothing to the understanding. We find it difficult properly to conceive true saintliness, since we cannot grasp that to which we give no thought.

Although saintliness is latent in the character of every normal person, yet without cultivation it is sure to remain dormant. Bear in mind that such qualities of character as saintliness, fear and love of God, and purity of heart are not so innate as to enable men to dispense with the effort needed to develop them. These traits are not so natural as being asleep or awake, being hungry or thirsty, or experiencing any other physical want. They can be developed only by means of special effort. Though there are many obstacles to the cultivation of these traits, there are various ways of overcoming those obstacles. . . .

We read in Scripture, "The fear of the Lord, that is wisdom" (Job 28:28). The fear of the Lord is thus identified with wisdom, and declared to be the only true wisdom. The term "wisdom" presupposes the use of the intellect. The truth is that the fear of God, to be properly understood, requires profound study, especially if one wants to comprehend it with the thoroughness necessary to make it part of oneself. Whoever pursues this inquiry realizes that saintliness has nothing to do with what foolish pietists consider to be essential, but rather with wisdom and true perfection.

This is the teaching of Moses, "And now, Israel, what doth the Lord thy God require of thee, but to fear the Lord thy God, to walk in all His ways and to love Him, and to serve the Lord thy God with all thy heart and with all thy soul, to keep the commandments of the Lord and His statutes which I command thee this day for thy good" (Deuteronomy 10:12ff.). Herein are included all the elements of perfect piety, which are considered acceptable to the Holy One, blessed be He, namely, fearing God, walking in his ways, loving Him, acting sincerely, and keeping all the commandments. . . .

I find that our Sages have followed a different arrangement and a more detailed classification of the virtues, giving at the same time the order in which those virtues should be cultivated. Thus we read in the oft quoted *baraita* of Rabbi Phineas ben Yair, "The knowledge of Torah leads to watchfulness, watchfulness to zeal, zeal to cleanness, cleanness to abstinence, abstinence to purity, purity to saintliness, saintliness to humility, humility to the fear of sin, and the fear of sin to holiness" (Avodah Zarah 20b).

OF WATCHFULNESS

A man should be watchful of his conduct. He should scrutinize and pass in review all his actions and habits to determine whether they are right or not, so that he may save his soul from the peril of destruction, and not grope about like a blind man. It is to this conclusion that reason impels us. . . .

A man who goes through life without regard to whether or not he follows a virtuous way is like a blind man who walks along the edge of a river. He is in constant danger and more likely to suffer harm than to escape it. It matters not to what a man's negligence be due, whether it be to natural blindness or to his deliberately shutting his eyes. . . .

Whoever wishes to keep watch over himself must comply with the following two requirements. In the first place, he must know what constitutes the true good, and is therefore to be striven after, and what is unquestionably bad, and therefore to be avoided. Second, he must be able to classify each of his actions as either good or evil. He should do this at all times, while he is active no less than when he is quiescent. . . .

I consider it necessary for a man to conduct himself like a merchant who always takes stock of his affairs so that he may not go wrong in his reckoning. He should set aside a special time each day for the practice of self-scrutiny. For this practice, carried on not sporadically but regularly, is fraught with consequences of great import. . . .

Watchfulness, which consists primarily of mental concentration, is naturally counteracted by levity, which distracts the mind from all rational and logical thinking and leaves the heart void of all feeling of reverence. Scoffing has a sinister and depraving effect. As a shield that is anointed with oil causes the arrows that strike it to glance off without touching the body, so scoffing renders reproof and chastisement ineffective. A single sarcasm or jest is liable to blight most of the spiritual zeal and enthusiasm which a man may have acquired from the experience that taught him to be particular and scrupulous in his actions. As a result of ridicule he is apt to cast off all that he has learned so that there is no sign of it left in him, not because it is not instructive, nor because he lacks, but because mockery has the power to destroy every vestige of conscience and reverence. . . .

OF ZEAL

After giving thought to the development of the trait of watchfulness, one should seek to develop the trait of zeal. Watchfulness pertains to the negative commandments, zeal to the positive commandments. Both traits are implied in the precept, "Depart from evil and do good" (Psalm 34:15). To be zealous means to attend promptly to the performance of the commandments, and to fulfill all their particulars. . . .

It should be borne in mind that it is the nature of man to be inert, and that the earthiness of the physical element in him acts as a weight upon him. Man, therefore, seeks to avoid all toil and effort. Accordingly, a man who desires the privilege of worshiping the Creator, blessed be He, must be able to prevail over his own nature, and act with strength and energy. If he yields to his inertia, he cannot possibly succeed. Thus a *Tanna* said, "Be as strong as a leopard, light as an eagle, fleet as a hart, strong as a lion, to do the will of thy Father in heaven" (Avot 5:20). Our Sages include the study of the Torah and good works among the things that require self-exertion (Berakhot 32b). This is explicitly stated in the verse, "Only be strong and very courageous to observe to do according to all the law which Moses my servant commanded thee" (Joshua 1:7). A man who would transform his nature into the opposite of what it is surely requires great strength.

Solomon warned us repeatedly against indolence and its evil consequences. "Yet a little sleep, a little slumber, a little folding of the hands to sleep—so shall thy poverty come as a runner and thy want as an armed man (Proverbs 6:10f.). Though the sluggard does not actively cause evil, his very inactivity is certainly the cause of evil. Thus Solomon added, "One that is slack in his work is brother to him that is a destroyer" (Proverbs 18:9). Though he is not actually a destroyer, do not imagine that he is far from being one: yea, he is very brother and companion to the destroyer. . . .

One of the greatest hindrances to zeal is excessive fear and undue anxiety as to what the future might bring. Some are afraid of cold or of heat, others of disease and epidemics, others of tempests, and so forth. "The sluggard sayeth, 'There is a lion in the way; yea, a lion is in the streets' " (Proverbs 26:13). Our Sages denounced such fear as characteristic of sinners . . .

To be sure, we are expressly commanded, "Take ye therefore good heed unto yourselves" (Deuteronomy 4:15, according to rabbinic interpretation). Hence, it follows that no one should carry confidence to excess, even in performing a commandment. It should be borne in mind, however, that there are different kinds of fear. There is fear that is warranted, and there is foolish fear; there is faith, and there is folly. When the Lord, blessed be He, created man, He endowed him with proper understanding and with the power of reasoning so as to enable him to lead a good life, and to avoid the injurious things that have been created as a means of punishing the wicked. But he who refuses to lead a life of prudence, and exposes himself to danger, displays not faith but folly. . . .

In the words of Scripture, "A prudent man seeth the evil and hideth himself, but the thoughtless pass on and are punished" (Proverbs 22:3). Yet to take unnecessary precautions, or to indulge in needless anxiety, is to display that foolish fear which hinders a man from worship and the study of the Torah.

The rule that our Sages have laid down with reference to fear is, "Where there is a possibility of danger, we should not depend upon a miracle" (Kiddushin, 39b). Wherever mishap commonly threatens, or may be reasonably apprehended, one must be on one's guard; but where no mishap is known to occur, one must not be afraid. . . .

This, indeed, is the thought underlying the verse, "A prudent man seeth evil and hideth himself." The allusion is to evil which one actually foresees, but not to evil of which there is only a remote possibility. A similar thought is conveyed in the other text that I have quoted. "The slothful man saith, 'There is a lion in the way, yea, a lion is in the streets' " (Proverbs 26:13). In interpeting that verse, our Sages have shown to what extent groundless fear may withhold a man from good works. "In that verse," they say, "Solomon has given us a sevenfold characterization of the sluggard. When a sluggard is told, 'Your teacher is in the city, go and learn Torah from him,' he replies, 'I am afraid I might meet a lion on the way to the city.' When he is told, 'Your teacher is in town,' he replies, 'I am afraid I might meet a lion in the street.' When he is told, 'He is in your house,' he replies, 'If I go to him, I shall find the door locked,' and so forth" (Deuteronomy R. 8:6).

OF CLEANNESS

The quality of cleanness consists in being free from evil traits as well as from sin. That applies not only to sin which is flagrant, but also to such as we are inclined to condone. If we were to look for the true reason why we condone certain sins, we should find that it is because the human heart is plagued as it were, with lust, of which it is with difficulty ever thoroughly cleansed. Therefore, we are inclined to be indulgent.

Only the man who is entirely free from that plague, and who is undefiled by any trace of evil that lust leaves behind it, will see clearly and judge truly. Desire cannot mislead him; he looks upon the most trifling sin as an evil to be shunned. Our sages designated the perfect men, those whose standard of purity was so high that there was not the least trace of evil in them, as "the clean-minded men of Jerusalem" (Sanhedrin 23a).

You may know the difference between one who is merely self-watchful and one who is clean, although the two resemble each other in certain respects. The former is merely watchful of his conduct and takes care not to commit any flagrant sin; but he has not yet achieved such mastery of himself as to ignore the voice of inclination when it tries to prove to him that he may commit certain acts, the evil character of which is not manifestly flagrant. . . .

The quality of cleanness finds expression in manifold ways. It assumes, indeed, as many forms as there are negative commandments, since to be clean means to be clean of transgressions in all its forms.

Although the Evil Desire endeavors to lead man into sin by all sorts of temptations, there are certain temptations which are stronger than others. Those are the ones to which the Evil Desire always helps us find a reason for yielding. Hence, it is against them especially that we must fortify ourselves. . . . We see that although most people are not outright thieves, that is, do not actually seize their neighbor's property and transfer it to their own premises, yet in their dealings with one another they have a taste of the sin of theft, insofar as they permit themselves to profit at their neighbor's expense, claiming that profit has nothing to do with theft. . . .

The laws against unchastity are second in importance only to those against theft. "The majority of men commit theft; a smaller number commit unchastity" (Baba Batra 165a). Whoever desires to be free from the latter sin must exert himself not a little. It is not the forbidden act alone that constitutes unchastity, but whatever approaches it in character. Thus, Scripture states explicitly, "None of you shall approach any woman near of kin to you to uncover her nakedness"

(Leviticus 18:6). In the words of our Sages, "Do not imagine that where cohabitation is sinful, it is no sin to fondle, caress, or kiss." As a Nazarite who has taken the vow is commanded to abstain not only from wine but also from grapes, whether they be fresh or dried, and from any product of grapes, so is it forbidden even to touch any woman except one's wife, and whoever touches a woman not his wife brings death upon himself (Exodus Rabbah 16:2). . . .

OF ABSTINENCE

Abstinence is the beginning of saintliness. All that we have thus far set forth is what a man must do in order to be righteous; henceforth, we shall speak of what a man must do in order to be saintly. We shall find that abstinence bears the same relation to saintliness as watchfulness does to zeal. Abstinence and watchfulness constitute merely the shunning of evil; but saintliness and zeal constitute the doing of good. . . .

We will now discuss the true kind of abstinence. It is evident . . . that all worldly affairs are a source of temptation. . . . Therefore, a man should avoid contact with worldly affairs as much as possible, and thus escape the evil which follows in their wake. There is no worldly pleasure but some sin follows close upon its heels. For instance, it is surely permitted to eat or drink anything that is not forbidden by the dietary laws. Yet filling oneself with food brings on licentiousness, and drinking wine leads to lust and other evils. When a man gets into the habit of eating and drinking heartily, he is in distress if he happens to miss his regular meal. He will enter into the most arduous transactions and moneymaking schemes in order to maintain the kind of table to which he has been accustomed. Thus result dishonesty and greed, which are followed by false swearing and all the other sins that go with it, to say nothing of the neglect of the ritual duties, of the study of the Torah, and of prayer. Yet he would have been free from all these sins had he not allowed himself to be lured by the love of pleasure. . . .

Since abstinence is an absolute prerequisite to saintliness, you will ask, why have not our Sages enacted definite laws with regard to it, in the same way as they have instituted certain "fences" and ordinances to forestall transgressing the precepts of the Torah? The answer is simple. Our Sages have prescribed only such laws as the majority of the people can obey; but the majority of the people cannot be saints. It is enough that they are pious. The few, however, who desire to earn the privilege of being near to God, and by their own merit to impute merit to the mass of the people spiritually dependent upon them, must live by that saintly code to which the average person cannot be expected to conform. . . .

The wrong kind of abstinence is that practiced by foolish Gentiles, who deny themselves not only those things which may bc dispensed with, but even those things which are absolutely essential, and who afflict their bodies with torments and strange practices which God abhors. Our Sages strongly deprecate such actions. "It is forbidden," they say, "for a man to afflict himself" (Ta'anit 22b). With regard to charity, our Sages remark, "He who in dire need refuses to take charity is as though he shed blood" (J. T. Pe'ah 8:9). . . .

The dictum, "Whoever observes a fast which is not prescribed by law is called a sinner" refers to one who fasts in order to torture himself (J. T. Pe'ah 11 a, b.). Hillel was wont to apply the verse, "The merciful man doeth good to his own soul" (Proverbs 11:17), to one who breakfasted early. Hillel was also wont to say of himself that he washed his hands and feet in honor of his Master. . . . You may accept as a true principle that a man should abstain from things in this world which are not absolutely necessary; but if, for any reason, a thing is physically indispensable, he who abstains from it is a sinner. To this there is no exception; and how each particular thing is to be regarded must be left to each man's discretion. "A man shall be praised according to his understanding" (Proverbs 12:8). It is impossible to set down a rule for all the possible cases, because these are innumerable, and the human mind, not being able to grasp all of them at the same time, must deal with each case as it presents itself.

OF PURITY

Purity consists in perfecting one's heart and one's thoughts. Thus David prayed, "Create in me a clean heart, O God" (Psalm 51:12). A man is pure when he does not give the Evil Desire an opportunity to influence his conduct; when wisdom and reverence rather than sin and lust govern all his actions, including those that pertain to the welfare of the body. A man may lead an abstinent life, insofar as he takes from the world only what is indispensable; but he must, in addition, purify his heart and his thoughts by seeking to derive from the little that he does take from the world, not pleasure and satisfaction of desire, but some intellectual and spiritual good. This teaching is conveyed in the verse, "In all thy ways acknowledge Him, and He will direct thy paths" (Proverbs 3:6). . . .

To acquire the trait of purity is an easy matter to one who has made an effort to possess the traits thus far described, and has succeeded. If a man would reflect and realize how worthless the pleasures and the goods of this world are, he would repudiate them and regard them as nothing more than evils and defects inherent in the things of nature, material, unillumined and gross in character. Once a man is convinced that the worldly pleasures are actually evils and defects, he finds it easy to keep aloof from them and to dismiss them from his mind. Therefore, the more attentively and the more frequently a man will note the futility of things earthly, and of the pleasures associated with them, the easier will it be for him to keep his thoughts and his heart pure, and to allow none of his actions to be influenced by the Evil Desire. Even his physical functions will be performed by him as though he were acting under compulsion.

OF SAINTLINESS

In truth, the nature of saintliness requires considerable explanation. There are numerous habits and practices which pass with many people for perfect saintliness, but which are in reality nothing more than the rude and inchoate forms of this trait. This is the case because those of whom these habits are characteristic lack the power of true understanding and reflection. They have neither troubled nor toiled to understand clearly and correctly the way of the Lord. They have practiced saintliness according to the course of conduct which they hit upon at first thought. They have not delved deeply into things nor have they weighed them in the scales of wisdom. Such people render the very savor of saintliness repellent to the average person, as well as to the more intelligent. They give the impression that saintliness depends upon foolish practices that are contrary to reason and common sense, like reciting numerous supplicatory prayers and long confessionals, or weeping and genuflections, or afflicting oneself with strange torments that are liable to bring one to death's door, such as taking ablutions in ice and snow. Though some of these practices may serve as an expiation for certain sins, while others may be fit for ascetics, they cannot form the basis of saintliness. The best of these practices may be associated with saintliness; nevertheless, saintliness itself, properly understood, is something far more profound. Saintliness should be reared upon great wisdom and upon the adjustment of conduct to the aims worthy of the truly wise. Only the wise can truly grasp the nature of saintliness; as our Sages said, "The ignorant man cannot be saintly" (Avot 2:5). . . .

Saintliness is only another form of abstinence, except that abstinence finds expression in negative precepts whereas saintliness expresses itself through positive precepts. Yet the same principle is implied in both, namely, that it is necessary to do much more than what we are explicitly commanded, and to do that which we believe will afford happiness to God, blessed be He. . . .

The practice of lovingkindness is essential to saintliness. The Hebrew word which denotes saintliness is derived from the same root as that which denotes kindness. The practice of lovingkindness is one of the three things upon which, according to our Sages, the world is based. Our Sages have also included deeds of lovingkindness among the meritorious deeds, the interest of which a man enjoys in this world, while the principal remains for him intact in the world to come (Pe'ah 1:1). . . .

Lovingkindness requires that we shall not inflict pain upon any living being, even an animal. We should be merciful and compassionate toward animals, as it is said, "A righteous man regardeth the life of his beast" (Proverbs 12:10). Some are of the opinion that cruelty to animals is prohibited even by the Torah. In any case, it is certainly prohibited by the Rabbis (Shabbat 128b). The sum of the matter is that in the saint's heart, compassion and benevolence must be firmly rooted. His striving must be always to increase the happiness of the world's creatures, and never to cause them any pain. . . .

OF HUMILITY

The principle of humility is that a man shall not think highly of himself for any reason whatsoever. This is the very opposite of what we understand by pride, and equally contrasted to each other are the consequences which follow from each of these traits respectively.

Upon examination, we find that humility depends upon both thought and action. A man must be humble at heart before he can adopt the ways of the meek. Whoever wishes to conduct himself humbly, without being humble at heart, is only an evil pretender, and of the company of those hypocrites who are the bane of mankind. . . .

The man of understanding will, upon reflection, realize that there is no justification for pride or vainglory, even if he was privileged to become very learned. A man of understanding, who has acquired more knowledge than the average person, has accomplished nothing more than what his nature impelled him to do, as it is the nature of the bird to fly, or of the ox to pull with all its strength. Hence, if a man is learned, he is indebted to natural gifts which he happens to possess; and any one gifted by nature with a mind like his would be just as learned. The man who possesses great knowledge, instead of yielding to pride and self-esteem, should impart that knowledge to those who are in need of it. As Rabbi Yohanan ben Zakkai said, "If thou hast learned much Torah, take not any merit, for thereunto wast thou created" (Avot 2:8). If a man is rich, let him rejoice in his portion and help those who are poor; if he is strong, let him help those who are weak, and redeem those who are oppressed. For indeed we are like the servants of a household. Every one of us is appointed to some task and is expected to remain at his post and do the work of the household as well as possible. In the scheme of life there is no room for pride. . . .

The habit of humility is acquired through training and reflection. The training consists in gradually habituating oneself to act humbly by always keeping in the background, and by dressing modestly; for a man's dress may be respectable without ostentation. In the very process of becoming habituated to these ways, humility gradually takes possession of a man's heart, until it is firmly established. For dispositions like pride and arrogance, inherent in human nature, cannot be eradicated except by means of outward actions. As we have explained with regard to zeal, these outward actions, being subject to control, gradually modify a man's inward nature, which is less subject to control. This truth is conveyed in the rabbinic adage, "Let a man always be resourceful in his piety" (Berakhot 17a), that is to say, let him contrive stratagems wherewith to overcome his natural inclinations. . . .

OF THE FEAR OF SIN

The very fact that the virtuous traits which we have thus far discussed are a prerequisite to the fear of sin should be sufficient to make us realize how important and fundamental a trait it is, and how difficult of attainment. It can be attained only by him who has first acquired all the other traits.

It is necessary to state at the outset that there are two types of fear, one that is extremely easy to acquire, and another that is extremely difficult to acquire and, when attained, is an evidence of moral perfection. There is the fear of punishment, and there is the sense of awe. It is with the latter that we should identify the fear of sin. . . .

The way to attain this sense of awe is to realize the following two veritable facts: first, that the Divine Presence exists everywhere in the universe; and second, that God exercises His providence over everything, both great and small. Nothing is hidden from His sight. Nothing is too great or too small for Him to see. He beholds and discerns equally all things, whether trivial or important. . . .

When a man is convinced that, wherever he is, he always stands in the presence of God, blessed be He, he is spontaneously imbued with fear lest he do anything wrong, and so detract from the exalted glory of God. "Know what is above thee," said our Sages, "a seeing eye and a hearing ear, and all thy deeds written in a book" (Avot 2:1).

OF HOLINESS

Holiness is of a twofold nature; it begins as a quality of the service rendered to God, but it ends as a reward for such service. It is at first a type of spiritual effort, and then a kind of spiritual gift. A man must first strive to be holy, and then he is endowed with holiness. . . .

The most that a man can do to achieve holiness by himself is to make a beginning and to persist in his efforts. Only after having attained all the traits that we have thus far discussed, from watchfulness to the fear of sin, may he "enter the sanctuary" (Leviticus 16:3). For, if he lacks any of them, he is like a stranger, or like one that has a blemish, both of whom are prohibited from entering the sanctuary, as it is said, "A stranger shall not come nigh" (Numbers 18:4). But, if after having passed through all these preliminary stages, he cleaves to God with an ardent love and profound awe by reason of his comprehending God's greatness and majesty, he will gradually break away from all that is physical. In all his doings he will succeed in centering his mind upon the mystery of the true communion, until there is poured upon him a spirit from on high, and the name of the Creator, blessed be He, will abide within him as it does within all the holy beings. He will then literally become a messenger of the Lord.

CONCLUSION

It is evident that every man has to be led and guided according to the calling which he pursues, or the business in which he is engaged. The method of attaining saintliness that applies to one whose calling is the study of the Torah does not apply to the manual laborer, and neither method applies to one who is engaged in business. Each man must be shown a method which fits his occupation. Not that there are different kinds of saintliness, since saintliness must consist for all alike in doing that which is pleasing to the Creator, but as there are different kinds of men, the means of accomplishing that purpose are bound to vary. The man who is compelled to labor at the meanest work is capable of being a perfect saint as one who never leaves off the study of the Torah; as it is written, "The Lord hath made all things for Himself" (Proverbs 16:4); and, elsewhere, "In all thy ways acknowledge Him, and He shall direct thy paths" (Proverbs 3:6). God, blessed be His name, will, in His mercy, open our eyes to His Torah, teach us His ways, and guide us in His paths, and we shall be privileged to honor His name and to afford Him delight.

CHAPTER 58

THE ADMONITIONS OF RABBI JOEL

The following passages are taken from another last will and testament, this one left by a Lithuanian scholar, Joel ben Abraham Shemariah, in 1773. The document was eventually published by a disciple with the exhortation: "My friends, despise silver, despise gold, and buy this little book, so small in size, so great in worth."[1]

Your first aim in life here on earth should be to be at peace with all men, Jew and Gentile alike. Contend with no one. Your home should be a place of quietude and happiness, where no harsh word is ever heard, but love, amity, modesty, and a spirit of gentleness and reverence reigns all the time. This spirit must not end with the home, however. In your dealings with the world you must allow neither money nor ambition to disturb you. Forego your rights, if need be, and envy no man. For the main thing is peace, peace with the whole world. Show all men every possible respect, deal with them in the finest integrity and faithfulness. . . .

It was oft my way at assemblies to raise my eyes and regard those present from end to end, to see whether in sooth I loved

[1]Translated by Israel Abrahams in his *Hebrew Ethical Wills*, vol. 2, p. 334 ff.

everyone among them, whether my acceptance of the duty to love my fellow-men was genuine. With God's help I found that, indeed, I loved all present. Even if I noticed one who had treated me improperly, then, without a thought of hesitation, without a moment's delay, I pardoned him. Forthwith I resolved to love him. If my heart forced me to refuse my love, I addressed him with spoken words of friendship, until my heart became attuned to my words. So, whenever I met one to whom my heart did not incline, I forced myself to speak to him kindly, so as to make my heart feel affection for him. What if he were a sinner? Even then I would not quarrel with him, for I wonder whether there exists in this age one who is able to reprove another! On the other hand, if I conceived that he would listen to advice, I drew near to him, turning toward him a cheerful countenance. If, however, I fancied that he would resent my advances, I did not intrude on him. As there is a duty to speak, so is there a duty to be silent.

CHAPTER 59

THE TESTAMENT OF ELIJAH DE VEALI

The author of this testamentary document was an eighteenth-century Italian rabbi of some repute both as a scholar and a poet.[1]

To my offspring I would gladly bequeath a gift over which they must stand at guard. This legacy is my exhortation to them to learn the fear of God all their days. . . .

Come listen unto me, my children, let not your minds despise my words! I would have you hold yourselves as men hired for the day's work, saying every morning: "Today I will be a faithful servant to the All-Master." Keep yourselves the whole day from anger, falsehood, hatred, contention, envy and incontinence. Forgive everyone who troubles you. For half an hour supplicate God's aid to bring you to repentance; do this in synagogue, this day, and on the morrow also! At least appoint one day a week for such exercise. I do not ask you to torture yourselves with fasting, although nowadays the whole world ought to repent with the sharpest rites of betterment. . . .

If your wealth increase, be not proud; unto the rich, more

[1] *Ibid.*

than others, is humility becoming. They that possess most should be the most lowly, gratefully recognizing that they have their all from God. Pride oft displays itself in men's dress; avoid this form of arrogance just as ye concern yourselves with your moral excellence. Be ye attired so that you and your garments harmonize. Let your dress be righteousness, wear modest stuffs, not embroideries or gold and silver. Grace is not shown by fine feathers, but is revealed by unobtrusive bearing.

Happy will ye be, my children, my disciples, and all who attend to my counsel, if ye keep strict account of your expenditure, avoiding all superfluities, acting parsimoniously to yourselves and generously to others! What ye save from frivolous outlays, add bountifully to your charities, and to your loans to the poor in the hour of their need. . . .

It has been a lifelong sorrow to me to behold how, on the contrary, so many, of whatever station, spend extravagantly on themselves and their own pleasures, sparing nothing on their soul's desires, but acting the most miserly part toward others, to whom they yield no services at all; not among such should be the portion of Jacob!

Beware of entering into obligations involving suretyship. I would not have you think that I myself avoided the mistake. I acted otherwise out of my willingness to help others. Often I paid. Often I became liable to serious troubles from which God delivered me; but miracles do not happen every day, and you must not rely on them. Therefore, flee from the act of becoming guarantor as from a sword. Never stand surety whether in written or verbal promises, and, in general, in your business transactions, examine before you sign any document or obligation, whatever it be. Do not rely on the skill of the official scribe or of any other writer. I am grateful to the cheats who opened my eyes by their wiles; and in this connection, I warn you against making promises for fulfillment at a future time. . . .

Love work, hate lordship, and the idleness which tires more

than toil itself. No rest excels that derived from labor in the Torah and in affairs of real import. Be ye kings, not slaves to your passions, rulers over your own spirit. True is the epigram: questioning is the half of wisdom. But questions may be inept, for inquisitiveness in itself is impudence. Judge ye therefore truly in your minds whether the question is a suitable one. . . .

If ye render a kindness to any man, do not recurrently remind him of it. This is a despicable habit. . . . Fix ye this maxim in your hearts: Do what you say, but say not what you do!

CHAPTER 60

THE COUNSEL OF THE VILNER GAON

Rabbi Elijah ben Solomon (1720–1797), better known as the "Vilner Gaon" ("Sage of Vilna"), was the foremost Talmudist of his day. He is reported to have been highly precocious as a child, knowing several tractates of the Gemara by heart when he was barely seven! In his late teens he was sent on the customary "student's tour" of the rabbinic centers in Germany and Poland, and on returning home at the age of twenty, was accepted as a full-fledged Master of the Law.

Unlike most of his contemporaries, however, he interested himself also in secular studies, especially mathematics and philology, and this inclined him to approach the Talmud in a scientific rather than scholastic spirit. He had no patience with the hair-splitting which had become the chief pursuit of the rabbinic pundits, and insisted on simple interpretation based on critical examination of the text. He surrounded himself with a small circle of disciples, and through them and his voluminous writings succeeded in giving the stream of Talmudism a totally new direction. In a sense, the Vilner Gaon was the founder of the "modernist" movement within Orthodox Judaism.

In his personal life he was given to asceticism, refusing all honors and denying himself most pleasures. Toward the close of his life he started out on a pilgrimage to the Holy Land, but for some reason turned back at Koenigsberg. (Perhaps it was because he learned there how impossible it would be to give strict observance to the dietary laws during the long sea voyage.) While on this journey he wrote a lengthy epistle to his family which he evidently intended to be his tzava'ah *("testament"), and it is from this that the following excerpts have been taken.*[1]

It is a familiar truth that this world is altogether vain, its delights ephemeral. Woe to them who pursue after vanity which profiteth nothing! Be not eager after wealth, for there are "riches kept by the owner thereof to his hurt." As a man came forth from his mother's womb, naked shall he return; as he entered, so shall he quit the world. What profiteth it him that he laboreth for the wind and, though he live a thousand years twice told, enjoy no good? Even if a man lives many years rejoicing in them all, yet must he remember the days of darkness, for they shall be many, all that cometh is vanity. As for mirth, what doth it accomplish? What gives you pleasure today will make you weep tomorrow. Neither be zealous after glory, which is likewise a vain thing. Time deceives, resembling a balance which raises the light and lowers the heavy.

Moreover, this world may be likened to one who drinks salt water; he seems to quench his thirst, but he grows thirstier from the draught. No man dies with half his desires attained, and what profit has he of all his toil? Remember the former generations, whose love and ambition and joy have already vanished, and who are enduring their manifold penalties. Destined to the worms, what is man's enjoyment, when the grave transforms all enjoyments into bitterness? Death is near and inevitable; it is no mere accident; life is a series of vexations and pains, and sleepless nights are the common lot. For every word judgment is exacted, no word (however light) is overlooked. Therefore, I urge you to make solitude your habit, for the sin of the tongue weighs as much as all sins put together. So, after enumerating the sins, the punishment for which man eats in this world (while the stock remains for the World-to-Come), our Sages add: "and slander equals them all."

But why need I dilate on this most serious of sins? "All a

[1] *Ibid.*

man's labor is for his mouth,"on which text our Sages remarked that all a man's pious acts and studies fail to compensate for his frivolous speech. What should be man's chief objective in this world? To make himself as one dumb, tightening his lips like the two millstones. The entire penalty of the "hollow of the sling" is due to man's idle words; for every vain utterance he must be slung from end to end of the world. All this applies to words which are merely superfluous, but with regard to forbidden speech–such as slander, scoffing, oaths, vows, dissensions, and curses (particularly in synagogue and on Sabbaths and festivals)–for all such must a man sink very deep into Sheol. 'Tis impossible, indeed, to estimate the chastisements and sorrows which a man bears because of a single utterance–every word of his is noted. . . .

On Sabbaths and festivals speak not at all of matters which are not absolutely essential, and even in such cases be very brief. For the sanctity of the Sabbath is great indeed, and only with reluctance did the authorities allow even the exchange of greetings–so severe were they regarding even a single utterance. Honor then the Sabbath to the utmost, as was done when I was with you. Be in no wise niggardly, for though God determines how much a person shall have, this does not apply to Sabbaths and festivals.

I also make an especial and emphatic request that you train your daughters to the avoidance of objurgations, oaths, lies or contention. Let their whole conversation be conducted in peace, love, affability and gentleness. I possess many moral books with German (versions); let them read these regularly; above all on the Sabbath–the holy of holies–they should occupy themselves with these ethical books exclusively. For a curse, an oath, or a lie, strike them; show no softness in the matter. For (God forbid!) the mother and father are punished for the corruption of the children. Even if you do your best to train them morally and fail, woe to your shame here and hereafter–"she profaneth her father." Therefore, use your utmost rigor in their moral training, and may heaven help you to success! . . .

The fundamental rule, however, is that they gad not about in the streets, but incline their ear to your words and honor you and my mother and all their elders. Urge them to obey all that is written in the moral books.

Furthermore, bring up your sons in the right way and with gentleness. Their teacher must be constantly in your house, and you must pay him generously. All a man's expenditure is appointed from the New Year, but (as the Talmud adds) this does not apply to expenditure on education. I have left the necessary books for tuition. Pay careful heed to the children's health and diet, so that they never lack anything. They should first study all the Pentateuch, learning it practically by heart. Let not the teacher impose his yoke heavily on them, for instruction is only efficient when it is conveyed easily and agreeably. Give the children small presents of money and the like, to please them–this helps their studies. To this apply your unfailing attention; all else is vanity. . . .

Say not: I will bequeath to my children money and means for their support. Know that the sons of man are like the grasses of the field, some flourish and others wither, each being born under his star, and under the providence of the Most High God. The heirs of a wealthy man rejoice at his death, to inherit his estate, while he descends to the grave and leaves his wealth to others. So it was said of Rabbi Simeon ben Lakish, who left behind him nothing more than a measure of saffron, that he applied to himself the text: "and leave their wealth to others." Woe and alas for the sins of men who toil and moil to leave their children money and goods and full houses! All this is vanity, for the only profit in sons and daughters is their Torah and their virtue. . . .

For slander once spoken there is no remedy. Therefore, the rule must be: Speak of no man to his praise, still less to his dispraise. For what has a man to do with slander? "The mouth of slander is a deep pit, he that is abhorred of the Lord falleth therein."

Against this offense the most effective hedge is solitude – to avoid ever leaving the house for the streets unless under pressure of extreme necessity or in order to perform an important religious duty. . . . Even in synagogue make but a very short stay and depart. It is better to pray at home, for in synagogue it is impossible to escape envy and the hearing of idle talk. . . .

It is also better for your daughter not to go to synagogue, for there she would see garments of embroidery and similar finery. She would grow envious and speak of it at home, and out of this would come scandal and other ills. Let her seek her glory in her home, cleaving ever to discipline, and showing no jealousy for worldly gauds, vain and delusive as they are, coming up in a night and perishing in a night. . . .

Among my books is the Book of Proverbs in German; for the Lord's sake let them read it every day, as it is chief of moral works. They should also read Ecclesiastes constantly, in your presence; for this book exposes the vanity of temporal concerns; but the end must not be a mere perusal of these books, for man does not thus gain incentive. Many a man reads moral words without rousing himself to moral works. Partly because they merely read, partly because they fail to understand – this renders the reading fruitless. This is shown in the parable of one who sows without plowing the soil, so that the wind snatches the seed and satisfies the birds. Because he cannot restrain himself or make himself a fence, he is like one who sows without fence, and the pigs consume it and tread it down. Sometimes one sows on stone, the stony heart into which no seed enters at all, and it is necessary to strike the stone until it is split. Therefore, I have bidden you to strike your children if they refuse to obey you. "Train up a child in the way he should go, and even when he is old he will not depart from it." This is the great rule!

CHAPTER 61

SAYINGS OF THE BAAL SHEM TOV

Israel ben Eliezer (1700–1760), who came to be called the Baal Shem Tov—commonly abbreviated to Besht—was one of the most extraordinary characters in Jewish history. Born in some village in southern Poland, and orphaned in childhood, he was reared on charity until his waywardness exhausted the patience of his benefactors. Instead of devoting himself to his studies, he was constantly going off alone into the woods or else idling in the barns of the neighboring peasants. He was a good lad, but inclined to be slightly daft, and showed every sign of growing up to be a thoroughgoing schlemiel. So he was made a helper in the village school, then janitor of the synagogue, and thus enabled to care for himself, and, at the age of eighteen, even for a wife.

However, his bride died soon after the wedding, and the young man took to wandering. He supported himself by teaching small children, but spent most of his time helping their parents. He gave them advice on all sorts of questions, prayed for them, settled their disputes, and brewed potions for their ailments. There were many such characters wandering about in Eastern Europe, especially in the Carpathian region, where the Jews were as ignorant and superstitious as they were poor and woebegone. This Israel, however, was unlike most of his colleagues, for he was obviously sincere and utterly selfless. He never asked pay for his incantations, but served out of love alone. That was why the people took to calling him the Baal Shem Tov, the Master of the Good Name.

Finally, settling in the little city of Medziboz, he became the leader of a cult which soon began to spread throughout Poland. It was called Hasidism *("Pietism"), and its central tenet was the belief that everything–mind and matter, good and evil, the birds and trees and rocks and rills–everything was a manifestation of God. From this it followed that God could be worshipped anywhere, and not necessarily according to a fixed formula, but with whatever words came into one's mind. The most ignorant man, therefore, could draw as near to God as the most learned; and since access to God was so easy, one ought to be full of joy; one ought to sing and dance. Hasidism was intensely fervid and comforting.*

The Besht left no books, but his utterances were remembered by many disciples, and eventually received publication in Hebrew, Yiddish, and German. The following are typical examples of the didactic sayings and anecdotes which came to be accepted as his.[1]

Men learned in the Law came to the Besht on an errand of dispute. "In times gone by," they protested, "there were pious men aplenty, fasting from Sabbath to Sabbath, and inflicting their own bodies with self-devised torments. Now your disciples proclaim it to all who care to listen that much fasting is unlawful and self-torment a crime."

The Besht made answer: "It is the aim and essence of my pilgrimage on earth to show my brethren by living demonstration how one may serve God with merriment and rejoicing. For he who is full of joy is full of love for men and all fellow creatures."

On another occasion, the Besht declared: "The strength thou wert willing to lose through fasting, devote to the Torah and to worship. Thereby wilt thou ascend to a higher state."

Man should know how to be proud, and yet not be proud; he should know how to be angry, and yet never feel angry. For

[1]My chief source for these excerpts has been *The Hasidic Anthology* by Louis J. Newman and Samuel Spitz (New York, Scribner, 1934). More material from the same source will be found below under "The Sayings of the Bratzlaver" (p. 573) and "Hasidic Tales and Teachings" (p. 581).

man should be a complete personality, possessing all human traits. Does not the Torah picture God as possessing both justice and mercy?

The Lord does not object even if a man misunderstands what he learns, provided he only strives to understand out of his love of learning. It is like a father whose beloved child petitions him in stumbling words, yet the father takes delight in hearing him.

The Turbiner Rabbi narrated the following tale: "Two hasidim were traveling to the Besht by horse and wagon. On a narrow road, they were compelled to slacken their pace because a nobleman's carriage ahead had developed a defect in one of the wheels. One hasid complained that with such slow going they would be unable to reach Medziboz for the Sabbath. The other hasid replied. 'What God brings to pass, is for good.' They soon came to a still narrower pass, and found it blocked by a milk wagon which had broken down. The nobleman ordered the milk cans to be transferred to another wagon, and the broken wagon to be pushed aside. Later the nobleman took a branch road, and the hasidim were able to drive ahead quickly. 'You see, now, that I was right,' said the hasid who had not complained. 'Had the nobelman not been ahead of us, we should have been forced to wait until the milk wagon had been repaired. The owner would never have bothered to transfer the milk cans for our sake.' "

In the hour of his death the Baal Shem Tov said: "Now I know the purpose for which I was created."

When you perceive the Satan diligently seeking to persuade you to commit an evil deed, understand that he is endeavoring to fulfill his duty as he conceives it. Learn from him diligence in performing your bounden duty–namely, to battle and overcome his persuasion.

When you eat and take pleasure in the taste and sweetness of the food, bear in mind that it is the Lord who has placed into the food its taste and sweetness. You will, then, truly serve him by your eating.

Several hasidim came to the Besht and said: "Our opponents, the sages of Brody, persecute us continually and accuse us, Heaven forbid, of disobedience to the Law and irreverence toward the traditions of our forefathers. We can endure it no longer, and we must answer them."

"Our adversaries," replied the Besht, "do this certainly out of pious zeal. They believe they are performing a good deed, and they take joy in oppressing us. Why should we seek to deprive them of their joy?"

Laugh not at the motions of a man who prays with fervor. He makes these motions in order to save himself from foreign thoughts which intrude upon him and threaten to engulf his prayer. Would you laugh at a drowning man who makes motions in the water in order to rescue himself?

The Besht once journeyed with his little son Hirsch to Medziboz to visit the ailing rabbi of the town. The rabbi was a man of means, and in his house there stood a cabinet of silverware which Hirsch admired greatly.

"My son," said the Bescht, "thou thinkest in thy heart that this silverware standeth in the wrong place and that it should be in thy father's house. You are right by half, and wrong by half. The silver truly stands in the wrong place, but not because it is not ours. It should rather be given away as charity, instead of glittering here as futile ornaments."

Said the Besht: "We read in the Talmud that forty-nine doors of understanding out of fifty were opened to Moses; but since man aspires always to know more, how did Moses continue? The answer is that when he found the fiftieth door closed to him as unapproachable to the human mind, he substituted faith and meditated again upon those phases of knowledge open to him.

"It is thus that every man should discipline his mind. He should study and reflect to the utmost of his ability. When he has reached a point where he is unable to comprehend further, he may substitute faith, and return to the learning within his grasp. Beyond a certain degree of research, both the sage and the ignorant man are alike. It may be that some will apply to you the verse: 'The simpleton believeth every word,' but you may remind the scoffers of another verse: 'The Lord preserveth the simple.' "

Said the Besht: "A hero promised to defend his city and showed the inhabitants his many weapons. He was met by the foe unexpectedly, however, when he had no weapons on his person; he was captured, and the undefended city fell. In the same way, people depend upon their rabbi to protect them against irreligion; but, if Satan succeeds in deceiving the rabbi, all of them fall into error. Each man should learn his duties for himself, and he should be able to prevent wrong deeds by indicating their falsity, if the leader should happen to be weaponless."

The Besht commented on the phrase: "Our God and God of our Fathers." He said: "Some persons have faith because their fathers taught them to believe. In one sense, this is satisfactory: no philosophical axioms will break their belief; in another, it is unsatisfactory, since their belief does not come from personal knowledge.

"Others come to belief through conviction after research. This is satisfactory in one sense: they know God from inner conviction; in another, it is unsatisfactory: if other students demonstrate to them the fallacy of their reasoning, they may become unbelievers.

"The best believers are those whose beliefs are satisfactory in every way: they believe because of tradition and also through their own reasoning. This is what we mean when we say: 'Our God and the God of our Fathers.' The Lord is our Master, both because we know He is our God, and because our fathers have taught us that He is God."

A father complained to the Besht that his son had forsaken God. "What, Rabbi, shall I do?"

Love him more than ever," was the Besht's reply.

The Besht commented on the verse: "As in the water, face answereth to face, so the heart of man to man" (Proverbs 27:19). He said: "When a man stands upright near the water, his shadow is reflected in enlarged form. But when he bends down his reflection is smaller in size. In like manner, when one man looks upon another with pride, the other is also prompted to a feeling of proud aloofness. When, however, a man is meek in his relationship with another man, the latter likewise feels friendship and goodwill toward him."

"Why does the Bible relate the wrongdoings of good men?" the Besht was asked. "Would it not encourage righteousness to teach that good men are invariably good?"

The Besht answered: "If the Bible failed to indicate the few sins of its heroes, we might doubt their goodness. Let me explain this by the following fable:

" 'A lion taught his cubs that they need fear no living creature, since they were the strongest on earth. One day the cubs went for a walk and came upon a ruin. They entered and saw on the wall of the deserted castle a picture of Samson breaking in twain a lion cub. In fright they ran to their father, crying out: "We have seen a creature stronger than ourselves, and we are in fear of him." The old lion questioned them, and on learning what they had seen in the ruin, he said: "This picture ought assure you that the race of lions is the strongest of creatures, for when once a stronger creature appears, it is pictured as a miracle. Exceptions prove the rule." ' "

A farmer held an egg in his hand, and mused: "I shall place this egg under a hen; I shall raise up the chick and it shall hatch other chicks; I will sell them, and purchase a cow and . . ." While planning thus, he squeezed the egg and it broke in his fingers.

In the same fashion some people are satisfied with the sum of holiness and knowledge they have attained and think constantly that they are superior to others; but they do not perceive that by doing this they lose even the little they have attained.

A king was told that a man of humility is endowed with long life. He attired himself in old garments, took up his residence in a small hut, and forbade anyone to show reverence before him; but when he honestly examined himself, the king found himself to be prouder of his seeming humility than ever before. A philosopher thereupon remarked to him: "Dress like a king; live like a king; allow the people to show due respect to you; but be humble in your inmost heart."

The Besht was asked: "What is the chief point in service to the Lord, if it be true, as you teach, that fasting and self-chastisement are sinful?"

The Besht answered: "The main thing is to encompass oneself in the love of God, the love of Israel, and the love of the Torah. A man may attain this if he secures enough nourishment to preserve his health, and if he makes use of his strength to battle against evil inclinations."

The influence of a leader is likened, in the Talmud, to a burning coal. Do not hold yourself aloof from your master; you will remain cold. Do not approach him too closely; you may be burned. This applies also to your relationship with your friends.

Mind is the foundation of man. If the foundation is solid, the building is secure. By the same token, if a man's mind is filled with holy thoughts, his actions will be sound. But if his mind is occupied with selfish thoughts, even his good actions are unsound, being built on a weak foundation.

The Besht was accustomed to send forth his disciples to endeavor to improve people. Once his disciple, Rabbi Mendel of Bar, returned to Medziboz from a journey. The Besht said to him: "A broom sweeps the courtyard clean, but it becomes soiled itself. Go now and cleanse yourself of any offenses in which you may be guilty."

The disciples of the Besht were told of a certain man who was known as truly wise. There were several of the disciples who were prompted to call upon this man in the town of his residence and to profit by his doctrine. The Besht gave them leave, but they inquired: "How shall we know him for a true *tzadik*?"

"Ask him to counsel you," said the Besht, "how to keep your thoughts from going astray when praying or learning. If he offers counsel, you will know that his wisdom is nought; for it is part of man's bondage, until the hour of his death, to wrestle with alien thoughts, time and again, and to subdue them in any ascent of the soul."

It is so natural for a gifted man to attain pride that he scarcely is aware of it. It is only when he strives to humble himself in his intercourse with people that he realizes how full of pride he has been. It is like a man who travels in a stagecoach and falls asleep. The driver has to ascend a hill; after he reaches the summit, there is a long stretch of smooth road. When the man awakes and is told he is now on a hill, he can hardly believe it. Only when the descent is made does he realize how high he had been.

False humility can be illustrated by this story: "A man was learned, gifted and charitable, but was afflicted with the blemish of pride. He was told that if he learned humility he would become a perfect man. He acted upon this counsel, and studied humility until apparently he had learned it by heart. One day a man failed to show him deference. Then the man of supposed humility turned to him and said: 'You fool! Do you now know that since I have learned humility, I am a man of perfect character?"

The Besht asked a man: "Why is a fast horse worth ten times as much as a slow one?"

"Because he runs ten times as fast," was the reply.

"Yes, but if he loses his way, he loses it ten times as fast."

"Yes?" queried the man, not knowing what the Besht would say next.

"Well, but do not forget that when he finds the right road, he makes up for lost time ten times as quickly."

"When a sagacious man repents, he attains his former state of righteousness much faster than the dull man."

The chief joy of the Satan is when he succeeds in persuading a man that an evil deed is a *mitzvah*. For when a man is weak and commits an offense, knowing it to be a sin, he is likely to repent of it; but when he believes it to be a good deed, does it stand to reason that he will repent of performing a *mitzvah*?

A man of piety complained to the Besht, saying: "I have labored hard and long in the service of the Lord, and yet I have received no improvement. I am still an ordinary and ignorant person."

The Besht answered: "You have gained the realization that you are ordinary and ignorant, and this in itself is a worthy accomplishment."

No true saint would be able to see wickedness in others. The real *tzadik* would not know if men and women are guilty of offenses. He could not, therefore, under these circumstances serve as an example to others, and could not teach the people. It is for this reason that there is no man on earth who does not sin. The sin makes the *tzadik* humane and enables him to guide others."

Do not consider the time you spend for eating and sleeping wasted. The soul within you is rested during these intervals, and is enabled to renew its holy work with fresh enthusiasm.

You may be free from sin, but if your body is not strong, your soul will be too weak to serve God aright. Maintain your health and preserve your strength.

The Besht was about to enter a synagogue, but he halted at the door and exclaimed: "This place is overfilled with prayers and learning!"

"Why, then, do you hesitate to enter such a holy place?" inquired his disciples.

"Were this a truly sacred place," replied the Besht, "the prayers and learning would have ascended heavenward, and this synagogue would be empty of them. Only the prayer and learning which does not come from the heart can fill an earthly abode."

Once the Baal Shem said: "There are precious stones beyond cavil; everyone can see the gleam and the lights they shed in their different colors; their genuineness can be recognized at once. These are the Jews who are true hasidim. There are also false gems: these are the hypocritical pietists. Finally there are stones, 'treasures concealed in the sand,' which cannot at once be identified as precious. These are the Jews who easily surrender to untrammeled desires and passions, and who do not follow the injunctions of the Law. Nevertheless, they, too, carry in their heart the treasure of abiding love for humanity."

He meditated for a moment, and then continued: "But they are all precious gems."

Think not that you are superior to your fellowman in your devotion. If he is not endowed with as fine an intellect as yours, he is equal to you when he serves God to the best of his ability. A worm may be as important as you in the eyes of the Creator, since it serves Him with all the strength granted to it.

Brood not upon your sin, for this leads to melancholy and prevents sincere service to God.

Express contrition in your heart for your wrongdoing; resolve not to repeat it, and serve God with joy. Make no response to one who ridicules your devotions. If he retorts in anger, your devotions will thus lead to quarrelsomeness and thereby become worthless.

Accustom yourself to keep constantly in mind the knowledge that whatever gives you pleasure derives its ability to please from God. Every pleasure will then become an act of praise to the Lord for endowing everything with His Spirit.

When a man squeezes wine grapes into a vessel, he must first use a sieve with large holes to strain it; later he uses a cheesecloth, but no matter how many times he will strain it, some sediment will still remain. It is the same with the *tzadik*. He must rid himself of his evil inclinations and continue to do so his entire life; but there are always a few dregs left over.

If the vision of a beautiful woman come suddenly to a man's eyes, or if he perceive any other fair and lovely thing, he should unhesitatingly ask himself: Whence comes this beauty except from the divine force which permeates the world? Consequently the origin of this beauty is divine, and why should I be attracted by the part? Better for me to be drawn after the All, the Source of every partial beauty! If a man taste something good and sweet, let the taster conceive that it is from the heavenly sweetness that the sweet quality is derived. Such perception of beauty then is an experience of the Eternal, blessed be He. . . . Further if he hear some amusing story and he derive pleasure from it, let him bethink himself that this is an emanation from the realm of love. . . .

Sometimes the evil spirit betrays a man, persuading him that he has committed a deadly sin. Possibly he has failed in some stringency of the law, possibly he had done no wrong at all. The spirit's purpose is to drive him into despondency over the supposed lapse, and by inducing a condition of gloom render him incapable of service. Let man beware of this dastardly trick! Let him retort on the spirit: "I perceive thy design to lure me from service. Thou speakest a lie! If indeed I have sinned a little, the more gratified will my Creator be if I refuse to let my offense interrupt the joyousness of my service. On the contrary, I will go on serving Him in a happy mood. For I serve not for my own ends but to give God pleasure. If I do not worry about this peccadillo, with which thou chargest me, God will not take it amiss. For I ignore it, that my service be not stayed for a single instant." This is the great rule of service: Bid melancholy avaunt!

Weeping is an exceeding great evil, for man must serve in joy. If, however, weeping comes through joy, then it is an exceeding great good . . .

Therefore, let a man desist from anxiety as to his conduct. . . . Let him not yield overmuch to paralyzing grief. Let him indeed sigh for his sin, but then let him turn again in joy to the Creator, blessed be He!

CHAPTER 62

THE SAYINGS OF THE BRATZLAVER

Nahman ben Simha (1770–1811), a great-grandson of Baal Shem Tov, the founder of Hasidism (see above on p. 561), was one of the chief sources of the early literature on that movement. The center of his activities was the small Ukranian town of Bratzlav, and he is, therefore, generally referred to as "the Bratzlaver." His endless table-talk was taken down by a tireless disciple and published in a series of volumes which Nahman himself seems to have regarded somewhat highly. He is reported to have said of them that they marked the "beginning of the Messianic Redemption," and that their mere presence in a household, even if left standing unread on the shelves, guaranteed protection against sickness, robbery, and disaster!

This report may have been invented by his Boswell, but whatever Reb Nahman himself may have thought of the worth of his words, we can see by the following examples that they were not without value.[1]

CONCERNING JOY

Even repentance should be attained through joy. We should rejoice so much in God that it will arouse in us regret for having offended Him.

[1]Translation by Newman and Spitz in their *Hasidic Anthology*.

Through zealous labor in the performance of a holy deed, we can acquire joy.

God dislikes melancholy and depressed spirits.

Joy is a cure for illnesses caused by melancholy.

It is the duty of the joyful person to endeavor to bring to those in sadness and melancholy a portion of his mood.

CONCERNING KNOWLEDGE

Lack of proper understanding is the cause of all tribulations; perfection of knowledge will banish them.

The essence of a man is his mind and understanding. Hence, wherever his thoughts are, there he is. Let him but think holy thoughts, and he will be in a holy place.

Anger and cruelty testify to a defect in man's knowledge. With increased understanding come calmness, peace, kindness, and contentment.

No one is entitled to excuse his lack of service to the Lord by affirming that he is engaged in business and must associate with vulgar folk. God is everywhere. He is among the most common of men; he is to be found in the lowliest occupation. Delve deeper and you will find a way to serve God in everything and in every work and place.

By the same token, no matter how low you may have fallen in your own esteem, bear in mind that if you delve deeply into yourself, you will discover holiness there. A holy spark resides there which, through repentance, you may fan into a consuming flame which will burn away the dross of unholiness and unworthiness.

Passion and desire surround understanding as the shell, the kernel; break through the shell, and thereby attain understanding.

He who is able to write a book and does not write it is as one who has lost a child.

Every author should weigh his work to determine whether it has any connection with the "Book of Humanity," namely, whether humanity will receive any benefit from it.

CONCERNING CHARITY

When you give aid to scholars, you gain a share in their learning.

He who restores to its owner a stolen object is like one who gives to charity.

He who gives a penny to a poor man receives six blessings; he who shows his sympathy with the poor man receives eleven blessings.

He who feels resentment when he beholds a man prospering who formerly was poor is a partner of Satan.

He who gives charity with a smile is truly a wholehearted man.

Charity is greater than the sacrifices brought to the altar; yet kindness is greater than charity.

Kindhearted folk should be watchful lest their kindness does not result in more evil than good.

CONCERNING PARENTS AND CHILDREN

Children will be healthy and well bred, if parents do not play with them overmuch and do not indulge them too generously.

A well-nourished mother has healthy children.

We have the kind of children we deserve.

One who adopts an orphan is like unto him who begot him.

One who displeases his parents will have disobedient sons.

If husband and wife quarrel, they cannot raise good children.

The strict leader will not have understanding sons.

When the father is quick-tempered, his sons are fools.

ON GOOD MANNERS

A man should eat slowly and with etiquette even if alone at the table.

He who never leaves his home is as if he sojourned in prison.

Drunkenness causes a man to fall from his high estate, to accept bribes, to deny truth, and to rely upon untruths.

God has no love for the Drunkard.

It is impossible for a drunkard to avoid harm to someone.

One who eats more than he needs is worse than an animal.

ON FAITH AND MEDITATION

The knowledge that whatever happens to you is for your good raises you to the heights of living in Paradise.

Better is the superstitious believer than the rationalistic unbeliever.

A man should believe in God by virtue of faith rather than miracles.

Be not discouraged by any tribulations which may assail you. The recognition that they are for the good of your soul will aid you to endure them.

If you are your own judge and regret your misdeeds, you will not be judged in Heaven.

Meditation and prayer before God is particularly efficacious in grassy fields and amid the trees, since a man's soul is thereby strengthened, as if every blade of grass and every plant united with him in prayer.

If a man finds that he cannot concentrate upon the theme of his meditation, he should express his thoughts in words. Words are like water which falls continually upon a rock until it breaks it through. In similar fashion they will break through a man's flinty heart.

CONCERNING HONORS

Do not pursue honors; rather flee from them. Then God will approve your honors, and people will not investigate or question whether you deserve your honors.

The Lord permits no durable leadership to those who accept a position of honor on the plea of reforming the community. The reformer's true desire is rather to attain the honor.

Be careful to give due honor to the sons of the lower classes who engage in the study of the Torah. Your honoring of them will serve to encourage them and bring forth their best abilities.

There are so-called leaders versed only in superficialities and outward values. They cannot lead even themselves, and yet their evil impulse prompts them to lead others. They are not so much to be blamed as those who vote for them and support them. These adherents will be called upon eventually to give an accounting for their action.

When a man is able to receive abuse smilingly, he is worthy to become a leader.

He who cannot accept reproof cannot become a great man.

The man whom you encourage in his service to God will love you. The way to encourage him is to love him.

God is present whenever a treaty of peace is signed.

CONCERNING AVARICE

Those sunk in desire for money are always in debt. They either borrow to make more money and carry the load of debt, or they fall into obligations to this desire for money. Oftentimes we perceive men of wealth toiling arduously and assuming risks in order to acquire more money, as if they were compelled to pay off a debt. This debt they owe to their desire, and since a man has not yet died who was half-satisfied with his possessions, they are always in debt to their own desire. These slaves to gold suffer irritation, bitterness, sadness, and anxieties because of their desire. The more gold they own, the more anxiety they feel. Their money consumes the days of their life.

He who dislikes superfluous money attains wisdom, intelligent understanding, and inspiration.

Those who are dissatisfied though they possess every necessity are those concerning whom it is written (Proverbs 13–25): "But the belly of the wicked shall want."

He who covets is guilty of robbery in thought.

Only the man of folly marries for money. He will pay for his sin by suffering through his wife and children.

The man and his money cannot both be in the same person. Either he loses his money and remains a man, or he loses his dignity as a man, and the money is left.

Poverty is worse than fifty plagues.

OTHER SAYINGS

Uncleanliness in the home leads to poverty.

When we wish to influence another person, we ought to begin by commending his good traits, and help him find excuses for his misdeeds. In this fashion we may hope to succeed in improving him.

To chop down a fruit-bearing tree is like unto murder.

Soiled clothing is an indication of the wearer's character. Ostentatious garments mark their wearer as an adherent of the Satan. His clothes are more important to him than his God.

Prayers are not heard where there is no peace.

Even the wicked who live in peace enjoy prosperity.

Philosophy may become dangerous when the development of the mind it encourages is not accompanied by a similar degree of self-improvement through the medium of good practice.

Before prayer, give to charity.

One who must fast and scourge his body is not yet a *tzadik,* since he has not yet rid himself of bodily desires.

A poor and lowly man who gives nothing to charity is preferable to a rich haughty man who gives to charity.

Sometimes a man pays no attention to his opponent in order to vex him the more by his silence. There is no holiness in this behavior. If you understand that a soft answer will calm your foe, do not withhold it from him.

He who keeps silence in the face of abuse is a true hasid.

Even though a quarrelsome man be learned, show him no honors.

The world stands firm because of the man who closes his lips during a quarrel.

He who is able to halt wickedness and fails to do so is considered as if he performed the evil himself.

Satan is like an urchin who teases his friends by asking them to guess what is in his closed hand. Each person guesses that the hand conceals whatever is particularly desirable to himself; but when the hand is opened, it is found to contain nothing.

A man should know even in study when he has attained sufficiency. He should not attempt to study too much lest he become confused; he cannot learn all there is to be known.

He who learns and does not review his studies is like one who sows and does not reap.

Learning for which a man spends money will be remembered longer by him.

He who is ready to steal is prepared to commit every offense.

He who cares not to prevent waste of another's property is equivalent to a thief.

A city where thieves abound is sure to possess judges who are bribed and police who are corrupt.

There is no room for more than one thought at a time. Think of a subject of Torah or even of a transaction of your business, and the unworthy thoughts will find no place in your mind.

In a family where the parents are untruthful, the children are unruly.

Lies are usually caused by undue fear of men.

He who possesses no confidence utters falsehoods, and he who utters falsehoods possesses no confidence.

How can you say: "It was mere talk; no harm was done by me"? Were this true, your words of prayer and kindness would be a waste of breath.

When the rays of the sun enter a house through a dusty window, they form illumined pillars; but if one tries to feel them, he discovers there is nothing there. Worldly desires are comparable to these seeming pillars fashioned by the sun.

He who repays good for evil will live many years.

CHAPTER 63

HASIDIC TALES AND TEACHINGS

Like all warmly idealistic movements, Hasidism fell prey eventually to practical organizers, and at their hands it suffered the usual fate. It became outwardly a success, winning converts throughout Eastern Europe, and acquiring an importance almost equal to that of Talmudism in that region. But this success was bought at a price that ultimately spelled utter failure.

Hasidism started out as a revolt against the learned ones who had obtruded themselves between God and the ordinary Jew. Those scholars had become a sort of religious bureaucracy, for they alone were profoundly versed in the Law, and through the Law alone was salvation believed to be obtainable. But the founder of Hasidism insisted that not the letter but the spirit of the Law was important, and since the spirit could be understood by the heart rather than the mind, learning was religiously inconsequential. What counted was prayer, and this could be indulged in as readily by an ignorant villager as by the most erudite rabbi in creation. No, even more readily.

Hasidism began, therefore, as a vehemently democratic movement, and so long as it remained that it served Israel well. But, as was seemingly inevitable, its character changed after a while. Dynasties of tzadikim arose, each with its own local following.

Rivalries characterized the movement. Individual hasidim proved themselves men of high worth: earnest, kindly, and in a deceptively naive way, profoundly wise. Their "miracles" were often conscious feats of therapeutic suggestion, and their "divine counsel" was in many instances merely distilled common sense. The following miscellany of some of their sayings and doings will indicate a little of the service they were able to render the poor, ignorant, woe-ridden folk whom they led.[1]

ANECDOTES

Once a poor hasid became so distraught because of the crowding in his hovel that he appealed to his tzadik for advice. "Rebee,"[2] he cried, "we have so many children (may no Evil Eye fall on them!) and so many relatives living with us, that my wife and I cannot turn around in the house!"

"Have you also a goat?" asked the tzadik.

"Why not?" answered the other. "What Jew doesn't own a goat?"

"Then my counsel is that you bring the animal into your dwelling."

This greatly mystified the hasid, but he did not dare argue. The next day, however, having done as he had been told, the unhappy man came running back to the tzadik. "Beloved Rebbe," he groaned, "things now are worse than ever!"

"Have you any chickens?" he was asked.

"What then? How can a Jew live without a few chickens in his yard?"

"My counsel is that you bring them likewise into your house."

Again the hasid could not bring himself to argue, but after a day with the chickens underfoot and on every rafter, he returned once more to the tzadik, this time half-crazed.

"So it is bad, eh, my son?" the other said calmly.

---

[1]The first ten anecdotes are drawn from various sources, and given in an abbreviated version of my own. The majority of the subsequent quotations are taken verbatim from the *Hasidic Anthology* by Newman and Spitz.

[2]This was the common term applied to a *tzadik* to distinguish him from an ordinary rabbi.

"It is the end of the world!" replied the hasid.

"Very well, then. Now go home, turn out the goat and the chickens, and come back to me on the morrow."

The following day the hasid showed up with his face beaming. "Rebbe!" he cried, "a thousand blessings on thee! My hut seems like a palace now!"

Two Jews, one poor and the other rich, sat waiting to consult a famous tzadik. The rich man was ushered in first, and his audience lasted fully an hour. But the poor man, when he was finally ushered in, was given merely a few moments.

He tried to protest, crying, "Rebbe, is this not unfair?"

"Foolish man!" the other chided him. "When you entered I could see at a glance that you were poor; but that other one–I had to listen to him for an hour to discover that he was even poorer than you!"

A tzadik who was renowned for his ability to get donations from the rich was once asked whether it was not beneath his dignity to stoop to those creatures even for the sake of the charity fund.

"My son," he replied, "it is all in the order of nature. See, there is no creature more excellent than man, and few more lowly than the cow. Yet does not man have to stoop before the cow in order to milk her?"

Once a tzadik was called on to arbitrate a dispute involving a large sum of money. When he performed the task, the litigants handed him a paltry ten *rubles* for his trouble. The tzadik looked at the coin with an air of innocence, and asked what it was.

"It is money," he was told.

"And what does one do with money?"

"One buys goods and sells them at a profit, thus acquiring more money."

"If that is so," said the tzadik, "I do not need it," and he made as if to return the coin.

"No," said the businessmen, "if you do not need it, give it to your wife."

"And what can she do with it?"

"She can buy food and clothing and things for the house."

"So?" cried the tzadik, suddenly appearing to brighten up. "If that is the case, you should give me more."

In a time of famine a tzadik took it upon himself to raise money enough to feed all the starving people in the community. In the course of his rounds he approached a certain rich man who was notoriously boorish and ill-tempered. Instead of receiving alms, however, all the tzadik got from him was a slap in his face. The holy man was dazed for a moment; but then, wiping the blood from his cheek, he said gently: "That, my son, was evidently meant for me. Now what will you give for my poor?"

A rich miser, having lost his purse, announced that he would give a generous reward to the finder. When a poor man showed up with it, the miser counted the contents and immediately cried: "There are a hundred *rubles* missing! Go away, man! Would you expect me to give you a reward yet?"

The other, knowing he had taken nothing out of the purse, complained to the local tzadik, who sent for the skinflint and demanded: "How much did your purse contain?"

"Five hundred *rubles*," came the brazen reply.

Turning to the poor man, the tzadik asked: "And how much was in the purse which you found?"

"Four hundred *rubles*," he answered meekly.

"Then it is clear," the tzadik decided, turning back to the miser, "that this purse was not the one you lost. You will, therefore, give it back to the finder and let him keep it until its rightful owner appears!"

A tzadik was once asked whether wisdom was more important than wealth. He replied, "Certainly." Whereupon he was asked, "Why then do the wise wait on the rich, and not the rich on the wise?" He answered, "Because the wise, being wise, understand the value of wealth, whereas the rich, being merely rich, are ignorant of the value of wisdom."

The tzadikim held regular sessions with their followers on Sabbath afternoons. At one of these a skeptic who happened to be present, thinking to make sport of the holy man at the head of the table, asked him: "Rebbe, if you know all things, tell us what Eve did whenever Adam returned home late."

"She counted his ribs," replied the tzadik.

One day a rich but miserly man came to consult a tzadik. Pointing to the window facing the street, the latter said, "What do you see out there?"

"People," answered the rich man.

The tzadik then took him by the hand and led him to a mirror. "What do you see now?" he asked.

"Now I see myself," answered the rich man.

Then the tzadik said: "Behold, in the window there is glass, and in the mirror there is glass; but the glass of the mirror is covered with a little silver, and no sooner is the silver added than you cease to see others, but see only yourself."

The wife of a tzadik said to him: "Your prayer was lengthy today. Have you succeeded in bringing it about that the rich should be more generous in their gifts to the poor?"

The tzadik replied: "Half my prayer I have accomplished. The poor are willing to accept them."

A hasidic exhorter decided to settle in a small town. When he met the rabbi of the community, he explained his purpose. The other was surprised and cried: "But the community pays even its rabbi an exceedingly small amount. How will you make a living here?"

The evangelist narrated the following parable by way of answer: "A goose belonging to the thoughtless owner often suffered from hunger because her master forgot to feed her. One day the man bought a rooster and placed him in the same coop with the goose. The goose was greatly concerned. 'Now I shall surely starve. There are two of us to eat from my small portion.'

" 'Do not worry,' retorted the rooster. 'I can crow when I feel hungry, and this will be a reminder to our owner. Then we shall both be fed.' "

A little farm boy, having been orphaned in infancy, was unable to read, but he had inherited a large, heavy prayer book from his parents. On the Day of Atonement he brought it into the synagogue, laid it on the stand, and cried out tearfully: "Lord of Creation! I do not know how to pray, so here I give Thee the entire prayer book." The Lord heard him and was more moved than by the prayers of all the rabbis.

Two young scholars were wandering from place to place, poorly dressed and unknown to fame. Halting one night in the town of Lodmir, no one would give them hospitality save a poor hasid named Reb Aaron. Some years later, when those two had both become noted, tzadikim, they arrived again in Lodmir, but this time in a fine equipage. The richest man in town invited them to stay in his home, but they went instead to the house of Reb Aaron. When the wealthy man protested, they replied:

"We are the same persons to whom you paid no attention when we stopped here a few years ago. Hence, it appears that it is not so much we who are welcome, as our coach and horses. We are, therefore, entirely willing to accept your hospitality for the horses."

SAYINGS OF THE NIKOLSBURGER[3]

A hasid asked Reb Schmelke of Nikolsburg (died 1778): "We are bidden to love our neighbors as ourselves. How can I do this when my neighbor does me ill?"

The rabbi answered: "Thou must understand the command aright. Thy neighbor is a spark from the Original Soul, and that Original Soul is in all mankind, just as thy soul is in all the limbs of thy body. It may sometimes happen that thy hand slips and strikes thee. Wouldst thou then take a rod and beat thy hand because of its blunder, and thus add to thy pain? So it is if thy neighbor, whose soul is part of thy soul, does thee ill in his blindness. If thou dost retaliate, thou merely injurest thyself."

Rabbi Schmelke once had no money to give to a beggar. He ransacked his wife's bureau, and found a ring which he gave to the destitute man. His wife returned, saw that the drawer was open and that her ring was missing. She raised a hue and cry, and when her husband explained his action, she asked him to run after the beggar, since the ring was worth fifty *thalers.*

The tzadik ran swiftly in pursuit, and, catching up with the beggar, said: "I have just learned that the ring is worth fifty *thalers*. Let no one cheat you by giving you less than its value!"

When Rabbi Schmelke came to Nikolsburg to assume his duties as tzadik, he locked himself in a room and began pacing back and forth. One of the welcoming party overheard him repeating again and again the many forms of greeting he anticipated. Later the man confessed that he had overheard Rabbi Schmelke, and begged the rabbi to explain his odd action.

Rabbi Schmelke said: "I dislike intensely honors which tend to self-pride; therefore, I rehearsed to myself all the words of

---

[3]It became the common practice to refer to a noted *tzadik* by the name of the town where he made his headquarters.

welcome. No one appreciates self-praise, and after becoming accustomed to these words of acclaim by frequent repetition, I no longer felt pride in hearing these very phrases uttered by the committee of welcome."

SAYINGS OF THE KORETZER

Rabbi Phineas Shapiro, the tzadik of Koretz (died 1791) said: "When a man injures or abuses you, it does not lie within your rights to revenge yourself. It is as if a man stood in the presence of a king, and another smote him on the cheek. The only course open to him is to keep silent. The king witnessed the blow, and if he believes the man deserved it at the hands of his neighbor, the injured person can hardly complain. If the king, however, believes the blow was undeserved, he himself will surely punish the offender. In the same way, remember that you are always in the presence of the King of Kings. He will inflict punishment upon your adversary if you are undeservedly abused by him."

The Koretzer was accustomed to say: "I am constantly in fear lest I become too wise to remain pious."

Said the Koretzer: "The Talmud declares that wine taken in moderation unfolds the brain of a man. He who is a total abstainer is rarely possessed of wisdom."

The Koretzer also said: "It is best to eat sparingly. Thereby a man tends to lengthen his life. We find among animals and reptiles that those which eat the least live the longest."

Said the Koretzer: "If a man honors you, he considers himself your inferior at the moment, and he thereby becomes your superior. The more he honors you, the more he grows at your expense. How then can you feel pride at being showered with honors?"

Said the Koretzer: "Man was created last for the following reason: if he is deserving, he shall find all nature at his service; if he is undeserving, he shall find all nature arrayed against him."

Said the Koretzer: "Satan is inconsistent. He persuades a man not to go to synagogue on a cold morning; yet when the man does go, he follows him into it."

This tzadik also said: "Gold and silver become purified through fire. If you feel no sense of improvement after your prayer, you are either made of base metal, or your prayer lacked heat."

The wife of the Koretzer once bought a gilded Sabbath goblet. When the tzadik saw the vessel, he called to his wife indignantly: "Since when do we have golden utensils in our house?"

His wife sought to justify herself, saying: "See it is not genuine, but only a gilded goblet!"

"Then," said the tzadik, "you have brought not alone arrogance, but also deceit and falsehood into the house," and he refused to use the goblet for the sacred ceremony.

SAYINGS OF THE ZBARAZER

The wife of Rabbi Wolf of Zbaraz (died 1800) accused her maidservant of having stolen a costly vessel. The girl denied the deed. The woman, being wroth, prepared herself to go out and appeal to the rabbinical court. Rabbi Wolf, seeing her preparations, put on his Sabbath garment also. His wife said that it was not fitting for him to go, and that she knew well enough how to conduct herself in the court's presence.

"Truly," replied the tzadik, "you do; but the poor orphan, your maid, as whose counsel I am going, does not, and who but I will see that justice is done her?"

The Zbarazer was told that certain Jews in the town had spent the entire night at the gaming table. He said: "Perhaps it is their intention to accustom themselves to the habit of remaining awake all night. After they acquire this habit, they may learn to devote the night to holy study and divine service."

SAYINGS OF THE SASSOVER

Moshe Leib Sassover (died 1807) sat at the bedside of all the sick boys of his city, nursing and tending them. Once he said: "He who cannot suck the matter from the boils of a child stricken with the plague has not yet gone halfway up the height of love for his fellow men."

Said the Sassover: Why is it written (Psalms 29:11): "The Lord will grant strength unto His people; the Lord will bless His people with peace"? Because it is customary for sick people to be quarrelsome and irritable. Hence, we implore the Lord to give us health and bodily strength so that we may be blessed with peace and tranquillity of spirit.

Sayings of Rabbi Moshe Leib Sassover:

Whether evil or good events betide, let it be the same to you, since you are a stranger and a sojourner on this earth.

A sigh breaks the body of a man.

Wherefore shouldst thou have anxiety over a world that is not thine?

If peace is absent, everything else is lacking.

Be patient in the enduring of insults, for what art thou and what is thy life?

Be deliberate and thou wilt have no regrets.

Do not reprove another unless thine own actions are correct.

A man may be an upright servant of the Lord until temptation comes to him. It is only the one who has withstood temptation who is truly righteous.

The main superiority of man over animals is in his power of speech; but if we speak vanity and folly, we are no better than animals.

SAYINGS OF THE BERDITSCHEVER

After Yom Kippur the Berditschever (died 1809) called over a tailor and asked him to relate his argument with God on the holy day.

The tailor said: "I declared to God: You wish me to repent of my sins, but I have committed only minor offenses. I may have kept left-over cloth, or I may have eaten in a non-Jewish home, where I worked, without washing my hands. But Thou, O Lord, hast committed grievous sins: Thou hast taken away babies from their mothers, and mothers from their babies. So let us be quits. If Thou wilt forgive me, I shall forgive Thee."

Said the Berditschever: "Why did you let God off so easily? You might have forced Him to forgive all of Israel."

A teamster sought the Berditschever's advice as to whether he should give up his occupation because it interfered with regular attendance at the synagogue.

"Do you carry poor travelers free of charge?" asked the rabbi.

"Yes," answered the teamster.

"Then you serve the Lord in your occupation just as faithfully as you would by frequenting the synagogue."

The wife of one of the Berditschever's enemies met him one day on the street and poured over his head a pail of water. He ran to the synagogue and prayed: "O Lord, do not punish that woman. She must have done this by the order of her husband, and she is, therefore, to be commended as an obedient wife."

The Berditschever insisted upon serving his guests himself. He would bring them food and prepare their beds for them. When asked why he did not leave these duties to his servant, he responded: "Hospitality is an excellent deed when performed without payment. The servant would do it for pay, and the intrinsic kindness of the deed would be lost."

SAYINGS OF THE LUBLINER

The Lubliner (died 1815) said: "I have greater love for the wicked man who knows that he is wicked than for the righteous man who knows that he is righteous. The first one is truthful, and the Lord loves truth. The second one falsifies, since no human being is exempt from sin, and the Lord hates untruth."

He also said: "A true hasid is very rare. Two hasidim are not likely to be found in one town, and one hasid is not enough. Every town must, therefore, contain a hasid and a half, and each should consider himself as the half, and the other as a whole."

Said the Lubliner: "The Talmud tells us that 'poverty becomes Israel as a red ribbon becomes a white horse.' When the horse is for sale, the owner decorates him to please the eye of the purchaser. Likewise when Jews look poor, it pleases the non-Jews, and they do not do us harm out of envy."

A man of wealth lost his fortune and was unable to provide for the marriage of his daughters. He complained to the Lubliner, who counseled him to go forth to ask for donations. The man said: "But, rabbi, if I do that I shall become a misanthrope. Every time a man gives me nothing, or less than I think he should, I will hate him in my heart."

"Here is a preventive," said the Lubliner. "Believe that the Lord has decreed how much you are to receive from each person, and you will bear no ill will toward anyone."

SAYINGS OF THE PARSISCHARER

Simchah Bunam, the tzadik of Parsischa (died 1827), sought to cause a sinner to improve his ways. He invited him to a game of chess and, while playing, the tzadik made an obviously false move. The man was about to take advantage of the error, but the other asked him to excuse the mistake. Soon the tzadik made another wrong move, and this time his opponent refused to overlook it. The tzadik turned to him and said:

"You refuse to condone two false moves in a game of chess, yet you expect the Lord to pardon you regardless of the number of your own transgressions."

The sinner was stricken with remorse and promised to mend his conduct.

A disciple reported that his father had appeared to him in a dream and counseled him to become a tzadik.

Hearing this, Simchah Bunam remarked: "The next time your father comes to you, ask him to appear in a dream to others, and persuade them to become your followers."

A man complained to Rabbi Bunam: "The Talmud (Eruvin 13a) tells us that when a man runs away from honors, honors run after him. Now I have run away from honors, but no honors pursue me."

"The reason," explained the rabbi, "is that you keep looking backwards."

Rabbi Bunam visited Germany and observed the conduct of the Jews there. Turning to a companion, he said: "It is concerning this land that Solomon said: 'Grace is deceitful and beauty is vain; but a woman who feareth the Lord, she shall be praised' (Proverbs 31:30). I paraphrase it thus: "In a land where deceit is considered as graceful, and vanity as beauty, a woman who feareth the Lord deserves indeed to be praised."

Said Rabbi Bunam: "No Jew, however learned and pious, may consider himself an iota better than a fellow Jew, however ignorant or irreligious the latter may be. This is confirmed by the law that if a learned and pious Jew were commanded to slay the ignorant and impious one, or be himself slain, he must accept death rather than kill the other. No one can tell whose blood is redder and whose life is more important in the eyes of God. If a man in this crucial moment has no right to deem himself superior to another, what right can he possibly have to do so on less critical occasions?"

He also said: "The Lord's kindness is attracted to gayety. A joyful person is usually blessed with plenty, even though he may be impious. A sad person is usually in want, even though he may be God-fearing."

When Rabbi Bunam was a young man, a friend borrowed a few dollars from the chest established for the repairing of damaged synagogue books in order to donate a gift to a poor man who was collecting funds for the marriage dowries of dowerless brides. This became known and the trustees summoned the borrower to a hearing. The defendant asked Rabbi Bunam to serve as his counsel.

Rabbi Bunam narrated the following well-known fable: "There was once an epidemic among the animals of the forest. The lion, the tiger, the wolf, and the fox held a consultation, and the fox affirmed his belief that the epidemic was due to a great sin committed by some resident of the forest. He advised that all the animals assemble and confess their transgressions. The beasts of prey were the first to confess, and their excuses were accepted. Finally a sheep timidly approached and confessed that she had eaten a little hay from her owner's mattress.

" 'Aha,' roared the lion, 'you are the great sinner. You have abused your master's confidence.' And the sheep was condemned to death."

Rabbi Bunam then turned to the judges, and said: "You, Reb Leo, have been guilty of this and this; and you, Reb Baer, have done so-and-so; you, Reb Wolf, have acted wrongly in this and this instance. Yet you dare sit in judgment against a kindhearted man because he has borrowed money for a highly worthy cause."

Everyone present felt ashamed and left without pronouncing judgment against the defendant.

When Rabbi Bunam was lying on his deathbed, his wife wept bitterly. Thereupon he said: "Why dost thou weep? All my life has been given me merely that I might learn to die."

SAYINGS OF THE YUD

The Yud (Yerachmiel of Parsischa, died 1836) became dangerously ill, and the inhabitants of his town proclaimed a fast for his speedy convalescence. A villager chanced to come to town and went to the tavern for a drink of brandy. Several townsfolk overheard him and informed him that drinking was prohibited for the day.

The villager at once went to the synagogue and prayed: "O Lord, please cure the holy rabbi so that I may have my drink."

Soon thereafter the Rabbi began to recover his strength, and he then declared to his followers: "The prayer of the villager was more acceptable than any of yours. His expressed the greatest longing, and the most earnest supplication, for my quick recovery."

Said the Yud: "We find that a father strives to help his son to become a learned man and pious Jew. When the son grows up, he in turn endeavors to make his own son become a good Jew. But will the time ever come when the father himself will strive to be a good Jew, instead of leaving this task to his son?"

The Yud told the following tale: "A thief in his old age was unable to ply his 'trade,' and was starving. A wealthy man, hearing of his distress, sent him food. Both the rich man and the thief died on the same day. The trial of the magnate occurred first in the heavenly court, and he was found wanting and sentenced to Purgatory. At the entrance, however, an angel came hurrying to recall him. He was brought back to the court and learned that his sentence had been reversed. The thief whom he had aided on earth had stolen the list of his iniquities!"

Said the Yud: "Accustom thyself to generosity by degrees. At first refuse not a request for a pinch of snuff, for the light of a match, or for other small gifts. Such petty kindnesses will broaden thy heart so that thou canst habituate thyself to helping thy fellow-men in great ways."

SAYINGS OF THE RIZINER

A young man came to the Riziner (died 1850) and asked to be ordained as a rabbi. The Riziner inquired regarding his daily conduct, and the candidate replied: "I always dress in white; I drink only water; I place tacks in my shoes for self-mortification; I roll naked in the snow; and I order the synagogue caretaker to give me forty stripes daily on my bare back."

Just then a white horse entered the courtyard, drank water, and began rolling in the snow.

"Observe," said the Riziner. "This creature is white, it drinks only water, it has nails in its shoes, it rolls in the snow, and it receives more than forty stripes a day. Still it is nothing but a horse."

Said the Riziner: "Coarse trades are held in contempt. A tinsmith is little esteemed, and a bricklayer less, because they handle crude materials. Now, how do matters stand with me? What is coarser than an oaf who balks at spiritual improvement? Yet is not that the material with which I have to labor all the time?"

The Riziner was asked by an opponent of Hasidism: "Why is it that after the prayer services we rigorists study the Talmud, and you hasidim drink brandy?"

The rabbi replied: "Your prayers are lifeless, and it is customary to study Talmud for the sake of the souls of the dead. The prayers of the hasidim, however, are alive and vital, and a drink of excellent brandy is beneficial to the living."

The Kobriner found the Riziner sitting in his chamber on a Friday before sunset, and smoking so furiously at his pipe that the room was filled with fumes. The smoker noticed his friend's displeasure, and narrated to him the following story:

"A man lost his way in a forest and chanced upon the hut of a brigand. Near the door stood a table on which a loaded gun was lying. The man seized the gun and thought to himself: 'If I kill the robber, I save myself; if I miss him, I may be able to escape in the smoke.'

"By the same token, in order to purify my brain for the Sabbath, I think holy thoughts and smoke my pipe. If my thoughts fail me, the tobacco fumes may at least dull my brain, so that I do not think unholy thoughts."

The Riziner lived in great luxury. A disciple inquired the reason, and the Riziner explained as follows:

"I have three kinds of funds. One is from the real hasidim, and this goes for my necessities. One is from the householders of middling piety, and this I give away to the needy. The third is from habitual sinners, and this goes for luxuries. Is it my fault that the third fund is the largest?"

A disciple complained to the Riziner that he lacked fine garments, a fine dwelling, and a beautiful wife–the three things which serve to broaden understanding according to the Talmud (Berakhot, 57).

"But," replied the Riziner, "these things serve only to broaden a man's understanding, not to create it in him. Therefore, of what use will they be to you?"

On one of his visits to a neighboring village, the Riziner sojourned at the home of a certain wealthy man. The latter complained that the multitudes who came to see the tzadik had mud on their shoes, and soiled his home. The guest thereupon related the following tale: "Once a poor villager came to town to earn money for the Passover. On his return home, laden with purchases, his horse and wagon fell into a pit made swampy by the spring rains. A rich man, passing by, heard his cries and helped his own driver extricate the villager.

He roped the latter's wagon to his carriage, and accompanied the poor man to his hut. On beholding the abject poverty in which the villager and his family lived, the magnate gave him several hundred rubles.

"When the wealthy man died and was brought before the Heavenly Tribunal, it seemed as if his demerits because of certain business dealings would result in his sentence to Purgatory. Suddenly an Angel of Mercy appeared and asked that the Heavenly Scales be used to determine whether the worth of the man's good deeds outweighed his sins. When consent was given, the Angel placed the poor villager and his family on the Scale of Good Deeds; but this did not suffice. The horse and the wagon were added, but even they were not enough. Then the Angel placed on the Scale the mud and mire out of which the rich man had helped rescue the villager, and lo, the Scale of Good Deeds dipped with its weight, and the magnate was saved from Purgatory."

The host understood the Riziner's hint, and complained no more of the mud on the shoes of his visitors.

SAYINGS OF THE PREMISLANER

Rabbi Aaron Leib Premislaner (died 1852) went to pay a visit to a neighboring tzadik. This became known and some hasidim went out on the highway to meet him. When he noticed them from afar, he speedily changed clothes with his driver, in order to avoid the undesired honor. His noble mien, however, betrayed him to the other tzadik, who was one of the welcoming party. Therefore, while the others shook hands with the disguised driver, this tzadik gave greeting to the real rabbi. When asked how he had detected the deception, he replied with a laugh, "One crook cannot fool another."

The Premislaner told the following tale: "I went up to heaven in a dream and stood at the Gates of Paradise in order to observe the procedure of the Heavenly Tribunal. A learned rabbi approached and wished to enter. 'Day and night,' he said, 'I studied the Holy Torah.' 'Wait,' said the Angel. 'We will investigate whether your study was for its own sake or whether it was a matter of profession, or for the sake of honors.'

"Then a tavern-keeper drew near. 'I kept an open door,' said he, 'and fed without charge every poor man who came to my inn.' The Heavenly Portals were opened to him without further investigation.

"I then said to myself: If charity opens the Gates of Paradise, whether it be practiced for its own sake or for honors, I vow to become a collector of funds for charity."

A storekeeper complained to the Premislaner that another man had opened a store near him and was taking away his livelihood. The rabbi answered: "Did you ever notice that when a horse is led to a pool of water to drink, he stamps his hoof in the water?"

"Yes," said the man.

"The reason is as follows," continued the rabbi. "When the horse lowers his head to drink, he sees his shadow. He imagines that another horse is also drinking, and fearing there will not be sufficient water for both, he tries to chase away the other horse. In reality, he is afraid of his shadow, and there is plenty of water for many horses. You, likewise, are afraid of an imaginary foe. God's abundance flows like a river, and there is enough for all."

SAYINGS OF THE ROPSHITZER

Said the Ropshitzer (died 1854): "To obtain a livelihood from a man is oftentimes like obtaining honey from a bee; it is accompanied by a sting."

The Ropshitzer wished to test whether a certain man, reputed to fast from Sabbath to Sabbath, and to spend all day in the synagogue, was truly pious or just merely a hypocrite. He ordered some boys to annoy him, and then went to the synagogue and called out to them: "Why do you harass a man who fasts on Mondays and Thursdays?"

The man turned to him and said: "Have you not heard that I fast from Sabbath to Sabbath?"

The Ropshitzer then knew the man was indeed a hypocrite.

Said the Ropshitzer: "Who is a sage? 'One who knows his place,' say our Sages (Pirke Avot, 6:6). I shall paraphrase it: 'Who is a sage? One who makes his place known.' A town becomes known throughout the entire world by the presence within it of an illustrious sage.

Said the Ropshitzer: "I was once loath to accept a rabbinical post, inasmuch as I believed I would be compelled to resort to flattery. I despise flattery. Then I observed that everyone must practice flattery, whether he be tailor, shoemaker, or storekeeper. Hence, I said to myself: "Since flattery is an unavoidable and universal necessity, I may as well become a rabbi.' "

A confirmed sinner visited the Ropshitzer, saying he had been sent by an erring friend who was too shy to come himself. His friend had committed certain offenses, and he desired to learn the appropriate means of repentance. The rabbi at once divined that the visitor was himself the sinner, and said: "What a foolish person is your friend! Could he not have come himself to me, and pretended that the sinner is a friend?"

SAYINGS OF THE KOBRINER

A villager lamented to the Kobriner (died 1857) that his evil desires constantly overcame him and caused him to fall into transgression.

"Do you ride a horse?" the rabbi inquired.

"Yes," answered the villager.

"What do you do if you happen to fall off?"

"I mount again," said the villager.

"Well, imagine the Evil Impulse to be the horse," remarked the rabbi. "If you fall, mount again. Eventually you will master it."

Said the Kobriner: "When a man suffers tribulation, he should not say: 'This is evil,' for the Lord sends no evil. He should rather say: 'I am undergoing a bitter experience.' It is like a bitter medicine which a physician prescribes in order to cure the patient."

The Kobriner commented upon Psalm 10:10: "He croucheth, he boweth down, and the helpless fall into his mighty claws." In explanation he told the following fable:

"An old mouse sent out her son to search for food, but warned him to be careful of the enemy. The young mouse met a rooster and hastened back to his mother in great terror. He described the enemy as a haughty being with an upstanding red comb. 'He is no enemy of ours,' said the old mouse, and sent her son out again.

"This time he met a turkey, and was still more frightened. 'O Mother,' he said, panting, 'I saw a great puffed-up being with a deadly look, ready to kill.'

" 'Neither is he our enemy,' replied the mother. 'Our enemy keeps his head down like an exceedingly humble person; he is smooth and soft-spoken, friendly in appearance, and acts as if he were a very kind creature. If you meet him, beware!' "

SAYINGS OF THE KOTZKER

Said the Kotzker (died 1859): "Take care of your own soul and of another man's body, not of your own body and of another man's soul."

An ignorant villager, having heard it is a good religious deed to eat and drink on the day before the Atonement Fast, drank himself into a stupor. He awoke late at night, too late for the evening services. Not knowing the prayers by heart, he devised a plan. He repeated the letters of the alphabet over and over, beseeching the Almighty to arrange them into the proper words of prayers. The following day he attended the synagogue of the Kotzker and confessed his transgression. Whereupon the tzadik declared: "Your prayer was more acceptable than mine because you uttered it with the entire devotion of your heart."

Said the Kotzker: "There are three ways in which a man can go about performing a good deed. If he says: 'I shall do it soon,' the way is poor. If he says: 'I am ready to do it now,' the way is of average quality. If he says: 'I am doing it,' the way is praiseworthy."

The Kotzker Rebbe also said: "Death is merely moving from one home to another. If we are wise, we will make the latter the more beautiful home."

SAYINGS OF THE GERER

Rabbi Isaaac Meyer of Ger (died 1866) lost every one of his thirteen sons. When the youngest died, the mother refused to be comforted. Her husband said to her: "Our sons have not died in vain. If a misfortune like ours should happen to another man, he will remember that we lost thirteen holy sons, and he will not feel angry against the Lord."

A hasid complained to the Gerer that he kept forgetting what he learned.

"Do you forget to place the spoon with food into your mouth?" asked the holy one.

"No, because I cannot live without food," was the reply.

"Neither can you live without learning. Remember this and you will not forget."

Said the Gerer: "If a man has fear of anything except the Creator, he is in some degree an idolator. For to fear is to worship the thing feared; and worship may be offered to the Lord alone."

The Gerer also said: "Many of us possess less fear of a transgression than of a fly. When a fly alights upon us, we at least take the trouble to brush it away. Likewise, many of us possess less willingness to perform a commandment than to obtain a small coin. If we see a small coin on the ground, we take the trouble to bend over and pick it up."

A young man was asked by the Gerer if he had learned Torah. "Just a little," replied the youth.

"That is all anyone ever has learned of the Torah," was the rabbi's answer.

SAYINGS OF OTHER TZADIKIM

The Pulnoer Rebbe (died 1769) said: "Jews are likened in the Torah to sand. Each particle of sand is distinct, and only through fire do they become fused into glass. Likewise the Israelites are usually divided among themselves, and it requires calamities to unite them."

The Mezeritzer (died 1772) said: "Let no one be discouraged by violent opposition. Brigands attack the one who carries jewels on his person, not the one who drives a wagonload of manure. Like the carrier of gems, we must be prepared to repel our assailants."

Jacob Krantz, the great *maggid* (preacher) of Dubno (died 1804), was famed for his parables. Arriving in a certain town one day, he stopped at the house of a rich man.

"Peace to you!" the host greeted him. "Sit down and tell me a good parable."

"With pleasure," replied the preacher. "A good man once brought home a goat which he had purchased at a fair, and his wife immediately began to try to milk it. Of course, she could not get out a drop. 'Pooh!' she cried. 'This animal cannot be a goat. There is no milk in her.' To which her husband replied: 'You are wrong, my beloved. It is a goat, and there is milk in her; but she has come a long distance, and is tired and hungry and thirsty. Supply her needs, and let her rest overnight, and you will see–tomorrow she will give plenty of milk.' "

The hasidim came to Rabbi Phineas of Frankfort (died 1805) with this question: "Master, who, if anyone, is to study Maimonides' *Guide for the Perplexed?*"

The master replied: "Know that the *Guide* is like an apothecary's shop. The chemist dwelling within prepares many useful remedies, for many ills, being licensed as a man of skill; but he who has no learning of remedies and diseases, let him beware how he meddles with the contents of the shop. The smallest error may kill a man. The least want of precaution may involve grievous punishment, and any mistake entails loss of reputation."

A terrible famine once occurred in the Ukraine, and the poor could buy no bread. Ten disciples assembled at the home of the "Spoler Grandfather" (died 1811) for a session of the Rabbinical Court. The Spoler said to them:

"I have a case in judgment against the Lord. According to rabbinical law, a master who buys a Jewish serf for a designated time [six years or up to the Jubilee year] must support not only him but also his family. Now the Lord bought us in

Egypt as his serfs, since He says: 'For to Me are the sons of Israel serfs,' and the Prophet Ezekiel declared that even in Exile, Israel is the slave of God. Therefore, O Lord, I ask that Thou abide by the Law and support Thy serfs with their families."

The ten judges rendered judgment in favor of the Spoler Rabbi. In a few days a large shipment of grain arrived from Siberia, and bread could be bought by the poor.

The Rimanover (died 1815) dreamed that he ascended to Heaven and heard an angel pleading with the Lord to grant Israel wealth, saying: "Behold how pious they are in poverty! Give unto them riches, and they will be many times as pious."

The rabbi inquired the name of the angel. The reply was: "He is called Satan."

The rabbi then exclaimed: "Leave us in poverty, O Lord. Safeguard us from the favors of Satan."

The Kariver (died 1813) said: "Do not hate your erring brother on the ground that you have not erred like him. Had he possessed your nature, he might not have sinned; and had you possessed his nature, you might have been the sinner. A man's transgressions depend not entirely upon his free choice, but oftentimes upon many other circumstances."

Said the Bershider (died 1816): "It is not easy to repent of the sin of melancholy. When a man begins to repent of it, he falls into deeper melancholy because he realizes that he has sinned."

Said the Radviller (died 1825): "The commandment: 'Thou shalt not covet,' is placed at the end of the Decalogue because he who has observed this commandment is certain to have observed all those which precede it. But he who has not sufficient self-discipline to fulfill this prohibition against coveting must commence anew with the first commandment which is belief in the justice of God. For had he sincerely believed in God, he would not be covetous of that which God had allotted as the share of others."

The Strelisker (died 1826) was asked: "Why is it that the tzadikim formerly were contented with small donations whereas the present-day tzadikim ask for large donations?"

He answered: "Because a natural rose is cheaper than an artificial one."

Rabbi Noah Lekhivitzer (died 1833) said: "Man is often called 'a small world.' This title is to be explained as follows: If a man is small in his own eyes, he is indeed a 'world.' But if a man is 'a world' in his own eyes, then he is indeed small."

He also said: "To worry is a sin. Only one sort of worry is permissible: to worry because one worries."

Rabbi Leib Dimimles of Lantzut (died 1834) was a wealthy merchant, and very learned in the Torah. It happened that he lost his money and was reduced to poverty. Rabbi Leib paid no heed to this calamity and continued his studies. His wife inquired: "How is it possible for you not to show the least anxiety?"

The rabbi answered: "The Lord gave me a brain which thinks rapidly. The worrying which another would do in a year, I have done in a moment."

Rabbi Mordecai of Tzernobil (died 1837) said: "If you wish to acquire the habit of truthfulness, make it a point when you catch yourself telling a falsehood to say unashamedly: 'I have just been guilty of a lie.' In this manner you will speedily discipline your tongue."

The Stretiner (died 1844) declared: "We say: 'And mayest Thou assemble the dispersed as one assembles grainstalks.'

Why do we not say: 'as one assembles pearls?' The reason is this: when we gather assembled pearls, we cleanse them of all impurities and select only those that are pure. Had we therefore said, 'Assemble us as pearls out of the Dispersion,' it would imply that we asked only for the Redemption of the pure tzadikim. But he who gathers grainstalks does so with hay clinging to them. We likewise petition that we may all be redeemed–the ears of grain with the haystalks, the tzadikim and the ordinary Jews."

Rabbi Mendel Libavitzer (died 1866) was accustomed to restrain an angry rebuke until he had searched through the Shulhan Arukh to learn whether anger is permissible in that particular instance. But how much genuine anger could he feel after searching all through that great tome?

The Tzupenester (died 1869) found his hasidim playing checkers. He said: "You may learn much wisdom from the rules of this game. You surrender one in order to capture two. You may not make two moves at one time. You must move up, but not down. When you reach the top, you may move as you like."

Rabbi Henoch of Alexander (died 1870) once said: "The real exile of Israel in Egypt was that they had learned to endure it."

The Amshinover (died 1877) said: "To sin against a fellow man is worse than to sin against the Creator. The man you harmed may have gone to an unknown place, and you may lose the opportunity to beg his forgiveness. The Lord, however, is everywhere and you can always find Him when you seek Him."

The Slonimer (died 1884) related the following story: "A commander-in-chief received a message telling him that his main line of defense had been broken by the enemy. He was greatly distressed and his emotions showed plainly on his countenance. His wife heard the nature of the message, and entering her husband's room, she said: 'I too at this moment have received tidings, and worse than yours.'

" 'And what are they?' inquired the commander with agitation.

" 'I have read discouragement on your face,' replied the wife. 'Loss of courage is worse than loss of an army.' "

The Gastininer (died 1888) made it a rule for himself never to express his displeasure with anyone on the same day that he was offended by that person. On the morrow he would say to the man: "I was displeased with you yesterday."

The Brisker (died 1892) remarked concerning a certain philanthropist who was known as an enthusiastic contributor to every charity: "He is a most admirable man, but he possesses one fault. He enjoys almsgiving so much that he desires people should always be in need, in order that he may aid them."

The Tzartkover (died 1903) failed to preach for a long time. He was asked his reason and replied: "There are seventy ways of reciting the Torah. One of them is through silence."

A hasid heard much regarding the renown of Rabbi Israel Meir HaCohen, the Radiner (died 1933), and asked one of the latter's followers: "Is it true that your tzadik performs miracles?"

The other answered: "You deem it a miracle when God does the will of your tzadik. We, however, deem it a miracle if it can be truthfully asserted that our tzadik does God's will."

ANONYMOUS HASIDIC SAYINGS

False friends are like migratory birds; they fly away in cold weather.

One who thinks he can live without others is mistaken. One who thinks others cannot live without him is more mistaken.

One who believes that anything can be accomplished by money is likely to do anything for money.

While pursuing happiness we are in flight from contentment.

It is easier to abandon evil traits today than tomorrow.

Want makes people better; luck makes them worse.

For the unlearned, old age is winter; for the learned, it is the season of the harvest.

Fear of a misfortune is worse than the misfortune.

Teach your children in youth, and they will not teach you in your old age.

A Jew came to a rabbi and said: "I encounter prejudice everywhere and, therefore, am thinking of becoming baptized. What difference would this make in me, seeing that I will not believe in Christianity?"

The rabbi replied: "You know that the Bible likens Jews to sand. As long as sand is dry, it is sand, but the moment water is poured over it, what happens? It becomes mud."

Woe to him whom nobody likes; but beware of him whom everybody likes.

Man should be master of his will and slave of his conscience.

Fear only two: God and the man who has no fear of God.

One who looks for a friend without faults will have none.

Fear the one who fears you.

One who has confidence in himself gains the confidence of others.

One who cannot survive bad times cannot see good times.

Let us be the lines leading to the central point of the circle: all come to one point and unite there; but let us not be like the parallel lines which are always separate.

A tzadik was asked: "Why is it that the pious man seems less eager to persuade others to become virtuous than the impious man to gain companions in wickedness?"

He replied: "The man of piety walks in light and is not afraid to walk alone, whereas the man of impiety walks in darkness and is anxious for company."

A king visited a prison and talked to the prisoners. Each asserted his innocence, except one who admitted he was a thief. "Throw this scoundrel out," exclaimed the king. "He will corrupt the innocents."

There are two kinds of readers of serious books. One is like the man who squeezes wine grapes with his fingertips. He secures only the watery juice from the ends of the grapes, and, inasmuch as it does not ferment, he complains that the grapes are poor. This type of reader glances hurriedly at the pages of a volume and finds no merit in the writings.

The other kind of reader is like the man who squeezes out the full juice from the grapes. It ferments and turns into pleasing wine. This type of reader delves deeply into the words he is reading, and finds delight in the thoughts they convey.

A hasid asked a Talmudistic rabbi why he lived in great luxury. The other replied: "We are told in the Talmud (Berakhot, 57) that a fine dwelling, fine clothes, and a beautiful wife broaden a man's understanding, and I need all the understanding I can acquire to serve my master fitly."

A certain tzadik was called on to pray for an impious Jew who was dangerously ill. He said: "It may be true that the patient deserves to die if judged by the rules of the strict justice; but it is only the judges of the lower tribunals who have no choice under the law and must sentence the offender according to his acts. The king, however, being the chief magistrate of the country, may issue a pardon in disregard of the law.

"Thou, O Lord, art like the king, the judge of all the earth, and mayest grant a pardon. I implore thee to exercise Thy right of mercy, as Abraham said (Genesis 18:25): 'The judge of all the earth need not exercise justice.' "

PART VI

THE MODERN PERIOD

INTRODUCTION

So far as the Jews were concerned, the Middle Ages lasted until near the close of the eighteenth century. As late as 1790 there was not a land in all of Europe where they enjoyed political equality; and even long after that date there were many in which they were denied the most elementary social rights. As a result, they were slow to abandon the wall of tradition and moat of mysticism which had kept them inwardly secure throughout the medieval night.

But once outward oppression began to wane, inward security ceased to seem so urgent; and then a break with the past became inevitable. No sooner were the ghetto walls torn down than the ghetto fears began to dwindle, and more and more Jews rushed to fling themselves into the life of their neighbors. Now that the vicious cycle of exclusion and seclusion seemed broken at last, the deepest hunger in Israel seemed to be for assimilation. First it was for assimilation in merely external ways: in speech, costume, deportment, and so forth. This, however, only whetted the appetite for profounder changes, and soon the Jews were assimilating inwardly. An increasing number of them began to identify themselves so completely with the culture of the lands they lived in that they ceased to be

Jews save in name alone. In all essential respects, in their convictions as well as their vocations, in their loyalties no less than their prejudices, they became children not of Israel but of the world.

That is why this section is not many times its present length. Most of the Jewish notables of the last two centuries had to be left out because they were Jewish solely by birth. Enough remain, however, to prove that the traditional lore of the Jews continued to be richly seminal during this latest period. The wisdom which it produced may seem less Jewish than in the past, but an objective reader will probably find it no less wise.

CHAPTER 64

CONVICTIONS OF MOSES MENDELSSOHN

The modern era in Jewish life may be said to begin with this extraordinary man. Born a hunchback in the ghetto of a provincial German town, Moses Mendelssohn (1729–1786) lived to triumph over poverty, sickness, and discrimination, and emerge one of the most honored and influential sages of his day. Learned Gentiles called him a "second Plato," and his own people proclaimed him—after Maimonides—the "third Moses." The following passages are taken from his epoch-making "treatise on ecclesiastical authority and Judaism" entitled Jerusalem *(Berlin, 1763), in which he dared to make the first lucid and outspoken plea for the separation of Church and State in Germany. The work was widely translated and aroused sharp controversy throughout Europe. Emanuel Kant hailed it "an irrefutable book . . . the proclamation of a great reform destined to affect not alone [Jewry] but all peoples."*[1]

THE IDEAL GOVERNMENT

"Which form of government is the best?" is a question which has hitherto been answered in many different ways, seemingly all equally correct. The fact, however, is: it is too

[1] *Jerusalem,* translated from the German by M. Samuels (London, 1838), pp. 17–23, 101, 170–173.

indefinite a question, nearly as much so as another of the same sort in medicine, that is, "Which kind of food is wholesomest?" Every constitution, every climate, every age, sex, profession, and so forth, requires a different answer; and so does our politico-philosophical problem. For every people, for every stage of civilization at which that people has arrived, another form of government may be the best. Many despotically-ruled nations would feel very miserable were they left to govern themselves; and so would high-spirited republicans if subjected to a monarch. Nay, many a nation, as improvements, general habits and principles undergo changes in it, will change also its form of government, and, in a course of ages, run the whole round from anarchy to absolutism in all their shades and modifications, and yet be found to have all along chosen the form of government which was best for them under existing circumstances.

But under every circumstance, and with every proviso, I think it an unerring standard of a good government, the more there is under it, wrought by morality and persuasions, and accordingly, the more the people are governed by education itself. In other words, the more opportunity there is given the citizen to see evidently that he foregoes some of his rights for the public good only; that he sacrifices part of his own interest to beneficence only; and that, therefore, he gains on the one side as much by acts of beneficence as, on the other, he loses by sacrifices. Nay, that by sacrificing he even profits in inward happiness, because it enhances the merit and dignity of the action, and, therefore, also increases the true perfection of the beneficent himself. So it is, for instance, not advisable for the state to charge itself with all offices of philanthropy, not even the distributing of charity excepted, and convert them into public establishments. Man feels his own worth when he is acting liberally; when it is obvious to him that by his gift he alleviates the distress of a fellow creature; that is, when he gives because he *pleases;* but when he gives because he *must*, he feels only his fetters.

It ought, therefore, to be the chief endeavor of the state to govern mankind by morals and persuasions. Now there is no other way of improving men's principles, and by means of them also their morals, but conviction. Laws will not alter persuasions. Arbitrary punishments or rewards generate no maxims, nor do they improve morals. Fear and hope are no criterions of truth. Knowledge, reasoning, convictions, they alone bring forth principles which, through credit and example, may pass into manner.

THE OFFICE OF RELIGION

Religion must step in to assist the state, and the church become the supporter of civil happiness. It behooves her to convince the people, in the most emphatic manner, of the truth of noble sentiments and persuasions; to show them that the duties to man are also duties to God, the transgressing of which is itself the greatest misery; that serving one's country is true religion; probity and justice the commandment of God; charity, His most holy will; and that a right knowledge of the Creator will not let misanthropy harbor long in the creature's heart. To teach this is the office, duty, and vocation of the Church; to preach it, the office, duty, and vocation of her ministers. How could it ever have entered men's thoughts to let the Church teach and her ministers preach quite the reverse?

But when the character of a people, the stage of civilization at which it has arrived, a population swelled along with its national prosperity, multiplied relations and alliances, overgrown luxury, and other causes render it impossible to govern it by persuasions only, the state has recourse to public institutions, compulsory laws, punishment of crime, and reward of virtue. If a citizen will not come forward in the defense of the country from an inward feeling of his duty, let him be either allured by rewards or compelled by force. If people have no longer a sense of the intrinsic value of justice; if they no longer acknowledge that uprightness of life and dealing is true happiness, let injustice be corrected; let fraud be punished.

In this manner, it is true, the state gains the object of society only by half. External motives do not render him happy on whom they do nevertheless act. He who escheweth fraud from love of honesty is far happier than he who only dreads the arbitrary penalty which the state attaches to fraud; but to his fellow man it is of little consequence from what motives evildoing is refrained, or by what means his rights and property are secured to him. The country is defended all the same, whether the citizen fight for it from patriotism, or from fear of positive punishment, although the citizen himself is happy in the former case, and unhappy in the latter. If the internal happiness of society cannot be entirely preserved, at least external peace and security must, at any rate, be enforced.

Accordingly, the state is, if need be, contented with dead works, with services without spirit, with consonance of action without consonance of thought. Even he who thinks nothing of laws must do as the law bids, when once it has been sanctioned. The individual citizen may be allowed the privilege of judging of the laws, but not that of acting up to his judgment; for, as a member of society, he was obliged to surrender that right, because without such surrender a social compact would be a chimera. Not so religion!

Religion knows of no actions without persuasion, of no works without spirit, of no consonance of acting without consonance of thought. Religious observances without religious thoughts are idle boys' play and no worship; this, as such, must, therefore, proceed from the spirit, and can neither be purchased by rewards nor enforced by punishments. But from civil actions also religion withdraws its auspices, so far as they are not produced by principle but by authority. Nor has the state to expect any further cooperation of religion when it cannot act otherwise than by rewards and punishments; for when that is the case, the duties toward God cease to be of any consideration; and the relations between man and his Creator have no effect. All the help religion can then lend the state consists in teaching and comforting. It instills, by its divine lessons, into the citizen, principles tending to public utility; and, with its superhuman consolations, supports the malefactor doomed to die for the public good.

CHURCH VS. STATE

There appears an essential difference between the state and religion. The state dictates and coerces; religion teaches and persuades. The state enacts laws; religion gives commandments. The state is armed with physical force, and makes use of it if need be; the force of religion is love and benevolence. The former renounces the undutiful, and thrusts him out; the latter receives him in its bosom, and yet, in the last moments of his present life, tries, not quite unavailingly, to instruct, or, at least, to console him. In one word: civil society, as a moral entity, may have compulsory power; nay, was actually invested with it by the social compact; religious society lays no claim to it; nor can all the compacts in the world confer it on it. The state possesses perfect rights; the church only imperfect rights.

OF HUMAN PROGRESS

In respect to the human race at large, you do not perceive a constant progress of improvement that looks as if approaching nearer and nearer to perfection. On the contrary, we see the human race, as a whole, subject to slight side swings; and it never yet made some steps forward but what it did, soon after, slide back again into its previous station, with double the celerity. Most nations of the earth pass many ages in the same degree of civilization, in the same crepuscular light, which appears much too dim to our spoiled eyes. Now and then, a particle of the grand mass will kindle, become a bright star, and run through an orbit which, now after a longer, now after a shorter period, brings it back again to its standstill, or sets it down at no great distance from it. Man goes on; but mankind is constantly swinging to and fro, within fixed boundaries; but, considered as a whole, retains, at all periods of time, about the same degree of morality, the same quantity of religion and irreligion, of virtue and vice, of happiness and misery; the same result, when the same is taken into account against the same; of all the good and evil as much as was required for the transit of individual man, in order that they might be trained here on earth, and approach as near to perfection as was allotted and appointed to every one of them.

ON FREEDOM OF CONSCIENCE

Brethren, if it be genuine piety you are aiming at, let us not feign uniformity when variety is, evidently, the design and end of Providence. None of us feels and thinks exactly alike with his fellowman; then wherefore impose upon one another by deceiving words? We are, alas, prone enough to do so, in our ordinary transactions, in our general conversation, comparatively of no material importance; but wherefore also in things involving our spiritual and temporal welfare, and constituting the whole purpose of our creation? God has not stamped on every man a peculiar countenance for nothing: why, then, should we, in the most solemn concerns of life, render ourselves unknown to one another, by disguise? Is not this resisting Providence so far as with us lies? Is it not frustrating the designs of creation, if it were possible, and purposely acting against our vocation and destiny, both in this life and that to come?

Regents of the earth, if an insignificant fellow inhabitant of it may be allowed to lift up his voice unto ye, O listen not to the counselors who, in smooth words, would misguide you to so pernicious an undertaking. They are either blind themselves and cannot see the enemy of mankind lurking in ambush, or they want to blind you. If you hearken to them, our brightest jewel, freedom of conscience, is lost. For your happiness' sake, and for ours, *religious union is not toleration;* it is diametrically opposite to it. For your happiness' sake, and for ours, lend not your powerful authority to the converting into a law any *immutable truth,* without which civil happiness may very well subsist; to the forming into a public ordinance any theological thesis, of no importance to the state. Be strict as to the life and conduct of men; make that amenable to a tribunal of wise laws; and leave thinking and speaking to us, just as it was given us, as an unalienable heirloom; as we were invested with it, as an unalterable right, by our universal father.

If, perhaps, the connection of privilege with opinion be too prescriptive, and the time have not yet arrived to do away with it altogether, at least endeavor to mitigate, as lies with you, its deleterious influence, and to put wise bounds to prejudices now grown too superannuated;[2] at least pave, for happier posterity, the way to that height of civilization, to that universal forbearance amongst men, after which reason is still panting in vain. Reward and punish no doctrine; hold out no allurement or bribe for the adoption of theological opinions. Let everyone who does not disturb public happiness, who is obedient to the civil government, who acts righteously toward

---

[2]We regret to hear also the Congress of the United States (1783) harp on the old string by talking of an established religion.

you, and toward his fellow countrymen, be allowed to speak as he thinks, to pray to God after his own fashion, or after that of his forefathers, and to seek eternal salvation where he thinks he may find it. Suffer no one to be a searcher of hearts, and a judge of opinions in your states; suffer no one to assume a right which the Omniscient has reserved to himself. "*As long as we are rendering unto Caesar the things which are Caesar's, render ye, yourselves, unto God the things which are God's. Love truth! Love peace!*"

CHAPTER 65

THE WORDS OF HEINRICH HEINE

Heinrich Heine (1797–1856), the great German lyric poet and essayist, belongs in this anthology because his career and temper were so profoundly influenced by his Jewish background. Reared in a day when the emancipation of his people seemed assured, he lived to see that promise balked by lingering prejudice and political reaction, and the disillusionment left its mark on all his work. He was a most tragic example of the maladjusted modern Jew, for though of Israel, he was no longer in it, and though already in the world, he could not feel himself of it. He belonged nowhere, and the consequent frustration helped to make him one of the supremely embittered geniuses of our era.

He is chiefly remembered today for his lyric poems, many of which have won a permanent place in the world's treasury of great literature. During his own lifetime, however, he was almost more renowned for his prose writings, which were as brilliantly phrased as they were passionately felt. A born iconoclast, and an instinctive hater of injustice and tyranny, he became the terror of the German reactionaries, and the inspiration of liberals throughout the world. The first is still true, as witness the fury with which the Nazis burned his books and tried to blot out his memory. So is the second, for Heine's prose writings continue to be widely read.[1]

---

[1]The following selections are taken in part from Lewis Browne's biography entitled *That Man Heine* (New York, Macmillan, 1927), and for the rest from Hermann Kesten's anthology, *Heinrich Heine – Works of Prose* (New York, L. B. Fischer, 1943).

WHEN GERMANY GOES BERSERK[2]

Some day there will awake that fighting folly found among the ancient Germans, the folly that fights neither to kill nor to conquer, but simply to fight. Christianity has – and that is its fairest merit – somewhat mitigated that brutal German lust for battle. But it could not destroy it; and once the taming talisman, the Cross, is broken, the savagery of the old battlers will flare up again, the insane berserk rage of which Nordic bards have so much to say and sing. That talisman is brittle. The day will come when it will pitiably collapse. Then the old stone gods will rise from forgotten rubble and rub the dust of a thousand years from their eyes; and Thor will leap up and with his giant hammer start smashing gothic cathedrals. . . .

Then when you hear the rumble and clatter – beware. . . . Don't smile at the visionary who expects the same revolution in the material world which has taken place in the realm of the spirit. The thought precedes the act, as lightning precedes thunder. True, our German thunder is a German too, and not very dexterous; it comes rolling up pretty slowly, but come it will – and when you hear a crash as nothing ever crashed in world history, you'll know that the German thunder has finally hit the mark. At that sound the eagles will fall dead from the sky and the lions in the farthest desert of Africa will pull in their tails and slink away into their royal caves. A play will be performed in Germany that will make the French Revolution seem like a harmless idyll in comparison. Now, of course, all is rather quiet. And if one or the other over there acts a little frisky, don't think these will soon appear as the real actors. They are the little dogs that run about the empty arena

---

[2]This is a passage from Heine's *Religion and Philosophy in Germany* (1834). Read in the light of what happened since the advent of Hitler, it seems almost uncannily prophetic.

barking and snapping at each other, before the hour strikes and the host of gladiators arrive who shall fight for life or death.

And the hour will come. As on the tiers of an amphitheater, the nations will range round Germany to watch the great games. I warn you, Frenchmen, keep very quiet then, and above all do not applaud. We might easily misunderstand that and hush you somewhat roughly in our impolite way; if in the past, in our servile sullenness, we were sometimes able to worst you, we could do it far better in the young elation of being drunk with freedom. You know yourselves what one can do in such a state—and you are no longer in it. Beware! I wish you well; that is why I tell you the bitter truth. You have more to fear from a "liberated" Germany than from the whole Holy Alliance with all its Croats and Cossacks. . . . We forget nothing. You see, if once we feel the urge to come to grips with you we shall not lack valid reasons. In any case, I advise you to stay on guard. No matter what happens in Germany, whether the Crown Prince of Prussia comes to power or Doctor Wirth, keep your powder dry and remain quietly at your posts, rifle on arm. I wish you well, and it almost frightened me recently to hear that your ministers were planning to disarm France.

Being born classicists, despite your present romanticism, you know Olympus. Among the naked gods and goddesses there, making merry over nectar and ambrosia, you see one who even amid such joy and sport always wears armor, and goes with helmet on head and spear in hand.

It is the Goddess of Wisdom.

ON THE COMING OF COMMUNISM

I confess frankly that communism, which is so inimical to all my interests and inclinations, yet exerts a magic influence over my soul. . . . Two voices move me in its favor, two voices which will not be silenced, and which in their essence may be quite diabolical. The first is logic . . . and the second . . . is hate–the hate which I feel for . . . the so-called Nationalist Party in Germany. . . . I have detested and fought the latter all my life, and now, as the sword falls from the hand of the dying man, I feel myself consoled by the conviction that Communism . . . will give them the *coup de grâce.* It will, however, be no blow with a club, but rather a crushing beneath a giant's foot. Communism will tread on aristocracy as one treads on a vile toad. . . . Out of hatred for the champions of nationalism I could almost love those Communists. . . . Howl away, ye nationalists! The time will come when the fatal tread of the giant's foot will grind ye to dust! With this conviction I can calmly leave the world. . . .

ISRAEL AMONG THE NATIONS

What we call today the proletarians' hate of the rich was once called hatred of the Jews. Indeed, the latter–barred from owning land and earning a livelihood by handicraft, and thus depending solely on trade and on the money business which the Church forbade to true believers–were legally condemned to be rich, hated, and murdered. True, in those days such murders still bore a religious cloak: it was said that one had to kill those who had killed our Saviour. Odd! The very race that gave the world a God, whose entire life breathed only devotion to God, was decried as deicide! We saw the bloody parody of this madness at the outbreak of the revolution in San Domingo–where a Negro band, devastating the plantations with fire and sword, was led by a black fanatic carrying a huge crucifix and screaming bloodthirstily: "The whites killed Christ, let us kill all the whites!"

To the Jews, to whom the world owes its God, it also owes His divine word, the Bible. They saved it out of the bankruptcy of the Roman Empire; and in the mad scuffles during the migration of peoples they preserved the cherished book, until Protestantism sought it out among them and translated the find into native languages and spread it throughout the world. This circulation has borne the most blessed fruit, lasting until this day when the propaganda of the Bible Society fulfills a providential mission – more important, and in any case apt to have other results, than the pious gentlemen of this British Christianity-exporting agency are dreaming. They mean to bring a small, narrow dogmatism to power, and to monopolize heaven as they did the sea, to turn it into a dominion of the Church of England – and lo! without knowing it, they speed the downfall of all Protestant sects, all of which live by the Bible and must dissolve in any universal Biblicism. They are promoting the great democracy where every man shall be not only king but bishop in the castle of his home; in distributing the Bible over the whole earth – in foisting it on all mankind, so to speak, by commercial tricks, smuggling or barter, and handing it over to the exegesis of individual reason – they are founding the great empire of the spirit, the empire of religious feeling, of neighborly love, of purity, and of the true morality that cannot be taught with dogmatic formulas but by parables and examples, as are contained in the beautiful, holy book for the education of little and big children: in the Bible.

For the contemplative thinker, it is a marvelous spectacle to regard countries where, ever since the Reformation, the Bible has exercised its formative influence on the natives, and marked their customs, ways of thought, and emotions with the stamp of the Palestinian life as it is manifested in both the Old and New Testaments. In the north of Europe and America – especially in the Scandinavian and Anglo-Saxon countries, in all Germanic and in some measure also in Celtic ones – Palestinism has permeated so far that one fancies himself to be among Jews. The Protestant Scots, for example – are they not

Hebrews whose names are biblical throughout, whose very cant has a somewhat Jerusalemitic-Pharisaic ring, whose religion is a mere pork-eating Judaism? The same is true in many North German provinces and in Denmark; to say nothing of most of the new communities in the United States, where the life of the Old Testament is aped pedantically. There, it looks as if daguerreotyped; the contours are scrupulously correct but everything is gray upon gray, and the sunny colorful luster of the Promised Land is lacking. But some day the caricature will vanish; the genuine, imperishable and true – the morality of ancient Judaism – will flourish as God-pleasingly in those lands as once along Jordan and on the heights of Lebanon. One needs no psalms and camels to be good, and goodness is better than beauty.

Perhaps it was not just because these nations were susceptible that they so easily took to the Jewish life, in customs and ways of thinking. Perhaps another cause of this phenomenon is to be found in the character of the Jewish people, which always had a strong affinity to the character of the Germanic and to some extent also of the Celtic race. To me, Judea always seemed like a piece of the West that had got lost in the middle of the East. With its spiritualistic faith, its severe, chaste, even ascetic ways – in short, with its abstract inwardness – this land and its people always formed the strangest contrast to neighbor countries and peoples devoted to the most luxurious and voluptuous cults of nature, and to a life spent in bacchantic revels. Israel sat piously under its fig tree, sang the praises of the invisible God and practiced virtue and righteousness, while in the temples of Babel, Nineveh, Sidon, and Tyre, those bloody and lascivious orgies were celebrated whose mere description still makes our hair stand on end. Considering these surroundings, we cannot marvel enough at Israel's early greatness.

Of Israel's love of freedom, while slavery was legal and thriving not in the vicinity alone but among all nations of antiquity, including the philosophical Greeks – of this love of freedom I will say nothing, so as not to compromise the Bible with the powers that be. Actually, there is no Socialist more terroristic than our Lord and Saviour; and in fact even Moses was such a Socialist, though as a practical man he only sought to remodel existing institutions, particularly in regard to property. Instead of wrestling with the impossible, instead of hot-headedly decreeing the abolition of property, Moses only strove for its moral reform. He sought to establish harmony between property and morality, the true law of reason, and effected it by introducing the "Year of Jubilee," when every alienated heritage–always consisting of land, in an agricultural nation–reverted to the original owner, no matter in what way it had passed from his hands. . . .

Moses did not want to abolish property. Rather, he wanted everybody to own some, so that poverty should make of no man a serf with servile thoughts. Freedom always was the great emancipator's final idea; it flames and breathes in all his laws on pauperism. Slavery itself he hated beyond measure, almost grimly, but he could not quite destroy this inhumanity either; it was still too deeply rooted in the life of that primitive age and he had to restrict himself to legal alleviation of the slaves' fate, to making the purchase of their freedom easier and limiting the period of their service. If, however, a slave whom the law finally set free refused absolutely to leave his master's house, Moses ordered the incorrigible servile wretch to be nailed by his ear to the house's gatepost, and after this shameful exhibition he was condemned to servitude for life. O Moses, our teacher–Moshe Rabbenu, august fighter against slavery–hand me hammer and nails, that I may nail our peaceful, black-red-and-gold-liveried slaves by their long ears to the Brandenburger Gate!

"It used to amuse Boerne," Heine wrote, "when his enemies could find nothing worse to say of him than that he was a descendant of a race that once had filled the world with its glory, and, in spite of all its degradation, had never altogether lost its sanctity. . . . Indeed, the Jews are of the dough whereof the gods are kneaded. If today they are trampled under foot, tomorrow they are worshipped; while some of them creep about in the filthiest mire of commerce, others ascend to the highest peaks of humanity–for Golgotha is not the only mountain on which a Jewish God has bled for the salvation of the world. The Jews are the people of the spirit, and whenever they return to their spirit they are great, splendid, and put to shame and conquer their rude oppressors. . . . It is remarkable how striking are the contrasts! While among the Jews there is to be found every possible caricature of vulgarity, there are among them also the ideals of the purest humanity. Just as they once led the world into new paths of progress, so the world has perhaps still to look for leadership from them."

CONCERNING THE MESSIAH

O dear, longingly-awaited Messiah! Where is he now, where does he tarry? Is he yet unborn or has he lain hidden for a thousand years, awaiting the great, the right hour of deliverance? Is he old Barbarossa sitting asleep in his stone chair in the Kyffhaeuser, so long asleep that his white beard has grown through the stone table? Sometimes drowsily shaking his head, blinking with half-closed eyes, reaching for his sword in a dream–and sinking back into the heavy thousand-year sleep?

No, it is not the Emperor Red-beard who will free Germany as the people believe–the German people, the sleepy, dreaming people who can imagine even their Messiah only in the shape of an old sleeper!

The Jews have a much better idea of their Messiah, and many years ago when I was in Poland and at Cracow met the great Rabbi Menasseh ben Naphtali, I always listened with a glad open heart when he spoke of the Messiah. I have forgotten which book of the Talmud contains the details given me quite faithfully by the great rabbi, and only the main features of his description of the Messiah are still in my memory. The Messiah, he said, was born on the day when Jerusalem was destroyed by the villain, Titus Vespasian, and ever since he has been living in the most beautiful palace in heaven, surrounded by brightness and joy, wearing a crown upon his head just like a king – but his hands are fettered with golden chains!

"What is the meaning of these golden chains?" I asked in amazement.

"They are necessary," replied the great rabbi with a wise look and a deep sigh. "Without these fetters the Messiah, losing patience, might suddenly plunge down and start his work of deliverance too early, at the wrong time. He is no quiet sleepyhead. He is a handsome, very slender, but immensely strong man, thriving like youth itself; and he leads a very monotonous life. He spends the best part of the morning with the customary prayers, or laughing and joking with his servants, angels in disguise who sing prettily and play the flute. Then he has his long hair combed, and is anointed with nard and dressed in his princely purple. All afternoon he studies the Kabbalah. Toward evening he sends for his old chancellor, another angel in disguise, as are the four strong councillors who accompany him. Then the chancellor must read to his master, from a large book, what has happened each day. There are all sorts of stories at which the Messiah smiles with pleasure, or shakes his head disapprovingly. But when he hears how his people are abused below, he gets most fearfully angry and cries out so that the heavens tremble – then the four strong councillors must hold back the enraged one lest he rush down to earth, and they truly would not overpower him if his hands were not fettered with the golden chains. In the end they soothe him, with gentle reminders that the time, the true hour of salvation, is not yet come, and he sinks down on is couch and veils his face and weeps. . . ."

This was about what Manasseh ben Naphtali told me in Cracow, referring to the Talmud in witness of his credibility. I often had to think of his tales, especially in the most recent times, after the July Revolution. On the worst days I even thought I heard with my own ears a rattling as of golden chains, and then a desperate sobbing. . . .

Do not lose heart, beautiful Messiah, you who will save not only Israel, as the superstitious Jews imagine, but all suffering humanity! Break not, you golden chains! Keep him fettered yet a little time, lest he come too soon, the redeeming King of the World.

OBITER DICTA

But what is the great question of the age? It is Emanicipation! Not merely the emancipation of the Irish, the Greeks, the Frankfurt Jews, the West-Indian Negroes, and other oppressed races, but the emancipation of the whole world . . . which now tears itself loose from the leading strings of the privileged class, the aristocracy.

The King of Prussia is a very religious man; he holds strongly to religion; he is a good Christian, firmly attached to the evangelical confession of faith; indeed,he has even written a liturgy and believes in holy symbols. But, ah, I wish he believed instead in Jupiter, the Father of the Gods, who punishes perjury–perhaps then the king would give us that promised constitution.

PERSONALIA

It is true that I was once baptized, but I was never converted. It is extremely difficult for a Jew to be converted, for how can he bring himself to believe in the divinity of–another Jew?

Ah, gone is my yearning for rest. I know now what I will, what I shall, what I must do. . . . I am the Son of the Revolution and I again take up the charmed weapons upon which my mother has breathed her magic words of blessing. . . . Flowers! Flowers! I will crown my head with flowers for the fight unto death. And my lyre, give me my lyre that I may sing a battle song. . . . Words like flaming stars that shoot from the heavens to burn palaces and illumine hovels . . . words like bright javelins, that go whizzing up to the seventh heaven and smite the pious hypocrites who have crept into the Holy of Holies. . . . I am all joy and song, all sword and flame!

Perhaps you are correct, and I am only a Don Quixote; and the reading of all manner of strange books has turned my head, even as that of La Mancha was turned. . . . (But) he desired to restore decaying chivalry, while I, on the contrary, would utterly destroy all that is left over from those days. . . . My colleague regarded windmills as giants; I, however, see in the giants of the day only noisy windmills. . . . He took beggars' pothouses for castles, ass-drivers for cavaliers, stablegirls for court-ladies; but I take our castles for mere lodging-houses for blackguards, our knights for ass-drivers, and our court-ladies for common wenches. And just as he mistook a puppet show for the deeds of a state, so do I regard our state deeds as mere puppet comedies. Yet just as bravely as the bold knight of La Mancha do I let drive into the wooden trash. . . .

I am no longer a divine biped; I am no longer the "freest German since Goethe," as I was called in better days; I am no longer the Great Heathen No. 2, another vine-crowned Dionysus, excelled only by my colleague, No. 1, to whom was given the title of Grand Duke Jupiter of Weimar; I am no longer a joyous Hellene, sound in body, smiling down gaily on the melancholy Nazarenes. I am now only a poor sick Jew.

CHAPTER 66

YIDDISH HUMOR

Since humor is so largely a vent for frustration, one can understand why it was peculiarly well developed among the Yiddish-speaking Jews. Forced to live on sufferance among people who were their cultural inferiors, humor served them in two potent though unconscious ways. First, it enabled them to exact a subtle vengeance for the gross injustices to which they were subjected, and thus produced a deep inward consolation. Second, it armored them against the insults which were always coming their way, and thus furnished them with an effective method of outward defense. This second factor helps to explain why so much of the humor was directed at themselves. Jibes were certain to come anyway, so why not let them be self-inflicted? Thus the jibes were not merely robbed of their sting, but actually made a source of perverse pleasure. They transformed the Jew from the victim of the mockery into its master.

For these and less recondite reasons the innumerable witty anecdotes current among the Jews of the old Russian Pale of Settlement certainly deserve to be considered part of the wisdom of Israel, and a few examples are, therefore, included in this anthology.[1]

---

[1]There are several English collections of such anecdotes, one of the best being Rufus Learsi's *Book of Jewish Humor* (New York, Bloch Publishing, 1941). The versions given here are for the most part my own. Several anecdotes belonging to this same genre will be found scattered through this anthology.

ANECDOTES ON THIS AND THAT

The best audience for a joke, say the Jews, is a Russian nobleman, for he laughs at it three times: first when you tell the joke, then when you explain it, and finally when he understands it.

A Russian official is not quite as good, for he laughs only twice: when you tell him the joke, and when you explain it. He never understands it.

A Russian peasant is still less good, since he laughs only on hearing the joke. He hasn't time to have it explained to him, and even if he did, he wouldn't understand it.

But the worst audience of all is a Jew of any sort, for he will not laugh even once. No sooner do you start telling the joke than he breaks in and sneers: "Pooh, I heard that one in my cradle!"

A "progressive" Russian Jew was bitterly distressed because his son kept failing in the provincial *gymnasium* (secondary school), and finally decided that the youth might be right in putting the blame on the prejudice of his Christian teachers. So in desperation he arranged to have the boy baptized, and then sent him back to try the examinations over again. Once more, however, the outcome was unfavorable; indeed the grade was even lower than in any previous report. Whereupon the father confronted the scapegrace and demanded sternly: "*Nu*, my son, what excuse can you give this time?"

The youth merely shrugged his shoulders. "After all, papa," he retorted, "haven't you always said that we Gentiles have no brains for study?"

Two traders who made the rounds of the provincial fairs selling the same sort of merchandise chanced to meet on a train.

"Where are you going?" asked the first.

"Me?" answered his rival with an air of innocence. "I'm on my way to Pinsk."

"Hh!" snorted the other. "You tell me you are going to Pinsk because you want me to believe you are going to Minsk. But I happen to know you really *are* going to Pinsk, so why do you have to tell me a lie?"

The pogroms in Russia at the turn of this century caused widespread migration, and a certain rabbi found himself roaming all over Europe, looking for a new post. Finally he crossed to New York, and there, after months of correspondence, he was informed of an opening in Argentina. When a friend tried to dissuade him from going, saying Argentina was too far away, the wanderer sighed: "Too far away? From where?"

Two young Polish Jews left their native village to seek their fortunes in the West. When they reached Berlin, one of them felt he had gone far enough, but the other wanted to push on to Paris. Lacking sufficient funds, however, he begged his friend to lend him an extra hundred marks, promising to return them with interest out of his very first earnings. Needless to add, he did not send them back even without interest.

Ten years later, the fellow who had settled in Berlin was sent to Paris by his employer, and while there he was amazed to discover that his old friend was reputed to be a highly successful stockbroker. So he went to him and said, "Look, Itzik, I'm still a poor man, and you're supposed to be very rich. Why haven't you ever paid me back my hundred marks?"

"*Quoi?*" cried the other, drawing himself up and suddenly lapsing into French. "Pay you back? First you Germans must give us back Alsace-Lorraine!"

A Jew was asked: "Why do you people always answer a question with another question?"

He answered: "Why shouldn't we?"

A Jew once boasted that he had four sons, and all of them "intellectuals." Two were doctors, one was a lawyer, and the fourth was a scientist.

"And you?" he was asked. "What do you do?"

"I'm just a businessman," he replied. "My shop isn't very big, but thank God it brings in enough for me to support all of them."

A priest and a rabbi fell to arguing the difference between believing in a God of Love and a God of Vengeance. The rabbi said: "It is true that ours is a God of Vengeance, for it is written: 'Vengeance is mine, saith the Lord.' This means that we must leave vengeance to Him. As for us, we must practice love, for it is written: 'Thou shalt love thy neighbor as thyself.' Now if in your case it is the other way around, would you say that yours is the better religion?"

It once happened that the Chief Rabbi of Warsaw was invited to attend a city banquet, and found himself seated next to the bishop. The latter, thinking to have some fun with the old Jew, urged him to try the hors d'oeuvres, which consisted chiefly of spiced ham.

"Thank you, your grace," said the other, "but do you not know that such food is prohibited by my religion?"

"So?" remarked the hierarch. "What a foolish religion! This ham is so delicious!"

When the banquet was ended, the rabbi bade a polite goodnight to his neighbor, adding: "And please, your grace, be so good as to pay my respects to madame, your wife."

"My wife?" cried the bishop in horror. "Do you not know that my religion forbids a priest to marry?"

"So?" murmured the rabbi. "What a foolish religion! A wife is so delicious!"

A man who had just married off his daughter came running to the rabbi to plead for a divorce.

"What is wrong with the groom?" asked the rabbi.

"He can't play cards."

"What?" cried the rabbi. "Would to God that not a one of our young men could play cards."

"True," said the unhappy father. "But this one does."

A young Jew who had gone to Vienna to study medicine, returned to practice among his own people in a small Polish town. Like all such "intellectuals," he was suspected at first of being a socialist, but his pious behavior coupled with his kindly ministrations soon convinced most of the community that he was really a "good" Jew. Shortly thereafter, however, an epidemic broke out in the neighborhood, and the doctor arose in the synagogue and pleaded that the Jews should burn their garbage instead of throwing it into the streets. Whereupon there was almost a riot. "You see?" stormed the old rabbi, who had never ceased to suspect the young man. "He *is* a socialist after all!"

ANECDOTES ABOUT SCHLEMIELS

Characteristically, Yiddish folklore has no Paul Bunyan, but it does have a Motke Habad. He is the Jew who is forever trying to make ends meet, but always in vain. Good-natured, well-intentioned, and desperately eager to get ahead in the world, fate seems to be constantly against him, and he fails no matter to what he turns. He is the archetypical schlemiel, *and the mock-pathetic hero of countless anecdotes. For example:*

It is related that on one occasion Motke Habad was reduced to such straits that he was forced to appeal to the heads of the community for help. "If you will not support me," he threatened, "I shall become a hat maker!"

"*Nu*," they laughed, "and what if you will?"

"But don't you see what that would mean?" he wailed. "If I turn hat maker, all the infants in this town will be born without heads!"

Almost next door to Motke Habad lived a very rich merchant who was exceedingly haughty. Poor Motke could not abide the latter's snubs, and he finally confronted him one day and cried: "Look, Reb Hayyim, I can't understand why you are so arrogant. Now, if *I* were arrogant, there would be some justification for it. After all, I am a person of importance, for *my* neighbor is the rich Hayyim Stoltz. But you? Pooh, *your* neighbor is that miserable Motke Habad!"

Motke Habad was once summoned by the local Polish landowner and told to go to the fair in a neighboring town to purchase a French poodle for the baroness.

"Certainly!" cried Motke, all eagerness. "And how much is Your Excellency willing to spend for a first-class French poodle?"

"Up to twenty *rubles*."

"Out of the question!" Motke snapped. "For a really first-class French poodle one must pay at least–at least fifty *rubles*!"

The nobleman tried to dispute this, but Motke was so positive that the other finally yielded. Handing over the fifty *rubles*, he told Motke to hurry off. Whereupon the schlemiel became covered with confusion and stammered: "Yes, Your Excellency, I go, I go. B-but please, Your Excellency, what exactly is a French poodle?"

A wealthy man was being laid to rest, and his relatives followed the bier with loud lamentations. Motke Habad, happening to see the cortege, joined the mourners and started weeping even more demonstratively than the rest.

"Are you too a relative of the deceased?" he was asked.

He shook his head, but continued weeping.

"Then why all your grief?"
"That's the reason," he replied.

One night Motke caught a burglar crawling through the window of his miserable hovel. When the rascal tried to escape, Motke cried: "No, please don't run away. Let me join you in your search. Perhaps your luck is better than mine!"

Motke became a teamster, but he found the horse consumed all the profits. He determined to wean the beast from the habit of eating, and began by depriving it of oats one day a week, then two days, then three. After a month the horse seemed well on its way to learning how to get along with almost no oats at all, when it suddenly collapsed and died.

Motke was beside himself with grief. Standing over the beast, he groaned, "Woe is me! Just when my troubles were almost over, you have to give up and die!"

Eager as Motke Habad was to get rich, every time he managed to make a little money he would give it away to someone in distress. So he repaired to his rich neighbor, and asked him the secret of his success.

"Motke," said the other, "you must stop being a schlemiel. Don't keep giving your money away. If you want to be rich, you must train yourself to behave like a hog for at least ten years."

"And then what happens?" asked Motke.

"Then," came the answer, "it grows to be second nature."

ANECDOTES ABOUT SCHNORRERS

The luckless schlemiel *is merely one of many stock characters in Yiddish humor. Even more fabled is the* schnorrer, *the professional mendicant. He is as importunate as the other is easygoing, and as cunning as the other is slow-witted. For instance:*

The tale is told of how a *schnorrer* once came to a community late on a Friday afternoon and found that the only house where there was not a poor man already billeted for the Sabbath was the one owned by the town miser. Undaunted, the beggar knocked on the door of that house and insisted on speaking with the host in private. "I have not come for charity," he cried. "This is a matter of business."

Admitted to the miser's office, the *schnorrer* closed the door carefully and whispered, "How much will you give me for a diamond as big as an egg?"

The other's cupidity was at once aroused, but he knew better than to betray any eagerness.

"You look weary," he said to the stranger. "Stay with me over the Sabbath, and when you are rested we can talk business."

All the next day he showered his guest with favors, and not until nightfall did he finally ask to see the diamond. Whereupon the beggar shrugged his shoulders and declared: "Did I ever say I had a diamond? I merely wanted to know what you would offer me for one as large as an egg if I should happen to find one!"

A strange beggar began making the rounds in a certain town, asking alms on the plea that all his possessions had been destroyed in a fire. To aid a Jew in such a plight was considered a bounden duty throughout the Russian Pale, but it was customary for him to carry a document signed by his rabbi attesting to the disaster. This *schnorrer,* however, showed no such document, and when asked for it, he drew himself up and cried: "Didn't I tell you that *all* my possessions were destroyed? That document was one of them!"

A rich man was sitting at his window when he saw a beggar across the street scratching his back against a fence. Learning from the poor fellow that he had not been able to afford a bath in many months, he gave him some money and also a change of underclothes.

When the news spread to the other beggars in the neighborhood, two of them rushed to the fence and began scratching themselves against it with all their might. Instead of giving them alms, however, the rich man started belaboring them with his stick.

"You can't fool me!" he cried. "You are impostors!"

"But why did you believe the other fellow?" they protested.

"Because he was alone, and naturally had to use the fence to relieve his itching. But you are two, and if you were not impostors, each of you would scratch the other's back."

A man who had just given a *schnorrer* a whole *ruble* found him seated in a restaurant a little later, eating caviar. "Shame!" he cried. "You beg money on the streets and then squander it on caviar!"

The *schnorrer* became indignant instead of abashed. "And why not?" he retorted. "Before I got your *ruble,* I *couldn't* eat caviar. Now that I have it, I *mustn't* eat caviar. At that rate, when in the world *will* I eat caviar?"

A rich Jew had his pet *schnorrer* to whom he gave a regular annual stipend. One year he sent only half the usual sum, and the beggar made loud complaint.

"But I have unusual expenses this year," the rich man explained. "My son has become friendly with a ballet dancer, and it is costing me a fortune."

"What has that to do with me?" cried the beggar, incensed. "If he wants to support a fancy lady, that's *his* affair. But let him do it with his own money, not mine!"

It was the regular custom for each pious householder to take a wandering beggar home with him from the synagogue on Friday evening, and give him shelter over the Sabbath. One such householder, returning from the prayer service with his poor guest in tow, noticed that a second *schnorrer* was trailing them.

"Who is that?" he asked.

"It's my son-in-law," answered the guest. "I am supporting him."

Returning home from a train journey, a *schnorrer* reported that the conductor had kept staring at him very peculiarly.

"What do you mean, 'peculiarly'?" he was asked.

"I mean," he explained, "as if I were traveling without a ticket."

"What did you do about it?"

"What should I do?" he replied. "I stared back at him as if I really did have a ticket!"

ANECDOTES ABOUT THE FOOLS OF HELM

The little town of Helm somehow became legendary for the extravagant stupidity of its inhabitants. The latter figure in a whole cycle of what would now be termed "moron stories," a few of which go as follows:[2]

The traditions of Helm relate that before the work of building began, the founders met in solemn assembly and deliberated a long time on the best site for their city. They decided finally to build it at the foot of a mountain.

The great day arrived and the builders began by climbing to the summit, where they cut down trees for their houses. But how were the logs to be brought down, seeing the Helmites had no vehicles or horses? Their amazing ingenuity came immediately to their aid. They lifted the logs to their shoulders and carried them down into the valley.

Now it happened that a stranger passed by and saw the Helmites toiling and panting.

[2]These anecdotes are all taken from Rufus Learsi's *Book of Jewish Humor*.

"Foolish people," said the stranger, "why do you needlessly puff and sweat?" And having spoken, he pushed one of the logs with his foot and it rolled down the mountain as if it knew exactly where to go.

The builders of Helm stood and marveled. "The man is a genius," they whispered to each other.

But Helmites are quick to learn. Without losing a moment, they went down into the valley, carried the logs back to the summit, and sent them rolling in the precise manner of the stranger.

Building the public bathhouse presented a grave problem to the Jews of Helm. It involved the benches on which the bathers stretched out and reveled in the steam and heat. The question was whether the planks for those benches should be smooth or rough.

Immediately two parties came into existence: smoothists and roughists. The smoothists maintained that rough planks would scratch the bodies of the bathers, not to speak of the splinters they would carry home. The roughists argued that smooth planks would make the bathers slip and fall and that some of them might be hurt, *holileh!*

The wise men of Helm called a meeting that lasted far into the night. But each party held its ground and the assembly was deadlocked. At last the rabbi proposed a compromise which was universally acclaimed and proved over again that Torah and wisdom go together.

"My decision is," said he, "that the boards should be planed on one side only. For fear, however, that this planed side should cause people to slip, I order that the boards be laid with that side downward!"

The superior mentality for which the Helmites were famous was not, it should be noted, confined to the men. The women, too, were distinguished for it, as the following tale illustrates.

A stranger once came to Helm and put up at the tavern. After eating a hearty meal, he asked the mistress of the inn for his account.

"The bread, the soup, and the dessert come to seven *kopeks*," said she. "For the roast, another seven *kopeks*. Altogether eleven *kopeks*."

"Pardon me," said her guest, "two times seven are fourteen."

For a moment the woman was puzzled, but only for a moment.

"No," said she. "Two times seven are eleven. I was a widow with four children. I married a widower who also had four children, and three more children were born to us. Now each of us has seven children, and altogether we have eleven. Two times seven are eleven."

The stranger paid his account, filled with admiration for the acumen of a mere woman.

On a Friday morning, immediately after prayers, the rabbi of Helm went to market and bought a live and handsome fish in honor of the Sabbath. Now having to carry his cane in one hand and the bag with his prayer shawl in the other, he slipped the fish head down into the inside pocket of his cloak and went his way. But the fish was a big one and the tail projected out of his pocket.

Suddenly the fish waved his tail and slapped the rabbi full in the face. The fact got around and the city was in an uproar. Such impudence on the part of a fish had never been known before!

At once the worthies of Helm came together and passed sentence of death upon the culprit. The sentence was carried out immediately. The fish was taken to the river and drowned.

What is most important in the character of a judge? All will admit that impartiality is most important. The impartiality of the rabbi of Helm was famous for miles around.

Two litigants came to him one day to settle their dispute. After listening long and patiently to the plaintiff, he said to him: "You are in the right."

Then he listened to the defendant and said to him: "You are in the right."

The litigants departed highly pleased, but the rabbi's wife, who was present, was puzzled. A mere woman, what would she understand of legal matters?

"How is it possible," said she, "that they should both be in the right?"

The rabbi pondered the question long and deeply. Finally he turned to his good wife and said: "Shall I tell you something? You are also in the right."

One Friday afternoon the first snowfall came down on Helm and the people rejoiced to see the clean white blanket covering the rutted streets and dingy houses of their city. But then they thought sadly: "The *shammes* will soon be passing through the town and call on the people to close their shops and prepare for the Sabbath. What will happen to the snow when he walks over it?"

Immediately the rabbi and the seven worthies came together to see what could be done. The snow, they decided, must at all costs be kept clean. But how will the merchants know when to close their shops for the Sabbath? They might, God forbid, violate the sanctity of the holy day! Finally the rabbi issued an edict as follows:

"The *shammes* is to proclaim the Sabbath as usual. But he is not to go on foot. He is to stand up on a table and be carried through the town by four of the worthies."

This tale is one of many that might be cited as evidence of the business acumen for which the Helmites were famous.

The story is about two of them who agreed to go into partnership and, between them, managed to find enough capital to buy a little keg of whiskey as their stock in trade.

"Berel," said Sholem to his partner, "I have seen many a business like ours ruined by credits. Let us sell for cash only."

"For cash only," Berel agreed.

They opened their business to the public and waited for customers. But no customers came and after a while Berel felt just a little bit discouraged.

"Sholem," said he to his partner, "I have five *kopeks* in my pocket. Pour me a little glass of whiskey. It's for cash, of course."

Sholem poured and Berel paid and drank. He felt and looked much better.

"Berel," said Sholem to his partner. "I see in your eyes that we have the right stuff. Now that I have five *kopeks*, I think I'll have a little also. It's for cash, of course."

Berel poured, Sholem paid and drank, and he too felt and looked much better.

"Sholem," said Berel to his partner after a rather long pause. "We'll not be so foolish as to sell on credit. Pour me another little glass–for cash, of course."

Berel drank and passed the five *kopeks* to Sholem. Then Sholem drank again and passed the five *kopeks* to Berel.

Still there were no customers, but were the partners discouraged? On the contrary! They were in a state of satisfaction bordering on joy!

"Another little glass for me!" said one and paid spot cash.

"Another little glass for me!" said the other and paid spot cash.

The day passed and the contents of the little keg as well. It was time to close up for the day.

"Look, Sholem!" said Berel to his partner, hugging the keg on one side. "In one day we–we sold out our stock–all of it!"

"Yes!" said Sholem, hugging the keg on the other side, "and for–for cash only!"

Now with regard to the schoolteacher of Helm it goes without saying that he was in every respect a true Helmite.

How could it be otherwise? Isn't every genuine schoolteacher, no matter where he may live and labor, a Helmite?

The one of Helm was particularly shrewd in matters economic and financial.

"You know," said he to his wife one day, "if I were the czar, I would be richer than the czar."

"How so?" she asked.

"I would do a little teaching on the side," he explained.

With regard to money, the schoolteacher of Helm had his feet completely on the ground. "It's a topsy-turvy world," he once declared to his wife. "The rich who have plenty of money buy on credit. The poor, who haven't a copper, have to pay cash. Isn't it common sense it should be the other way: the rich to pay cash and the poor to get credit? What's that you say? A merchant who gives credit to the poor will become a poor man himself? Very well! What if he does? He'll be able to buy on credit, won't he?"

That good man laid no claim to a knowledge of the latest pedagogic methods, nevertheless he had his own way of impressing his teachings on his pupils. Consider, for example, the following discourse he once held to acquaint his pupils with the differences that exist among the social classes.

"An ordinary man," he said, "puts on a clean shirt on Friday for the Sabbath. A rich man changes his shirt every day. Rothschild changes his shirt three times a day, in the morning, at noon, and in the evening. The czar is attended by two generals, one of whom takes off the shirt he wears and the other puts on a clean one, off and on, off and on, without interruption, night and day.

"An ordinary man takes a nap and who takes care he should not be awakened? His wife. A rich man is protected by a vestibule before his sleeping room. Rothschild has twelve men stationed before his bedroom to guard his sleep. The czar has an army of soldiers before his door who cry continually and all together: 'Quiet! His Majesty is sleeping!'

"An ordinary man gets up early in the morning and eats his breakfast. A rich man sleeps until ten o'clock, then he gets up and has his breakfast. Rothschild sleeps until Afternoon Prayers, and eats his breakfast toward evening. The czar sleeps all day and all night, and has his breakfast the following day."

Once it happened that the schoolteacher of Helm was given a post in a neighboring town. Arriving there, he discovered he had forgotten to pack his slippers, so he wrote to his wife a letter reading as follows:

"Be sure to send me your slippers with this messenger. I have put down 'your slippers,' because if I wrote 'my slippers' you would read my slippers, and would send me your slippers. And what would I do with your slippers? Therefore, I say plainly 'your slippers' so that you would read your slippers and send me my slippers."

Foremost among the philosophers of Helm was a certain Lemach ben Lekish. No question was too deep for him. Take the following as mere illustrations:

"Why," he was asked, "does a dog wag his tail?"

"Because," Lemach answered without hesitation, "the dog is stronger than the tail. Were it the other way, the tail would wag the dog."

Again he was asked why the hair on a man's head turns gray sooner than his beard.

"It's because," Lemach replied, "the hair on his head is twenty years older than his beard."

"And why," he was further asked, "are the waters of the seas salty?"

"Don't you know?" he said. "It's because so many thousands of herring live in them."

It is related that one day Lemach ben Lekish and a fellow philosopher were strolling outside the town of Helm discoursing on the wonders of creation. One of them stopped and became lost in thought.

"The ways of Heaven are mysterious," said he finally. "Consider the birds and the cows. The bird is small and his needs are modest. Nevertheless, he has been given wings and he has access to the sky as well as the earth. The cow is big and her needs are much greater. Nevertheless, she is held down to the earth alone."

Now, as the speaker looked up toward the sky, a flock of birds flew by and something fell on his nose. Hastily he turned aside and wiped his face with his sleeve.

"What is it?" asked his companion.

"I have found the solution to the mystery!" declared the other joyfully.

"Indeed! What have you found?" asked the other thinker.

"I have been shown the reason why the Lord in His wisdom and mercy thought it best not to give wings to the cow."

It was once observed that Lemach's face became as though illumined, and his brother philosophers realized that he had made a new discovery.

"What is it? What is it?" they asked.

"Thank Heaven!" he answered. "From now on every poor man will eat cream and every rich man drink sour milk. I've discovered how to do it.

"It's very simple," he continued solemnly as they crowded around him. "Let a decree be issued in Helm that from now on sour milk shall be called cream and cream, sour milk!"

CHAPTER 67

YIDDISH PROVERBS

The Yiddish language is peculiarly rich in proverbs. Here are a few.[1]

GOD AND THE WORLD

God waits long, but pays with interest.

God strikes with one hand and heals with the other.

Man strives and God laughs.

Whom God would regale, man cannot quail.

If thou intend a thing, God will help thee.

God gives naught for nothing.

One path leads to paradise, but a thousand to hell.

Better to receive from God by the spoonful than from man by the bushel.

The world can be changed by neither scolding nor laughing.

A man can bear more than ten oxen can draw.

God forbid that we should experience all that we are able to bear.

Ten enemies cannot do a man the harm that he does to himself.

---

[1] *Jewish Encyclopedia* (New York, 1905), vol. 10, pp. 228–229.

A man can eat alone but not work alone.

Comrades are needed both for joy and for sorrow.

Better a fool who has traveled than a wise man who has remained at home.

If folk knew what others intended for them, they would kill themselves.

To know a man you must ride in the same cart with him.

MAN AND WOMAN

Give thine ear to all, thy hand to thy friends, but thy lips only to thy wife.

A third person may not interfere between two that sleep on the same pillow.

Women persuade men to good as well as to evil, but they always persuade.

Fools generally have pretty wives.

Love tastes sweet, but only with bread.

FAMILY LIFE

Small children, small joys; large children, large annoys.

There is no bad mother and no good death.

Parents may have a dozen children, but each one is the only one for them.

A boy, a blessing; a girl, a care.

A married daughter is as a piece of bread that is cut off.

One father supports ten children, but ten children do not support one father.

The mother-in-law and the daughter-in-law do not ride in the same cart.

MONEY

Though money has a dirty father, it is regarded as noble.

A golden nail drops from a golden cart.

He who saves is worth more than he who earns.

Shrouds have no pockets.

The way most valued leads to the pocket.

In hell an ox is worth a *groschen*, but no man has that *groschen*.

The poor are ever liberal.

He that is sated believes not the hungry.

If a poor man eats a chicken, either he is sick or the chicken was sick.

SELF-CRITICISM

If a Jew breaks a leg, he says, "Praised be God that I did not break both legs"; if he breaks both, he says, "Praised be God that I did not break my neck."

When a Jew is hungry, he sings; when the master (Polish nobleman) is hungry, he whistles; when the peasant is hungry, he beats his wife.

If the Jew be right, he is beaten all the more.

The master (nobleman) thinks of his horse and dog, the Jew of his wife and child.

FATE

Intelligence is not needed for luck, but luck is needed for intelligence.

Dowries and inheritances bring no luck.

Nothing is so bad but that good may come of it.

He with whom luck plays the game hits the mark without even taking aim.

LIFE AND DEATH

The angel of death always finds an excuse.

Better ruined ten times than dead once.

No man dies before his time.
Every man knows that he must die, but no one believes it.
Better a noble death than a wretched life.

CHAPTER 68

THE WIT OF SHOLOM ALEICHEM

Sholem Rabinowitz (1859–1916), who wrote under the pen name of Sholom Aleichem (literally "Peace to you," but more idiomatically "Hello") was one of the giants of modern Yiddish literature. He succeeded better than any other man in depicting the humor, heartbreak, grandeur, and pain of life in the Russian Jewish Pale. The following slections are taken from Maurice Samuel's admirable volume entitled The World of Sholom Aleichem.[1] *The first is a typical soliloquy by one of this author's best-known characters, Tevyeh the Dairyman–the irrepressible little village Jew who is at once optimist and cynic, devotee and skeptic, dreamer and man of endless, though always hapless, enterprise. Tevyeh is riding through a forest with a wagonload of wood and addressing his poor nag:*

"Pull, miserable monster! Drag, you wretched beast in the likeness of a horse! You're no better than I am! If it's your destiny to be Tevyeh's horse, then suffer like Tevyeh, and learn like Tevyeh and his family to die of hunger seven times in the day and then go to bed supperless. Is it not written in the Holy Book that the same fate shall befall man and beast? . . . No! That is not true. Here I am at least talking, while you are dumb and cannot ease your pain with words. My case is better

[1]New York, 1943, pp. 9–12, 114–115.

than yours. For I am human, and a Jew, and I know what you do not know. I know that we have a great and good God in heaven, who governs the world in wisdom and mercy and lovingkindness, feeding the hungry and raising the fallen and showing grace to all living things. I can talk my heart out to Him, while your jaws are locked, poor thing. However, I must admit that a wise word is no substitute for a piece of herring or a bag of oats. . . ."

(Tevyeh suddenly realizes it is already time for Minchah, *the afternoon service, so he hastens to recite the prescribed prayers. But while his lips piously mumble the words, his mind keeps interjecting gently impious comments. For instance:)*

"Blessed are they that dwell in Thy house (Good! But I take it, O Lord, that Thy house is somewhat more spacious than my hovel!). . . . I will extol Thee, my God, O King (What good would it do me if I didn't?). . . . Every day I will bless thee (on an empty stomach, too). . . . The Lord is good to all (And suppose He forgets somebody now and again, good Lord, hasn't He enough on His mind?). . . . The Lord upholdeth all that fall, and raiseth up all that are bowed down (Father in Heaven, loving Father, surely it's my turn now, I can't fall any lower). . . . Thou openest Thy hand and satisfiest every living thing (So You do, Father in Heaven, You give with an open hand–one gets a box on the ear, and another a roast chicken, and neither my wife nor I nor my daughters have even smelt a roast chicken since the days of creation). . . . He will fulfill the desire of them that fear Him; He will also hear their cry and will save them. (But when, O Lord? When? . . .)"

The following passage is characteristic of Sholom Aleichem's wry wit, and also of the wry spirit bred in the Jews by ghetto confinement.

"When a man gives an account of what befell him at the fair, he must always be considerate of the feelings of his neighbors. He must be careful not to wound his fellow Jews, but strive rather to be at one with them. For it is written in the Ethics of the Fathers: 'Separate not thyself from the community,' which means, among other things, do not break in thoughtlessly and selfishly with something that jars on your listeners. . . . Unity in Israel! Let us never forget that principle. So, for instance, if I went out to the fair–in a manner of speaking, of course, for I never attended fairs except as a child, with my father–when I went out to the fair and did well, sold everything at a good profit, and returned with pocketfuls of money, my heart bursting with joy, I never failed to tell my neighbors that I had lost every *kopek* and was a ruined man. Thus, I was happy, and my neighbors were happy. But if, on the contrary, I had really been cleaned out at the fair, and brought home with me a bitter heart and a bellyful of green gall, I made sure to tell my neighbors that never since God made fairs had there been a better one. You get my point? For thus, I was miserable, and my neighbors were miserable with me."

CHAPTER 69

A TALE BY PERETZ

Isaac Leib Peretz (1851–1915) ranks with Sholom Aleichem as one of the "classic" Yiddish writers. His early education was confined to Hebraic lore, and he seemed destined to become a rabbi. Instead, succumbing to the wave of "enlightenment" which had begun to sweep the Russian Pale, he turned in his late youth to secular studies, and became an attorney-at-law. His liberal views soon brought him into conflict with the czarist government, and he was forced to abandon his profession. Moving to Warsaw, where he secured a minor post in the offices of the Jewish community, he began to devote himself entirely to literature. Somewhat of a mystic by nature, he took especial delight in elaborating the hasidic tales which had become so large a part of the folklore of East European Jewry. The following story–one of his best known–is well worth quoting in an anthology of wisdom.[1]

THE RABBI OF NEMIROV

Round about the penitential days, shortly before the New Year, when Jews the world over pray for the remission of sins and for a happy year to come–round about those days, early

[1]Translated by Maurice Samuel in Fleg's *Jewish Anthology* (New York, 1925), p. 348 ff.

in the morning, the Rabbi of Nemirov was wont to disappear. Simply vanish!

He was nowhere to be seen; neither in the synagogue, nor in the study rooms, nor making one in a group at prayer – least of all, of course, was he to be found at home. The door of his home stood open and men and women went in and out at will: nothing was ever stolen from the rabbi's house. But not a living thing was to be seen there.

Where could the rabbi be?

Where, indeed, if not in heaven? Busy days, these, for the rabbi, the days before the New Year. Are there not Jews enough, bless them all, in need of a livelihood, of peace, health, husbands for their daughters? Are there not Jews who want to be good, and would be good if it were not for the Evil Spirit, who looks with his thousand eyes into every nook and cranny of the world, tempts and then tells, reports it in heaven that such and such a one has fallen. . . . And who is to come to the rescue, if not the rabbi himself?

Everybody understood that.

But once there came into Nemirov a Litvak, a Lithuanian Jew. He thought otherwise. He laughed at the whole story. You know these Litvaks, enemies of the hasidim, cold-blooded and exact. It's little enough they care about anything but what's written in black and white, proof positive, and no mistake about it. They want chapter and verse before they believe anything, and their heads are crammed chockful of texts, the whole Talmud by heart. They'll prove to you, beyond the veriest shadow of a glimmer of a doubt that Moses himself, while he lived, couldn't get into heaven: he had to stop ten levels below – the book says so. How then shall the hasidim mount into heaven? Can you argue with a man like that?

"Well, where do *you* say the rabbi goes during those days?" we ask him angrily.

"No business of mine," says he, shrugging his shoulders.

And, believe it or not, he made up his mind to get to the bottom of the business – for that's what a Litvak is like.

And that very same evening, soon after prayers, this fellow steals into the rabbi's bedroom, hides himself under the bed, and . . . waits. He was ready to wait all night just to find out what became of the rabbi in the early mornings of those penitential days.

Anyone else would have dozed off and fallen asleep. A Litvak has a way of getting round it. He kept awake just by repeating in his mind a whole tractate of the Talmud – Hullin or Nedarim – I don't remember which.

In the early dawn he hears the beadle going the rounds, waking good Jews to penitential prayers.

But the rabbi had been awake for something like an hour already, lying there and moaning to himself.

Whosoever has heard the Rabbi of Nemirov when he moans in his affliction knows what burden of grief, of anguish for his people, he bears. No one could hear him, and not weep with him. But the heart of a Litvak is every bit of it iron. He heard, but he lay there, under the bed, while the rabbi, God be with him, lay on the bed.

Then the Litvak heard how the beds throughout all the house began to creak, as the household woke from sleep. He heard the murmuring of words, the splash of water, the closing and opening of doors. Then, when the household had departed, the house was silent and dark once more, except where a moonbeam broke through a crack in the shutters. . . .

He confessed afterwards, did the Litvak, that when he found himself alone in the house with the rabbi, he was seized with fear. He felt a creeping in his skin, and the roots of the hair of his beard tingled and pricked like thousands of needles.

And reason enough, too. Can you imagine it – he alone in the house with the rabbi, in the early morning, on a day of penitentials? But a Litvak is a Litvak . . . he trembled like a caught fish—and endured.

At last the rabbi, God bless him, began to get up.

He dresses himself first, then he goes to the clothes-closet and takes out a bundle, and out of the bundle stumbles a heap of peasant clothes, a smock, a huge pair of boots, a big fur cap with a leather strap studded with brass buttons.

The rabbi puts these on, too.

From one of the pockets in the smock there stuck out the end of a thick rope—a peasant's rope.

The rabbi leaves the room. The Litvak follows.

Going through the kitchen the rabbi stoops, picks up a hatchet, hides it under his smock and goes on.

The Litvak trembles—and persists!

The dread of those days of judgment, before the beginning of the New Year, lies on the dark streets. Here and there you could hear the cry of Jews at prayer; here and there you heard a moaning from a sickbed at an open window. The rabbi sticks to the shadows, flits from house to house, the Litvak after him.

The Litvak hears the beating of his own heart keeping measure with the heavy footsteps of the rabbi. But he persists, follows—and is with the rabbi when the end of the town is reached.

There's a little forest at the end of the town.

The rabbi, God bless him, plunges into the forest. Thirty or forty paces within the forest he stops near a young tree, and the Litvak nearly drops with amazement when he sees the rabbi take out his hatchet and begin to chop at the tree.

And the rabbi chops steadily at the tree until it begins to give, creaks, bends, and then cracks. And the rabbi lets it fall, and begins to chop it up, first into logs, then into chips. He gathers up the chips into a bundle, binds it round with the rope which he takes from his pocket, throws the bundle over his shoulder, shoves the hatchet back under his smock, and begins to walk back to the town.

He stops in one of the poorest alleys at that end of the town, at a broken-down hut, and knocks at the window.

A frightened voice asks from within: "Who's there?" The Litvak recognizes the voice of a sick woman.

"*Jo,*" answers the rabbi, in the accent of a peasant.

"*Kto jo,* who's there?" the same frightened voice asks, in Russian.

"It's I, Vassil," answers the rabbi, in the same language.

"Which Vassil? I don't know you. What do you want?"

"Wood," answers Vassil, "I've got wood to sell–very cheap, next to nothing. . . ."

He waits for no answer and makes his way into the house.

The Litvak steals after him, and, by the gray light of the dawn, looks round the room, broken, poor, unhappy. . . . A sick woman lies in bed, wrapped in rags, and in her sick voice she says, bitterly: "Buy? What shall I buy, and how? What money have I, a widow, and sick."

"I'll give it to you on credit," says Vassil, "six *groschen* in all."

"And where shall I ever get the money to pay you back? The sick woman moans.

"Foolish woman," the rabbi rebukes her, "see, you are a sick woman, and a widow, and I am willing to lend you this wood. I will trust you. I am certain you will pay for it some day. And you have a great and mighty God in heaven, and will not trust Him. You will not trust Him to the extent of six *groschen*. . . ."

"And who will light the fire for me?" she moans again. "I am sick and have not the strength to rise, and my son is away at work."

"I'll light it for you," says the rabbi.

And the rabbi bent down to the fireplace, and began to light the fire, and as he arranged the wood he repeated, in a low voice, the first of the penitential prayers, and when the fire was well lighted he was repeating the second of the penitential prayers. . . .

And he repeated the third of the penitential prayers when the fire had died down – and he covered the oven. . . .

The Litvak, who had seen everything, remained in Nemirov, became one of the most passionate adherents of the Rabbi of Nemirov.

And later, when the adherents of the Rabbi of Nemirov told how, every year, in the dread penitential days before the New Year, it was the custom of their rabbi to leave the earth, and to ascend upward, as high as heaven, the Litvak would add quietly, "And maybe higher, too."

CHAPTER 70

THUS SPAKE ASHER GINZBERG

Asher Ginzberg (1856–1927), the most noted of modern Hebrew publicists, was born in the Russian Pale, and sedulously schooled in the hasidic tradition. Married off at the age of sixteen to a maiden of excellent rabbinic lineage, he continued to devote himself to talmudic studies, but with increasing restiveness. Finally, when already in his late twenties, he left his family to seek a worldly education in Vienna, Berlin, and Breslau, and on his return home became a confirmed secularist. Settling in Odessa, he identified himself actively with Zionism, and won recognition as the most brilliant and logical theoretician of that movement. Toward the close of his life he migrated to Palestine, and he died in Tel Aviv.

Ginzberg's essays exercised a deep influence on his fellow workers in the cause of Zion. Published under the nom de plume of Ahad Ha-Am ("One of the People"), and written in a singularly chaste and fluent modern Hebrew, they insisted that Jewish nationalism must be fundamentally cultural rather than political. This brought their author into sharp conflict with the extremists in the movement, many of whom had succumbed to the Nietzschean delusions which were destined–as we now know–to lead straight to Fascism. The following essay, though pointed at these Jewish extremists, contains truths which all peoples might well take to heart.[1]

[1]Translated by Leon Simon in *Selected Essays by Ahad Ha-Am* (Philadelphia , Jewish Publication Society, 1912), p. 217 ff.

Amid the confused Babel of voices that are heard in the prevailing chaos of modern Jewry there is one angry, strident, revolutionary voice which gains the public ear occasionally, and leaves a most extraordinary impression. The younger men, ever on the alert, ever receptive of new ideas, drink in the new gospel which this voice proclaims; they are thrilled by it, attracted by it, without inquiring very deeply as to its ultimate worth, or whether the idea which it contains is really a new truth, worthy of all this enthusiasm.

The new gospel is that of "the transvaluation of values," and we may perhaps describe it thus:

The whole life of the Jews from the time of the Prophets to the present day has been, in the opinion of those who propound this new gospel, one long mistake; and it demands immediate rectification. During all these centuries, Judaism has exalted the abstract, spiritual ideal above real, physical force: it has exalted the "book" over the "sword." Now, therefore, that the desire for a national rebirth has been aroused in us, it behooves us first of all to transvaluate the moral values which are accepted among us at present; to overthrow, mercilessly and at a single blow, the historic edifice which our ancestors have left us, seeing that it is built up on this dangerously mistaken idea of the superiority of spirit to matter, and of the subordination of the individual life to abstract moral laws. We must, then start again from the beginning, and build up a new structure on a foundation of new values. We must put the body above the spirit; we must unfetter the soul, which craves for life, and awaken in it a passion for power and mastery, so that it may satisfy all its desires by force, in unlimited freedom.

Like all the other new gospels which run riot in our literature, this gospel of the "transvaluation of values" is not a Jewish product. It is of German origin, being the handiwork of a certain philosopher-poet named Friedrich Nietzsche. According to him, it is wrong to regard that as good which brings welfare to the human race in general, and lessens the amount of suffering, and to call that evil which has the reverse effect. The moral law, working on this basis, has turned the world upside down; it has degraded the high, and exalted the low. The few strong men are made subordinate to the many weaklings. . . . They are actually commanded by morality to serve the despicable and worthless multitude. The inevitable result is that the human type, instead of producing in each successive generation stronger and nobler examples, does in fact progress downwards, dragging down even the chosen few of every generation to the low level of the multitude.

In order to restore the power of self-perfection to the human type, we need a complete change of moral values. We must give back to the idea of good the meaning which it had of old, before "Jewish morality" overthrew Greek and Roman culture. "Good" is to be applied to the strong man, who has both the power to expand and complete his life, and the will to be master of his world (*der Wille zur Macht*), without considering at all how much the great mob of inferior beings may lose in the process. For only he, only the "Superman" (*Ubermensch*), is the fine flower and the goal of the human race; the rest were created only to subserve his end, to be the ladder on which he can climb up to his proper level.

This is the fundamental idea of the doctrine of the "transvaluation of values" in its original German form. It desires not merely to change morality in certain details–to pronounce some things evil which were regarded as good, and the reverse–but to alter the very foundation of morality, the actual standard by reference to which things are pronounced good or evil. Hitherto, the standard has been the lessening of pain and increasing of happiness among the mass of human beings.

Now we are told that there is one thing which is essentially good, and that is the free development of individuality in the elect of the human race, and the ascent of the specific type in them to a level higher than that of the generality of men.

So we see whence our own literary men got the idea of the "transvaluation of values." They found a new doctrine, universal in its scope, and its attraction for them produced a desire to propound a similar new doctrine, of special application to the Jews. So far I have no fault to find with them. The same thing has often been done before, from the Alexandrian period to our own day; and Judaism has more than once been made richer in new conceptions and stimulating ideas.

Nietzsche exalts physical force and external beauty; he longs for "the fair beast" (*die blonde Bestie*)–the strong, beautiful beast which shall rule the world, and act in all things according to its will. . . . Israel, on the contrary, has always exalted spiritual force and moral splendor.

This same Nietzsche, if his taste had been Hebraic, might still have changed the moral standard, and made the Superman an end in himself; but in that case he would have attributed to his Superman quite different characteristics–the expansion of moral power, the subjugation of the bestial instincts, the striving after truth and righteousness in thought and deed, the eternal warfare against falsehood and wickedness. In a word, that moral ideal which Judaism has impressed on us. And what is there to prove that the change in the moral standard necessarily involves changing the Hebraic outlook, and substituting the Aryan: that man becomes Superman not through moral strength and the beauty of the soul, but only through the physical strength and the external beauty of the "fair beast"?

Those who are at all expert in this matter do not need to be told that there is no necessity now for the creation of Jewish Nietzscheism of this kind, because it has existed for centuries. Judaism has never based itself on mercy alone, and has never made its Superman subordinate to the mass of men, as though the whole aim and object of his existence were simply to increase the happiness of the multitude. We all know the importance of the tzadik, the "righteous man," in our ethical literature, from the Talmud and the Midrashim to the literature of Hasidism; we know that, so far from his having been created for the sake of others, "the whole world was only created for his sake," and that he is an end for himself. Phrases like this, as is well known, are of frequent occurrence in our literature; and they did not remain mere expressions of individual opinion, mere philosophic tags, but obtained popular currency, and became generally accepted principles of morality. . . .

It is almost universally admitted that the Jews have a genius for morality, and in this respect are superior to all other nations.[2] It matters not how this happened, or in what way this trait developed: we certainly find that in the very earliest times the Jewish people became conscious of its superiority in this respect over the surrounding nations. This consciousness found its expression, in accordance with the spirit of that age, in the religious dogma that God had chosen out Israel "to make him high above all nations." But this election of Israel was not to be a domination based on force, for Israel is "the fewest of all peoples." It was for moral development that Israel was chosen by God, "to be a peculiar people unto Himself. . . . and to keep all His commandments"; that is, to give concrete expression in every generation to the highest type of morality, to submit always to the yoke of the most exacting moral obligations, and this without any regard to the gain or loss of the rest of mankind, but solely for the sake of the existence of this supreme type. This consciousness of its moral election has been preserved by the Jewish people throughout its history, and has been its solace in all its sufferings. . . .

One can understand – and one can tolerate – the individual Jew who is captivated by the Superman in Nietzsche's sense; who bows the knee to Zarathustra, throws off his allegiance

---

[2] Nietzsche himself often admits this: see, for instance, *Zur Geschichte der Moral* (Leipzig, 1894), p. 51.

to the Prophets, and goes about to regulate his own private life in accordance with these new values. But it is difficult to understand, and still more difficult to tolerate, the extraordinary proceeding of these men, who offer such a new law of life as this to the whole nation, and are simple enough to think that it can be accepted by a people which, almost from the moment of its first appearance in the world's history, has existed only to protest vehemently and unceasingly on behalf of the rights of the spirit against those of the strong arm and the sword; which, from time immemorial to the present day, has derived all its spiritual strength simply from its steadfast faith in its moral mission, in its obligation and its capacity to approach nearer than other nations to the ideal of moral perfection. This people, they fondly imagine, could suddenly, after thousands of years, change its values, forgo its national pre-eminence in the moral sphere, in order to become "the tail of the lions" in the sphere of the sword; could overthrow the mighty temple which it has built to the God of righteousness, in order to set up in its place a mean and lowly altar (it has no strength for more) to the idol of physical force.

CHAPTER 71

THE SONGS OF BIALIK

The late Hayim Nahman Bialik (1873–1934) was the most distinguished poetic talent to use the Hebrew language in well over a thousand years. Born and reared in an Ukrainian village, his mother tongue was, of course, Yiddish; but, like so many other gifted youths of his generation, he became a devotee of Jewish nationalism, and in consequence a resolute Hebraist. His first poems, written when his spirit was still steeped in the gloom of ghetto life, were prevailingly tearful. The world he describes is a stark and terror-haunted waste in which the one source of strength and hope is the rabbinic House of Study. Typical of his verse during this period is "The Fountain."

But the stirring events of the early 1900's, the swift spread of Socialism and Zionism throughout the Russian Pale, set fire to his soul, and his songs suddenly began to grow lusty, rebellious, unbridled in their hunger for life and love and earthy prowess. It was in 1902 that he wrote "The Dead in the Desert," a poem in praise of those froward Israelites who dared mutiny against God and Moses, and join battle with the Amalekites in the wilderness. Bialik sees them asleep now in the sand, giants turned to stone, and summoning a tempest to wake them up, he sets them singing a hymn of revolt against submissiveness. His purpose was to stir his fellow Jews to throw off their age-old docility, to cease being mice, and fight like men.

The same thought animates the third poem here partially quoted. This, "In the City of the Slaughtered," was prompted by the Kishinev pogrom at Easter 1903, and heaps scorn on the Jews who meekly submitted to that outrage. Published originally in Hebrew, then translated by its author into Yiddish, this poem had an enormous effect on the harried folk penned in the czarist ghettos. "Self-defense" corps sprang up everywhere, and when the next pogrom-wave came in 1905, the Jews resisted with matchless courage.

Bialik was, thus, one of the most potent influences in reviving Israel's will to live. If his doctrine seems reactionary, teaching men to meet hate with hate and violence with violence, it nevertheless belongs in such an anthology as this. There are times, it would seem, when a righteous wrath can be the truest expression of wisdom.

THE FOUNTAIN[1]

And shouldst thou wish to know the Source
From which thy tortured brethren drew
In evil days their strength of soul
To meet their doom, stretch out their necks
To each uplifted knife and axe,
In flames, on stakes to die with joy,
And with a whisper, "God is One,"
To close their lips?

And shouldst thou wish to find the Spring
From which thy banished brethren drew,
'Midst fear of death and fear of life,
Their comfort, courage, patience, trust,
An iron will to bear their yoke,
To live bespattered and despised,
And suffer without end?

And shouldst thou wish to see the Lap
Whereon thy people's galling tears
In ceaseless torrents fell and fell,
And hear the cries that moved the hills,
And thrilled Satan with awe and grief,

---

[1]Translated from the Hebrew by P. M. Raskin.

But not the stony heart of man,
Than Satan's and than rock's more hard?

And shouldst thou wish to see the Fort
Wherein thy fathers refuge sought,
And all their sacred treasures hid,
The Refuge that has still preserved
Thy nation's soul intact and pure,
And when despised, and scorned, and scoffed,
Their faith they did not shame?

And should thou wish to see and know
Their Mother, faithful, loving kind,
Who gathered all the burning tears
Of her bespattered, hapless sons,
And when to her warm bos'm they came,
She tenderly wiped off their tears,
And sheltered them and shielded them,
And lulled them on her lap to sleep?

If thou, my brother, knowest not
This mother, spring, and lap, and fort,
Then enter thou the House of God,
The House of Study, old and gray,
Throughout the sultry summer days,
Throughout the gloomy winter nights,
At morning, midday, or at eve;
Perchance there is a remnant yet,
Perchance thy eye may still behold
In some dark corner, hid from view,
A cast-off shadow of the past,
The profile of some pallid face,
Upon an ancient folio bent,
Who seeks to drown unspoken woes
In the Talmudic boundless waves;
And then thy heart shall guess the truth
That thou hast touched the sacred ground
Of thy great nation's House of Life,

And that thy eyes do gaze upon
The treasure of thy nation's soul.

And know that this is but a spark
That by a miracle escaped
Of that bright light, that sacred flame,
Thy forbears kindled long ago
On altars high and pure.

THE DEAD IN THE DESERT[2]

Yonder great shadow–that blot on the passionate glare of the desert–
'Tis not an army of lions couched in the sun with their young ones,
'Tis not the pride of the forests of Bashan uprooted and fallen:
Those are the dead of the wilderness under the sunlight recumbent.
Hard by their tents are they laid, like children of Anak for stature,
Stretched on the desolate sands like numberless lions in slumber;
Under the might of their limbs the floor of the desert is hollowed.
Armed as for battle they sleep and clad in the armor of giants;
Swords like to crags at their heads and spears twixt their shoulders protruding,
Sound to their girdle the quiver and firm in the sand is the lance thrust.

Deep in the earth are their heads sunk, heavy with tangles neglected,
Matted and monstrous and vast, and uncouth as the mane of a lion;

[2]Translated by Maurice Samuel in *Selected Poems of Chaim Nachman Bialik* (New York, New Palestine, 1926), p. 27 ff.

Matted and monstrous and vast are their beards like to tangles of serpents.
Strong are their faces and burnished and darkened to bronze are their eyelids,
Targets to arrows of sunlight and rocks to the fury of tempests.
Hard are their foreheads and grim and changeless upturned to the heavens,
Eyes that are cruel and terrible peer through the tangle of eyebrows.
Cast as of lava upthrown from volcanos and hardened their breasts are
Lifted like anvils of iron that wait for the blow of the hammer;
Yet though the hammer of time beats long and unceasing upon them
Like to the stone that enfolds it the strength of their hearts sleeps for ever.
Only the faces unmoving, the breasts multitudinous, naked,
Strangely are covered, like ancient memorials, with runes of the desert
Graven by arrows and swords which the tempests have tossed and uplifted.
And when the eagle descends in his flight to behold he shall read there,
Graven on breast and on brow, the tale of unbroken endurance,
How many arrows and spears these breasts have encountered and shattered.

Sunlight and darkness revolve and cycle succeeds unto cycle,
Storm winds awake and are stilled and the desert turns back to its silence.
Far stand the crags, as amazed in beholding the first things created,
Clothed by the silence with splendor, the proud, the eternally-lonely,

Limitless stretches the wilderness, lifeless and soundless.
Lost to the end of all time is the jubilant voice of the giants,
Laid into stillness for ever the tumult that followed their footsteps;
Where they once trod are now lifted the sandhills and crags of the desert.
Silence has breathed on the mighty and cast into slumber their fierceness,
And the hot winds of the desert eaten their strength and their beauty. . . .

Deep is the sleep of the heroes . . . and cycle succeeds unto cycle.
But there are moments when, tortured too long by the silence eternal,
Wild with unbearable sickness of aeons, the desert uprises,
Wakens and rages for vengeance against the inhuman Creator,
Raises a column of sand to ascend to the fastness of heaven,
Once and for ever to meet Him and shatter the throne of His glory,
Once for the torture eternal to loose the floods of its fury,
Sweep his whole world into darkness and bring back the kingdom of chaos. . . .
Then the Creator is stirred, and His anger envelops the heavens.
Like a great cover of iron, He bends them to blot out the desert.
Red from the blast of His breath, the flame of His anger outbreaking
Wraps the desert in fury and scatters its crags in a furnace.
Stubborn and bitter the desert responds, and new furies are loosened,
Rise from the bowels of hell, and all earth is in fury confounded.
Seized by the madness that spins like a vehement wheel in the vastness

Tigers and lions, with manes uplifted and eyeballs aglitter,
Join in the riot infernal, and howl with the voice of the tempest,
Lifted and torn by the strength of the tempest like gossamer insects.
And in that instant–
Wakes the terrible power that slumbered in chains,
Suddenly stirs and arises the old generation of heroes,
Mighty in battle: their eyes are like lightning, like blades are their faces.
Then flies the hand to the sword.
Sixty myriads of voices–a thunder of heroes–awaken,
Crash through the tempest and tear asunder the rage of the desert.
Round them is wildness and blindness:
And they cry
"We are the mighty!
The last generation of slaves and the first generation of freemen!
Alone our hand in its strength
Tore from the pride of our shoulders the yoke of bondage.
We lifted our heads to the heavens, and behold their broadness was narrow in the pride of our eyes,
So we turned to the desert, we said to the Wilderness: "Mother!"
Yea, on the tops of the crags, in the thickness of clouds,
With the eagles of heaven we drank from her fountains of freedom.
And who is lord of us?
Even now, though the God of Vengeance has shut the desert upon us,
A song of strength and revolt has reached us, and we rise.
To arms! To arms! Form ranks! Forward!
Forward into the heavens and the wrath thereof.

Behold us! We will ascend
With the tempest!
Though the Lord has withdrawn His hand from us,
And the Ark stands moveless in its place,
Still we will ascend–alone!
Even under the eye of His wrath, daring the lightning of His countenance,
We will carry with storm the citadels of the hills,
And face to face in combat encounter the armed foe!
Listen!
The storm, too, calls unto us–"Courage and daring!"
To arms! To arms! Let the hills be shattered and the mountains blasted into dust,
Or let our lifeless bodies be heaped in countless cairns.
Forward!
On to the hills!
And in that instant the desert is wild with a fierce anger–
And who shall conquer it?
In the storm goes up a terrible voice, a mingling of cries.
It must surely be
That the desert is bringing to birth a deed of evil,
A bitter thing, a cruel and a terrible . . ."

Passed is the tempest. The desert is silent and pure is the silence.
Bright is the broadness of heaven, and marvelous quiet beneath it.
Now from their terror awaking, the caravans trapped in the tempest
Rise from their crouching and call on their God and adore Him and praise Him.
Still in the sand are the sixty myriads of heroes aslumber.
Darkened their faces, for death has brought them to peace with their Maker. . . .

THE CITY OF SLAUGHTER[3]

. . .Look, here and here, and in between the rafters,
Are eyes and eyes that gaze at thee in silence,
The eyes of martyred souls,
Of hunted, harried, persecuted souls,
Who've huddled all together in the corner,
And press each other closer still and quake;
For here it was the sharpened axes found them,
And they have come to take another look,
And in the apple of each staring eye
To glass once more the picture of their end,
Of all the terror of their savage death,
Of all the suff'ring of their dreary lives
And, trembling like a crowd of startled doves,
They flutter in a cluster to the ceiling,
And thence they gaze at thee with dumb, wild eyes,
That follow thee and ask the old, old question,
The one that never yet has reached to heaven,
And never will:
For what, for what? and once again, for what?
Yes, came thy neck . . . behold, there is no heaven!
There's nothing but a roof of blackened tiles.
Thence hangs a spider – go and ask the spider!
She saw it all, and she's a living witness,
The old gray spider spinning in the garret.
She knows a lot of stories – bid her tell them!
A story of a belly stuffed with feathers,
Of nostrils and of nails, of heads and hammers,
Of men who, after death, were hung head downward,
Like geese, along the rafter.
A story of a suckling child asleep,
A dead and cloven breast between its lips,
And of another child they tore in two,
Thus cutting short its last and loudest scream,
For "Ma – ," was heard, but "Mama" never finished.

[3]Translated from the Yiddish version by Helena Frank, *op. cit.,* p. 68 ff.

And many, many more such fearful stories
That beat about thy head and pierce thy brain,
And stab the soul within thee, does she know.
And, stifling down the sob within thy throat,
Thou rushest headlong down the stairs and out–
To see again the world of ev'ry day,
The usual sun, outpouring unashamed
A wealth of beams at every guilty threshold,
And lavish of its store on worse than swine. . . .

Now go without the town when none may see thee,
And steal thee softly to the place of burial;
And stand beside the martyrs' new-made graves,
And stand and look and let thine eyelids fall–
And turn to stone.
Thy heart shall fail within thee, but thine eye
Burn hot and tearless as the desert sand.
Thy mouth shall open to shriek aloud for vengeance,
And dumb as are the tombstones shalt thou stand.
Go, look and look, behold them where they lie
Like butchered calves, and yet thou hast no tear
To give to them, as I, the Lord, have no reward.
For I have hither come, O ye dead bones,
To beg of you, forgive *me!*

Aye, forgive your God, you that are ashamed forever!
For all your dark and bitter lives forgive me,
And for your ten times dark and bitter death!
For when you stand tomorrow at my threshold,
When you remind me, when you ask for payment,
I shall but answer you: "Come, see, I've nothing."
It cries to heaven, I hear it, but I've nothing.
For I am poor myself, I'm beggared also.
And woe and woe and woe is all my worlds!
Let all the seven heavens moan for pity.
To bring such sacrifices all for nothing,
To live such lives and die such deaths for nothing,
Not knowing to what end, for what, for what!

Her head enwrapped in clouds, my old Shechinah
Shall sit for evermore and weep for shame;
And night by night I too will lean from heaven
And mourn myself upon your graves.
The shame is very great and great the anguish,
And which is greater, say thou, son of man!
No, best keep silent, be a speechless witness,
Nor testify with words to having found me
In poverty and having seen my woe.
Yet, son of man, departing take with thee
A portion of my sorrow and my care,
And mingle it with wrath and cast it from thee
To fill the lap of corpses still alive.

What now? go back and gaze on leaves and grass?
The fresh and fragrant message of the spring
Steals in upon thine heart and there awakes
A longing for a new and freer life . . .
The grass is grave-grass, man, and smells of death.
Tear out a handful, fling it down behind thee,
And say, with closed eyes:
"My people is as grass plucked up, and how
Shall that which has no root revive and live?"
Come, look no more, come back to those yet living.
Today's a fast day, come where stands the *Shool,*
And plunge thy soul in tears, their sea of tears.
Thou hear'st the lamentations and the moans
From open mouths, from out between locked teeth.
The rent and quiv'ring sounds, like things alive,
Unite, and–hearken! now they rise again
In one despairing wail of misery,
That tosses still between a damp, dark ceiling
And upturned faces all awry with pain.
A sudden horror chills you to the bone:
Thus wails a people only that is lost,
Whose soul is dust and ashes, and their heart
A scorched desert. . . .
No root of hatred, not a blade of vengeance,

For hark, they beat the breast and cry, "Forgive us!"
They pray of me forgiveness for their sin.
Their sin? The sin of shadows on the wall,
The sin of broken pots, of bruised worms!
What will they? Why stretch out their hands to me?
Has none a fist? And where's a thunderbolt
To take revenge for all the generations,
To blast the world and tear the heavens asunder
And wreck the universe, my throne of glory?
And hear, thou son of man!
When next the reader cries upon the platform,
"Arise, O God, avenge the slaughtered victims,
Avenge thy holy ones, the pious graybeards,
The suckling children, God, the little children!"
And all the people cry with him together,
And when, like thee, the very pillars tremble,
I will be cruel to thee, very cruel,
For thou shalt have no single tear to shed;
And should a cry arise in thee, I'll choke it,
Between thy teeth, if need be, I will choke it.
I will not have thee mourn as do the others.
The tear unshed, that bury in thyself,
Deep down within thy heart, and build a tower
Of gall and hatred round it; let it lie
A serpent in a nest (and men shall suck
And pass its venom on),
With thirst and hunger still unsatisfied.
And when the day of retribution comes,
Then break the wall and let the serpent out,
And like a poisoned arrow shoot it forth
With hunger raging and with thirsty fang,
And pierce thy race, thine own race, through the heart!

Tomorrow, son of man, go pace the street:
Behold a market full of living ware,
Of bruised and beaten, half-dead human cattle,
With bent and twisted backs,
Of skin and bones tied up in rags,

Of maimed and crippled children, and of women
All fagged and parched, and these,
Like locusts or the latter summer flies,
Besieging doors and windows, ev'ry gateway,
And stretching out crooked hands with fest'ring wounds
(The hands have only lately learned to beg),
And crying each his merchandise of woe:
"A groschen for a wound, a groschen for a wound!
A groschen for a violated daughter!
A groschen for a grandsire done to death,
And for a son, a boy just less ripe for marriage!"
Go, tramping pedlars, seek the field of victims,
And dig white bones from out your new-made graves,
And fill your baskets, ev'ry one his basket.
Go out into the world, and drag them with you,
From town to town, wherever there's a market,
And spread them out before the strangers' windows,
And sing hoarse beggar-songs, and ask for pity!
And beg your way, and trade as heretofore
In flesh and blood, your own. . . .
Now flee, O son of man, for ever flee,
And hide thee in the desert–and go mad!
There rend thy soul into a thousand pieces,
And fling thy heart to all wild dogs for food!
The burning stones shall hiss beneath thy tears,
And stormy winds shall swallow up thy cry!

CHAPTER 72

THE PHILOSOPHY OF FELIX ADLER

The career of Felix Adler (1851–1933) strikingly exemplifies the trend toward assimilation which swept American Jewry during the late nineteenth century. He came of a long line of noted rabbis, and was himself educated to follow that calling. On being invited, however, to occupy his father's pulpit–in New York's Temple Emanu-El, the foremost Reform Jewish congregation in America–his theological radicalism gave rise to so much controversy that he was hastily shunted off into an academic siding. A chair of Hebrew and Oriental Literature was established for him at Cornell University; but after two years even this became untenable owing to his advanced views. Returning to New York (1876), he gathered a group of sympathetic laymen–Gentile as well as Jewish–and organized a Society for Ethical Culture which aimed to promote right living without invoking dogmatic or sectarian sanctions. The movement enjoyed a considerable local success, and eventually established local branches in other American cities, and in London and Cambridge, England. Similar societies arose also in Berlin and Frankfurt-am-Main.

True to his slogan, "Deed, not Creed," Dr. Adler devoted himself ardently to social and educational reforms. He agitated for slum-clearance, labor arbitration, public-health service, and similar liberal causes. He established the first free kindergarten, and pioneered the progressive-school movement in America. Gentle by nature, and always somewhat intellectual in his approach, he nevertheless succeeded in exercising a considerable influence on the religious thought and civic life of his generation.

The following passage is taken from the last of his Hibbert Lectures delivered at Oxford University in May 1923.[1]

There are three needs of our time and generation, and three problems arising out of these needs: the problem of the insignificance of man in the face of the innumerable worlds, the problem of the man who perishes in the meanwhile, and the problem of the divided conscience.

Nothing has been effectually said in these chapters if the answer to the first problem is not now evident. The sense of man's utter nothingness is relieved, the heavy pall of the consciousness of insignificance is lifted by self-knowledge—man's knowledge of himself as a spiritual being. Gazing at night upon the star-sown firmament he is not dwarfed into littleness. Stars and suns are lesser lights compared with those supra-solar luminaries that constitute the spiritual universe. And the magnitudes of space and time, far from overwhelming him, are useful as supports to lean on in rising to the conception of the transcendent magnitude of the infinite host of spirits whereof man is one—an infinitesimal one (hence, his humility), an indispensable one (hence, his dignity).

The solution of the second problem concerning the fate of the man who perishes in the meantime; he has worth and he can affirm it under no matter what material conditions. His worth demands, indeed, that the conditions under which he lives be incessantly improved, but he is not the helpless victim of his conditions for all that. He can exercise the spiritual rule of promoting the best in others, his wife and children, for instance, thereby honoring the best in himself, in the meanest hovel of the slums. The problem of the divided conscience—

[1] *The Reconstruction of the Spiritual Ideal* by Felix Adler (New York, Appleton, 1924), p. 211 ff.

the moral law recognized in the private relations and the law of strife prevailing in business and politics–ceases to exist under the spiritual ideal as stated. There are no longer two laws; the conscience is no longer distracted by opposite tendencies. There is one law, that runs through all the human relations, the family, the vocation, the state, and so forth. These are successive stages on the road toward the supreme goal. One and the same rule obtains in all, only blossoming into richer meanings as man passes out of the nearer into the more remote–out of the narrower into the wider groups.

Spinoza has truly said that wisdom consists not in the contemplation of death but in the contemplation of life. Nevertheless, it is well at times in imagination to think of oneself as facing death, in order then to turn back and form a juster estimate of the aims and ends of life that really count. It is not too much to say that most men live provisional lives, absorbed in the pursuit of merely provisional ends, such as to build up a business, or to carry through a scheme of reform, or to see their children happily married or successful in some profession; and they forget that these same children, now young perhaps, will presently stand where they stand–at the brink–the few decades allotted to human beings passing for them also with incredible swiftness. The activities and the provisional ends seem futile enough unless they are linked to some ulterior ultimate end.

Standing then at the terminus, I should say that one guiding thought for me would be continued interest in the progress of the human race to which I belong. A youth thinks of his mature age as the continuation of his present life, so I think of future generations as continuing my earthly life, and as I desire progress for myself, so I desire it for mankind. Progress means advance toward a society which shall more adequately reflect in all its relations the pattern of the spiritual world. To see God as reflected in the face of Christ is the theological way of putting this idea; to see the world of spiritual perfection as reflected in the face of humanity is the turn I give to the same thought.[2]

And the second crucial thought that touches me is that of the persistence of the spiritual part. Do we live merely in the effect we leave behind upon the life of future generations on this earth? Is the spiritual part of us obliterated? The doctrine of immortality as commonly understood means that the psychophysical organism will continue to exist in some attenuated fashion in another sphere. The departed will be recognizable, their arms will be outstretched to welcome us, and the like. Or again, the psychic is supposed to be clothed with, to assume (a vague form of speech to which no definable meaning whatever can be attached) new organs unlike the bodily. These evidently are projections of temporal conditions into the admittedly non-temporal; the last outreachings of human tenderness striving to keep hold of the beloved as a concrete object.

With the doctrine in this version of it I am not concerned. What is required of me is the valiancy of truth. I must train myself to relinquish tranquilly and *in toto* the psychophysical self. What I retain is the conviction that the spiritual self is the eternal self and cannot perish. And secondly, that this spiritual self of mine, being social or suprasocial, is inseparably bound up with other spiritual selves, and in this sense that those I have loved and I cannot be parted in eternity. And if I seek communion with them while I still live here, I must produce the best in myself in order to encounter the best in them which is their very being.

[2]That there actually is progress in human history it is impossible to prove. I rest my belief in progress, not on the fact that it is demonstrable, for it is not demonstrable, but on the moral pronouncement that it ought to be, that therefore it can be, and must be.

CHAPTER 73

THE SENTIMENTS OF ISRAEL ZANGWILL

Israel Zangwill (1864–1926), born in London of immigrant parents, lived to become one of the most notable English literary figures of his generation. His considerable learning, keen intelligence, dazzling style, and remorseless sense of humor won him a wide audience both at home and abroad. Though a prolific writer on general themes, he was at his best when dealing with the life and problems of his own people, especially those transplanted from Eastern Europe to London's East End. He is most renowned for his Children of the Ghetto, *a narrative work which first described the immigrant Jewish milieu, and* The Melting Pot, *a play which was one of the first to advocate intermarriage between Jews and Gentiles. Himself a devoted Jew, and for many years an active Zionist, Zangwill was a firm believer in assimilation.*

The following passages, taken from various of his works, will indicate the broad character of his sentiments as well as the brilliance of his style.

THE AMERICAN CENTURY[1]

The twentieth century will be America's critical century. Will she develop on the clear lines laid down by her great

[1]From an article published originally in 1899, and quoted in *The War for the World* (New York, Macmillan, 1916), pp. 36–37.

founders, or will she survive, like most human institutions, as a caricature and contradiction of the ideals of her creators? Will she fall back into outworn feudalisms, accepting second-hand ideals from the Europe she has outgrown? Small as is the significance of aristocracy in the modern world of Europe, it is at least the petrifaction of what was once living and significant. The original adoration of nobility was not snobbery but respect for real superiority. But the modern American love of a lord is the worship of a withered leaf. That all men are created free and equal is a nobler proposition, if "free" be interpreted as having a right to one's own body and soul and "equal" as having a right to develop one's own body and soul to their highest. America became the exponent of these ideals; every other conception has been tried and found wanting. And for America to hash up again hereditary aristocracy and militarism would be a ridiculous anti-climax. If America breaks away from her ideals, humanity's last chance will be gone–at least for the white races: for perhaps–who knows?–destiny would seek its next instrument among the despised colored races. O if America were less conscious of her own greatness, and more conscious of the greatness of her opportunity!

The eighteenth century saw the dawn of generous ideals of the Brotherhood of Man. What the Jewish prophets had dreamed twenty-five centuries before became the dream of the noblest spirits of Europe. The nineteenth century, which, by its electric links, has brought the nations nearer to one another physically than ever before, yet closes on the tableau of their spiritual separation–each armed to the teeth and fearfully watching the others, anxious to outstrip them not in greatness but in bigness. The nineteenth century has set aside the ideas of the eighteenth, but I dare to hope it has not destroyed them. They will return–but purified of whatever dross of false idealism was in them, and more equated to the facts of life. But let it be remembered that Liberty, Equality, Fraternity, do not belong to the world of facts but to the world of ideals. They are the way man's aspiration shapes the facts, as man's will cuts tunnels through the dumb mountains and lays cables beneath the blind seas.

The nineteenth century's own idols have not proved so worshipful as it imagined. If the Press diffuses light, it can also – as Bismarck discovered – diffuse darkness. If Science as a maid-of-all-work is a success, Science as an interpreter of the mystery of the Universe is a dismal failure. Even her immense practical boons only serve to amplify our senses and increase our speed: they cannot increase our happiness. Giants suffer as well as dwarfs, and the soul may sit lonely and sad, surrounded by mechanical miracles.

As ever, the soul is the true center of things, and if America remembers this, she may steer safely through the immense spiritual perils of the coming century toward her old goal of a noble democracy, and may yet point the true path of civilization to the feudal nations and exhibit the divine element in the long procession of the centuries.

ON THE WARRING OF SECTS[2]

Why, indeed, quarrel over religions when all men agree; all men, that is, at the same grade of intellect! The learned busy themselves classifying religions – there are reviews at Paris and Tuebingen – but in the crude working world religion depends less on the belief than on the believer. All the simplest minds believe alike, be they Confucians or Christians, Jews or Fantees. The elemental human heart will have its thaumaturgic saints, its mapped hells, its processional priests, its prompt answers to prayer, and if deprived of them will be found subtly to reintroduce them. Mohammed and the Koran forbade the worship of saints, yet the miracles and meditations of the *walis* and the pilgrimages to their tombs – with

[2] *Italian Fantasies* (New York, Macmillan, 1910), pp. 13–14.

Mohammed himself as arch-*wali*—are inseparable from Islam. The Buddha who came to teach a holy atheism was made a god, the proclaimer of natural law a miracle-monger, his revolution turned into a revolution of prayer-wheels and his religion into the High Church Romanism of Lamaism. The Hebrew Torah which cried anathema on idols became itself an idol, swathed in purple, adorned with golden bells, and borne round like a Madonna for reverent kisses. The Madonna herself, overgrown with the roses of a wayside shrine, perpetuates the worship of Flora. On the very gates of St. Peter's, Europa, Ganymede, and Leda show their brazen faces. Not Confucius nor Christ can really expel devils. What grosser idolatry than the worship of those dressed wax dolls which make many an Italian church like a theological Madame Tussaud's! The Church has its Chamber of Horrors too, its blood and nails and saintly skulls; the worship of Moloch was not more essentially morbid. At the base of the intellectual mountain flourishes rank and gorgeous vegetation, a tropic luxuriance; higher up, in the zone of mediocrity, there are cultivated temperate slopes and pruned gardens, pleasant pastures and ordered bowers; at the snowy summits, in the rarefied aether, flash white the glacial impersonal truths, barely a tuft of moss or lichen. Hark! peak is crying unto peak: "Thy will be done."

ON RELIGIOUS FANATICISM[3]

In the real universe pestilences and earthquakes are not due to the wrath of God. The physical universe proceeds on its own lines, and the religious motives of the Crusaders did not prevent a Christian host from dying of the putrefying infidel corpses which it had manufactured so abundantly. Nor did heaven endorse the theory of the Children's Crusade—that

[3] *Ibid.*, pp. 107–109.

innocence could accomplish what was impossible for flawed manhood. The poor innocents perished like flies, or were sold into slavery. These things take their course as imperturbably as Halley's Comet, which refused to budge an inch even before the fulminations of Pope Callixtus III. Nor is the intermission of earthquakes or pestilence to be procured by the intercession of the saints or by the efficacy of their relics. A phial of the blood of Christ was carried about in Mantua during the plague of 1630, but there were not enough boats to carry away the corpses to the lakes. It was those marshes round Mantua that should have been drained. But it is in vain God thunders. "Thus and thus are My Laws. I am that I am." Impious Faith answers, "Not so. Thou art that Thou art not."

Pestilence – we know today – can be averted by closing the open cesspools and opening the sunless alleys of medievalism; malaria can be minimized by minimizing mosquitoes, and earthquakes can be baffled by careful building. . . . Where reliance is placed on paternosters and penitence, how shall there be equal zeal for antiseptics or structural precautions? The censer tends to oust the fumigator, and the priest the man of action. "Too easily resigned and too blindly hopeful," says the *Messagero* of Rome, commenting on the chaos that still reigns among the population of Messina.

"Trust in God and keep your powder dry," was the maxim of a Protestant. Cromwell but echoed the Psalmist, "Blessed be the Lord my strength, which teacheth my hands to war and my fingers to fight." This is the spirit that makes the best of both cosms. The too trustful denizen of the Catholic autocosm with his damp powder and his flaccid fingers risks falling a prey to the first foe.

But the balance sheet is not yet complete. For it may be better to live without sanitation or structural precaution and to die at forty of the plague or the earthquake, after years of belief in your saint or your star, than to live a century without God in a bleak universe of mechanical law. True the believer has the fear of hell, but by a happy insanity it does not interfere with his *joie de vivre.* He has had, indeed, to pay dearly for the consolation and courage the Church has sold him–since we are at the balance sheet let this be said too–and seeing how in the last analysis all this overwhelming ecclesiastic splendor has come out of the toil of the masses, I cannot help wondering whether the Church could not have done the thing cheaper. Were these glittering vestments and soaring columns so absolutely essential to the cult of the manger-born God?

THE WICKEDNESS OF SAINTS[4]

There is nothing which at first sight seems more puzzling than the wickedness of good people. For it has often been said that the truly devout and respectable Christians are the very ones who would crucify Christ afresh if he appeared again, as indeed Arnold of Brescia, who had a touch of his spirit, was crucified by emperor, pope, and church. And St. Bernard, the inspirer of the Second Crusade to recover the dead bones of Christ, played a leading part in hounding him down, as the Franciscans played a leading part in hounding down Savonarola.

Now why was St. Bernard–that *santo sene* who was chosen by Dante to induct him into the last splendors of the Paradise, and whose noble hymns to Jesus still edify the faithful–so blind to the divine aspects of his victim? And why is it that the citizens of Ferrara, whose excellent statue and eloquent tribute to their illustrious townsman, Savonarola, faced my hotel window, could not be trusted not to stone their next prophet in a cruder sense of the words?

A converse question will conduct us to the answer. Why is the hooligan in the gallery of the theatre ever the chief friend of virtue? Why is the wife-bruiser the most fervid applauder of

[4] *Ibid.*, pp. 337–339.

the domestic sentiment? Because the man in the gallery looks down on the tangle of life like the god his name implies: he sees it in as clear perspective as the aeronaut sees the network of alleys through which the pedestrian blunders; the plot is straightened out for him, the villain duly colored, virtue in distress plainly marked by beauty and white muslin, and through no mists of prejudice or interest or passion he beholds the great outlines of right and wrong. 'Tis to the credit of human nature that, confronted with the bare elementals of ethics, and freed from egoistic bias, the human conscience, even the conscience most distorted in life, reacts accurately and returns a correct verdict with the unfailingness of a machine. This it is that preserves the self-respect of the blackest of us, this capacity of ours for seeking our neighbors' sins, which is the chief bulwark of public virtue. Wherefore, could St. Bernard have seen Arnold of Brescia as history sees him, or as a dramatist of insight would have drawn him, St. Bernard would have been the first to be horrified at St. Bernard's behavior. But a saint, no more than a hooligan, is free from passions, interests, and prejudices of his own, especially an ecclesiast and theologian and a founder of monasteries. Wilful and obstinate as are all the saints of my acquaintance, the most domineering are the clerical.

JUDAISM VS. GERMANISM[5]

If I were asked to sum up in a word the essential difference between Judaism and Germanism, it would be the word "Recessional." While the prophets and historians of Germany monotonously glorify their nation, the Jewish writers as monotonously rebuke theirs. "You only have I known among all the families of the earth," says the message through Amos. "*Therefore* I will visit upon you all your iniquities." The Bible is

[5]*Chosen Peoples* (New York, Macmillan, 1919), pp. 95–101.

an anti-Semitic book. Israel is the villain, not the hero, of his own story. Alone among epics, it is out for truth, not high heroics. To flout the Pharisees was not reserved for Jesus. "Behold, ye fast for strife and contention," said Isaiah, "and to smite with the fist of wickedness." While some German writers, not content with the great men Germany has so abundantly produced, vaunt that all others, from Jesus to Dante, from Montaigne to Michelangelo, are of Teuton blood, Jewish literature unflinchingly exposed the flaws even of a Moses and a David. It is this passion for veracity unknown among other peoples–is even Washington's story told without gloss?–that gives false color to the legend of Israel's ancient savagery. . . .

If in Germany a voice of criticism breaks the chorus of self-adoration, it is usually from a Jew like Maximilian Harden, for Jews, as Ambassador Gerard testifies, represent almost the only real culture in Germany. I have been at pains to examine the literature of the German synagogue, which if Germanism were Judaism, ought to show a double dose of original sin. But so far from finding any swagger of a Chosen People, whether Jewish or German, I find in its most popular work–Lazarus's *Soziale Ethik im Judentum*–published as late as November, 1913, by the League of German Jews–a grave indictment of militarism. For the venerable philosopher, while justly explaining the glamour of the army by its subordination of the individual to the communal weal, yet pointed out emphatically that what unites individuals separates nations. "The work of justice shall be peace," he quotes from Isaiah. I am far from supposing that the old Germany of Goethe and Schiller and Lessing is not still latent–indeed, we know that one professor suggested at a recent Nietzsche anniversary that the Germans should try to rise not to Supermen but to Men, and that another now lies in prison for explaining in his *Biologie des Krieges* that the real objection to war is simply that it compels men to act unlike men. So that, when moreover we remember that the noblest and most practical treatise on "Perpetual Peace" came from that other German professor, Kant, the hope is not altogether *ausgeschlossen* that in the internal convulsion that must follow the war, there may be an upheaval of that finer Germanism of which we should be only too proud to say that it is Judaism.

CHAPTER 74

SOME OPINIONS OF LUDWIG LEWISOHN

The career of Ludwig Lewisohn (1882–1955) is a straw in the wind of reaction which appeared to sweep the world–and Israel. Born of "emancipated" parentage in Berlin, and reared in South Carolina, his early tendencies were all toward assimilation. Until well in his forties he struggled to identify himself completely with the world at large; but finally he gave up. Sensitive by nature, the slights and rebuffs to which he found himself increasingly subjected drove him at last to turn in his course, to become one of the most eloquent partisans of Jewish nationalism. Though never a convert to Christianity, he was, nevertheless, in essence, a revert to Judaism–or, more accurately to Jewishness–and his writings betray this by their often excessive vehemence.

Despite his intense particularism–he himself would say because of it–Lewisohn had much to say that had universalistic import, as can be seen from the following quotations.[1]

TWO VIEWS OF JEWS

A man came to a Polish magnate and asked him: "What do you think of the Jews?" The answer was: "Swine, Christ-killers, usurers, not to be trusted." "But what do you think of

[1]Most of these passages will be found in an anthology of Lewisohn's writings entitled *A Jew Speaks,* edited by James Waterman Wise (New York, Harper, 1931).

Isaac?" "A man after my own heart. An honorable man. A kind man. He saved me from bankruptcy." "And what do you think of Berl?" "I have known Berl all my life. He's one of the best." "And of Shmuel? "Shmuel is a saint as everyone knows."

The same man went to a rich and pious Jew and asked him: "What do you think of the Jews?" The pious man answered: "A kingdom of priests and a holy nation, the elect of the Eternal, blessed be his name." "And what do you think of Isaac?" "That thief? That scoundrel? May his bones be broken. He looks at you and you are robbed!" "And of Berl?" "A fellow of the same kind, without truth or justice." "And of Shmuel?" "Do you think I am taken in by his piety? A pretentious idiot."

Reb Moshe hid his hands in his sleeves: "Avoid both errors." (The Island Within)

THE DUTY OF THE JEW

. . . The salvation of Israel and the salvation of mankind are one. Hence, the duty of the Jew to himself as well as to his Gentile fellowmen is overwhelmingly clear: to be as a Jew always on the side of the oppressed and disinherited, to be unfalteringly in league with those who work for peace anywhere in the world, to give and expect no return, to resist war and the call to war and the propaganda of war to the uttermost, to do all this as a normal self-expression of his Jewishness, to build up in Palestine a state that abstains from power, that knows nothing of rivalry, that will suffer injustice rather than seek to share political responsibility, a state that shall not only restore the preserved of Israel but be a light to the Gentiles. (Israel)

HOW TO BE A JEW

It is not easy to be a Jew. It will be easier when the Jew is content to be himself. He must listen to his own soul. It is futile for him to try to cultivate the chivalric virtues – love of combat, uncritical acceptance of standardized objects of loyalty, an artificial sense of honor, an acceptance of life as a game to be played according to rules. The Aryan gentleman asks concerning an action: Is it honorable according to a code? Is it correct? Is it gentlemanly? Is it "quite cricket"? The Jewish gentleman asks: Is it righteous? What is its relation to an eternal justice, to an eternal mercy? It is perfectly true that, according to the standards of chivalric Europe and the analogous tradition in America, the Jew is no gentleman. How could he be? Why should he strive to be? He cannot say, for instance, "my country, right or wrong." His historic experiences are not rooted in the Germanic institutions of nobles and retainers, of fealty as an abstract virtue. He missed not only by actual exclusion but as a matter of character and instinct the whole experience of the feudal world. As a romantic curiosity he can appreciate the devotion of Aryan gentlemen to a royal nonentity, to the mediocre occupant of an exalted office. Personally he can never share these emotions. His democracy, his passion for reasoned justice, are bone-deep and thousands of years old. In the moral world he does not understand compromise. When the great oppressed the humble, the prophets of Israel sought to destroy the state even unto obliteration, even unto foreign captivity. The Jew has not changed. It was inevitable that modern socialism should be largely the creation of Jews. It does not matter whether the precise doctrines of any group of them are likely to prevail. They acted out of an immemorial and unchangeable Jewish instinct. "He judged the cause of the poor and needy; then it was well. Was not this to know me? saith Jehovah." (Israel)

THE JEW OF THE FUTURE

. . . The Jew of the future will understand both himself and the world better. That world cannot be saved, cannot be redeemed from chaos except through cooperation and peace. Liberals and pacifists and the truly ethically minded see that. They know that the chivalric instincts must fall into disuse, that the gallant barbarisms of the North will end by destroying civilization unless they are curbed. Men must return to the ideals which Jesus derived from the prophets and teachers of his people. The world must be Christianized, the world must be Judaized. The two are one. . . .

The Jew who sees these truths, who strives to build the state of peace and justice first in Palestine, next to cooperate with all men who seek to build it elsewhere – that Jew will be calmly and serenely himself. Being a Jew is what he owes mankind. It may be that he will fail. It may be that all those thousands of fine and erect spirits among the Gentiles who are at one with him will fail. It may be that the black reaction now upon the world will overwhelm the great civilizations of the West. It may be. . . . Then at least we shall have been among the least guilty; we shall have tried; we shall have clung to the saving doctrines of our people. With Elijah and Amos, with Jeremiah and Jesus we shall have stood unafraid before the powers of earth; we shall have loved the sojourner and judged righteously between a man and his brother; we shall not have brought vain oblations to the idols of the marketplace; we shall have striven that violence shall no more be heard in the land, nor desolation nor destruction within its borders, but that its walls shall be called salvation and its gates praise. (Israel)

CONCERNING ASSIMILATION

The days of propitiatory assimilation are coming to an end. Our loftiest minds see the vision of that end. It is not easy for them to consent to that vision. For the material in which they work is the speech and life of the Gentiles. They have given their gifts, they cannot take these gifts back. They cannot relive their lives and give these gifts in another spirit–give them proudly as the gifts of Jews to mankind, instead of pretending to give them as Germans to Germany, Frenchmen to France, Englishmen to England. Thus they pretended to give them. And the pretense was discovered first by the Gentiles, then–by themselves. . . . Perhaps these creative spirits always harbored a profound suspicion that in the calculation of the assimilatory theory there was some gross if deeply hidden error. Early or late they were driven to speak of the Jew and of Jewish history and life. . . .

Our assimilationist may never think a Jewish thought or read a Jewish book. In the essential character of all his passions as well as of all his actions he remains a Jew. . . . The groundwork of Jewish character is his; the terrible post-exilic experience is his; he remains a strange mixture of passionate prophet and beaten cur, leader and outcast. If he has forgotten the call to "restore the preserved of Israel," he throws himself into the business of giving "a light to the Gentiles." He is liberal, reformer, practitioner, or patron of the arts; he makes discoveries in medicine or, as a lawyer, pleads the causes of those for whom none will plead. If he does none of these things he is a sordid scoundrel. But the sordid scoundrels are a minority. The average decent Jew in business, in the professions, in journalism or the arts sustains a perceptible relation to the prophets of his people. . . .

But assimilation is bankrupt. Germany was the great laboratory of the experiment. I think that the experiment was necessary. It was an unescapable part of the modern historic process. But the experiment has failed. It is not necessary that several American generations be sacrificed to foreknown humiliation and predictable disaster. (Israel)

HOW CAN ONE BE SAVED?

The Jewish religion, though it has had its periods of mild proselytizing, has never had to be, like either Mohammedanism or Christianity, a missionary religion. For since it does not hold man and nature to be corrupt, it does not consider men damned automatically and thus in need of a specific nostrum of metaphysical salvation. To become a Jew, which is as much a matter of nationality as of religion, of naturalization as of custom and belief, the non-Jew must undergo ceremonies and tests. But it is not necessary to be a Jew in order to be saved or, in the Jewish phrase, to be a partaker either of the Messianic age or of the world to come. It is merely necessary to be righteous, to be a bringer of peace. (Mid-Channel)

WHO IS A GENTLEMAN?

The Christian command not to judge is, of course, a Jewish command and antedates Christianity by centuries. Of many specific applications of the command, one of the happiest in tone is this: "If you see a learned and pious man commit a sin on a night, think of it no more on the morrow. Perhaps he has repented. Nay, to say so is not enough. He has surely known penitence." But what is true of the learned is equally true of the simple and the inclusive principle is this: "Judge every man according to his better self, literally, according to that scale which holds his merits." Upon this point the sages are uncompromising and declare that whoever invokes God's judgment against his neighbor will be the first to be punished, irrespective of the merits of the case. It follows from all this that the so-called Christian gentleman of Anglo-American tradition is a Jewish gentleman. He is not knightly in the Nordic, pagan, belligerent sense. He is never truculent; his great aim is to spare his neighbor shame and pain; he is commanded by the sages to "let his language and his relations with his neighbor always be gentle and gracious." His character is defined once and for all in the tractate *Kiddushin,* "Sanctifications": "If two men quarrel, watch him who gives in and is silent first. You may be sure that he is of gentler birth than the other." (Mid-Channel)

CHAPTER 75

REFLECTIONS OF JACOB KLATZKIN

Jacob Klatzkin (1882–1948) is one of the more noted polylingual Jewish intellectuals who wrote with felicity as well as facility in a modernized Hebrew. Descended from a line of distinguished Polish rabbis, he received a thorough grounding in Talmudic lore, and published a legalistic treatise at the age of sixteen. He became increasingly attracted, however, to secular learning, especially philosophy, and he left Poland to become a student of the great Professor Hermann Cohen at the University of Marburg.

Like so many other "emancipated" young Jews of the middle class, he became an ardent Zionist, and devoted much of his time to the cultural development of that movement. Though reared to speak Yiddish, and educated to use German, he preferred to write in Hebrew–a language in which he published, among many other works, an impressive biography of Spinoza. He was living in Berlin, engaged in editing a voluminous Hebrew encyclopedia, when the advent of Hitler compelled him to leave Germany in 1933. He settled in the United States.

This work is a striking collection of reflections and aphorisms entitled In Praise of Wisdom, *and it is from this that the following excerpts have been taken.*[1]

---

[1]Translated from the Hebrew (with exceptional brilliance) by Abraham Ragelson, and published by L. B. Fischer (New York, 1943).

TO EACH GENERATION ITS LAUGH

When I visualize the coming generations and imagine how these will wonder at our life and make mockery of it; how they will jest at our wars and conquests, our pleasures and torments, even as we stand and wonder at the life of past generations, and regard it with derision–I become aware of the hollowness and pitiableness of our being. Yet one comforting thought puts me at ease: Those who come after us will in turn be accounted savages in comparison with those who come after them.

THE TASK OF CULTURE

One of the great tasks of culture is to convert necessity into freedom. Its mission is to educate human beings to enjoy their obligatory acts, so they may discharge them with a sense of inner freedom, as though they themselves had willed them. A man should enjoy the labor of his hands and not feel it as a curse. A worker who crushes stones and builds a house should enjoy the processes of toil and construction quite apart from the enjoyment of the prospective pay. This, then, is the purpose of education: to increase within us the innocence of enjoyment.

Just as art is commissioned to give us life, with all its sorrows and pains, as a gift for enjoyment (in a stage play, even the martyred death of the just offers a species of enjoyment), so all culture is commissioned to convert, as far as lies within its power, pain into enjoyment, necessity into freedom.

OUR LOST SOUL

A Hebrew legend tells: What is an embryo like? It is like a scroll all rolled up in its place, with a candle burning at its head.

It looks forth and can see from one end of the world to the other. Never has a person any better time than that time. He is taught the entire Law. As soon as he goes forth into the air of the world, an angel comes, slaps him on his mouth, and makes him forget the entire Law. . . .

Even after the moment of birth, that legendary angel stands ready to slap us, and make us forget our own selves. We are perpetually tossed back and forth between forgetting and remembering, loss of soul and recovery of soul. Hence, the lack of peace in ourselves.

WHAT IS POWER?

Some say: Power is the only reality. Hence, all moral laws that are intended for the protection of the weak create unreal and imaginary values.

However, if we examine the character of dominant power, we discover that often it is itself a mythical thing, owing its existence to imagination. In essence, it is a psychological phenomenon; all the reality it has is illusory in character.

We see one person ruling a people, dictating to an entire nation. Multitudes of human beings serve him with fear. Whom do they fear? In actual power the slaves are immeasurably superior to their master. But each slave sees himself as an individual against his fellow slaves. If they are impelled to rebel, they are afraid of each other. Sometimes one of them does rebel; then his fellows are forced to punish that one, though in their hearts they wish or scheme to do as he had done.

It is not the ruler whom they fear, but the host of slaves who do his bidding. In other words, they fear themselves. Their weakness is a fiction, an error, a slave's error.

The ruler derives his power from the fact that he adds the power of others to his own. He does this through obliterating from the consciousness of his slaves the fact of their common interests. The multitude sees itself as individuals opposed to each other. Each enslaved creature regards himself as enslaved by the community of his fellow slaves. It is through this common error, the error of many, that the power of one is upheld.

The many come back into their proper power the moment they see through this secret of mutual fear. The abolition of error in the hearts of slaves marks the end of the fictitious power of tyranny.

The emancipation of slaves is, first of all, their liberation from this small error. All great revolutions are really the correction of an error, a trifling error in the minds of the enslaved.

UNCONSCIOUS VENGEANCE

If you look deeply into the events of history, you will find that the gravest acts of vengeance were perpetrated unconsciously. Illustrations in point are Heine's revenge upon the Germany that was so far from him and so near to him, Hermann Cohen's revenge upon German culture, which he knowingly praised to the utmost, and unknowingly undermined. We may explain the preeminence of Jewish participation in the great revolutions of the world as unconscious acts of vengeance. It is as though an angel, say, the Angel of History, stood behind the backs of Jews and urged them: "Take your revenge! Sacrifice yourselves for others!"

This is the character and the beauty of our history-making vengeance. It brings blessing to the nation upon whom the vengeance is wreaked, and sacrifices no one but the avenger. Thereby he, too, is blest.

When I see many, many writers, who had their origin in

the Jewish fold, most powerful in negation and destructiveness, I think to myself: Haply, this is Israel's revenge upon the Gentile nations–a revenge which begets blessing.

LOGIC VS. MYSTICISM

Logic is, seemingly, an impudent faculty. It dares plunge a cold scalpel into the warm vitals of existence, cut up the universe piecemeal, peer into its saps. On the other hand, it might seem that mysticism is modest. It never dares (so it seems) to remove the veil and touch what is hidden and occult.

But observe the writers of our time. The gross-spirited and impudent among them are the very ones who wrap themselves in a cloak of mysticism and make a boast of occult knowledge. "See, we float above the realm of logic! Logic cannot touch us!" they cry out in boastful humility; "Ours the mystery, ours the secret, ours the subjection to the Divine Will."

The boastfulness with which modern mysticism reeks is the child of an unconscious fear which dwarfs-in-spirit feel in the presence of the strong truths of logic. They seek escape in a dark, intoxicating blindness. From this comfortable hiding, they may prattle forth "mysteries." They are possessed by a fear of clarity, a fear of solutions. They, therefore, deck themselves out with a veil, flatter themselves with vague wonderings, and that is sufficient unto them. Yet this fear of theirs and this boldness of theirs is at the extreme opposite pole of true mysticism.

The boldness of logic, however, is its natural right and leads only to salutary results.

A SHIELD AGAINST AMBITION

If you wish to conquer the urge of ambition, just let this strange thought pass through your mind at least once a day: What would I have been, if I hadn't been what I am?

After a time, you will thus learn to be a fugitive from self and at one with the world and the fullness thereof.

THE VALUE OF LAZINESS

Because people are too lazy to live, too lazy to think and feel, they tend to escape soul-tempests and spiritual adventure, and to steep themselves instead in labors that make them oblivious of their inner world. That is good for them. In this way, those too lazy to live become truly industrious. That is good for the world.

DOUBLE EGO

When you think, "How I envy Shakespeare's genius! How I wish I were like him!" you are wishing a thing and its opposite. You want to have your own ego and Shakespeare's ego simultaneously. In fact, you are lying to yourself. You would not wish to exist as Shakespeare, for in that case Shakespeare would exist, and not yourself.

LIAR AND GUNMAN

There is none so mean as the liar. A liar is worse than a gunman. Murder is usually committed in a state of excitement, and may have mitigating circumstances. The liar does his work composedly, calmly; his is an unforgivable crime. One can protect one's self against a gunman. There is no protection against a liar. A gunman kills a mortal. A liar would assassinate Divinity itself. He forges God's royal seal–the truth. No sin can be greater than that.

EQUALITY AS A BASIS FOR INEQUALITY

The social ideal of equality for all human beings is not to be conceived as an end in itself. It is but a means toward the development of inequality along desirable lines. By an equalization of classes in the material and economic fields, human opportunities will be enlarged to permit the development—under equal conditions—of unequal talents (of a profound natural and spiritual kind) in all their varieties and degrees. When the artificial inequality of wealth is removed, then we shall see the efflorescence of the natural inequalities obtaining among men in all their delicate and beautiful variations.

NEGATIVE STANDARD

Ere you judge your neighbor for all the ugly things he has done, judge him for all the ugly things a human being is capable of doing, by which he has not been tainted. We may put it this way: Evaluate a man's morality by a negative, rather than by a positive, standard—not by the good or evil things he has done but by the good or evil things he is *incapable* of doing. The actual deeds of a man are in great part the result of accident or external compulsion. The deeds which he is incapable of doing testify to his character, to his inner being. . . .

THE VALUE OF REVOLUTIONS

Never ask: Are the sacrifices required by a revolution worth the gains it offers? Does it build at least as much as it destroys? If we ask them, we should conclude that no revolution is worthwhile. Measured by moral standards, by balancings of human loss and human gain, no revolution that intends to save great masses of people from destruction, or to free nations from their oppressors, or to institute a kingdom of Heaven on earth, or to save religion or civilization or morality itself, would have a claim on our conscience, that we grant it the right to murder, plunder, destroy property, and break contracts. No future world of righteousness would justify present unrighteousness. We must comprehend, therefore, that revolution derives its right from other, nonmoral sources, though its professed aims be allied morality. As likely as not, its justification is derived from aesthetic impulses: anger and bitterness against a wrong order, the rebellion of what is beautiful in the human soul against what is ugly in society. Revolutionary pathos expands the limits of morality, broadens conscience to countenance, yea, even to demand, acts that violate normal moral considerations. Revolutions testify to the *metaphysical* nature of life, to life's heroic and sublime character. They permit life to leap at intervals beyond the bounds of morality; beyond the weighing of bundles of virtues against bundles of sins; beyond the drawing of parallels between constructive and destructive agencies, between sacrifices and gains. During revolutions, life stands under the star of a categorical command to destroy what ought to be destroyed, never mind the cost.

SUNDRY APHORISMS

If your neighbor has insulted you and you lift yourself so high above him that you easily forgive the insult, you are indeed among the proud. A higher degree is for you to be so far above all matters of honor that you are not even aware of the insult.

If a man tells you that he is of high moral character or that he is a true idealist–well, button your coat tightly if you have a gold watch on you.

Hate is a greater tie than love. The person we hate occupies our mind far more than the person we love. Therefore, if it is incumbent upon us to be careful in choosing our friends, we should be doubly careful in choosing our enemies. However, it is far easier for a person to find enemies and opponents worthy of him and befitting him than to find friends of that caliber.

A thinker who cannot set forth weighty thoughts in simple and clear language should be suspected, primarily, of lacking talent for thought and only secondarily of lacking talent for expression.

Art has no excellence higher than true simplicity. Art has no abomination baser than artificial simplicity.

Generally speaking, the clever are not wise. Neither are the wise clever; they are innocent. But there is a type of innocent cleverness – a combination which resides only in the mansions of superior wisdom.

He who cannot at times hate himself or despise himself must needs be lacking in conscience.

The weak-minded change their opinions because they are easily influenced by others, and the strong-minded change their opinions because they have complete mastery of their opinions.

Perforce we live and perforce we die, perforce we do evil and perforce we do good – and perforce we deem ourselves free agents.

TESTAMENT

May this be my testament:

Play with life, O mortal. Play with thine own self and thy desires. What is above and what is below shall be a game to thee, a pleasantry unto thee the height and the depth. Mount unto the pinnacle of reason to behold her smile, then laugh thou with her laughter. Rise beyond her, and laugh even at her laughter – then descend to life.

Life hath two gates. By one gate enters he who is full of awe before existence, he who is spanned to lofty aspirations and loves duties and commandments, he who rejoices in the joy of subjection: serious-minded he climbs and ascends, while bundles of purpose weigh down his back. By the other gate enters he who has risen above all purposes and above all the petty eternities of purpose, he who has cast off the yoke of reason, the handmaid of life, and has freed himself from her chains of morality, he who has reigned for one hour over knowledge and has observed her ignorance: light-minded he descends and smiles.

I hold the descending one more praiseworthy than the ascending one.

Play with life, O mortal. Seek danger, and if thou findest it not, create it. Gaze into the deeps – and fear. Whoever has not feared the great fear, that one has not lived the great life. Fear and laugh.

CHAPTER 76

THE RELIGION OF SHOLOM ASCH

The most renowned of all Yiddish writers is Sholom Asch (1880–1957), a native of Poland who became a citizen of the United States in 1914. Reared in the intensely religious atmosphere of the Russian Pale, the "yoke of the Torah" was laid on him at an early age, and he acquired an excellent Hebrew education. Drawn to literature, he decided—on the advice of his elder contemporary, I. L. Peretz—to write in Yiddish rather than Hebrew; and his many novels, plays, and essays have since done much to give that jargon a world importance. Asch is best known for his historical novels, The Nazarene *and* The Apostle, *which have provoked much curiosity as to his own religious beliefs. These, though sprung from sectarian seed, have so flowered out that they are almost entirely universalistic in character—as the following passages will reveal.*[1]

JEWS AND GENTILES

Who dares maintain that the Jewish God is against the Gentiles? Did not the prophets take all the nations into the Kingdom of the Messiah? From first to last they widened the skirts of the tent for all peoples, making them equal with the

[1]These excerpts are all taken from Asch's *What I Believe,* translated by Maurice Samuel (New York, Putnam, 1941).

Jews. Egypt and Assyria were given the same ultimate privileges as Israel: "In that day shall Israel be the third with Egypt and Assyria, even a blessing in the midst of the land: whom the Lord of hosts shall bless, saying, Blessed be Egypt my people, and Assyria the work of my hands, and Israel mine inheritance" (Isaiah 19:24–25). The prophets speak in the same spirit to the Gentile and the Jewish nations. Jonah is sent to Nineveh, other prophets to Damascus, with tidings of God. It is not the heathen nations whom God would destroy, but their heathendom, "not the sinners shall be destroyed, but sin." Amalek is the archenemy, because Amalek is the symbol of the demonic heathendom in its extremest form. For abomination has its spokesmen in heaven, not less than purity: Samael and Asmodeus, the enemies of all that is sacred and good. The enemy of man watches him with a thousand eyes; he lies in ambush to avail himself of every opportunity, no matter how trivial, to exploit every weakness for his undoing. The abomination, which is heathendom, is locked in a death-struggle with God, or Judaism; but it is not a struggle between Gentiles and Jews.

JEWS AS PERSECUTORS

God be thanked that the nations have not given my people the opportunity to commit against others the crimes which have been committed against it. I say, God be thanked, for had that opportunity been given it, who can doubt that it would have conducted itself against strangers in the same manner as the other peoples? To be sure, remembering the attitude of the Jewish faith toward "strangers" and "God-fearing" Gentiles, I simply cannot imagine it succumbing to the same frightful beastliness. But perhaps in the same way a genuine Christian believer, remembering the high ethical concepts of the Christian faith, cannot imagine that his Church lit the fires of the

Inquisition. The undeniable fact remains, however, that within the narrow limits of their power the Jewish rabbis did not fail to make use of repressive measures; they issued excommunications; they condemned sinners against the faith to the lash, or to lie in chains at the entrance of the synagogue; they persecuted unbelievers and burned the "unclean" books found among Jews. In Amsterdam, the Marranos who had fled from Spain invoked some of the methods of the Inquisition against those noble spirits, Uriel Acosta and Baruch Spinoza. It is not impossible, I repeat, that if the Jewish faith had been tempted by opportunity, it would have wrung from the words of Moses and the Prophets and the Mishnah the right or the duty to do unto others as others had done unto them. If the Inquisition could find such warrant in the New Testament, the Jewish faith could have found it in the Old.

But, when all is said and done, it was *not* my faith which applied the tinder to the faggots about the stake; it was not my faith which erected the Inquisitorial courts, haled before them innocent people, and condemned them to the most fantastic tortures in the hope of squeezing out of them "confession" and "acceptance." It was not the rabbis who forced priests to debate with them in the attentive presence of the Inquisition. It was not my faith, or my people, which descended on others with fire and sword, compelling them to abandon the ways of their fathers, reject and condemn their ancient sanctities, and adopt modes of worship alien to their religious nature. And therefore I thank and praise God that my faith had not the opportunity to visit upon other faiths the crimes which the other faiths visited upon her.

THE DEFECTS OF ATHEISM

The seeming marriage of atheism with humanitarianism was only a temporary liaison, a passing affair. It was a device to win the recognition and loyalty of the oppressed and the wretched of the earth. Once this object had been achieved, the union was repudiated; atheism took possession of the house and expelled humanitarianism.

Nor was it easy to reproach atheism with treachery. Had atheism ever undertaken to serve a God? Had it accepted any form of authority which would compel it to do this, or refrain from doing that? Atheism was its own god; good and evil were measured by its standards; whatever it called justice was justice, whatever it condemned as evil was evil.

Can this be taken as an attack on humanism? I cannot fell the tree of humanism, lest I destroy the branch to which I cling, the justice which was brought forth by humanism. It is very far indeed from my mind to anoint the old chains of physical and spiritual slavery with the oil of faith, so that they may be slipped on our limbs again. How would it be with me, today, if not for the work of the humanists? How would it be with all of us Jews if not for the emancipation of the liberal movement? Where would we be if not for liberators like Reuchlin, Rousseau, and even Voltaire? It was they who fought on the side of God when the Church was arrayed against Him. They picked up the essential good in faith, the liberation of man, when the Church contemptuously rejected it.

But is it not obvious that with all their seeming opposition to God and authority, the humanists – however little they may have understood this at the time – were nourished by the highest moral good which the faith had brought forth, namely, the love of one's fellowmen? It was not intelligence which inspired the idealism of the fighters and martyrs on the humanistic side; it was that deep-rooted passion for justice which faith had planted in man as a second nature. What the humanists failed to realize was that their quarrel was not with the Church, to whatever extent that body had still retained the inspiration of the Prophets. From the beginning they placed man on a level which made him the center of human events, so that he found again, in his high election, his mystic bond with the divinity. This apotheosis and election was later to stick in the throats of the rationalists, who saw humanity as an aggregation of maggots; the mystic value of man was denied in the slogan of "bread and work" which was the sum total of the vision of Marxism.

Yet side by side with this outburst of creative passion informed by inner faith, there was to be observed in man a suicidal impulse, a fury directed against himself. One noted on the faces of certain scholars of the monistic period a murderous kind of grinning, evoked when they succeeded in proving that man was not a separate creation but merely a highly developed animal.

They used every possible and impossible device to fasten man down to his animal condition; and every attempt to raise man above that condition, and to accord him a place above the animals, was regarded very definitely as a betrayal of the high principles of equality and fraternity; it was also denounced as a manifestation of backwardness and of a theological world-outlook, as an adulteration of the purity of science for the benefit of clericalism and the Church.

This materialistic view eventuated in the condition to which man has been reduced wherever the view has triumphed and become a reality: the herring-collectivism of Bolshevism and the mass enslavement of Nazism. In both instances the magic name of a god of social liberation is invoked for the suppression of all personal value and the destruction of that individual creative power to which, and to which alone, we can credit all our progress. Methods of the utmost cruelty and savagery were applied to the end that the human species might be violently torn away from whatever represented growth and progress and flung back into the condition which characterizes the animal world.

Even more powerful than these external methods, contrived

by physical force, was the eternal reiteration of the suggestion that the goal of our liberation is to be sought in the dissolution of our personality; as though, in a literal sense, our social needs could be met only after we had sloughed off our human skins and covered ourselves with the hides of beasts.

The condition to which the materialistic world-outlook has reduced man–that is, the herring-collectivism of Bolshevism and the mass slavery of Fascism–marks, I believe, the close of the atheistic period. Vengeance against God wound up in vengeance against man, in the obliteration of his personality. Today the men who are responsible for the unhappy results of the storm of the atheistic period see that a humanity which has lost its only privilege, that of personality, can become only that which the species is by nature: a herring-collective.

The lash may force men to physical labor; it cannot force them to spiritual creativity. If the protagonists of materialism want to become creative, they must take up again what they have so contemptuously rejected–the individual personality. I would call the personality of man the gland of creativity.

MAN'S SIN

We have all sinned. We are all guilty in the calamity which has come upon us. We have all contributed to the elevation of the demon of evil to the throne of God. Have we Jews lived according to all the prescriptions thoughtfully provided by our wise men for every foreseeable and unforeseeable situation, or according to the ethical concepts of the Jewish faith? Were we the holy people, the people of the election, which we were bidden to be, and which we persuade ourselves that we are? What shall I answer? We have commissioned our rabbis to make a "settlement" for us with the Accountant on High, while we ourselves pursued earthly well-being as the highest good. It may be, indeed, that we have been somewhat more generous than others in our philanthropies, simply because our peculiar position, our common suffering, has awakened in us a strong feeling of mutual responsibility as a means of self-preservation. But as against this we have been too noisy, lacking in reserve and modesty both in our acts and in our contacts with others. I take upon myself the right to say this to my people, because I am of it, and bear part of the guilt. I have no right to preach to others than Jews – if, indeed, to them! – but I have the right to address this question to the Christians: has Christian man, to whatever faith or division of faith he belongs, lived according to his faith? Has he suffered, surrendered, died, and been purified in the spirit of Jesus? Have the limbs of the Christian been the vessels of Christ? How can Christian man lift his hand to do evil if he believes that he is a part of the suffering Messiah and the Messiah is a part of him?

All of us must beat our breasts in confession. A great Day of Atonement must come over the world. Life must be remolded. Jew and Christian alike must turn back to the origins of faith. We must choose a path of which we can say with the utmost certainty that it is the good path, God's path, the only one to be followed. More than at any other time in our history we must be armed morally, so that every one of us may be conscious that he is a defender of those moral goods without which life is not worth the living. Our house must be put in order, and the order must be a just one, so that every one of us is prepared to lay down his life for it.

Such a change within us, such conviction that we stand on the side of God, cannot be the result of ideals emanating solely from the intelligence. One ideal alone can save us, that which is coterminous with faith in God and which is the sum of ideals, excluding from its grace no member of the human race. There is no measure of justice other than the justice of God; for justice is truth, and there is one truth, and one truth only.

WHAT I BELIEVE

(1) It is my deepest belief that just as I have a share in the God of Israel through my faith in Him, that I stand under His authority and am included in the promise of redemption, so my Christian brother has his equal share in the God of Israel, stands equally under the authority and is included equally in the promise of redemption. For he is a son of Israel equally with me. His faith has made him a son of Abraham, Isaac, and Jacob. My rights are his, and I have a share in his religious values as he has a share in mine.

Basing themselves on this concept of equality, the sons of every faith must justify themselves in works. Man's ladder to God is a ladder of works. God must be the ultimate expression of our relationship to each other on earth.

(2) It is my deepest belief that man has been chosen by God's grace from among all creatures. Apart from the intelligence, which nature has given to every creature, and which is included in nature and limited to the objective and conditioned, man—alone among creatures—possesses a soul which is a part of the endowment from above. Through his soul man stands in mystic contact with heaven. By means of his soul man can acquire intellectual and intuitive powers which are outside the competence of nature, derive from the highest inspiration of the divinity, and are not limited to the objective and conditioned. God guides every individual destiny through the inspiration of the soul. This soul-inspiration is given to each one, and not only to the elect, so that everyone may, in the exercise of his free will, reach to the higher reason which is the supreme level of the holy spirit.

Each one of us can follow in the footsteps of Amos, abandon the flocks, and become a prophet in Israel. In keeping with Jewish doctrine I believe in the democracy of divine election; each one of us can become even a Moses.

(3) Accepting this point of view, it is further my

profoundest conviction that the democratic principle–in the social system not less than in faith–is God's especial gift to man and resides in the act of grace which God performed for man in choosing him among all creatures. The democratic principle is interwoven with faith and cannot be separated from God. In having been chosen by God we became the children of God: "For sons are ye of the Lord God"–all of us, and not just a few individuals. Any other relationship as between us and God, or as between ourselves, would contradict the will of the divinity, and would be incompatible with all that has been given to the Jews by Moses and the Prophets, and all that has been given to the Christians by Jesus and the Apostles. The democratic principle is "all the law fulfilled in one word, even in this: Thou shalt love thy neighbor as thyself." (Galatians 5:14) This is the foundation which, together with the love toward God, was given through Moses, the Prophets, the Pharisees, Jesus of Nazareth, and the Apostles.

"Love thy neighbor as thyself" does not mean that you must be mild in your dominion over him; it means that you shall not have any dominion over him. He is a son of liberty not less than you, and the relationship between you and him can be built only on a system which assumes the identity of your rights. This is the democratic principle.

And as the democratic principle is the will of God in relationship between man and man, it is equally his will in the relationship between man and God. "It is not in the heavens." The divine law was not given to the angels, but to us, who are of the earth. It lies before us like an open book. The measure is in our hand.

Hence I believe profoundly that there is no love of God without love of men. Service to mankind is in my view the higher service of the divinity. But service to mankind must not be seen in the throwing of crumbs to the poor; as we are equal in our faith in God, so we must be equal in our faith in man.

We must work out a world order which shall rest upon equal distribution of labor and rewards. "The right to happiness" must not remain an empty gesture in our Declaration of Independence; it must be incorporated in the administrative duties of the state. It must be interpreted in the material sense to which men are bound by their nature: in food and clothing and shelter, in the care for the aged, in our regard for widows, for the sick and the weak. All this must become a cardinal obligation for the state, in its administration. The inner security of our citizens must become the cornerstone of our independence and freedom; it must become a tacit obligation, like external security; not because we regard social injustice as the most potent instrument of the devil–though it is, indeed, exactly that–but because without that tacit obligation our professions of faith are as empty as dicers' oaths.

"Though I speak with the tongues of men and of angels, and have not charity, I am become as sounding brass, or a tinkling cymbal. And though I have the gift of prophecy, and understand all mysteries, and all knowledge; and though I have all faith, so that I could remove mountains, and have not charity, I am nothing. And though I bestow all my goods to feed the poor, and though I give my body to be burned, and have not charity, it profiteth me nothing" (I Corinthians 13:1–3).

(4) It is further my profoundest belief that we must lead a life in faith; that is, we must become that which we undertook to be–a holy people. We can be a holy people only in a pure, ethical life, a life ruled by laws and commandments. But no laws and commandments, though they have a thousand eyes, and though they seem to control all our acts, can purify and sanctify us if the heart of man does not sanctify his life. The heart of man is a filter for all his acts and thoughts. If the heart is sound, man knows that his highest joy is bound up not with dissoluteness and the free play of uncontrollable passion, but with purity, with modesty, and with restraint.

There is no level of corruption from which man cannot redeem himself, by the exercise of his free will. And whenever he makes an effort at such redemption, he can be certain of help from above. For God's act of creation was not single and unique; it is a continuity of relationship through the individual destiny.

I believe, therefore, that for every individual there is salvation, no matter how low he has sunk. "Have I any pleasure at all that the wicked should die? saith the Lord God; and not that he should return from his ways, and live?" (Ezekiel 8:23). The heart of man is bound with the divinity through the radiations of divinity. To the darkest and most horrible retreats to which men have withdrawn from the divinity, a ray of the divinity penetrates. And for this reason we must never despair of a man, much less of a group which is temporarily lost to the divinity. However deep a group has sunk, we must continue to pray for it, and to help it with our desires and sympathies. And no matter how deeply we feel that we have been wronged by such a group, we must exert ourselves to purify our hearts from bitterness.

We were worms in our physical creation; we have become human in our hunger for the divinity. The drink of God, which was lifted to our lips by the authority, has enabled us to mount the ladder of Jacob which rises from earth to heaven. If we will endure, and continue the upward path, we will attain to the true salvation of a world which stands under the authority of God through a single, universal redeemer.

The renewal of faith in the divine force of our moral values, as our sole hope in the darkness of our night, is what I would wish to submit to a suffering humanity.

It is America, which has been saved from the worst terrors of the night, which has not been corrupted with the cynicism which has been the undoing of Europe; it is America, young and powerful, blossoming in the virginity of faith, which must become the leading spirit among the nations. It is America, the land which has taken me in, among so many other homeless ones, as a child of her own, which I would like to see as a "light to the Gentiles," leading the world back out of the night into the authority of the one and only God.

CHAPTER 77

PRACTICES OF ORTHODOX JUDAISM

The religion of Israel is now manifested in at least four different forms—Orthodox, Conservative, Reconstructionist, and Liberal or Reform. Of these the Orthodox continues to retain the largest number of nominal adherents, especially in the Old World. It is fundamentally ritualistic, insisting that the practices ordained in the Pentateuch, and amplified in the Talmud and the later rabbinic Codes, are still sacrosanct and binding. It recognizes a distinction between dinim *(laws), which are mandatory, and* minhagim *(customs), which are volitional; but it tends to lay equal emphasis on both. This is because the basic aim is to keep the Jew from yielding to the gravitational forces exerted by his Gentile environment, and such an aim can best be served by making his personal conduct ubiquitously distinctive. Orthodox Judaism is thus more than a creed; it is a way of life.*

Certain of its teachings are of far more than merely sectarian value, and they deserve consideration here. The following excerpts are taken from a publication intended for use in the homes of English-speaking Orthodox Jews. It is a popular digest based on the Shulhan Arukh *and summarizes all the ritual observances incumbent on the pious.*[1]

---

[1]*Laws and Customs of Israel,* compiled by Gerald Friedlander (London, 1915), 3 vols.

SOME MORAL PRECEPTS

Everyone is commanded to love all human beings as one loves himself, provided they are good and upright. . . . One is obliged to love strangers and look after orphans and widows even though they be very wealthy. Anyone who vexes them or provokes them to anger or grieves them or domineers over them or wastes their fortune transgresses the law; this applies much more if one smite them or curse them. All this applies when one afflicts them for his own advantage, but if it be for their benefit, for example, to teach the orphans the Torah or a trade or to train them in the right path, it is permitted. Nevertheless, one must lead them with love and mercy. They are considered to be orphans in this matter until they no longer need the assistance of another and are able to keep themselves. One must not put a stumbling block in the way of a person who is ignorant of the good and righteous way, lest he transgress the Law.

The following are general moral rules: Not to talk about other people except for some good cause. Neither to utter or to listen to idle words which serve no useful purpose. To cultivate a silent tongue and not to talk except to acquire wisdom or to satisfy the needs of one's physical life. To speak gently with one's fellow creatures. Not to talk of material things in the House of Study. To learn from every man and to accept the truth from all who speak it. To be anxious to promote the welfare of his fellow and to pursue peace. To remember the day of death and continually to have in one's mind the purpose of his creation in this world.

Men differ according to their natures: some are jocular and happy, others are sad and mournful; some are gentle, others are hardhearted; some are boastful whose desires are never satisfied, others lack all desires even for the actual needs of life; some constantly pursue material gain, whilst others are idle, not even seeking their daily needs. Likewise is it with all ethical principles.

The right course for a man to accustom himself to pursue is the golden mean, and he should avoid any extreme. Nevertheless, if he should accustom himself to some evil habit, so that he has gone to one extreme, the best counsel for this person is to go to the opposite extreme, until he can eradicate this vice from his nature; thereafter he should pursue the golden mean. Pride is an extremely bad vice, and, therefore, the proud should pursue the opposite extreme and become humble in spirit. Likewise with anger, all those addicted thereto must strive to avoid becoming angry in any circumstance. But when one has to exercise his authority over his children, he may pretend to be angry in their presence, whilst in his heart he is quite composed.

A man must not pray to God to punish his fellow, and even though he cannot obtain redress on earth he should not adopt such a course without informing him of his intention.

A man must not accustom himself to indulge in flattery or deception, saying one thing with his tongue and thinking otherwise in his mind. . . . One must not urge his fellow to be his guest, when he knows that he will not accept. A man must not offer gifts with importunity, knowing they will not be accepted. One must not pretend to open casks of wine with the intention of deceiving anyone as though it were done to show him honor, whereas he opens them in order to sell the wine. Any similar action is prohibited; even one word of dissimulation or deceit is forbidden. One's word must be true and one's spirit honest and one's heart free from all works of deceit. One must avoid doing anything which might lead others to suspect him of transgressing the Law.

ON ARISING FROM BED

The first daily thought of man should be concerning the God of his salvation and His many loving kindnesses, because He has restored to him his soul and health, making him like a new creature. Let him thank God for this with all his heart, and whilst on his bed let him say: "I thank Thee, O eternal King, because Thou hast graciously restored my soul to me, great is Thy faithfulness." This prayer may be said, although he has not yet washed his hands, because the name of God is not mentioned therein. Let him strengthen his will to rise quickly and eagerly. If he accustom himself to do this four or five times, he will find no difficulty thereafter.

When he arises he must not walk four cubits unless he has washed his hands, except in cases of emergency. Prior to his ablution he must not touch his mouth, nostrils, eyes or ears, nor may he touch any food. Water must be poured three times on each hand alternately as far as the wrist or at least to the joints of the fingers, then the face and mouth must be washed and whilst drying his hands he says the benediction. The water with which he washed must not be used for any other purpose.

On the following occasions the hands must be washed: on awakening from sleep in the morning, on coming from the lavatory or bath, after cutting the nails or hair, after taking off one's boots, after attending a funeral or going into the house where the corpse lies, or after touching anything unclean or any part of the body usually covered.

Purity is a very important principle which everyone must seek and observe even when alone in one's secret chamber. . . . One's garments must not be torn or soiled, for even though a person be indifferent to his own sense of shame, the honor due to humanity must be respected. . . .

As soon as it is dawn, when the time of prayer commences, a man must not begin any work or occupation, or start on a journey before he has prayed. One is likewise forbidden to eat or drink before reciting the morning prayer, except in case of sickness or extreme hunger. . . .

It is permitted to take the *tallit* (prayer shawl) of anyone who is a casual companion even without his knowledge and to pray therewith and to say its benediction. But it must not be taken out of the house where it happens to be. If it be folded, the user must fold it again. . . .

CONCERNING THE SYNAGOGUE

The inhabitants of a place compel one another to build a synagogue or House of Study, to buy books for study. . . . The sanctity of the synagogue and of the House of Study is very great, and we are warned concerning them to fear the One who dwells therein. . . . It is, therefore, forbidden to eat, drink, sleep, or even to doze in a synagogue. We should not kiss our little sons therein, because it is not meet to distract one's attention from the love of God.

It is permitted to make a House of Study out of a synagogue. It is forbidden to see a synagogue unless there is another; if it be the only one, it must not be sold or demolished until they have another one ready, unless it be in danger. . . .

We say neither the public prayers nor do we read the Torah (with benedictions) unless there be a *minyan* (ten male adults) present. An adult is one who has passed his thirteenth year . . . .

Some authorities allow, in a case of emergency, such prayers (permitted only when a *minyan* is present) to be said when nine adults and a boy more than six years old are present. But the later authorities do not approve this. . . .

It is necessary that all the ten should be in one room and the Reader should be with them. . . . Only a fit person is appointed as a Reader. A fit person is one who has a good reputation, and is not known as a transgressor, even as a youth. He must be modest and pleasing to the congregation. He must have a pleasant and sweet voice which touches the heart. He must be accustomed to read the Law, the Prophets and the Hagiographa, so that the Scripture texts in the prayers may be fluent in his mouth. If they do not find a person with all these qualifications, they must select from among the candidates the best as regards knowledge and morals.

A beardless person may not be appointed permanently, but may be appointed temporarily. Any male who is more than thirteen years old may read the prayers.

It is accounted disgraceful for a Reader to prolong the service so that the congregation may hear his voice; it is said of such: "She hath uttered her voice against me; therefore I have hated her" (Jeremiah 12:8). He should pray with decorum and stand in awe and dread. The service must not be unduly prolonged.

If one's garments be torn and the elbows be bare, one must not officiate. A blind man may officiate.

A Reader may not be dismissed unless he be guilty of some fault. Even if he take an oath that he will not continue in his evil ways, he must not officiate until he has sincerely repented. He must not be dismissed because of gossip.

RULES FOR READING THE LAW

It is a tradition of our sages that our teacher Moses instituted the custom in Israel of reading the Law in the congregation at fixed times, and that Ezra the Scribe extended this custom, which it is necessary to observe very carefully.

We do not read in the Scroll of the Law unless it be written according to the proper rules. If three mistakes be found therein, it is prohibited to read it until it be corrected, for the presumption holds good that it contains other mistakes. . . .

RULES FOR THE STUDY OF THE LAW

Every Israelite must fix a certain time by day and by night to study the Torah. At least after his prayers he should study the laws which are essential for every Israelite to know. If one cannot study through inability to learn or by reason of his many distractions, he should support others who devote themselves to study and this will be accounted unto him as though he himself had studied. When one studies and must interrupt his reading, he must not leave his book open. Whatsoever he studies he should read audibly and attentively. . . .

If sacred books be placed on the bench it must not be used as a seat. . . . It is, of course, forbidden to put the books on the ground. . . . In an emergency one may sit on a chest containing sacred books, but it is forbidden to do so if a Scroll be therein. . . . One must not do anything objectionable before these books nor should they be turned upside down, and if they be thus found, they must be put in their proper position. If the Scroll or any sacred book or anything used for divine worship be worn out, it must be hidden away.

One must not use a sacred book for a personal benefit, for example, to use it as a screen against the sun, unless he should do this for the purpose of study, when it is permitted to do so.

RULES OF HYGIENE

Since it is God's will for man to keep his body healthy and sound, because it is impossible for a man, if he be ill, to understand anything concerning the Creator, it is necessary, therefore, to avoid aught that injures the body but rather to accustom oneself to such actions which promote physical well-being, namely: A man should eat only when he is hungry, and drink only when he is thirsty. He should not neglect for a moment the calls of nature, but he should arise forthwith and attend thereto. One must not eat overmuch, but rather leave off eating before he has quite satisfied his appetite. He should drink only a little water mixed with wine during the meal. He may drink as much as he needs when his food has commenced to be digested and even when it has been digested he should not drink too much water. He must not begin his meal until he has attended to the calls of nature.

A man should not eat unless he has had exercise and made his body fairly warm, or unless he has done some work which has made him tired. As a general rule, one should take physical exercise every morning until the body becomes fairly warm, thereupon he should rest until he has regained his normal condition and then he should eat. It is good to take a warm bath when one is tired; then let him rest awhile and then eat.

When one has eaten one's meal, he should continue to be seated or recline on his left side, but he should neither go for a walk nor ride, nor weary himself, nor excite his body, nor move about until his food has been digested. If one should move about or weary oneself directly after eating, he renders himself liable to serious illnesses.

The day and night have twenty-four hours; it is enough for a man to sleep a third part thereof, that is, eight hours. These hours should be at the end of the night, so that from the beginning of his sleep until sunrise, eight hours should intervene, consequently he will get up just before sunrise.

A man should sleep neither on his face nor on his back but on his side; at the beginning of the night on his left side and at the end of the night on the right side. He should not go to sleep directly after eating, but he should let three or four hours elapse. He should not sleep by day.

Such things which possess laxative qualities, for example, grapes, figs, and so forth, should be eaten before the meal. . . . After partaking thereof, he must wait awhile until they have been partly digested and then he should take his meal. Fruits with costive qualities, for example, pomegranates, quinces, and so forth, may be eaten immediately after the meal, but in moderation.

In summer one should eat cooling food, avoiding too much spice but rather using vinegar. In winter one should partake of heating food with plenty of spices and a little mustard and asafoetida. One should observe similar rules according to the climate of the place where he lives. . . .

As long as a person works and takes plenty of exercise, and does not eat to satiety, and his bowels are regular, he is sure to escape illness, and he will find his strength increasing, even if he should eat unwholesome food. . . .

The following are the rules for bathing: one should take a bath at least once a week, but never immediately after meals, nor when one is hungry. . . .

He who conducts himself according to the rules, which we have laid down, can be assured that he will not suffer illness all his days until he reaches a ripe old age and dies. He will not need a physician, and he will always enjoy good and perfect health, unless he had an unhealthy constitution from his birth, or had given way to evil habits from early youth, or owing to extraordinary calamities, such as an epidemic or famine.

All these rules, which we have mentioned, are for the guidance of the healthy only; but a person who is ill, or who has led for many years an irregular life, must follow other rules and prescriptions according to the nature of his malady, as it is explained in the book on medicine; change of the regular course of life is the root of all illness.

Where there is no physician, it behooves both the healthy and the sick not to depart from any of the rules mentioned in this chapter, inasmuch as each of them leads to a beneficial result.

In a town where the following are not to be found, a wise man ought not to reside, namely, a physician, a surgeon, baths, public convenience, water supply from the river or a spring, a synagogue, a teacher, a scribe, an overseer of the poor, and a court of law.

A person should endeavor to dwell in a locality where the air is clear and pure, on elevated ground, and in a house of ample proportions. If possible he should not reside in the summer in a place facing north or east, and it should be free from all decayed refuse. It is very beneficial continually to purify the air of the house with good disinfectants. One should see that the atmosphere of the house is maintained at an even temperature, neither too hot nor too cold, but so as neither to chill a person nor to make one too warm.

Our sages of blessed memory have said that one . . . should not eat any food which had been partly eaten by a mouse, rat, or any other animal.

To preserve the sense of sight one should not do the following: not to go suddenly from a dark place to a well-illuminated place, or vice versa, for the sudden change is very injurious to the optic nerve; therefore, the eyes should become accustomed gradually to the change. Light reflected by the sun is injurious to the eyes, that is, the light reflected from a surface upon which the sun shines affects the eyesight. One should not strain his eyes in the dusk of twilight nor in the sunshine of midday nor at night by lamplight. He should neither gaze steadily at white or bright red colors nor at the glare of fire. Smoke and sulphurous odors are injurious to the eyes.

RULES OF ETIQUETTE

One should not eat or drink like a glutton, one should neither eat nor drink whilst standing, and even if one had but poor fare, still his table should be clean and nicely covered. . . . One should not drink a glass of wine at one draught, for one who does so is a tippler. It is the correct thing to drink one's wine in two draughts, but one who finishes his wine in three draughts, behold he is haughty. If, however, the glass be extra large, one may finish it in several draughts; likewise, if it be very small, one may finish it in one draught.

One should not place upon the table the piece of bread which he had bitten, neither should he give it to his neighbor, nor should he put it in the dish, as his neighbor may find it loathsome. One should not hand a cup, the contents of which he has partly drunk, to one's neighbor, as the latter may through bashfulness drink against his will. The utmost care should be taken not to drink of the leavings of the cup of which one's neighbor had partaken. . . .

A man should not be hot-tempered at his meal lest the guests and members of his household be ashamed to eat, thinking that he rages and is angry because they are eating. One should neither stare in the face of a person who is eating or drinking, nor look at the portion set before him, so that he put him not to shame. . . .

When two eat at one table, even if each one have his separate plate before him or if they partake of fruit and each one have his portion before him, it is meet for the elder of the two to begin to eat first, and he who stretches forth his hand before his elder or superior is a glutton. . . .

A woman should not drink wine during her husband's absence even in her own home, and at any other place, even in her husband's presence, she is forbidden to drink wine or any other intoxicating beverage; if, however, she be accustomed to drink wine in her husband's presence, she is permitted to partake of a little thereof during his absence.

One should not give food to an Israelite unless he knows him to be of those who wash their hands and say the appropriate benediction. This, however, applies only to him who provides one with food as a part of his pay, but if the recipient be a poor man, he should provide him with food as an act of charity without making any inquiry as to his piety.

Guests must not give to the children of their host aught of what had been set before them, as the host may have no more food than that which was set before them. Therefore, if they do not leave enough for themselves he will be ashamed on account of his poverty. If the table were richly supplied, it is permissible for them to do so.

One who enters a house should not say, "Give me to eat"; but he should wait until he is invited to eat. It is forbidden to partake of a repast which does not suffice for the host, for this would be akin to robbery. Moreover, the host invites him to dine with him only as an act of politeness.

LAWS OF BUYING AND SELLING

It is necessary to be most careful not to deceive one's neighbor, either in buying or selling, or with reference to hiring, contracts, or exchange. . . .

Just as there is the prohibition of wrongdoing (i.e., deception) with reference to buying and selling, so also with regard to money-changing. . . .

If one have something to sell, he is forbidden to make it look better than what it really is in order to deceive thereby, for example, to give an animal bran-water which helps to distend its bulk and makes its hair stand erect so that it seems to be fat and healthy. It is also forbidden to paint over old utensils so that they appear to be new, and all such devices are prohibited.

Likewise it is forbidden to mix a little bad fruit with plenty of good fruit to sell the same as though they were good, or to mix inferior liquor with superior liquor, but if the taste of the former predominate, the mixing is permitted for the purchaser will notice this.

A shopkeeper is permitted to distribute parched grain and nuts among children in order to accustom them to buy of him. He may also sell cheaper than the market price for the same reason, and the other tradesmen cannot prevent this.

He who gives short measure or weight to his companion or to an idolater transgresses a precept of the Divine law.

It is necessary to measure and to weigh with a generous eye; this means that he should give more than the exact quantity demanded, as it is said "A perfect and just measure shalt thou have" (Deuteronomy 25:15).

LAWS CONCERNING LOANS

It is an affirmative precept to lend to a poor Israelite. . . . A poor man who is a relative takes precedence before other poor people and the poor in one's city take precedence before the poor of another city. The religious act of lending to the poor is greater than the act of giving charity to the poor. . . .

It is forbidden to lend money even to a scholar without having witnesses, unless a pledge be forthcoming. The best course is to have a deed drawn up referring to the loan.

It is forbidden to exact payment from the borrower when it is known that he is unable to pay, even to confront him is prohibited lest he be put to shame since he cannot repay.

CHAPTER 78

THE ETHICS OF MORDECAI KAPLAN

Professor Mordecai M. Kaplan recruited numerous rabbinical disciples to "reconstruct" Jewish life so that it conformed to modern exigencies without losing its traditional sanctions. Essentially sectarian, many of Professor Kaplan's teachings are nevertheless highly universalistic in character, as the following passages from his best-known work will indicate.[1]

THE ETHICAL MOTIVATION

The worth of a civilization depends not only upon the ideals and values it professes, but upon its ability to energize them. Judaism formerly possessed that ability to an eminent degree. The concept of divine revelation reinforced the moral standards of Judaism so that they acquired the potency of physical causes. At a time when the disintegration of the ancient religions and loyalties shook men's faith in the values and standards essential to the stability of the social order, Judaism performed a much-needed service to mankind. the nations were far less prepared than they are even today to be

[1] The excerpts are taken from Chapter XXX of his *Judaism as a Civilization* (New York, Macmillan, 1934).

governed by an ethical code which is based on man's recognition of his spiritual nature. Men were still accustomed to look to extraneous authority for the sanction of the right. They were too heteronomously minded to be spiritually self-reliant. The philosophers and their schools were not able to inspire sufficient confidence in what they offered as sustaining certitudes, because they had no way of proving the objectivity and imperativeness of the moral law. It was at that juncture that Judaism saved civilization by supplying a transcendent sanction not only to the moral law as such, but even to some of the specific laws for the regulation of human conduct.

In place of the reasoned conclusions of the philosophers which pointed to the objective and categorical character of the ethical standards of human life, Judaism affirmed as a sanction of the higher life the historic fact of supernatural revelation. The fact that supernatural revelation is now questioned might mean that the human race will once more be plunged into the hopeless skepticism characteristic of the Roman world at the beginning of the Common Era, unless the human mind learns to free itself from dependence upon supernatural authority to validate moral law. It is imperative that men break away from the habit of identifying the spiritual with the supernatural. The reality of the spiritual should be conceived in terms of the supersensible which interacts with and functions through the sensible and perceptible world. The human mind, in sensing that reality, has with some already attained a mature form of spiritual grasp, the product of a firsthand realization that the world is not characterless, that it acts with a uniformity which gives meaning to existence, and that the salvation for which man strives is to live in rapport with that meaning. But this spiritual maturity is far from being general. The majority of mankind are still in the stage of spiritual adolescence. They have outgrown the traditional ideology, but they have not yet acquired an ideology which, taking into account the new knowledge, might help them achieve an affirmative and spiritual adjustment to life. The Jews ought to realize the seriousness and extent of the spiritual maladjustment in their own lives and in those of the rest of mankind, and take a leading part in effecting the new orientation which is the only means of preventing the eruption of a new barbarism.

Modern religiously minded thinkers are striving to construct a foundation of ethical values upon which the social structure might henceforth be reared. Kant inaugurated the movement in modern times to find in "practical reason" a sanction for values. But like the movement inaugurated by Socrates and Plato, or the school of the Stoics, this too will fail as long as it remains confined to the limited class of intellectuals.

The nations of the world are so preoccupied with their anxieties and ambitions that they do not realize that the very foundation of civilized life is being undermined. Though their traditional religious sanctions are decaying, there is no concerted effort on the part of their leaders to forestall the crash which must ultimately come. It is nothing more than fitting that the Jews should be among the first to reckon with this spiritual crisis. The rich residue of ethical passion and inspiration latent in the Jewish heritage should be called into action once more.

The spiritual reconstruction in which Jews of ethical enlightenment ought to engage should not be conceived merely as a task in rethinking the problem of spiritual adjustment along lines familiar to philosophers. The ethical teacher who promulgates his intuitions and experiences, as though they belonged to man or mankind in the abstract, may develop a system of formal but not of living ethics. The ethical teachers who left the deepest impress upon mankind were those who came to save their own peoples, not mankind in general. By addressing themselves to their own civilization, their message had a concreteness and dynamic character which compelled attention. This explains why prophets have succeeded where ethical philosophers have failed. The ethical philosopher taught in abstract terms and failed to move men because he addressed himself to civilization in general. The prophet taught in concrete terms and moved men to action, because he addressed himself to his people's civilization, trying to change its course, opposing its idols and putting up before it new ideals. Ethical philosophers are dreamers and creators of Utopias. Prophets are practical revolutionaries. Only when the ethical reconstruction is incorporated into Jewish civilization will that reconstruction affect the lives of all Jews who want to remain Jews. They will want to remain Jews as soon as they feel that the best in them is being definitely challenged by and elicited through their civilization.

The only kind of ethical movement that is compatible with the genius of the Jewish civilization is a movement of the prophetic and not of the philosophic type. . . .

ECONOMIC JUSTICE

The future of Judaism, even more than that of the other historical civilizations, depends upon its having the courage to commit itself to the cause of social idealism. The various religious traditions have by this time managed to come to terms with the challenge of the modern scientific and philosophic approach to reality. But a new and more serious challenge is either implied or expressed in the movements for the reconstruction of the economic order. Traditional religion, by its emphasis upon the ephemeral and relative worthlessness of the material aspect of human life, has at least indirectly condoned the evils of the present economic order. So imperious nowadays is the demand for economic justice that, if Judaism were to find itself without a message, and unable to canalize the trend of social and economic changes into a more equitable distribution of wealth, it would veritably admit its moral impotence.

Jews have become so implicated economically in the fortunes and misfortunes of the non-Jewish environment that the truth of Judah HaLevi's designation of Israel as the heart of mankind has been all too tragically demonstrated of late. As the heart responds to the least disturbance of the equilibrium of the body, so is Israel sensitive to the least that goes wrong in the life of the nations. Both collectively and individually, the Jews have been among the worst sufferers in the calamities that have befallen humanity since the World War. To no people has the world-depression which mankind has brought upon itself through its sins of avarice, exploitation, and cruelty been so disastrous as to the Jews. This should be sufficient reason for the Jews to realize that the only kind of a world which can be safe for them is one built on economic justice.

The ethical contribution which Jews can make to the economic aspect of human life is to counteract the tendency to treat economic activity as though it were independent of considerations of right and wrong. Modern economics, whether of the individualist or the socialist type, is largely responsible for the dehumanization of economical problems. In former days men interpreted earthquakes and tidal waves as afflictions sent by God for the sins they had committed. The knowledge since acquired of the working of natural law has negated any connection between human sin and the tremors of the earth. But unfortunately this tendency to deny any relationship between human misery and human sin has been carried over to the domain of men's dealings with one another where the relationship is inextricable. Nineteenth-century economists of the individualistic school of thought, wishing to pose as masters of an exact science, sought to treat the process of exchange of goods and services as though it were fatalistically determined by external laws of nature, as are the forces of gravitation, heat, and light. This conception of the economic activities, which constitute the major part of human conduct, has been humbly accepted as gospel truth by the teachers of morality and religion, and therefore as not within their sphere of judgment or guidance. Thus, the producing, distributing, and consuming of things have come to be regarded as inevitably subject to the law of the jungle. Accordingly, if there is to be such a thing as a law of the spirit, it has to be realized in those interstices of our life in this world which are not preempted by the economic struggle, or in some form of spiritual existence not bound up with the needs of the body. It is no wonder, therefore, that modern capitalism has been aptly described as being absolutely irreligious.

CAPITALIST ETHICS

All who take the ethical view of life seriously must vigorously oppose the popular notion that business is essentially a struggle for advantage, in which considerations of right and wrong can play at best only a secondary role. They should even have the courage to question the economists' assumption that the law of supply and demand, with its corollary, the profit motive, is beyond human control. The professional economists still operate with the mid-Victorian doctrine, "Let each inform his mind, behave reasonably and look after his own interests; a society of such persons, each successfully minding his own business, will be a successful society." Current events have proved those sages mistaken who said that to take the attitude of "Mine is mine and thine is thine" is to take a middle course, and I have vindicated the opinion of those who maintained that such an attitude is worthy of the inhabitants of Sodom.

Those who are interested in the improvement of human life

must learn to emancipate themselves from the domination of economic stereotypes which have been used to bolster up the profit system. One of these is the so-called law of supply and demand, which merely makes a law of lawlessness. In itself it is as likely to make for order and security as allowing the desire of each car driver to get to his destination as quickly as possible to govern present-day traffic. So long as the lawlessness and anarchy of supply and demand will be permitted to govern the production of goods and the employment of workers, it is futile to keep on urging what is termed "a just wage" in the exchange of services, and "a fair price" in the exchange of goods. Even a child ought to be able to understand that with the infinite complexity of factors which enter into the making of any product, or the buying and selling of any article, there is no possible way of determining what is fair or just from the standpoint of exchange based on *quid pro quo.* It may be that the whole price and wage system has become morally untenable and should be scrapped. What is true of price and wage is equally true of interest on capital, or rent on land. Surely there must be some justice to the contention of Henry George that rent on land is inherently indefensible from an ethical standpoint. A civilization which calls itself moral or ethical should delve beneath the surface of the commonly accepted standards and habits of our social order. It should ascertain whether the profit motive which is the fundamental source of most of the corruption and misery, and against which all teaching and preaching have spent themselves in vain, is the indispensable stimulus to humane effort and productivity that it is trumped up to be. Such an assumption virtually implies that humanity is doomed to lead forever a life of violence, and that all the dreams and hopes of the great visionaries of mankind are a mirage. Such nihilism would confirm the description of man's world given by a modern economist who said that "in a universe of transmigrating souls, our particular planet must have been assigned to be the lunatic asylum of the universe."

SOCIALIST ETHICS

No less unmoral than the thesis of the individualist economists is that of the socialist economists. Karl Marx, who was the implacable enemy of religion and philosophy, regarded all moral judgments and religious doctrines as the result rather than the cause of economic conditions. For him they were changing concepts, determined entirely by the economy at any particular time. Indeed, he said, all social values are the products of economic forces and the reflection of the economic system. Every "ought" is the outgrowth of an "is." This is known as the theory of "economic determinism," based, as Marx believed, upon true "science," and it is intended to demonstrate that far from being the source of sanctions and guidance, ethics and religion are no more than the passive by-product of social forces which can be controlled only through the scientific study of their operation.

Are the means of making a livelihood the only conscious movers in one's conduct? Nothing could be further from the truth. The case of the Jews and of all religious groups that sacrifice opportunities of making a livelihood out of loyalty to their historic tradition are cases in direct refutation of this contention. The fallacy of economic determinism is that it confuses effective cause with indispensable condition. A foundation is indispensable to a house, and may even be responsible for certain features of the house; but it by no means explains the entire house. The exaggerated claims that Marx made for the economic factor may be explained by the tendency that has always prevailed to overestimate the significance of a discovery. Marx's outstanding discovery was the determining influence that economic factors have on human life. To Marx we are indeed indebted for his discovery that economic relationships play a great part in determining not alone the nature of the economic practices and institutions but of all social and creative activities. Nevertheless, the careful analyst of history cannot conscientiously accept Marx whole. . . .

To interpret the entire history of civilization in terms of class struggle is to see nothing in the history of music, sculpture, religion, philosophy, education but evidences of the contest between exploiter and exploited. This is arrant dogma. What is perhaps true is that the struggle between exploiter and exploited that has always marked the life of peoples accounts for most of the political history and for many of the laws and mores of mankind. It is true that those who possessed a greater degree of power and cunning than their fellows always took advantage of every opportunity to seize political authority and tried to translate their interests into laws and mores and religion. But to imply that the creative activity in religion and in the arts and sciences reflects merely class antagonism is to fail to realize that man does not live by bread alone.

JUDAISM AND SOCIAL JUSTICE

Ultimately, the forces for good that inhere in the world and in human nature will give rise to a just social order, one in which every human being will be able to achieve the full measure of self-realization and accord to his neighbor the same right and opportunity. The evolution of mankind, though marked by frequent and disheartening reactions, moves irresistibly in the direction of universal security and freedom. From the standpoint of the Jewish religion, ethical purpose does not emerge merely as an incident of social history, but is a directive and creative force. The social changes that occur as a result of mechanical inventions may be viewed as part of the divine plan. Achieved through the use of intelligence, the divine spirit at work in man, the machine precipitates the conditions that will create abundance, and thereby will remove forever the fear of scarcity and insecurity, which is the main cause of all social conflict. The machine is thus the instrument of the divine will. Through it God's attribute as provider will be completely fulfilled. If in the meantime it has given the exploiters added power to enslave the masses, it is only that they might overreach themselves as did all the arrogant rulers of mankind who set themselves up as gods, and thus brought about their own downfall.

Whether the security and abundance for all made physically possible by the creative intelligence and cooperative will of man is to come in our day or in some distant future is for us to decide. "All things are foreseen, yet freedom of choice is given," said Rabbi Akiva. This means that the ethical choice of man operates within the framework of a morally determined world. And it is in these areas of voluntary action that religion as a social force must fire the zeal of men and bring them to work ardently for the new day.

The Jewish interpretation of history, therefore, regards the contest between the exploiter and exploited not as a blind and purposeless one, nor does it regard the many changes in the social structure of mankind as meaningless and vain. It sees in them the striving for human equality progressively intensified and brought nearer than ever to realization by the industrial revolution. But whether this realization will be near or far, the inexorable law of God will prevail.

The only way in which any culture or civilization can come to possess significance and relevance in our day is by bravely grappling with all these problems. If Jews are in search of a mission, do they need one more urgent and imperative than the promulgation of economic justice? The behest of Jeremiah to the Jews who had been exiled to Babylon takes on an entirely new meaning in our day. When he urged them to seek the welfare of the city in which they dwelt because their welfare depended upon that of the city, he did not mean, as some interpret his words, that they should be demonstrative in their loyalty to the political regime. What he urged upon them was a participation in the furtherance of all those forces which made for the welfare of the general community. Translating Jeremiah's teaching into the duty for our day, it should be regarded by Jews as a plea to participate in all the forces and movements which make for the reconstruction and betterment of the social order to which they belong.

CHAPTER 79

PRAYERS OF REFORM JEWS

Liberal or Reform Judaism arose in Germany during the first half of the nineteenth century, but attained its fullest development in the United States. It started out as a movement to reform merely the synagogue ritual, but eventually went on to recast the entire character of the religion. The avowed aim was to rid Judaism of all doctrines and practices which seemed untenable and intolerable in a world committed to intellectual enlightenment and social progress. It therefore abjured the belief in a personal Messiah who would one day restore Israel to Zion, and abandoned most of the ritual observances calculated to keep Israel secluded until that day arrived. Like the Unitarians in Christendom, the Reform Jews were intensely optimistic, believing that bigotry was swiftly becoming a thing of the past, and that reason was certain soon to prevail universally and forever.

Animated by this cheerful notion, the movement was able to flourish in America, and even throw up shoots in England, France, and other lands. Until the close of the 1920s it was qualitatively the most impressive religious force in Israel.

The vital spark in the movement was its aspiration toward universalism, and that spark cannot possibly survive unless society succeeds in outgrowing rabid nationalism.

To what extent the aspiration was realized—at least in words—can be judged by the following prayers. The first is taken from a highly nonconformist service adopted by the Newark (N.J.) Free Synagogue, in 1924. The remainder will be found in editions (Part I, 1940; Part II, 1942) of the Union Prayerbook.

HEAR, O ISRAEL!

Brethren, let us bethink ourselves of our past, of our common heritage as children of Israel. A strange folk have we been all these years, a riddle and bewilderment to men. Through centuries without tale we have wandered about on earth, fleeing from eternal Egypt through a shoreless Red Sea. We have seen far-flung empires crack and crumble, and mighty peoples dwindle to naught. Armies beyond counting have marched by us in pomp and glory; with kings and priests, with tyrants and princelings, have they marched by us in pride. Yet of them all is no sign left, for they fell and died by the roadside.

But we, the Jews, still march on. Obstinately we fight off Time and Man, contending at each step with a thousand foes, yet ever marching, marching on.

O may there be sense in our persistence, and reason in our tenacity. May our constancy as Jews not be deemed an end in itself, but solely a way and a means. May we live our lives as Jews only to keep alive our heritage, to keep ablaze the fires our Prophets lit. May we, like our fathers, still stand out against the multitude, protesting with all our might against its follies and its fears. May a divine discontent give color to our dreams, and a passion for holy heresy set the tone of our thoughts. May the soul of the rebel still throb in us as it throbbed in our forefathers, that today and forever we may still be a light unto those who stumble in darkness.

And in that hope let us repeat the cry our people uttered when a thousand idols were still worshipped by man:

HEAR O ISRAEL, THE LORD IS OUR GOD.
THE LORD IS—ONE!

PRAISED BE HIS NAME WHOSE GLORIOUS KINGDOM IS FOREVER AND EVER!

PRAYERS FOR GUIDANCE

Almighty and merciful God, Thou hast called Israel to Thy service and found him worthy to bear witness unto Thy truth among the peoples of the earth. Give us grace to fulfill this mission with zeal tempered by wisdom and guided by regard for other men's faith. May our life prove the strength of our own belief in the truths we proclaim. May our bearing toward our neighbors, our faithfulness in every sphere of duty, our compassion for the suffering and our patience under trial show that He whose law we obey is indeed the God of all goodness, the Father of all men, that to serve Him is perfect freedom and to worship Him the soul's purest happiness.

O Lord, open our eyes that we may see and welcome all truth, whether shining from the annals of ancient revelations or reaching us through the seers of our own time; for Thou hidest not Thy light from any generation of Thy children that yearn for Thee and seek Thy guidance.

May the time not be distant, O God, when Thy name shall be worshipped in all the earth, when unbelief shall disappear and error be no more. Fervently we pray that the day may come when all men shall invoke Thy name, when corruption and evil shall give way to purity and goodness, when superstition shall no longer enslave the mind, nor idolatry blind the eye, when all who dwell on earth shall know that to Thee alone every knee must bend and every tongue give homage. O may all, created in Thine image, recognize that they are brethren, so that, one in spirit and one in fellowship, they may be forever united before Thee. Then shall Thy kingdom be established on earth and the work of Thine ancient seer be fulfilled: The Lord will reign forever and ever.

PRAYERS FOR BROTHERHOOD

O Lord, though we are prone to seek favors for ourselves alone, yet when we come into thy presence, we are lifted above petty thoughts of self. We become ashamed of our littleness and are made to feel that we can worship Thee in holiness only as we serve our brothers in love.

How much we owe to the labors of our brothers! Day by day they dig far away from the sun that we may be warm, enlist in outposts of peril that we may be secure, and brave the terrors of the unknown for truths that shed light on our way. Numberless gifts and blessings have been laid in our cradles as our birthright.

Let us then, O Lord, be just and great-hearted in our dealings with our fellowmen, sharing with them the fruit of our common labor, acknowledging before Thee that we are but stewards of whatever we possess. Help us to be among those who are willing to sacrifice that others may not hunger, who dare to be bearers of light in the dark loneliness of stricken lives, who struggle and even bleed for the triumph of righteousness among men. So may we be co-workers with Thee in the building of Thy kingdom which has been our vision and goal through the ages.

We thank Thee, O God, that Thou has permitted us to be co-workers with Thee in the unfolding of Thy divine plan. Thou has set Thy blessing upon labor, and hast enabled us to promote the well-being of all by the faithful work we do. Strengthen in us, O God, the spirit of service and sacrifice. May we never be tempted to profit by impoverishing and degrading the lives of others. Make us realize the wrong of letting others hunger while we are surfeited with the bounties of nature. Implant in our hearts, we pray Thee, a sense of responsibility and comradeship. Reveal to us the divine glory that abides in every soul, and the high dignity that invests all honest labor. Help us so to live that, by our own endeavors, we may hasten the day when all shall toil and serve side by side as brothers; when love and sympathy shall stir every heart, and greed and want no longer mar the beauty of Thy creation. Amen.

God of freedom, Thy children still groan under the burden of cruel taskmasters. Slavery debases their bodies and minds, and robs them of the enjoyment of Thy bounties. The fear of cruelty and the peril of death blight the souls of men. O break Thou the irons that bind them. Teach men to understand that by forging chains for others they forge chains for themselves, that as long as some are in fetters no one is truly free. Help them to see that liberty is the very breath of life and that only in the atmosphere of freedom can truth, prosperity, and peace flourish. Imbue us with courage to guard our heritage of freedom above all material goods and to preserve it for others so that all men shall dwell together in safety and none shall make them afraid.

Fervently we pray for the universal springtide in the life of mankind when the long winter of intolerance and hatred shall have passed, the vision of the prophets fulfilled and the glory of Thy kingdom acknowledged of all men. Amen.

On this day, we pray Thee, O Father, that we may learn to labor in Thy spirit and to live in harmony with Thy law. When tempted to hoard Thy blessings, to impoverish others that we might prosper, open Thou our eyes to the wrong and privation we would thus inflict on our own brothers. When, goaded by selfishness and greed, we would ignore the rights of the weak and forget the common kinship of all men, reveal Thou unto us, we beseech Thee, the divine pattern of life shown to the seers of old. The earth is Thine and the fullness thereof; help us to realize that the blessings we enjoy are but tokens of Thy love, and that when we use Thy gifts in the service of our fellowmen we offer thanksgiving unto Thee. Turn Thou our strength to tasks of justice, mercy, and peace, so that, in our labors for the common good, we may find the joy and exaltation of the righteous life. We live in the shelter of Thy protection; teach us to serve Thee in truth, in humility, and in love.

We pray Thee, O Father, that in the presence of cruelty and wrong our hearts remain steadfast and true. When evil men plot against us and seek to uproot us, let no despair drain our strength nor fear chill our faith. Teach us to meet enmity with courage and hope, and to battle against adversity with resolute will and unyielding self-possession. Keep alive within us the vision of our higher purposes and nobler destiny, and renew our zeal for the divine tasks of life. Open our hearts to the cry of the persecuted and the despoiled. Hasten the day when hate and strife shall cease to divide the family of men, and justice and love reign supreme in the world.

CONGREGATIONAL PRAYERS

Our God and God of our fathers, we stand before Thee on this day, as the community of Israel. . . . We have declared to the world that we were sent by Thee to teach justice and lovingkindness, brotherhood, and peace. And yet, even in our own household, petty prejudices, class enmities, and the envious conflicts for the prizes of worldly gain, have not ceased. They have not been overcome by the belief that Thou art our Father, that Thou hast created us all, and that therefore, we should not deal treacherously one man against his brother. Preaching peace to the world, we have not established it, even in the midst of Israel. . . .

We have proclaimed to the world, even as law-giver and prophet taught, that we were Thine own treasure, a chosen people, Thy servant, upon whom Thou didst put Thy spirit. But we have not always lived so as to show ourselves worthy of this high and holy charge. Alas, we have contemned our holy heritage and made it minister to our own pride. Our sacred obligations we have turned into an oblation of incense to our racial vanity.

Also, the world's injustice, and the persecution of Israel, have forced upon us the task of self-defense to such a degree as not to leave us strength enough to examine our own lives with impartial search for the truth. We have not made our sufferings a discipline for our souls. We have found excuses for our own sin in the iniquity of the persecutor. We lacked the moral power, which our heroic forefathers had, even in the face of unjust hate, to point to our own breasts and say, we too, have sinned, have committed iniquity, have transgressed. . . .

O Lord, hasten the day when all evil shall be destroyed and wickedness shall be no more. Quicken us to work with the righteous of all nations and creeds, to bring about Thy kingdom upon earth, so that hatred among men shall cease, that the walls of prejudice and pride, separating peoples, shall crumble and fall, and war, the weapon of man's hate, be destroyed forever. . . .

When Solomon dedicated the Temple, he prayed: "Moreover concerning the stranger that is not of Thy people Israel, when he shall come out of a far country for Thy name's sake—for they shall hear of Thy great name, and of Thy mighty hand, and of Thine outstretched arm—when he shall come and pray toward this house, hear Thou in heaven, Thy dwelling place, and do according to all the stranger calleth to Thee for; that all the peoples of the earth may know Thy name, to fear Thee, as doth Thy people Israel, and that they may know that Thy name is called upon in this house which I have builded."

In this spirit we too pray for all men. Grant that wherever a heart sighs in anguish under the burden of guilt, wherever a soul yearns to return to Thee, it may feel the effect of Thy pardoning love and mercy. Let superstition, falsehood, and malice vanish everywhere. Send forth Thy light and Thy truth to those who grope in darkness, and the knowledge of Thee to those who follow after strange gods; and may Thy house be called the house of prayer for all peoples. Hasten the time when the mountain of thy house shall be established as the top of the mountains and shall be exalted above the hills and peoples shall flow unto it; when they shall beat their swords into plowshares and their spears into pruning hooks; when nation shall not lift up sword against nation, neither shall they learn war any more; but they shall sit every man under his vine and under his fig tree; and none shall make them afraid.

Then shall Thy kingdom be established upon earth, and upon all the nations shall rest Thy spirit, even the spirit of wisdom and understanding, the spirit of counsel and might, the spirit of knowledge and fear of Thee. Then as one great family shall all Thy children exclaim:

The Lord will reign for ever, thy God, O Zion, from generation to generation. Hallelujah.

A PRAYER FOR MOURNERS

To you, who mourn the loss of loved ones, let there come the comfort of the hope that, though the dust returns to the earth as it was, the spirit returns to God who gave it. Death is not the end. Our dear ones have passed through the gateway of the grave into the peace of life that endureth always. We know that all of us must tread the same path, though we know not when the hour may strike. Let us so live that the coming of that hour shall find us unafraid. May our deeds do honor to the memory of our beloved whom Thou has taken unto Thyself. In unshaken trust in Thy wisdom and lovingkindness, we give praise unto Thy name.

A PRAYER FOR THE AGED

The earnest meditations of this sacred day, O God, awaken my soul to grateful acknowledgment of Thy grace which has bestowed upon me the gift of life; of Thy loving providence, which has prolonged my days. By Thy mercy I have been permitted to pass through the dangers and difficulties that beset my pathway and have come in safety to the coveted goal of a ripe old age.

And now as I look back over the years that have gone, the whole past shines out before me revealing my inmost self. I humbly confess before Thee in this solemn hour the sins and errors that cast their shadows over my life – the willfulness of childhood, the waywardness of youth, the selfishness and vanity of mature years, and the frailties of even these later days. How far, alas, have I fallen from those noble ideals and pure motives in character and conduct which Thou hast set as the aim of life! How often have I failed to make use of those divine powers which Thou hast implanted within me! In the lengthening shadows of life's decline, all my sins and failures loom up reprovingly, and I devoutly pray for thy pardoning favor and forgiveness.

Grant me clearness of vision to see life as a whole from youth to age and to be comforted in the faith that the best is yet to be. In moments of doubt and despondency when, like the patriarch, I count my days as few and evil and when the waning of my bodily powers makes me declare with the sage, I have no pleasure in them, O then sustain me with a realization of these blessings which the maturity of age alone can bring and the ripeness of experience alone can yield. Give me the sweetness of that joy which is reserved for those who serve others through the counsel and guidance learned in the school of life's experience. . . .

Enable me to hold fast, however old I may grow, to the spirit of youth. Suffer me not to lose that sense of wonder which stirs within me in the presence of Thy creation. O quicken me from day to day with that power of communion with Thee which restores my soul.

I crave the power to see ever more clearly that other half of life's plan, which youth cannot discern. Sustain me with the faith that wrong, cruelty, and injustice cannot prevail, but that the right, the pure, and true shall endure. And may the imperishable worth of life uphold me in the deathless hope of the hereafter.

Let me not be afraid! As one by one my bodily powers weaken, may my soul enter into greater freedom and be purified and atoned in Thy sight. Let me die the death of the righteous and let mine end be like his. Amen!

A PRAYER FOR YOUNG PEOPLE

O my Maker, I pray unto Thee!

There are moments when I dream of what I would like to make of my life. The vision of manhood and character and a life of worth and service fill me with joy. But, alas, for the hours of temptation and struggle. The vision fades and the will weakens. I realize that I need Thee, O my Maker, so to strengthen me that I may achieve all the fine potentialities of heart and mind and soul with which Thou hast endowed me.

God, I need Thee!

In the environment of my daily life, in the pressure of things and business, in the pursuit after pleasure, I lose sight of my best self. Temptations assail me. Thoughts which I abhor terrify me by their power. I feel myself in the grip of forces before which I am too weak to stand alone.

God, I need Thee!

Be with me in these hours. Grip me by a sense of the holiness of my life. I do not ask that my path be made easy. I do not ask that all temptation and struggle be removed from my way. But I pray Thee, strengthen within me the conviction that I can make of my life what I will! Cause me to feel that if Thou art with me, sustaining, encouraging me, no victory of the spirit is impossible. O let me know the joy of moral conquest!

O my God! Life looms up before me, so terrifying, so enthralling, I seem so pitifully small that at times a great heartsickness seizes me. I cannot seem to find my place in all this vast scheme of things. My work seems void of usefulness and my life meaningless.

Let me feel that in Thine eyes my efforts are worthwhile. Deepen within me the consciousness of the obligation I owe to my friends, my loved ones; the responsibility I have to my fellowmen and to Thee. Give me strength so to mould and purify my character that my life may be counted as a blessing!

MEDITATION FOR THE NEW YEAR

The solemn advent of the New Year calls me, O God, to the quiet of Thy sanctuary to commune with Thee in fellowship with my brethren. Here, under the inspiration of our sacred traditions, I would open my innermost self to those deeper thoughts and feelings which I have only too often shut from mind and heart in my day-by-day preoccupation with worldly pursuits and pleasures. May a real responsiveness of spirit be stirred within me and may I be enabled to consecrate my mood of the moment by influences and sentiments that will outlast the moment.

Do Thou, Almighty, help me to this end. Quicken my memory that I may draw lessons from the past before the old year is wholly gone. Give me of Thy light that I may see my varied experiences in their true meaning. As I look backward, may there be revealed to me how much richer, how much more abundant were my blessings than my privations, and how even my losses, my trials, my sorrows had within themselves the possibilities of higher good. And even more, I pray Thee, teach me how small and insignificant were many of the things which at the time seemed all important, and how needlessly I permitted my soul to be troubled sorely and my heart to be fretted by cares which proved to be of no moment. Bring home to me the folly and futility of all this, and the need of ever holding before myself the standard of true values. Let no self-deception hide from me the record of sin and shortcoming, of opportunities neglected, of time misspent, of abilities and powers perverted to lower purposes against my own better impulses and knowledge.

O Thou who knowest the secrets of the heart, make all this to pass in solemn review before my inner vision. Arouse my conscience to a deep sense of guilt and inspire and strengthen my will to high and holy resolves. Grant that, like Jacob of old, wrestling with the adversary in the dark, I may not let the departing year go from me until I shall have wrested a blessing from its trials and mistakes.

And O that I may also be enabled by Thy divine grace to turn into blessing the possibilities of the new year which stretches out before me in solemn mystery! Let its message of time and eternity make me indeed mindful of the uncertainty of human life and the passing nature of all things earthly–but let not the thought of my frailty awaken unwholesome fear of death or unworthy thoughts of life. Imbue me with the conviction that my times are in Thy hands, that Thou wilt be with me whithersoever I may go and that, relying on Thy wise and loving providence, I may face the unknown future with courage and hope.

Trustfully, I confide myself and those dear to me to Thy

keeping for the year upon which we are now entering. We are strangers to it and know not the way which we should go. We need Thy light and leading. Guide Thou us in paths of safety for Thy name's sake. Bless us in our home and in all our wider relationships, sanctifying our affections, strengthening our loyalties and enlarging our powers of helpfulness.

As I implore Thee to inscribe me in the Book of Life, help me to understand that life is to be measured in terms of character and usefulness, and that more than mere length of days are breadth of sympathies, loftiness of ideals and greatness of service. Aid me to utilize rightly whatever added span of time Thou, in Thy grace and goodness, shalt accord to me. May the beauty of the Lord our God be upon us and establish Thou the work of our hands–yea, the work of our hands establish Thou it. Amen.

EXHORTATION FOR A TROUBLED AGE

While the problems of livelihood have always been urgent, never before have they pressed upon us so insistently and with such disquieting effects. What disturbs one now is not the fear that God's earth might cease to yield, but the unhappy realization of the growing discontent with the manner in which the earth's increase is shared and enjoyed by the human family. The world of commerce and industry is filled with threatening suspicions and antagonisms. Great plenty and abject poverty, limitless power and utter weakness exist side by side. These disparities are forcing themselves upon the attention of men and women as they have never done before. Everywhere earnest minds are seeking to know whether these inequalities are justified and permanent, or whether a way may not be found that shall lead to more contentment and greater mutual respect and confidence the world over.

In seeking a solution to these problems we, the children of

Israel, should hold foremost in our minds the belief of our fathers, that human life is of the utmost value and that all duties and responsibilities have for their purpose the safeguarding of the life of man and the furtherance of his nature as a child of God. To Israel, man has always been the center of our obligations. We have been taught for ages that whatever does not serve to make our neighbor happy and confident and whatever does not dispose him to become kindly and trustful and helpful cannot receive the sanction of God and of His moral law. If our world is torn by great divisions and suspicions due to what is believed to be an unfair and unjust distribution of the world's goods, we cannot and must not regard such a condition as inevitable and normal. Surely we cannot find in such a state of human affairs the promise of mutual appreciation and love. No peace of mind is possible when one lives in the shadow of unwarranted economic uncertainty and in the fear of industrial power that is felt to be used arbitrarily.

It is well to be reminded that even if these fears and suspicions are groundless, they yet remain unsettling influences in the lives of men. They yet disturb them and rob them of confidence in themselves and faith in their fellowmen. But the fears of great masses of men have a foundation, and the recurrent protests of thousands upon thousands of men and women are justified. Upon this day, when our hearts are searched by Him who sees and knows all, it is for each one of us to summon his own conscience to help rectify the wrong according to his power.

Our fathers have always been specially sympathetic with the hardships of those that toil. Lawgiver and prophet have warned over and over again that wealth and the possession of power tended to make men insensible to the needs and struggles of others. On the very threshold of our history, we were reminded not to forget how we felt when we were in Egypt as strangers, and how the oppression and injustice of our taskmasters made us suffer. Labor is man's very life. Nothing comes into the world ready-made. The things that we daily enjoy must first be conceived and planned by the human mind, and fashioned and formed by the human hand. Let none of us, therefore, in the pride of possession forget the true nature and source of human wealth and be unmindful of the responsibilities of power. It is not possible for any of us, however strong and however wise, to control the destinies of our own lives single-handed. Whether we will or no, human life is a cooperative venture and the business of life is carried on whenever and wherever two persons transact any enterprise whatsoever. If there is fair dealing between them, then so much good issues from it and the whole world is enriched thereby. If, however, one man should take advantage of the other, then out of this transaction must inevitably come hatred, strife, and possibly violence.

In thinking over industrial problems and struggles let us be on our guard against believing that the things that constitute the difficulties are in the order of nature beyond the control of man himself, for in the end, whatever troubles us in the world of business and industry has issued from personal covetousness, arrogance, and cold indifference to the welfare of others.

On this day of self-examination let us search and examine our ways, and in genuine integrity of mind and humility of spirit make acknowledgment that we ourselves have not been sufficiently mindful of the interest and rights of our fellowmen. We have been too ready to seize upon any excuse to hold what we have and even to multiply it without due regard to the welfare of our brothers and sisters, who depend upon us.

In this solemn hour let us resolve to be helpful to the men and women who earnestly and sincerely strive to make a better world and let us on our own part seek to establish this world by such justice as shall be stimulated by generous sympathies and by such righteousness as shall be based upon genuine sacrifice.

A PRAYER FOR PEACE

Grant us peace, Thy most precious gift, O Thou eternal source of peace, and enable Israel to be its messenger unto the peoples of the earth. Bless our country that it may ever be a stronghold of peace, and its advocate in the council of nations. May contentment reign within its borders, health and happiness within its homes. Strengthen the bonds of friendship and fellowship among all the inhabitants of our land. Plant virtue in every soul, and may the love of Thy name hallow every home and every heart. Praised be Thou, O Lord, Giver of peace.

GLOSSARY

ARAMAIC: The popular dialect used by the Palestinian Jews after the return from the Babylonian Exile (536 B.C.E.).

BEN: Hebrew for "son."

ELOHIST: Name given by scholars to those portions of the Pentateuch which refer to the deity as *Elohim*, and which are presumed to have originated in the (Northern) Kingdom of Israel.

GAON: Hebrew for "Brilliant One." Head of the chief rabbinical academy in Babylonia during the early Middle Ages.

GEMARA: Hebrew for "Learning." The Talmudic amplification of the legal decision in the Mishnah.

HASID (pl. *hasidim*): Hebrew for "Pietist." A follower of Hasidism, the mystical religious movement which arose among the Polish Jews in the eighteenth century.

HEBREW: From the Hebrew root-word *ivri*, which may originally have meant "one from the other side (of the Jordan)." Properly the word should be applied only to Israelites and Judeans *before* the Babylonian Exile (586 B.C.E.). After that date the term *Jew* (from *Judah*) became the accepted one.

HELLENISM: From the Greek *Hellas*, meaning Greece. The word is used to describe the culture of ancient Greece.

IBN: Arabic for "Son (of)."

ISRAEL: Hebrew meaning "Champion of God." Properly the term should be applied solely to the Northern Kingdom, where dwelt the so-called "Ten Tribes of Israel." General acceptance, however, has made it synonymous with Jewry.

JAHVEH: Original name of the Hebrew deity. The word is now usually spelled *Jehovah*.

KABBALAH: Hebrew for "tradition." A system of mystical thought that was popular among the Jews during the later Middle Ages.

LITVAK: Yiddish for "Lithuanian." It is often used to connote shrewdness and also skepticism, because the Lithuanian Jews were inclined to doubt the powers of the hasidic leaders.

MIDRASH (pl. *Midrashi*): Hebrew for "homily." The Midrashic compilations contain the non-legal rabbinic literature of the Talmudic period.

MISHNAH: Hebrew for "Repetition." The civil and religious law code compiled around 200 B.C.E.

MOREH NEVUHIM: Hebrew for "Guide for the Perplexed," by Moses Maimonides (Rambam).

PENTATEUCH: The first five books in the Bible, known to the Jews as the Five Books of Moses.

RABBI: Hebrew for "my master." Originally the title of respect applied to a teacher of the Law. Later it came to mean the spiritual leader in a synagogue.

REBBE: Yiddish for rabbi.

SANHEDRIN: Greek for "assembly." The Parliament and Supreme Court of the ancient Jews.

SCHLEMIEL: Yiddish for an unlucky person.

SCHNORRER: Yiddish term of reproach for a beggar who makes pretensions to respectability.

SHULHAN ARUKH: Hebrew for "Prepared Table." Title of the

most popular compilation of the rabbinic laws regulating the practice of Judaism. It was compiled by Joseph Karo in 1555.

SYNAGOGUE: Greek for "convocation." A Jewish religious organization, or the building in which such an organization worships.

TORAH: Hebrew for "Law." Specifically the Five Books of Moses, but often a synonym for all Jewish Law, for all Jewish learning.

TZADIK (pl. *Tzadikim*): Hebrew for "Righteous One." A hasidic rabbi claiming the power to work miracles.

YAHVEH: See Jahveh.

YIDDISH: From the German *juedisch,* meaning Jewish. The vernacular of East European Jews. It is the Middle High German of the sixteenth century with an admixture of Slavic and Hebrew.

ZOHAR: Hebrew for "Radiance." Title of a kabbalistic work introduced into Spain by Moses de Leon in the thirteenth century.

INDEX OF AUTHORS